Encyclopedia of Crime & Justice

Second Edition

EDITORIAL BOARD

Encyclopedia of Crime & Justice

Second Edition

Joshua Dressler, Editor in Chief

Volume 4
Schools & Crime—
Wiretapping & Eavesdropping

MACMILLAN REFERENCE USA

GALE GROUP
TM
THOMSON LEARNING

New York • Detroit • San Diego • San Francisco
Boston • New Haven, Conn. • Waterville, Maine
London • Munich

Macmillan Reference USA
An imprint of the Gale Group
300 Park Avenue South   27500 Drake Road
New York, NY 10010   Farmington Hills, MI 48331

Library of Congress Cataloging-in-Publication Data
Encyclopedia of crime and justice.—2nd ed. / Joshua Dressler, editor in chief.
     p. cm.
    Includes bibliographical references and index.
    ISBN 0-02-865319-X (set: alk. paper)—ISBN 0-02-865320-3 (v. 1: alk.
paper)—ISBN 0-02-865321-1 (v. 2: alk. paper)—ISBN 0-02-865322-X (v. 3:
alk. paper)—ISBN 0-02-865323-8 (v. 4: alk. paper)
    1. Criminology—Encyclopedias. 2. Criminal justice, Administration of—
Encyclopedias. I. Title: Crime and justice. II. Dressler, Joshua.
HV6017 .E52 2002
364'.03—dc21   2001042707

Portions of "Delinquent and Criminal Subcultures" have been adapted in part
from "The Code of the Street" by Elijah Anderson by permission of W. W.
Norton & Company Inc.

Printed in the United States of America
Printing number
 2 3 4 5 6 7 8 9 10

S

SCHOOLS AND CRIME

Most school crime, like crime outside the school, is nonviolent. Teachers and students report thefts of money and valuables from unattended desks; student lockers are broken into; teachers' pocketbooks are snatched; bicycles are stolen. Other nonviolent offenses include such acts by students as using and selling drugs, drinking alcoholic beverages, defacing walls and desks, and setting minor fires in wastebaskets and toilet bowls. Violations of rules specific to schools also occur: walking the corridors without a pass, cursing a teacher, cutting a class, and truanting.

Less frequent but more disturbing offenses are violent crimes: assaults, robberies, and, occasionally, rapes and murders. Violent offenses create anxiety in students and teachers out of proportion to their frequency. They are unusual in private, parochial, and rural schools but occur with greater frequency in suburban schools, the secondary schools of small cities, and the junior and senior high schools of large cities. Some secondary schools in large cities have so much violent crime that students and teachers regard the schools as war zones. Students sometime claim that they stay away from such schools out of fear, and teachers refer to some of their nominal sick-day absences as "mental health" days. In addition to encountering violence *inside* school buildings, students, teachers, and other school employees are vulnerable to violence traveling to and from school, in parking lots, and in school-yards.

Sources of information about school crime

There are several main sources of information about school crime. One source consists of the informal observations of participants in the educational process, especially teachers and former teachers (for example, see Gerson). Since the schools are part of a major social institution involving millions of people in diverse roles, such observations are constantly issued in both personal and organizational reports. Teachers' unions have school safety committees that collect and tabulate the crime incidents in which teachers are victimized; they are especially interested in assaults on and robberies of teachers (United Federation of Teachers).

Boards of education also collect from principals and teachers information about school offenses, especially violent ones. Journalists are another source, since they visit schools; interview students, teachers, crime victims, and perpetrators; and report their conclusions in the media. Finally, there is systematic survey research. In 1976 the National Institute of Education of the Department of Health, Education, and Welfare obtained questionnaire responses from 31,373 public-school students and 23,895 public-school teachers about their victimization experiences in 642 junior and senior high schools (U.S. Department of Health, Education, and Welfare). The results, published in a 1978 report to Congress, provided the first quantitative comparisons of the rates of robbery, assault, and larceny in public secondary schools across the United States. Somewhat surprisingly, students were victimized to about the same extent in large and small communities except for a somewhat higher rate in cities of a million or more; however, within large school systems some schools were much more dangerous than others. Teacher victimization, on the other hand, increased overall in proportion to the size of the community. The main deficiency of this landmark study was that it did not ask student respondents about their own violent behavior because raising this crucial issue would have jeopardized access to some school systems.

The Bureau of the Census administered the National Crime Survey (later renamed the National Crime Victimization Survey) in twenty-six large American cities in 1974 and 1975. Data were obtained on various types of victimization covering approximately ten thousand households in each city. These were later analyzed to provide information about offenses committed inside big-city schools (U.S. Department of Justice). Whereas the National Institute of Education study collected reports of personal victimization from both students and teachers, the twenty-six-city National Crime Survey also contained data about the victimization of school staff members other than teachers. However, these data were limited to school crime in very large cities. Several states have conducted statewide studies of school violence and vandalism, such as the Hawaii Crime Commission's analysis of six thousand questionnaires completed by principals, counselors, teachers, and students in 1979 (Hawaii Crime Commission).

The School Crime Supplement to the National Crime Victimization Survey collected national data on school crime in 1989 and 1995, as reported by students (Bastian and Taylor; Chandler et al.). Then, after a series of highly publicized school murders in 1997–1998, President Bill Clinton called on the Departments of Justice and Education to produce an annual report on school violence. One response of the statistical agencies of the two departments was to plan a more regularly conducted School Crime Supplement to the National Crime Victimization Survey, beginning in 1999 and scheduled for every two years thereafter. Another is a new biennial school-based survey starting in 2000 that collects data on crime and discipline problems in U.S. schools. Still another is an annual statistical report on a broad range of indicators of school crime and safety that will supplement the annual report on school safety aimed at the general public; these reports were first produced in 1998 (Kaufman et al.).

The victims

Since the systematic data on school crime were mainly derived from surveys of *personal* victimization, less is known about school crimes in which the victim was the school collectively than about crimes against students or teachers. The National Institute of Education estimated the annual cost of vandalism in American schools at $200 million, but these reports from principals about vandalism in the late 1970s were less complete and less trustworthy than the data from students and teachers about their own experiences with crimes (U.S. Department of Health, Education, and Welfare). The principals' accounts of offenses against public order known to them—drug sales, intoxication, false fire alarms, and bomb threats—and of theft of school property, including larcenies that resulted from burglaries, were also less reliable than victim reports on personal experiences.

The following conclusions can be drawn from the available data about the characteristics of individual victims:

1. Students are more frequently the victims of violent crimes in school than are teachers. However, "robbery" of a student may mean extortion of lunch money or bus passes by fellow students, whereas robbery of a teacher is more often perpetrated by youthful intruders and accompanied by gratuitous violence.
2. Male students are more than twice as likely to be victims of both robbery and assault than female students.
3. In 1976, when data for the nationwide Safe Schools study was being collected, the rate of violent victimizations in junior high schools was twice as high as the rate of violent victimizations in senior high schools (U.S. Department of Health, Education, and Welfare). In 1989 and 1995 the Bureau of Justice Statistics found that violent victimizations continued to occur at twice the rate in junior as in senior high schools (Bastian and Taylor; Chandler et al.). But the notion that high schools are safer than junior high schools from everyday school violence has been challenged by a small study of school violence by Louis Harris and Associates, conducted in 1993, which contradicted the findings of the larger studies; it indicated that high school violence was at least as prevalent as junior high school violence and perhaps worse

(Louis Harris and Associates). Even assuming that the larger studies are correct and that there is more violence in junior high schools, without detailed self-report data it is not possible to choose between two inferences that might be drawn from the differential rate of victimization at different school levels: first, that junior high school is a violent stage of youth development and that youngsters grow more peaceful as they pass into the high school years; and second, that some junior high school youngsters are violent but that these antisocial youngsters tend to drop out gradually so that high schools are safer, on the average, than junior high schools.

4. Younger, less experienced teachers are more likely to be attacked or robbed than older colleagues.
5. Minority students are more likely to be attacked or robbed at school than white students. This is probably because they are more likely to attend schools with higher rates of violence, located in less affluent neighborhoods. The greater the proportion of minority students in a school, the higher the rate of attacks on, and robberies of, both students and teachers.
6. The larger the school, the more extensive the vandalism. The bigger pool of potential perpetrators and the anonymity in a large school may explain the relationship between the dollar value of school property losses and school size.

The perpetrators

Although we lack self-report data from perpetrators, victims of school crime have been able to provide some descriptive information about perpetrators because, especially with violent offenses, victims have close and memorable contacts with those who prey on them. Conclusions about offenders, based on victim reports, include the following:

1. The majority of perpetrators of violent school crimes are recognized by their victims. This suggests that most of the offenders are fellow students, not intruders from the outside community. However, when the victims of school crime in large cities are considered separately, the majority of the perpetrators are unknown to the victims, partly because of the anonymity of large

urban schools where even enrolled students attend irregularly and partly because intruders contribute significantly to school violence in large cities. Intruders are not much older, on the average, than students, as nearly as the victims can judge.
2. A greater proportion of the violence directed at teachers than at students is committed by intruders, especially in inner-city schools. Parents and other relatives of students are a special category of intruder and are responsible for some assaults on teachers and other staff members.
3. The bulk of the perpetrators of school crime are male youths.
4. An appreciable portion of the robberies and assaults of both teachers and students (about 25%) is perpetrated by groups of three or more offenders.
5. The majority of perpetrators of school violence in large cities in the 1979 study were identified by the teacher and student victims as black males, even though in the twenty-six cities surveyed, blacks comprised only 29 percent of the general school population at that time.
6. According to student reports in the 1995 survey, only 0.1 of 1 percent of male students (and virtually no female students) said that they brought guns to school. However, more than 12 percent of the students of both sexes said that they knew students who brought guns to school and about half that number actually saw a student with a gun in school. Public schools in the central cities had considerably more guns than private schools or public schools outside of central cities, as might be expected.
7. The School Crime Supplements to the National Crime Victimization Survey of 1989 and 1995 went beyond victimization questions to ask respondents about bringing weapons to school themselves as well as knowledge of other students who brought them. But apart from the weapons questions, this large-scale survey, like the other earlier school victimization surveys, avoided asking student respondents self-report questions about their own rule violations or criminal behavior.
8. Only about 40 percent of sixth-grade students reported in both 1989 and 1995 that illegal drugs are readily available in their schools, but by the seventh grade a majority report easy availability of illegal drugs, and

the proportion rises monotonically until the twelfth grade, where it exceeds 80 percent. These same studies reported more violent victimizations in junior high schools than in senior high schools. Drug availability and violence do not necessarily go hand in hand.

9. According to teacher unions and the reports of big-city boards of education, 5 to 10 percent of enrolled students produce almost all of the violence. If indeed a small proportion of the student population is responsible for the school crime problem, identifying such troublemakers and putting them into special schools or special programs could make all schools safe (Shanker).

The causes of school crime

Any specific offense stems from both the personality of the offender and his sociocultural milieu. In addition, those sociocultural factors conducive to school crime tend to operate more strongly on disturbed personalities.

Personality causes. The personalities of some children predispose them to rule-violative behavior in the school setting, and especially to aggressive violence. Formerly, such children were expelled or given lengthy suspensions from public schools. This is less likely to happen today, for two reasons. First, the Education for All Handicapped Children Act of 1975 (Pub. L. 94–142, 89 Stat. 773, codified in scattered sections of 20 U.S.C.) stipulates that every handicapped child is entitled to a free public education and also that such an education shall be provided in the least restrictive educational setting (Hewett and Watson). Since emotionally disturbed children are considered handicapped, they are entitled to education in the mainstream along with physically handicapped children. Second, the Supreme Court held in *Goss v. Lopez* (419 U.S. 565 (1975)) that a state enacting a compulsory attendance law is obliged to educate children until the age specified in the law is reached; and that the school's obligations are greater for students in danger of expulsion or suspension for more than ten days than for students subject to less severe disciplinary penalties. The combined impact of the Education for All Handicapped Children Act and the Court ruling is that it became difficult to remove violent students younger than sixteen years of age from public schools (Toby, 1983). Such students therefore continue contributing to school crime.

Sociocultural causes. In the 1990s, public schools probably contained a higher proportion of violence-prone emotionally disturbed children than was the case a generation earlier. But contemporary schools also contained a higher proportion of students without diagnosed emotional handicaps who behaved in a manner that would have been unacceptable a generation earlier. Both changes were facilitated by a more liberal cultural climate that placed greater emphasis on children's rights, including the rights of children accused of school crimes (Toby, 1980).

This liberal cultural climate complicates the general problem of social control over potential misbehavior. The larger the school and the more anonymous its students and teachers, the less affected the students are by expressions of disapproval from teachers and even from classmates (Toby, 1998). In addition, schools in modern societies tend to be isolated physically and psychologically from parents and others in the local community whose reactions are important to students. Paradoxically, the professionalization and specialization of education increase the isolation of schools from local communities and thereby increase the probability of student misbehavior.

Furthermore, the trend has been to raise the age to which school attendance is compulsory, on the assumption that all children need a longer period of education in order to participate in an information-oriented society. However, there may be a downside to compulsory attendance. While some kids are unhappy in school for academic reasons, others, such as those who perpetrated violence at Columbine High School, in a middle-class suburb of Denver, experience acute social and personal crises. After Eric Harris and Dylan Klebold shot to death a teacher, a dozen of their schoolmates, and themselves at school in the spring of 1999, newspapers and TV stations speculated on where responsibility for this tragedy lay. But an obvious question was not raised: Why, if these two students were so miserable at school, did they not drop out and get jobs? A fresh setting just might have given them a new lease on life. Apparently the social stigma of dropping out of high school makes that option unthinkable in middle-class suburbs.

Kids in inner-city high schools are more likely than kids in middle-class suburbs to drop out when schoolwork does not enjoy sufficient parental or peer group support or when individual circumstances interfere with acquiring academic skills. In a sense they are less trapped than middle-class kids in suburban schools. But the high dropout rate of the inner city is deplored and inner-city kids too are under pressure—formal pressure from compulsory attendance laws and informal dropout-prevention arguments from teachers, parents, and the larger society—to remain enrolled whether they find school meaningful or not. Thus, inner-city and suburban schools both contain unwillingly enrolled students. In inner-city secondary schools the main consequence of containing a substantial population of involuntary students who lack a stake in behavioral conformity (Toby, 1957) is an undermining of the educational process. This increases the likelihood of low-level chronic crime and violence in such schools: everyday school violence rather than the explosive violence that sometimes erupts in middle-class schools.

Everyday school violence is fostered by the disorganized educational process of inner-city schools. When students do not perceive school as contributing to their futures, they have little incentive to be respectful to their teachers or to try to please them; they cope in various ways with being compelled to spend a good part of their time in an environment they dislike. Some truant. Some clown around for the amusement of their friends and themselves. Some come to school drunk or high on illegal drugs. Some wander the halls looking for friends to speak with or enemies to fight. Some assault other kids or extort money or valuables from them, partly for profit but also for kicks.

Unlike a prison, where a prisoner participates in the program willy-nilly, education in any meaningful sense depends on a cooperative relationship between teacher and student, not on the occasional presence of an enrolled student in a classroom. Professors Laurence Steinberg of Temple University, Bradford Brown of the University of Wisconsin, and Sandford Dornbusch of Stanford University conducted a massive study of twelve thousand students in nine high schools in Wisconsin and northern California from 1937 to 1990. They described a substantial minority of students in American high schools as being "disengaged" from the educational enterprise, which they defined as follows:

Disengaged students . . . do only as much as it takes to avoid getting into trouble. They do not exert much effort in the classroom, are easily distracted during class, and expend little energy on in-school or out-of-school assignments. They have a jaded, often cavalier attitude toward education and its importance to their future

success or personal development. When disengaged students are in school, they are clearly just going through the motions. When they are not in school, school is the last thing on their mind. (Steinberg, p. 15)

Steinberg, Brown, and Dornbusch were primarily interested in academic achievement, not in school violence, but the two are related. When the proportion of disengaged students in a high school is small, the educational process suffers but teachers are able to maintain control in the classrooms, corridors, and lunchrooms. When the proportion of disengaged students in a school is high, the school tips into disorder, and everyday school violence becomes endemic.

A complementary problem in schools with high proportions of disengaged students is disengaged teachers. One consequence of having disengaged students still enrolled in high schools but making no effort to learn anything is that teachers get discouraged. It is difficult to teach a lesson that depends on material taught yesterday or last week when an appreciable number of students are not in class regularly or fail to pay attention when they do come. Eventually these circumstances lead some teachers to "burn out," that is, to despair at the seemingly hopeless task of stuffing ideas into the heads of uninterested students (Dworkin). Others retire early, change to another profession, or take jobs in private or parochial schools at a cut in pay. Thus, teacher turnover rates are high, especially in inner-city schools with substantial proportions of internal dropouts, sometimes called "stayins" (Toby, 1989). New York City, for example, constantly has to hire new teachers (or substitute teachers) to replenish those who abandon their jobs. Of course some public school teachers hold on grimly, taking as many days off as they are entitled to.

But burned-out teachers lose effectiveness at teaching those in their classes amenable to education; this probably partly explains the greater satisfaction of students and their parents with charter schools and with private and parochial schools available through voucher programs than with public schools (Coleman, Hoffer, and Kilgore; Coleman and Hoffer; Peterson and Hassel). Burned-out teachers are also ineffective at preventing student misbehavior. The public thinks of teachers primarily as educators, not as agents of control. Teachers themselves tend to downplay their disciplinary role. Some object to hall or cafeteria duty on the grounds that they are not policemen. If pressed, however, teachers will agree that control of the class is a prerequisite for education.

Whatever the reasons for the reluctance of individual teachers to admonish misbehaving students, partly out of fear for their own safety, partly out of the desire to be popular, this reluctance implies at least partial abandonment of their role as guardians of school order. When teachers see student misbehavior and turn away to avoid the necessity of a confrontation, adult control over students diminishes at school, thereby encouraging student misbehavior that might otherwise not occur. In short, teachers' reluctance to admonish misbehaving students may be partly the *cause* of the high level of disorder in some schools as well as its effect. The *formal* controls that have developed in big-city schools are a partial result of the breakdown of *informal* social controls over students, such as the expression of teacher approval or disapproval. Informal controls still work quite well in the smaller schools of smaller communities.

Instead of the natural peacekeepers, teachers, preventing disorder and even violence from breaking out, many school systems have resorted to security guards, and some schools also have metal detectors to screen for knives and guns. In the mid 1990s, the District of Columbia school system employed 250 security officers—along with metal detectors in place in 31 schools. A few years later, New York City employed 3,200 security officers, as well as metal detectors. Security guards and metal detectors *are* useful for inner-city schools that need protection against invading predators from surrounding violent neighborhoods and to break up fights that teachers are afraid to tackle. But security programs cannot be the *main* instrument for preventing student misbehavior in public secondary schools because security guards are not ordinarily in classrooms where teachers are alone with their students. Furthermore, there are never enough security guards to maintain order in hallways or gyms or cafeterias or to prevent assaults or robberies by their mere presence. In January 1992, while Mayor Dinkins was at Thomas Jefferson High School in Brooklyn, New York, to deliver a speech, accompanied by bodyguards and security guards, two students were fatally shot by an angry fifteen-year-old classmate (Toby, 1992). In short, security guards constitute a second line of defense; they cannot by themselves provide a disciplined environment within which the educational process can proceed effectively.

Involuntary students and a paucity of effective adult guardians help to explain why everyday school violence is so difficult to control in public secondary schools in the United States. But there is a third factor: the official curriculum sponsored by boards of education, principals, and teachers does not monopolize student activity. A large public secondary school is not only an educational institution; for students without strong academic interests it is more like a bazaar, a place where a multiplicity of activities are available for students interested in them: history and geography, yes, but also football, basketball, the student newspaper, chess, romance, sex, extortion from fellow students, and opportunities to make teachers' lives as difficult as possible. Although adults think of the school as an educational opportunity, the education that students take advantage of may be quite different from that envisioned in the formal curriculum. At school students learn lessons that teachers do not teach them.

The term "extracurricular" presupposes that clubs and sports supplement rather than displace the paramount academic pursuits of enrolled students. For most students, especially those who anticipate applying to college, extracurricular interests show that they are well-rounded persons. However, for some students the extracurricular activities take the place of the academic curriculum; the football or basketball player who has no interest in academic subjects is the usual example, but interests in drama or the chorus or the newspaper can also come at the expense of academic achievement. But at least these activities are recognized as legitimate by school authorities. There are, however, other offerings that are by no stretch of the imagination legitimate.

Certainly no school would say that armed robbery is a curriculum offering in its school. But insofar as there is a tradition of predatory extortion by gangs or cliques against weak and fearful schoolmates, some students rehearse the process of preying on their fellows until they become quite skillful at it. In effect, they learn to rob at school. Alcohol and drugs constitute another illegitimate curriculum among the many that compete for student attention. Student interest in drugs and alcohol feeds a counterculture hostile to academic effort, which in turn undermines the authority of teachers and reduces their ability to control student misbehavior.

The effects of school crime

An obvious effect of school crime is a fear reaction from persons who study or work in school buildings. Although crime is a problem in the neighborhoods from which students, teachers, and other staff members come, it seems worse in the schools, especially in the case of violent offenses. This is partly because members of the school community must expose themselves daily to whatever threats exist, since their obligations require their presence in the school. In response, teachers, students, and parents urge boards of education to allocate funds for collective protection: for security guards, for intercoms to facilitate the summoning of help, and for related technological resources. Thus, another effect of school crime is to increase the cost of operating the school system. Less measurable than the additional expense is the reduced morale of students, teachers, and staff members exposed to personal danger and potential theft. As a result, schools with serious crime problems have difficulty in retaining students and teachers. Parents enroll their children elsewhere—in parochial, private, charter, and suburban schools. The loss of students is a serious problem because those students who transfer tend to be more educationally oriented and consequently their departure lowers the academic standards of the schools they leave. But the loss of experienced, effective teachers is worse. Additionally, substitutes are difficult to recruit in a low-morale, high-crime school (Archibold).

Since school crime is concentrated in public schools, one of its effects is to contribute to dissatisfaction with public education. This dissatisfaction is partly a direct consequence of crime—parents dislike sending their children to unsafe schools—and partly an indirect consequence: it is more difficult to maintain order in schools with high crime rates, and disorder means that students do not learn as much. A study of students at more than a thousand public, parochial, and private high schools throughout the United States revealed that students at public high schools learned less on the average than students at parochial and private schools (Coleman, Hoffer, and Kilgore). The study attributed this difference to the less orderly atmosphere in public schools, which had more truancy, more cutting of classes. Thus, school crime contributes to dissatisfaction with the public schools by making the schools more expensive and by creating a disorderly, fear-ridden atmosphere that undermines academic achievement.

Remedial measures to reduce school crime

A possible strategy for reducing school crime and violence builds on three sociocultural facilitators of crime that may be amenable to change:

1. *Giving high-school-age youngsters a choice between attending high school and dropping out with an option to return later.* This deals with the entrapment problem. Students disengaged from school might go to work and return to a regular high school program more amenable to school discipline when they recognize that they need more education. A voluntary high school population will learn more, be happier, and is less likely to behave violently toward teachers and fellow students. Japanese high schools are voluntary and are not only successful in promoting academic achievement and school safety; they influence Japanese junior high school students to take schoolwork seriously because junior high school students must demonstrate by performance their admissibility into high school (Rohlen).

2. *Introducing adults with more conventional values into high schools to buttress the authority of teachers and thereby to serve as guardians of order.* Chicago's DuSable High School, an all-black school close to a notorious public housing project, demonstrated the practicality of offering the opportunity for repentant dropouts from the neighborhood to enroll as regular students (Wilkerson). Some of these adult students were embarrassed to meet their children in the hallways; some of their children were embarrassed that their parents were schoolmates; some of the teachers at the high school were initially skeptical about mixing teenagers and adults in classes. But everyone agreed that the adult students took education seriously, worked harder than the teenage students, and set a good example. These adult students were not in school to bolster the authority of teachers. That was merely a by-product of their presence. Although most adults who wish to return to school will not be able to do so during the regular school day, much can be gained by encouraging even a handful of adult dropouts to return to regular high school classes, especially in inner-city high schools where student disengagement is frequent.

Teachers who have a serious adult student or two in their classes are not alone with sullen or mutinous teenagers.

3. *Crowding out everyday school violence by increasing the vitality of the traditional academic curriculum.* At present the average number of hours of homework done by students each week in public high schools in the United States is much less than the average number of hours of homework done by private high school students (Coleman, Hoffer, and Kilgore, p. 104). Since by comparison with Japanese high school students, American students do hardly any homework at all, it seems feasible to increase the amount of homework expected of American public high school students. The most important reason for doing so is academic. But an incidental effect might be to reduce everyday school violence by competing more effectively with illegitimate curricula like substance abuse and crime.

JACKSON TOBY

See also EDUCATION AND CRIME; EXCUSE: INFANCY; JUVENILE AND YOUTH GANGS; JUVENILE JUSTICE: HISTORY AND PHILOSOPHY; JUVENILE JUSTICE: COMMUNITY TREATMENT; JUVENILE JUSTICE: INSTITUTIONS; JUVENILE JUSTICE: JUVENILE COURTS; JUVENILES IN THE ADULT SYSTEM; JUVENILE STATUS OFFENDERS; JUVENILE VIOLENT OFFENDERS; POLICE: HANDLING OF JUVENILES; PREVENTION: JUVENILES AS POTENTIAL OFFENDERS.

BIBLIOGRAPHY

ARCHIBOLD, RANDAL C. "Worst Schools Still Seeking 400 Teachers." *New York Times,* 22 August 1999. Section 1, p. 35.

BASTIAN, LISA D., and TAYLOR, BRUCE M. *School Crime: A National Crime Victimization Survey Report.* Washington, D.C.: Bureau of Justice Statistics, 1991.

CHANDLER, KATHRYN A., et al. *Students' Reports of School Crime: 1989 and 1995.* Washington, D.C. : U.S. Department of Education and U.S. Department of Justice, March 1998.

COLEMAN, JAMES S.; HOFFER, THOMAS; and KILGORE, SALLY. *High School Achievement: Public, Catholic, and Private Schools Compared.* New York: Basic Books, 1982.

COLEMAN, JAMES S., and HOFFER, THOMAS. *Public and Private High Schools: The Impact of Communities.* New York: Basic Books, 1987.

DWORKIN, ANTHONY G. *Teacher Burnout in the Public Schools: Structural Causes and Consequences for Children.* Albany, N.Y.: State University of New York Press, 1987.

GERSON, MARK. *In the Classroom: Dispatches from an Inner-City School That Works.* New York: Free Press, 1997.

HARRIS, LOUIS and Associates. *The Metropolitan Life Survey of the American Teacher 1993: Violence in America's Public Schools.* New York: Metropolitan Life Insurance Company, 1993.

Hawaii Crime Commission. *Violence and Vandalism in the Public Schools of Hawaii: A Report to the Hawaii State Legislature,* Vol. 1. Honolulu: The Commission, 1980.

HEWETT, FRANK M., and WATSON, PHILIP C. "Classroom Management and the Exceptional Learner." In *Classroom Management.* Edited by Daniel L. Duke. University of Chicago Press, 1979. Pages 301–332.

KAUFMAN, P., et al. *Indicators of School Crime and Safety, 1998.* Washington, D.C.: Departments of Education and Justice, 1998.

PETERSON, PAUL E., and HASSEL, BRIAN C., eds. *Learning from School Choice.* Washington, D.C.: Brookings Institution Press, 1998.

ROHLEN, THOMAS P. *Japan's High Schools.* Berkeley: University of California Press, 1983.

SHANKER, ALBERT. "Classrooms Held Hostage: The Disruption of the Many by the Few." *American Educator* (Spring 1995): 8–13, 47–48.

STEINBERG, LAURENCE. *Beyond the Classroom: Why School Reform Has Failed and What Parents Need to Do.* New York: Simon & Schuster, 1996.

TOBY, JACKSON. "Social Disorganization and Stake in Conformity: Complimentary Factors in the Predatory Behavior of Young Hoodlums." *Journal of Criminal Law, Criminology and Police Science* 48 (May–June 1957): 12–17.

———. "Crime in American Public Schools." *The Public Interest* 58 (1980): 18–42.

———. "Violence in School." *Crime and Justice: An Annual Review of Research,* Vol. 4. Edited by Norval Morris and Michael Tonry. University of Chicago Press, 1983. Pages 1–47.

———. "Of Dropouts and Stayins: The Gershwin Approach." *Public Interest* 95 (spring 1989): 3–13.

———. "To Get Rid of Guns in Schools, Get Rid of Some Students." *Wall Street Journal,* 3 March 1992. Section A, p. 14.

———. "Getting Serious about School Discipline." *Public Interest* 133 (fall 1998): 68–83.

United Federation of Teachers. "Report of the School Safety Department for the 1997–1998 School Year." New York: United Federation of Teachers, 1998.

U.S. Department of Health, Education, and Welfare. *Violent Schools—Safe Schools: The Safe School Study Report to the Congress.* Washington, D.C.: National Institute of Education, 1978.

U.S. Department of Justice. *Criminal Victimization in Urban Schools*. Prepared by Joan McDermott. Washington, D.C.: Department of Justice, 1979.

WILKERSON, ISABEL. "In School with Their Children, Parents Try Again." *New York Times*, 28 November 1993. Section 1, p. 1.

SCIENTIFIC EVIDENCE

The first American crime laboratories were established about 1930. The principal techniques used in these laboratories were fingerprinting, handwriting comparisons, toolmark and firearms ("ballistics") identifications, drug analysis, blood tests, and trace analysis (hair, fiber, and glass). However, by the late 1960s the nature of scientific evidence had changed dramatically; new techniques had been developed, and courts faced decisions about the admissibility of testimony based upon a much wider array of scientific techniques: sound spectrography ("voiceprint"), neutron activation, atomic absorption, electrophoretic blood testing, scanning electron microscopy, mass spectrometry, gas chromatography, and bite mark comparisons. Even fingerprint identification had moved into the high-tech age with laser technology for visualizing latent prints and powerful computers for searching databases including millions of sets of prints.

Contributing factors

Funding. Several factors may have contributed to this increased use of scientific evidence. At one time there was substantial funding for "forensic" science research—the application of science in a legal setting. The creation of the Law Enforcement Assistance Administration (LEAA) in 1968 undoubtedly played a significant role. In the 1970s the LEAA underwrote a number of research projects designed to encourage the forensic application of scientific knowledge, and the development of some techniques can be traced directly to this research. Voiceprint analysis is the most prominent example. Other funded projects dealt with blood analysis, blood flight characteristics (blood spatter evidence), trace metal detection, and the polygraph. Later, the F.B.I. spent considerable resources refining the forensic application of DNA, and the Bureau of Alcohol, Tobacco, and Firearms joined the F.B.I. in establishing computerized firearms comparison systems.

Supreme Court decisions. Some commentators attribute the expanded use of scientific evidence to another factor, namely, U.S. Supreme Court decisions of the 1960s, in which the Warren Court severely restricted the acquisition of evidence for criminal cases by traditional crime-solving techniques such as interrogations and lineups. There is some suggestion in the Supreme Court's own cases that the Court deliberately encouraged greater reliance on scientific techniques. For example, in one case the Court wrote: "Modern community living requires modern scientific methods of crime detection lest the public go unprotected" (*Breithaupt v. Abram*, 352 U.S. 432, 439 (1957)). In *Escobedo* the Court observed: "We have learned the lesson of history, ancient and modern, that a system of criminal law enforcement which comes to depend on the 'confession' will, in the long run, be less reliable and more subject to abuses than a system which depends on extrinsic evidence independently secured through skillful investigation" (*Escobedo v. Illinois*, 378 U.S. 478, 488–89 (1964)).

Interestingly, at the same time the Court was erecting constitutional barriers to the use of confessions and lineups, it was removing Fourth and Fifth Amendment obstacles to the use of scientific evidence. The most important case was *Schmerber v. California*, 384 U.S. 757 (1966). The Court, in an opinion by Justice Brennan, held that the privilege against compulsory self-incrimination applies only to testimonial evidence and not to physical evidence. Thus, the police could extract blood from Schmerber for blood-alcohol analysis without violating the Fifth Amendment privilege. This ruling had broader significance; the ruling also meant that handwriting exemplars, fingerprints, voice exemplars, and, later, biological samples for DNA testing could be compelled from a suspect without running afoul of the self-incrimination clause. Justice Brennan likewise authored *Warden v. Hayden*, 387 U.S. 294 (1967), in which the Supreme Court overruled its prior cases prohibiting the seizure of "mere evidence." Under the "mere evidence" rule the police could seize only contraband, instrumentalities of a crime, or fruits of a crime. Most scientific evidence, such as blood, hair, gunshot residues, and blood-stained clothing, would have been "mere evidence" and hence immune from seizure.

Technology. It is unclear that either of these reasons—research funding or Supreme Court decisions—fully explains the increased use of scientific evidence. The answer may be more basic. It is simply expectable that a society so dependent on science and technology should turn to such knowledge as a method of proof. With computer technology running modern businesses, magnetic resonance imaging (MRI) aiding medicine, and Nintendo and other electronic devices captivating children, no one should be surprised to see DNA evidence in the courtroom.

Novel scientific evidence

In any event, what is clear is that reliance on scientific proof has increased. One survey concluded: "About one quarter of the citizens who had served on juries which were presented with scientific evidence believed that had such evidence been absent, they would have changed their verdicts—from guilty to not guilty" (Peterson et al., p. 1748).

Voiceprints. During the last quarter of the twentieth century, each decade seemed to produce its own "novel" technique for identification. In the 1970s the admissibility of voice identification by spectrographic examination of speech samples, often referred to as "voiceprint" evidence, divided the courts. The technique was designed to identify a person's voice, often an important fact in telephone threats, extortion, and kidnaping cases. Even the name "voiceprint," which was initially used to describe this technique, sparked controversy because it suggested an unwarranted comparison with fingerprint identification. Some speech scientists concluded that the differences between these techniques "seem to exceed the similarities" (Bolt et al., p. 599). Although numerous early cases had admitted voiceprint evidence, a National Academy of Sciences report undermined the scientific basis for the technique: "Estimates of error rates now available pertain to only a few of the many combinations of conditions encountered in real-life situations. These estimates do not constitute a generally adequate basis for a judicial or legislative body to use in making judgments concerning the reliability and acceptability of aural-visual voice identification in forensic applications" (National Research Council, 1979, p. 60). This report, however, has not rendered voiceprint evidence inadmissible in all jurisdictions (*State v. Coon*, 974 P.2d 386 (Alaska 1999)).

Hypnotically-refreshed testimony. In the early 1980s hypnotically enhanced testimony became the focal point of the admissibility battles. The courts had rejected hypnotic evidence when first offered at trial (*People v. Ebanks*, 49 P. 1049, 1053 (Cal. 1897)). The issue remained dormant until the 1970s when "a dramatic rise in the use of hypnotism as an aid in criminal investigations"

occurred (*People v. Lucas*, 435 N.Y.S.2d 461, 462 (Sup. Ct. 1980)). After traumatic crimes, victims often experience difficulties recalling the details. Police decided to resort to hypnosis to help victims retrieve the memories. Indeed, it was "hailed as a major breakthrough in police investigation" (Orne et al., p. 171).

Several factors may have accounted for this trend. First, the leading case permitting hypnotically refreshed testimony was decided in 1968. (*Harding v. State*, 246 A.2d 302 (Md. App. 1968), *cert. denied*, 395 U.S. 949 (1969)). Second, by the 1960s professional organizations, notably the American Medical Association and the American Psychiatric Association, had recognized the validity of hypnosis for therapeutic purposes, such as psychotherapy, treatment of psychosomatic illnesses, and amnesia. Third, hypnotic induction is easily learned. "A police officer can become a reasonably skilled hypnotist in a few hours of practice, with or without formal instruction" (Diamond, p. 314). Fourth, a number of books and articles on hypnosis had advocated its use, often claiming that hypnosis yielded valuable leads in many investigations: "In 77% of cases, important information was elicited that had not been available by routine interrogation" (Reiser and Nielson, p. 76).

The early judicial decisions that considered the admissibility of hypnotically refreshed testimony took the position that hypnosis affects the credibility of the testimony but not its admissibility. Under this view, the use of hypnosis to stimulate recall is treated no differently than other methods of refreshing recollection. Accordingly, cross-examination, the presentation of expert testimony on the dangers of hypnosis, and cautionary instructions are thought adequate to both protect the defendant against unreliable evidence and enable a jury to evaluate the credibility of previously hypnotized witnesses. In retrospect, there seems little dispute that this approach rested on dubious scientific grounds, and by the early 1980s courts began to more closely scrutinize this type of testimony. In rejecting hypnotically enhanced testimony in *State v. Mack*, 292 N.W.2d 764, 768 (Minn. 1980), the Minnesota Supreme Court recognized that for hypnosis to be "therapeutically useful, it need not produce historically accurate memory." In therapy, the mental health expert is often more concerned about what the patient believes than in what actually occurred.

Two years later, the California Supreme Court identified several dangers of hypnotically enhanced testimony (*People v. Shirley*, 641 P.2d 775, *cert. denied*, 459 U.S. 860 (1982)). These dangers include hypersuggestibility and hypercompliance. In addition, there is an inability to distinguish accurate from inaccurate recall; neither the subject nor the hypnotist can differentiate between true memories and pseudomemories. Moreover, "a witness who is uncertain of his recollections before being hypnotized will become convinced by that process that the story he told under hypnosis is true and correct in every respect" (p. 803). There is, however, no correlation between confidence and accuracy in this context. The jury may find the testimony convincing precisely because the witness displays (unjustified) confidence in his or her demeanor on the stand. Finally, the danger of confabulation—filling in details from the imagination in order to make a memory more coherent and complete—is present. After much litigation, the majority of courts concluded that the dangers outweighed any possible benefit and adopted a per se rule of exclusion, albeit with some exceptions. Other courts left the admissibility decision to the trial judge, under what became known as the "totality of the circumstances" approach.

Many of these issues resurfaced in the 1990s with "repressed memory" cases. Perhaps the most publicized case was *Franklin v. Duncan*, 884 F. Supp. 1435 (N. Cal.), *aff'd*, 70 F.3d 75, 78 (9th Cir. 1995), where the defendant was convicted of a 1969 murder based on the testimony of his daughter. She did not recall the event until twenty years later following hypnosis. The conviction was overturned on constitutional, not evidentiary, grounds.

Social science research. During the 1980s, expert testimony based on social science research found its way into American courtrooms. The first inroad was evidence of battered wife syndrome (BWS). While being a battered woman by itself is no defense to homicide, the syndrome may assist a jury in understanding two elements of a self-defense claim: (1) the defendant's subjective fear of serious injury or death, and (2) the reasonableness of that belief. For example, the evidence may explain why a battered woman has not left her mate. According to the New Jersey Supreme Court, "[o]nly by understanding these unique pressures that force battered women to remain with their mates, despite their long-standing and reasonable fear of severe bodily harm and the isolation that being a battered woman creates, can a battered woman's state of

mind be accurately and fairly understood" (*State v. Kelly*, 478 A.2d 364, 372 (N.J. 1984)).

Another illustration is rape trauma syndrome (RTS), a phrase coined by Burgess and Holmstrom to describe the behavioral, somatic, and psychological reactions of rape and attempted rape victims. Other studies elaborated on the initial research, sometimes confirming the earlier studies and occasionally providing additional insights. "Subsequent research, which is much more rigorous, conceptualizes rape trauma in terms of specific symptoms rather than more general stages of recovery" (Frazier and Borgida, p. 299).

While BWS was primarily used by defense attorneys, RTS became an important tool for prosecutors. By the early 1980s prosecutors had begun to use this research in rape trials. RTS evidence was offered at trial for two different purposes: (1) to prove lack of consent by the alleged victim, and (2) to explain postincident conduct by a victim, such as delayed reporting of the incident, that a jury might perceive as inconsistent with the claim of rape and therefore impeaching. The courts divided over the first use but generally accepted the second use. In 1982 the Kansas Supreme Court in *State v. Marks*, 647 P.2d 1292, 1299 (Kan. 1982), became the first state supreme court to uphold the admission of RTS evidence. The court concluded: "An examination of the literature clearly demonstrates that the so-called 'rape trauma syndrome' is generally accepted to be a common reaction to sexual assault." Many other courts followed this precedent.

In contrast, courts rejecting RTS as proof of lack of consent disputed the scientific validity of the syndrome when offered for the first purpose. For example, in *People v. Bledsoe*, 681 P.2d 291 (Cal. 1984), the California Supreme Court noted that "rape trauma syndrome was not devised to determine the 'truth' or 'accuracy' of a particular past event—i.e., whether, in fact, a rape in the legal sense occurred—but rather was developed by professional rape counselors as a therapeutic tool, to help identify, predict and treat emotional problems experienced by the counselors' clients or patients" (p. 300). Thus, according to the court, although generally accepted by the scientific community for a therapeutic purpose, expert testimony on RTS was not generally accepted as a fact-finding technique "to prove that a rape, in fact, occurred" (p. 301).

Although the California Supreme Court rejected RTS evidence offered to prove lack of consent, it approved prosecution use of RTS evidence where the defendant attacked the victim's credibility and suggested to the jury that the victim's conduct after the incident was inconsistent with the claim of rape. In this situation, the court wrote, "expert testimony on rape trauma syndrome may play a particularly useful role by disabusing the jury of some widely held misconceptions about rape and rape victims, so that it may evaluate the evidence free of popular myths" (p. 298). Most courts accepted this position, admitting expert testimony to account for a victim's (1) passive resistance during a rape, (2) delay in reporting the crime, (3) failure to attempt to escape, and (4) calm demeanor after an attack. RTS evidence has also been introduced to explain that "in the context of a trust relationship, such as a doctor-patient relationship, some victims may return to the trusted relationship for further contact with the perpetrator of the assault" (*Commonwealth v. Mamay*, 553 N.E.2d 945, 951 (Mass. 1990)).

DNA profiling. We turn now to the late 1980s and 1990s. DNA (deoxyribonucleic acid) is a chemical messenger of genetic information, a code that gives both common and individual characteristics to people. Except for identical twins, no two individuals share the same DNA pattern. DNA is found in every body cell with a nucleus. Red blood cells lack a nucleus. However, blood may still be used as evidence because white cells and other components of blood have DNA. With few exceptions, DNA does not vary from cell to cell. Each cell contains the entire genetic code, although each cell reads only the part of the code that it needs to perform its job. Thus, blood obtained from a suspect can be compared with semen or hair cells from a crime scene. In the World Trade Center bombing prosecution, an F.B.I. expert matched saliva on an envelope sent by the terrorists to the *New York Times* with the DNA of one of the defendants.

In effect, the United States imported DNA typing from the United Kingdom. In 1985 Dr. Alec Jeffreys of the University of Leicester, England, recognized the utility of DNA profiling in criminal cases. Its first use in American courts came the following year. The initial appellate case, *Andrews v. State*, 533 So. 2d 841 (Fla. App. 1988), *rev. denied*, 542 So. 2d 1332 (Fla. 1989), was reported in 1988. By January 1990, forensic DNA evidence had been admitted in at least 185 cases by 38 states and the U.S. military. At the close of the twentieth century, DNA evidence, in one form or the other, was admissible in every state and federal circuit. These developments are

remarkable. No other scientific technique had gained such widespread acceptance so quickly. No other technique had been as complex or evolved so rapidly. DNA profiling raised issues at the cutting edge of modern science. New DNA technologies were introduced even as cases litigating the older procedures worked their way through the court system; there have already been three generations of tests—Restriction Fragment Length Polymorphism, Polymerase Chain Reaction, and the current state of the art, Short-Tandem Repeat (STR) analysis.

Finally, no other technique has been as potentially valuable. One court called DNA evidence the "single greatest advance in the 'search for truth'. . . since the advent of cross-examination" (*People v. Wesley*, 533 N.Y.S.2d 643, 644 (Co. Ct. 1988), *aff'd*, 633 N.E.2d 451 (N.Y. 1994)). Even its critics acknowledged that "[a]ppropriately carried out and correctly interpreted, DNA typing is possibly the most powerful innovation in forensics since the development of fingerprinting in the last part of the 19th Century" (Lewontin and Hartl, p. 1746).

Yet, much of the initial euphoria that accompanied the introduction of DNA was dispelled by *People v. Castro*, 545 N.Y.S.2d 985, 996 (Sup. Ct. 1989), the first reported case to successfully challenge DNA evidence. In *Castro* the court accepted the general validity of the DNA technique but ruled that the test results in *Castro* were inadmissible. The court found fault with the specific manner in which the analysts applied the technique and conducted the test. Later, the F.B.I.'s top DNA expert conceded these deficiencies: "The initial outcry over DNA typing standards concerned laboratory problems: poorly defined rules for declaring a match; experiments without controls; contaminated probes and samples; and sloppy interpretation of autoradiograms. Although there is no evidence that these technical failings resulted in any wrongful convictions, the lack of standards seemed to be a recipe for trouble" (Lander and Budowle, p. 735).

After *Castro* was decided, the National Academy of Science's National Research Council convened a committee to study the forensic use of DNA. That committee's 1992 report recommended stringent laboratory procedures—written laboratory protocols, objective and quantitative procedures for identifying patterns, clearly defined procedures for declaring a match, and methods for identifying potential artifacts (National Research Council, 1992, pp. 52–55). The report bemoaned the fact that there was no mandatory proficiency testing. The NAS report added: "No laboratory should let its results with a new DNA typing method be used in court, unless it has undergone such proficiency testing via blind trials" (p. 55). The publication of the National Academy of Science report did not resolve all the issues. Indeed, it sparked a heated controversy, which an experienced prosecutor would later describe as follows: "[S]cientists fighting for principle displayed an intensity, even a savagery, unmatched by the most aggressive lawyers" (Levy, p. 106). The report recommended statistical techniques designed to ensure that any random match probabilities quoted in court were relatively conservative. Critics charged that these techniques were nothing more than policy judgments masquerading as science. The criticisms of its first report were so forceful that the NAS commissioned a second report, published in 1996. The 1992 "report did not eliminate all controversy. Indeed, in propounding what the committee regarded as a moderate position [for dealing with the statistical issues] the report itself became the target of criticism from scientists and lawyers on both sides of the debate on DNA evidence in the courts" (National Research Council, 1996, p. 1).

This episode illustrates the difficulties courts face when trying to understand complicated scientific procedures and their suitability for forensic use. In 2000, DNA evidence is routinely admitted at trial. The importance of DNA profiling was underscored by a Department of Justice report that discussed the exoneration of twenty-eight convicts through the use of DNA technology—some of whom had been sentenced to death (Connors et al.). By mid-1999, more than seventy convicts had obtained postconviction relief based on exculpatory DNA test results.

Frye v. United States

When the courts began confronting new and more sophisticated scientific evidence in the late 1960s and early 1970s, they needed a legal test for determining admissibility. Three different approaches emerged. One treats the validity of the underlying principle and the validity of the technique as aspects of relevancy. A second approach, ultimately adopted by the U.S. Supreme Court, is known as the reliability test. (The relevancy and reliability approaches are discussed below.) A third approach, which requires the proponent of a novel technique to establish its general acceptance in the scientific community,

is based on *Frye v. United States*, 293 F. 1013 (D.C. Cir. 1923), a federal case decided by the District of Columbia Circuit in 1923. In *Frye* the D.C. Circuit considered the admissibility of testimony based on the systolic blood pressure test, a precursor of the modern polygraph. The court announced that a novel scientific technique "must be sufficiently established to have gained general acceptance in the particular field in which it belongs" (p. 1014). The court found that the systolic test had "not yet gained such standing and scientific recognition among physiological and psychological authorities" (ibid.). Thus, under the *Frye* standard, it is not enough that a qualified individual expert, or even several experts, testify that a particular technique is valid. *Frye* imposes a special burden: the technique must be "generally" accepted by the relevant scientific community.

The *Frye* court's brief two-page opinion offered no explanation for adopting the "general acceptance" test. As a federal decision, it did not apply to state courts; for that matter, it was not binding on any of the other federal circuit courts. For the next five decades, *Frye* remained largely dormant; it was rarely cited, and then, mostly in polygraph cases. As late as 1972, a federal district court correctly observed that "[t]here is notably an absence of any discussion of the 'general acceptance' standard in federal decisions" (*United States v. Zeiger*, 350 F. Supp. 685, 687 n. 6 (D.D.C.), *rev'd*, 475 F.2d 1280 (D.C. Cir. 1972)).

This state of affairs was understandable. For most of the period between the rendition of *Frye* and the 1970s, the scientific techniques confronting the courts did not raise significant *Frye* issues—the admissibility of novel scientific evidence. A 1966 amendment to Federal Criminal Rule 16, which governs the pretrial disclosure of scientific reports in criminal litigation, provides some insight into the types of expert testimony used during this period. The accompanying committee note mentioned reports of "fingerprint and handwriting comparisons." Ballistics, blood tests, paint, fibers, and autopsies could be added to this list. None of these techniques presented *Frye* issues; they were traditional techniques, long accepted by the courts.

Over the years, the general acceptance standard gradually became the overwhelming majority rule in both federal and state courts until 1993 when the U.S. Supreme Court rejected *Frye* in *Daubert v. Merrell Dow Pharmaceuticals, Inc.*, 509 U.S. 579 (1993). By 1993, *Frye* had been applied to voiceprints, neutron activation, gunshot residue tests, fingerprints, bite mark comparisons, psycholinguistics, truth serum, scanning electron microscopic analysis, hypnosis, blood analysis, hair analysis, intoxication testing, instrumental analysis, and numerous other forensic techniques. Later, the *Frye* test would be applied to DNA evidence as well as to social science techniques such as the battered woman syndrome, rape trauma syndrome, child abuse accommodation syndrome, profile evidence, and psychiatric testimony.

Rationale. The stated justification for the general acceptance standard is that it tends to indirectly ensure the reliability of scientific evidence. The D.C. Circuit, the progenitor of the *Frye* test, later stated in rejecting voiceprint evidence that the "requirement of general acceptance in the scientific community assures that those most qualified to assess the general validity of a scientific method will have the determinative voice" (*United States v. Addison,* 498 F.2d 741, 743–44 (D.C. Cir. 1974)).

Application of *Frye* test. The *Frye* rule was not without its detractors. One criticism focused on the difficulties involved in applying the test. The general acceptance test requires a two-step analysis: first, identifying the field in which the underlying principle falls, and second, determining whether that principle has been generally accepted by members of the identified field. Neither step is free of difficulties.

The first step can be problematic. Many scientific techniques do not fall within the domain of a single academic discipline or professional field. Consequently, selecting the proper field may prove troublesome. For example, "voiceprint" analysis requires a knowledge of anatomy, physiology, physics, psychology, and linguistics. Similarly, DNA involves several disciplines— molecular biology, genetics, environmental biology, physical anthropology, evolutionary biology, population genetics, and statistics. The selection of the field, moreover, will often affect whether a novel technique satisfies the general-acceptance test. If polygraph examiners are selected as the relevant field, polygraph results would be admissible.

Once the relevant field has been identified, the second step requires determining whether the technique has been "generally accepted" by members of that field. The percentage of those in the field who must accept the technique has never been clearly specified. For instance, one court has defined general acceptance as "widespread; prevalent; extensive though not universal" (*United States v. Zeiger,* 350 F. Supp. 685, 688 (D.D.C.), *rev'd,* 475 F.2d 1280 (D.C. Cir. 1972)). Another court conceded that "a degree of scientific divergence of view is inevitable," without elaborating on how much divergence would be fatal to admissibility (*Commonwealth v. Lykus,* 327 N.E.2d 671, 678 n.6 (Mass. 1975)).

An additional issue arises in multiple-step procedures such as DNA profiling, which consists of a molecular biology component (declaring a match) and a population genetics component (statistical calculations). Are both aspects subject to the general-acceptance requirement? A related issue concerns subsequent developments or variants of a technique. For example, the general acceptance of stationary radar should not automatically lead to the admissibility of moving radar, in which the patrol car as well as the suspect car is in motion. Similarly, general acceptance of RFLP(DNA) does not mean that PCR(DNA), or even a particular type of PCR such as DQalpha, is necessarily admissible.

Moreover, some jurisdictions following *Frye* do not apply the general-acceptance test to all types of "scientific" evidence. For example, a California appellate court refused to apply the *Frye* test to bitemark comparisons (*People v. Marx,* 126 Cal. Rpt. 350, 355–56 (App. 1975)). The court reasoned that bite mark evidence did not require blind acceptance by the jury. The basis on which the expert reached his conclusions— models, photographs, and X rays—are shown to the trier of fact, and the trier could therefore independently second-guess the expert's conclusions. Similarly, the Arizona Supreme Court has ruled that the "*Frye* analysis is not applicable to footprints [comparisons]" (*State v. Murray,* 906 P.2d 542, 562 (Ariz. 1995), *cert. denied,* 518 U.S. 1011 (1996)). In short, many jurisdictions that profess adherence to *Frye* exempt some techniques from scrutiny under *Frye.*

Criticisms. In addition to the attacks concerning the difficulties of applying the *Frye* test discussed above, the test has been criticized on other grounds. Another criticism of the general-acceptance test is that it exacts too high a cost and often bars the admission of reliable evidence. Critics of *Frye* assert that the delay to permit the technique to win general acceptance "precludes too much relevant evidence for purposes of the fact determining process" (*United States v. Sample,* 378 F. Supp. 43, 53 (E.D. Pa. 1974)). In contrast, courts favoring the general acceptance test recognize its conservative nature but believe that this aspect does not exact an "unwarranted cost" (*United States v. Addison*, 498 F.2d 741, 743 (D.C. Cir. 1974)). The California Supreme Court has stated that the "primary advantage. . .of the *Frye* test lies in its essentially conservative nature" (*People v. Kelly*, 549 P.2d 1240, 1245 (Cal. 1976)). The criticism that the *Frye* test is too conservative begs a question. The question is not whether the *Frye* test is conservative (which it is), but whether other standards would better accomplish the objective of preventing the admission of unreliable scientific evidence.

Still another criticism of *Frye* is that it rests upon an invalid assumption, namely, that jurors are overwhelmed by scientific evidence. For example, in excluding voiceprint evidence under the *Frye* test, the D.C. Circuit asserted that scientific evidence may "assume a posture of mystic infallibility in the eyes of a jury of laymen" (*United States v. Addison*, 498 F.2d 741, 744 (D.C. Cir. 1974)). Commentators, however, have argued that the available empirical research on jury reaction to different types of scientific evidence does not support the D.C. Circuit's assertion (Rogers and Ewing; Imwinkelried, 1983).

Finally, "[p]erhaps the most important flaw in the *Frye* test is that by focusing attention on the general acceptance issue, the test obscures critical problems in the use of a particular technique" (Giannelli, 1980, p. 1226). There is a great diversity in the underlying bases of expert testimony, varying from the complexity of DNA to the social science–based research of rape trauma syndrome. The *Frye* "one-test-fits-all" approach is too blunt an instrument.

Relevancy test

One alternative approach to *Frye* is to treat scientific evidence in the same way as other evidence, weighing its probative value against countervailing dangers and considerations. Charles McCormick, a noted evidence scholar, advocated this position. In his 1954 text, he wrote that "Any relevant conclusions which are supported by a qualified expert witness should be received unless there are other reasons for exclusion. Particularly, its probative value may be overborne by the familiar dangers of prejudicing or misleading the jury, unfair surprise and undue consumption of time" (pp. 363–364).

In practice, however, the relevancy test affords inadequate assurance of the reliability of scientific evidence; this test often means that qualifying the expert automatically renders testimony about the technique admissible. Even if the expert is qualified, the expert may be relying on a bogus theory or technique. "The major flaw in the relevancy analysis . . . is its failure to recognize the distinctive problems of scientific evidence. . . . [T]he judge frequently is forced to defer to an expert, thereby permitting admissibility based on the views of a single individual in some cases" (Giannelli, 1980, p. 1250).

Barefoot v. Estelle. *Barefoot v. Estelle*, 463 U.S. 880 (1983), a capital murder case decided by the Supreme Court in 1983, illustrates the weakness of the relevancy approach even though the case was decided on constitutional, rather than evidentiary, grounds. In the penalty phase, the prosecution offered psychiatric testimony concerning Barefoot's future dangerousness, a qualifying factor under the Texas death penalty statute. One psychiatrist, Dr. James Grigson, without ever examining Barefoot, testified that there was a "'one hundred percent and absolute' chance that Barefoot would commit future acts of criminal violence" (463 U.S. at 919). Barefoot challenged the admission of this evidence on constitutional grounds due to its unreliability.

In an amicus ("friend of the court") brief, the American Psychiatric Association (APA) stated that the "large body of research in this area indicates that, even under the best of conditions, psychiatric predictions of long-term future dangerousness are wrong in at least two out of every three cases" (p. 9). In a later passage, the brief noted that the "unreliability of psychiatric predictions of long term future dangerousness is by now an established fact within the profession" (p. 12). A substantial body of research supported the APA position.

Nevertheless, the Court rejected Barefoot's argument. According to the Court, "[n]either petitioner nor the [APA] suggests that psychiatrists are always wrong with respect to future dangerousness, only most of the time" (p. 901). In one passage the Court virtually adopts McCormick's relevancy approach. As a result, the *Barefoot* Court admitted evidence "at the brink of quackery" (Dix, p. 172). Justice Blackmun, who later authored the *Daubert* opinion, dissented. He noted that "[i]n the present state of psychiatric knowledge, this is too much for me. One may accept this in a routine lawsuit for money damages, but when a person's life is at stake . . . a requirement of greater reliability should prevail. In a capital case, the specious testimony of a psychiatrist, colored in the eyes of an impressionable jury by the inevitable untouchability of a medical specialist's words, equates with death itself" (p. 916). Even a proponent of capital punishment believed that the execution of Thomas Barefoot on 24 October 1984 was based on "junk science." One could favor the death penalty and "yet still recoil at the thought that a junk science fringe of psychiatry . . . could decide who will be sent to the gallows" (Huber, p. 220).

Reliability Test

A third admissibility test eventually emerged from the *Frye* debates; the new test rejected the *Frye* standard but demanded proof of reliability. The Supreme Court adopted this approach in 1993, ruling that the Federal Rules of Evidence had displaced the *Frye* test. The case, *Daubert v. Merrell Dow Pharmaceuticals, Inc.*, involved the admissibility of expert epidemiological testimony concerning whether Bendectin, an anti-nausea drug, causes birth defects. In place of *Frye*, the Court substituted a reliability test. The test, in the Court's view, derived from a federal statute, Evidence Rule 702, which uses the terms "scientific" and "knowledge." The Court embraced a classically Newtonian understanding of scientific methodology—the process of formulating a hypothesis and then engaging in experimentation or observation to falsify or validate the hypothesis. "[I]n order to qualify as 'scientific knowledge,' an inference or assertion must be derived by the scientific method. Proposed testimony must be supported by appropriate validation—i.e., 'good grounds,' based on what is known. In short, the requirement that an expert's testimony pertain to 'scientific knowledge' establishes a standard of evidentiary reliability" (p. 590). In performing this "gatekeeping role," the trial court may consider a number of factors. First, the court should determine whether the scientific theory or technique has been tested. Citing scientific authorities, the Court recognized that a hallmark of science is empirical testing. Second, whether a theory or technique had been subjected to peer review and publication is "a relevant, though not dispositive, consideration in assessing . . . scientific validity." The peer review and publication process increase the likelihood that flaws will be revealed. They thus serve as circumstantial evidence that the hypothesis has been validated by sound scientific methodology. Third, a technique's "known or potential rate of error" is a pertinent factor. Fourth, the "existence and maintenance of standards controlling the technique's operation" is another indicia of trustworthiness. Finally, "general acceptance" remains an important consideration. Although the Court rejected "general acceptance" as the sole criterion for admissibility as in the *Frye* test, it recognized its relevance in assessing the reliability of scientific evidence. Again, this factor can be important circumstantial evidence of the soundness of the research underlying the expert's hypothesis.

Although the *Daubert* decision was a civil case, it applied to federal criminal trials as well. Its ancestry can be traced to civil litigation concerning toxic torts (asbestos, Agent Orange, and silicone breast implants) in the 1980s. *Frye* had rarely been applied to civil cases until the 1980s. At this point, the *Frye* test, which had previously been championed by the criminal defense bar, was adopted by big business in their battle against "junk science." A plank against junk science appeared in the Republican platform in 1988; and President George Bush, by executive order, imposed a modified *Frye* test on Justice Department lawyers in civil cases. Inconsistently, the same Justice Department was advocating a lower standard, the complete rejection of *Frye*, in criminal DNA cases (Giannelli, 1993).

Application in the states. *Daubert*'s effect on state jurisdictions depends on several factors. As previously stated, *Daubert* rests on an interpretation of the Federal Rules of Evidence, a federal statute. As a statutory rather than a constitutional case, *Daubert* is not binding on the states, which are therefore free to continue to follow *Frye*. The state courts have that freedom even in the forty jurisdictions with evidence codes modeled after the Federal Rules, some of which still adhere to the *Frye* test. Although numerous jurisdictions have rejected *Frye* in favor of the *Daubert* approach, other courts have retained the *Frye* test. For example, the Arizona Supreme Court declined to follow *Daubert*, noting that it was "not bound by the United States Supreme Court's non-constitutional construction of the Federal Rules of Evidence when we construe the Arizona Rules of Evidence" (*State v. Bible*, 858 P.2d 1152, 1183 (Ariz. 1993), *cert. denied*, 511 U.S. 1046 (1994)). Indeed, *Frye* still has adherents in some of the most populous states—California, New York, Pennsylvania, Michigan, and Florida. Courts retaining *Frye* have found *Daubert* wanting. The Washington Supreme Court declared: "While *Frye* may be difficult to apply in some contexts, this is a result of the complexity of the particular science at issue, the extent to which the scientific community has made its view known, and the extent of any dispute in the scientific community. . . . Questions of admissibility of complex, controversial scientific techniques or methods, like those involving DNA evidence, are going to be difficult under either standard" (*State v. Copeland*, 922 P.2d 1304, 1314 (Wash. 1996)).

Post-*Daubert* issues. Although the *Daubert* decision resolved a number of significant issues, like most landmark cases, it left many questions unanswered. One question raised by the *Daubert* opinion is whether the Supreme Court intended its reliability test to be more permissive than the *Frye* test. There is some language in the opinion that points in this direction, and a number of courts have embraced this position. The polygraph cases are a good example. In *United States v. Posado*, 57 F.3d 428, 429 (5th Cir. 1995), the Fifth Circuit stated that "the rationale underlying this circuit's per se rule against admitting polygraph evidence did not survive *Daubert*." The court did not hold that polygraph evidence was admissible but only that admissibility should be left to the discretion of the trial judge.

There is, however, another view—that *Daubert* sets forth a different, but not necessarily less stringent, standard. Some language in *Daubert* supports this position, particularly the Court's emphasis on the "gatekeeper" function of the trial judge. Federal courts examining handwriting and hair analysis have questioned the admissibility of testimony based on these traditional techniques, thereby undercutting the notion that *Daubert* is a more liberal standard.

Technical evidence. In interpreting Rule 702, the Supreme Court in *Daubert* dealt only with "scientific" evidence. The epidemiological testimony offered in *Daubert* was purportedly scientific. Rule 702, however, also includes the terms "technical" and "specialized" knowledge. That alternate phrasing raised two issues: (1) whether *Daubert*'s reliability requirement extended to these other types of nonscientific expert testimony, and (2) if so, whether the factors set forth in *Daubert* for judging reliability applied in this context. In 1999, the Supreme Court in *Kumho Tire Co. v. Carmichael*, 526 U.S. 137 (1999), answered both questions in the affirmative. *Kumho* involved a civil case—a tire blowout accident, in which the Court upheld the trial court's decision to exclude engineering testimony concerning the cause of the blowout. The Court acknowledged that some of the *Daubert* factors might prove inappropriate in assessing the reliability of certain types of nonscientific testimony. The Court accorded trial judges discretion to select the factors to employ in evaluating the specific type of non-

scientific expertise. *Kumho* applies to criminal cases as well. Accordingly, the *Daubert* reliability requirement applies across the board to all expert evidence, for example, handwriting and hair comparisons.

Other developments

At the same time that DNA evidence was being closely scrutinized by the courts and *Kumho* was prompting renewed judicial interest in nonscientific expert testimony, several notorious cases of scientific malfeasance received extensive treatment in the news media (Giannelli, 1997). One case is illustrative. Fred Zain, the former head serologist of the West Virginia State Police crime laboratory, falsified conventional serological test results in as many as 134 cases from 1979 to 1989. Defendants, since exonerated, were sentenced to long prison terms based upon his testimony. A judicial inquiry concluded that "as a matter of law, any testimonial or documentary evidence offered by Zain at any time in any criminal prosecution should be deemed invalid, unreliable, and inadmissible" (*In re Investigation of the W. Va. State Police Crime Lab., Serology Div.*, 438 S.E.2d 501, 520 (W. Va. 1993)). In 1989, Zain accepted a serologist position with the County Medical Examiner's laboratory in San Antonio, where he performed DNA profiling and testified in death penalty cases. Another instance of misconduct involved New York State Troopers who tampered with fingerprint evidence.

Despite the publicity that the cases of intentional misconduct generated, there is good reason to believe that in at least some crime laboratories simple incompetence is a more prevalent problem—often traceable to inadequate funding (Giannelli, 1988). There is a widespread feeling that courts should rigorously police the reliability of proffered expert testimony to give the laboratories an even greater incentive to select trustworthy scientific tests and to use meticulous care in conducting the tests.

Conclusion

Scientific evidence is often superior to other types of evidence, such as eyewitness identifications and confessions. The Justice Department report of twenty-eight convicts released from prison during the 1990s due to exculpatory DNA evidence dramatizes this point. Most of these convictions were based on eyewitness identifications. One involved a mentally limited defendant who falsely confessed and then pled guilty to avoid the death penalty.

However, if the introduction of expert testimony is to enhance the fact-finding process, the courts must separate the wheat from the chaff. Forensic science is being scrutinized as never before. The "junk science" debate emanating from the civil docket is having a spillover effect on criminal litigation. The Supreme Court in *Daubert* and *Kumho* affirmed its determination to improve the quality of expert testimony in federal trials. In *Kumho*, the Court declared that the "objective of [*Daubert*'s gatekeeping] requirement is to ensure the reliability and relevancy of expert testimony. It is to make certain that an expert, whether basing testimony upon professional studies or personal experience, employs in the courtroom the same level of intellectual rigor that characterizes the practice of an expert in the relevant field" (526 U.S. at 152). One of the benefits of the DNA litigation is that these cases set high standards for the evaluation of scientific proof. Finally, Zain and similar misconduct cases have further fueled the drive for crime laboratory accreditation, examiner certification, and the standardization of forensic procedures.

PAUL C. GIANNELLI
EDWARD J. IMWINKELRIED

See also CIVIL AND CRIMINAL DIVIDE; CRIME CAUSATION: BIOLOGICAL THEORIES; CRIME CAUSATION: PSYCHOLOGICAL THEORIES; DIMINISHED CAPACITY; DOMESTIC VIOLENCE; EYEWITNESS IDENTIFICATION: PSYCHOLOGICAL ASPECTS; RAPE: BEHAVIORAL ASPECTS; RAPE: LEGAL ASPECTS; VIOLENCE.

BIBLIOGRAPHY

American Psychiatric Association. Brief Amicus Curiae, *Barefoot v. Estelle,* 463 U.S. 880 (1983).
BOLT, RICHARD H.; COOPER, FRANKLIN S.; DAVID, EDWARD E.; DENS, PETER B.; PICKETT, JAMES M.; and STEVENS, KENNETH N. "Speaker Identification by Speech Spectrograms; A Scientist's View of Its Reliability for Legal Purposes." *Journal of the Acoustical Society of America* 47 (1970): 597–612.
BURGESS, ANN WOLBERT, and HOLMSTROM, LYNDA LYTLE. "Rape Trauma Syndrome." *American Journal of Psychiatry* 131 (1974): 981–986.
CONNORS, EDWARD; LUNDREGAN, THOMAS; MILLER, NEAL; and MCEWEN, TOM. *Convicted by Juries, Exonerated by Science: Case Studies in the Use of DNA Evidence to Establish Innocence After Trial.* Washington, D.C.: National Institute of Justice, U.S. Department of Justice, 1996.
DIAMOND, BERNARD L. "Inherent Problems in the Use of Pretrial Hypnosis on a Prospective Witness." *California Law Review* 68 (1980): 313–349.
DIX, GEORGE E. "The Death Penalty, 'Dangerousness,' Psychiatric Testimony, and Professional Ethics." *American Journal of Criminal Law* 5 (1977): 151–215.
FRAZIER, PATRICIA A., and BORGIDA, EUGENE. "Rape Trauma Syndrome: A Review of Case Law and Psychological Research." *Law and Human Behavior* 16 (1992): 293–311.
GIANNELLI, PAUL. "The Admissibility of Novel Scientific Evidence: *Frye v. United States,* a Half-Century Later." *Columbia Law Review* 80 (1980): 1197–1250.
———. "The Admissibility of Laboratory Reports in Criminal Trials: The Reliability of Scientific Proof." *Ohio State Law Journal* 49 (1988): 671–701.
———. "'Junk Science': The Criminal Cases." *Journal of Criminal Law and Criminology* 84 (1993): 105–128.
———. "*Daubert*: Interpreting the Federal Rules of Evidence." *Cardozo Law Review* 15 (1994): 1999–2026.
———. "The Abuse of Scientific Evidence in Criminal Cases: The Need for Independent Crime Laboratories." *Virginia Journal of Social Policy and Law* 4 (1997): 439–478.
GIANNELLI, PAUL, and IMWINKELRIED, EDWARD. *Scientific Evidence.* 3d ed. Charlottesville, Va.: Lexis Law Publishing, 1999.
HUBER, PETER W. *Galileo's Revenge: Junk Science in the Courtroom.* New York: Basic Books, 1991.
IMWINKELRIED, EDWARD. "The Standard for Admitting Scientific Evidence: A Critique from the Perspective of Juror Psychology." *Villanova Law Review* 28 (1983): 554–571.
———. "The Next Step after *Daubert*: Developing a Similarly Epistemological Approach to Ensuring the Reliability of Nonscientific Expert Testimony." *Cardozo Law Review* 15 (1994): 2271–2294.
JEFFREYS, A. J.; WILSON, V.; and THEIN, S. L. "Individual-Specific 'Fingerprints' of Human DNA." *Nature* 316 (1985): 76–79.
LANDER, ERIC S., and BUDOWLE, BRUCE. "DNA Fingerprinting Dispute Laid to Rest." *Nature* 371 (1994): 735–738.
LEVY, HARLAN. *And the Blood Cried Out: A Prosecutor's Spellbinding Account of the Power of DNA.* New York: Basic Books, 1996.

LEWONTIN, RICHARD C., and HARTL, DANIEL L. "Population Genetics in Forensic DNA Typing." *Science* 254 (1991): 1745.

MALETSKOS, CONSTANTINE J., and SPIELMAN, STEPHEN J. "Introduction of New Scientific Methods in Court." In *Law Enforcement, Science & Technology.* Edited by S. A. Yefsky. U.S. Office of Law Enforcement Assistance. Washington, D.C.: Thompson Book Company, 1967. Pages 957–964.

McCORMICK, CHARLES T. *Law of Evidence.* St. Paul, Minn.: West Publishing Company, 1954.

National Research Council. *On the Theory and Practice of Voice Identification.* Washington, D.C.: National Academy Press, 1979.

———. *The Evaluation of Forensic DNA Evidence.* Washington, D.C.: National Academy Press, 1996.

———. *DNA Technology in Forensic Science.* Washington, D.C.: National Academy Press, 1992.

Office of Technology Assessment, U.S. Congress. *Genetic Witness: Forensic Uses of DNA Tests.* Washington, D.C.: U.S. Government Printing Office, 1990.

ORNE, MARTIN T.; SOSKIS, DAVID A.; DINGES, DAVID F.;, and ORNE, EMILY CAROTA. "Hypnotically Induced Testimony," In *Eyewitness Testimony: Psychological Perspectives.* Edited by Gary L. Wells and Elizabeth Loftus. Cambridge, U.K.: Cambridge University Press, 1984. Pages 171–213.

PETERSON, JOSEPH L.; RYAN, JOHN P.; HOULDEN, PAULINE J.; and MIHAJLOVIC, STEVEN. "The Use and Effects of Forensic Science in the Adjudication of Felony Cases." *Journal of Forensic Science* 32 (1987): 1730–1753.

REISER, MARTIN, and NIELSON, MICHAEL. "Investigative Hypnosis: A Developing Specialty."*American Journal of Clinical Hypnosis* 23 (1980): 75–85.

ROGERS, RICHARD, and EWING, CHARLES PATRICK. "Ultimate Opinion Proscriptions: A Cosmetic Fix and a Plea for Empiricism." *Law and Human Behavior* 13 (1989): 357–374.

WECHT, CYRIL H. "Introduction." In *Legal Medicine Annual.* Edited by Cyril H. Wecht. New York: Meredith Corp., 1972. Pages 1–2.

CASES

Andrews v. State, 533 So.2d 841 (Fla. App. 1988), rev. denied, 542 So. 2d 1332 (Fla. 1989).

Barefoot v. Estelle, 463 U.S. 880 (1983).

Breithaupt v. Abram, 352 U.S. 432 (1957).

Commonwealth v. Lykus, 327 N.E.2d 671 (Mass. 1975).

Commonwealth v. Mamay, 553 N.E.2d 945 (Mass. 1990).

Daubert v Merrell Dow Pharmaceuticals, Inc., 509 U.S. 579 (1993).

Escobedo v Illinois, 378 U.S. 478 (1964).

Franklin v. Duncan, 884 F. Supp. 1435 (N. Cal.), aff'd, 70 F. 3d 75 (9th Cir. 1995).

Frye v. United States, 293 F. 1013 (D.C. Cir. 1973).

Harding v. State, 246 A.2d 302 (Md. App. 1968), cert. denied, 395 U.S. 949 (1969).

In re Investigation of the W. Va. State Police Crime Lab., Serology Div., 438 S.E.2d 501 (W. Va. 1993).

Kumho Tire Co. v. Carmichael, 526 U.S. 137 (1999).

People v. Blesdoe, 681 P.2d 291 (Cal. 1984).

People v. Castro, 545 N.Y.S.2d 985 (Sup. Ct. 1989).

People v. Ebanks, 49 P. 1049 (Cal. 1897).

People v. Kelly, 549 P.2d 1240 (Cal. 1976).

People v. Lucas, 435 N.Y.S.2d 461 (Sup. Ct. 1980).

People v. Marx, 126 Cal. Rpt. 350 (App. 1975).

People v. Shirley, 641 P.2d 775, cert. denied, 459 U.S. 860 (1982).

People v. Wesley, 533 N.Y.S.2d 643 (Co. Ct. 1988), aff'd, 633 N.E.2d 451 (N.Y. 1994).

Schmerber v. California, 384 U.S. 757 (1966).

State v. Bible, 858 P.2d 1152 (Ariz. 1993), cert. denied, 511 U.S. 1046 (1994).

State v. Coon, 974 P.2d 386 (Alaska 1999).

State v. Copeland, 922 P.2d 1304 (Wash. 1996)

State v. Kelly, 478 A.2d 364 (N.J. 1984).

State v. Mack, 292 N.W.2d 764 (Minn. 1980).

State v. Marks, 647 P.2d 1292 (Kan. 1982).

State v. Murray, 906 P.2d 542 (Ariz. 1995), cert. denied, 518 U.S. 1011 (1996).

United States v. Addison, 498 F.2d 741 (D.C. Cir 1974).

United States v. Posado, 57 F.3d 428 (5th Cir. 1995).

United States v. Sample, 378 F. Supp. 43 (E.D. Pa. 1974).

United States v. Zeiger, 350 F. Supp. 685 (D.D.C.), rec'd, 475 F.2d 1280 (D.C. Cir. 1972).

Warden v. Hayden, 387 U.S. 294 (1967).

SEARCH AND SEIZURE

In any free society, the police must be constrained. The constraint can come from a variety of sources—politics, bureaucratic culture, administrative sanctions, and so forth. It need not necessarily come from the law. And in most Western democracies, it does not come from the law; outside the United States, police seem to be regulated, where they are regulated, mostly through nonlegal means.

For much of its history—until 1961, to be precise—the same held true of the United States.

Since that date, however, American law has played a very large role in regulating the police and reining in police misconduct. And the chief source of legal restraint is the law of search and seizure.

That law has three key features. First, it is constitutional. The basic standards that limit police investigation of crime—the standards that define when police can search a home, or seize a suitcase believed to contain drugs, or arrest a suspect for some crime—derive from the Fourth Amendment to the federal constitution. Because judges are the prime interpreters of the constitution, this means search and seizure law is basically judge-made. Because constitutional law is binding on popularly elected legislatures and executives, it means search and seizure law cannot be altered by elected politicians, state or federal. In the United States, to a degree that probably has no parallel elsewhere, judges—especially Supreme Court Justices—decide what rules the police must follow. Congress, state legislatures, and the police themselves must live with the rules these judges and Justices create.

Second, its chief business is protecting privacy. The dominant focus of the law of search and seizure is to limit what police can see and hear, to limit their ability to invade spaces people prefer to keep private. That is not the only interest the law protects, but it clearly is the interest that the law protects most. Other concerns—the potential for police violence, the harm to individual liberty that comes from arrest or street detention, discriminatory treatment of black and white suspects—receive much less attention from judges and Justices in Fourth Amendment cases.

Third, it is police-focused. Government gathers information about people in a variety of ways, through a variety of agents. Grand juries subpoena witnesses and documents; prosecutors interview suspects; administrative agencies inspect wetlands and workplaces. These things receive only slight legal regulation; with few exceptions Fourth Amendment law ignores them. That law's clear focus is on police searches and arrests. It is not too much to say that Fourth Amendment law is a kind of tort law for the police; it is the body of civil liability rules that limit day-to-day police activities. Police must therefore pay close attention to Fourth Amendment rules; other government officials can usually ignore them.

The Fourth Amendment: origins, text, and history

Origins.   Like most of the rest of the Bill of Rights, the Fourth Amendment has its origins in seventeenth- and eighteenth-century English common law. Unlike the rest of the Bill of Rights, the Fourth Amendment's origins can be traced precisely—it arose out of a strong public reaction to three cases from the 1760s, two decided in England and one in the colonies.

The two English cases are usefully treated as a pair. Both *Wilkes v. Wood*, 19 Howell's State Trials 1153 (C.P. 1763), and *Entick v. Carrington*, 19 Howell's State Trials 1029 (C.P. 1765), involved pamphleteers charged with seditious libel for criticizing the king's ministers and, through them, the king himself. In both cases, agents of the king issued a warrant authorizing the ransacking of the pamphleteers' homes and the seizure of all their books and papers. (An aside is necessary at this point: Warrants are means of giving government officials permission to search or arrest someone whom they otherwise might not be allowed to search or arrest. In American practice, warrants are issued only by judges or magistrates after reviewing an application from a police officer. In eighteenth-century England, warrants were sometimes issued by agents of the Crown on their own initiative.) These searches were duly carried out. Wilkes and Entick sued for damages, claiming that the warrants were void and that the searches pursuant to them were therefore illegal. Both Wilkes and Entick won, with powerful opinions issued by Lord Camden, the judge in both cases. These decisions made Camden a hero in the colonies; a number of towns and cities were named after him because of his opinions in *Wilkes* and *Entick*.

The third case was the *Writs of Assistance Case* (see Dickerson, 1939). British customs inspectors seeking to stamp out smuggling in colonial Boston were given blanket search warrants, called writs of assistance, that permitted them to search anyplace where they thought smuggled goods might be. (The writs also allowed the inspectors to compel private citizens to help them carry out the searches—hence the writs' name.) Some Boston merchants, represented by James Otis, sued, seeking a holding that the writs were invalid. The merchants lost, but Otis's argument, with its ringing defense of individual privacy, became famous and strengthened opposition to British rule. John Adams later said of Otis's argument that "then and there the child Independence was born."

Historians generally agree that the Fourth Amendment was designed to affirm the results in *Wilkes* and *Entick*, and to overturn the result in the *Writs of Assistance Case*. Three principles seem to follow. First, the government should not be allowed to search without some substantial justification, some reason to believe the place being searched contains the evidence being sought. That was the problem with the writs of assistance—they authorized searches based on no more than the unsupported suspicion of the inspector. Second, searches, particularly of private homes, should not go beyond their justification. That was the problem with the searches in *Wilkes* and *Entick*—the authorities did not simply search for and seize illegal writings, but took all the books and papers in the suspects' houses. Third, the government should not use blanket warrants to evade the first two principles. That was a problem in all three cases. English common law held it a trespass to invade someone's home without some kind of authorization; the warrants in *Wilkes* and *Entick* and the writs of assistance looked like efforts to evade that common law right. This explains why, at the time of the Founding era, search warrants—now viewed as a protection against police overreaching—were seen as more of a danger than a safeguard.

Notice that none of these three cases involved ordinary criminal law enforcement. None stemmed from the investigation of a murder, or a robbery, or a rape. Rather, each involved the investigation and prosecution of what might fairly be called dissidents—ordinary law-abiding citizens who disagreed strongly with the laws they were disobeying, and who enjoyed some substantial support among the citizenry. It is not at all clear from the Fourth Amendment's history that James Madison and his contemporaries wished to restrict the investigation of ordinary crimes; indeed, it is not clear that they even thought about the investigation of ordinary crimes.

Notice, too, that none of these cases involved searches by people whom we would recognize today as police officers. Police forces did not exist in the eighteenth century, either in England or in the colonies. It follows that the Framers could not possibly have thought about how best to regulate them. The Fourth Amendment's central role—reining in the police— is a role that it assumed much later. This point counsels in favor of a certain modesty when seeking to extract contemporary lessons from the Fourth Amendment's historical context.

The Fourth Amendment's text.   The Fourth Amendment, along with the other provisions of the Bill of Rights, was proposed by James Madison. The version that was ultimately ratified (Madison's original version was slightly different) reads as follows:

The right of the people to be secure in their persons, houses, papers, and effects, against unreasonable searches and seizures, shall not be violated, and no Warrants shall issue, but upon probable cause, supported by Oath or affirmation, and particularly describing the place to be searched, and the persons or things to be seized.

The first clause—lawyers usually call it the "reasonableness clause"—contains a simple prohibition: unreasonable searches and seizures are forbidden. It leaves the key term, "unreasonable," undefined. The second clause, usually called the "warrant clause," places a set of limits on the issuance of search or arrest warrants. Three limits are listed: the warrants must be supported by probable cause, they must define where the search is to take place, and they must define what the object of the search is—who or what is to be seized.

This text nowhere requires the government to get search or arrest warrants—the second clause limits the use of warrants, but never says when, if ever, the government must use them. So far as the text of the Fourth Amendment is concerned, the police apparently may search or seize without a warrant, as long as the search or seizure is reasonable. This is unsurprising given the Fourth Amendment's origins. Madison and his contemporaries were chiefly concerned with preventing a recurrence of searches like the ones in *Wilkes* and *Entick;* the safest way to do that was to severely limit the use of warrants. Requiring them was apparently not on the Framers' agenda.

Subsequent history to 1961.   For a century and a half after it was ratified, the Fourth Amendment (like the rest of the Bill of Rights) applied only to the federal government; state and local police were not bound by it. During most of this period, federal criminal investigation and prosecution was rare—there was no F.B.I., and no army of federal prosecutors—so there was little opportunity for Fourth Amendment litigation. As a consequence, Fourth Amendment law basically lay dormant until Prohibition in the 1920s, which for the first time produced a large and active federal enforcement bureaucracy. By that time, three important changes had taken place. First, the Supreme Court had adopted the exclusionary rule (in *Weeks v. United States*, 232 U.S. 314 (1914)), which held that illegally seized evidence ordinarily could not be used in criminal trials. The source and rationale of that rule are discussed in a separate entry. Second, during the course of the nineteenth century search warrants had come to be seen as a way of limiting police authority, not as means by which the government could evade legal restriction. This is a natural development: once the Fourth Amendment placed stringent limits on warrants, requiring warrants became a good way to ensure that police had good reasons for searching. Accordingly, one sees frequent discussion in Prohibition-era cases of the importance of requiring police to get advance permission from a magistrate, in the form of a warrant, before searching. Third, probable cause had become the generally applicable legal standard for searches. "Reasonable" searches meant searches supported by probable cause—which meant, roughly, a fair likelihood that the evidence searched for would be found in the place searched.

Thus, by the end of the 1920s, Fourth Amendment law had assumed the following structure. Probable cause was required for all searches or arrests. A warrant, obtained in advance, was required at least for searches of homes, and possibly for many other searches as well. (Curiously, arrests for serious crimes were not thought to require warrants, a rule that still holds today.) And these rules were enforced primarily by an exclusionary rule, so that when the police violated the rules, any evidence they found would be inadmissible in a subsequent criminal trial.

These rules still applied only to the federal government. That state of affairs changed when, in *Wolf v. Colorado*, 338 U.S. 25 (1949), the Supreme Court held that the Fourth Amendment was part of the liberty protected by the Fourteenth Amendment's due process clause against infringement by state and local officials. Twelve years later, in *Mapp v. Ohio*, 367 U.S. 643 (1961), the Supreme Court gave teeth to *Wolf* by imposing the exclusionary rule on the states. Henceforth local police, who are the primary enforcers of American criminal law, would be subject to the same search and seizure rules as F.B.I. agents, and to the same penalty for violating those rules.

It is not too much to say this worked a revolution in the way American police are themselves policed. Before 1961, local police were subject to state constitutional limits and could be sued for common law trespass (just like the offending officials in *Entick* and *Wilkes*). But these limits were illusory: state constitutions went unenforced, and common law claims against police officers virtually were never brought. Consequently, there was no working law of search and seizure, no body of rules that officers felt bound to obey, outside the federal system. Local police were restrained, if they were restrained at all, by local custom or politics. Law played no real part in their regulation.

This posed more of a danger to some suspects than to others. At the time *Mapp* was decided, it was widely (and surely correctly) believed that local police, especially in the South, treated black suspects much more harshly than white ones. And blacks could not protect their interests through the political process, because they were often either denied the right to vote or frozen out of governing coalitions. Although the opinions in *Mapp* do not make this point explicitly, it seems likely that one of the reasons—perhaps the primary reason—for the Supreme Court's assertion of regulatory control over local police was the desire to protect black suspects from unfair treatment at the hands of nearly all-white police forces. In this way, Fourth Amendment law, which began as a tool for protecting upperclass pamphleteers and smugglers, had become a means of protecting a poor minority against oppression by police forces dominated by a middle-class (white) majority.

After 1961. The law *Mapp* imposed on local police forces was basically the same law that had been imposed on federal agents enforcing Prohibition in the 1920s: probable cause for searches and arrests, with warrants required for searches unless the police had a good excuse for not getting one. Perhaps because of a coincidence in timing—at about the time *Mapp* was decided, crime rates began skyrocketing, with the number of serious felonies trebling in the course of the next decade—these rules came to seem too burdensome for increasingly busy local police. (Rising crime also meant rising public hostility to the Supreme Court's efforts to regulate the criminal process, which was seen as "handcuffing" police and prosecutors.) Beginning in 1968, the Supreme Court moved to relax these rules in two key ways. First, in *Terry v. Ohio*, 392 U.S. 1 (1968), the Court permitted police to "stop and frisk" suspects on the street based on reasonable suspicion of criminal activity, a lesser standard than probable cause. *Terry* involved suspicion of an about-to-be-committed robbery, but the Court soon applied its reasonable suspicion standard to past crimes and, most importantly, to drug crime. With these extensions, *Terry* meant that officers could briefly detain people, but not arrest them, based on fairly low-level suspicion of crime—the sort of suspicion that might come from spending time in the company of "known" drug dealers at places where drug trafficking is believed to be common.

The second change involved the warrant requirement. In a series of decisions stretching from the early 1970s to the early 1990s, the Court created or expanded various exceptions to the warrant requirement. For example, searches of cars were exempt, as were searches incident to arrest, as were inventory searches (these involved the inspection and cataloging of a suspect's belongings when he is taken into custody). These various exceptions, taken together, meant that the warrant requirement applied to searches of houses and apartments, but almost never applied to anything else. For searches and seizures outside private homes, police were still bound by the probable cause or reasonable suspicion standards, but no advance permission to search was required.

The creation and expansion of "stop and frisk" doctrine and the contraction of the warrant requirement were both contentious; Fourth Amendment decisions in the 1970s and 1980s gave rise to some of the most heated arguments the Supreme Court has ever seen. Defenders of Fourth Amendment law's classical structure, primarily Justices William Brennan and Thurgood Marshall, argued passionately that it was important to preserve probable cause, not the softer reasonable suspicion standard, as the primary standard for searches and seizures; they also argued for a broad warrant requirement to provide an extra check on police overreaching. But these arguments generally lost, and the structure that had emerged by the early 1990s is now fairly stable. The key characteristics of that structure are the subject of the next part.

The current structure of search and seizure law

Search and seizure law today is built around three key questions. First, did the police "search" or "seize" anyone or anything? If not, the law leaves police action basically unregulated. If so, what justification must the police have—probable cause, reasonable suspicion, or (in rare cases) something else? Finally, what process must the police follow—must they seek permission in advance from a magistrate, or can they search first and defend themselves in a suppression hearing later?

The definition of "search" and "seizure." The most important of these questions may be the first one, for if a given police tactic is not a "search" or "seizure" within the meaning of the Fourth Amendment, the police are free to use that tactic when and on whom they wish, free of legal constraint.

"Searches," in Fourth Amendment law, are police tactics that infringe a "reasonable expectation of privacy." A reasonable expectation of privacy is the kind of expectation any citizen might have with respect to any other citizen. A fair translation of this standard might go as follows: Police can see and hear the things that any member of the public might see and hear, without fear of Fourth Amendment regulation. Only when police cross that line, only when they see and hear things that members of the public would not be allowed to see and hear, has a "search" taken place.

A few examples might clarify the standard. Eavesdropping on telephone conversations is a "search." Overhearing a conversation on the street is not. Climbing over a backyard fence is a "search." Observing the same backyard from the window of an airplane is not. Hiding in the bushes outside a house and looking inside is a "search." Standing on a public street and looking through open curtains into a living room is not. Opening a briefcase to inspect its contents is a "search." Observing someone carrying a briefcase on the street is not.

When applying the reasonable-expectation-of-privacy standard, courts ask whether, at the moment the police officer observed the illegal behavior, he was in a position any member of the public might have been in. The duration and intensity of police observation does not matter. Thus, police officers can stake out a private home, taking up residence across the street and watching all comings and goings for a period of days or even weeks, and that behavior does not constitute a "search," because at any given moment, any member of the public might have been looking. And police can follow a suspect's movements along public streets, in shops or restaurants, and so forth; once again, such behavior is not a "search" (even though it amounts to something like stalking), because any member of the public might have seen any given transaction in public.

One other feature of the definition of "search" bears mention. Consensual transactions are not "searches," even if consent was given under false pretenses. So if a police officer poses as a drug buyer, and a suspect lets him into the suspect's house in order to sell him drugs, anything the officer sees and hears in the house is fair game—no Fourth Amendment "search" has taken place. The use of undercover agents is thus routinely permitted by search and seizure law, whether or not the police have good reason to suspect the person with whom the undercover agent is dealing of any crime. Also, if a police officer asks permission to look in a suspect's car or briefcase, and the suspect says yes, once again no "search" has taken place. This last point is particularly important. Police officers exert a certain amount of force just by virtue of their status. For many, perhaps most, a request from a police officer will sound like a command; the tendency will be to say yes whether one wants to or not. Nevertheless, if the police officer asks, and the suspect says yes, that almost always amounts to consent. Only if the officer behaves unusually coercively—if he pulls his weapon, or grabs hold of the suspect, or the like—will a court find that the consent was involuntary.

All these rules sound complicated; in practice, they are relatively simple. In general, the police are "searching" when they are either committing some kind of trespass—grabbing a suspect's briefcase and looking inside, breaking into a house or apartment, climbing over a backyard fence—or are engaged in some kind of electronic eavesdropping—for example, wiretapping a phone. Most of the rest of what police do to gather information falls outside the Fourth Amendment.

"Seizures" are harder to define. The Supreme Court says that a suspect has been "seized" if a reasonable person in the suspect's shoes would not feel free to leave. If the Court took its own language seriously, every conversation between a police officer and a citizen would be a "seizure." After all, few people, when approached on the street by an officer, feel free to turn on their heels and walk away. The consequences of that position would be huge; the police would need some adequate justification for every interaction.

Not surprisingly, the law does not operate that way in practice. The working standard seems to be roughly the same as the standard for consent. The dispositive question is this: Did the police officer behave coercively (not counting the coercion that is inherent in a police officer questioning a suspect)? If so, the encounter is a "seizure." If not, it is not. Compared to the definition of "search," which has acquired a good deal of definition over the years, the definition of "seizure" remains remarkably vague and open-ended. Conversations on the street between police officers and citizens often begin as consensual conversations; at some point the encounter often becomes a "seizure." Neither the officer nor the suspect—nor, for that matter, courts—know precisely when that point is.

Probable cause and reasonable suspicion. When the police have searched or seized someone, the Fourth Amendment requires some justification. With rare exceptions, the justification takes one of two forms: either the police must have probable cause, or they must have reasonable suspicion. The following paragraphs explain what these standards mean, and to what cases each standard applies.

Probable cause has never received a clear definition in the cases; the Supreme Court has said, unhelpfully, that an officer has probable cause to arrest when "the facts and circumstances within [the officers'] knowledge and of which they had reasonably trustworthy information [are] sufficient in themselves to warrant a man of reasonable caution in the belief that an offense has been or is being committed" *Brinegar v. United States*, 338 U.S. 160, 175–76 (1949). What that means in practice seems to be, roughly, more likely than not. Thus, probable cause to arrest requires enough information to show that the suspect probably committed the crime. Probable cause to search requires enough information to show that evidence of crime can probably be found in the place to be searched.

One issue that regularly arises in the cases is whether police can rely on tips from informants to establish probable cause. Informants are sometimes ordinary citizens who call into police stations with useful information; more commonly they are criminals themselves who report information about other criminals in return for some favors—sometimes leniency, sometimes cash—from the police. Informants are common in police work, and especially in the policing of drug markets. (The leading study of search warrants shows that jurisdictions with the most drug cases also make the most use of informants' tips.) Such tips are clearly useful to the police; they equally clearly pose significant problems. Informants may have some incentive to frame rivals, or to concoct whatever information will get them the greatest reward from the police. And since the identity of the informant is almost always confidential—for obvious reasons, informants tend to insist on anonymity—there is some risk that police will make up phony informants to justify their own hunches. For these reasons, the Supreme Court in the 1960s and 1970s placed serious restrictions on the use of informants' tips to generate probable cause.

Those restrictions were largely removed in 1983, in *Illinois v. Gates*, 462 U.S. 213 (1983). The Court in *Gates* held, basically, that informants' tips were to be treated like any other information. And the Court specifically approved findings of probable cause where an informant's tip is partially corroborated—as where the informant says a suspect will be driving a certain car at a certain time and place and will be carrying drugs, and the officer confirms that the suspect was indeed driving that car at that time and place.

Like probable cause, reasonable suspicion is not well defined in the cases. Indeed, the only thing one can confidently say about it is that reasonable suspicion means something less than probable cause. Just how much less is unclear. A good indication of the kind and level of information required is the following common fact pattern. A police officer, on foot or in his car, turns a corner on a city street in an area known as a locale for drug trafficking. A young man standing on a street corner sees the officer, turns, and runs in the other direction. The officer knows nothing about the young man other than that he was in a place where crime was common, and that he ran when he saw the police. Does the officer have reasonable suspicion?

In *Illinois v. Wardlow*, 120 S.Ct. 673 (2000), the Supreme Court said the answer is yes. Likewise, if police see a suspect in a place where drugs are often sold, and if the suspect has a series of brief conversations with people the police know to be drug users, most courts would say the police have reasonable suspicion. In these cases the police have some ground for suspecting criminality, but not a great deal. Reasonable suspicion is meant to capture that intermediate condition.

To what cases do these standards apply? Probable cause is the governing standard for arrests, and for searches of homes, cars, or personal effects. For arrests, the standard is probable cause to believe the suspect has committed a crime; for searches it is, with one important ex-

ception, probable cause to believe evidence will be found in the place sought. The exception is for searches "incident to arrest." When the police make a valid arrest, they are permitted to search the suspect's person, any belongings he has with him, and his car; if the arrest occurs at home, they may search the area within his immediate control. These searches incident to arrest are legal if the arrest is legal. Thus, probable cause to arrest authorizes not only arrests but also a good many searches.

Reasonable suspicion is the governing standard for brief stops, as where an officer detains a pedestrian for a few minutes or pulls over a car in order to ask the driver a few questions. Reasonable suspicion of the presence of a weapon is the standard for very brief searches, such as a pat-down or frisk of a suspect's outer clothing. In practice, reasonable suspicion of the presence of a weapon tends to follow from reasonable suspicion of criminal activity. At least for serious crimes, judges tend to find that suspicion of the crime entitles the police to frisk the suspect in order to detect any weapons. The officer is, of course, entitled to check the contents of the pockets if this frisk turns up anything that might be a weapon. Naturally, the line between lumps that might be weapons and lumps that might be evidence of crime (drugs, for example) is a fine one. As a result, frisks for weapons tend to turn into frisks for either weapons or evidence.

The authority to frisk, or conduct a brief search, based on reasonable suspicion extends beyond the suspect's clothing. If the suspect is in a car, the officer is entitled to briefly look through the car's interior. If the suspect is carrying a purse or briefcase, the officer can briefly look inside, long enough to ensure that it does not contain a gun. And any evidence the officer finds during the course of such inspections is admissible.

Thus, given reasonable suspicion, officers can briefly detain pedestrians or pull over drivers of cars. Given reasonable suspicion of the kind of crime often associated with weapons, officers can briefly look around the car's interior, frisk a suspect's outer clothing, and open any containers (such as a purse or bag) that the suspect might reach to check for weapons. More extensive searches and seizures require probable cause.

Special cases—police use of force and group seizures. There remain two important categories of cases where neither probable cause nor reasonable suspicion applies. The first is police use of force, where the standard is higher than probable cause. The second is group seizures such as roadblocks, where the standard is lower than reasonable suspicion.

At common law, the police could use whatever force necessary to apprehend suspects and to bring them under control. If suspected of a felony, and if he fled, the suspect could be killed. These doctrines were still in force as late as the 1980s; not until 1985 did the Supreme Court decide that a higher standard was required for police use of force against suspects.

In that case, *Tennessee v. Garner*, 471 U.S. 1 (1985), the police shot and killed a fleeing burglary suspect; there was no reason to believe the suspect was armed or had threatened serious physical harm to anyone. The Court concluded that the shooting was unreasonable, and hence violated the Fourth Amendment. The Court ruled that deadly force was permissible only given some immediate danger of death or serious physical injury. Immediate danger is presumed if the police have probable cause to believe the suspect has caused or threatened death or serious injury, and if the suspect has been warned to stop but refuses to do so. The standard for using nondeadly force is both less demanding and less certain: the Supreme Court says only that officers must behave reasonably, taking account of the danger the suspect poses, the kind of crime he is suspected of committing, and the amount of force necessary to bring him under control.

These standards governing police use of force receive much less attention in the courts than the standards governing police frisks or house searches, because use-of-force claims are litigated much less frequently. The reason has to do with remedies. The primary remedy for Fourth Amendment violations is the exclusionary rule; the huge majority of Fourth Amendment claims arise as efforts by criminal defendants to suppress illegally obtained evidence. But when police beat or shoot a suspect, they are not looking for evidence. Thus, excessive force claims only rarely lead to efforts to suppress evidence; the exclusionary rule is essentially irrelevant to these claims.

Instead, excessive force claims arise either as claims for damages by the victim (or the victim's next-of-kin), or as criminal prosecutions of the offending officers. The latter happen only very rarely. Damages claims are more frequent, but still amount to a very small fraction of the number of exclusionary rule claims. Which explains

why the law of excessive force is so much less developed than, say, the law of car searches or street stops.

Group searches and seizures are the second category of cases that fall outside the probable cause and reasonable suspicion standards. Here the law is both complex and unclear. In *United States v. Martinez-Fuerte*, 428 U.S. 543 (1976), the Supreme Court permitted the use of highway checkpoints near the border to check for illegal immigrants; at these checkpoints all cars were stopped and all drivers seized, even though the government had no reason to suspect any particular driver of harboring illegal aliens. Similarly, in *Michigan Highway Department v. Sitz*, 496 U.S. 444 (1990), the Court ruled that officers may set up roadblocks to catch drunk drivers, even though the officers have no ground for suspecting any particular driver of any wrongdoing. But in *Indianapolis v. Edmond*, 121 S.Ct. 447 (2000), the Court barred the use of roadblocks designed to catch drug violators. For now, the government can apparently seize (and perhaps search) all members of a group in pursuit of goals other than ordinary criminal law enforcement (border control in *Martinez-Fuente*, highway safety in *Sitz*). But it cannot use power as a routine crime control tactic.

Drugs may fall on either side of this boundary. In *Edmond*, drug checkpoints were banned. But the result has been different in a number of cases involving drug testing. Government agencies sometimes seek to require periodic testing of employees, without any showing that any given employee was reasonably suspected of drug use or other misconduct. These testing programs have sometimes prevailed in the courts and sometimes not; the usual approach is to ask whether there is some "special need" to test the category of employees in question. The idea is similar to the idea behind *Martinez-Fuerte* and *Sitz:* In support of these testing programs, the government often claims suspicionless testing is permissible as long as many people are tested; that is, as long as no one person is singled out. If that argument were applied to tactics like group fingerprinting or DNA testing, it would considerably expand the scope of police authority. For now, *Edmond* is holding the line against such an expansion. But the line is unstable. The government can argue, with some force, that its interest in fighting drug crime is at least as strong as its interest in catching drunk drivers. If so, it seems odd that the police would be granted substantially greater power in the latter setting than in the former.

The role of substantive law.   Probable cause and reasonable suspicion both refer to a level of probability, a likelihood that some asserted fact— the suspect committed a crime, or evidence of crime will be found in a particular place—is true. The asserted fact always involves crime. It follows that the meaning of probable cause or reasonable suspicion depends on what counts as a crime. To put it another way, to say that the police have probable cause to arrest a given suspect is to say they have reason to believe that the suspect probably violated some criminal statute. Whether the claim is right depends in part on just what behavior criminal statutes forbid. If enough criminal statutes forbid enough conduct, the police will have probable cause to arrest a large portion of the population.

Something much like this was true before the late 1960s. Loitering statutes made it a crime to hang around on street corners; vagrancy statutes made it a crime to be able-bodied but unemployed, or to be a "rogue" or "vagabond." These open-ended prohibitions plausibly covered a large fraction of ordinary street behavior, at least by people the police might wish to arrest or search. Consequently, the police had something close to blanket authority to arrest or search a large portion of the population. The probable cause standard mattered little.

In the late 1960s and early 1970s, most loitering and vagrancy statutes were declared unconstitutional on the ground that they were unacceptably vague. States and cities responded with a wave of statutes and ordinances criminalizing loitering with intent to commit acts of prostitution or drug use; some jurisdictions went farther, passing laws forbidding loitering in the presence of members of gangs that themselves were involved in various sorts of criminal activity. In *Chicago v. Morales*, 119 S.Ct. 1849 (1999), the Supreme Court struck down one such law, declaring that it was, like older loitering and vagrancy laws, too vague, and that it infringed on individuals' liberty to wander about on public streets free of official interference.

Morales was not a Fourth Amendment decision; the Court relied on the due process clause of the Fourteenth Amendment instead. But the Court's decision may have a large impact on the scope of Fourth Amendment protection. Again, if "crime" covers enough territory, police will have reasonable suspicion or probable cause with respect to most people, and Fourth Amendment standards will, as a practical matter, cease to operate. *Morales* may suggest that, at least with respect to pedestrians, the Court will not permit that state of affairs to recur.

The story is different when it comes to automobile traffic. In many states, moving violations—speeding, changing lanes without using a turn signal, running a stop sign, and the like— are, technically, crimes. Since such rules are not strictly enforced in most places (to the extent that speeding is the norm on many roads), most drivers are, technically, committing crimes most of the time, which gives the police authority to stop a large fraction of drivers.

That authority can be exercised strategically. If police believe a given suspect is transporting drugs, but they lack the kind of support needed to satisfy the probable cause or reasonable suspicion standards, they can wait for the suspect to run a stop sign, or speed, or violate some other traffic regulation, then pull the suspect over, arrest him for the traffic offense, and search him and his car incident to the arrest—all the while looking for drugs. In *Whren v. United States*, 517 U.S. 806 (1996), the Supreme Court held that this sort of pretextual police search is permissible. As long as the police have probable cause to believe the suspect is doing something the state defines as a crime, an arrest is legal, and if an arrest is legal, so is a search incident to arrest.

Whren and *Morales* are thus in some tension. *Whren* gives police near-blanket authority to stop vehicles; *Morales* seems to forbid near-blanket authority to stop pedestrians. In both cases, the primary determinant of the scope of police authority is not Fourth Amendment law, but the law that defines crimes.

The warrant requirement.   All police searches and seizures are subject to legal challenge, but the challenge ordinarily comes after the fact. The officer searches, the defendant moves to suppress evidence found in the search, and the court holds a hearing to determine whether the search was legal. Where a search or arrest warrant is required, by contrast, judicial evaluation of the search or arrest happens in advance. The officer fills out a brief warrant application, with a sworn affidavit stating the facts in support of the application; a magistrate reviews the application, sometimes questioning the officer, and then decides whether to issue the warrant. If the warrant is issued and the search turns up evidence, the defendant can still seek to suppress it, but the court will give substantial deference to the magistrate's judgment. Thus, Fourth Amendment law knows two procedures for testing the legality of a search: the warrant process before the search, and the suppression hearing after.

In form, the law requires the first of these procedures—warrants—unless some special exception applies. In practice, the exceptions swallow the rule. Warrants are not required for (among other things) arrests outside the suspect's home, searches incident to arrest (which, remember, cover the suspect's clothing, car, and belongings at the time of arrest), searches of cars whether or not anyone is arrested, and brief stops or frisks of suspects. These categories encompass the large majority of searches and seizures.

Warrants are required for wiretaps, for searches of homes, and for arrests that take place in a home. Even here, there is an exception for cases where "exigent circumstances" exist— where getting a warrant is impractical because of the danger that suspects will flee or evidence will be destroyed.

The warrant requirement thus applies chiefly when police wish to enter a private home. Elsewhere, police generally are allowed to search first, and face judicial scrutiny afterward. Fourth Amendment law purports to have a warrant requirement with a few narrow exceptions. The true rule is no warrant requirement, with an exception for homes and wiretaps.

In theory, this regime offers an extra measure of protection for house searches. Forcing police to ask permission in advance of a search, and requiring that permission come from a neutral magistrate, should weed out potential searches based on thinly supported police hunches. In practice, it is unclear how much the warrant requirement accomplishes. Most reviews of warrant applications are cursory, and magistrates only hear from one side—the police officer. Not surprisingly, most applications are granted. That, one might think, suggests warrants are something of a sham, a process by which discretionary decisions by police officers are rubber-stamped by magistrates. On the other hand, the leading study of the warrant process suggests the large majority of searches pursuant to warrants turn up evidence of crime. That, one might suppose, suggests warrants work, that they serve as an effective screen. The truth may be somewhere in between these two views, or it may be different in different jurisdictions.

Two problems

The basic structure of search and seizure law seems fairly stable; large changes are unlikely, at least in the near future. In assessing that structure, it is helpful to focus on two issues. The first goes to the interests the law of search and seizure protects. The second goes to an interest that, for the most part, the law of search and seizure ignores.

Privacy. The dominant focus of the law of search and seizure is protecting privacy. "Privacy" here has a particular meaning—it is not some generalized right to be let alone; rather, it is the interest in being free from observation, the interest in not being seen or heard. That the law protects privacy in this limited sense is shown by the cases that define "searches," which cover only police conduct that permits officers to see or hear things that ordinary citizens would not be able to see or hear.

Notice that the interest in liberty receives less protection. Searches of private homes require probable cause and a warrant. Probable cause, with no warrant, suffices for an arrest outside the home—even though an arrest can lead to detention in the police station. The interest in being free from police violence receives, if not less protection, less attention, which may amount to the same thing: The number of excessive force claims brought against police officers is but a small fraction of the number of suppression motions based on allegedly illegal car searches.

The law's focus on privacy sits uncomfortably together with its focus on regulating the police. Administrative agencies like the Internal Revenue Service arguably invade people's privacy more than the police—think about the kinds of information people must supply on their tax forms. If one really wished to protect privacy, then, a natural way to do so would be to regulate with some care what questions the IRS can ask and how it can ask them. Yet Fourth Amendment law has almost nothing to say about those topics. At the same time, it has a great deal to say about questions like when the police can inspect the inside of a paper bag, or look inside the glove compartment of a car—trivial privacy invasions, one might think, compared with tax forms. In other words, search and seizure law protects privacy, but only when the police infringe it. That seems an odd way to protect privacy.

And protecting privacy may be an odd way to regulate the police. Police do two things that other government agents—grand juries, prosecutors, or administrative agencies—do not. Police arrest people, which means removing them from their homes and locking them up. And police beat, sometimes shoot, people as a means of obtaining and maintaining control over them. If one were to imagine a body of law whose goal was specially to regulate the police, one might expect that law to focus on those two things: on regulating police ability to deprive suspects of their liberty and, perhaps especially, on limiting police ability to injure or kill suspects. Fourth Amendment law does some of that. But it focuses more on privacy interests, on searches of homes and cars and paper bags, and less on other, perhaps more important goals.

Race discrimination.   One of those goals might be to eliminate police discrimination on the basis of race. African Americans suffer a disproportionate share of arrests and prison sentences. Much of that disproportion flows from differences in crime rates across population groups, but some of the disproportion may be a consequence of discriminatory targeting of suspects by the police. Perhaps surprisingly, Fourth Amendment law does little to stop that sort of discrimination. Given the breadth of criminal law, police have probable cause to arrest or reasonable suspicion to stop a large portion of the population—when it comes to vehicular traffic, a large majority of the population. Within this pool of potential suspects, police can target whom they wish; Fourth Amendment law basically says nothing about their exercise of enforcement discretion. So if police officers stop large numbers of black drivers, ostensibly for speeding but primarily to check for drugs, and stop few whites, the black drivers have no legal claim.

This is true notwithstanding the fact that a number of courts forbid the use of race as a factor in police "profiles." Such profiles are common in drug investigations; they basically list factors common to drug couriers in particular markets at particular times. Officially, race is a forbidden factor, but officers can easily take race into account without acknowledging that they do so, and for now, the law tolerates that.

Another form of potential discrimination involves the targeting of some kinds of crimes, and some neighborhoods, more severely than others. In the late 1980s and early 1990s, urban crack markets received more police attention than suburban markets in cocaine powder. Most crack defendants were black; most cocaine powder defendants were white. One could argue that the strong tilt against crack was, on balance, a good thing; one could also argue that it was socially harmful, in part because of the racial composition of the two pools of defendants. Whichever answer is right, the current law of search and seizure leaves the question wholly to the police.

There may be no good alternative to that position. Courts are poorly positioned to direct the allocation of police resources across crimes and neighborhoods, and any serious effort to eliminate discriminatory policing would require precisely that. Still, it seems strange that Fourth Amendment law—the body of law most clearly devoted to regulating the police—has so little to do with what may be the most serious regulatory problem in the world of policing: stamping out race discrimination.

WILLIAM J. STUNTZ

See also CRIMINAL PROCEDURE: CONSTITUTIONAL ASPECTS; CRIMINAL PROCEDURE: COMPARATIVE ASPECTS; EXCLUSIONARY RULE; POLICE: CRIMINAL INVESTIGATIONS; POLICE: POLICE OFFICER BEHAVIOR; WIRETAPPING AND EAVESDROPPING.

BIBLIOGRAPHY

AMAR, AKHIL REED. "Fourth Amendment First Principles." *Harvard Law Review* 107 (February 1994): 757–819.
AMSTERDAM, ANTHONY G. "Perspectives on the Fourth Amendment." *Minnesota Law Review* 58 (1974): 349–477.
DICKERSON, O. M. "Writs of Assistance as a Cause of the Revolution." *The Era of the American Revolution.* Edited by Richard B. Morris. New York: Columbia University Press, 1939. Pages 40–75.
KENNEDY, RANDALL. *Race, Crime, and the Law.* New York: Pantheon Books, 1997.
LAFAVE, WAYNE R. *Search and Seizure: A Treatise on the Fourth Amendment.* 5 vols. St. Paul, Minn.: West, 1995.
LIVINGSTON, DEBRA. "Police Discretion and the Quality of Life in Public Places: Courts, Communities, and the New Policing." *Columbia Law Review* 97 (April 1997): 551–672.
SKLANSKY, DAVID A. "Traffic Stops, Minority Motorists, and the Future of the Fourth Amendment." *Supreme Court Review* (1997): 271–329.
STEIKER, CAROL S. "Second Thoughts About First Principles." *Harvard Law Review* 107 (February 1994): 820–857.
STUNTZ, WILLIAM J. "Warrants and Fourth Amendment Remedies." *Virginia Law Review* 77 (August 1991): 881–942.

———. "The Substantive Origins of Criminal Procedure." *Yale Law Journal* 105 (November, 1995): 393–447.

TAYLOR, TELFORD. *Two Studies in Constitutional Interpretation.* Columbus: Ohio State University Press, 1969.

VAN DUIZEND, RICHARD, et al. *The Search Warrant Process: Preconceptions, Perceptions, Practices.* National Center for State Courts, Williamsburg, Va., 1985.

WASSERSTROM, SILAS J., and SEIDMAN, LOUIS MICHAEL. "The Fourth Amendment as Constitutional Theory." *Georgetown Law Journal* 77 (October 1988): 19–112.

CASES

Brinegar v. United States, 338 U.S. 160 (1949).
Chicago v. Morales, 119 S.Ct. 1849 (1999).
Entick v. Carrington, 19 Howell's State Trials 1029 (C.P. 1765).
Illinois v. Gates, 462 U.S. 213 (1983).
Indianapolis v. Edmond, 121 S.Ct. 447 (2000).
Mapp v. Ohio, 367 U.S. 643 (1961).
Michigan Highway Department v. Sitz, 496 U.S. 444 (1990).
Tennessee v. Garner, 471 U.S. 1 (1985).
Terry v. Ohio, 392 U.S. 1 (1968).
Weeks v. United States, 232 U.S. 314 (1914).
Whren v. United States, 517 U.S. 806 (1996).
Wilkes v. Wood, 19 Howell's State Trials 1153 (C.P. 1763).
Wolf v. Colorado, 338 U.S. 25 (1949).
Writs of Assistance

SEDITION AND DOMESTIC TERRORISM

The crime of sedition consists in any attempt short of treason to excite hostility against the sovereign. Most commonly, the crime takes the form of expression, and in such form it is known as seditious libel. Because the substantive contours of seditious libel have shifted over time, there is no simple definition of the doctrine. In its most expansive form, however, seditious libel may be said to embrace any criticism—true or false—of the form, constitution, policies, laws, officers, symbols, or conduct of government. Prosecutions for seditious libel have routinely been used on both sides of the Atlantic to suppress opposition to the dominant political order.

The early English experience

Seditious libel first entered Anglo-American jurisprudence in a statute enacted by Parliament in 1275. This statute outlawed the telling or publishing of "any false news or tales whereby discord or occasion of discord or slander may grow between the king and his people or the great men of the realm." Violations were punished by the King's council sitting in the "starred chamber" (Slander and Sedition Act, 1275, 3 Edw. 1, C. 34 (England)).

In a 1606 decision, the Star Chamber dramatically transformed the concept of seditious libel (The Case *De Libellis Famosis,* 77 Eng. Rep. 250 (K.B. 1606) (Coke)). The Star Chamber ruled, first, that a libel against a private person might be punished as a crime, on the theory that it might provoke revenge and, hence, a breach of the peace. Second, the Star Chamber held that a libel against the government might also be punished criminally and was especially serious because "it concerns not only the breach of the peace, but also the scandal of government." Third, although the statute of 1275 had insisted upon proof of falsity, the Star Chamber ruled that the truth or falsity of the libel was immaterial under the common law; thus, even a true libel of government could now be the subject of criminal prosecution.

The rationale of the Star Chamber decision was straightforward: If government is to govern effectively, it must command the respect and allegiance of the people. Since any utterance critical of government necessarily undermines this respect and allegiance, it must inevitably tend, however remotely, toward disorder. Moreover, a true libel is especially dangerous, for unlike a false libel, the dangers of truthful criticism cannot be defused by mere disproof. It was thus an oft-quoted maxim after 1606 that "the greater the truth the greater the libel." The potential benefits to be derived from bringing governmental shortcomings to light were not seen as sufficiently valuable to justify the exclusion of true libels from the reach of the criminal law. The Star Chamber's open-ended formulation of the crime opened the door to essentially unchecked suppression of dissent. During the seventeenth and eighteenth centuries, prosecutions for seditious libel ran into the hundreds.

The procedures employed in the prosecution of seditious libel were especially problematic. By the seventeenth century, the use of general warrants in felony cases had been sharply curtailed. Such warrants were used virtually without restraint, however, in cases of seditious libel, a mere misdemeanor. General warrants routinely authorized government officers to arrest and to search the homes and offices of anyone even suspected of seditious libel. Such arrests and searches were frequently used to harass critics of the government even when the evidence against them was clearly insufficient to warrant a trial.

Moreover, prosecutions for seditious libel did not require the attorney general to obtain an indictment from the grand jury. Long regarded as a fundamental safeguard against the power of government unjustly to prosecute its political enemies, the grand jury consists of a body of laymen who may issue an indictment (a necessary predicate for a felony prosecution to proceed) only if they are persuaded that there is a reasonable probability that the suspect is actually guilty. Because seditious libel was a mere misdemeanor, however, the attorney general could evade the protections of the grand jury and proceed instead by information. This procedure required only that the attorney general present his suspicions to the King's Bench, obtain a warrant for the suspect's arrest, and then bring the suspect before the bar of the court for trial.

The trial was structured so as to leave most of the critical decisions in the hands of government officials. In prosecutions for seditious libel, the common law jury was permitted to decide only whether the defendant had actually published the words in question. The judges reserved to themselves the central issues of malicious intent and bad tendency. Although the intent and tendency concepts had the potential to limit significantly the doctrine of seditious libel, in the hands of the judges they were of no appreciable consequence. The judges simply inferred bad intent and bad tendency from the very fact of the libel. In practical effect, then, the criticism itself became criminal. And, of course, truth was no defense.

During this era, the prosecution of seditious utterances was not left entirely to the common law courts. Parliament, too, took an active role. Although Parliament, after a long struggle, finally won freedom of speech for its members in the English Bill of Rights of 1689, it denied this same freedom to ordinary citizens. Parliament interpreted its power to punish any contempt of its authority or reputation as encompassing the power to punish aspersion of either House, any of its members, or the government generally. The procedures employed by Parliament were even more summary than those used by the courts.

The American colonial experience

Although it is popularly believed that colonial writers were engaged in a continual struggle with royal judges over the right to criticize the government, actually there were no more than half a dozen common law trials for seditious libel in colonial America. The most famous of those trials was that of John Peter Zenger in New York in 1735 (Alexander). Zenger, publisher of the *New York Weekly Journal,* was charged with seditious libel by the governor-general of New York, whom he had criticized. The grand jury refused to indict, and the prosecution was thus begun by the filing of an information. Because he was unable to post the high bail imposed, Zenger spent almost a year in jail awaiting trial.

Zenger was brilliantly represented by Andrew Hamilton and James Alexander, who challenged the established doctrine of seditious libel on two basic grounds. First, although conceding that a false libel of a government official might be punished, they maintained that the truth of the libel should be an absolute defense. Second, they argued that the jury, rather than the judge, should decide the ultimate question of intent and bad tendency. These two propositions, which played a central role in eighteenth-century criticism of seditious libel, were flatly rejected by the trial judge. The jury, however, responding to the eloquence of Hamilton's oratory and the popularity of Zenger's cause, ignored the judge's instructions and returned a verdict of not guilty. Although the Zenger case had no precedential effect on the substantive law, it signaled a potential shift in the political climate.

Although common law prosecutions for seditious libel were infrequent, the popularly elected colonial assemblies assumed and vigorously exercised the power to punish as contempt any expression of criticism of their members, their laws, or their policies. The Virginia House of Burgesses, the first popularly elected colonial assembly, first punished a "treasonable" utterance in 1620. Thereafter, hundreds of persons were brought before the various colonial assemblies and summarily tried for similar breaches of parliamentary privilege.

Adoption of the First Amendment

Scholars have long puzzled over the actual intentions of the framers of the First Amendment's guarantee that "Congress shall make no law . . . abridging the freedom of speech, or of the press." According to one theory, the framers intended to enact Blackstone's statement that under the common law "the liberty of the press . . . consists in laying no *previous* restraints upon publications and not in freedom from censure for criminal matter when published" (Blackstone, *151). In other words, the amendment prohibited censorship in the form of licensing but did not restrict the power of government to punish expression *after* publication. Under this theory the amendment left the common law of seditious libel intact.

A competing theory maintains that the primary intention of the framers was to abolish seditious libel. Supporters of this theory point out that licensing had been abandoned in England in 1695 and in the colonies by 1725, and that it was highly unlikely that the framers would have bothered to enact an amendment to deal with so moot an issue. Supporters of this theory thus argue that it was the seditious libel issue, as manifested in controversies like the *Zenger* prosecution, that was paramount in the minds of the framers.

In the end, the framers' actual intentions remain obscure. Indeed, the framers themselves seem not to have had any shared understanding about the precise meaning of the First Amendment.

The Sedition Act

The first serious challenge to freedom of political expression in the newly formed nation came with the Sedition Act of 1798, ch. 74, 1 Stat. 596. The United States was on the verge of war with France, and many of the ideas generated by the French Revolution aroused fear and hostility in segments of the American population. At the same time, a bitter political and philosophical debate raged between the Federalists, then in power, and the Democratic Republicans. The polemics hurled by both sides were violent in tone and frequently scurrilous.

Against this backdrop, the Federalists enacted the Sedition Act. The act prohibited the publication of "false, scandalous, and malicious writings against the government of the United States, or either house of the Congress of the United States, or the President of the United States, with intent to defame the said government, or either house of the said Congress, or the said President; or to bring them, or either of them, into contempt or disrepute." The act provided further that truth would be a good de-

fense, that malicious intent was an element of the crime, and that the ultimate question of guilt or innocence was for the jury to decide.

The Republicans questioned the validity of this legislation on two grounds. First, they maintained that since the Constitution did not expressly delegate to the Congress the power to pass a law against sedition, the law was adopted without constitutional authorization and was therefore null and void. The Federalists responded that Congress was specifically given the power to make all laws "necessary and proper" for carrying into execution its delegated powers and that the government could not function effectively if seditious utterances were to pass unpunished.

Second, the Republicans argued that even if the Constitution as originally drafted gave Congress an implied power to prohibit seditious speech, that power was expressly removed by the First Amendment. To the Federalists, however, "the freedom of speech" and "the freedom of the press" were terms that could be defined only by the English common law. Relying upon Blackstone's definition, they maintained that such freedom is nothing more than an exemption from all previous restraints. Moreover, the Federalists observed with pride that the Sedition Act made truth a defense, required proof of malicious intent, and, like Fox's Libel Act, 1792, 32 Geo. 3, C. 60 (Great Britain), made the jury the ultimate judge of the libel. Thus, the Sedition Act eliminated those elements of the English common law that had previously been the focus of attack.

The Republicans were unpersuaded. In their view, the First Amendment must have been intended not only to preserve the abolition of prior restraints but also to guarantee free and unimpaired discussion of public men and measures. In a political system which presumes that the ruler can do no wrong, the doctrine of seditious libel may be defensible. But it is wholly indefensible, they argued, in a system in which governmental officials are elected by, and are responsible to, the people.

The Sedition Act was vigorously enforced, but only against members or supporters of the Republican Party. Republican newspapers were scanned for seditious material, and prosecutions were brought against the four leading Republican papers as well as against some of those less influential. The number of arrests made under the act is uncertain but totaled at least twenty-five, with at least fifteen indictments. The cases, often tried before openly hostile Federalist judges, resulted in ten convictions and no acquittals. Moreover, in the hands of these judges, the "protections" of the act, such as the defense of truth and the requirement of proof of malicious intent, proved largely illusory.

Consider, for example, the plight of Matthew Lyon, a Republican congressman from Vermont and a staunch opponent of the Federalists. During his reelection campaign, Lyon asserted in a published article that under President John Adams "every consideration of the public welfare was swallowed up in a continual grasp for power, in an unbounded thirst for ridiculous pomp, foolish adulation, and selfish avarice." For this and similar statements, Lyon became the first person indicted under the act. At his trial, the jury was instructed to find malicious intent unless the statement "could have been uttered with any other intent than that of making odious or contemptible the President and the government, bringing them both into disrepute." In effect, the jury was instructed to infer malicious intent from the statement itself. Moreover, given the nature of the statement, Lyon could hardly prove its "truth." Mere expressions of opinion or political hyperbole cannot be proved true. Lyon was convicted and sentenced to a fine of $1,000 and four months in prison. Although the Federalist press rejoiced, Lyon became an instant martyr and was reelected while in jail (*Trial of Matthew Lyon* (1798), F. Wharton, State Trials of the United States 333 (Philadelphia 1849)).

Although the Supreme Court did not at the time rule upon the constitutionality of the Sedition Act, the act was upheld without dissent by the lower federal courts and by three Supreme Court justices sitting on circuit. The act expired of its own force on March 3, 1801. President Thomas Jefferson thereafter pardoned all those who had been convicted under the act, and Congress eventually repaid most of the fines.

Sedition from 1800 to 1917

Between the close of the Sedition Act controversy and enactment of the Espionage Act of 1917 (ch. 30, title 1, § 3, 40 Stat. 217) during World War I, there were three significant developments in the history of sedition.

Suppression of abolitionist expression in the South. After 1830, the Southern states embarked upon a pervasive campaign to suppress the expression of antislavery opinion. Fears of Garrisonian abolitionism and slave revolt led one state after another to enact stringent prohibitions on the dissemination of abolitionist doctrine. Virginia, for example, made it a crime merely to deny the right to own slaves; South Carolina declared it unlawful to possess, receive, or publish abolitionist literature; and Louisiana rendered it a crime to write, publish, or speak anything that tended "to destroy that line of distinction which the law established between the several classes of this community."

These laws curtailed, but did not entirely suppress, antislavery expression. Many of the laws had loopholes, legal processes were slow, and the courts often were lenient. To remedy these defects, highly structured "vigilance committees" were organized throughout the South. These committees, representing a form of quasi-official mob rule, took enforcement of the law into their own hands. They regularly meted out punishments ranging from the infliction of such indignities as head-shaving to manhandling and transportation by various means out of the community.

The Civil War. Throughout the Civil War, there was open and widespread opposition to the war and the draft. The government recognized that any attempt to suppress seditious and disloyal utterances generally would be seen as simply another example of the despotism so often charged against Abraham Lincoln by his opponents. Thus, largely for pragmatic political reasons, the government did not enact legislation modeled on the Sedition Act of 1798. The government did attempt to minimize seditious expression, however, by limiting the privileges of hostile war correspondents and by restricting the right of anti-administration newspapers to use the telegraph system and the mails.

Criminal anarchy. In the second half of the nineteenth century, the activities of anarchists and other radicals reignited the controversy over sedition. Along with other, less dramatic events, the Haymarket Square bomb explosion in Chicago in 1886 and the assassination of President William McKinley in 1901 resulted in 1902 in New York's enactment of the first criminal-anarchy statute, 1902 New York Laws, ch. 371. The act prohibited advocacy of the overthrow of organized government by force, violence, assassination, or any other unlawful means. Although several states soon followed New York's lead, there were relatively few prosecutions under these criminal-anarchy laws until after World War I.

The Espionage Acts of 1917 and 1918

Two months after America's entry into World War I, Congress enacted the Espionage Act of 1917. The act made it a crime, among other things, willfully to make false statements with the intent to interfere with the war effort; willfully to cause or attempt to cause dissension in the armed services; or willfully to obstruct the recruitment or enlistment services of the United States. Violations were punishable by fines of up to $10,000, prison sentences of up to twenty years, or both.

Not satisfied that the 1917 act sufficiently protected the interests of the nation, Congress eleven months later enacted the Espionage Act of 1918 (ch. 75, §§ 3–4, 40 Stat. 553), which declared it criminal, among other things, for any person to say anything with intent to obstruct the sale of war bonds; to utter, print, write, or publish any disloyal, profane, scurrilous, or abusive language intended to cause contempt or scorn for the form of government of the United States, the Constitution, the flag, or the uniform of the army or navy; to urge the curtailment of production of war materials with the intent to hinder the war effort; or to utter any words supporting the cause of any country at war with the United States or opposing the cause of the United States. The 1918 act was repealed in 1921, but the Espionage Act of 1917 remains in force "when the United States is at war."

Most of the approximately two thousand Espionage Act prosecutions initiated during World War I involved the provisions of the 1917 act. Mere statements of opinion critical of the war were treated as statements of fact and then condemned as "false" because they were inconsistent with presidential or congressional declarations. Moreover, through the use of the doctrines of bad tendency and constructive intent, the courts transformed the prohibitions against causing insubordination and obstructing recruiting into prohibitions against criticizing the war and the draft generally. Any such criticism, the courts reasoned, might have the tendency to induce insubordination or refusals of induction. That the speaker or author did not intend to bring about such consequences was irrelevant, for every person, the courts maintained, is held to intend the natural and foreseeable consequences of his acts. Under the twin doctrines of bad tendency and constructive intent, even the most innocuous criticism could be deemed a crime (*Albers v. United States*, 263 F. 27 (9th Cir. 1920), *rev'd*, 256 U.S. 706 (1921); *Shaffer v. United States*, 255 F. 886 (9th Cir. 1919); *Kirchner v. United States*, 255 F. 301 (4th Cir. 1918); *United States v. Nagler*, 252 F.217 (W.D. Wis. 1918)). The one shining exception to the dominant view was the opinion of Judge Learned Hand in the *Masses* case, in which Hand interpreted the act as applying only to speech that expressly advocated unlawful conduct (*Masses Publishing Co. v. Patten*, 244 F. 535 (S.D.N.Y. 1917), *rev'd*, 246 F. 24 (2d Cir. 1917)).

The constitutionality of the Espionage Act of 1917 was first addressed by the Supreme Court in *Schenck v. United States*, 249 U.S. 47 (1919). Charles Schenck, the secretary of the Socialist Party, was convicted under the 1917 act for helping to prepare and distribute a leaflet sharply critical of the war and the draft. Although using the "clear and present danger" rubric for the first time in *Schenck*, the Supreme Court gave short shrift to Schenck's First Amendment argument, holding that the conviction was constitutionally permissible in light of Schenck's "intent" and the "tendency" of the leaflet. In effect, the Court construed the First Amendment as having little if any real impact in this context, and in an unbroken series of decisions in the next few years the Court upheld a stream of convictions under the 1917 and 1918 acts (*Frohwerk v. United States*, 249 U.S. 204 (1919); *Debs v. United States*, 249 U.S. 204 (1919); *Abrams v. United States*, 250 U.S. 616 (1919)).

Beginning with *Abrams*, however, Justices Oliver Wendell Holmes and Louis Brandeis launched a powerful attack upon the Court's analysis. From *Abrams* onward, Holmes and Brandeis argued persistently and eloquently that the First Amendment sharply curtailed the power of government to suppress seditious expression. Under the First Amendment, they maintained, such expression may be restricted only if it posed a clear and present danger of harm. Although Holmes and Brandeis failed to persuade their brethren, these dissenting opinions laid the foundation for the contemporary understanding of the First Amendment. Examples were *Abrams* (Justice Holmes dissenting), *Schaefer v. United States*, 251 U.S. 466 (1920) (Justice Brandeis dissenting), and *Pierce v. United States*, 252 U.S. 239 (1920) (Justice Brandeis dissenting).

Subversive advocacy in the 1920s

In the years immediately after World War I there was widespread concern that such radical political doctrines as anarchism and Communism could lead to social, economic, and political upheaval. The federal government used the immigration laws, as amended in 1918, to deport aliens holding radical political views, and this fear of alien ideas initiated the Palmer Raids of 1920, in which some four thousand aliens suspected of membership in the Communist Party were rounded up and held without warrant.

Two-thirds of the states enacted criminal-syndicalism or criminal-anarchy laws between 1917 and 1921. These laws, which were modeled on the 1902 New York criminal-anarchy statute, prohibited any person from advocating or teaching that organized government should be overthrown by force, violence, or other unlawful means and from organizing or becoming a member of any organization whose purpose was to advocate or teach this doctrine. In addition, some thirty-three states enacted laws prohibiting the display of "red flags." In this period approximately fourteen hundred persons were arrested, and about three hundred convicted, under these state sedition and red-flag laws. In two major decisions, the Supreme Court upheld state sedition laws as consonant with the First Amendment (*Gitlow v. New York*, 268 U.S. 652 (1925); *Whitney v. California*, 274 U.S. 357 (1927)).

The Smith Act

In the late 1920s and the 1930s, there were relatively few governmental efforts to suppress seditious utterances. Moreover, the Supreme Court in this era reversed several convictions for seditious expression, although these decisions did not significantly alter prior doctrine (*DeJonge v. Oregon*, 299 U.S. 353 (1937); *Herndon v. Lowry*, 301 U.S. 242 (1937); *Fiske v. Kansas*, 274 U.S. 380 (1927)).

In 1940, however, Congress enacted the Smith Act, 18 U.S.C. § 2385 (2000), which declared it unlawful for any person to advocate or teach the "duty, necessity, desirability, or propriety of overthrowing" by force or violence the government of the United States or of any state or to organize or knowingly become a member of any society or group "of persons who teach, advocate or encourage the overthrow" of any such government. Violations were punishable by imprisonment of up to twenty years, fines of up to $20,000, or both.

In the first major prosecution under the act, the government in 1948 indicted twelve members of the Central Committee of the Communist Party of the United States for conspiring to violate the act. After a trial lasting eight months, the defendants were convicted. In a confusing set of opinions, a divided Supreme Court upheld the convictions (*Dennis v. United States*, 341 U.S. 494 (1951)). The plurality opinion in *Dennis*, written by Chief Justice Fred Vinson, embraced a modified version of the clear-and-present-danger formula, holding that the critical question was whether the gravity of the evil, discounted by its improbability, justified the restriction on expression. Since the evil sought to be avoided—overthrow of government—was especially grave, even a remote danger of its occurrence, Vinson held, was sufficient to sustain the convictions.

After the decision in *Dennis*, Smith Act prosecutions were instituted against the secondary leadership of the Communist Party. By 1957, the government had secured convictions of ninety-six Communist Party members in addition to the *Dennis* defendants. In a 1957 decision, however, the Supreme Court retreated sharply from *Dennis*, holding that the Smith Act prohibited only express incitement to *specific* unlawful conduct (*Yates v. United States*, 354 U.S. 298 (1957)). *Yates* had a decisive effect upon the administration of the act. In all pending cases but one, the indictments were either dismissed by the courts or dropped by the government, and no further prosecutions were brought.

Sedition and the First Amendment

Since the 1960s, the Supreme Court has sharply defined and limited the constitutionally permissible contours of seditious libel. With respect to false statements critical of the government, the Court has announced that "under the First Amendment there is no such thing as a false idea. However pernicious an opinion may seem, we depend for its correction not on the conscience of judges and juries but on the competition of other ideas" (*Gertz v. Robert Welch, Inc.*, 418 U.S. 323, 339–340 (1974)). Moreover, although false statements of *fact* about a governmental official may give rise to a civil or criminal action for libel, the Court has held that such actions require proof that the speaker acted either with knowledge of falsity or with reckless disregard for the truth (*New York Times Co. v. Sullivan*, 376 U.S. 254 (1964)).

Finally, the Court has held that mere criticism of government may not be suppressed. The First Amendment permits punishment of seditious utterances only if they expressly advocate immediate unlawful action and are likely to produce such action imminently (*Brandenburg v. Ohio*, 395 U.S. 444 (1969)). In effect, the Court's affirmation of our "profound national commitment to the principle that debate on public issues should be uninhibited, robust, and wide-open" renders the traditional crime of seditious libel unconstitutional (*New York Times Co.*, 270).

After a nearly thirty-year hiatus, the crime of "seditious conspiracy," 18 U.S.C. § 2384 (2000), made a surprising reappearance in the 1980s and 1990s as an instrument for combating domestic terrorism. The most notorious case arose from the bombing of the World Trade Center in New York City by a group of individuals who perceived themselves to be involved in a Muslim holy war (or "jihad") against the United States. Some commentators reacted with dismay, arguing that the decision to prosecute under § 2384 rather than under general prohibitions against violence conveyed that the World Trade Center defendants were being condemned for their political and religious motivations and not just for the harms they caused. Nevertheless, the United States Court of Appeals for the Second Circuit rejected a First Amendment challenge patterned on this objection (*United States v. Rahman*, 189 F.3d 88 (1999)).

GEOFFREY R. STONE
DAN M. KAHAN

See also CONSPIRACY; FEDERAL BUREAU OF INVESTIGATION: HISTORY; FEDERAL CRIMINAL JURISDICTION; LIBEL, CRIMINAL; TREASON.

BIBLIOGRAPHY

ALEXANDER, JAMES. *A Brief Narrative of the Case and Trial [in the Supreme Court of the Judicature of the Province of New York, 1735] of John Peter Zenger, Printer of the "New York Weekly Journal."* 2d ed. Edited by Stanley Nider Katz. Cambridge, Mass.: Harvard University Press, 1972.

BLACKSTONE, WILLIAM. *Commentaries on the Laws of England (1765–1769)*, vol. 4. Reprint. University of Chicago Press, 1979.

BRENNAN, WILLIAM J. "The Supreme Court and the Meiklejohn Interpretation of the First Amendment." *Harvard Law Review* 79 (1965–1966): 1–20.

CHAFEE, ZECHARIAH. *Free Speech in the United States.* Cambridge. Mass.: Harvard University Press, 1948.

DONNER, FRANK J. *The Age of Surveillance: The Aims and Methods of the American Intelligence System.* New York: Knopf, 1980.

EMERSON, THOMAS I.; HABER, DAVID; and DORSEN, NORMAN. *Political and Civil Rights in the United States.* Boston: Little, Brown, 1967.

GRINSTEIN, JOSEPH. "Note, Jihad and the Constitution: The First Amendment Implications of Combating Religiously Motivated Terrorism." *Yale Law Journal* 105 (1996): 1347–1381.

GUNTHER, GERALD. "Learned Hand and the Origins of Modern First Amendment Doctrine: Some Fragments of History." *Stanford Law Review* 27, part 1 (1974–1975): 719–773.

HUDON, EDWARD GERARD. *Freedom of Speech and Press in America.* Foreword by William O. Douglas. Introduction by Morris L. Ernst. Washington. D.C.: Public Affairs Press, 1963.

KALVEN, HARRY, JR. "The *New York Times* Case: A Note on the Central Meaning of the First Amendment." *The Supreme Court Review.* Edited by Philip B. Kurland. University of Chicago Law School, 1964, pp. 191–221.

LEVY, LEONARD WILLIAMS. *Legacy of Suppression: Freedom of Speech and Press in Early American History.* Cambridge. Mass.: Harvard University Press, Belknap Press, 1963.

NYE, RUSSEL BLAINE. *Fettered Freedom: Civil Liberties and the Slavery Controversy, 1830–1860.* East Lansing: Michigan State University Press, 1964.

SIEBERT, FREDRICK SEATON. *Freedom of the Press in England,1476–1776: The Rise and Decline of Government Controls.* Urbana: University of Illinois Press, 1952.

SENTENCING, PURPOSES OF

See PUNISHMENT.

SENTENCING: ALLOCATION OF AUTHORITY

In the United States there are now a wide range of legal approaches to the sentencing of criminal offenders. These include indeterminate sentencing systems in many states, statutory determinate systems in a few others, and a growing number of sentencing guideline systems among the states and in federal law. The diversity in legal structure for punishment decisions has brought with it a great deal of experimentation concerning which decision-makers hold meaningful authority—or discretion—over sentencing outcomes. Allocations of sentencing discretion can be remarkably different as one moves from one American jurisdiction to another.

Definition of sentencing discretion

Sentencing discretion, as the term is used in this entry, exists whenever a participant in the design or operation of the criminal justice system can exercise choice in a way that dictates, places limits upon, or contributes to the sentencing outcome of a particular criminal case or whole categories of cases.

This is a broad definition that stretches familiar usages of the word "discretion." For one thing the definition of sentencing discretion embraces both public and private actors who take part in the processes leading up to final punishment outcomes. For another, the definition of sentencing discretion extends to acts of rulemaking by legislatures, sentencing commissions, and appellate courts, just as the definition extends to individualized decisions that affect only one defendant at a time. The expansive definition is necessary, however, to capture the complex and multilayered accumulation of human choices that eventuate, ultimately, in sentencing outcomes.

The term *sentencing outcome* also bears definition: As used here, it refers to the total of all sanctions as experienced by a criminal offender up until the moment that the legal system relinquishes jurisdiction over the offender.

Most sentencing outcomes build up over time and are the products of cumulative decisions by multiple actors. The sentencing process is "not over until it's over." For example, in most jurisdictions, a trial judge's pronouncement of a five-year sentence on a convicted offender would hardly qualify as a sentencing outcome. At the day of sentencing, we may still be at a relatively early point in the chronology of discretionary decisions affecting the punishment to be experienced by the offender. A parole board, together with officials in the department of corrections, might still hold enormous authority to fix the offender's actual release date from incarceration. (In some states, early release is possible after a small fraction of the judge's pronounced sentence has been served.) In many systems, we cannot guess the sentencing outcome in a prison case until the offender finally has been released on parole, perhaps years after the judge's decision in the courtroom—and additional years may elapse before the offender has successfully completed any term of supervised post-prison re-

lease. When this moment finally comes, we can look back and say what the total sentencing outcome has been.

A discretion diagram

A pictorial *discretion diagram* can be used to visualize many of the important relationships that exist in real-world sentencing systems. Figure 1, "A Discretion Diagram for Sentencing Systems," is a generic diagram that is not tailored to any up-and-running system. It introduces a cast of characters who may or may not possess meaningful sentencing authority in a given punishment structure. These include, at the "systemic level," the legislature (important in all U.S. jurisdictions) and a sentencing commission (chartered in more than twenty U.S. jurisdictions as of 1999). At the "case specific-level," Figure 1 begins with the parties (meant to include the defendant, the defense lawyer, and the prosecutor), adds various judicial actors, and concludes with corrections and parole officials.

From the perspective of a designer of sentencing systems, Figure 1 might be seen as a basic palette of primary colors from which the designer may work to create the fundamental discretionary relationships within a new system. As we shall see below, there are a great variety of design options for the power relationships that can be fashioned among the players shown in Figure 1.

Indeterminate sentencing systems

For most of the twentieth century, the indeterminate sentencing system was the dominant legal structure for punishment decisions in the United States. Through the 1940s, 1950s, and 1960s it was virtually the universal approach in this country, and remains (with adjustments here and there) the basic system followed by nearly half of the American states.

The original philosophy of indeterminate sentencing structures was that most criminals could be rehabilitated, and that this goal required an individualized inquiry into the life history, behavioral deficits, and "treatment" needs of each offender. In order to carry out an individualized program of "correction," legislatures granted judges unconstrained authority to impose punishments within a broad range of statutory options. It was not unusual, for example, for judges to have discretion to select any punishment (or none at all) within statutory maximum penalties as severe as ten, twenty, or thirty years in prison.

Figure 1

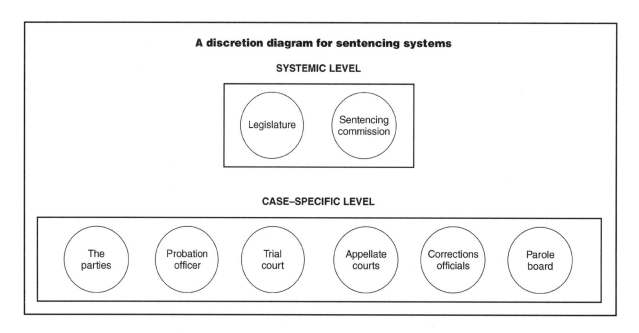

Broad judicial discretion was merely one facet of the case-specific paradigm of indeterminate sentencing. Figure 2 depicts some key features of the allocation of sentencing discretion in a typical indeterminate structure. At the systemic level only the legislature is shown in Figure 2, because traditional indeterminate systems had no sentencing commissions. Moreover, the oval depicting the legislature is shrunken in comparison with most of the other shapes on the diagram. This is meant to illustrate that legislatures play some role in defining punishment outcomes in an indeterminate system, but this role is limited generally to providing the outer boundaries of permissible sanctions. For many if not most serious crime categories in indeterminate systems, the statutorily authorized ceilings on punishment are far in excess of the sanctions most sentencing judges would normally dream of imposing. In this respect, the legislature has opted to make itself a marginal discretionary player as compared with downstream decision-makers. And because, in traditional indeterminate systems, there is no entity such as a sentencing commission to share systemic discretion with the legislature, such jurisdictions are marked by the relative paucity of systemic oversight by anyone.

The defining feature of indeterminate sentencing structures is their diffusion of meaningful sentencing discretion across numerous actors at the case-specific level. Prosecutors most of the time enjoy unregulated charging discretion; plea bargains between the parties (sometimes including sentence bargains) can have sizable impact on punishment; probation officers, at least in some jurisdictions, make sentence recommendations that are highly influential with judges; the judges themselves usually have a boggling array of choices remaining open to them on the day of sentencing; and, following a judicially pronounced prison sentence, correctional officials and parole boards retain impressive powers to fix actual release dates. (However, in some jurisdictions, parole guidelines have been adopted, in an attempt to at least partially structure release decisions.)

The only case-specific actor without meaningful sentencing discretion in traditional indeterminate systems is the appellate judiciary. For reasons of historical practice, deference to trial courts, and caseload pressures, appellate courts almost universally have resisted responsibility to participate in sentencing outcomes in such systems. This state of affairs persisted despite a vigorous reform movement to inculcate "sentence review" in the 1950s and 1960s, and remains a stable feature of indeterminate systems today.

The abdication of systemic authority in indeterminate sentencing structures, and the concentration of sentencing discretion among case-specific actors, originally reflected a deliberate

Figure 2

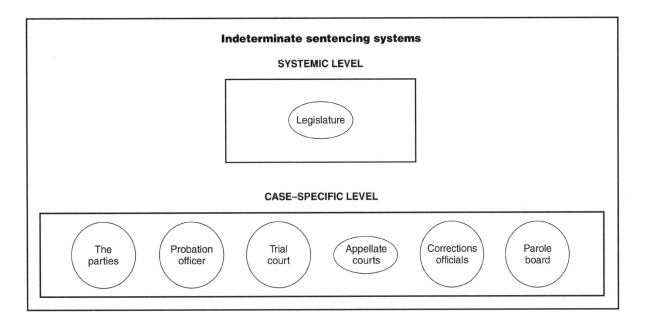

policy judgment that offender treatment could best be pursued on a case-by-case basis. The correctional process was expected to unfold slowly, as authorities monitored each criminal's progress toward rehabilitation. Parole boards, last in the chronology of case-specific actors, were charged with looking the offender in the eye, examining the full case history, and discerning when the magic moment of rehabilitation had finally arrived.

The most important question to be asked about indeterminate systems today is not whether their configurations of discretion are a fair reflection of an articulable plan. (They are.) Rather, the pertinent question is whether the plan itself is sufficiently sound to justify the bottom-heavy and diffuse allocations of decision-making power that characterize indeterminacy. For those who believe that uniformity of punishment is an important goal, or that systemwide policymaking should not be sacrificed wholly to ad hoc individualization, doubts about the wisdom of the indeterminate ideal have become pronounced. This perhaps is inevitable in a world that no longer believes in the widely achievable rehabilitation of offenders, yet continues to operate with the machinery of the damaged theory.

Statutory determinate sentencing

In the 1970s, a handful of states including Arizona, California, Colorado, Illinois, Indiana, and North Carolina modified their former indeterminate sentencing schemes to provide for greater specificity and certainty in authorized punishments as a mailer of statutory command. (Colorado reverted back to indeterminacy in the 1980s, while North Carolina went on to adopt sentencing guidelines in the 1990s.)

The best known statutory determinate sentencing plan is California's. In 1976 the state adopted, and still follows, a "multiple choice" approach under which most serious offenses carry three designated punishments. For example, the current provision concerning first-degree burglary specifies that the sentencing options for the offense include "imprisonment in the state prison for two, four, or six years" (California Penal Code, § 461). In a normal case, the trial judge is expected to impose the middle, or "presumptive," sentence laid out for each crime. As alternatives, the judge may select the "mitigated" or "aggravated" term, provided the judge can cite adequate reasons on the record. Although prison terms are subject to limited reduction at the discretion of corrections authorities, California's determinate sentencing legislation abolished the parole board's authority to decide release dates.

Figure 3 represents California's version of statutory determinacy. It indicates graphically that the legislature is an important discretionary actor in the California system when compared to legislatures in indeterminate systems. (Compare Figure 2.) Instead of writing capacious punishment options into the criminal code, as in indeterminate structures, the California legislature has chosen to be far more directive in its penalty prescriptions. In one sense, therefore, discretionary actors within the trial court system (the parties, probation officers, and trial judges) enjoy a restricted field of sentencing discretion vis-à-vis the legislature. On the other hand, California's abolition of parole release, plus statutory limitations on the release authority of corrections officials, ensure that the sentencing decisions made by the trial court working group will bear predictable relation to the final sentencing outcomes of particular cases. Much more so than in indeterminate sentencing systems, in other words, the sentences pronounced in courtrooms matter in California. Thus, in Figure 3, courtroom actors are represented as discretionary players with meaningful authority. As in most states, however, the California appellate courts exert modest authority over the propriety of sentences; a trial judge's sentence will not be overturned on appeal unless the appellate court finds an "abuse of discretion."

The theory behind California's determinate sentencing reform was that rehabilitative sentencing had proven a failure, and the legislature elected to pursue a new vision that "the purpose of imprisonment for crime is punishment." Further, the California legislature concluded that "the elimination of disparity and the provision of uniformity in sentences can best be achieved by determinate sentences fixed by statute in proportion to the seriousness of the offense as determined by the Legislature to be imposed by the court with specified discretion" (California Penal Code, § 1170). Consistent with these views, sentencing discretion is now concentrated at the "front end" of the discretionary chronology—in the legislature and court system. There is no perceived need to wait months and years for a determination of when offenders have become rehabilitated, so "back end" authorities are granted limited discretionary roles, or eliminated entirely, from the discretionary equation.

Other statutory determinate sentencing reforms of the 1970s, such as those still surviving in Arizona, Illinois, and Indiana, followed a somewhat different scheme from that in California. The criminal codes in such states were amended to set forth narrowed "ranges" of potential punishment for each offense, as opposed to the fixed integers in California law. Still, the overall plan was similar: Typically such statutes provide a "presumptive" range for ordinary cases, with the bookends of "aggravated" and "mitigated" ranges available for unusual circumstances. In addition, Arizona, Colorado (temporarily), Illinois, and Indiana joined California in the elimination of parole release. Thus, these states effectuated a net shift of sentencing discretion toward the "front end" of the decision-making chronology, quite similar to that shown in Figure 3 for the California system.

The defining strength and weakness of statutory determinate sentencing reforms is that they rely on legislatures to choose specific penalties (or narrowed ranges of penalties) for specific crimes. Jurisdiction-wide uniformity in sentencing can be promoted in this way, but state legislatures do not have the time or expertise to ponder exact punishments with care. Nor do legislatures have the attention span needed to monitor their sentencing systems in operation, and to make periodic adjustments in the matrices of presumptive sentences. Indeed, most jurisdictions that enacted statutory determinate laws have found that their legislators tend to pass crazy-quilt amendments over time. In addition, legislative determinacy has proven a weak tool to manage prison population growth. The prison population in states like California, Colorado, and North Carolina grew even more quickly under new determinate laws than before such sentencing reforms were instituted. In part, these developments can be attributed to changes in the political climates of the individual states, but they led many to conclude that legislative determinacy was too blunt an instrument for the administration of a statewide sentencing system. The reform impetus toward statutory determinacy appears to have run its course. No jurisdiction has adopted such a structure since 1980.

Mandatory penalties

An important variation on the theme of statutory determinate sentencing occurs when legislatures fix exact penalties, or exact minimum penalties, for particular crimes. For example, some states have laws stating that the sentence for first-degree murder must be a life term in prison without the possibility of parole. This is an instance of a mandatory penalty. In other states,

Figure 3

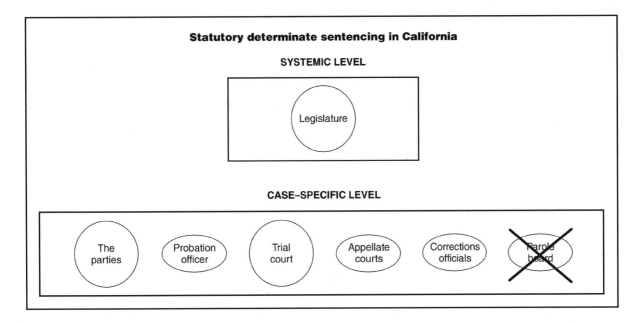

the authorized punishments for first-degree murder may include a death sentence or, at a minimum, a life term in prison without possibility of parole. This is an instance of a mandatory minimum penalty: Following a conviction of the designated offense, no one at the case-specific level holds sentencing discretion to impose a punishment any less severe than a life term of incarceration. Case-specific sentencing discretion exists to exceed the mandatory minimum penalty, but not to undercut it.

Since the 1970s, federal and state legislatures have enacted large numbers of mandatory penalty provisions, and the public popularity of such measures remains high. Such laws commonly apply to crimes involving serious violence, drugs, or firearms. Another species is keyed to criminal record: "habitual offender" laws have long been used to require heavier-than-normal sentences for criminals with substantial prior convictions. In the 1990s a new incarnation of the habitual-offender approach appeared in the form of "three-strikes" laws. Congress and many states have now adopted such laws, which operate on a similar plan: Upon conviction for a third serious felony (these are defined differently from place to place), the judge must sentence the offender to a life term of imprisonment without parole.

As opposed to statutory determinate sentencing, mandatory penalty provisions do not at-

tempt to rework a jurisdiction's overall sentencing structure. They apply to one offense at a time. Mandatory sentencing statutes have been adopted in jurisdictions that otherwise use indeterminate sentencing for the bulk of offenses, in jurisdictions that follow the statutory determinacy approach for most crimes, and in jurisdictions with sentencing commissions and guidelines. In other words, American legislatures have regarded mandatory penalties as a desirable means to produce zones of hyper-determinacy within every available structural environment.

Suppose that a legislature has passed a statute providing that anyone convicted of a designated offense (e.g., possession of a weapon in connection with a drug transaction) must be sentenced by the trial judge to five years in prison, and may not be granted parole or good time credit toward release. Figure 4 attempts to capture the most salient discretionary features of such mandatory penalty schemes in operation.

At the systemic level, Figure 4 depicts the legislature as an important discretionary actor. The legislature has exercised an especially direct form of sentencing discretion because it has pronounced that, for all defendants convicted of *crime x*, the punishment shall be *sentence y*. Indeed, the legislature means to be the one-and-only sentencer for such cases, and has sought to bring about this result by eliminating other dis-

Figure 4

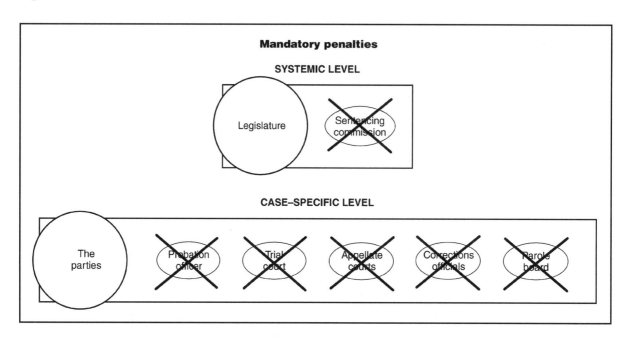

cretionary actors from the decisional process. In contrast, the sentencing commission, even if one exists in the jurisdiction, typically holds no authority to modify or soften the statutory punishments in a mandatory penalty scheme. Thus, the commission is crossed out in Figure 4.

Jumping down to the case-specific level, the probation office and courts are also canceled in the discretionary diagram. Following a conviction for the specified crime, nothing is left for such players to do beyond the rote motions of functionaries. Similarly, any parole authority that may exist in the jurisdiction for other crimes is no longer in force for this offense. And corrections officials, under the imagined statute, have lost their discretion to award or withhold good time credits.

Turning our attention to the enlarged shape in Figure 1 that indicates "the parties," experience has shown that the legislative enactment of mandatory penalties, intentions aside, does not succeed in removing the parties' capabilities to make discretionary choices that carry enormous impact on sentences imposed. For example, in cases where the prosecutor has evidence that an offender has committed the kind of gun-and-drug crime covered by the law, the prosecutor may still decline to bring the charge. If the government charges a lesser offense, out of a sense that five years is too much for this particular case, or from a belief that the required facts will be dif-

ficult to prove, or as part of a plea bargain, the outcome is almost certain to be a sentence well below that required by the statute. Thus, charging discretion, while not formally a part of sentencing proceedings, can exert a powerful impact on the sentencing outcome. Similarly, the plea bargaining process, in which both parties participate, can and frequently does operate to avoid the force of a mandatory penalty.

Taking stock of the discretionary configurations of mandatory penalty provisions, it is apparent that legislatures have succeeded in part, and have failed in part, in bringing about the structural adjustments attempted in such laws. Legislatures have surely succeeded in eliminating the decision-making authority of many familiar players in the sentencing structure. This much comports exactly with the theory of mandatory sentencing: the legislature is trying to impose its own judgments about appropriate sentences on everyone else in the system. Getting rid of the input of sentencing commissions, probation officers, judges, corrections officials, and parole boards is consistent with such a purpose.

At the same time, mandatory penalties greatly heighten the importance of discretionary decisions by the parties. Through charging and plea bargaining discretion, the parties have become the only actors at the case-specific level who may pass upon the application of the mandatory sentence. Moreover, their choices are effectively unreviewable. In most other discretionary arrangements, the parties' authority is diluted by the later-in-time discretions of other case-specific players, such as trial courts, departments of corrections, and parole boards. Mandatory sentencing—which at first glance would appear to privilege the discretion of legislatures—instead produces a hegemony of the charging and plea bargaining decision points. It is hardly surprising that empirical studies of mandatory penalties have concluded that such laws actually work to increase arbitrariness and disparities in sentencing.

Sentencing commissions and guidelines

Since the 1980s, the most popular form of "sentencing reform," among jurisdictions that have wished to move away from the traditional approach of indeterminate sentencing, has been the creation of a sentencing commission empowered to promulgate sentencing guidelines. The first sentencing commissions were chartered in Minnesota and Pennsylvania in the late 1970s; their guidelines went into effect in the early 1980s. Today, there are more than twenty sentencing commissions across the United States, and sixteen jurisdictions with some form of sentencing guidelines in operation. Most of the remaining commissions are at work formulating guideline proposals that have not yet been adopted by their state legislatures.

The amount of sentencing discretion held by sentencing commissions varies widely across American guideline jurisdictions. In some jurisdictions, such as Washington and North Carolina, the guidelines and guideline amendments authored by the commission do not take effect unless affirmatively enacted into law by the state legislature. This might be called a "legislative adoption" model. In other jurisdictions, such as Minnesota and in the federal system, the commission's guidelines and amendments automatically become effective within a specified time period after their promulgation by the commission—unless the legislature acts affirmatively to *disapprove* the commission's proposals. This might be called a "legislative veto" model. All other things being equal, the share of discretion held by a sentencing commission vis-à-vis the legislature is greater in the legislative-veto model than in the legislative-adoption scheme.

In addition to the commission's relationship to the legislature, the discretionary interrelationships of all actors within guidelines systems have

differed dramatically from jurisdiction to jurisdiction since guidelines were first created in 1980. Some sentencing commissions are very powerful players when compared with trial judges in their systems and, in some other places, trial court discretion eclipses the authority of the commission. In a handful of U.S. guideline jurisdictions, the appellate bench exerts meaningful discretion in the realm of sentencing decisions, but in the majority of guidelines states, the appellate courts remain marginal discretionary players. Most guideline jurisdictions have abolished the release authority of the parole board and have limited the release discretion of corrections officials, but in some guideline systems these "back-end" release discretions remain fully intact.

Discretion diagrams can be useful tools to capture these and other permutations of decision-making authority across guideline jurisdictions. The diagrams allow the major discretionary features of different systems to be summarized visually, so that policy makers may compare the advantages and disadvantages of alternative structures.

The federal system

The current federal guidelines system, in effect since 1987, attempts to concentrate sentencing discretion at the systemic level and constrain such discretion at the case-specific level. In both respects, the federal system differs sharply from most guideline structures that have been adopted at the state level.

Although there is a great deal of variation across the country in the operation of the federal sentencing laws, Figure 5 attempts to capture a number of general observations that have been made about the system. First, at the systemic level, both Congress and the U.S. Sentencing Commission are pictured in Figure 5 as highly efficacious discretionary players. Through the adoption of many mandatory penalties, and through close oversight of the commission, Congress has assumed a major role in the determination of sentencing outcomes. The U.S. Sentencing Commission has also exerted great authority over sentences at the case-specific level through the creation of highly detailed guidelines and provisions that give federal district court judges only narrow authority to "depart" from penalties prescribed by the guidelines.

At the case-specific level, the most obvious discretionary effects of the new federal system

Figure 5

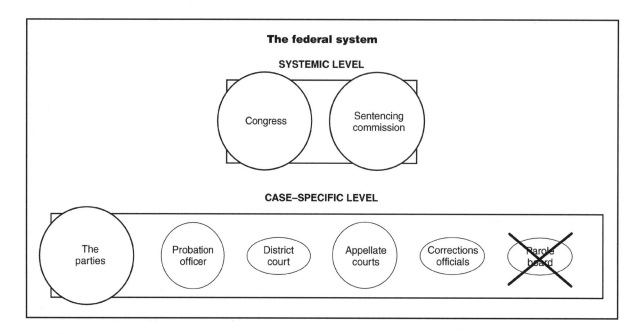

are at the back end of the decision-making chronology. The release authority of the parole board has been abrogated entirely (indicated by an "X" in Figure 5), and the good-time credits that may be granted by federal corrections officials have been cut back to a maximum of 15 percent of the pronounced prison term (thus only a small shape for "corrections officials" in Figure 5). At the case-specific level, most sentencing authority has been removed from the back end of the system and is clustered among the actors who participate in the litigation process.

Among litigation players, the parties have probably assumed the lion's share of sentencing discretion in the federal system. Under either mandatory penalties or the tightly restrictive federal guidelines, the charge(s) of conviction can have forceful if not determinative impact upon what the punishment in a given case will be. Thus, the charging decisions of prosecutors, plus the plea agreements consummated by both parties, will often deliver cases to the judiciary with very little room to move punishments up or down from that prescribed by statute or guideline.

As between the two parties in federal litigation, it has generally been said that the prosecutor holds considerably greater power over sentencing outcomes than the defense attorney. While it is true that roughly 90 percent of federal cases are resolved through a guilty plea—and

both sides must agree to such resolutions—prosecutors are perceived as enjoying a much stronger bargaining position than defense counsel.

The heightened authority of federal prosecutors might be ascribed to three sources. First, given the large number of mandatory penalties in federal law, the prosecutor's charging authority can determine by itself whether a heavy mandatory punishment will be at issue in a given case. Given the prosecutor's sole discretion in such charging decisions, the government may also use the threat of bringing such a charge, or the promise to dismiss such a charge, as bargaining leverage in plea negotiations.

Second, it is widely acknowledged that the severity of penalties in the federal system has increased substantially since before guidelines were enacted in 1987, in part because the guidelines themselves are more punitive than the pre-guidelines sentencing practices of federal judges, and in part because of the proliferation of mandatory penalties. As a result, many federal defendants who go to trial today face heavier sentences following a conviction than would have been the case before 1987. This unappetizing prospect can compel defendants to accept plea bargains that are less favorable than those to which they would have assented before the guidelines. This is clearly a net gain to the prosecution—although it is also a direct outgrowth of the sizable sentencing discretions exercised by Congress and the sentencing commission. If those systemic decision-makers had not decided that heavier sanctions were wanted as a matter of public policy, the bargaining position of federal prosecutors would not have eclipsed that of defense lawyers to the extent we have seen.

Third, prosecutors in the federal system have gained a unique boost to their sentencing discretion under the "relevant conduct" provision of the federal guidelines (United States Sentencing Guidelines, § 1B1.3). The provision requires that sentences be increased at the sentencing hearing when the government proves, by a preponderance of the evidence, that the defendant committed certain offenses in addition to those of which the defendant was convicted. Thus, for offenses within the scope of the relevant conduct provision, a federal prosecutor has two opportunities to secure punishment: The prosecutor may seek a formal conviction by trial or guilty plea, or the prosecutor may wait to prove the offense at the sentencing hearing, under a reduced standard of proof, and where the defendant may not claim such rights as trial by jury, the exclusionary rule, double jeopardy, or the protections of the federal rules of evidence. No state guideline system has yet created an analogue to the relevant conduct provision, so it may be viewed as a source of prosecutorial sentencing authority that is entirely unique to the federal guidelines.

At least once in a while, in some but not all federal districts, the relevant conduct provision has also worked as a source of sentencing discretion enjoyed by probation officers. Under federal law, probation officers are required to bring evidence of all offenses included within the provision to the attention of the sentencing court—whether or not the prosecutor has chosen to do so. In theory, this requirement was intended to cut back on prosecutorial discretion by ensuring uniform sentencing for all relevant conduct even when the United States attorney would prefer to procure a plea bargain by agreeing to drop some or all relevant conduct allegations. In practice, however, federal probation officers do not routinely "upset the applecart" of negotiated guilty pleas by exposing facts at sentencing that the parties had agreed to keep out. But anecdotal accounts tell us that this has happened in some federal cases, perhaps depending on the individual probation officer's talents and predilections, and perhaps occurring in some districts more than others. Even though this form of probation

officer sentencing discretion does not appear to be a stable feature of guideline sentencing in the federal system, it does suggest that the probation officer in Figure 5 should be depicted with more than minimal power to influence sentences.

Last, but by no means least important in Figure 5, are judicial actors. Here, the most remarkable feature of the federal system is how little sentencing discretion is left in the hands of district court judges. Under mandatory penalties, as we have seen, trial judges often have no discretion at all. In addition, district court judges are permitted small latitude to "depart" from the narrow sentencing ranges calculated under the federal guidelines. When district courts have chosen to deviate from the guidelines, the federal appellate courts have been vigilant in upholding the literal terms of the guidelines. Indeed, one recent study found that the chances of a trial court sentence being reversed on appeal in the federal system were ten times weaker than under the guidelines in Minnesota, and nearly fifty times greater than in Pennsylvania's guidelines system. Thus, federal district court judges are often heard to complain that their function has been reduced to "sentencing by computer."

In contrast to the shrunken sentencing discretion of district courts, the federal appeals bench has assumed a vigorous role in the new system. It is important to emphasize, however, that the discretion exercised by the U.S. Courts of Appeals has not been in the direction of creating new judge-made principles for the punishment of offenders. Instead, the powers of the appellate bench have been devoted heavily toward the strict enforcement of the commission's guidelines. This behavior on the part of the appeals courts is in fact a linchpin of the entire discretionary structure of federal sentencing. If the courts of appeals were more relaxed in their review of district court sentences, then the sentencing discretion of district court judges would swell immediately. As a consequence, the systemic powers of Congress and the U.S. Sentencing Commission would deflate (because their prescriptions were less enforceable). And, very likely, if the guidelines were to lose some of their constraining power over trial courts, the importance of the parties' charging and plea bargaining discretions would drop off as well. The appellate courts in the federal system are like a finger in the dike, preventing the trial courts from exercising meaningful discretion over sentencing outcomes, while at the same time allowing great quantities of discretion to pool among actors earlier in the decision-making chronology.

The discretionary relationships surveyed here are complex to grasp, despite the visual aid of Figure 5. Most of the allocations of discretion in the federal system make sense, however, in light of the policies the system was designed to achieve. As recounted by Kate Stith and José A. Cabranes, one major goal of federal sentencing reform was to stiffen punishments for a host of crimes, and to take away the discretion of district court judges to mete out penalties that Congress and the U.S. Sentencing Commission perceived were too lenient. Certainly, to date, these objectives have largely been achieved. Strict enforcement of the federal guidelines was also supposed to promote uniformity in sentencing and, once again, the planned reduction of trial court discretion is consistent with this purpose. However, just as we saw earlier in the case of mandatory penalties (see Figure 4), the federal guidelines system has not solved the riddle of prosecutorial and plea bargaining discretion at the case-specific level.

The Delaware system

The Delaware guidelines system, as it has been in operation since 1990, is illustrated in Figure 6. The Delaware system utilizes the same basic array of institutions as those at work in the federal system (legislature, commission, guidelines, courtroom actors, correctional officials, the abolition of parole release), but to very different effect. A comparison of Delaware with the federal structure is a vivid way to contrast the allocations of discretion that are possible in different guidelines systems.

The greatest distinction between Delaware's guidelines and those in federal law is that, while the federal guidelines are tightly binding on federal judges, Delaware's guidelines are merely "voluntary"— to be used, or not used, by trial judges as they wish. To indicate the weak legal force of the Delaware guidelines, both the legislature and sentencing commission are pictured in Figure 6 as diminutive discretionary players. When these systemic actors speak through guidelines, they utter no more than advisory statements concerning what punishments should be.

At the case-specific level, the current Delaware approach to back-end decision makers is quite similar to federal law. As of 1990, parole release was abolished in Delaware and the release authority of corrections officials was placed under new limitations. Also like the federal system, the sharp confinement of discretion at the back end of the system tends to shift authority toward actors at the adjudication stage.

Among the litigation players, however, the Delaware structure could hardly be more different from the federal arrangement. Because guidelines are only advisory, trial courts may impose any punishment authorized in the criminal code—and Delaware's statutory penalties are expressed in broad statutory ranges left over from the days of indeterminate sentencing. Also like indeterminate schemes, the appellate courts in Delaware exercise virtually no review of the sentencing decisions of trial judges. The result of advisory guidelines and the near absence of sentence review, however, is the creation of far more sentencing discretion in Delaware's trial courts than that possessed by trial judges in indeterminate systems. This is because, under indeterminacy, the trial court's discretion is diluted by the later-in-time discretions of corrections officials and parole authorities. (Compare Figure 6 with Figure 2.) In the Delaware system, however, the trial judge is the last decision-maker to hold meaningful power over punishment outcomes.

It is especially interesting to compare the discretionary power of trial courts under the Delaware guidelines with that in the federal structure. Although both jurisdictions purport to be "sentencing guidelines" jurisdictions, and both systems operate with a similar cast of institutional players, the legal structure of the federal system brings all pressure to bear on choking off the sentencing discretion of trial judges, while Delaware has oriented its system to removing all checks upon the sentencing authority of its trial bench. The comparison of Delaware and the federal system illustrates the following point: As the sentencing discretion of the legislature or sentencing commission is inflated (as in federal law), the sentencing discretion belonging to trial courts tends to deflate—and vice versa. In Delaware, the weak and advisory powers exercised by systemic decision-makers are important complements to the very appreciable powers held by trial judges.

There have been no formal studies of prosecutorial discretion or plea bargaining practices under the Delaware guidelines, but it is clear that the case resolution presented by the parties cannot "tie the judge's hands" to the same extent as in the federal system. Significantly in Delaware, one does not hear the complaints so often voiced

Figure 6

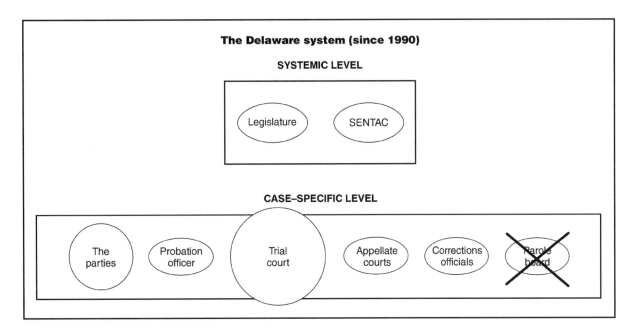

in the federal system that prosecutors have gained huge reservoirs of sentencing discretion under guidelines. It is difficult structurally to have a powerful trial bench and, at the same time, a system in which prosecutors hold determinative authority over sentencing outcomes. In Delaware, if the guideline sentence attending a plea agreement is not to a trial judge's satisfaction, the judge may depart from the voluntary guidelines at will.

Given the realities of courtroom operations, it is probable that plea agreements in Delaware are honored in spirit by trial courts much of the time. (Otherwise the courts, along with everyone else, would have to bear the costs of more frequent trials.) Therefore, the parties surely have substantial impact on sentencing decisions in Delaware, just as the recommendations of trusted probation officers may influence some judicial decisions. But the overall structure of Delaware law places the greatest and most definitive sentencing discretion directly in the trial judges. The discretionary allocations under Delaware's guidelines are so different from those under the federal guidelines, that the Delaware system might be described as the federal system "inside-out."

The Minnesota system

Minnesota, the oldest of all guideline systems in the United states, has taken a middle course between the polar discretionary arrangements illustrated in the federal system and the Delaware system. Where the federal system attempts to concentrate most sentencing discretion at the systemic level, and where the Delaware system attempts to collect very little authority at the systemic level, the approach in Minnesota has been to balance the discretion exercised at the systemic level (by legislature and commission) with discretion discharged at the case-specific level (by the judiciary). Figure 7 attempts to capture this equilibrium in the apportionment of discretion with shapes of similar size for the major discretionary players at both levels.

Less concerned with enforced uniformity than the architects of the federal system, the designers in Minnesota saw the case-specific discretion of trial judges as a desirable feature in the overall system. The original set of guidelines promulgated by the Minnesota Sentencing Commission purported to govern only "ordinary" or "typical" cases. The theory was that trial judges would follow the guidelines prescriptions in the majority of cases, but would retain discretion to depart from the guidelines in cases that were sufficiently atypical. Such a departure decision, however, would have to be explained on the re-

Figure 7

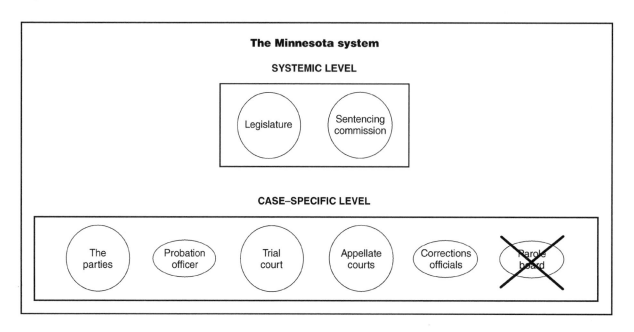

cord, and the trial judge's reasoning made subject to appellate review.

As in the federal system, the actual operation of the Minnesota guidelines has been greatly dependent upon the behavior of the state's appellate courts. If Minnesota's appellate judiciary had chosen to enforce the guidelines to their strict letter, as the federal appeals bench often has done, then trial judges in Minnesota might have become marginal discretionary players in the new system. Instead, however, the Minnesota Supreme Court and Court of Appeals have taken a measured approach to guideline enforcement. Soon after guidelines were enacted, the appellate courts declared that the guidelines were legally binding on trial judges (not merely voluntary, as in Delaware), yet the appellate courts said they would allow sentencing judges to select non-guideline punishments in cases where "substantial and compelling reasons" could be set forth on the record. In practice, trial court sentences below the guideline range have almost always been upheld on appeal in Minnesota and sentences somewhat above the range are usually affirmed as well, but sentences greatly above the range are hard-pressed to survive on appeal in the absence of compelling justification. One study of sentencing appeals rendered in 1995 found that, overall, a sentence handed down by a trial judge in Minnesota had only one-tenth the

chances of being reversed on appeal as in the federal system.

The appellate bench in Minnesota has enforced a kind of give-and-take arrangement between the sentencing commission and trial judges. The commission's guidelines are expected to govern most of the time, but a sentencing court sufficiently moved by the circumstances of an individual case can work around the guidelines, subject to review. As among Minnesota's sentencing commission, the trial bench, and the appellate bench, it would be hard to say which has been the dominant player within the sentencing structure since guidelines were enacted in 1980. Indeed, the three institutions are constantly jostling within a framework of shared powers.

To fill out the description of discretionary relationships shown on Figure 7, it should be noted that the Minnesota legislature has not played a consistently powerful role in the determination of punishment outcomes. When the Minnesota Sentencing Commission was first created in the 1970s, the legislature gave it few specific instructions about what its mission should be. Thus, the initial shape of Minnesota's guidelines was more the result of commission discretion than legislative directive. Over time, however, state legislators have learned that they can exert immediate influence over sentencing policy by instructing the commission to amend its guidelines in specific ways. Such legislative interventions have not been an annual event in Minnesota, but they testify to the power of systemic governance available to the legislature should the legislature choose to use it.

On the case-specific level, Minnesota, like many other guidelines jurisdictions, chose to eliminate parole release when sentencing guidelines went into operation, and also cut back on the early release authority of corrections officials. As we have seen in both the federal system and in Delaware, such changes shift discretion toward the litigation players at the case-specific level. Indeed, one selling point among Minnesota's trial judges, when the state's guidelines were first proposed, was that judicial sentencing authority would actually be increased in comparison with the prior system of indeterminate sentencing. While trial judges are more constrained than formerly by authorities at the systemic level, new controls on the back-end release of prisoners ensure that judicially pronounced punishments bear predictable relationship to sentences actually served.

The full-sized shape on Figure 7 for "the parties" represents the continued importance of plea bargaining within the Minnesota system. Richard Frase, in a 1993 study, found that the pre-guidelines practices of plea negotiation seemed alive and well in Minnesota's guideline structure, but there is no reason to believe that there has been an unintended exacerbation of the importance of charging decisions and plea bargains, as many perceive to have occurred in federal law. The experience of Minnesota, like Delaware, disproves any notion that guidelines structures inevitably enlarge the sentencing discretion of prosecutors. The track record of both states, in comparison with the federal structure, suggests that the best remedy for an undue bulging of discretion in the prosecutor is a system that preserves meaningful sentencing authority in the hands of trial judges. Where trial courts are marginalized, as in the federal system pictured in Figure 5, or as under mandatory penalties as pictured in Figure 4, charging and plea bargaining discretions tend to gain enormous importance.

Guidelines with parole release

The three guideline systems highlighted above are sufficiently different from one another that they give the reader a fair sense of the diverse permutations of sentencing discretion that are possible under guidelines—depending on how the overall guidelines system is designed.

The discussion above has not been comprehensive, however, for the sixteen guidelines systems currently up and running in America are all different from one another, and the new guidelines proposals on the table in several additional states promise still more experimentation.

Seven of the existing guidelines states, for example, have not abrogated the release authority of the parole board. Pennsylvania, which adopted guidelines in 1982, is one such jurisdiction. Much like Delaware, Pennsylvania's guidelines are advisory and are not enforced by the state appellate courts, so sentencing discretion at the systemic level does not have many teeth. At the case-specific level, the release authority of the corrections department has been abolished in Pennsylvania, but the parole board still has discretion to release prisoners after a minimum of one-half of their sentence has been served (Pennsylvania Consolidated Statutes, § 9756). Thus, trial judges and representatives of the sentencing commission in Pennsylvania claim that the most important ultimate decision-maker, for prison cases, is the parole board. Certainly, when significant back-end release discretion exists to modify trial-court prison sentences, the power of trial judges is diminished. Although Pennsylvania's structure is in many ways similar to the Delaware system shown in Figure 6, the major differences between Delaware and Pennsylvania occur in the relative powers of the parole board and the trial judiciary. An overview of these discretionary effects in Pennsylvania is presented in Figure 8.

Discretionary actors elsewhere in the process

There are a number of decision-makers who, in some cases, and in some jurisdictions, hold and exercise discretion to influence punishment outcomes, but who are not represented on the discretion diagrams featured above. A number of these decision-makers will be noted in this section.

First, victims of offenses in the 1980s and 1990s have increasingly become a part of the formal criminal process, including sentencing proceedings. Victims commonly submit "victim impact statements" to sentencing courts, in writing, in the form of oral statements at sentencing hearings, or both. Earlier in the process, victims in many states now consult with prosecutors concerning the charges that will be filed in their cases, and whether or not they approve of plea agreements contemplated by prosecutors. Earli-

Figure 8

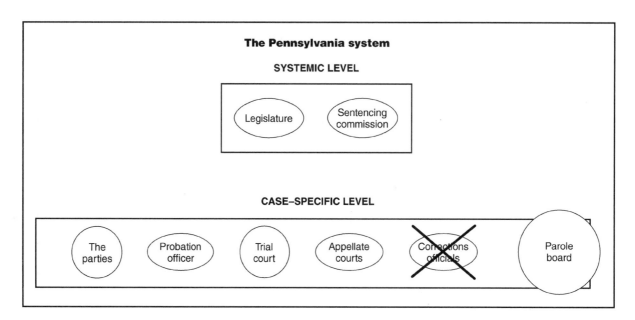

er still, victims might be said to exercise a form of discretion when they decide in the first instance whether or not to report a crime committed against them. A crime that is not reported stands small chance of being punished. We have little empirical knowledge concerning the actual effect upon sentences that has resulted from the growing input from crime victims, but the trend across the country remains one of an increasingly important role for victims.

Second, executive clemency was once an extremely important form of sentencing discretion in the United States—it was a major feature of criminal justice before parole was invented in the late nineteenth century. The president and the governors of most states hold power to pardon offenders, before or after conviction, or to commute sentences (that is, to reduce the severity of sentences). In some jurisdictions this executive power is exercised in conjunction with an agency such as a board of pardons, and in other jurisdictions it remains within the sole discretion of the chief executive. The clemency power continues to exist in all U.S. criminal justice systems, but was probably used less often in the latter twentieth century than in previous times. In the 1980s and 1990s, many elected officials became wary of taking action that could identify them as "soft on crime." Executive clemency has hardly disappeared from the legal horizon, but it is seldom a factor in run-of-the-mill criminal prosecutions.

Third, at least in a handful of states, voters can now exert direct impact upon state sentencing laws through the initiative process. Three-strikes laws, for example, appeared on the ballots of a number of states in the 1990s. The voters in Washington State passed a number of mandatory penalties, including a three-strikes law, that have had real impact on prison growth in the state. Such adjustments in the punishment structure can affect other decision-makers at the systemic level. For instance, if mandatory penalties created through the initiative process result in a significant drain upon prison bed spaces, less flexibility remains in the hands of the legislature and sentencing commission to determine priorities in incarceration policy.

Fourth, a small number of states employ jury sentencing in noncapital cases that go to jury trial, and a majority of jurisdictions with the death penalty rely upon juries to make capital sentencing decisions. In such instances, juries possess the kind of sentencing discretion that is familiarly reposed in trial judges. Where such practices thrive, it is often because jurors are considered to be better representatives of community sentiment than a single member of the judiciary, and thus better positioned to render just punishments. Jury sentencing is often criticized, however, on the ground that jurors lack experience across the full range of criminal prosecutions, and are handicapped in their abilities to compare one case with another for purposes of rendering proportional sanctions. Jury sentencing tends to be politically popular where it exists, but there is no trend to introduce jury sentencing, particularly in noncapital cases, to jurisdictions that have not had such a tradition.

Fifth, in some types of cases, police officers or other law enforcement officers are said to have a new kind of sentencing discretion. Of course, the police have always had considerable discretion over whom to arrest, and a decision not to arrest usually forecloses any possibility of later punishment for the crime at hand. In recent years, however, a number of cases have arisen under sentencing guidelines and mandatory penalties in which the law enforcement decision concerning when to make an arrest has acquired new importance. If, for example, a mandatory penalty requires that a drug offender buy or sell a specified quantity of drugs, some defendants have alleged that the police have prolonged their undercover operations until charges entailing the triggering quantity of drugs can be brought. In the case of undercover sales, it is possible for the police to engineer a number of transactions, waiting for the drug amount to exceed the statutory threshold. This behavior has sometimes been called "sentencing entrapment." To date, there is no legal remedy for a defendant who claims to have been the target of such police behavior, nor is there consensus that there is anything wrong with such law enforcement activity, despite its deliberate impact upon punishment consequences.

Finally, the offender himself might be seen as one of the most important discretionary actors in the criminal process. Barring a miscarriage of justice, the offender's provable criminal conduct places boundaries on the potential punishment in every case, simultaneously creating and restricting the discretions of all downstream decision-makers. It is sometimes said that the prosecutor has the power to select punishment in a case involving a mandatory minimum penalty, or in a restrictive guidelines system, through the decision of what charge to file. There is much truth to the claim that prosecutors have sizable discretion not to charge (or to drop charges in return for a guilty plea or other cooperation), thereby lowering the punishment range available to the court and later system actors. But prosecutors have much less power to increase the punishment range; they cannot "select" a more severe punishment by filing more serious or additional charges unless there is a realistic chance of proving those charges beyond a reasonable doubt (or in federal system, at least proving such charges by a preponderance of evidence, as "relevant conduct" for sentencing purposes). Thus the prosecutor's power derives directly from the offender's underlying guilt.

Kevin R. Reitz

See also Amnesty and Pardon; Criminal Justice System; Guilty Plea: Plea Bargaining; Probation and Parole: Procedural Protection; Probation and Parole: Supervision; Prosecution: Prosecutorial Discretion; Punishment; Sentencing: Disparity; Sentencing: Guidelines; Sentencing: Mandatory and Mandatory Minimum Sentences; Sentencing: Presentence Report; Sentencing: Procedural Protection.

BIBLIOGRAPHY

Alschuler, Albert W. "Sentencing Reform and Prosecutorial Power: A Critique of Recent Proposals for 'Fixed' or 'Presumptive' Sentencing." *University of Pennsylvania Law Review* 126 (1978): 550.

American Bar Association. *Standards for Criminal Justice: Sentencing*, 3d ed. Chicago: ABA Press, 1994.

Bureau of Justice Assistance. *National Assessment of Structured Sentencing*. Washington, D.C.: Office of Justice Programs, 1996.

————. *National Survey of State Sentencing Structures*. Washington, D.C.: Office of Justice Programs, 1998.

Frankel, Marvin E. *Criminal Sentences: Law Without Order*. New York: Hill and Wang, 1973.

Frase, Richard S. "Implementing Commission-Based Sentencing Guidelines: The Lessons of the First Ten Years in Minnesota." *Cornell Journal of Law and Public Policy* 2 (1993): 279–337.

————. "Sentencing Guidelines in the States: Lessons for State and Federal Reformers." *Federal Sentencing Reporter* 6 (1993): 123–126.

Gebelein, Richard. "Sentencing Reform in Delaware." In *Sentencing Reform in Overcrowded Times: A Comparative Perspective*. Edited by Michael Tonry and Kathleen Hatlestad. New York: Oxford University Press, 1997. Pages 88–91.

Knapp, Kay A. "Allocation of Discretion and Accountability Within Sentencing Structures." *University of Colorado Law Review* 64 (1993): 679–705.

Nagel, Ilene H., and Schulhofer, Stephen J. "A Tale of Three Cities: An Empirical Study of Charging and Bargaining Practices Under the Federal Sentencing Guidelines." *Southern California Law Review* 66 (1992): 501–566.

PARENT, DALE G. *Structuring Criminal Sentences: The Evolution of Minnesota's Sentencing Guidelines.* Stoneham, Mass.: Butterworth Legal Publishers, 1988.

REITZ, KEVIN R. "Sentencing Guideline Systems and Sentence Appeals: A Comparison of Federal and State Experiences." *Northwestern Law Review* 91 (1997): 1441–1506.

———. "Modeling Discretion in American Sentencing Systems." *Law & Policy* 20 (1998): 389–428.

ROTHMAN, DAVID J. *Conscience and Convenience: The Asylum and Its Alternatives in Progressive America.* Boston: Little, Brown and Company, 1980.

STEIGER, JOHN C. "Taking the Law into Our Own Hands: Structured Sentencing, Fear of Violence, and Citizen Initiatives in Washington State." *Law & Policy* 20 (1998): 333–356.

STITH, KATE, and CABRANES, JOSÉ A. *Fear of Judging: Sentencing Guidelines in the Federal Courts.* Chicago: University of Chicago Press, 1998.

TONRY, MICHAEL. *Sentencing Matters.* New York: Oxford University Press, 1996.

———. *Reconsidering Indeterminate and Structured Sentencing.* Washington, D.C.: Office of Justice Programs, 1999.

U.S. Sentencing Commission. *Special Report to the Congress: Mandatory Minimum Penalties in the Federal Criminal Justice System.* Washington, D.C.: U.S. Sentencing Commission, 1991.

ZIMRING, FRANKLIN E. "A Consumer's Guide to Sentencing Reform: Making the Punishment Fit the Crime." *Hastings Center Report* 6 (1976): 13–17.

SENTENCING: ALTERNATIVES

The United States has relatively little intermediate punishment for crime. Offenders are either incarcerated or they are given routine probation, which sometimes equates with perfunctory supervision. Because seriousness of crime does not fall into two neat compartments, sentencing often errs in one direction or another. It is either too harsh, putting behind bars people whose crimes and criminality do not warrant it, or too lenient, giving routine probation to people whose crimes and criminality deserve stronger punishment or supervision.

These realities have encouraged states to consider sentencing alternatives (or "intermediate sanctions") that punish but do not involve incarceration. There are two basic arguments for sentencing alternatives. One is practical—many prisons and some local jails are overcrowded, and resources are constrained. Some advocates argue that sentencing alternatives can alleviate prison and jail crowding at less cost than expanding incarceration capacity and without jeopardizing public safety. The second argument is from principle—alternatives provide more latitude for making the punishment fit the crime, thus achieving the sentencing objective of just deserts (Tonry).

The practical argument has been most often used to support sentencing alternatives. Their increasing popularity reflects an impression that they meet their objectives of alleviating prison crowding, costing less than incarceration, and controlling crime. Intermediate sanctions reflect the realization that prisons are crowded, partly because in some states everyone from first-time welfare cheats to repeat robbers are sent to prison, without consideration of the different risks they present to the community. National statistics show that about half the offenders admitted to prison each year are there for property or public order offenses, not violent crimes (Beck). While nonviolent offenses must be taken seriously, it is not obvious that a prison term is necessary. Lawmakers hope that when properly structured, intermediate sanctions may prevent new crimes, but do so without the expense of prison.

These alternative sentencing strategies require finer distinctions among criminal offenders and create, de facto, a continuum of sanctions that reflect the range of criminality. These alternatives are also commonly referred to as "intermediate" or "middle-range" sanctions, since they are tougher than traditional probation but less stringent—and expensive—than imprisonment. Intermediate sanctions offer an alternative to the "either/or" sentencing policy found in many states, that is, either prison or probation. They are seen as a major means to curb prison crowding, while at the same time delivering punishment and protecting the public.

Beginning in the 1980s, states began experimenting with "new" alternative sentencing programs (Tonry and Hamilton). In one sense, alternatives to prison have long been a staple of the justice system through the granting of probation. But conventional probation was shown to be ineffective with felons (Petersilia et al., 1985), and the medical model on which probation was founded also fell out of favor with the public after Robert Martinson's now-famous review claiming that rehabilitation did not work (Lipton et al.). The new sentencing alternatives and the newer name (intermediate sanctions) did not prioritize the offender's need for services, but rather focused primarily on the community's need for protection. This philosophical shift from an offender-rehabilitation focus to a community protection-punishment focus spurred the wide proliferation of intermediate sanctions during the 1980s (for a complete review, see Petersilia).

Enthusiasm for modern sentencing alternatives was generated by early reports from programs like that of the Georgia Department of Corrections. Georgia's self-evaluation claimed that their Intensive Supervision Program (ISP) had saved at least $10,000 per year for each offender who was sentenced to it. Their ISP assigned probationers to a team of officers who had a reduced caseload of not more than twenty-five probationers (normal caseloads in the United States average one hundred). Georgia reported that these ISP participants had extremely low recidivism rates, maintained employment, and paid a monthly supervision fee.

These positive findings attracted national attention and such alternatives were touted as being the future of American corrections. Proponents argued that such programs could relieve prison crowding, enhance public safety, and rehabilitate offenders—and all at a cost savings. Probation staff was also enthusiastic, saying that such programs gave them the opportunity to do probation work the way it ought to be done.

State and federal governments were encouraged by the early evidence, and as Clear and Hardyman wrote about this period, "State legislators were virtually falling over each other" in an effort to sponsor legislation to implement these programs (Clear and Hardyman, 1990). In the ensuing years, every state experimented with a variety of sentencing alternatives, and hundreds of programs were implemented. Today, virtually every state has a variety of intermediate sanction programs (ISPs) in place, as do many countries around the world (for a review, see Petersilia, 1997; Tonry and Hatlestad).

Development and characteristics of alternative sentencing programs

In and of themselves, intermediate sanctions programs (ISPs) do not imply any particular type of program. Rather, ISP is a generic term, and

programs take a variety of forms. The most popular are intensive probation or parole, house arrest, electronic monitoring, boot camps, drug courts, day reporting centers, community service, and specialized (mostly drug-related or sex offender) probation and parole caseloads.

While these alternative sentencing programs differed in detail, they were all designed to be tough, and less expensive than incarceration. Since the voters are not about to endorse "soft" social programs, these new alternatives had to be sold foremost as punitive, rather than as rehabilitative. In fact, some of the older, first-generation "intensive supervision" programs (which had focused on providing intensive rehabilitation services) changed their name to "intensive surveillance" programs, and "alternatives to incarceration" were renamed "intermediate punishments."

The most popular intermediate sanctions are the following.

Intensive supervision probation or parole.   ISP programs are currently the most popular intermediate sanction. They exist in all fifty states, and offenders sentenced to them are closely supervised on small caseloads (twenty-five to forty offenders), usually pay victim restitution and perform community service, must hold a job, submit to random urine and alcohol testing, and pay a probation/parole supervision fee. Statewide ISP programs now operate in Arizona, Connecticut, Florida, Georgia, Illinois, Massachusetts, New Jersey, New York, Oklahoma, Texas, Utah, and Vermont.

House arrest and electronic monitoring.   In many respects, house arrest and electronic monitoring programs are identical to ISP programs, except they are often more stringent in terms of conditions and revocation policies. In house arrest programs, offenders are legally ordered to remain in their residences for the duration of sentences (or portions thereof). House arrestees may be allowed to leave their homes for medical reasons, employment, and approved treatment programs. They may also be required to perform community service and to pay victim restitution and supervision fees. House arrest may also be enforced with electronic supervision that includes the use of an electronic monitoring device such as an ankle bracelet, pager, voice verification telephone, or other electronic technology that assists probation and parole officers in ascertaining an offender's whereabouts.

Shock incarceration and boot camps.   There are basically two types of shock incarceration programs: (a) programs that simply combine a period of incarceration with a period of probation/parole supervision, and (b) programs that introduce offenders to a "boot camp," which may or may not be followed by a period of probation supervision. The duration of the "shock" and the subsequent supervision component varies from state to state, but it is usually a few months in prison, jail, or boot camp followed by a year in the community. Boot camps are facilities in which young first-time offenders are confined for short periods under rigid standards and strict military discipline.

Residential community corrections programs and day reporting centers. Halfway houses or residential community corrections programs are not new but are enjoying revitalization under the intermediate sanctions concept. These programs sentence offenders to serve their sentences in small residential facilities, operated by private agencies under the jurisdiction of the courts. Residents are sometimes permitted to work or attend treatment during the day, returning at night to the facility. Day reporting centers do not hold offenders overnight; the offenders simply report to the center (usually staying from morning until early evening) and participate in work and/or treatment programs for the day.

Day fines, restitution, and community service. Day fines are a relatively new concept whereby monetary fines are meted out that take into account not only the seriousness of the offender's crime and criminal record, but also his or her ability to pay. Judges first determine the number of fine units an offender should be assigned based on the seriousness of the crime and criminal record. After determining the number of fine units, the judge then reviews the offender's financial circumstances in order to set a monetary value for each of these fine units. Usually this amount is based on some proportion of the defendant's daily income (hence, the term "day fines"). While fairly new, courts in Phoenix, Arizona, and Staten Island, New York, have experimented with this sentencing option. Restitution is compensation for financial, physical, or emotional loss caused by the offender; it usually involves payment of money to the victim, but offenders are sometimes ordered to repair damage or perform other work or service for the victim or the victim's family. Community service requires the offender to work without pay for the community, supervised by either probation/parole staff or by private agency personnel.

Table 1

Average sanction cost per year, per adult offender, 1997

Boot camps	$22,995
Prison	$20,297
Jail	$19,892
Halfway houses	$17,885
Electronic monitoring	$4,073
Intensive probation	$2,865
Regular probation	$1,534

The costs of alternative sentencing programs

Most of the enthusiasm for alternative sanctions in modern times comes from its presumed cost-effectiveness. Dollars might be saved if enough prison-bound offenders are diverted to alternatives. The costs per day per offender for imprisonment are much higher than costs per day for intensive supervision. As shown in Table 1, for example, the annual costs of housing a prisoner in the United States is more than $20,000, compared to the annual costs of intensive probation, which are just below $3,000. Such comparisons fuel the popular notion that alternative sanctions are much cheaper than prison. (Table 1 contains the average annual costs of various correctional options, computed from Camp and Camp).

Of course, there is much more to comparing corrections costs than simply comparing per capita costs of sanctions. Intensive probation will be more expensive than most people expect if, for example, greater surveillance and more drug testing increase technical violations, court appearances, and revocations to prison. Or, cost savings will not be realized if program participants come from regular probation caseloads, rather than being diverted from the more expensive jail or prison sentences. In fact, this is exactly what the research evidence shows often happens—programs begun as prison or jail diversion programs end up being probation-enhancement programs (Petersilia and Turner).

The effectiveness of alternative sentencing programs

Dozens of program evaluations have documented the performance of intermediate sanctions. Researchers were primarily interested in learning how participation in these programs affected offenders' subsequent criminal behavior (that is, its impact on recidivism). A secondary but important issue, however, was whether these alternative sanctions could reduce prison crowding and save justice system costs.

The findings are profound in their importance because they are so consistent, despite differences in the programs, the agencies that implemented them, and the characteristics of offenders who participated (see Petersilia, 1998; Sherman, 1997).

First, and critically important, very few offenders participated in such alternative sentencing programs, and few overall dollars were spent on new program initiatives:

- As of 2001, virtually all states and the federal government report having intensive supervision programs, but fewer than 6 percent of the 2.7 million adult probationers and parolees are estimated to be participating in them (although this number is higher than in the past) (Camp and Camp).
- All fifty states report using electronic monitoring; yet despite what has often been characterized as "explosive growth," the actual number of probationers and parolees monitored electronically—now at its highest ever—is estimated to be only about 1 percent (Camp and Camp).
- Thirty-five states report operating boot camps, but the daily census of all of them combined has never exceeded ten thousand participants (Camp and Camp).
- By comparison, there were over 1,200,000 inmates in the state and federal prisons in June 1998, and almost 600,000 inmates in local jails (Bureau of Justice Statistics, 1999).
- At latest count, there were nearly 125 day-reporting centers operating in the United States, but the estimated daily population of all of them combined is less than fifteen thousand (Parent et al.).

From these rough estimates it appears that, at most, 10 percent of all U.S. adult probationers and parolees are participating in alternative sentencing programs—a figure that is probably higher than at any point in the past. And, knowing that felons being granted probation have increasingly serious prior records and substance abuse problems, we can safely say that intermedi-

ate sanction has not touched the bulk of those for whom it might be appropriate.

Second, by and large, intermediate sanction program participants did not come from that group of offenders who were prison bound, but rather those who were high-end probationers. In state after state, well-meaning program developers wrote guidelines for prison "diversions," and just as well-meaning judges and prosecutors ignored them, and filled up the programs with high-risk probationers. From the perspective of those who created these programs to save money and prison space, judges "misused" intermediate sanctions. But from the perspective of judges, they had endorsed the concept of a continuum of sanctions, and preferred to use these options to increase supervision and accountability for felony probationers. The "alternatives" experiment was definitely "widening" the net of social control, but given earlier evidence about the lax supervision of serious felons on probation, some instead characterized it as "net repairing."

Third, offenders were watched more closely, but intensive supervision did not decrease subsequent arrests or overall justice system costs. It did, however, increase technical violations. Offenders on ISP, electronic monitoring, boot camps, day fines, and drug testing programs were watched more closely—as evidenced by a greater number of contacts—but the programs did not reduce subsequent (officially recorded) arrests.

For example, the intensive supervised probation/parole national demonstration evaluated by Turner and Petersilia, which involved fourteen counties in nine states (Petersilia and Turner), found:

- No difference in arrests at one year (38 percent for ISP, and 36 percent for routine probationers);
- More ISP than control offenders had technical violations (70 percent vs. 40 percent), and as a result;
- More were returned to prison or jail by the end of one year (27 percent of ISPs, compared with 19 percent of the controls).

Since it is doubtful whether they committed more violations, close surveillance meant that officers uncovered more technical violations. When this happened, many ISP managers believed they needed to take punitive actions—often revocation to prison—to maintain the program's credibility in the eyes of judiciary and the community. Therefore, programs that were started primarily to save money and avoid the costs of prison often ended up costing their counties more in the long run.

ISPs also tend to attract "law and order" types of probation and parole officers who, in turn, generate higher rates of technical violations (Paparozzi). More technical violations lead to more returns to prison. Importantly, research has yet to show evidence that technical violations are precursors to more serious offending (Petersilia and Turner).

These results bring into question a basic premise of intermediate sanctions, that is, that increased surveillance will act as a constraint on the offender, and that the likelihood of detection will act as a deterrent to crime. A recently completed meta-analysis of the impact of intermediate sanctions on recidivism concluded: "On average, there was no difference in percentage recidivism rates between the ISP and control groups. In summary, the unmistakable conclusion is that the new 'get tough' revolution in probation and parole has been an abject failure when it comes to reducing recidivism" (Gendreau, Goggin, and Fulton, p. 6).

The fourth main finding is important and tantalizing, and has been found consistently across all of the evaluations regardless of program design. The finding points to the importance of combining surveillance and treatment program participation. The RAND national evaluation found that offenders who participated in treatment, community service, and employment programs—or prosocial activities—had recidivism rates 10–20 percent below that of those who did not have such additional activities.

Researchers have found similar findings in Massachusetts, Oregon, and Ohio, and a recent meta-analysis of 174 evaluations of intermediate sanctions programs concluded that the combination of surveillance plus treatment is associated with reduced recidivism (Gendreau and Little). Gendreau and Little conclude: "In essence, the supervision of high risk probationers and paroles must be structured, intensive, maintain firm accountability for program participation and connect the offender with prosocial networks and activities." ISPs that employed more treatment reported a 10 percent decrease in recidivism (Gendreau, Goggin, and Fulton). The empirical evidence regarding ISPs is decisive: without a rehabilitation component, reductions in recidivism are exclusive. With a treatment component, significant reductions in recidivism are possible.

The changing face of sentencing alternatives

Today we still face the same questions that motivated the alternative sentencing movement of the 1980s—prison crowding, probation overload, few resources, and a public demand for accountability and punishment. But some program administrators are using evaluation evidence to redesign programs so that they integrate surveillance with treatment opportunities. There is also evidence that the public is willing to support, both politically and financially, effective offender treatments (Applegate, Cullen, and Fisher). This is particularly true in the area of juvenile justice programming, but also applies to adults, particularly drug offenders.

The OJJDP Comprehensive (COMP) Strategy for Youth endorses graduated sanctions, and incorporates two principle components: increasingly strict supervision and a continuum of treatment alternatives (Howell). Many states are adopting the COMP's strategy, a program for delinquent youth that requires both surveillance and treatment and draws heavily upon the intermediate sanctions program evaluations.

Most boot camps are enhancing the therapeutic parts of their programs and shifting away from their total reliance on physical, militaristic programming. The state of Maryland has adopted a "coerced abstinence" initiative, which will provide drug testing (a main ingredient in surveillance programs) plus treatment in and out of prisons, followed by intensive aftercare upon release. A key component of this program is swift and certain response to drug use violations.

Wisconsin has called for the elimination of probation for felons. They recommend that felony probation be replaced with an arrangement called Community Confinement and Control or CCC. CCCs would include mandatory electronic monitoring, mandatory urine testing, mandatory work or community service, and eighteen to twenty contacts a month, with a probation officer who has a caseload of seventeen offenders. CCC officers would do "community-oriented probation" (similar to community-oriented policing), where they would provide "active" as opposed to "passive" supervision, and be required to engage the offender's community, family, employers, and neighborhoods to create a support and supervision network (Dickey). The Wisconsin legislature is piloting the project in two jurisdictions.

The state of Washington is experimenting with "community" probation, where probation officers partner with the police and community members to reduce the public safety threats posed by offenders in their midst. This is accomplished by having probation officers take an active role in community building, and not just offender restraint. Some have referred to this emerging model as "community justice" or "neighborhood probation," and the probation and parole officers who were involved in alternative sentencing programs are emerging as key players.

These are just a few of the ways in which the ISP research results are directly influencing the design of future programs, and there are several others. It is safe to say that most involved in corrections are keenly aware of the ISP findings, and are using them to design local programs.

But the legacy of the intermediate sanctions experiment is likely to be far more important than simply the redesign of individual programs. ISPs, it seems, have set the stage for an emerging model of "community" probation similar to the Washington experiment described above. Interestingly, as community corrections officers were moving toward a "tougher" form of probation that some likened to police work, police officers were embracing community-based policing, which some likened to probation or social work. Both of them were getting out from behind their desks, out of their cars, and into the community. "In-your-face probation" meant home visits, stopping by the offender's work site, and working with community agencies to develop and supervise community service obligations—a much more "active" probation.

Police, too, were getting out in communities, holding neighborhood meetings, trying to take the pulse of neighborhoods they served—under comparatively well-funded community policing programs. One of the keys of community policing is getting to know the persons on the beat—offenders as well as law-abiding citizens. Police kept hearing over and over again about the residents' fear of offenders, and the lack of justice and accountability for persons who were arrested and placed on probation or released on parole. Victims felt their crimes had been trivialized by a justice system that simply slapped the wrist of offenders and sent them home—or imposed conditions that were not monitored. Repeat victimization was common, and the community wanted serious criminals taken off their streets . . . and once that was done, they wanted programs to help the next generation become responsible citizens.

Police came to realize that to truly reduce crime they had to get out in front of it—not merely react to crime reports. They needed to be *proactive* rather than simply reactive. But to be proactive, they needed a variety of sources of information—and much of that information (and as it turns out, legal authority) existed in probation departments that were operating intensive supervision programs. Historically there has been animosity between police and probation officers—police believe they catch criminals, and probation lets them out. But the new "community justice" model creates a three-part collaboration among the police, probation, and members of the community.

Early program results of these community-based collaborative efforts are positive, and it is likely that the next generation of "sentencing alternatives" will be modeled after them. Judges report having greater confidence in probation terms—feeling that curfews and geographical restrictions might be enforced. Police now have information on conditions of probation, and feel they can count on probation to hold offenders accountable when police report violations of probation conditions.

By combining police and probation resources, probation supervision has become a twenty-four-hour-a-day reality. So what was impossible for probation to do alone (even in the most intensive ISP programs) has become possible once they began partnering with the police and the community.

Initially, probation officers were reluctant to partner with police, and police did not want to connect with "social workers." Over time, however, they have begun to realize that each has something to gain from the other. Police have begun to learn from community corrections and others about community resources—employment programs, school prevention, and so on. Police officers in Boston have started attending joint training seminars, participating in strategic planning sessions at the others' organizations, and jointly participating in research projects. The police, probation, clergy, and laypeople now attend monthly community meetings—and most recently, gang members and street workers have begun to attend as well. And the Boston program is expanding. New initiatives have begun that involve the "teamed" approach. For example, police now help probation officers monitor high-risk domestic violence cases, and operate school programs to reduce truancy. Probation absconders now receive priority arrest status by police.

The program has now spread from Boston to a dozen other probation jurisdictions throughout Massachusetts (for a full description, see Corbett, Fitzgerald, and Jordan).

These programs mainly provide more surveillance. But study after study has shown that both probation and police officers, once they become familiar with individual communities and the persons who live there, tend to develop less hardened attitudes.

These and other alternative sentencing programs show promise as part of a comprehensive strategy for sentencing criminal offenders. We have become so preoccupied with debating whom to imprison, for how long, and under what conditions that we often ignore sentencing alternatives and community-based sanctions. It is currently true—and has always been so—that three-fourths of all convicted criminals will continue to reside in the community. And for those who are initially sent to prison, they, too, will return to the community, usually within a period of less than two years. So the development of effective alternative sentencing program has major implications for public safety and the offender's prospects for rehabilitation. We now have evidence that alternative sanctions can balance the goals of costs, safety, and accountability—and give the public what they most want, which is increased public safety.

JOAN PETERSILIA

See also PRETRIAL DIVERSION; PUNISHMENT; SENTENCING: ALLOCATION OF AUTHORITY; SENTENCING: DISPARITY; SENTENCING: GUIDELINES; SENTENCING: MANDATORY AND MANDATORY MINIMUM SENTENCES; SENTENCING: PRESENTENCE REPORT; SENTENCING: PROCEDURAL PROTECTION; SHAMING PUNISHMENTS.

BIBLIOGRAPHY

APPLEGATE, B. K.; CULLEN, F. T.; and FISHER, B. S. "Public Support for Correctional Treatment: The Continuing Appeal of the Rehabilitation Ideal." *The Prison Journal* 77 (1999): 237–258.

BECK, ALLEN. "Trends in U.S. Correctional Populations." In *The Dilemmas of Corrections.* Edited by Kenneth Haas and Geoffrey Alpert. Prospect Heights, Ill.: Waveland Press, 1999. Pages 44–100.

Bureau of Justice Statistics. "Bulletin: Prison and Jail Inmates at Midyear 1999." Washington D.C.: Office of Justice Program, 1999.

CAMP, CAMILLE, and CAMP, GEORGE. *The Corrections Yearbook 1998.* Middletown, Conn.: Criminal Justice Institute, 1999.

CLEAR, TODD, and HARDYMAN, PATRICIA. "The New Intensive Supervision Movement." *Crime and Delinquency* 36 (1990): 42–61.

CORBETT, RONALD; FITZGERALD, BERNARD; and JORDAN, JAMES. "Boston's Operation Night Light: An Emerging Model for Police-Probation Partnerships." In *Community Corrections: Probation, Parole, and Intermediate Sanctions.* Edited by Joan Petersilia. New York: Oxford University Press, 1998. Pages 180–189.

DICKEY, WALTER. "Governor's Task Force on Sentencing and Corrections." Madison, Wisc.: Wisconsin Department of Corrections, 1996.

GENDREAU, PAUL; GOGGIN, CLAIRE; and FULTON, BETSY. "Intensive Supervision in Probation and Parole Settings." In *Handbook of Offender Assessment and Treatment.* Edited by C. R. Hollin. Chichester, U.K.: John Wiley, 1999.

GENDREAU, PAUL, and LITTLE, T. "A Meta-Analysis of the Effectiveness of Sanctions on Offender Recidivism." Saint John, N.B., Canada: University of New Brunswick, 1993.

HOWELL, JAMES C. "Guide for Implementing the Comprehensive Strategy for Serious, Violent, and Chronic Juvenile Offenders." Washington, D.C.: Office of Juvenile Justice and Delinquency Prevention, 1995.

LIPTON, DOUGLAS; MARTINSON, ROBERT; and WILKS, JUDITH. *The Effectiveness of Correctional Treatment and What Works: A Survey of Treatment Evaluation Studies.* New York: Praeger, 1975.

MORRIS, NORVAL, and TONRY, MICHAEL. *Between Prison and Probation: Intermediate Punishments in a Rational Sentencing System.* New York: Oxford University Press, 1990.

PAPAROZZI, M. A. "A Comparison of the Effectiveness of an Intensive Parole Supervision Program with Traditional Parole Supervision." New Brunswick, N.J.: Rutgers University, 1994.

PARENT, DALE; BYRNE, JAMES; TSARFATY, V.; VALDAE, L.; and ESSELMAN, J. "Day Reporting Centers." Washington, D.C.: National Institute of Justice, 1995.

PETERSILIA, JOAN; TURNER, SUSAN; KAHAN, JAMES; and PETERSON, JOYCE. "Granting Felons Probation: Public Risks and Alternatives." Santa Monica, Calif.: RAND Corporation, 1985.

PETERSILIA, JOAN, and TURNER, SUSAN. "Intensive Probation and Parole." In *Crime and Justice: An Annual Review of Research.* Edited by Michael Tonry. Chicago: University of Chicago Press, 1993.

PETERSILIA, JOAN, ed. *Probation in the United States*. Chicago: University of Chicago Press, 1997.

PETERSILIA, JOAN. "A Decade of Experimenting with Intermediate Sanctions: What Have We Learned?" *Perspectives on Crime and Justice 1997–1998 Lecture Series*, vol. II. Washington, D.C.: National Institute of Justice, 1998.

SHERMAN, LAWRENCE. *Preventing Crime: What Works, What Doesn't, What's Promising*. College Park, Md.: University of Maryland, 1997.

TONRY, MICHAEL, and HAMILTON, KATE. *Intermediate Sanctions in Overcrowded Times*. Boston: Northeastern University Press, 1995.

TONRY, MICHAEL. "Intermediate Sanctions in Sentencing Guidelines." Washington, D.C.: National Institute of Justice, 1997.

TONRY, MICHAEL, and HATLESTAD, KATHLEEN. *Sentencing Reform in Overcrowded Times: A Comparative Perspective*. New York: Oxford University Press, 1997.

SENTENCING COUNCILS

See SENTENCING: ALLOCATION OF AUTHORITY.

SENTENCING: DISPARITY

Critics of the sentencing process contend that unrestrained discretion results in sentencing disparity. They contend that judges who are not bound by sentencing rules or guidelines, but who are free to fashion sentences as they deem appropriate, often impose different sentences on similarly situated offenders or identical sentences on offenders whose crimes and characteristics are substantially different. As Judge Marvin Frankel charged in his influential book *Criminal Sentences: Law Without Order*, unstructured discretion leads to "lawlessness" in sentencing.

Allegations of "lawlessness" in sentencing reflect concerns about discrimination as well as disparity. Although these terms are sometimes used interchangeably, they are significantly different. *Disparity* refers to a difference in treatment or outcome, but one that does not necessarily result from intentional bias or prejudice. As the Panel on Sentencing Research noted, "[Sentencing] disparity exists when 'like cases' with respect to case attributes—regardless of their legitimacy—are sentenced differently" (Blumstein et al., p. 72). *Discrimination*, on the other hand, is a difference that results from differential treatment based on illegitimate criteria, such as race, gender, social class, or sexual orientation. With respect to sentencing, discrimination exists when illegitimate or legally irrelevant defendant characteristics affect the sentence that is imposed after all legally relevant variables are taken into consideration. It exists when black and Hispanic offenders are sentenced more harshly than similarly situated white offenders or when male offenders receive more punitive sentences than identical female offenders.

Types of disparity

Sentencing disparities reveal both intra- and inter-jurisdictional differences. Judges in a particular jurisdiction, for example, may have differing perceptions of crime seriousness or may give greater or lesser weight to legally relevant factors such as the seriousness of the crime and the offender's prior criminal record, with the result that similar offenders sentenced by different judges receive substantially different sentences. If, for example, some judges routinely send all armed robbers with no previous felony convictions to prison while others typically sentence all such offenders to probation, the result would be intra-jurisdictional sentencing disparity. A similar outcome would result if some judges routinely hand out either substantially harsher or substantially more lenient sentences than their colleagues on the bench. In both cases, the severity of the sentence the offender gets rests in part on the judge who imposes it.

The sentencing patterns of judges in different jurisdictions also may vary. Certain categories of crimes may be viewed as more serious, and certain types of offenders perceived as more dangerous, in some jurisdictions than in others. For example, offenders convicted of serious felonies may be sentenced more leniently in large urban court systems, where such crimes are fairly common, than in rural areas, where misdemeanors and less serious felonies dominate the court docket. Similarly, blacks who victimize whites may be sentenced more harshly than other categories of offenders in southern jurisdictions, no differently than other offenders in non-southern jurisdictions. These geographic or regional variations in sentence outcomes signal inter-jurisdictional disparity. The harsher sentences imposed on black offenders in southern jurisdictions also may be indicative of racial discrimination in sentencing.

A third type of sentence disparity is intra-judge disparity. This type of disparity occurs when an individual judge makes inconsistent sentencing decisions; that is, he or she imposes different sentences on equally culpable offenders whose crimes are indistinguishable. Although these sentence variations might be attributable to subtle, and thus not easily observed or measured, differences in crime seriousness and offender blameworthiness, they also might be due to intentional bias on the part of the judge. An individual judge who believes that black and Hispanic offenders are particularly dangerous and especially likely to recidivate may impose harsher sentences on these types of offenders than on otherwise identical white offenders. Similarly, a judge who is concerned about the "social costs" of incarcerating female offenders with young children may refuse to send such offenders to prison, but may not hesitate to incarcerate similarly situated male offenders. These types of intra-judge sentencing disparities, then, may signal the presence of discrimination based on race, gender, social class, or other legally irrelevant defendant characteristics.

Not all sentencing disparities are unwarranted. Although one might question the fairness of a system in which the sentence an offender receives depends upon the jurisdiction where the case is adjudicated, jurisdictional differences in values and in attitudes toward crime and punishment might foster sentencing disparity. Variations in laws and in criminal justice resources might have a similar effect. At the state level, the judge's discretion at sentencing is constrained by the penalty range established for crimes of varying seriousness by the state legislature. In one state, for example, the presumptive sentence for burglary might be five to seven years, while in another state the range might be from seven to ten years. The fact that an offender convicted of burglary in the first state received five years, while a seemingly identical offender convicted of burglary in the second state got seven years, is not indicative of unwarranted disparity. In each instance, the judge imposing the sentence determined that the offender deserved the minimum punishment specified for the particular crime.

Within-state sentencing disparities also are to be expected. Judges, many of whom are elected or appointed by the governor or some other public official, share at least to some degree the values and attitudes of the communities in which they serve. The fact that sentences for minor drug offenses are harsher in some jurisdictions than in others may simply reflect the fact that different communities (and thus the judges on the bench in those communities) have differing beliefs about the appropriate penalty for this type

of crime. Principled and thoughtful judges sitting in different jurisdictions, in other words, might come to different conclusions about the appropriate punishment for identical offenders.

The legitimacy of intra-jurisdictional sentencing disparities is more questionable. One might argue that some degree of disparity in the sentences imposed by judges in a particular jurisdiction is to be expected in a system that attempts to individualize punishment and in which there is not universal agreement on the goals of sentences. As long as these differences resulted from the application of legitimate criteria and reflected fundamental differences regarding the purposes of punishment, they might be regarded as warranted. Alternatively, it could be argued that justice demands that similarly situated offenders convicted of identical crimes in the same jurisdiction receive comparable punishments. To be fair, in other words, a sentencing scheme requires the evenhanded application of objective standards. Thus, the amount of punishment an offender receives should not depend on the values, attitudes, and beliefs of the judge to whom the case is assigned.

Regardless of how this issue is resolved, it is clear that sentencing disparities that result from the use of *illegitimate* criteria are unwarranted. This would be true of sentencing disparities between jurisdictions as well as those within jurisdictions. In fact, much of the criticism of sentencing disparity centers on the issue of discrimination based on race, ethnicity, gender, and social class. Allowing judges unrestrained discretion in fashioning sentences, it is argued, opens the door to discrimination, with the result that racial minorities are sentenced more harshly than whites, men are sentenced more harshly than women, and the poor are sentenced more harshly than the non-poor.

Studies documenting illegitimate disparities

The evidence regarding the extent of discrimination in sentencing is equivocal. With respect to discrimination based on the race/ethnicity of the offender, for example, some studies find that blacks and Hispanics are sentenced more harshly than whites, while others conclude that racial disparities disappear once crime seriousness and prior criminal record are taken into consideration. Still other studies reveal that the effect of race/ethnicity is confined to certain types of offenders, certain types of crimes, and certain types of circumstances. One study, for example, found that young, black males received substantially more severe sentences than any other type of offender (Steffensmeier et al.). Researchers also have concluded that blacks who murder or sexually assault whites are singled out for harsher treatment (Baldus et al.; LaFree), that black and Hispanic drug offenders are sentenced more harshly than white drug offenders (Albonetti), and that pretrial detention and going to trial rather than pleading guilty increase sentence severity more for racial minorities than for whites (Chiricos and Bales; Ulmer). Racial/ethnic discrimination in sentencing, in other words, is contextual rather than systematic.

The evidence with respect to gender discrimination is less contradictory. In fact, theoretically informed and methodologically rigorous studies conducted in diverse jurisdictions and focusing on a variety of offenses consistently find that women are less likely than men to be sentenced to prison; a number of studies also find that the sentences imposed on women are shorter than those imposed on men (for a review of this research, see Daly and Bordt). Although some studies conclude that preferential treatment is reserved for white females, others find that all female offenders, regardless of race/ethnicity, are sentenced more leniently than male offenders. Explanations for the more lenient treatment of female offenders generally focus on the fact that judges tend to view male offenders as more blameworthy, more dangerous, and more threatening than female offenders. There also is evidence that judges' assessments of offense seriousness and offender culpability interact with their concerns about the practical effects of incarceration on children and families to produce more lenient sentences for "familied" female defendants (Daly).

Allegations of disparity and discrimination have been leveled at aspects of the criminal justice system other than sentencing. In fact, some commentators contend that sentencing disparities are merely "the tip of the iceberg" and emphasize the importance of examining discretionary decisions made earlier in the process. The police officer's decision to arrest or not and the prosecutor's decision to file charges or not are both highly discretionary decisions that typically are not subject to review. Although the plea bargaining process may be governed by the informal norms of the courtroom workgroup or by formal office policies, it, too, is characterized by a considerable amount of discretion. Decisions regarding bail and pretrial release, while structured to some extent by bail guidelines or schedules and by statutes or policies concerning preventive detention, also are discretionary. At each of these decision points, discretion creates the potential for disparity and discrimination. This is particularly troublesome, given the fact that these early decisions themselves affect the sentence that is eventually imposed. Defendants arrested for and charged with more serious crimes are sentenced more harshly, as are those who are unable to negotiate a favorable plea or who are detained prior to trial. Disparity and discrimination at the front end of the criminal justice system, in other words, can result in "cumulative disadvantage" (Zatz) for certain categories of defendants at sentencing.

Sentencing disparity and sentence reform

Concerns about disparity and discrimination in sentencing led to a "remarkable burst of reform" (Walker, p. 112) that began in the mid-1970s and continues today. The focus of reform efforts was the indeterminate sentence, in which an offender received a minimum and maximum sentence and the parole board determined the date of release. Under indeterminate sentencing, which is still used in about half of the states, the judge was to individualize punishment by tailoring the sentence not just to the seriousness of the offense but also to the offender's unique characteristics and circumstances, including his or her potential for rehabilitation. Likewise, the parole board's determination of when the offender should be released rested on its judgment of whether the offender had been rehabilitated or had served enough time for the particular crime. Under indeterminate sentencing, in other words, discretion was distributed not only to the criminal justice officials who determined the sentence, but also to corrections officials and the parole board. The result of this process was "a system of sentencing in which there was little understanding or predictability as to who would be imprisoned and for how long" (Bureau of Justice Assistance, p. 6).

Both liberal and conservative reformers challenged the principles underlying the indeterminate sentence, and called for changes designed to curb discretion and reduce disparity and discrimination. Liberal reformers argued that judges and corrections officials should not be given unfettered and unreviewable discretion in determining the nature and extent of punishment; they were particularly apprehensive about the potential for racial bias under indeterminate sentencing schemes. They asserted that "racial discrimination in the criminal justice system was epidemic, that judges, parole boards, and corrections officials could not be trusted, and that tight controls on officials' discretion offered the only way to limit racial disparities" (Tonry, 1995, p. 164). Political conservatives, on the other hand, argued that sentences imposed under indeterminate sentencing schemes were too lenient and championed sentencing reforms designed to establish and enforce more punitive sentencing standards. Their arguments were bolstered by the findings of research demonstrating that most correctional programs designed to rehabilitate offenders and reduce recidivism were ineffective (Martinson).

After a few initial "missteps," in which jurisdictions attempted to eliminate discretion altogether through flat-time sentencing (Walker, p. 123), states and the federal government adopted determinate sentencing proposals designed to control the discretion of sentencing judges. Many jurisdictions adopted presumptive sentence structures that offered judges a limited number of sentencing options and that included enhancements for use of a weapon, presence of a prior criminal record, or infliction of serious injury. These systems vary widely in the amount of discretion allotted to judges. California's Uniform Determinate Sentencing Law, which was adopted in 1976, is one of the more restrictive laws. It classified offenses into four categories of seriousness and established a presumptive sentence, an aggravated range, and a mitigated range for each category. In the absence of aggravating or mitigating circumstances, the judge is to impose the presumptive sentence. At the other extreme, the determinate sentencing statutes adopted in Maine and Illinois give judges wide discretion to determine the appropriate sentence. The legislation enacted in Illinois in 1977 established a fairly wide sentence range for each of six categories of offenses. Offenders convicted of Class X offenses (the most serious offenses, excluding murder), for example, could be sentenced to prison for anywhere from six to thirty years, and enhancements for aggravating circumstances such as use of a weapon could result in a sentence that ranged between thirty and sixty years. The determinate sentencing laws enacted in other states generally fall between these two extremes.

During this early stage of the reform movement, parole release also came under attack. A number of states and the federal system initially adopted guidelines that parole boards were to use in determining whether an offender should be released or not. These guidelines typically were based on the seriousness of the offense and the offender's prior criminal record, and on an assessment of the offender's risk of recidivism. Other states (and eventually the federal system) abolished parole release altogether. In these jurisdictions the offender is automatically released at the end of the term, less credit for good behavior.

Other sentence reforms include voluntary and presumptive sentencing guidelines. During the late 1970s and early 1980s a number of states experimented with voluntary or advisory guidelines, so-called because judges are not required to comply with them. Michael Tonry, a professor of law at the University of Minnesota, notes that "voluntary guidelines were often created by judges in hopes that by putting their own houses in order they would forestall passage of mandatory or determinate sentencing laws" (Tonry, 1996, p. 27). Evaluations of the impact of voluntary guidelines found low compliance by judges and, consequently, little if any effect on the type or severity of sentences imposed. Most jurisdictions eventually abandoned voluntary guidelines in favor of determinate sentencing or presumptive sentencing guidelines.

The movement toward presumptive sentencing guidelines began in the late 1970s when Minnesota, Pennsylvania, and a number of other states created sentencing commissions and directed them to develop rules for sentencing that judges would be required to follow. By the mid-1980s, commission-based guidelines had been adopted in Minnesota, Pennsylvania, and Washington. In 1984, the U.S. Congress enacted legislation that abolished parole release and directed the U.S. Sentencing Commission to develop guidelines for federal sentencing; the guidelines took effect in 1987. Experimentation with commission-based guidelines continued into the 1990s. By 1996, at most half of the states had created sentencing commissions; ten states had adopted presumptive sentencing guidelines, six had implemented voluntary guidelines, and several were in the process of developing either presumptive or voluntary guidelines.

Although the guidelines adopted in different jurisdictions vary on a number of dimensions, most incorporate crime seriousness and prior criminal record into a sentencing "grid" that judges are required to use in determining the appropriate sentence. The statutes spell out the aggravating and mitigating circumstances that justify departures from the presumptive sentence. In presumptive systems, the judge must provide written justification for a departure and either the defense or the prosecution can request appellate review of sentences that do not conform to the guidelines.

Other reforms enacted at both the federal and state levels included mandatory minimum penalties for certain types of offenses, habitual offender and "three strikes" laws, and truth-in-sentencing statutes. All states have adopted mandatory sentencing provisions that apply to repeat or habitual offenders or to offenders convicted of crimes such as drunk driving, possession of drugs, and possession of weapons. These laws generally require the judge to sentence the offender to prison for a specified period of time; nonprison sentences, such as probation, are not allowed. A handful of states adopted "three strikes" laws that mandated life sentences for offenders convicted of a third serious felony. Other states enacted so-called "truth in sentencing" statutes designed to increase the certainty and predictability of sentencing; under this system, parole release discretion is abolished, and the sentence imposed reflects the actual amount of time an offender will serve, with very limited time credited for good behavior in prison.

The attack on indeterminate sentencing and the proposals for reform reflect conflicting views of the goals and purposes of punishment, as well as questions regarding the exercise of discretion at sentencing. The National Research Council's Panel on Sentencing Research characterized the sentencing decision as "the symbolic keystone of the criminal justice system," adding that "It is here that conflicts between the goals of equal justice under the law and individualized justice with punishment tailored to the offender are played out. . ." (Blumstein et al., p. 39). Proponents of retributive or just deserts theories of punishment, such as Andrew von Hirsch, argue that sentence severity should be closely linked to the seriousness of the crime and the culpability of the offender. Thus, those who commit comparable offenses should receive similar punishments, and those who commit more serious crimes should be punished more harshly than those who commit less serious crimes. Like cases, in other words, should be treated alike. Proponents of utilitarian rationales of punishment, including special (or

individual) deterrence, incapacitation, and rehabilitation, argue that the ultimate goal of punishment is to prevent future crime and that the severity of the sanction imposed on an offender should serve this purpose. Thus, the amount of punishment need not be closely proportioned to crime seriousness or offender culpability but can instead be tailored to the defendant's unique characteristics and circumstances. (The utilitarian goal of general deterrence, like just deserts, requires that punishment be at least roughly proportional to crime seriousness (Bentham, pp. 322–338; Minnesota Sentencing Guidelines Commission, p. 12), but the need for other utilitarian measures such as incapacitation must also be considered.)

These conflicting views of the goals of punishment incorporate differing notions of the amount of discretion that judges and juries should be afforded at sentencing. A sentencing scheme based on utilitarian rationales would allow the judge or jury discretion to shape sentences to fit individuals and their crimes. The judge or jury would be free to consider all relevant circumstances, including the offender's degree of dangerousness, potential for rehabilitation, and need for deterrence, as well as "the importance of the behavioral norms that were violated, the effects of the crime on the victim, and the amalgam of aggravating and mitigating circumstances that make a defendant more or less culpable and make one sentence more appropriate than another" (Tonry, 1996, p. 3). A retributive or just deserts sentencing scheme, on the other hand, would constrain discretion more severely. The judge or jury would determine the appropriate sentence using only legally relevant considerations (essentially crime seriousness and, to a lesser extent, prior criminal record) and would be precluded from considering individual characteristics or circumstances, which are unrelated to offense seriousness and offender culpability.

The reforms enacted during the sentencing reform movement reflect both retributive and utilitarian principles. Sentencing guidelines, for example, generally are based explicitly or implicitly on notions of just deserts: punishments are scaled along a two-dimensional grid measuring the seriousness of the crime and the offender's prior criminal record. The Minnesota Sentencing Commission decided that "Development of a rational and consistent sentencing policy requires that the severity of sanctions increase in direct proportion to increases in the severity of criminal offenses and the severity of criminal histories of convicted felons" (Minnesota Sentencing Guidelines Commission, p. 1). The commission thus adopted a "modified just-deserts" model of sentencing (pp. 7–14). Other sentencing commissions are mandated to accomplish utilitarian as well as retributive goals. For example, legislation adopted in Arkansas states that the goals of the sentencing guidelines include retribution, rehabilitation, deterrence, and incapacitation. Because these goals may conflict with one another and because legislatures rarely prioritized them, sentencing commissions generally "developed guidelines using measures of offense seriousness and criminal history, leaving to the courts the discretion to aggravate and mitigate the sentence as a means of considering rehabilitation and other sentencing purposes" (Bureau of Justice Assistance, p. 42). Even in Minnesota, the commission gave sentencing judges substantial discretion to consider rehabilitation and other utilitarian sentencing rationales; moreover, the importance of these nonretributive goals has grown steadily since guidelines first became effective (Frase).

Although the sentencing reforms promulgated during the past three decades were based on diverse and sometimes contradictory principles, the overriding goal of reformers was to reduce disparity and discrimination, including racial and gender discrimination, in sentencing. The Minnesota sentencing guidelines, for example, explicitly state that sentences should be neutral with respect to the gender, race, and socioeconomic status of the offender. Reformers hoped that the new laws, by structuring discretion, would make it more difficult for judges to take these legally irrelevant factors into account when determining the appropriate sentence. They also anticipated that the reforms would produce greater consistency in the sentences imposed on comparable offenders convicted of similar crimes.

Evidence concerning the effectiveness of the sentencing reforms adopted during the past three decades is mixed. An examination of sentences imposed by judges in Minnesota before and after the implementation of guidelines, for example, showed that the impact of race, gender, and socioeconomic status declined, but did not disappear (Miethe and Moore). A series of studies conducted in Pennsylvania produced similar results. This research also demonstrated that judges were more likely to depart from the guidelines—that is, to impose probation when

the guidelines called for prison or to impose a shorter sentence than called for by the guidelines—if the offender was white or was a woman (Kramer and Ulmer). Research findings such as these, coupled with the inconsistent findings of research designed to evaluate the effect of the federal sentencing guidelines, have led scholars to question the degree to which reforms have reduced sentencing disparity and discrimination. As Tonry (1996, p. 180) notes, "There is, unfortunately, no way around the dilemma that sentencing is inherently discretionary and that discretion leads to disparities."

CASSIA SPOHN

See also CRIMINAL JUSTICE SYSTEM; GUILTY PLEA: PLEA BARGAINING; POLICE: COMMUNITY POLICING; POLICE: CRIMINAL INVESTIGATIONS; POLICE: HANDLING OF JUVENILES; POLICE: POLICE OFFICER BEHAVIOR; POLICE: POLICING COMPLAINANTLESS CRIMES; PROBATION AND PAROLE: HISTORY, GOALS, AND DECISION-MAKING; PROSECUTION: PROSECUTORIAL DISCRETION; SENTENCING: ALLOCATION OF AUTHORITY; SENTENCING: ALTERNATIVES; SENTENCING: GUIDELINES; SENTENCING: MANDATORY AND MANDATORY MINIMUM SENTENCES; SENTENCING: PRESENTENCE REPORT; SENTENCING: PROCEDURAL PROTECTION; URBAN POLICE.

BIBLIOGRAPHY

ALBONETTI, CELESTA A. "Sentencing Under the Federal Sentencing Guidelines: Effects of Defendant Characteristics, Guilty Pleas, and Departures on Sentence Outcomes for Drug Offenses, 1991–1992." *Law & Society Review* 31 (1997): 789–822.

AUSTIN, THOMAS. "The Influence of Court Location on Types of Criminal Sentences: The Rural-Urban Factor." *Journal of Criminal Justice* 9 (1981): 305–316.

BALDUS, DAVID C.; WOODWORTH, GEORGE; and PULASKI, CHARLES. *Equal Justice and the Death Penalty: A Legal and Empirical Analysis.* Boston: Northeastern University Press, 1990.

BENTHAM, JEREMY. *The Theory of Legislation.* New York: Harcourt, Brace, 1931.

BLUMSTEIN, ALFRED; COHEN, JACQUELINE; MARTIN, SUSAN; and TONRY, MICHAEL, eds. *Research on Sentencing: The Search for Reform,* Vol. 1. Washington, D.C.: National Academy Press, 1983.

Bureau of Justice Assistance. *National Assessment of Structured Sentencing.* Washington, D.C.: Bureau of Justice Assistance, 1996.

CHIRICOS, THEODORE G., and BALES, WILLIAM D. "Unemployment and Punishment: An Empirical Assessment." *Criminology* 29 (1991): 701–724.

DALY, KATHLEEN. "Neither Conflict nor Labeling nor Paternalism Will Suffice: Intersections of Race, Ethnicity, Gender, and Family in Criminal Court Decisions." *Crime & Delinquency* 35 (1989): 136–168.

DALY, KATHLEEN, and BORDT, REBECCA. "Sex Effects and Sentencing: A Review of the Statistical Literature." *Justice Quarterly* 12 (1995): 143–177.

FRANKEL, MARVIN. *Criminal Sentences: Law Without Order.* New York: Hill & Wang, 1972.

FRASE, RICHARD S. "Sentencing Principles in Theory and Practice." *Crime & Justice: A Review of Research* 22 (1997): 363–433.

HAWKINS, DARNELL. "Beyond Anomalies: Rethinking the Conflict Perspective on Race and Criminal Punishment." *Social Forces* 65 (1987): 719–745.

KRAMER, JOHN H., and ULMER, JEFFERY T. "Sentencing Disparity and Departures from Guidelines." *Justice Quarterly* 13 (1996): 81–106.

LAFREE, GARY D. *Rape and Criminal Justice: The Social Construction of Sexual Assault.* Belmont, Calif.: Wadsworth, 1989.

MARTINSON, ROBERT. "What Works? Questions and Answers About Prison Reform." *Public Interest* 35 (1974): 22–54.

MIETHE, TERANCE D., and MOORE, CHARLES A. "Socioeconomic Disparities Under Determinate Sentencing Systems: A Comparison of Preguideline and Postguideline Practices in Minnesota." *Criminology* 23 (1985): 337–363.

Minnesota Sentencing Guidelines Commission. *The Impact of the Minnesota Sentencing Guidelines: Three Year Evaluation.* St. Paul, Minn., 1984.

STEFFENSMEIER, DARRELL; ULMER, JEFFERY; and KRAMER, JOHN. "The Interaction of Race, Gender, and Age in Criminal Sentencing: The Punishment Cost of Being Young, Black, and Male." *Criminology* 36 (1998): 763–797.

TONRY, MICHAEL. *Malign Neglect: Race, Crime, and Punishment in America.* New York: Oxford University Press, 1995.

———. *Sentencing Matters.* New York: Oxford University Press, 1996.

TONRY, MICHAEL, and HATLESTAD, KATHLEEN, eds. *Sentencing Reform in Overcrowded Time: A Comparative Perspective.* New York: Oxford University Press, 1997.

ULMER, JEFFERY T. *Social Worlds of Sentencing: Court Communities Under Sentencing Guidelines.* Albany, N.Y.: State University of New York Press, 1997.

VON HIRSCH, ANDREW. *Doing Justice: The Choice of Punishments.* New York: Hall & Wang, 1976.

WALKER, SAMUEL. *Taming the System: The Control of Discretion in Criminal Justice, 1950–1990.* New York: Oxford University Press, 1993.

WILSON, JAMES Q. *Thinking About Crime.* Rev. ed. New York: Basic Books, 1983.

ZATZ, MARJORIE S. "The Changing Forms of Racial/Ethnic Biases in Sentencing." *Journal of Research in Crime and Delinquency* 24 (1987): 69–92.

SENTENCING: GUIDELINES

"Sentencing guidelines" are rules or recommendations created by judges or an expert administrative agency, usually called a "sentencing commission," which are intended to influence, channel, or even dictate the punishment decisions made by trial courts in individual cases. Since the early 1970s, commission-based guideline structures have emerged as the principal alternative to traditional practices of "indeterminate sentencing," under which judges and parole boards hold unguided and unreviewable discretion within broad ranges of statutorily authorized penalties. Sentencing guidelines in operation have varied widely in their form, content, legal authority, and even in their nomenclature. (Not all guidelines are called guidelines.) It is thus treacherous to assume that "all guidelines are created equal."

Origins of sentencing commissions and guidelines

The idea of a "commission on sentencing" can be traced to Marvin Frankel's influential writings of the early 1970s, most notably his 1973 book *Criminal Sentences: Law Without Order.* Frankel wanted to replace what he saw as the "lawless" processes of indeterminate sentencing with an alternative model that would promote legal regularity. His chosen vehicles were chiefly *procedural* innovations, and it is possible to identify three fundamental procedural goals in Frankel's plan: (1) The creation of a permanent, expert commission on sentencing in every jurisdiction, with both research and rulemaking capacities; (2) the articulation of broad policies and more specific regulations (later called guidelines) by legislatures and sentencing commissions, to have binding legal authority on case-by-case sentencing decisions made by trial judges; and (3) institution of meaningful appellate review of the appropriateness of individual sentences, so that a jurisprudence of sentencing could develop through the accumulation of case decisions.

Along with these procedural elements, Frankel advocated for two major *substantive* goals: (1) Greater uniformity in punishments imposed upon similarly situated offenders, with a concomitant reduction in inexplicable disparities, including racial disparities in punishment and widely varying sentences based simply on the predilections of individual judges; and (2) a substantial reduction in the overall severity of punishments as imposed by courts throughout the United States, including a general shortening of terms of incarceration, and the expanded use of intermediate punishments.

Frankel's suggestions that U.S. jurisdictions should create permanent sentencing commissions, which in turn should author sentencing guidelines, have been enormously productive of institutional changes. In the early 1970s, commissions and guidelines were wholly new ideas, and existed nowhere. By midyear 1999, as summarized in Figure 1, sixteen American jurisdictions were operating with some form of sentencing guidelines (including fifteen states and the federal system). In four additional states, fully developed guideline proposals are under consideration by the state legislatures, and at least three more jurisdictions were in the early stages of deliberations that may eventually lead to commission-based sentencing reform. In nearly thirty years since Frankel's seminal writings, this is a remarkable record indeed, unrivaled by nearly any other work of criminal-law-related scholarship over the same period.

Design features of guideline structures

Up-and-running guideline systems have differed substantially from one another, and not all guidelines systems have conformed closely to Marvin Frankel's ambitions. As of 1999, we can identify a menu of choices faced by policymakers who undertake to create a new sentencing guideline structure, or who are interested in amending an existing structure. We will begin here by identifying a number of the most important "design features" of existing guideline systems. These are also salient attributes for assessing operational distinctions among guideline jurisdictions.

Guideline grids

Most sentencing guideline systems in America in the late twentieth century used the format of a two-dimensional "grid" or "matrix." Figure 2 provides an illustration of the popular grid approach, taken from the Minnesota Guidelines (see Minnesota Sentencing Guidelines Commission, 1997, p. 43). Along one axis of the grid, such guidelines rank offense severity on a hierarchical scale. On the other axis, a similar scale reflects the seriousness of the offender's prior criminal history. The guideline sentence in a particular case is derived by moving across the row designated for the offense to be punished, and down the column that corresponds to the offender's past record. Thus, for example, the guideline sentence under Minnesota's current grid for a conviction of residential burglary ("severity level V") by someone with a "criminal history score" of 4 (calculated by the number of prior felony sentences and their severity levels) is thirty-six to forty months of incarceration in a state prison.

The tightness or looseness of such "sentencing ranges" has differed greatly among American guideline jurisdictions, from a bandwidth of several months to as much as several years. For instance, the Pennsylvania guidelines in the early 1990s recommended penalty ranges as expansive as three to ten years for third degree murder and twenty-seven months to five years for rape and robbery with serious injury. (See Commonwealth of Pennsylvania Commission on Sentencing, *Sentencing Guideline Implementation Manual,* 3d ed., 9 August 1991, p. 12(a).) Thus, when comparing different systems, we may speak in terms of *fine-toothed* or *broad-gauged* sentencing guidelines, depending on the specificity with which the sentencing commission has articulated its punishment ranges.

Most guideline grids differentiate explicitly between sentences to incarceration and to non-prison sanctions. In Figure 2, the heavy black line that runs diagonally though the Minnesota grid is called the "in-out" line. For cases above the in-out line, the "presumptive" sentences in Minnesota are all prison terms. Offenders who fall within the guideline cells below the in-out line are subject to a "presumptive stayed sentence," which can include probation or any available intermediate sanction (although, in the Minnesota system, a "stayed" sentence may also include up to a year in jail at the discretion of the sentencing judge). For such cases, the number

Figure 1

American sentencing guidelines systems in 1999		
Jurisdiction	**Effective date**	**Features**
Minnesota	May 1980	Presumptive guidelines for felonies; moderate appellate review; parole abolished; no guidelines for intermediate sanctions
Pennsylvania	July 1982	Voluntary guidelines for felonies and misdemeanors; minimal appellate review; parole retained; guidelines incorporate intermediate sanctions
Maryland	July 1983	Voluntary guidelines for felonies; no appellate review; parole retained; no guidelines for intermediate sanctions; legislature created permanent sentencing commission in 1998
Washington	July 1984	Presumptive guidelines for felonies; moderate appellate review; parole abolished; no guidelines for intermediate sanctions; juvenile guidelines in use
Delaware	October 1987	Voluntary guidelines for felonies and misdemeanors; no appellate review; parole abolished in 1990; guidelines incorporate intermediate sanctions
Federal Courts	November 1987	Presumptive guidelines for felonies and misdemeanors; intensive appellate review; parole abolished; no guidelines for intermediate sanctions
Oregon	November 1989	Presumptive guidelines for felonies; moderate appellate review; parole abolished; guidelines incorporate intermediate sanctions
Tennessee	November 1989	Presumptive guidelines for felonies; moderate appellate review; parole retained; no guidelines for intermediate sanctions; sentencing commission abolished effective 1995
Kansas	July 1993	Presumptive guidelines for felonies; moderate appellate review; parole abolished; no guidelines for intermediate sanctions
North Carolina	October 1994	Presumptive guidelines for felonies and misdemeanors; minimal appellate review; parole abolished; guidelines incorporate intermediate sanctions; dispositional grid for juvenile offenders to become effective July 1999
Arkansas	January 1994	Voluntary guidelines for felonies; no appellate review; parole retained; guidelines incorporate intermediate sanctions; preliminary discussion of guidelines for juvenile cases
Virginia	January 1995	Voluntary guidelines for felonies; no appellate review; parole abolished; no guidelines for intermediate sanctions; study of juvenile sentencing underway
Ohio	July 1996	Presumptive narrative guidelines (no grid) for felonies; limited appellate review; parole abolished and replaced with judicial release mechanism; no guidelines for intermediate sanctions; structured sentencing for juveniles under consideration by legislature
Missouri	March 1997	Voluntary guidelines for felonies; no appellate review; parole retained; guidelines incorporate intermediate sanctions
Utah	October 1998	Voluntary guidelines for felonies and selected misdemeanors (sex offenses); no appellate review; parole retained; no guidelines for intermediate sanctions; voluntary juvenile guidelines in use
Michigan	January 1999	Presumptive guidelines for felonies; appellate review authorized; parole restricted; guidelines incorporate intermediate sanctions
Alaska	Early 1980s	Judicially-created "benchmark" guidelines for felonies; moderate appellate review; parole abolished for most felonies (retained for about one-third of all felonies); benchmarks do not address intermediate sanctions; no active sentencing commission
Massachusetts	Proposal Pending	Presumptive guidelines for felonies and misdemeanors; appellate review contemplated; parole to be retained; guidelines would incorporate intermediate sanctions
Oklahoma	Proposal Pending	Presumptive guidelines for felonies; appellate review contemplated; parole to be limited; guidelines would not incorporate intermediate sanctions
South Carolina	Proposal Pending	Voluntary guidelines for felonies and misdemeanors with potential sentence of one year or more; no appellate review contemplated; parole to be abolished for all felonies; guidelines would incorporate intermediate sanctions
Wisconsin	Proposal Pending	Voluntary guidelines for felonies; no appellate review contemplated; parole to be eliminated; guidelines would not incorporate intermediate sanctions; new permanent sentencing commission to be created
Washington, D.C.	Under Study	Temporary sentencing commission, currently scheduled to report to City Council in April 2000
Iowa	Under Study	Legislative commission to study sentencing reform, currently scheduled to report in January 2000
Alabama	Under Study	Study committee has requested that Alabama Judicial Study Commission create a permanent sentencing commission in 2000

Figure 2

| \multicolumn{9}{c}{**The Minnesota "Sentencing Guidelines Grid"**} |||||||||
| Severity level of conviction offense (common offenses listed in italics) | | \multicolumn{7}{c}{**Criminal history score**} |||||||
		0	1	2	3	4	5	6 or more
Murder, 2nd degree *(intentional murder, drive-by-shooting)*	X	306 *299–313*	326 *319–333*	346 *339–353*	366 *359–373*	386 *379–393*	406 *399–413*	426 *419–433*
Murder, 3rd degree Murder, 2nd degree *(unintentional murder)*	IX	150 *144–156*	165 *159–171*	180 *174–186*	195 *189–201*	210 *204–216*	225 *219–231*	240 *234–246*
Criminal sexual conduct, 1st degree Assault, 1st degree	VIII	86 *81–91*	98 *93–103*	110 *105–115*	122 *117–127*	134 *129–139*	146 *141–151*	158 *153–163*
Aggravated robbery, 1st degree	VII	48 *44–52*	58 *54–62*	68 *64–72*	78 *74–82*	88 *84–92*	98 *94–102*	108 *104–112*
Criminal sexual conduct, 2nd degree (a) & (b)	VI	21	27	33	39 *37–41*	45 *43–47*	51 *49–53*	57 *55–59*
Residential burglary Simple robbery	V	18	23	28	33 *31–35*	38 *36–40*	43 *41–45*	48 *46–50*
Nonresidential burglary	IV	12	15	18	21	24 *23–25*	27 *26–28*	30 *29–31*
Theft crimes (over $2,500)	III	12	13	15	17	19 *18–20*	21 *20–22*	23 *22–24*
Theft crimes ($2,500 or less) Check forgery ($200-$2,500)	II	12	12	13	15	17	19	21 *20–22*
Sale of simulated controlled substance	I	12	12	12	13	15	17	19 *18–20*

appearing in the grid cell is the presumptive duration of a stayed sentence. The Minnesota guidelines, it should be noted, do nothing to communicate to the judge which among the array of nonprison sanctions are appropriate in individual cases. Thus, no guidance is given to courts concerning the selection among such options as regular probation, intensive probation, in-patient or out-patient treatment programs, halfway houses, home confinement, community service, fines, victim restitution, and so forth. Such choices below the in-out line remain discretionary with the sentencing judge in Minnesota's structure.

Guidelines for intermediate punishments

Some sentencing guidelines do provide at least limited direction to courts concerning the selection among intermediate punishment options. This is still an experimental undertaking, however, and one that has been attempted with ambition in only two or three states. The current North Carolina "Felony Punishment Chart," reproduced as Figure 3, illustrates one promising innovation in operation since 1994. For the most serious cases (such as all of those in offense classes A through D on the chart), North Carolina's guidelines prescribe an "active punishment," designated by the letter "A" in each guideline

Figure 3

The North Carolina "Felony Punishment Chart"

Prior record level

Offense class		I 0 Pts	II 1-4 Pts	III 5-8 Pts	IV 9-14 Pts	V 15-18 Pts	VI 19+ Pts	
A		Death or life without parole						
B1		A 240-300	A 288-360	A 336-420	A 384-480	A Life without parole	A Life without parole	Disposition Aggravated range
		192-240	230-288	269-336	307-384	346-433	p384-480	Presumptive range
		144-192	173-230	202-269	230-307	260-346	288-384	Mitigated range
B2		A 157-196	A 189-237	A 220-276	A 251-313	A 282-353	A 313-392	
		125-157	151-189	176-220	201-251	225-282	251-313	
		94-125	114-151	132-176	151-201	169-225	188-251	
C		A 73-92	A 100-125	A 116-145	A 133-167	A 151-188	A 168-210	
		58-73	80-100	93-116	107-133	121-151	135-168	
		44-58	60-80	70-93	80-107	90-121	101-135	
D		A 64-80	A 77-95	A 103-129	A 117-146	A 133-167	A 146-183	
		51-64	61-77	82-103	94-11"	107-133	117-146	
		38-51	46-61	61-82	71-94	80-107	88-117	
E		I/A 25-31	I/A 29-36	A 34-42	A 46-58	A 53-66	A 59-74	
		20-25	23-29	27-34	37-46	42-53	47-59	
		15-20	17-23	20-27	28-37	32-42	35-47	
F		I/A 16-20	I/A 19-24	I/A 21-26	A 25-31	A 34-42	A 39-49	
		13-16	15-19	17-21	20-25	27-34	31-39	
		10-13	11-15	13-17	15-20	20-27	23-31	
G		I/A 13-16	I/A 15-19	I/A 16-20	I/A 20-25	A 21-26	A 29-36	
		10-13	12-15	13-16	16-20	17-21	23-29	
		8-10	9-12	10-13	12-16	13-17	17-23	
H		C/I/A 6-8	I/A 8-10	I/A 10-12	I/A 11-14	I/A 15-19	A 20-25	
		5-6	6-8	8-10	9-11	12-15	16-20	
		4-5	4-6	6-8	7-9	9-12	12-16	
I		C 6-8	C/I 6-8	I 6-8	I/A 8-10	I/A 9-11	I/A 10-12	
		4-6	4-6	5-6	6-8	7-9	8-10	
		3-4	3-4	4-5	4-6	5-7	6-8	

A = Active punishment   I = Intermediate punishment   C = Community punishment

cell. This is defined as a state prison sentence. For less serious cases, other cells within the guidelines authorize "intermediate punishments," denoted by the letter "I," and defined to include split sentences (prison then probation), boot camp, residential programs, electronic monitoring, intensive probation, and day reporting centers. Finally, and for those offenses and offenders lowest on North Carolina's severity scale, "community punishments" become available, indicated by the letter "C," which include supervised or unsupervised probation, outpatient drug or alcohol treatment, community service, referral to the federal TASC (drug treatment) program, restitution, and fines (North Carolina Sentencing and Policy Advisory Commission, Structured Sentencing for Felonies: Training and Reference Manual, 1995, pp. 21–22). Many of the cells on the North Carolina chart allow the judge to select from more than one category of sentence disposition—such as the first four cells at Offense Class G—which indicate the propriety of either an "active" or "intermediate" punishment, in the court's discretion. (Examples of offenses classified at level G are domestic abuse, burglary in the second degree, causing death by impaired driving, and various drug trafficking crimes; p. 51).

The North Carolina grid is an advance over the Minnesota system in that the guidelines direct judges to relevant clusters of punishment options, rather than committing the choice among sanctions to free-form judicial discretion. Further, instead of utilizing a firm and unambiguous in-out line, North Carolina has substituted a diagonal swath of cells in which judges are free to select interchangeably among "active" and "intermediate" punishments (see the cells marked "I/A" in Figure 3). This follows a suggestion made by Norval Morris and Michael Tonry in their 1990 work *Between Prison and Probation*, that the in-out line should be a "blurred" line instead of a hard-and-fast demarcation—in recognition of a policy judgment that intermediate punishments should sometimes be viewed as the functional equivalents of incarceration, and should be available for offenders who otherwise would be prison-bound (pp. 29–30).

At least two other states employ scaled clusters of punishment options within their guidelines. The Pennsylvania sentencing matrix, as revised in 1997, specifically directs courts toward "state or county incarceration," "boot camp," "restrictive intermediate punishments," and "restorative sanctions," depending upon the position of individual cases within five zones of the guideline matrix (Commonwealth of Pennsylvania Commission on Sentencing, *Sentencing Guidelines Implementation Manual*, 5th ed. 13 June 1997, p. 33). Delaware's sentencing guidelines, although not expressed in a grid format (see below), designate five graduated levels of recommended sanctions to sentencing judges: "full incarceration," "quasi-incarceration," "intensive supervision," "field supervision," and "administrative supervision" (Delaware Sentencing Accountability Commission, 1997, pp. 2–3).

The "grading" distinctions in guidelines

Another central design feature of a sentencing guideline system is the number of severity (or grading) distinctions that the system attempts to capture within the guidelines themselves—as opposed to allowing trial judges discretion to sort among shadings of offense gravity. As Albert Alschuler noted in a classic 1978 article, there is something ridiculous about having 132 grades of robbery—but how far should guidelines go in such a direction? The number of formal classifications written into guideline grids has differed greatly across jurisdictions, but most guidelines have been modest in their attempts at grading precision. The grids in state jurisdictions have generally incorporated nine to fifteen levels of offense severity, and four to nine categories for offenders' prior records. The Minnesota grid in Figure 2 is representative: Its ten-by-seven format contains a total of seventy guideline "cells" or "boxes." The North Carolina chart in Figure 3, also representative, features a total of fifty-four cells.

The current federal sentencing guidelines system, inaugurated in 1987, opted for a much more intricate matrix than those used by the states, reflecting a philosophy that the U.S. Sentencing Commission can and should make precise distinctions among cases in advance of adjudication in the courts. The federal grid incorporates forty-three levels of crime seriousness and six categories for prior criminal history, yielding a total of 258 guideline cells. If anything, however, the visual complexity of the federal grid understates the degree to which the federal system attempts to draw fine distinctions among specific cases. Unlike all state guideline systems, offense severity under federal law is not fixed by the crime(s) of conviction. The conviction offense is merely one factor among many fed into a multistep calculation, including "relevant conduct" (other related crimes the defendant probably committed, but for which convictions were not obtained), a point-scale scoring of the "base offense level" (which can go up or down depending on such things as the weight of the drugs involved in a narcotics offense or the amount of money lost in a fraud case), and further point "adjustments" for surrounding circumstances (for example, two points off for "acceptance of responsibility," or two points added for "more than minimal planning"). In these and other respects (mentioned below), the federal guidelines are the most "fine-toothed" and rigid of any guideline system now in operation across the country. For all of its size and complexity, however, the federal grid does nothing to assist sentencing judges in the selection among intermediate punishments.

Narrative guidelines

In two U.S. jurisdictions (Delaware and Ohio), the sentencing commissions have eschewed the grid apparatus and have elected to communicate their guidelines in narrative form—expressing punishments though verbal exposition rather than a numerical table. For example, in Delaware, the "presumptive" sentence for first-degree burglary by a first-time offender is written out in a "Truth in Sentencing Benchbook" as twenty-four to forty-eight months at "Level V." (In the Delaware guidelines, Level V is a prison sentence.) Longer presumptive prison terms are indicated for defendants with prior records. For instance, a first-degree burglar with "two or more prior violent felonies" receives a presumptive sentence of 60 to 120 months (or five to ten years) in the Delaware Benchbook (Delaware Sentencing Accountability Commission, Truth in Sentencing Benchbook, March 1997, p. 23). Delaware's guidelines look more like a series of statutes or textual regulations than most other guidelines, and rely less on visual aids. To date, however, the distinction between narrative guidelines and those distilled into grid form has been largely stylistic. With small ingenuity, the current narrative guidelines in use in Delaware or Ohio could be summarized pictorially in a grid or matrix. Conversely, all "grid jurisdictions" supplement their guideline matrices with narrative provisions, which can be quite voluminous, addressing such topics as the purposes of punishment, the permissible grounds for departure for the guidelines, the treatment of multiple convictions, and the computation of criminal history scores. Overall, the design choice between grid and non-grid formats has mattered much less than substantive choices about sentence severity, guideline specificity, intermediate punishments, and other central policy issues.

The legal force of guidelines

Perhaps the most important design feature of existing guideline systems has been the degree of binding legal authority assigned to the sentencing ranges laid out in the guidelines. On one extreme, seven states presently operate with guidelines that are "voluntary," or merely "advisory," to the sentencing judge. In such systems, the court is free to consult or disregard the relevant guideline, and is permitted to impose any penalty authorized by the statute(s) of conviction. For example, a given case may be subject to a guideline range of forty-two to fifty months, yet otherwise be subject to a statutory maximum sentence of fifteen years (180 months). The full incarceration range available in the criminal code could be as wide as zero to 180 months—with the terms and conditions of any nonincarcerative

penalty often left to the discretion of the judge, as well. In *voluntary* guideline systems, the specific guideline range of forty-two to fifty months is merely a recommendation within the much broader range of statutory options freely available to the judge.

There is one variation on this voluntary-guideline approach that exerts light pressure upon trial courts to stay within the guideline ranges: A number of states with voluntary guidelines require sentencing courts to produce a written explanation whenever they opt not to employ the suggested guideline penalty. This supplies at least a mild incentive for courts to abide by guideline provisions, since no similar burden of explanation attends a guideline-compliant decision. The required explanations also provide data to the sentencing commission, allowing the commission to identify frequently cited reasons for judicial noncompliance.

In a bare majority of current guideline structures (nine of sixteen jurisdictions in 1999, including the federal system), the stated guideline range carries a degree of enforceable legal authority. Under the Minnesota scheme, which has been emulated in a number of other states (including Washington, Oregon, Kansas, and the pending proposal in Massachusetts), trial courts are instructed that they must use the presumptive sentences in the guideline grid in "ordinary" cases—which in theory include the majority of all sentencing decisions. However, the trial judge retains discretion to "depart" from the guidelines in a case the judge finds to be atypical in some important respect. In the Minnesota model, the formal legal standard for a guideline departure is that the sentencing judge must find, and set forth on the record, "substantial and compelling reasons" why the presumptive guideline sentence would be too high or too low in a given case. Provided an adequate justification exists, the trial court is potentially freed from the guidelines and may choose a penalty from the broader range of options authorized by the statute(s) of conviction. A judge's departure sentence, however, may be appealed by the defendant (where there has been an "aggravated" departure) or by the government (following a "mitigated" departure). Ultimately, the appellate courts review whether the trial court has given sufficient reasons for a departure, and whether the degree of departure is consistent with those reasons. In almost all jurisdictions with legally enforceable guidelines, however, a sentence that *conforms* to the guidelines requires no explanation by the sentencing court and may not be appealed. Thus, in such systems, trial judges have a dual procedural incentive to honor the guidelines: when they do so, they need not justify their action with a statement of reasons, and there is no prospect of reversal by a higher court.

Two jurisdictions have built sentencing structures in which the guidelines are more tightly legally confining upon trial judges than in the Minnesota model. The federal guideline system bears surface similarity to the Minnesota approach, except that the "departure power" retained by trial courts is more strictly limited under federal law than in Minnesota and most other states. By federal statute, district court judges may impose a departure sentence only when "there exists an aggravating or mitigating circumstance of a kind, or to a degree, *not adequately taken into consideration* by the Sentencing Commission in formulating the guidelines that should result in a sentence different from that described" (emphasis added). The same statute further provides that, "In determining whether a circumstance was adequately taken into consideration, the court shall consider only the sentencing guidelines, policy statements, and official commentary of the Sentencing Commission" (18 U.S.C. § 3553(b)). As interpreted by the federal courts of appeals, this departure standard has been used regularly and often to reverse district court sentences outside the guidelines. A 1997 study found that the chances of a trial court's sentence being reversed on appeal were ten times greater in the federal system than in Minnesota, and fifty times greater than in Pennsylvania (Reitz, 1997). Thus, the federal guidelines are probably the most restrictive of judicial discretion of any yet created in the United States—because of their narrow ranges, the number of fine grading distinctions they draw among cases, and their unusually high degree of legal enforceability.

The only state guidelines to rival the federal system in legal authority are the North Carolina guidelines. Alone among guideline systems so far invented, there is no departure power in North Carolina. By statute, the trial court must impose a guideline sentence in every case. In effect, the guidelines have replaced the former maximum and minimum penalties that used to exist as a matter of statutory law.

Offsetting the forceful legal punch of the North Carolina guidelines, the sentencing ranges available to judges are generally broad in comparison with the federal system and the guidelines in many other states. A judge in North Carolina may select a sentence in the "presumptive range" as depicted in the "Felony Punishment Chart" (Figure 3), but the judge has unreviewable discretion to elect a sentence from the "aggravated" or "mitigated" ranges that are also set out on the chart. Thus, for example, in box E(I) on the North Carolina chart, the judge could impose an "active" (prison) sentence of any length between fifteen and thirty-one months, or the judge could substitute one or more "intermediate punishments." No appellate court may second-guess the trial judge across this continuum of possibilities. Appellate review exists only for "unlawful" sentences that reach beyond the aggravated or mitigated ranges.

The North Carolina model is unique among existing guideline structures. In the run-of-the-mill cases, North Carolina trial judges have more discretion (because of the breadth of available sentencing ranges) than judges in other jurisdictions where guidelines are legally binding. However, the North Carolina law cuts off sentencing options at the extreme high and low ends that remain available to judges in other jurisdictions, at least in sufficiently unusual cases, through the vehicle of the departure power.

In summary, the degree of real authority exerted by a set of guidelines upon trial judges depends upon a combination of factors: whether the guidelines are characterized by the legislature as legally binding or as advisory to the courts; whether the stated sentencing ranges are fine-toothed or broad-gauged; how many grading distinctions are built into the guidelines; whether the "departure power" retained by judges is defined in a broad or stingy fashion—if it exists at all; and whether the appellate courts are vigilant or lax in their guideline-enforcement function. Even a quick review of established sentencing guideline structures reveals a full spectrum of possibilities on all of these dimensions: Some guidelines are wholly advisory, some exert an exceedingly light touch on judicial authority, some are legally enforceable yet flexible when a sentencing judge feels strongly about a case (and can provide a reasoned basis for the feeling), and some guidelines are tightly restrictive—even mandatory—in their effects on sentencing outcomes. As noted earlier, all guidelines are not created equal.

Guidelines and parole release

The workings of any set of sentencing guidelines are interrelated with the sentencing authority held by other institutional actors in the punishment system. The impact of sentencing guidelines on prison terms can be greatly affected by the presence or absence of a parole board with authority to set release dates for incarcerated offenders. Marvin Frankel argued in the early 1970s that parole release should be cut back once sentencing commissions had brought rational uniformity to the penalties imposed by judges, and Frankel joined other voices decrying the standardless, arbitrary, and unreviewable nature of parole board decision-making. Among guideline systems as of 2001, nine of sixteen legislatures have chosen to abolish parole release in conjunction with guideline reform—usually under the banner of "truth in sentencing." (See Figure 1.) In such systems, the guideline sentence pronounced by the trial judge, allowing for good-time reductions by prison authorities, will bear close resemblance to the sentence actually served by the convicted offender.

The remaining seven guideline jurisdictions, however, have retained parole release discretion in some form. Thus, for example, in Pennsylvania, the guidelines for prison cases set forth minimum terms of incarceration. Under state law, the maximum must then be set equal to at least double the minimum. The Pennsylvania parole board enjoys authority to release prisoners who have served the minimum sentence, but the board may also in its discretion require the prisoner to serve out the full sentence (with adjustment for good time credits). On the other side of the scale, Congress's Sentencing Reform Act (authorizing the federal guidelines) abolished parole release and limited the availability of good time to 15 percent of an offender's pronounced sentence. Thus, in the federal system, incarcerated offenders serve a minimum of 85 percent of imposed penalties.

Facts relevant to sentencing

All guideline jurisdictions have found it necessary to create rules that identify the factual issues at sentencing that must be resolved under the guidelines, those that are potentially relevant to a sentencing decision, and those viewed as forbidden considerations that may not be taken into account by sentencing courts. One heated controversy, addressed differently across jurisdictions, is whether the guideline sentence should be based exclusively on crimes for which offenders have been convicted ("conviction offenses"), or whether a guideline sentence should also reflect additional alleged criminal conduct for which formal convictions have not been obtained ("nonconviction offenses"). Nonconviction offenses, as cataloged by Reitz in 1993, may include crimes for which charges were never brought, charges dismissed as part of a plea bargain, and even charges resulting in acquittals at trial. Sentencing based freely upon both conviction and nonconviction crimes is often called *real-offense sentencing*.

As noted earlier, the federal sentencing guidelines require trial judges to base guideline calculations upon conviction offenses and nonconviction offenses in some circumstances. Under the federal guidelines' "relevant conduct" provision, if a nonconviction crime is related to the offense of conviction (that is, if it is similar in kind or arose from the same episode), and if the defendant's guilt has been established by a preponderance of the evidence during sentencing proceedings, then the trial judge must compute the guideline punishment as though the defendant had been convicted of the nonconviction charge. Real-offense sentencing in such cases is mandatory in the federal system. To give one striking example, in *United States v. Juarez-Ortega*, 866 F.2d 747 (5th Cir. 1989), a defendant convicted at a jury trial of a drug charge but acquitted of a related gun charge was sentenced as though convictions had been returned on both counts. The trial judge found by a preponderance of the evidence that—despite the jury's acquittal—the defendant was guilty of the nonconviction gun offense.

State guideline systems have all gone in a different direction than the federal system on this issue. Instead of mandating real-offense sentencing, the consideration of nonconviction crimes is usually restricted to *departure cases* in the states or, in a few jurisdictions, is prohibited outright. All guideline grids set out presumptive sentences based on conviction offenses and prior convictions; no state follows the federal example of adding or substituting nonconviction offenses for purposes of the initial guideline calculation. Thus, presumptive sentences, intended to govern all typical cases, are oriented solely toward conviction crimes. In some guideline states, including all voluntary-guideline jurisdictions, a trial court may deviate from the guidelines in the belief that the defendant's "real" offenses were more numerous or more serious than those reflected in the verdict or guilty plea. Unlike the federal system, however, such consideration of nonconviction crimes is discretionary with the court rather than mandatory, and is limited to departure cases. In at least three states, even departure sentences based on nonconviction conduct are legally forbidden. Thus, for example, a sentence such as the one imposed in the *Juarez-Ortega* case above would be struck down on appeal in Minnesota, Washington, and North Carolina.

Another difficult issue of fact-finding at sentencing for guideline designers has been the degree to which trial judges should be permitted to consider the personal characteristics of offenders as mitigating factors when imposing sentence. For example: Is the defendant a single parent with young children at home? Is the defendant addicted to drugs but a good candidate for drug treatment? Has the defendant struggled to overcome conditions of economic, social, or educational deprivation prior to the offense? Was the defendant's criminal behavior explicable in part by youth, inexperience, or an unformed ability to resist peer pressure? Most guideline states, once again including all jurisdictions with voluntary guidelines, allow trial courts latitude to sentence outside of the guideline ranges based on the judge's assessment of such offender characteristics. Some states, fearing that race or class disparities might be exacerbated by unguided consideration of such factors, have placed limits on the list of eligible concerns. For example, in Minnesota, judges are not permitted to depart from the guidelines because of a defendant's employment history, family ties, or stature in the community. (However, such factors may indirectly affect the sentence, since judges are permitted to base departures on the offender's particular "amenability" to probation (Frase, 1997).)

Once again, the federal system is an outlier among guideline jurisdictions in its sweeping proscriptions of the consideration of offender characteristics. All of the personal attributes mentioned in the preceding paragraph are treated as forbidden or discouraged grounds for departure in federal law. If a federal judge wishes to tailor a sentence to a defendant's old age and infirmity, youth and inexperience, family obligations, or amenability to rehabilitation, the case law has required that the trial judge may do so only in truly "extraordinary" cases—and the federal courts of appeals have been vigilant in re-

versing lower court sentences deemed too easily responsive to sympathetic offender attributes (on the ground that, however sympathetic, the attributes are not sufficiently extraordinary). In contrast to the experience of state judges under state guidelines, U.S. District Court judges complain loudly that the federal guidelines have excised the human component of sentencing decisions.

Evaluations of guidelines in operation

So far we have been concerned with the structural and procedural architecture of sentencing guideline systems. A different set of issues arises when we ask how well or poorly the new guidelines have performed in operation. While the guideline evaluation literature is shockingly thin, especially that focused on the states as opposed to the federal system, twenty years of experience under guidelines permits a number of observations about their successes and failures.

Uniformity in sentencing

First, it is probably fair to say that "uniformity in sentencing" has proven to be a more elusive commodity than sentencing reformers foresaw in the 1970s. For one thing, the past few decades have not yielded a consensus on what counts as uniformity. Nearly all guideline systems report that, in the great majority of cases, trial judges follow the applicable guidelines when imposing sentences. Surprisingly, high rates of guideline compliance are reported by a number of commissions with voluntary guidelines (including Delaware, Pennsylvania, and Virginia), as well as in jurisdictions with legally enforceable guidelines. Many people accept such reports as evidence of marginal improvements in sentencing uniformity when comparing guidelines with traditional indeterminate sentencing systems.

Critics, of the federal guidelines in particular, argue that high rates of guideline compliance show nothing more than false uniformity in sentencing. Such claims, in part, go to the very definition of uniformity: If one believes that federal guidelines mandate lock-step punishments that exclude consideration of important offender characteristics, then the federal guidelines will appear to demand rigidly disparate sentences (e.g., the person who committed crime x for reasons of economic deprivation gets the same sentence as the person who committed crime x out of pure avarice). On the other hand, if one believes that most personal characteristics of defendants should be removed from the sentencing calculus, and that punishment should be matched closely to criminal conduct, then current federal sentences tend to look both more appropriate and more uniform in application. Uniformity (as against what baseline) tends to be in the eye of the beholder.

Aside from such fundamental disagreements, which do not promise to dissipate any time soon, evaluators of existing guideline systems have discovered, or strongly suspected, that the plea bargaining process can work to undermine the goal of sentencing uniformity. A sophisticated study by Nagel and Schulhofer in 1992 of the federal guidelines in three cities found that the parties were "circumventing" the guidelines as often as 35 percent of the time through plea negotiations. Richard Frase's 1993 assessment concluded that plea bargaining remained a major force in sentencing outcomes after Minnesota's guidelines were implemented, as well—although perhaps no more so than before the guidelines. Again, there are different ways to assess the meager evidence in hand: It seems likely that plea negotiations are channeled by the parties' expectations of what the ultimate sentences in their cases would be under guidelines, and that negotiated resolutions thus treat the guidelines as a meaningful point of departure. However, the empirical evidence is far too slight to permit anyone to prove it, so the controversy will remain pending additional research.

Racial disparities in punishment

On the issue of racial disproportionalities in sentencing, observers of guideline reforms have so far rendered a mixed verdict. For the nation as a whole, racial disparities in incarceration have become more pronounced since the early 1980s, when guidelines were first introduced. Forceful charges have been leveled that the federal guidelines, particularly for drug offenses, and in conjunction with mandatory penalties for drug crimes enacted by Congress, have exacerbated preexisting racial disparities in sentencing. The story appears to be a bit different at the state level. Among state guideline systems, the evaluation literature is scanty on this issue, but most state commissions have reported a modest reduction in racially disparate sentencing following the enactment of guidelines. No guideline jurisdiction claims to have made major headway on the problem of racial disproportionalities in punish-ment. So far, even under the best case scenario, it appears that sentencing commissions and guidelines can achieve small advances in problems of racial disparity, but commissions and guidelines (as in the federal example) can also act to make such problems worse. No one, in other words, should support guideline reform in the belief that racial equity in sentencing will automatically follow.

Guidelines and prison populations

Marvin Frankel hoped that the rationalizing process of commission-based sentencing reform would ultimately lead to what he viewed as more humane sentencing outcomes overall: a reduced reliance on incarceration and increased creativity in the use of intermediate punishments. Writing in the early 1970s, Frankel could hardly have predicted that prison and jail confinement rates in America would in fact increase by more than a factor of four in the next twenty-five years, with most of the confinement explosion occurring after 1980. We must ask how much of the incarceration boom has been attributable to the advent of sentencing guidelines.

Some of it clearly has been. In the federal system, where our knowledge base is deepest, U.S. District Court judges complain regularly that the guidelines (or Congress's mandatory minimums, or both) force them to impose heavier sentences than they would otherwise have chosen. These claims are consistent with the original legislative and commission intents in promulgating the federal guidelines, as outlined in a 1998 book by Stith and Cabranes: there was widespread political sentiment during the Reagan administration that federal judges had been meting out sentences of undue leniency for many crimes, and the federal guideline reform was directed in large part to preventing that from happening by curtailing the judges' discretion.

Raw statistics suggest that the designers of the federal system got what they wanted. In the first ten years under the new federal guidelines, from 1987 to 1997, the federal imprisonment rate increased by 119 percent. This growth surge was 25 percent greater than the average increase in imprisonment rates for the nation as a whole during the same period (Bureau of Justice Statistics, 1998, p. 491, table 6.36). In contrast, in the decade prior to the advent of the guidelines, the federal prison system had been expanding at a much slower pace (23 percent growth in imprisonment rates from 1977 to 1987), far below the national average (77 percent). There is good reason to conclude that the federal sentencing guidelines, in combination with congressional mandatory penalties, ushered in an era of deliberately engineered increases in punitive severity, and shifted gears in federal imprisonment from a slow-growth pace to a fast-growth pace virtually overnight.

At the state level, the relationship between guideline reform and sentencing severity has been mixed, but more consistent with Frankel's original vision than the federal experience. A number of state legislatures and commissions have created guideline structures with the express purpose of containing prison growth. Minnesota was the first jurisdiction to attempt this, beginning in 1980, by crafting its guidelines with the aid of a computer simulation model to forecast future sentencing patterns. Over the first ten years under the state's guidelines, imprisonment rates in Minnesota did incline upward, but only by 47 percent—in a period when the nationwide imprisonment rate more than doubled (plus 110 percent). This pattern of some incarceration growth, but slower than the national average, was also seen during the first ten years of the Washington and Oregon guidelines, respectively. Washington's imprisonment rates increased by 29 percent from 1984 to 1994, while national rates increased by 107 percent. Oregon's imprisonment rates rose by only 11 percent from 1989 to 1998, while national rates went up 70 percent over the same period. In a 1995 study of sentencing commissions operative in the 1980s, Thomas Marvell identified six state commissions that were instructed to consider prison capacity when promulgating guidelines. In all six jurisdictions, Marvell found "comparatively slow prison population growth," prompting him to write that "These findings are a refreshing departure from the usual negative results when evaluating criminal justice reforms" (p. 707).

In the 1990s, newer commissions in Virginia and North Carolina have also had notable success in restraining the incarceration explosion. Virginia's guidelines, for example, were created early in the administration of a new governor who had promised to crack down on violent crime and abolish parole. While allowing the governor to keep his campaign commitments, the new Virginia guidelines have coincided with a 3 percent decrease in the state's imprisonment rate from 1995 to 1998 (a period in which national rates climbed by 12 percent).

In North Carolina, the state's imprisonment rate (inmates with sentences over one year, per 100,000 state residents) grew at a fast (19 percent) pace during the first year of the new guidelines, from year-end 1994 to year-end 1995. This can largely be attributed to sentences still being handed down under pre-guidelines law, however, and the temporary growth surge was predicted by the state's sentencing commission. In the three successive calendar years of 1996 through 1998, as guideline cases have entered the system in greater numbers, North Carolina's imprisonment rates have fallen every year. Perhaps just as significantly, the state's guidelines have ushered in deliberate changes in the proportionate share of convicted felons sent to prison and those routed to intermediate punishments. In the first three years under guidelines, the total confinement rate for felony offenders fell from 48 to 34 percent, reflecting the state's policy judgment that an increased share of nonviolent felons should be sentenced to intermediate punishments. In order to accommodate this change, the commission successfully lobbied the state legislature to provide increased funding for intermediate-punishment programming. At the same time, however, North Carolina's guidelines have substantially increased the use of prison bed space for violent offenders. In the state's political arena, the North Carolina commission has won widespread support for its tripartite agenda of severe punishment for violent criminals, the expanded use of intermediate punishments for less serious offenses, and the introduction of planned "resource management" of prison growth.

Slow-growth policy has not been the whole story under state guidelines, however. Like the federal commission, the Pennsylvania sentencing commission was instructed by its legislature to write guidelines that would toughen prison sentences as compared with prior judicial practice—and Pennsylvania's prisons have grown steadily under the guidelines regime. In sixteen years under guidelines, between 1982 and 1998, Pennsylvania's imprisonment rate has increased by 244 percent, while the national rate increased by "only" 171 percent. Even in the pioneering states of Minnesota, Washington, and Oregon, the state legislatures (and sometimes the voters, through the initiative process), have acted to toughen sentencing guidelines and other sentencing provisions. In the late 1980s, the Minnesota legislature ordered the state sentencing commission to retool its guidelines to provide harsher sentences for violent crimes, beginning a period of planned prison growth. Accordingly, during the 1990s, Minnesota's prisons have grown slightly faster than the national average. Washington and Oregon steered similar courses in the late 1980s and the early 1990s.

Two conclusions on guidelines and prison growth emerge from two decades of experience. First, guidelines and computer projections have proven to be surprisingly effective technologies for the deliberate resource management of incarcerated populations—but they are tools that may be used with equal facility to push aggregate sentencing severity up or down. As Michael Tonry noted in 1993, virtually all sentencing guideline systems have been "successful" on this score, if we measure success against what the commission and legislature were trying to achieve. Second, the overall experience of guidelines to date has been that they have sometimes been used to retard prison growth (measured against national trends) and they have sometimes been used to parallel or even exceed the course of prison expansion observable in non-guideline jurisdictions. It is thus difficult to attribute independent causal significance to guidelines as a driving force of the prison boom in the past quarter century. In a number of instances, and whenever called upon to do so, guidelines have been an effective force in the opposite direction.

Purposes at sentencing

There is little question that sentencing guidelines have succeeded in injecting system-wide policy judgments about the goals of punishment into case-by-case decision-making. How one assesses this achievement turns in part upon whether one agrees with the goals that have been effectuated. For example, the earliest guideline innovations of the 1980s (such as those in Minnesota, Washington, and Oregon) all built their systems on a "just deserts" rationale, scaling punishment severity to the blameworthiness of offenders as measured by current crimes and past convictions. Some observers, like Andrew von Hirsch (an influential proponent of the just deserts theory), would rate such guidelines as enlightened reforms. Others, like Albert Alschuler and Michael Tonry, have charged that the just deserts model is an intolerably one-dimensional approach to punishment decisions.

Moving forward into the 1990s, several states have broadened the menu of underlying purposes that can be written into guidelines. For example, the current Virginia guidelines incorporate the criminological research of criminal careers in pursuit of a policy of selective incapacitation of the most dangerous offenders. Pennsylvania's guidelines, as revised in the mid-1990s, are driven by changing policies through five "levels" of the sentencing matrix. At Level 5 (the most serious cases), retribution and public safety are dominant concerns. Moving downward through the other levels, priorities of victim restitution, community service, and offender treatment become increasingly prominent. And in a recent study, Richard Frase has argued that the Minnesota guidelines, as modified by appellate court decisions and system actors, have come to exemplify the theory of "limiting retributivism" propounded by Norval Morris in which an offender's blameworthiness sets loose boundaries on available penalties, but consequential concerns such as the prospects for rehabilitation may be used to select a punishment within those boundaries (Frase, 1997). Even the federal guidelines, which claim to be agnostic as to sentencing purposes, can be said to embody a "philosophical" position that most criminal sentences under guidelines should be harsher than those imposed before the guidelines were created.

Data concerning big-picture sentencing patterns reinforce the gathering impression that sentencing commissions have had impact upon jurisdiction-wide punishment policy. Many state guideline systems since the 1980s have reported that, since guidelines were implemented, penalties for violent crimes have been deliberately increased, often at the same time that penalties for nonviolent offenses have been deliberately reduced. Because nonviolent offenses are so much more numerous than nonviolent crimes, even small cutbacks in punishment at the low end of the seriousness scale can free up many prison beds for the more serious criminals. Such results might be applauded on grounds of just deserts, deterrence, or incapacitation. Moreover, the fact that a number of states have had success in manipulating sentencing patterns in this way is one indicator that the policies subsumed in guidelines can have appreciable effects upon sentencing outcomes across the system.

Future horizons

Sentencing commissions and guidelines are still at an early stage in their institutional history. (Indeterminate sentencing, in contrast, has roots that reach back more than a full century.) Twenty years of experience with sentencing guidelines have not yielded a single model of reform, nor have guidelines yet replaced the indeterminate sentencing structures that remain at work in a bare majority of the American states. In the coming decades, there will almost certainly be continued experimentation and diversification in approach among existing guideline jurisdictions, as among the additional states that will come "on line" with new guidelines in the early twenty-first century.

It is likely that the proven ability of sentencing guidelines (plus computer projections) to manage the growth of correctional populations will induce a steadily increasing number of jurisdictions to invest in some version of guideline reform. But the future of guidelines will also depend heavily upon demonstrable improvements in existing guideline technology along a number of dimensions: system designers will have to solve the problem of finding the right balance between the legal enforceability of guidelines and the role for judicial discretion in sentencing determinations. Guideline drafters must also continue their experiments with incorporating consequential purposes of punishment into sentencing systems, if the policy community is to become convinced that guidelines can do more than instantiate a "one-note" just deserts program. Guideline designers will also continue to be faced with the unsolved riddle of addressing the array of intermediate punishments with guideline prescriptions—building upon a small store of promising initiatives from the late 1990s. Sentencing commissions will also be crucial forums for the ongoing struggle to combat racial disproportionalities in criminal punishment—although these efforts are likely to reinforce our understanding that the sentencing process is only one part of a much larger problem. Finally, the next generation of guideline evolution will depend on far better assessment research than has yet been performed, so that we may better approach such conundrums as the dynamics of charging and plea bargaining within guideline systems, the degree to which guidelines provide room for values of both uniformity and discretion, and the successes or failures of guidelines in furthering their underlying policy objectives. All of these issues, and others, will play out in numerous jurisdictions and in varying permutations in the coming years. Those interested in sentencing guidelines, their established viability, and their potential, must of necessity become

"comparativists"—with curiosity and knowledge extending outward across multiple systems.

KEVIN R. REITZ

See also CRIMINAL JUSTICE SYSTEM; GUILTY PLEA: PLEA BARGAINING; PROBATION AND PAROLE: HISTORY, GOALS, AND DECISION-MAKING; PROBATION AND PAROLE: PROCEDURAL PROTECTION; PROSECUTION: PROSECUTORIAL DISCRETION; PUNISHMENT; SENTENCING: ALLOCATION OF AUTHORITY; SENTENCING: ALTERNATIVES; SENTENCING: DISPARITY; SENTENCING: MANDATORY AND MANDATORY MINIMUM SENTENCES; SENTENCING: PRESENTENCE REPORT; SENTENCING: PROCEDURAL PROTECTION.

BIBLIOGRAPHY

ALSCHULER, ALBERT W. "Sentencing Reform and Prosecutorial Power: A Critique of Recent Proposals for 'Fixed' or 'Presumptive' Sentencing." *University of Pennsylvania Law Review* 126 (1978): 550–577.

———. "The Failure of Sentencing Guidelines: A Plea for Less Aggregation." *University of Chicago Law Review* 58 (1993): 901–951.

American Bar Association. *Standards for Criminal Justice: Sentencing*, 3d ed. Chicago: ABA Press, 1994.

Bureau of Justice Assistance. *National Assessment of Structured Sentencing*. Washington, D.C.: U.S. Government Printing Office, 1996.

Bureau of Justice Statistics, U.S. Department of Justice. *Sourcebook of Criminal Justice Statistics, 1997*. Washington, D.C.: U.S. Government Printing Office, 1998.

Delaware Sentencing Accountability Commission. *Truth in Sentencing Benchbook*. Wilmington, Del.: Delaware Sentencing Accountability Commission, 1997.

FRANKEL, MARVIN E. *Criminal Sentences: Law without Order*. New York: Hill and Wang, 1973.

FRASE, RICHARD S. "Implementing Commission-Based Sentencing Guidelines: The Lessons of the First Ten Years in Minnesota." *Cornell Journal of Law and Public Policy* 2 (1993): 279–337.

———. "Sentencing Principles in Theory and Practice." In *Crime and Justice: A Review of Research*, vol. 22. Edited by Michael Tonry. Chicago: University of Chicago Press, 1997.

FREED, DANIEL J. "Federal Sentencing in the Wake of Guidelines: Unacceptable Limits on the Discretion of Sentencers." *Yale Law Journal* 101 (1992): 1681–1754.

MARVELL, THOMAS B. "Sentencing Guidelines and Prison Population Growth." *Journal of Criminal Law and Criminology* 85 (1995): 696–707.

Minnesota Sentencing Guidelines Commission. *Minnesota Sentencing Guidelines and Commentary.* St. Paul, Minn.: Minnesota Sentencing Guidelines Commission, 1997.

Morris, Norval, and Tonry, Michael. *Between Prison and Probation: Intermediate Punishments in a Rational Sentencing System.* New York: Oxford University Press, 1990.

Nagel, Ilene H., and Schulhofer, Stephen J. "A Tale of Three Cities: An Empirical Study of Charging and Bargaining Practices Under the Federal Sentencing Guidelines." *Southern California Law Review* 66 (1992): 501–566.

National Center for State Courts. *Sentencing Commission Profiles.* Williamsburg, Va.: National Center for State Courts, 1997.

Reitz, Kevin R. "Sentencing Facts: Travesties of Real-Offense Sentencing." *Stanford Law Review* 45 (1993): 523–573.

———. "Sentencing Guideline Systems and Sentence Appeals: A Comparison of Federal and State Experiences." *Northwestern Law Review* 91 (1997): 1441–1506.

Schulhofer, Stephen J. "Assessing the Federal Sentencing Process: The Problem is Uniformity, Not Disparity." *American Criminal Law Review* 29 (1992): 833–873.

Stith, Kate, and Cabranes, José A. *Fear of Judging: Sentencing Guidelines in the Federal Courts.* Chicago: University of Chicago Press, 1998.

Tonry, Michael. "The Success of Judge Frankel's Sentencing Commission." *University of Colorado Law Review* 64 (1993): 713–722.

———. *Sentencing Matters.* New York: Oxford University Press, 1996.

———. "Intermediate Sanctions in Sentencing Guidelines." In *Crime and Justice: A Review of Research,* vol. 23. Edited by Michael Tonry. Chicago: University of Chicago Press, 1998.

University of Colorado Law Review. "A Symposium on Sentencing Reform in the States." *University of Colorado Law Review* 64 (1993): 645–847.

von Hirsch, Andrew. *Censure and Sanctions.* Oxford, U.K.: Clarendon Press, 1993.

von Hirsch, Andrew; Knapp, Kay A.; and Tonry, Michael. *The Sentencing Commission and Its Guidelines.* Boston: Northeastern University Press, 1987.

SENTENCING: MANDATORY AND MANDATORY MINIMUM SENTENCES

Supporters of mandatory sentencing assert that these laws achieve deterrence and incapaci-tation with more certainty than sentencing under other structures. Mandatory penalties are designed to eliminate judicial discretion in choosing among various punishment options, under the assumption that judges are too lenient and that offenders are therefore neither generally deterred from crime nor specifically deterred because some are not incarcerated long enough to prevent persistent criminality (Shichor and Sechrest).

Mandatory sentencing laws require judges to sentence the convicted offender to specific prison term of a fixed number of years. Usually this means that an offender must serve at least some absolute minimum prison term before becoming eligible for parole (some laws also preclude parole). The requirement is triggered when the offender is convicted of a particular charge. Although this approach may appear simple and straightforward, there is wide variation in how these laws are applied. The variation is mostly attributable to the exercise of discretion by criminal justice actors other than judges: prosecutors and parole boards. A prosecutor's decision whether to charge a crime to which a mandatory sentence will attach varies depending on local prosecutorial charging policies and plea bargaining practices, and the actual charge of conviction is somewhat flexible in a plea bargain. Decisions to release an offender from prison can depend on whether the particular statute allows parole reductions to apply to the mandatory sentence once it is handed down, and on whether "good time" or work release credits may apply. It is often said that discretion removed from one component of the justice system will reappear elsewhere, and mandatory sentencing is the prime example (McCoy).

Types of mandatory penalties

Mandatory sentences differ from determinate or guidelines sentences because they include no range of years, however narrow, within which a judge has discretion to set a prison sentence. Upon conviction, the judge is required to set the exact sentence enunciated in the law. This can be a prison term required for committing a particular offense, or it may be an "add on" term of years appended to a normally determined prison term. An example of the former type of mandatory minimum is the common *three-strikes law*, in which a third felony conviction means that the "three time loser" will automatically be imprisoned for life. State laws vary significantly as to which offenses count as "strikes" and whether parole from a life term is permissible (Clark, Austin, and Henry). An example of an "add-on," or enhancement of the base sentence, is a requirement that a person who has used a gun to commit a felony will receive a prison term for the "predicate" felony, and then have an extra year of prison time added for use of the firearm. Another type of law regarded as mandatory sentencing requires each offender to serve a set percentage—usually 85 percent to 100 percent—of whatever prison term the judge imposed under the existing sentencing law (Ostrom et al.).

The concept of mandatory minima usually refers to prison terms, with the "minimum" understood as referring to months or years of incarceration. However, the approach can also be seen in laws that forbid judges to grant probation, and/or which mandate jail terms. An example is a law from the Northern Territory of Australia requiring judges to send juveniles to jail, forbidding probation or any alternative correctional program, upon conviction for any felony. In March 2000, a report from the United Nations Human Rights Commission stated that mandatory jailing of juveniles violates the Convention on the Rights of the Child. The United States has not signed these international treaties and is thus not bound by them, nor by legal standards in most developed nations, which regard mandatory sentencing as a violation of due process or as punishment disproportionate to the crime.

History and legality of mandatory minima

Mandatory sentencing is not new. Sentencing "enhancements" for habitual felons have been used in most states for decades (Austin et al.) and the idea can be easily traced back to Dickensian England and, no doubt, earlier (Simon). The difference, if any, lies in the fact that modern mandatories often purport to eliminate discretion; by contrast, mercy from the judiciary or executive was explicitly possible, historically. In a particularly stark application of the modern notion of mandatory sentencing, several states enacted mandatory death penalty statutes after the U.S. Supreme Court had placed a moratorium on capital punishment in *Furman v. Georgia*, 408 U.S. 238 (1972). The Court struck these down as a violation of individualized justice in favor of a system in which death would be imposed on a convicted murderer only if an "aggravating factor" was alleged and proven to the trial court's

satisfaction (*Woodson v. North Carolina*, 428 U.S. 280 (1976); *Roberts v. Louisiana*, 428 U.S. 325 (1976)). In a line of case law that seems contradictory, however, the Supreme Court upheld a Texas mandatory three-strikes law when it required that life imprisonment be imposed on an offender who had committed three minor thefts (*Rummel v. Estelle*, 445 U.S. 263 (1980)). Perhaps the contradiction is resolved by the fact that, as Chief Justice Rehnquist pointed out in the majority opinion, parole from the life term was possible under the Texas statute. Contemporary three-strikes laws, however, have withstood individualized justice/due process and disproportionality challenges based on the Eighth Amendment's prohibition of cruel and unusual punishment, even though these statutes seldom permit parole (Zeigler and Del Carmen).

Soon after *Rummel* was decided in 1980, political campaigns and popular sentiment in favor of mandatory sentencing laws became widespread throughout the nation. In the 1980s and 1990s, demands for harsher and more certain sentencing became extremely popular. A grassroots campaign by Mothers Against Drunk Driving in the early 1980s, which successfully changed laws nationwide so as to require mandatory jail terms for drunk drivers, began the trend. Recognizing an emotionally appealing way to establish themselves in electoral politics as tough hard-liners, and thus to harness popular alarm over the high crime rates of the 1970s, political candidates promised to pass tougher and tougher sentencing laws if they were elected. They were and they did (Tonry, 1996).

Media portrayals of crime and criminals heightened the fears. Media outlets may encourage "moral panics" by demonizing offenders, drumming up widespread anxiety, and riding the wave of public concern with high viewership ratings and ad revenues. Although the media's influence on policy is not clearly causal—many factors influence lawmaking and public opinion—it is almost always present to some degree in the development of mandatory sentencing legislation. A news cycle can begin with "a preexisting social construction of predator criminals" from the entertainment media (Surette, p. 194) to which is added news of a horrific crime in some locality, which is widely reported nationally and thus dramatized everywhere as an ongoing firsthand threat. The media coverage can create "victim heroes" and build politicians' careers when they promise tough sentencing (Surette, 1996). (The instantaneous spread of three strikes law in twenty-four states is attributed to such a cycle, sparked by the kidnap/murder of young Polly Klaas in Petaluma, California.) Sometimes the furor addresses sensational crimes that were indeed very serious but that already had very heavy punishments on the books; in such cases, reformers have demanded abolition of parole or additional controls such as community notification when an offender is released. Examples include the Washington state sexual predator law and "Megan's Law" in New Jersey.

Sometimes the crimes at issue, however, had not previously been regarded as sufficiently serious as to deserve lengthy imprisonment, and these are the most controversial. The prime example is the federal requirement that a person convicted of possessing a half kilogram (500 grams) or more of powder cocaine will be sentenced to five years in prison with no parole eligibility. In comparison, just five grams of crack cocaine qualifies for the five-year mandatory term, and this increases to ten years for 50 grams of crack. In the federal criminal justice system, mandatory minima provisions for drug-related activities carry penalties ranging from five years to life (United States Sentencing Commission). These laws emerged from the cocaine scare of the late 1980s, as did many state statutes, but they presented a somewhat different legislative dynamic than the mandatories that were sparked by sex crimes or repeat offending. Although the cocaine-induced death of Maryland basketball star Len Bias in 1986 served perhaps as the horrific event that galvanized this media frenzy, drug use and trafficking is a market whose victims are in some sense consenting. Punishing these criminals with very harsh prison sentences, at least those who are cocaine users and small-time dealers, initially was regarded as too heavy-handed. But here the issue of race as "the demonizer" enters into the lawmaking equation. Crack cocaine was disproportionately used and sold in minority neighborhoods, while a higher percentage of white suburbanites favored the powder form. Critics of the federal mandatory sentencing drug laws claim that the severely harsher penalties for using/dealing crack versus powder cocaine—a defendant must have possessed one hundred times more powder than crack to be eligible for the five-year or the ten-year mandatory sentence—are correlated with probabilities that an arrested user or dealer will be a member of a racial minority (Tonry, 1995). One study concluded that black offenders received longer sentences than whites not because they were sentenced differently under identical conditions, but because they, not whites, were the ones charged and convicted of trafficking in crack (McDonald and Carlson).

Vigorous criticism of mandatory sentencing has come from scholars, news commentators, groups like Families against Mandatory Minimums, and even the U.S. Sentencing Commission itself when it asked Congress to amend the laws applying to cocaine use. But repealing these penalties is almost impossible politically. Any politician who would do so would immediately be attacked as "soft on crime." In practice, however, the laws have not necessarily had the draconian impact their drafters said they would, at least not in all cases.

Impact of mandatory minima on prosecution and sentencing severity

Any evaluation of how sentencing laws work must take into account how they affect pretrial procedures. This is so because mandatories apply only when an offender is convicted of crimes specified in the legislation, while investigation or evidentiary challenges might point to charges that do not carry the mandatory. Nearly unanimously, studies of the impact of mandatory minima have concluded that their most severe aspects are often moderated in pretrial decisions by prosecutors and defenders who do not believe all offenders deserve the heaviest punishments (Tonry, 1996). For their part, accused defendants are reluctant to plead guilty when the probable sentence will be the harshest possible. Still other impact studies have noted that under some mandatory sentencing laws (for example, some states' three-strikes laws) the justice system can continue functioning mostly as it had before the laws were passed, because the legislation in question did not make drastic changes. Despite the political campaigning surrounding their passage, offenders to whom they applied would have been required to serve very long prison sentences under already existing laws, so the mandatory minima added only a small amount of additional incarceration for a fairly small number of offenders. This is so in states with three-strikes laws that apply only to serious felons, but others, such as California's, cover all felonies of any degree of seriousness and thus have been the subject of prosecutorial discretion (Austin et al.).

Many important issues of equity and proportionality remain, because the conditions and criteria under which prosecutors agree not to seek the harshest penalties are mostly unreviewable and might produce racially or economically disparate outcomes. Furthermore, the role of the judiciary becomes weakened while that of prosecutors, whose decisions about charging determine the applicability of the mandatories, becomes dominant. In the majority of U.S. jurisdictions, judges do not participate in guilty plea negotiations, so the judiciary has little influence over charging (Feeley and Kamin). When a defendant is brought into court charged with a particular crime that carries exposure to a mandatory sentence, the role of the judge is generally limited to accepting the guilty plea or presiding over a trial, and upon conviction imposing the prescribed sentence. Under such a system, the prosecutor's charging decision usually determines the sentence. However, some impact studies from the late 1970s on the application of "add-ons" found that "by a mix of constitutional challenges, motions to quash the charge, sentence negotiations, and adjustments, waiver trials, and other techniques," the system managed to produce sentences roughly similar to those that had prevailed prior to passage of the mandatory sentencing law (Heumann and Loftin, p. 426). Occasionally, the most rigid features of a mandatory sentencing law are loosened when experience indicates that judges should have some discretion. This was the case in California, when the state Supreme Court decided in 1996 that judges had the discretion to determine what should count as a prior felony under the 1994 three-strikes law (*People v. Romero*, 917 P.2d 628 (1996)). Generally, however, the intent of these laws is to eliminate or at least severely constrain judicial discretion, and to a great extent this has indeed been their impact.

One way to conceptualize the effect of mandatory minima on criminal court procedures is to imagine the timing of major decisions shifting from the time of conviction and sentencing to much earlier stages of case processing. Often, police are interested primarily in certain convictions and short jail terms for lower-level drug dealers—which effectively disrupt the economy of open-air drug markets—but are not necessarily willing to endure paperwork and trial testimony to achieve mandatory punishments. Under those conditions, they choose to book suspects for crimes that do not carry a mandatory sentence, such as simple possession of small amounts of drugs. Prosecutors may agree more readily to diversion programs and even outright case dismissal when defendants are not as dangerous as

the incapacitative sentencing policy apparently assumes they are (Parent et al.). The most significant procedural stage in terms of numbers of cases affected and potential impact on sentencing outcomes is plea negotiation and the defendant's decision to plead guilty or go to trial. Few defendants will plead guilty to charges carrying mandatory life sentences, but will instead go to trial under the assumption that they have nothing to lose and a jury might find fault with some aspect of the prosecution's case. (Jury nullification of mandatory sentencing is seldom an issue, however, because under the law in most states juries decide on guilt and judges set the sentence.) In some jurisdictions, for some types of mandatories, trial rates increased dramatically. However, in most scenarios the effects of the mandatory minima requirements are blunted in plea negotiations. The factors that trigger a mandatory minimum—use of a gun, amount of drug possessed or sold, a third felony conviction, and so on—must be proven beyond a reasonable doubt in order for a mandatory to be held to apply. In plea bargaining, these factors are somewhat flexible depending on how strong the proof is and what the punishment would be if the defendant were convicted of a crime not covered by the mandatory (Parent et al.). In the case of three-strikes laws, for instance, defenders vigorously advocate for their clients when the prior felony is of low seriousness, if it was committed when the offender was a juvenile, or when it was committed a long time ago. Under these circumstances, prosecutors often agree to allow the defendant to plead to a misdemeanor requiring jail time but not triggering the "strike," especially when the process of getting the criminal records and proving the priors is quite labor intensive (Cushman).

Another significant impact of mandatory minima on plea bargaining is inducement of defendant cooperation. A prosecutor who wishes to obtain incriminating evidence often turns to the most accurate source: the criminals themselves. A defendant who will "snitch" on co-defendants will be rewarded with sentencing concessions. Often, the most efficient and easily understood reward a prosecutor can offer a "cooperator" is the promise not to charge crimes that carry the mandatory sentence. This practice is widespread in the federal system especially, where about half the offenders now sent to federal prison have been convicted of drug crimes, and the mandatories for gun use also often apply. However, a 1993 General Accounting Office report determined that 15 percent of cases involving offenders actually convicted of violating a federal statute carrying a mandatory minimum did not receive the prison time, because they had given "substantial assistance to government authorities" (Caulkins et al.). Moreover, the percentage of suspects who negotiate a "pre-bargain" to charges not carrying a mandatory, in return for testimony or other evidence, is even larger but cannot be measured from public databases.

Finally, one type of mandatory minimum influences the "end" of the system, that is, the parole decision, by requiring that offenders serve a minimum of 85 percent of any term of imprisonment. These *truth in sentencing* laws proliferated after Congress promised in the 1994 Crime Act to give money for prison construction to any state that would pass an 85 percent law (Ostrom et al.). Many did, though their statutes vary as to which crimes carry the 85 percent requirement. The impetus for these laws was quite different from the typical "horrific crime/media coverage/lawmaker embrace" background of many state mandatory minima laws. Advocacy from the federal government sparked the movement, modeled on the 1984 Sentencing Act, that instituted the federal sentencing guidelines and also remodeled the parole system by requiring 85 percent of every prison term be served. As might be predicted from experience with other mandatory sentencing laws, 85 percent truth in sentencing has not been applied mechanically. In New Jersey, prosecutors and judges often agreed to sentence offenders at lower base terms of imprisonment than had been typical prior to the law's passage, but when the 85 percent requirement was then calculated the final mandatory sentences to be served were longer on average than before (McCoy and McManimon). In sum, the effect of the law was to increase sentencing severity, but not as much as its supporters had expected.

The latter statement is a fair summary of the effect of all these laws. Mandatory minimum sentencing laws have drastically affected the operation of the various components of the justice system, which have adapted so as to ameliorate their harshest aspects. However, this also means that these laws have not caused the full incarcerative effect that their drafters apparently wanted. A great proportion of offenders eligible for mandatory sentences do not receive them; however, on the whole, these offenders are probably punished more severely than they would have been had the mandatory sentences not acted as threats

hanging over their guilty pleas. A much smaller proportion of offenders are actually sentenced under these laws. For them, there is no doubt that punishments are more severe than had been typical prior to these laws' implementation.

Effects of mandatory minima on crime

Of course, the entire point of mandatory minimum sentencing is crime reduction. To these laws' supporters, their narrower applicability than expected or their adverse impact on the justice system matter little as long as the laws serve the greater good of preventing serious crime. But it is difficult to prove a deterrent effect, and it is hard to know definitely whether any observed drops in the crime rate were caused by strict laws, strong economies, age-crime curves, or some other factors that have been said to influence crime. Furthermore, what we do know about the general deterrent effect of legislation is that it works best on people who have something to lose if they are punished; the rational choice is to be deterred, unless one is so poor or emotionally disturbed as to have nothing to lose by breaking the law. We also know that rational criminals are deterred more by the likelihood that they will be caught at all than by the severity of possible punishment. Finally, the deterrent effect of severe mandatory minimum laws is predicted to be weak because the people against whom they apply—recidivists, drug users and dealers, violent felons—are the type of offenders whose criminality defines their lifestyles and choices. Thinking about possible punishments deters few of them from the much more powerful daily rhythms of a way of life (von Hirsch and Ashworth).

The incapacitative as opposed to general deterrent effects of mandatory sentencing are probably more powerful. A felon in prison cannot commit crimes at the same rate as before, and this rate is measurable (Wilson). Economic models based on data from actual offenders demonstrate that the incapacitative effects of three-strikes laws, for example, reduce felony crime. The reductions vary depending on which crimes are covered as "strikes" and how often they will actually be applied (Greenwood et al.). However, over time the incapacitative effects diminish because older offenders serving life terms would not have been involved in crime at that point of their lives (Schmertmann et al.). Furthermore, these benefits are only one part of a traditional cost/benefit analysis. The very high costs of incarcerating so many offenders, and also ancillary social costs—impoverishing families when parents go to prison for life, fostering resentment and distrust of the justice system when mandatories are perceived as needlessly harsh and racially discriminatory—go a long way toward erasing the benefits (Tonry, 1995).

An important study of the effect of mandatory minimum drug sentences reached similar conclusions (Caulkins et al.). Although extremely severe punishments against drug traffickers does disrupt their businesses and prevent them from dealing, the researchers found that conventional enforcement casting a wider "net" of drug confiscation from all levels of drug users and dealers, and much less prison time, would also have incapacitative effects and be more cost-effective. Combining traditional enforcement and sentencing with mandatory drug treatment, they said, would produce the most crime reduction at the least cost (Caulkins et al.).

Such rational arguments have not been the basis for mandatory minima legislation in the past, and politicians are unlikely to embrace them publicly in the future. However, if mandatory sentences over time are applied only to the most serious felons and other correctional options are developed for mid-level offenders, the worst features of these laws may eventually erode.

CANDACE MCCOY

See also GUILTY PLEA: PLEA BARGAINING; PROSECUTION: PROSECUTORIAL DISCRETION; SENTENCING: ALLOCATION OF AUTHORITY; SENTENCING: ALTERNATIVES; SENTENCING: DISPARITY; SENTENCING: GUIDELINES; SENTENCING: PRESENTENCE REPORT; SENTENCING: PROCEDURAL PROTECTION.

BIBLIOGRAPHY

AUSTIN, JAMES; CLARK, JOHN; HARDYMAN, PATRICIA; and HENRY, D. ALAN. "The Impact of 'Three Strikes and You're Out.'" *Punishment and Society: The International Journal of Penology* 1, no. 2 (1999): 131–162.

CAULKINS, JONATHAN P.; RYDELL, C. PETER; SCHWABE, WILLIAM L.; and CHIESA, JAMES. *Mandatory Minimum Drug Sentences: Throwing Away the Key or the Taxpayers' Money?* Santa Monica, Calif.: RAND, 1997.

CLARK, JOHN; AUSTIN, JAMES; and HENRY, D. ALAN. *"Three Strikes and You're Out": A Review of State Legislation*. Washington, D.C.: U.S. Department of Justice, National Institute of Justice Research in Brief, September, 1997.

CUSHMAN, ROBERT C. "Effect on a Local Criminal Justice System." In *Three Strikes and You're Out: Vengeance as Public Policy*. Edited by David Shichor and Dale K. Sechrest. Thousand Oaks, Calif.: Sage Publications, 1996.

FEELEY, MALCOLM. *Court Reform on Trial: Why Simple Solutions Fail*. New York: Basic Books, 1983.

FEELEY, MALCOLM, and KAMIN, SAM. "The Effect of 'Three Strikes and You're Out' on the Courts: Looking Back to See the Future." In *Three Strikes and You're Out: Vengeance as Public Policy*. Edited by David Shichor and Dale K. Sechrest. Thousand Oaks, Calif.: Sage Publications, 1996.

GREENWOOD, PETER; RYDELL, C. PETER; ABRAHAMSE, ALLAN F.; CAULKINS, JONATHAN P.; CHIESA, JAMES; MODEL, KARYN E.; and KLEIN, STEPHEN P. "Estimated Benefits and Costs of California's New Mandatory-Sentencing Law." In *Three Strikes and You're Out: Vengeance as Public Policy*. Edited by David Schicher and Dale K. Sechrest. Thousand Oaks, Calif.: Sage Publications, 1996.

HEUMANN, MILTON, and LOFTIN, COLIN. "Mandatory Sentencing and the Abolition of Plea Bargaining: The Michigan Felony Firearm Statute." *Law and Society Review* 13 (1979): 426.

HUMPHRIES, DREW. *Crack Mothers: Pregnancy, Drugs, and the Media*. Columbus: Ohio State University Press, 1999.

MCCOY, CANDACE. "Determinate Sentencing, Plea Bargaining Bans, and Hydraulic Discretion in California." *Justice Systems Journal* 9 (1984): 256.

MCCOY, CANDACE, and MCMANIMON, PATRICK. *The Impact of New Jersey's '85 percent Truth in Sentencing Law' on Victims' Satisfaction, Prosecution, and Sentencing: Final Report*. Washington, D.C.: U.S. Department of Justice, National Institute of Justice, 2000.

MCDONALD, DOUGLAS C., and CARLSON, KENNETH E. *Sentencing in the Courts: Does Race Matter?* Washington, D.C.: U.S. Department of Justice, Bureau of Justice Statistics, 1993.

OSTROM, BRIAN; CHEESMAN, FRED; JONES, ANN; PETERSON, MEREDITH; and KAUDER, NEIL. *Truth-in-Sentencing in Virginia: Evaluating the Process and Impact of Sentencing Reform*. Williamsburg, Va.: The National Center for State Courts, 1999.

PARENT, DALE; DUNWORTH, TERENCE; MCDONALD, DOUGLAS; and RHODES, WILLIAM. *Key Legislative Issues in Criminal Justice: Mandatory Sentencing*. Washington, D.C.: U.S. Department of Justice, National Institute of Justice, 1997.

SCHMERTMANN, CARL P.; ADANSI, AMANKWAA A.; and LONG, ROBERT D. "Three Strikes and You're Out: Demographic Analysis of Mandatory Prison Sentencing." *Demography* 35, no. 4 (1998): 445–463.

SHICHOR, DAVID, and SECHREST, DALE K. "Introduction." In *Three Strikes and You're Out: Vengeance as Public Policy.* Edited by David Shichor and Dale K. Sechrest. Thousand Oaks, Calif.: Sage Publications, 1996.

SIMON, JONATHAN. "Criminology and the Recidivist." In *Three Strikes and You're Out: Vengeance as Public Policy.* Edited by David Shichor and Dale K. Sechrest. Thousand Oaks, Calif.: Sage Publications, 1996.

SURETTE, RAY. "News From Nowhere, Policy to Follow: Media and the Social Construction of 'Three Strikes and You're Out.'" In *Three Strikes and You're Out: Vengeance as Public Policy.* Edited by David Shichor and Dale K. Sechrest. Thousand Oaks, Calif.: Sage Publications, 1996.

TONRY, MICHAEL. *Malign Neglect: Race, Crime and Punishment in America.* New York: Oxford University Press, 1995.

———. *Sentencing Matters.* New York: Oxford University Press, 1996.

United States Sentencing Commission. *Special Report to Congress: Mandatory Minimum Penalties in the Federal Criminal Justice System.* Washington, D.C.: U.S. Sentencing Commission, 1991.

VON HIRSCH, ANDREW, and ASHWORTH, ANDREW. *Principled Sentencing.* Boston, Mass.: Northeastern University Press, 1992.

WILSON, JAMES Q. *Thinking About Crime.* New York: Vintage, 1985.

ZEIGLER, FRANK A., and DEL CARMEN, ROLANDO V. "Constitutional Issues Arising from 'Three Strikes and You're Out' Legislation." In *Three Strikes and You're Out: Vengeance as Public Policy.* Edited by David Shichor and Dale K. Sechrest. Thousand Oaks, Calif.: Sage Publications, 1996.

CASES

Furman v. Georgia, 408 U.S. 238 (1972).
People v. Romero, 917 P.2d 628 (1996).
Roberts v. Louisiana, 428 U.S. 325 (1976).
Rummel v. Estelle, 445 U.S. 263 (1980).
Woodson v. North Carolina, 428 U.S. 280 (1976).

SENTENCING: PRESENTENCE REPORT

Considered among the most important documents in the criminal justice field, the presentence investigation report (PSI) has been the central source of information to sentencing judges since the 1920s. Its original purpose was to provide information to the court on the defendant's personal history and criminal conduct in order to promote individualized sentencing. With the advent of more punitive sentencing policies in recent years, the PSI has become more offense-focused and less individualized. Despite current trends, the PSI will likely remain a critical component of the American criminal justice system.

Origins of the PSI

The origins of the modern presentence investigation began in the 1840s with the crusading efforts of Boston shoemaker John Augustus (1841–1859). It was Augustus's belief that the "object of the law is to reform criminals and to prevent crime, and not to punish maliciously or from a spirit of revenge" (p. 12). In his efforts to redeem selected offenders, Augustus gathered background information about the offender's life and criminal history. If he determined that the person was worthy, Augustus provided bail money out of his own pocket. If he succeeded in winning the person's release, he helped them find employment and housing. Later he appeared at the sentencing hearing and provided the judge with a detailed report of the person's performance. Augustus would then recommend that the judge suspend the sentence and release the person to his custody.

Considered the father of modern probation, Augustus's leadership led the Massachusetts legislature to establish the nation's first probation law in 1878. By authorizing the mayor of Boston to appoint a member of the police department to serve as a paid probation officer, this statute formalized the practice of extending probation to individuals deemed capable of being reformed. The law was expanded in 1891 with the creation of an independent statewide probation system. By the time that the National Probation Act was passed in 1925 creating a federal probation service, the majority of states had probation statutes.

The evolution of the presentence investigation was given further impetus by the reformatory movement of the 1870s. Because reformatory movement proponents advocated an individualized approach toward the redemption of the criminal, indeterminate sentencing became a popular sentencing reform throughout the later half of the nineteenth century and became the standard form of sentencing throughout the United States until the 1980s.

Simultaneously with the development of probation and the indeterminate sentence, the evolution of the social sciences gave rise to the medical model of corrections during the 1920s and 1930s. The medical model was founded on the belief that crime was the result of individual pathology that could be diagnosed and treated like a disease. Judges simply needed to know the problem in order to prescribe treatment.

As these systems and approaches evolved, the need for more information about the defendant became critical. By the 1930s, one of the primary tasks of probation officers throughout the country was the preparation of the presentence investigation report.

Content of the PSI

Offender-based reports. The traditional PSI was intended to provide the judge with comprehensive background information about the offender. Under this model, the PSI was intended to promote individualized sentencing by giving information specific to the offender's potential for rehabilitation and community reintegration and allow judges to tailor their sentence accordingly. The offender-based PSI is integral to a sentencing system founded on rehabilitation.

The elements of an offender-based report includes a summary of the offense, the offender's role, prior criminal justice involvement, and a social history with an emphasis on family history, employment, education, physical and mental health, financial condition, and future prospects. Based on this thorough background analysis, a probation officer renders a sentencing recommendation. A 1978 publication by the Administrative Office of the United States Courts described the essential elements of a typical offender-based PSI. It specifies that the presentence report shall contain "any prior criminal record of the defendant and such information about his characteristics affecting his behavior as may be helpful in imposing sentence and such other information as may be required by the court" (p. 3). In this type of PSI, little consideration is given to the offense or victim concerns.

Figure 1

Elements of an offender-based presentence report

1. Offense
   Official version
   Defendant's version
   Codefendant information
   Statement of witnesses, complainants, and victims
2. Prior record
   Juvenile adjudications
   Adult arrests
   Adult convictions
3. Personal and family data
   Defendant
   Parents and siblings
   Marital
   Education
   Employment
   Health
      Physical
      Mental and emotional
   Military services
   Financial condition
      Assets
      Liabilities
4. Evaluation
   Alternative plans
   Sentencing data
5. Recommendation

Instead, the primary role of the probation officer is to investigate the offender's background.

Although standards differ from jurisdiction to jurisdiction, Figure 1 provides an outline of the federal probation system's format for a typical offender-based PSI.

Offense-based reports. In recent years, as the indeterminate sentence and its rehabilitative ideal was replaced by determinate sentencing and the punishment ideology, the PSI has undergone major transformations. The primary purpose of determinate sentencing is not to rehabilitate, but to impose a predetermined range of fixed sentences. Such sentencing laws can take many forms—such as statutory determinate sentencing and guideline sentencing.

Statutory determinate sentencing requires a judge to choose from a narrow range of statutorily mandated sentencing options. For example, when imposing a prison sentence under California's sentencing system, a judge must choose one of three potential periods of confinement. Periods of confinement might include two, four, or six years of imprisonment, with the PSI providing information on the defendant's culpability.

Decisions on culpability are based on the defendant's actions and motivations in carrying out the offense. If the defendant was a primary instigator who inflicted excessive harm or damage, an aggravated term would likely be justified. In contrast, a defendant who participated in the offense under duress and did not occupy a leadership role may be eligible for the mitigated term. Under this sentencing system the primary role of the probation officer in preparing the PSI is to determine the mitigated and aggravating circumstances that apply.

Guideline sentencing further restricts the range of sentencing options by requiring judges to base their sentence on numerical formulas of offense severity and criminal history. In most guidelines systems these scores are calibrated on a sentencing grid, with judges given limited discretion in deviating from the guidelines. In order to deviate from the guidelines, judges must state their reasons in writing. The federal government instituted guideline sentencing in the late 1980s. At that time the federal probation system shifted from an offender-based PSI to a offense-based PSI. Because of the restrictive nature of guideline sentencing, PSIs are no longer required in some states where guidelines sentencing was adopted. Probation officers in these jurisdictions simply complete a guideline worksheet that calculates the prescribed sentence.

In other guidelines states, however, judges retain a considerable amount of sentencing discretion, for one or more of the following reasons: the guidelines are voluntary rather than legally binding; the prescribed guidelines sentence permits a broad range of choices as to the type or severity of punishment for a given case; or the guidelines recognize a wide variety of permissible justifications for deviating from the prescribed sentence. In these jurisdictions, PSIs continue to provide much information about the offender (as well as details of the offense and the application of guidelines rules to the instant case).

Offense-based PSIs are concerned with the offender's culpability and prior record. As a result, offense-based PSIs are more succinct and less concerned with the offender's personal background. The elements outlined in Figure 2 constitute an offense-based PSI.

PSI case law

The U.S. Supreme Court has ruled that PSIs are mandated only in death penalty cases; in

Figure 2

Elements of an offense-based presentence report

1. The offense
   Charge(s) and conviction(s)
   Related cases
   The offense conduct
   Adjustment for obstruction of justice
   Adjustment for acceptance of responsibility
   Offense level computation

2. The defendant's criminal history
   Juvenile adjudications
   Criminal convictions
   Criminal history computation
   Other criminal conduct
   Pending charges (included if pertinent)

3. Sentencing options
   Custody
   Supervised release
   Probation

4. Offender characteristics
   Family ties, family responsibilities, and community ties
   Mental and emotional health
   Physical condition, including drug dependence and alcohol abuse
   Education and vocational skills
   Employment record

5. Fines and restitution
   Statutory provisions
   Guidelines provisions for fines
   Defendant's ability to pay

6. Factors that may warrant departure from sentence guidelines

7. The impact of plea agreement (if pertinent)

8. Sentencing recommendations
   Offender characteristics
   Fines and restitution
   Factors that may warrant departure
   Impact of the plea agreement
   Sentencing recommendations

other cases, there is no right to a PSI unless such a right is granted by statute. State laws vary, with some requiring PSIs for all felony cases or if the defendant faces a period of incarceration.

Other critical legal issues include the defendant's right to review the PSI, the means of addressing inaccuracies, the use of hearsay, and the use of evidence excluded from trial proceedings. Although the U.S. Supreme Court in two landmark cases (*Williams v. Oklahoma*, 358 U.S. 576 (1959) and *Williams v. New York*, 337 U.S. 241 (1949)) determined that there is no denial of due process when a court considers a PSI without disclosing its contents, most states and the federal system allow the defendant to review the report's content except in certain circumstances. For example, under *Federal Rules of Criminal Procedure*, Rule 32(c) (3), the defendant has access to the PSI except when the disclosure will disrupt the rehabilitation process, the information was obtained on a promise of confidentiality, or when disclosure could cause potential harm to the defendant or other individuals. However, when information is withheld the court must provide a written summary and give the defendant the opportunity to respond.

Recent federal case law has also established that inaccuracies in the PSI are not sufficient grounds for revocation of an imposed sentence if the error is "harmless." The burden is on the defendant to prove the error was harmful. If the information is proven harmful, the courts have ruled that the court is obliged to vacate the sentence. In regard to hearsay evidence, the courts have determined that, while not admissible during trial, hearsay evidence can be included in a PSI. Discretion is left to the judge to determine which information is acceptable and what should be excluded. In the case *Gregg v. United States*, 394 U.S. 489 (1969), the Supreme Court held "there are no formal limitations on contents, and they may rest on hearsay and contain information bearing no relation whatever to the crime with which the defendant is charged" (p. 18).

In the case of *United States v. Schipani*, 435 F.2d 26 (2d Cir. 1970), the Second Circuit Court of Appeals ruled that the exclusionary rule's prohibition against illegally obtained evidence at the trial stage is not applicable at the sentencing stage. As of the year 2000, the courts had still not addressed the issue of evidence illegally gathered solely for use in the PSI.

The U.S. Supreme Court, in the case *Minnesota v. Murphy*, 465 U.S. 420 (1984), established that probation officers are not obligated to provide Miranda warnings when interviewing defendants. With the exception of Oregon, defendants do not have the right to have an attorney present at the PSI interview.

Defense-based presentence reports

Historically, responsibility for the development and presentation of the PSI was solely the role of the probation officer. However, PSIs produced by probation departments have long been criticized for being routinized and biased against the defendant. This issue was compounded by the failure of defense attorneys to properly prepare their clients for the probation interview and adequately plan for the sentencing hearing.

In the 1960s a new era in the history of the PSI emerged with the pioneering efforts of Dr. Thomas Gitchoff, a professor of criminal justice at San Diego State University. To improve the quality of defense representation at the sentencing hearing, Dr. Gitchoff introduced the privately commissioned PSI. Gitchoff's reports, known as the Criminological Case Evaluation and Sentencing Recommendation, provided a comprehensive analysis of the offender's background and motivations that exceeded the typical PSI generated by probation departments.

At the time Gitchoff was introducing his methods to California courts, the Offender Rehabilitation Project of the Legal Aid Agency for the District of Columbia also began offering defense-based PSIs to indigent clients. This program is considered the oldest ongoing defense-based PSI program in the country.

The use of privately commissioned defense-based PSIs swelled in the late 1970s and 1980s as a result of efforts by correctional reformer Jerome Miller and the National Center on Institutions and Alternatives (NCIA). Miller recognized the potential of the PSI while commissioner of youth corrections in Pennsylvania, where he used individualized disposition recommendations to remove four hundred youths from Pennsylvania's notorious Camp Hill Prison.

Through his "Client Specific Planning" (CSP) model, Miller promoted the use of defense-based PSIs to public defender offices and nonprofit legal aid and offender-advocacy groups around the country. Criticism of the defense-based PSI are centered on the belief that it is available only to those defendants with financial resources. However, in recent years nonprofit agencies such as the Center on Juvenile and Criminal Justice have emphasized court-appointed or public defender cases with sliding scale rates. In addition, the Washington, D.C.–based Sentencing Project has made the promotion of defense-based PSI reports an integral part of its efforts to improve the quality of defense representation. Because of the increasing role of defense-based PSIs, a number of law schools, led by the University of Minnesota, are integrating sentencing advocacy into their curricula.

The potential for defense-based PSIs to reduce prison commitments within a jurisdiction was demonstrated in San Francisco's juvenile justice system during the 1980s and 1990s. With the hiring of two social workers to prepare PSIs for the juvenile division of the public defender's office, and the introduction of defense-based PSIs for court-appointed attorneys, prepared by the Center on Juvenile and Criminal Justice staff, the county registered a 73 percent reduction in commitments to state juvenile correctional institutions.

With the growing acknowledgment for improved defense attorney representation in the sentencing process, it is likely that the use of private defense-based sentencing reports will continue to expand.

Conclusion

Despite the current trend toward offense-based sentencing, the PSI will continue to be an essential element of the American criminal justice system. The information contained in the PSI is critical in assisting judges in rendering sentencing decisions and providing vital information to correctional officials in determining classifications and release decisions. While its content and emphasis have changed in recent years, the PSI remains the most influential document in the sentencing of criminal defendants.

DANIEL MACALLAIR

See also CAREERS IN CRIMINAL JUSTICE: CORRECTIONS; PREDICTION OF CRIME AND RECIDIVISM; PROBATION AND PAROLE: HISTORY, GOALS, AND DECISION-MAKING; PROBATION AND PAROLE: PROCEDURAL PROTECTION; PROBATION AND PAROLE: SUPERVISION; SENTENCING: ALLOCATION OF AUTHORITY; SENTENCING: ALTERNATIVES; SENTENCING: DISPARITY; SENTENCING: GUIDELINES; SENTENCING: MANDATORY AND MANDATORY MINIMUM SENTENCES; SENTENCING: PROCEDURAL PROTECTION.

BIBLIOGRAPHY

ABADINSKY, HOWARD. *Probation and Parole: Theory and Practice.* 6th ed. Upper Saddle River, N.J.: Prentice Hall, 1997.

CHAMPION, DEAN J. *Probation, Parole, and Community Corrections.* 3d ed. Upper Saddle River, N.J.: Prentice Hall, 1999.

CLEAR, TODD R., and DAMMER, HARRY R. *The Offender in the Community.* Belmont, Calif.: Wadsworth, 1999.

CROMWELL, PAUL F., and DEL CARMEN, ROLANDO V. *Community-Based Corrections.* Belmont, Calif.: West/Wadsworth, 1998.

FERRIS, G. "The Case History of Probation Service." In *Probation and Criminology.* Edited by S. Glueck. New York: Arno Press.

GITCHOFF, T., and RUSH, G. "The Criminological Case Evaluation and Sentencing Recommendation: An Idea Whose Time Has Come." *International Journal of Offender Therapy and Comparative Criminology* (1989): 77–83.

John Augustus, First Probation Officer. New York: National Probation Association, 1939.

KLEIN, ANDREW R. *Alternative Sentencing, Intermediate Sanctions, and Probation.* 2d ed. Cincinnati, Ohio: Anderson Publishing Co., 1997.

LATESSA, EDWARD J., and ALLEN, HARRY E. *Corrections in the Community.* Cincinnati, Ohio: Anderson Publishing Co., 1999.

MACALLAIR, DAN. "Disposition Case Advocacy in San Francisco's Juvenile Justice System: A New Approach to Deinstitutionalization." *Crime and Delinquency* 40, no. 1 (1994): 84–95.

The Presentence Investigation Report. Monograph 105. Washington, D.C.: Administrative Office of the Courts, 1978.

YEAGER, MATTHEW G. *Survey of Client-Specific Planning Programs and Their Feasibility as an Alternative to Incarceration in Canada.* Ottawa, Canada: Office of the Soliticitor General, 1992.

CASES

Gregg v. United States, 394 U.S. 489 (1969).

Minnesota v. Murphy, 465 U.S. 420 (1984).

United States v. Schipani, 435 F.2d 26 (2d Cir. 1970).

Williams v. New York, 337 U.S. 241 (1949).

Williams v. Oklahoma, 358 U.S. 576 (1959).

SENTENCING: PROCEDURAL PROTECTION

Both the provisions of the U.S. Constitution and an array of statutes and court rules govern sentencing procedures in the United States. In considering sentencing procedures, it is important to note at the outset that sentencing is an area in which American jurisdictions vary considerably, and to recognize that differences in sentencing systems may have an important bearing on the applicable procedures.

Jurisdictions vary a great deal in the degree of discretion accorded to the sentencing judge. In jurisdictions where traditional rules apply, the judge has virtually unfettered discretion to set the sentence for an individual offender within a broad range established by statute for each offense. In many other jurisdictions, however, the sentencing judge's discretion has been channeled or restricted by various sentencing reforms. In these jurisdictions, provisions such as sentencing guidelines or mandatory minimum sentencing statutes require the judge to impose a particular sentence or to impose a sentence within a more limited range, depending upon the facts of the offense and the offender. One key issue in jurisdictions that have restricted the sentencer's discretion is whether these reforms also affect the procedures that apply at the sentencing phase.

Another important distinction among American jurisdictions concerns the type of information that may be considered at sentencing. Some jurisdictions employ *charge offense* sentencing, others *real offense* sentencing. In a charge offense jurisdiction, the sentence is based primarily upon the offense of conviction. In these jurisdictions, the defendant's conviction (at trial or by guilty plea) establishes most or all of the facts upon which the sentence will be based. The most notable example of real offense sentencing is the federal sentencing guidelines, which employ many elements of real offense sentencing. Real offense sentencing allows consideration of facts that are not elements of the offense to play a major role in determining an individual offender's sentence. Where real offense sentencing is permitted, the procedural and evidentiary rules that govern fact-finding at the sentencing phase assume greatly increased importance, since many key issues are not resolved by the guilty verdict.

It should also be noted that the requirements for the imposition of a capital sentence raise separate issues under the Eighth Amendment's cruel and unusual punishment clause. The remainder of this entry focuses on the requirements for noncapital sentences.

Constitutional requirements at sentencing

The Supreme Court has drawn a sharp distinction between the constitutional requirements applicable to the guilt/innocence stage of the trial, and those applicable to the sentencing phase. Although a few of the constitutional rights traditionally associated with the trial of criminal cases apply at sentencing, the Court has held that many others do not.

Right to counsel. Perhaps the most important constitutional right afforded a defendant at the sentencing phase is the right to counsel. In *Mempa v. Rhay*, 389 U.S. 128 (1967), the Supreme Court held that the sentencing hearing is a part of the "criminal proceedings" for purposes of the Sixth Amendment right to the assistance of counsel. Accordingly, a defendant who cannot afford a lawyer is entitled to the assistance of counsel provided by the state during the sentencing hearing. The Supreme Court reasoned that defense counsel can play an important role in ensuring the accuracy of the information put before the sentencing judge. Counsel is needed at sentencing both to present evidence on the defendant's behalf and to respond to adverse information.

Privilege against self-incrimination. Another right that applies at the sentencing phase is a facet of the Fifth Amendment privilege against compelled self-incrimination. The Supreme Court has long held it is improper to penalize a defendant for invoking the privilege against self-incrimination, and for that reason the trier of fact in a criminal trial may not draw any adverse inference from the fact that the defendant has invoked the privilege. In *Mitchell v. United States*, 526 U.S. 314 (1999), the Supreme Court held that the rule against drawing such negative inferences applies with equal force to the sentencing phase; accordingly, the sentencing judge was prohibited from drawing any adverse inference, as to the amount of drugs the defendant conspired to sell, from the defendant's exercise of the Fifth Amendment privilege at sentencing. The Court reasoned that the stakes at the sentencing phase, where an adverse inference might warrant many years of additional imprisonment, are quite different (and more severe) than those in a civil proceeding where adverse inferences are permissible. The practical importance of the *Mitchell* decision is unclear. The Court pointedly declined to express a view on the possibility that the defendant's silence might be relied upon at sentencing to support an inference of lack of remorse. Such an inference might be nearly as damning as an inference of guilt.

Consideration of the exercise of other procedural rights. Although the Supreme Court has held that due process is violated by sentencing that punishes the defendant for the exercise of his procedural rights, such prohibited vindictiveness must be distinguished from the inferences a sentencing judge is permitted to draw from trial-related conduct that reveals a defendant's character and bears on his prospects for rehabilitation. In *North Carolina v. Pearce*, 395 U.S. 711 (1969), the Supreme Court held that due process would be violated by the vindictive imposition of a higher sentence at retrial to punish a defendant for the successful appeal of his first conviction. The Court stated that it would presume vindictiveness whenever a trial judge imposed a higher sentence following an appeal that set aside an earlier conviction for the same offense. Later decisions indicate that this presumption can be rebutted by objective information justifying an increased sentence (LaFave and Israel, pp. 1128–1134). Subsequent decisions have also determined that *Pearce* does not apply where the defendant's conduct during the trial involves perjury, which bears on the defendant's character and prospects for rehabilitation. In *United States v. Grayson*, 438 U.S. 41 (1978), the Supreme Court held that the sentencer could properly give weight to his conclusion that the defendant had perjured himself at the trial, since that conduct provided important information about the defendant's character. The Court rejected the argument that this would chill the exercise of the right to testify, commenting that there is a right to testify truthfully, but no protected right to commit perjury.

Evidentiary reliability. There is considerable support in the cases for the principle that due process requires that the evidence upon which a criminal sentence is based must meet minimal standards of reliability, though it is unclear how far this principle extends. Two decisions of the Supreme Court recognized a due process requirement of evidentiary reliability, though they do little to clarify its scope. In *Townsend v. Burke*, 334 U.S. 736 (1948), the Supreme Court reversed the defendant's state sentence because it was premised, in part, on the sentencing judge's erroneous belief that the defendant had several previous convictions. The Court emphasized that its decision did not mean that any error in resolving a question of fact at sentencing would be a due process violation. In the case before it, however, an uncounseled defendant pleaded guilty, and the sentence rested upon an error that counsel could easily have corrected. In a later decision, *United States v. Tucker*, 404 U.S. 443, 447 (1972), the Court held that a new sentencing proceeding was necessary because the sentence was founded "at least in part upon misinformation of constitutional magnitude." In *Tucker* the sentencing court relied upon the fact that the defendant had three prior convictions, and was unaware that the defendant has been unconstitutionally imprisoned for more that ten years (some of them on a chain gang) after being convicted in proceedings in which he was not represented by counsel.

Many decisions in the state courts and the lower federal courts rely upon *Townsend v. Burke* and *Tucker* for the principle that a sentence may not be based upon misinformation of a constitutional magnitude, or that the evidence upon which a sentence is based must show indicia of reliability. These decisions do not, however, establish sharp criteria for the determination of such reliability, and they do not equate the standards for sentencing with the standard applicable to the evidence supporting a conviction.

Constitutional protections that are not applicable at sentencing

Many constitutional rights afforded at the trial stage no longer apply once the sentencing phase begins. In *Williams v. New York*, 337 U.S. 241 (1949), the Supreme Court decisively rejected the claim that due process limits the sentencing judge to considering the same sources and kinds of evidence that would be admissible at trial. The Court distinguished the function of the trial and that of sentencing. At trial, the issue is the defendant's guilt or innocence of the elements of the offense and rules of evidence are used to limit the fact-finder to information that is material to these limited issues. At sentencing, in contrast, the judge traditionally had a wide range of discretion in setting an individual defendant's punishment, and in making that discretionary determination the judge should be permitted to consider a broad spectrum of information regarding the defendant's life and characteristics. The Court concluded that the judge should not be limited to considering only evidence provided in open court by witnesses who would be subject to cross-examination, but should also be permitted, for example, to consider the reports prepared by probation officers. Although the Court referred to modern efforts to employ sentencing for rehabilitative purposes intended to benefit offenders, the issue in *Williams* was the trial judge's reliance on hearsay evidence in the presentence report that the defendant had committed thirty burglaries for which he had never been convicted. Even though this evidence would not have been admitted at trial, the Supreme Court upheld Williams's death sentence.

Williams was a landmark decision that set the pattern for much of the analysis in the next half century. In *Williams* the Supreme Court drew a sharp distinction between the trial itself—with its full panoply of constitutional protections for the accused—and the sentencing hearing, at which relaxed procedures are permitted and perhaps desirable. Later decisions dealing with a number of other constitutional guarantees followed this pattern. The one exception, *Specht v. Patterson*, 386 U.S. 605 (1967), involved a state statute allowing the imposition of a life sentence on a defendant convicted of certain sexual offenses who was also found to be mentally ill and a habitual offender. The Supreme Court distinguished *Williams* on the ground that the sex offender act required the invocation of a separate criminal proceeding under a different statute. *Specht* has been largely limited to the particular statutory scheme involved in that case, and has not been extended to sentencing proceedings in general.

Proof beyond a reasonable doubt. In the trial itself, due process requires that the prosecution prove each fact necessary for conviction beyond a reasonable doubt. The Supreme Court has repeatedly recognized, however, that the reasonable doubt standard is not constitutionally required at the sentencing phase. In *McMillan v. Pennsylvania*, 477 U.S. 79 (1986), the Supreme Court noted that traditionally sentencing courts heard evidence and found facts without being required to observe any particular burden of proof. Declining to constitutionalize the burden of proof at sentencing, the Court rejected the argument that a sentencing factor that subjected a defendant to a mandatory minimum sentence must be proven by more than a preponderance. In *McMillan* the sentencing factor in question required that the defendant receive a mandatory minimum sentence within the authorized sentencing range for the offense. As noted below, a more recent decision of the Supreme Court raises the question whether *McMillan* will be applied when the sentencing fact in question increases the range of the sentence to which a defendant is subject above that ordinarily applicable to the offense of conviction.

Since the government's burden of proof at trial is far higher than it is at sentencing, evidence that would not meet the standard of proof beyond a reasonable doubt may meet the preponderance ("more likely than not") standard applicable at the sentencing phase. Given this difference in the burden of proof, the Supreme Court concluded in *Watts v. United States*, 519 U.S. 148 (1997), that the government may rely at sentencing on conduct of which the defendant had been acquitted. The Court rejected the argument that reliance on acquitted conduct would be inconsistent with the jury's verdict or violate the double jeopardy clause. It reasoned that a jury acquittal is not a finding of innocence, but only a finding that the government has not established guilt beyond a reasonable doubt. Accord-

ingly, an acquittal should not preclude the government from relitigating an issue in a subsequent proceeding, such as a sentencing hearing, where it need only meet a lower standard of proof. This issue arises principally in real offense sentencing systems, where facts that are not elements of the conviction offense can have a major impact on the severity of the sentence.

Trial by jury. In *McMillan v. Pennsylvania*, the Supreme Court also considered and rejected the claim that the Sixth Amendment right to trial by jury applies to the sentencing phase. The issue in *McMillan* was whether the defendant visibly possessed a firearm during the commission of his offense. The defendant argued that the Sixth Amendment requires the necessary findings should be made by the jury, rather than the court, at least where the factor relates to the commission of the offense of conviction. The Supreme Court rejected this claim with the comment that "there is no Sixth Amendment right to jury sentencing, even where the sentence turns on specific findings of fact." Later decisions by the Court have reaffirmed this principle, which is consistent with the traditional Anglo-American allocation of sentencing authority to the court. Indeed, even in the context of capital punishment the Supreme Court has repeatedly rejected the argument that the Constitution requires that a jury impose the sentence of death or make the findings prerequisite to imposition of such a sentence. It should be noted, however, that many jurisdictions that authorize the death penalty provide for jury sentencing in capital cases, and a few states authorize jury sentencing (or jury recommendations) in noncapital cases as well.

Confrontation and cross-examination. As noted above, in the *Williams* case the Supreme Court rejected a claim that due process was violated by the introduction of evidence, such as a probation report, that presented adverse information in a form that provided the defendant with no opportunity for confrontation and cross-examination in open court. Subsequent cases in the lower courts raised the same general arguments under the confrontation clause of the Sixth Amendment. Although this issue has not been addressed by the Supreme Court, nearly every federal circuit has relied upon the sharp distinction between the guilt phase of the trial—where full rights of confrontation are accorded—and the sentencing phase, which begins once the fact finder concludes that the defendant's guilt has been established. However, many of these decisions also recognize that due process is violated if a defendant is sentenced on the basis of "misinformation of a constitutional magnitude," and accordingly that the evidence upon which a conviction is based must show some indicia of reliability. It should be noted that many of these decisions, such as *United States v. Wise*, 976 F.2d 393 (8th Cir. 1992) (en banc), were rendered by divided courts, and that the dissenting judges would have required confrontation.

The Fourth and Fifth Amendment exclusionary rules.   The Supreme Court's decisions outlining the scope of the exclusionary rules under the Fourth and Fifth Amendments focus on the guilt-innocence phase of the criminal trial, and the Court has not ruled on the question whether the exclusionary rules apply to sentencing proceedings. In general, the lower federal courts have concluded that the exclusionary rules do not apply to federal sentencing. These decisions follow the approach employed by the Supreme Court to determine whether the exclusionary rule should be applied to other kinds of proceedings (such as immigration deportation proceedings, grand jury proceedings, and civil tax proceedings) where the Supreme Court balanced the likelihood of deterring constitutional violations against the cost of withholding relevant and reliable information. Although recognizing the possibility that government investigators might have an incentive to illegally seize evidence in order to increase a suspect's sentence, the lower courts have generally concluded that the potential for deterrence is outweighed by the need for the sentencing judge to have access to a wide range of information in tailoring individual sentences.

On the other hand, several state courts have concluded that their state constitutions provide greater protection and bar the admission at sentencing of evidence obtained by an illegal search or by a confession obtained from a suspect who was not given his Miranda warnings. It should also be noted that some courts that do not generally apply the exclusionary rule to sentencing proceedings have indicated that illegally seized evidence will be suppressed at sentencing if it can be shown that it was seized in order to increase the defendant's sentence.

The critique of *Williams* and its progeny

Williams and its progeny have been criticized as affording insufficient procedural protection at a critical stage of the criminal process. In *Williams*

the sentencing judge made the decision to impose a capital sentence on the basis of information contained in reports that the defendant never had a chance to see. The defendant in *Williams* had no precise knowledge about the information in these reports, and he had no opportunity to challenge it by the usual mechanism of confronting and cross-examining the persons who provided the information. *Williams* appears to be an outgrowth of the traditional definition of the court's role in discretionary sentencing. The Supreme Court emphasized the latitude historically afforded to courts at the sentencing phase, and the opinion expresses concern that burdensome procedures would prevent courts from obtaining important information that could assist them in exercising their discretion and tailoring the sentences to the offenders.

There are two lines of criticism of *Williams* and its progeny. Many scholars and jurists have argued that even discretionary sentencing judgments should be made in a forum that provides most or all of the procedural protections afforded at the trial, in order to ensure fairness to the defendant as well as the reliability of any information upon which the court relies in imposing the sentence. As previously noted, *Mempa v. Rhay* held that traditional discretionary sentencing is part of the "criminal proceeding" for purposes of the Sixth Amendment right to counsel. The first critique of *Williams* is that the Court failed to follow *Mempha* in extending other procedural protections as well.

A second line of criticism argues that even if *Williams* is appropriate in discretionary sentencing jurisdictions, it should not be extended to modern sentencing regimes where the legislature has fundamentally reformed and altered the sentencing process to follow legal rules with prescribed legal consequences. Under the traditional sentencing scheme in *Williams* the sentence did not rest on any particular factual findings; indeed, the judge was not required to make any findings. In jurisdictions that have instituted greater restrictions on judicial discretion, in contrast, factual findings are ordinarily required, and they drive the sentencing process. Under a mandatory minimum statute or sentencing guidelines, the court does not have discretion to give whatever weight seems appropriate to the broadest possible range of factors. Rather, the legislature (or the sentencing commission) has designated the legal effect to be given to certain facts about the offense or the offender (especially his or her prior record). For example, many jurisdictions have statutes that require the sentencing judge to impose an increased sentence if a weapon was used in the commission of an offense, or if a victim was injured. It has been argued that under a sentencing regime of this nature the sentencing phase should be subject to some or all of the same procedural protections afforded at the trial, such as proof beyond a reasonable doubt and the right to confront and cross-examine witnesses. This argument is especially cogent under the federal sentencing guidelines because many of the facts being considered at the sentencing phase are not elements of the offense, and thus were not established by the fact of conviction, yet such facts can greatly increase the guidelines' sentence.

Despite the strength of the critiques of *Williams*, to date they have not been persuasive in most jurisdictions. Accordingly, as noted above, most constitutional protections afforded at the trial stage are not presently applicable at sentencing.

Rules of evidence and procedure at sentencing

The rules of evidence and procedure that govern sentencing vary from jurisdiction to jurisdiction. Although these rules must meet constitutional standards, they may also provide additional procedural protections for the accused.

Evidentiary rules. Although privileges (such as the attorney-client privilege) generally are observed at the sentencing phase of a criminal trial, in most jurisdictions the rules of evidence do not otherwise apply to sentencing. Federal Rule of Evidence 1101 follows this rule, providing that the rules of privilege are applicable to all proceedings in the federal courts, but that otherwise the rules are not applicable at sentencing. Most states have similar rules. These rules reflect practices that developed when sentencing in all jurisdictions was discretionary and the judge was given the widest possible latitude to hear evidence he deemed relevant, without the evidentiary restrictions employed to restrict the jury (Young, pp. 305–309).

In many jurisdictions mandatory minimum sentences or guidelines have been adopted, and sentencing is no longer discretionary. In these jurisdictions the sentence is based upon a series of factual findings about the offense and the offender. This fundamental change in the nature of the sentencing process makes the sentencing

hearing more like the trial; in both proceedings the determination of particular historical facts requires the application of particular legal rules. This is especially true in the federal system, which has adopted key features of real offense sentencing. In the federal system and in states that employ real offense sentencing many of the facts upon which the sentence depends are not elements of the offense, and they will not have been established by the finding of the defendant's guilt. The case for the application of the rules of evidence is the strongest in the federal system and in any states that employ nondiscretionary real-offense sentencing. For example, in a federal drug prosecution the key determinant of the defendant's sentence will be the quantity and type of drug. These facts are not currently deemed to be elements of the offense, and therefore they are not established by the conviction. They are determined, instead, at sentencing. If these findings are unreliable, then the offender will not receive the appropriate sentence.

It is therefore surprising that the U.S. Sentencing Commission has been unwilling to require that the rules of evidence be applied to ensure the reliability of fact-finding upon which the whole guidelines scheme depends, and to provide greater procedural fairness. Instead, the guidelines provide that "[i]n resolving any dispute concerning a factor important to the sentencing determination, the court may consider relevant information without regard to its admissibility under the rules of evidence applicable at trial, provided that the information has sufficient indicia of reliability to support its probable accuracy" (U.S.S.G. § 6A1.3(a) (Policy Statement)). This provision seeks to strike a balance between the need for accurate findings as a basis for guidelines calculations and the need to streamline the sentencing process and reduce the burden on the sentencing court. The commentary to the guideline notes that in many cases written statements by counsel or affidavits may be sufficient, though in some cases an evidentiary hearing will be required.

Procedural rules. Most jurisdictions have formal procedural rules governing sentencing. These rules govern matters such as the preparation of a presentence report to assist the court and the conduct of the sentencing hearing. For example, Rule 32 of the Federal Rules of Criminal Procedure governs the time for sentencing, the preparation and contents of the presentence report, and the sentencing hearing.

Rule 32 provides that the probation officer shall generally make a presentence investigation and prepare a report before sentence is imposed. This report is intended to include information about the defendant's history and characteristics as well as information necessary to make the determinations required to impose a sentence under the federal sentencing guidelines. Because the federal guidelines are a modified real offense system, this requires the probation officer to make numerous determinations about "relevant conduct" beyond the elements established by the defendant's conviction. For example, the probation officer may have to determine what quantity and type of drug was involved in a narcotics case. In contrast, in jurisdictions involving charge offense sentencing there would be less focus on fact-finding that goes beyond the elements of the offense, except as it bears on the defendant's personal characteristics and history. Rule 32 provides that the probation officer shall serve the presentence report on the prosecution and defense before the sentencing hearing, in order to permit the parties to raise any objections to the report prior to the hearing.

At the hearing itself, Rule 32(c) provides that the court shall afford counsel for the defendant (and the government) an opportunity to comment on the probation officer's determinations, and that the court may, at its discretion, permit the parties to introduce testimony or other evidence on the objections. Before imposing sentence the court is also required to afford the defendant's counsel an opportunity to speak on the defendant's behalf, and the court must address the defendant personally to determine whether he or she wishes to make a statement or present any evidence in mitigation.

Except in systems employing sentencing guidelines, or permitting appellate review of sentences, judges are generally not required to give reasons for the sentence imposed. Even in guidelines systems, such reasons are usually only required if the judge "departs" from the sentence recommended by the guidelines. Perhaps surprisingly, the U.S. Supreme Court has held that due process does require a written decision, and reasons for the decisions, in postsentencing proceedings resulting in the revocation of probation or parole release, and the incarceration of the offender (*Morrissey v. Brewer*, 408 U.S. 471 (1972); *Gagnon v. Scarpelli*, 411 U.S. 778 (1973)). It would seem that the initial sentencing decision—particularly when it involves incarceration—

should also be accompanied with a statement of reasons.

There is also no general constitutional right to appellate review of the sentence initially imposed, but such review is available by statute or rule in some jurisdictions (particularly those, such as the federal system, that have sentencing guidelines). In addition, defendants may sometimes be able to gain appellate review of the procedures used to impose the sentence (but not the sentence itself); of course, a sentence that was not authorized by law can also be appealed. One likely reason for the traditional lack of appellate review of sentences is that sentencing decisions were, until fairly recently, highly discretionary, and were supposed to be tailored to the particular offense and offender; such highly fact-dependent decisions could not, it was assumed, be made subject to legal "rules" that appellate courts could articulate and enforce. (In the American legal system, appellate courts generally only decide issues of law, not issues of fact.) It is therefore not surprising to find that appellate review of sentences is more likely to be granted—and to be effective—in those jurisdictions that have adopted sentencing guidelines; such guidelines seek to define and enforce specific sentencing rules, and limit judges' discretion.

What factors—and facts—may be considered at sentencing?

Given the sharply reduced procedural protections that are available at sentencing, a good deal turns on the question whether particular facts will be established at the trial or only at the sentencing phase. The Supreme Court has considered this issue in a series of cases that vary somewhat in their analysis, but taken together establish that the legislature has a wide range of discretion in deciding whether to designate a particular fact as an element of the offense or as merely a sentencing factor.

In *McMillan v. Pennsylvania*, the Supreme Court held that the legislature ordinarily has the discretion to designate certain facts as an element of the offense (which must be proven beyond a reasonable doubt at trial) or as a sentencing factor (which may be proven by a preponderance at the sentencing phase). The Court noted, however, that due process might be violated in a case where the sentencing factor increased punishment out of proportion to the offense of conviction (where the "tail" of sentencing "wagged the dog" of the offense of conviction). In one sense,

McMillan was an easy case: it involved setting the sentence within the range provided for by the offense of conviction, not increasing the sentence above that range. In *Almendarez-Torres v. United States,* 523 U.S. 224 (1998), a sharply divided Supreme Court extended *McMillan* to a case where the facts at issue were used to subject the defendant to a significantly enhanced sentence. Based upon this decision, it appeared that the legislatures had virtually unfettered discretion to designate particular facts as elements of a crime or merely sentencing factors.

However, in *Jones v. United States,* 526 U.S. 227 (1999), a different five-justice majority stated a sharply different view that would impose some limitations on legislative discretion. Writing for the majority, Justice David Souter stated—in dicta—that the due process clause of the Fifth Amendment and the notice and jury trial provisions of the Sixth Amendment require that "any fact (other than prior conviction) that increases the maximum penalty for a crime must be charged in an indictment, submitted to a jury, and proven beyond a reasonable doubt" (p. 243, n.6). If the Court follows the *Jones* dicta in later cases, it will allow the legislature largely unfettered leeway in designating certain facts as sentencing factors, rather than elements defining the crime, as long as those facts merely determine the sentence within the general sentencing range. Thus if the sentence for robbery is two to ten years, the legislature may provide that an offender who used a firearm shall receive any sentence up to and including ten years. However, if the fact in question is used to increase the sentencing range to more than ten years, then under *Jones* the facts in question must be treated as elements, at least to the extent that they must be charged in the indictment, and proved beyond a reasonable doubt at trial before a jury.

Given the shifting 5–4 majorities in *Almendarez-Torres* and *Jones,* it seems likely that this issue will be the subject of additional consideration in both the Supreme Court and the lower courts.

SARA SUN BEALE

See also BURDEN OF PROOF; CAPITAL PUNISHMENT: LEGAL ASPECTS; CRIMINAL PROCEDURE: CONSTITUTIONAL ASPECTS; PRISONERS, LEGAL RIGHTS OF; PROBATION AND PAROLE: PROCEDURAL PROTECTION; SENTENCING: ALLOCATION OF AUTHORITY; SENTENCING: DISPARITY; SENTENCING: GUIDELINES; SENTENCING: MANDATORY AND MANDATORY MINIMUM SENTENCES; SENTENCING: PRESENTENCE REPORT.

BIBLIOGRAPHY

BEALE, SARA SUN. "Procedural Issues Raised by Guidelines Sentencing: The Constitutional Significance of the 'Elements of the Sentence.'" *William and Mary Law Review* 35 (Fall 1993): 147–162.

Federal Rules of Evidence Committee, American College of Trial Lawyers. "The Law of Evidence in Federal Sentencing Proceedings." *Federal Rules Decisions* 177 (1998): 513–529.

FORDE, MICHAEL K. "Note, The Exclusionary Rule at Sentencing: A New Life Under the Federal Sentencing Guidelines?" *American Criminal Law Review* 33 (Winter 1996): 379–409.

GREENWALD, LAUREN. "Note, Relevant Conduct and the Impact of the Preponderance Standard of Proof Under the Federal Sentencing Guidelines: A Denial of Due Process." *Vermont Law Review* 18 (Winter 1994): 529–563.

HERMAN, SUSAN N. "The Tail That Wagged the Dog: Bifurcated Fact-Finding Under the Federal Sentencing Guidelines and the Limits of Due Process." *Southern California Law Review* 66 (November 1992): 289–356.

HOFFMAN, DAVID A. "Note, The Federal Sentencing Guidelines and Confrontation Rights." *Duke Law Journal* 42 (November 1992): 382–418.

JOH, ELIZABETH E. "Comment, 'If It Suffices to Accuse': *United States v. Watts* and the Reassessment of Acquittals." *New York University Law Review* 74 (June 1999): 887–913.

LaFAVE, WAYNE R., and ISRAEL, JEROLD. *Criminal Procedure,* 2nd ed. St. Paul, Minn.: West Publishing, 1992.

MAVEAL, GARY M. "Federal Presentence Reports: Multi-Tasking at Sentencing." *Seton Hall Law Review* 26, no. 2 (1992): 544–596.

Note. "An Argument for Confrontation Under the Federal Sentencing Guidelines." *Harvard Law Review* 105 (June 1992): 1880–1899.

Note. "Awaiting the Mikado: Limiting Legislative Discretion to Define Criminal Elements and Sentencing Factors." *Harvard Law Review* 112 (April 1999): 1349–1366.

PRIESTER, BENJAMIN J. "Sentenced for a 'Crime' The Government Did Not Prove: *Jones v. United States* and the Constitutional Limitations on Fact-finding by Sentencing Factors Rather than the Elements of the Offense." *Law and Contemporary Problems* 61 (Autumn 1998): 249–298.

REITZ, KEVIN R. "Sentencing Facts: Travesties of Real-Offense Sentencing." *Stanford Law Review* 45 (February 1993): 523–573.

SALKY, STEVEN M., and BROWN, BLAIR G. "The Preponderance of Evidence Standard at Sentencing." *American Criminal Law Review* 29 (Spring 1992): 907–918.

SLATKIN, STEPHANIE C. "Note, The Standard of Proof at Sentencing Hearings Under the Federal Sentencing Guidelines: Why the Preponderance of the Evidence Standard is Constitutionally Inadequate." *University of Illinois Law Review* 1997, no. 2 (1997): 583–609.

YOUNG, DEBORAH. "Fact-Finding at Federal Sentencing: Why the Guidelines Should Meet the Rules." *Cornell Law Review* 79 (January 1994): 299–373.

CASES

Almendarez-Torres v. United States, 523 U.S. 224 (1998).
Gagnon v. Scarpelli, 411 U.S. 778 (1973).
Jones v. United States, 526 U.S. 227 (1999).
McMillan v. Pennsylvania, 477 U.S. 79 (1986).
Mempha v. Rhay, 389 U.S. 128 (1967).
Mitchell v. United States, 526 U.S. 314 (1999).
Morrissey v. Brewer, 408 U.S. 471 (1972).
North Carolina v. Pearce, 395 U.S. 711 (1969).
Specht v. Patterson, 386 U.S. 605 (1967).
Townsend v. Burke, 334 U.S. 736 (1948).
United States v. Grayson, 438 U.S. 41 (1978).
United States v. Tucker, 404 U.S. 443 (1972).
United States v. Wise, 976 F.2d 393 (8th Cir. 1992).
Watts v. United States, 519 U.S. 148 (1997).
Williams v. New York, 337 U.S. 241 (1949).

SENTENCING: REFORM

See CORRECTIONAL REFORM ASSOCIATIONS; SENTENCING: ALLOCATION OF AUTHORITY; SENTENCING: ALTERNATIVES; SENTENCING: DISPARITY; SENTENCING: GUIDELINES.

SEX OFFENSES: CHILDREN

Crimes against children did not develop into a recognizable class of the criminal law of the United States until the latter half of the twentieth century. As societal recognition of both physical and sexual abuse of children increased in the 1960s and 1970s, legislatures throughout the United States revised criminal codes to more precisely define crimes against children. Although statutes describing sexual offenses against children are far from uniform, the development of the laws demonstrates societal recognition of the existence of such crimes and legislative acknowledgment of the need to define the crimes with specificity.

Historical developments

Early English laws defining sexual offenses against children provided the foundation upon which later American laws were constructed. The first such law, the Statute of Westminster I from 1275 A.D., stated that none should "ravish, nor take away by force, any Maiden within Age, neither by her own consent, nor without." The offense was a misdemeanor punished by "two years imprisonment and fine at the king's pleasure," and applied only to sexual intercourse with a female "within Age"—defined by most commentators as under twelve years old. Forms of sexual activity with a female child that did not involve sexual intercourse were not prohibited by English statute until late in the nineteenth century.

Jurisdictions in the United States incorporated into the common law and statutes of the states variations on the Statute of Westminster I and its successors. Thus, from their inception until the first half of the twentieth century, all states recognized sexual intercourse between an adult male and a female child as a crime, commonly labeling the offense *carnal knowledge of a child* or *statutory rape.* However, most states did little beyond this to proscribe sexual conduct between adults and children.

Fundamental elements of modern statutes

All modern statutes defining child sex crimes contain two essential elements: the sexual conduct at issue and the age of the child. Sexual conduct is classified by statute into acts of *sexual penetration* or acts of *sexual contact.* No longer limited to sexual intercourse between a male adult and a female child, acts of sexual penetration in most states include any intrusion of the sexual organ of one person into the sex organ, mouth, or anus of another person. The offenses are nearly uniform in the use of gender-neutral language, thus including acts committed by both male and female perpetrators against both male and female children.

The term sexual contact refers to virtually all other forms of sexual conduct that fall short of sexual penetration. Sexual contact includes any acts in which an adult touches the intimate parts of a child with sexual intent, or allows, with sexual intent, the child to touch the intimate parts of the adult. Most states define *intimate parts* to include the sexual organs, groin area, or buttocks of any person and the breasts of a female. Because not all touching of the intimate parts of a child is inherently sexual, proof of the adult's sexual intent in the touching is an element of sexual contact offenses. A few states broadly prohibit taking immodest, immoral, or indecent liberties with a child, an offense often comparable to sexual contact offenses in the level of punishment imposed, but encompassing by its broad language both acts of penetration and acts of sexual contact.

The early English model of creating one simple age of consent has been almost universally abandoned in the United States, with the vast majority of states creating multiple tiers of offenses in which the severity of the offense varies depending on the age of the child. First tier offenses apply to sexual acts with younger, typically prepubescent children, an age most commonly identified by the states as children younger than twelve, thirteen, or fourteen years old.

Second tier—and in some states third tier—offenses apply to sexual acts with older children, generally those children who have reached the age at which puberty commonly begins. In Virginia, for example, the most serious penetration offense, a felony, applies when the victim is under thirteen years old; a lesser offense, also a felony, applies to children thirteen and fourteen years old; and a misdemeanor offense applies when a child is between the ages of fifteen and seventeen years old.

A state with a tiered system for penetration offenses is likely to apply the same age categories to sexual contact offenses, although several states with tiered age categories for penetration offenses establish only a single age for sexual contact offenses.

The upper end of the age categories identifies the point at which age is no longer a barrier to consensual sexual activity. As of December 1999, the age of consent for sexually penetrative activity between adults and children was sixteen years old or older in all but one state. A substantial minority of states establish either seventeen or eighteen years old as the age of consent. When offenses involving abuse of a special relationship are considered, a strong majority of states establish eighteen years old as the age of consent.

Sexual penetration offenses with young children uniformly receive felony-level punishments, as do most such offenses involving older

adolescents. Sexual contact offenses against prepubescent children are typically, but not necessarily, felonies; when committed against older children, sexual contact offenses are likely to be misdemeanors.

Variable elements

A feature found in a majority of states is a separate offense or an enhanced penalty when an offender is in a position of trust or authority with respect to the child victim. Consistent with psychological literature demonstrating that significant harm is caused by a violation of trust, these offenses establish stronger penalties when a person exploits an authority relationship to sexually abuse a child. In some states a position of authority is limited to one in a parental role, while other states more broadly include teachers, clergy, and others in a position of authority with respect to the victim.

Another common innovation is language exempting from the scope of the criminal law sexual relations between children who are both below the age of consent. One method of accomplishing this goal requires proof of an age differential between perpetrator and victim. Many states have adopted a four-year age differential recommended by the Model Penal Code "to reflect the prevailing pattern of secondary education," though the age gap is smaller in a few states and larger in others. A different method of addressing the same concern is to create as an element of the offense a minimum age the offender must have attained. In Alaska, for example, a nonfamily offender who has sexual intercourse with a child under thirteen must be sixteen years of age or older; if the victim is sixteen or seventeen years old, the offender must be eighteen years or older. Some states combine the two approaches, requiring both a minimum age for the offender and an age differential between participants.

A handful of states create an offense for the continuous abuse of a child. A child who is abused repeatedly over a period of time may not be able to recall with specificity individual acts of abuse. Continuous abuse statutes eliminate the requirement that prosecutors prove a series of discrete acts, requiring only that the prosecutor prove a specified number of acts occurring within a designated time frame.

During much of the 1900s, several states required proof of a female victim's chastity, particularly when the victim was an older adolescent. This element is now rejected by nearly every

Figure 1

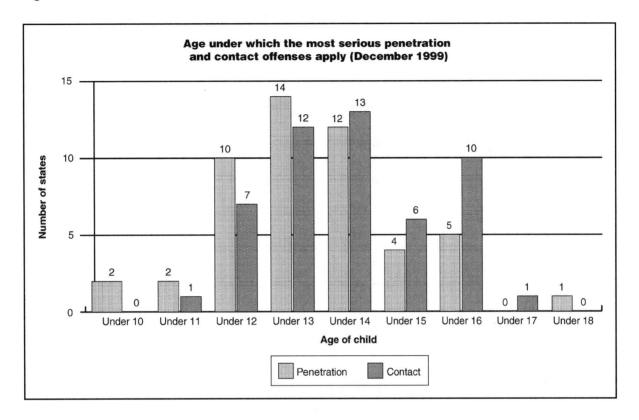

state, allowing prosecution regardless of a child's virginity. A large minority of states, however, require proof that the child is not married to the adult, thus allowing a defense in some of these states if the defendant marries the child prior to the prosecution.

The Model Penal Code

The Model Penal Code represents a modest advance in the American definition of sex crimes against children. The Model Penal Code, for example, advocates the tiered system, adopted in some form by nearly every state, in which separate offenses are created for acts committed against children at different ages. Similarly, the Model Penal Code introduces the widely accepted concepts of an age differential between victim and perpetrator and a separate offense for the abuse of a position of authority.

On the other hand, the Model Penal Code is, in many respects, archaic when compared to state laws. For example, the most serious sexual penetration offense in the Model Penal Code applies to children under ten years old, a model adopted by only two states. A clear majority of states set the age for the most serious offense much higher, reflecting a broader view of the age at which children are in need of expanded protection. Further, the Model Penal Code creates a reasonable mistake-of-age defense for acts committed against children as young as ten years old and applies the most serious sexual penetration offense only to girls, deeming sexually penetrative conduct with boys less likely to occur and less significant when it does occur. In these instances, the Model Penal Code does not reflect the policy judgments made by the vast majority of states.

Relationship to other sex crimes

Both federal and state laws establish a large number of sexual crimes against children addressing acts related to, but not directly involving, sexual touching between an adult and a child. For example, crimes such as child prostitution and child pornography—commonly referred to as child sexual exploitation offenses—target manipulation of a child for an adult's sexual gratification. The prohibited conduct in child exploitation offenses, however, is the taking of pictures or selling of a child's body rather than

Table 1

Age of consent (sexual penetration between an adult and a child under this age is a crime)

Alabama	16	Louisiana	17*	Ohio	16*
Alaska	16*	Maine	16*	Oklahoma	16
Arizona	18	Maryland	16*	Oregon	18
Arkansas	16*	Massachusetts	16	Pennsylvania	16
California	18	Michigan	16	Rhode Island	16
Colorado	17*	Minnesota	16*	South Carolina	16
Connecticut	16*	Mississippi	16*	South Dakota	16**
Delaware	18	Missouri	17	Tennessee	18
Florida	18	Montana	16*	Texas	17
Georgia	16	Nebraska	16	Utah	18
Hawaii	14	Nevada	18	Vermont	16*
Idaho	18	New Hampshire	16*	Virginia	18
Illinois	17*	New Jersey	16*	Washington	16*
Indiana	16*	New Mexico	17	West Virginia	16*
Iowa	16	New York	17	Wisconsin	18
Kansas	16*	North Carolina	16*	Wyoming	18
Kentucky	16	North Dakota	18		

* Sexual penetration between an adult and a child remains a crime until the child is 18 years old if the adult is in a special relationship to the victim.
** Sexual penetration between an adult and a child remains a crime until the child is 21 years old if the adult is a relative.

NOTE: This table reflects only clear legislative pronouncements and not interpretive case law of the age below which a child cannot consent to sexual activity with an adult. The information reflects statutes in effect December 1999.

the direct sexual contact between an adult and a child.

Offenses such as incest, sodomy, fornication, and the crime against nature—commonly classified as crimes against morality—condemn particular sexual acts regardless of the age of the participants or the consensual nature of the act. These offenses are largely obsolete and do not constitute a significant weapon in the modern child abuse prosecutor's arsenal. Statutes designed to protect children from adult sexual manipulation are better suited and more frequently used to prosecute an adult for engaging in sexual activity with a child.

A few states retain the designation *statutory rape* to refer to a sexually penetrative act between an adult and a child, and in casual usage the term often refers to sexual intercourse between an adult and an older adolescent. By definition, however, the term applies to any sexual activity between an adult and a child in which a statute removes the element of force otherwise required by the common law definition of rape. Most child sex crime statutes avoid the term altogether and are more likely to designate sexual crimes against children as *aggravated rape, sexual assault of a child,* or *sexual abuse of a child.*

CHARLES A. PHIPPS

See also CONTRIBUTING TO THE DELINQUENCY OF MINORS; FAMILY ABUSE AND CRIME; RAPE: LEGAL ASPECTS; SEX OFFENSES: CONSENSUAL; SEXUAL PREDATORS.

BIBLIOGRAPHY

American Law Institute. *Model Penal Code and Commentaries,* vol. 1, part 2. Philadelphia: American Law Institute, 1980.

BRIERE, JOHN, et al., eds. *The APSAC Handbook on Child Maltreatment.* Thousand Oaks, Calif.: Sage, 1996.

FINKELHOR, DAVID. *Child Sexual Abuse: New Theory and Research.* New York: Free Press, 1984.

HEFLER, MARY EDNA, et al., eds. *The Battered Child.* 5th ed. Chicago: The University of Chicago Press, 1997.

LEVINE, MORTIMER. "A More than Ordinary Case of 'Rape,' 13 and 14 Elizabeth I." *American Journal of Legal History* 7 (1963): 159–163.

MYERS, JOHN E. B. *Legal Issues in Child Abuse and Neglect Practice.* Thousand Oaks, Calif.: Sage, 1998.

PHIPPS, CHARLES A. "Children, Adults, Sex, and the Criminal Law: In Search of Reason." *Seton Hall Legislative Journal* 22 (1997): 1–141.

Regina v. Ferguson, 36 CCC3d 507 (Brit. Colum. Ct. App. 1987).

SEX OFFENSES: CONSENSUAL

Sex crimes that are sometimes labeled *consensual* are numerous. They include adultery, bigamy, fornication, incest between adults, obscenity, prostitution, and sodomy. In each case, criminalization is controversial, at least in part because of the consent issue. If two adults agree to participate in a private sex act, what *harm* can justify state intervention to criminalize that conduct? At first blush the notion of criminalizing consensual conduct is repugnant to many people raised during the late twentieth century in the liberal tradition. This reaction may be called the *libertarian* approach to sexual regulation: if the parties to the sex act consent, the act should not be a crime.

There is a deep history of criminalization of each of these sexual activities, first by dominant religious authority, and later by law as well. Before the twentieth century, sexual expression was not conceived widely as a human right important to individual identity. Instead, it was a social act with significant religious restriction that enjoyed social and legal legitimacy only in forms widely approved by the community. The community's right to approve or disapprove of sexual conduct was not widely questioned until the twentieth century. Before then, the community granted to itself a legitimate stake in the sexual conduct of others. The community thus marked itself harmed by the sexual actions of others; harmed by moral offense, banned by rifts in the social fabric of the community as relationships realigned, harmed by the injection of doubt into the identification of a child's father, and harmed by association as members of the same community as the sexual actors. It is against that backdrop that historically there have been prohibitions on the sexual acts that comprise all of the crimes discussed in this entry.

Over the course of the twentieth century, however, there was a significant shift in the conception of sexual conduct. Only during this period did we create a zone of privacy in law and culture around sexual conduct that included a claim of legitimacy to freely chosen sexual expression that does not affect third parties. It was only in the late twentieth century that we thought to tie these criminal prohibitions together under the heading of consensual crimes. The term *consensual sex crimes*, therefore, carries with it more than a descriptive character. The term connotes a claim of legitimacy for the sex acts in question, meaning a claim of right to engage in the acts without interference from the community in the form of legal prohibition, or even in most cases social prohibition. The term *consensual*, more precisely, is used to negate the notion that the crimes cause a *harm*, making them *victimless crimes*. Without a *cognizable* harm, criminalization may be illegitimate.

The concept of consensual crimes, however, does not lend itself to easy definition. The equation of *consent* with *harmlessness* is not as perfect as it appears at first blush. There are two disturbances to the concept of a consensual sex crime that account for most of the regulation in the area. There are two corresponding types of harm claimed. The change over the course of the twentieth century has come in the judging of the *legitimacy* of the harm in question.

The first harm that might arise from a consensual sex crime is to one or both of the parties themselves. The second is harm to third parties from consensual sex crimes—to *nonconsenting* parties whose existence requires us to sharpen what we mean when we call an act consensual and put boundaries around who is in fact a party to the act. Both parties to an act of political bribery are consenting, for example, but there are third parties who do not consent and may be harmed by the act; therefore bribery is a crime.

The first challenge to the concept of consensual sex acts questions the meaning of an individual's consent given some set of social circumstances. Here the community asks about the quality of consent surrounding a sexual act, even where no one holds the proverbial gun to the head of the parties. This applies, for example, to the regulation of incest between legal adults. Legislators may believe that power disparities within families make the consent of a significantly younger party who is nonetheless a legal adult suspect. Is father-daughter incest between a seventeen year old and her forty-five-year-old father, who lives in the same household, consensual? A seventeen year old is in most states old enough to consent legally to sex with nonfamily members. But the position of authority held by her father may make the quality of the consent suspect, as the father has significant power by virtue of his family position to coerce his daughter psychologically and materially. This question of whether consent is meaningful enough to dispel any public interest in an activity under certain social conditions affects the regulation of prostitution and pornography as well. If an adult prostitute was first induced into prostitution while she was a young minor, or she experiences periodic violence from a pimp, is her consent to the activity given under conditions that warrant complete legal deference to her choice? If consent is compromised, or if there is reasonable disagreement over the quality of consent under given circumstances, then there is a potential harm to the party whose consent is in some sense reluctantly given. Criminalization may seek to limit that harm by taking an undesirable option off of the table. Paternalism is the motivation, then, for some regulation of sexual conduct. Some commentators believe that there is never a justification for paternalism. They argue that a person ought to be entitled to make the best choice from among a set of bad choices; for example, a poor person may need to do something menial to earn money, and selling sex might seem to her the best choice from among other bad choices. Others think that paternalism is necessary under some circumstances, because choice occurs on a spectrum ranging from perfectly free to very constrained, rather than operating as an off and on switch. Some arguments then, for making consensual sex acts into crimes are based on the quality of the consent.

But harm to the parties is not the only, or even the primary, potential harm raised against consensual sex acts. The second challenge to the notion of a consensual sex crime accounts for more of the regulation of sexual conduct. That is a claim that nonconsenting third parties are harmed by the sex act between the consenting parties. Every consensual sex act that is criminal has as one major justification harm to third parties. The real controversy over criminalizing consensual sex acts, then, is over the legitimacy of that third party harm, or more precisely, whether the third party harm is cognizable—whether it legitimately justifies criminalization. The question is whether moral, religious, emotional, or ethical harms should be cognizable, whether nuisances to third parties may be regulated, and in some cases, whether the prevention of violence may be pursued through the indirect channels of regulating stimulus to violence.

Consider obscenity laws. In the case of photographic obscene materials, it is plausible that the photographer, the person being photographed, and the consumer of the obscene pictures all consent to the conduct. However, there are several claims by third parties to harms from this transaction. Suppose that the obscene pictures cause the consumer to become sexually violent (a causal connection about which there is substantial controversy, discussed below). The third party victim of the sexual violence claims a

legitimate or cognizable harm caused by the consensual sexual conduct. Suppose also that the obscene materials are distributed at a grocery or video store. Many third parties must in some limited form come across the materials in passing during the distribution process. If those parties are offended morally or ethically by the materials, they may claim a harm from involuntary contact with the materials. Few deny that a third party could experience such contact as a harm, but the legitimacy of addressing that harm and giving it a legally protected status by prohibiting the distribution of obscene materials is deeply contested. In other words, the existence of a harm is accepted, but the existence of a cognizable harm is contested. The same analysis applies to the criminalization of prostitution. In some percentage of cases, acts of prostitution are simply voluntary exchanges between individuals (how many cases is contested, as will be discussed below). But third parties claim a number of harms from such acts, and the legitimacy of each as a basis for legal regulation has to be weighed independently. Those third-party harms include the moral or ethical offense from coming in contact with the distribution system, harms to third parties from the spread of disease that may result from prostitution, harms from related racketeering offenses associated with prostitution organizations, and perhaps most controversially, harms to the public at large from the *commodification* of sex.

The perceived legitimacy of third-party moral and religious objections to consensual sexual activity waned somewhat in the second half of the twentieth century. This was in response to a number of social forces, ranging from the sexual revolution of the 1960s and 1970s and technological improvements in birth control, to the development of a constitutionally protected sphere of privacy. As those moral and religious harms have been delegitimized as grounds for criminalization, the legal landscape has shifted in a variety of ways. In some cases, the legal prohibitions on consensual sex crimes were repealed, as was the case with some adultery and fornication statutes at mid century, and later in the century with some sodomy statutes. In other cases, enforcement of some laws has dropped off completely, leaving them as almost (but not completely) dead letters. And finally, in some cases new justifications have arisen for old laws, as in the case of disease control as a justification for the regulation of prostitution, and the enforcement of the laws has been shifted somewhat to reflect those new concerns.

What legal historian Lawrence M. Friedman has termed the Victorian compromise warrants attention here. The most enduring complaint about consensual sexual activity has been the offense to those who come into incidental contact with it. At the same time, even before the sexual revolution of the 1960s there was widespread acceptance of the inevitability of frequent sexual activity, such as adultery and prostitution, considered immoral according to religious and community norms. Thus criminal law has developed the "Victorian compromise": the law would criminalize only that conduct that was actually visible to the outside world, and would leave alone conduct with no public facet. This compromise appears in the details of a number of criminal statutes governing sexual conduct. For example, some prostitution statutes are crafted so that solicitation and streetwalking are illegal, but the actual private exchange of sex for money is not mentioned in the law. This reflects the English common law approach to prostitution. Many adultery and fornication statutes in the United States require that the conduct be "open and notorious," or prohibit cohabitation with a member of the opposite sex rather than actual sex acts. This reflects the concern with outward appearances, and the protection of the sensibilities of third parties is the primary goal. The Victorian compromise has been viewed both as pragmatic on the one hand, and as hypocritical on the other. The compromise also removes from the table the specter of law enforcement snooping in bedrooms—if evidence of the crime is not apparent in public, then there is no crime to be investigated.

Prostitution and obscenity laws are routinely enforced. However, the rest of the consensual sex crimes discussed in this entry—incest between adults, fornication, bigamy, adultery, and sodomy—are not. Laws that are rarely enforced are often called *dead-letter* laws, and they give rise to problems in both the criminal and the civil law. In the criminal law context, rarely used laws provide opportunities for prosecutorial abuses through *selective prosecution*. Criminal laws are supposed to be invoked even-handedly, based only on the violators commission of the prohibited activity, and not on a particular prosecutor's dislike of any one individual. Violations of dead-letter laws may be prosecuted occasionally when the perpetrators are famous or unpopular. A person suspected of more serious crimes is some-

times prosecuted for a lesser crime that is easier to prove than the real offense. For example, a case of sexual assault or a case of prostitution that is difficult to prove may include a lesser charge of adultery, fornication, or sodomy. The Victorian compromise is alive and well in the enforcement of laws that are not formally limited to public activity; sodomy laws, for example, are most frequently invoked against acts that take place in public bathrooms or other visible forums. The Victorian compromise in enforcement can operate as a shaming device, then.

In the civil law context, dead-letter laws can still be invoked to justify discrimination against presumed law violators. So, for example, while fornication prosecutions are exceedingly rare, a landlord may argue successfully that housing laws that prohibit discrimination based on marital status do not require the landlord to rent to an unmarried couple who are presumed to be in violation of the fornication statute. The same arguments have been used in the employment, child custody, and adoption contexts as well.

Though we have lumped all of the consensual sex crimes together for analysis thus far, each has its own particular history, operation, legal definition, and constitutional limits. We will examine them in turn below.

Adultery and fornication

As the twenty-first century begins, adultery is still a crime in approximately half of the United States, and fornication is a crime in about one-third of the states. Reflecting the Victorian compromise, however, a substantial minority of the adultery statutes require a degree of visibility to the conduct, requiring the adultery to be habitual or open and notorious, or accompanied by cohabitation. Likewise, a majority of fornication statutes also require that the conduct be in some sense open and notorious.

The elements of fornication are straightforward: either it requires open and notorious cohabitation, or it is defined simply as intercourse between two unmarried people, depending on the jurisdiction. In almost every state where it's prohibited, the crime is a misdemeanor carrying a trivial punishment. The elements of adultery are more varied. Adultery was originally an offense punished by ecclesiastic law in England, and became a secular offense in the United States as an incident of Puritanism. The elements of the offense in its original form at common law, however, reflect a goal of preventing men from raising and providing inheritance to offspring who are not their own. The offense protected against the corruption of bloodlines. Therefore, it was an offense that married women could be convicted of when they engaged in sex with a man not their husband, but not an offense for married men. Minnesota's adultery statute takes this form even at the dawn of the twenty-first century, but it is alone in this sex-specific language, which would probably not survive a gender-based constitutional challenge. The ecclesiastical courts, however, punished any married person, male or female, for sex with someone other than a spouse. The remaining states now follow this lead, although they vary as to whether they can punish only the married party to adultery, or both parties even where one is single. In a few states, only a criminal complaint by the aggrieved spouse can lead to a prosecution for adultery. Adultery is also a misdemeanor in the majority of states where it is prohibited, but a few felony classifications remain. Ample Supreme Court dicta suggests that these laws are constitutional.

Of all of the statutes governing consensual sexual conduct, adultery and fornication are the most complete dead-letter crimes, meaning nonenforcement is the most long-standing and pervasive. The Model Penal Code recommends against criminalizing this conduct altogether, and nonenforcement preceded the sexual revolution of the 1960s. However, these statutes still have a force in the law. The abuses that can accompany dead-letter statutes are in play with each. Those include selective prosecutions, use of these statutes in place of crimes that are more difficult to prove, and most commonly, reference to these statutes as an excuse for civil law discrimination.

There are rare selective prosecutions of these crimes. For example, one prosecutor in the mid-1990s used a fornication statute to prosecute the sex partners of pregnant unwed teenagers. The statutes are more commonly used when prosecutors are interested in a more serious crime, but are not certain they will succeed on all of the elements of that crime. For example, a prostitution charge against a john could also be an adultery or fornication charge, and the exchange of money would not need to be shown. The threat of this kind of prosecution can be used to induce a potential defendant to testify against a prostitute on the prostitution charge. An adultery or fornication charge can also accompany a sexual assault charge where some difficulty of proof accompanies the more serious

charge. In those rare adultery or fornication charges that still occur, there is some explanation of this sort that goes beyond the crime itself, as when the adultery occurs in a public place.

The most significant application of these statutes, however, does not come in the form of criminal prosecution at all. Rather, these statutes are cited in civil cases as a justification for action against the offender, who by violation of an adultery or fornication statute is considered a criminal despite the lack of prosecution. For example, fornication statutes have served to excuse landlords who violate housing discrimination laws, with courts agreeing that the landlord need not rent to criminals. Or fornication and adultery charges may justify child custody awards that disfavor presumed criminals. Since the 1980s, however, fornication and adultery statutes have been invoked less frequently in child custody cases than they were prior to that time, and have had little effect on the outcomes of custody cases. Finally, adultery is a ground for divorce in many states today. Prior to the no-fault divorce revolution of the 1970s, adultery was routinely litigated in family courts as the ground for a fault-based divorce. But the no-fault revolution has not extinguished its use in divorce cases. In a number of states, though the no-fault ground of *irreconcilable differences* is used in most cases, adultery still exists as an alternative ground for divorce. It is still regularly used as the ground for divorce either because a state grants a faster divorce on the ground of adultery than on the ground of irreconcilable differences, or because the state is one of the minority that takes adultery into account in dividing property or awarding alimony.

Finally, military law is authorized to punish adultery among military personnel severely. Historically, the military looked the other way on completely private cases of adultery. But in the late 1990s, a flurry of high-profile adultery prosecutions in the military led to the dismissal or reduction in rank of several military officers, and generated public discussion of adultery laws, without leading to repeals. This discussion illustrated the extent to which these dead-letter laws are not quite dead.

Incest

Incest between consenting adults is a crime in virtually every state. In addition, incestuous marriages are void, and a crime in their own right. There are a number of different approaches to defining incest. Some prohibitions are *con-*

sanguinity-based, prohibiting sexual relations or marriage between individuals who are related by blood, to a degree of relation that varies from state to state. Other states also include relations by *affinity*, prohibiting sexual relations between individuals related through marriage, such as a stepparent and stepchild, or an in-law relationship.

While all cultures have some form of incest taboo, its contours vary widely. In fact, some cultures routinely practice affiliations that fall within the taboo in other cultures. The pairing of first cousins gives rise to the greatest difference in approaches. In parts of the world, the pairing of first cousins accounts for between 20 and 50 percent of all marriages (Gibbons). In the United States, however, the majority of states treat first-cousin unions as a felony. However, the incest taboo at least against parent-child and sibling relations is so strong as to put in question the need for a criminal prohibition, with self-sanction an effective alternative. Several reasons for the prohibition have been offered.

The most frequently offered explanation is the risk of genetic defects in the offspring of consanguineous relationships. There are several weaknesses to this justification for criminalization. First, the majority of criminal sexual liaisons will lead to no offspring, as the majority of sexual acts do not. In some cases reproduction will be impossible for one or both of the parties to the union, as when a woman is postmenopausal or either is infertile. Second, scientists are split on the extent of the risk of genetic defects. While closely related individuals are more likely to carry a negative recessive gene, giving it an opportunity to express itself, they also may carry a positive recessive gene. In addition, the expression of negative recessive genes provides the opportunity to eliminate them. The longer they stay recessive, the more widely distributed throughout the population they become. Though there is some increased mortality in the children of close offspring, the effect is not dramatic. Third, even if there is a significant genetic threat, criminalizing sexual unions may not be the most effective remedy, given that counseling, genetic testing, and contraception are available. Finally, genetic issues cannot explain the prohibition on sexual activity between relatives by affinity.

The weaknesses of the genetic explanation for criminal laws against incest lead us to the more plausible explanations for the law. Those are of two sorts. The first relates to the re-

enforcement of the cultural taboo, which may promote the cohesion of the family unit by preventing sexual jealousies and competition. Reinforcement of a cultural taboo may even be reason in itself; some people may expect the criminal law to respond to conduct that is universally disparaged. The second justification is the prevention of sexual imposition within families. While children are presumed unable to consent to sexual relations, and therefore fall outside the scope of this entry, sexual imposition among adults is still possible. Most efforts to enforce incest statutes are addressed to situations of abuse of authority, as in the case of a parent or parent substitute such as a stepparent and a child just over the age of consent.

Bigamy

Bigamy was another crime originally punished by ecclesiastical authorities. At the beginning of the seventeenth century, it became a part of the secular law in England, and has been a part of the criminal law of every state. It is generally the crime of having more than one spouse simultaneously. The second or both marriages become void, but in addition, the offense is punishable as a crime, ordinarily as a felony. There are two unusual elements to the crime. First, at common law, a spouse absent on the high seas for seven years could be presumed dead, and a remarriage at that point could not be bigamous even if the first spouse later returned from sea. Some states have a similar statutory provision, usually permitting a presumption of death after a five-year unexplained absence. Second, bigamy at common law was a *strict liability* crime. This means that a person with a perfectly reasonable belief either that a first spouse was dead or that a divorce from a first spouse was valid, could still be convicted of bigamy if that good-faith belief was in fact in error. However, states in the second half of the twentieth century have generally added a defense of reasonable mistake with respect to those two facts. The Model Penal Code recommends allowing that defense, arguing that there was no apparent reason for the common law strict liability tradition.

To understand bigamy prosecutions better, it may help to understand the reasons a person may commit bigamy. It may be as a matter of right or principle, as where a person's religion or culture practices open bigamy. While bigamy (or any other form of polygamy) is prohibited in most of the Judeo-Christian tradition, in the Islamic faith, which accounts for a substantial portion of the world's population, there is no traditional prohibition on polygamy. Bigamy is part of the criminal law of the United States apparently because it is an offense to Judeo-Christian faiths. The argument that codifying this perspective constitutes impermissible religious bias has been rejected twice by the U.S. Supreme Court (*Reynolds v. United States, Cleveland v. United States*). The Court considered the issue as early as 1878 in light of a now defunct Mormon practice of polygamy. That Mormon practice has been the cause for the only sustained controversy over polygamy in U.S. history. The federal government effectively conditioned Utah's entry into the union on Mormon retreat from the practice, in light of substantial public fervor against the Mormon marriage practices. The Model Penal Code actually proposes that states consider ordinary bigamy a misdemeanor, but a felony if it is done "in purported exercise of the right of plural marriage," pointedly singling out those few remaining Mormons who believe in polygamy, as well as those from other cultures who accept polygamy. Those from cultures accepting polygamy would receive more severe treatment than one who simply commits a fraud on a spouse who is unaware of a prior marriage. No state actually adopted the misdemeanor/felony distinction proposed in the Model Penal Code, but the proposal indicates one of the factors animating the criminal law in this area. The harm, then, is presumably moral offense to nonparties.

A person might instead practice bigamy because that person wishes to commit a fraud on one or both spouses, by disappearing from a spouse's life with joint assets, and later contracting a new marriage without either spouse knowing of the other's existence. There are even occasional cases of spouses conducting both marriages simultaneously and secretly, each family believing that the bigamist's job requires frequent travel away from home. In these cases there are real financial and emotional victims in the person of the unknowing spouse, and bigamy prosecutions have been used to protect these individuals from confidence men. Or a person may commit bigamy because a first marriage is over and a second is desired, but the first marriage is difficult to dissolve legally for some reason. This final reason accounted for many cases of bigamy before the availability of no-fault divorce. Bigamy, then, was simply serial marriage relationships parallel to divorce and remarriage. Now that divorce can be easily obtained in almost every state, this bigamous practice is less prevalent.

Sodomy

Sodomy was first prohibited by English common law in the sixteenth century. As recently as 1960, all states had a criminal provision governing consensual sodomy. The legal language used to describe the prohibition was, and in some cases still is, both oblique and severe; several states decree that "the infamous crime against nature" is a felony, others call it "the detestable and abominable crime against nature." Early prohibitions applied just to anal intercourse, but in the United States the definition has been interpreted as including oral sex as well.

Since 1960, there has been dramatic change in sodomy laws, concurrent with the rise of the gay and lesbian civil rights movement. By the end or the twentieth century, half of the state laws prohibiting private consensual sodomy had been repealed formally. A handful more had been struck down by state courts as violating state constitutional rights of privacy, though the U.S. Supreme Court decided in 1986 that sodomy laws do not violate the privacy guarantees in the U.S. Constitution (*Bowers v. Hardwick*). Despite the successes of gay rights organizations in effecting repeals, approximately twenty sodomy statutes remained on the books at the close of the twentieth century.

Though the language of most statutes does not limit the reach of the law to same-sex activity but would seemingly apply to heterosexual acts as well, the impact of the law is felt almost entirely by gays and lesbians. First, in several states, the language is explicitly limited to same-sex conduct, or judicial interpretation has narrowed broader language to have that effect. But in the majority of jurisdictions where the language appears to apply to heterosexual activity as well, the practical consequences of the law are limited to same-sex activity. These consequences include both enforcement of the criminal prohibitions, and significant civil law discrimination against individuals presumed to violate the statutes based on their sexual orientation.

Though largely thought to be dead letters, the use of these criminal statutes is slightly more common than is the case for the adultery and fornication statutes. They are frequently used when the conduct in question occurs in public, or when there is public solicitation to engage in same-sex activity. While laws against public sexual activity apply to heterosexual activity as well, there are two ways in which same-sex conduct receives harsher treatment. First, law enforcement officials routinely target specific public areas where gay solicitation is known to occur when organizing sting operations against solicitation or public sex. Further, sodomy charges are often tacked onto a gay or lesbian solicitation charge, whereas adultery or fornication charges are not as frequently tacked onto a heterosexual solicitation charge. In fact, it is inconceivable that law enforcement would set up a heterosexual sting operation in a public restroom with a police officer inducing someone to commit adultery, yet that kind of sting operation in the case of same-sex conduct leading to a sodomy charge is common. However, prosecution of completely private same-sex sexual activity is rare, though not entirely defunct.

More significantly, the sodomy laws, despite their apparent applicability to heterosexuals, are invoked exclusively against gays and lesbians in the civil law context. Presumed violation of a sodomy statute by a gay or lesbian parent is too frequently offered as justification for denying that parent child custody. Courts place restrictions on visitation with a gay parent in the presence of that parent's partner, relying on the criminality of the same-sex association as a justification for the restriction. But sodomy laws are not invoked against a heterosexual parent in custody or visitation proceedings, despite the frequency with which heterosexual couples engage in the same prohibited activities. The practical application of these statutes, then, if not the actual words, amounts to status discrimination. Gays and lesbians have been denied employment based on their presumed violation of sodomy statutes, and these actions have been upheld in courts. Sodomy statutes have been used in legal argument against civil rights laws designed to prevent sexual orientation discrimination. Sodomy laws can be used to justify housing discrimination as well. In other words, sodomy statutes have become in effect a license to discriminate. Without a criminal conviction, a person engaged in a same-sex relationship can be considered a criminal nonetheless for purposes of civil law. Thus the sodomy laws provide an incentive to conceal same-sex affiliations, despite the paucity of actual prosecutions of private consensual same-sex sexual activity.

The states where sodomy laws remain on the books tend to be some of the most conservative

in the nation, with a few exceptions. These statutes will probably be more difficult to repeal than they have been in other states. This is because these laws represent one piece of a wider legal battle over the status of sexual orientation discrimination, a legal battle that includes issues ranging from same-sex marriage to employment discrimination protection to military service to adoption laws. Conservatives in many states are opposed to the repeal of sodomy statutes despite their disuse, primarily because their repeal could signal an improvement in the political status of gays and lesbians, still a controversial concept for many.

Prostitution

Prostitution differs greatly from the consensual sex crimes discussed thus far, in that criminal prohibitions are routinely enforced, and the crime engages substantial law enforcement resources. It is, therefore, a theoretical concern. However, there is no shortage of theory surrounding the criminal law response to prostitution; whether and how to respond to prostitution has generated enormous debate from many quarters.

In the United States, prostitution was not directly prohibited by the criminal law during most of the nineteenth century, but prostitution activities were prosecuted under public lewdness, vagrancy, or nuisance statutes that ordinarily led to fines without imprisonment. Toward the end of the nineteenth century, most states passed laws prohibiting prostitution. These laws applied only to the women who worked as prostitutes, and not to their customers, or *johns*.

Not until the second half of the twentieth century were laws extended to cover the activities of johns, and not every state today criminalizes the patron of a prostitute at all. A number of states criminalize the conduct of both the prostitute and the john, but provide for more severe penalties for the prostitute. With a few exceptions, these statutes survive court challenges. By the 1980s, the official law on the books had come closer to equal treatment of prostitute and john. But in practice, the enforcement still has been extremely lopsided, with the vast majority of arrests and prosecutions brought against prostitutes. Studies of some jurisdictions have shown that virtually all of the thousands of prostitution arrests made each year in a given city have been of women prostitutes, not of the johns who are their compatriots in crime (Kandel). In the 1990s, however, there were sporadic attempts in some jurisdictions to arrest johns. These efforts included novel and controversial penalties, such as the publication of pictures and names of johns for the purpose of shaming them and thereby deterring others, and the seizure of automobiles driven by johns when those cars were used in the commission of the crime.

At common law, acts of prostitution were not crimes themselves, but solicitation was; this is the classic expression of the Victorian compromise. A number of states today continue this approach: they have no criminal prohibition of the actual exchange of money for sex where all aspects of the transaction are conducted in private. Instead, the criminal law in those states addresses solicitation, pandering, living in a house of prostitution, engaging in prostitution as a business (a single incident of prostitution is not enough to gain a conviction under these provisions), procuring a prostitute for another, inducing a person into a life of prostitution, or profiting from the prostitution of another. The majority of states do criminalize the private exchange of sex for money, but provide for trivial penalties, reserving the more severe sanctions for the organizational crimes associated with pimping. Finally, though it is widely believed that prostitution is not a crime in Nevada, in fact the state of Nevada simply delegates prohibition and regulation of prostitution to county governments, a few of which permit highly regulated prostitution.

The arguments in favor of criminalizing prostitution are numerous. They include the suppression of other crimes and harms that are incidental to prostitution, including organized crime activities, drug trading, violence against prostitutes and among pimps, as well as violence or offense to nonparticipant passersby, and emotional harm to the spouses of johns. These are about third party harms in some cases, and in some cases about harms to participants that are not easy to prosecute independently. For example, it is extremely difficult to obtain a conviction for sexual assault against a prostitute, though in study after study prostitutes report a high rate of nonconsensual sexual violence against them by both pimps and johns.

Underlying some of the dispute over the practice of prostitution is a dispute over facts. Libertarians often portray prostitutes as savvy entrepreneurs who have decided to capitalize on their sexuality. The contrasting picture, however, is of prostitutes who begin the work at an average age of fourteen, well below the age of consent, who are subject to routine sexual violence by pimps and johns, and who often have drug dependencies (that are sometimes encouraged by pimps) that drive their desperate need for cash. All three of these factors—early entry into the work, regular violence, and drug dependency—put in question the quality of the *consent* that would form the basis of the libertarian argument.

It is important to note that most of the criminal law response to prostitution has nothing to do with the protection of prostitutes themselves from these conditions. The response stems instead from the bargain struck in the Victorian compromise: seedy sexuality can take place without interference but anything that brings with it harms to bystanders in the form of criminality, violence, or offense in the neighborhood will not be tolerated. Therefore, some argue that we have the worst possible system: one that does not protect prostitutes themselves from the difficult conditions in their lives, but instead contributes a new difficulty in the form of arrests and fines aimed at the prostitutes themselves and not at the customers who create the demand for their work. Proponents of decriminalization argue that it would reduce some of these harms, specifically those associated with the black market corruption of law enforcement or organized crime involvement. They argue that it is the illegality itself that provides the opportunity for exploitative and violent behavior on the part of pimps and johns. Though the argument has become popular, it has not led to any actual changes in the law, or at least not to any decriminalizations.

There is a significant difference between the concept of decriminalization and the concept of legalization. Decriminalization makes the practice free from legal punishment. Legalization gives the practice all the protections of civil law. These include the legal enforcement of contracts, the protections of labor laws such as occupational safety laws, antidiscrimination laws, and Social Security, workers' compensation, and unemployment laws. Few libertarian advocates for decriminalization go so far as to advocate legalization. Decriminalization would remove police harassment from the lives of prostitutes and johns. However, it would not necessarily improve the conditions of prostitutes in other ways, or not to the extent that legalization would. Decriminalization would still permit violence by pimps and johns, and prostitutes would still need pimps to enforce contracts with johns were they unable to rely on the court system to do so instead.

An objection raised to complete legalization is that it would legitimize fully commodified sex. The argument continues that where the sale of sex is completely legitimate, a change would occur in the conception of sex among those who do not buy and sell it, as that noncommercial exchange would occur with the knowledge that the acts have a specific market price and availability.

Obscenity and pornography

The laws regulating obscenity are extremely complex and far-reaching, but are narrowed here through the lens of the consensual aspects of the crimes. Obscenity, like most moral sexual regulation, was first regulated by ecclesiastical authorities. It was first criminalized in England in the eighteenth century. Obscene materials are a subset of sexually explicit materials. Materials that fit within the legal definition of obscenity are not protected as speech by the First Amendment to the U.S. Constitution (*Roth v. United States, Miller v. California*). The legal definition of obscenity has particular contours that will be discussed below. It is important to understand that the absence of free speech protection simply means state and federal governments are permitted to develop criminal law responses to the materials; it does not by itself mean that the materials are banned. They may not, however, develop criminal law responses to sexually explicit materials that fall outside the constitutional definition of obscenity, as those materials would be protected by the free speech clause of the First Amendment.

The most interesting question to the lay reader will be what this legal definition of obscenity is—which sexually explicit materials lack free speech protection. But arguably the question of how materials, once they are judged obscene, are then regulated, ought to inspire as much curiosity. The prior question, the definition of obscenity, does not really involve the question of consent as the concept is used in this entry. Free speech can be protected without being consensual; a person may speak about politics freely in the public square to nonconsenting listeners, or may advocate civil disobedience or trespassing against individuals or nations that clearly do not consent to the effects of such speech. That speech is protected by free speech principles despite its harmful third-party effects, and lack of consent does not remove legitimacy from the legal protections of speech. Whether sexually explicit materials enjoy this protection depends on the purpose,

extent, and meaning of our free speech guarantee, and since obscene materials do not receive that protection, the legal definition of obscenity is one of the legal limits of the free speech guarantee. Consent is not a relevant question to this inquiry. However, consent is relevant to the question of how unprotected obscene materials are legally regulated. The definition of obscenity will be touched on briefly first, and then discussion will turn to the method of regulation.

The Supreme Court has determined that obscenity is not speech. *Speech* as the Court uses it must be understood not in its lay sense, but by reference to the reasons legal speech is protected by the Constitution: to promote the exchange of ideas. Obscene materials are not considered speech on the theory that they do not communicate ideas. They are instead deemed to be sexual aids, no more deserving of free speech protection than any other form of sexual aid. The Supreme Court has defined obscenity as all material that the average person, applying contemporary community standards, would find (1) taken as a whole, appeals to the prurient interest; (2) depicts or describes, in a patently offensive way, sexual conduct specifically defined by state obscenity law; and (3) taken as a whole, lacks serious literary, artistic, political, or scientific value. Implicit in the notion that this is not speech at all is that it does not communicate ideas, but is instead a form of sexual activity itself. If materials are sexually explicit but nonetheless convey a serious idea, they are speech and cannot be prohibited by obscenity laws (*Miller v. California*). Subject to some judicial scrutiny at the outer limits, juries decide whether allegedly obscene material meets the *Miller* definition of obscenity.

The individual consumption of obscene materials within one's home is constitutionally protected under the First Amendment as well as on privacy grounds (*Stanley v. Georgia, United States v. Orito*). This protection does not extend to carrying obscene materials across state borders or viewing obscene materials in movie theaters, for example, but remains confined to the home. This constitutional protection does not extend to the consumption of child pornography in the home (*Osborne v. Ohio*).

The private possession in the home of obscene materials that do not depict children cannot be prohibited. So what are the mechanisms for regulating obscenity? We will find that examination of the modes of regulation reveal the Victorian compromise: distribution and production with the intent to distribute is regulated, but not simple possession of obscene materials. An act that can be kept entirely private, then, and has no commercial gain involved, tends not to be a crime. But production and distribution of obscene materials is in fact prohibited almost everywhere in some form, and is usually punished as a misdemeanor. This is in part because commercial gains from obscenity may have third-party effects. For example, distribution areas may be associated with crime. In addition, production and distribution are crimes because the profit motive may lead to coercion in the production of obscene materials. Dissemination of obscene materials may offend those who inadvertently come into contact with the distribution system. Accordingly, many jurisdictions regulate which areas may sell obscene materials, keeping them out of the regular pathways of commercial activity and residential neighborhoods. Wide dissemination of these materials is thought to cause public desensitization to graphic sex, thereby affecting public morals. In the case of violent obscene materials, it is argued that they desensitize consumers to sexual violence, thereby inducing some individuals to commit such acts of violence. All of these potential harms affect third parties who are not the ones consenting to the sexual acts themselves.

No discussion of the regulation of obscenity is complete without attention to the feminist debate over pornography and its legal manifestations. Some feminists have argued that pornography, defined as sexually explicit materials that are degrading or dehumanizing to women, causes a number of harms that should be legally cognizable. Those include: (1) harms to individuals who are coerced to appear in pornographic materials; (2) harms to individuals who are victims of sexual assault perpetrated by one who has been incited to act after viewing pornography; and (3) a more diffuse harm to all women caused by the deterioration of the image of women through pornographic representations. The extent of each of these effects is debated fiercely. Some respected researchers have found that when sexually explicit images also depict violence, there is a causal connection between exposure to that aggressive pornography and propensity to commit violence against women (Malamuth and Donnerstein). Some have questioned the applicability of their work, performed under laboratory conditions, to real world crime, while others have argued that their laboratory work is supported by anecdotal evidence from the field.

In the mid-1980s, feminist legal reformer Catherine MacKinnon, along with feminist activist Andrea Dworkin, advocated in several cities for the passage of a local ordinance that would create a civil cause of action allowing monetary damages for anyone who could demonstrate that they had been harmed as a result of pornography. The statute would not prohibit the consumption or distribution of pornographic materials, and did not employ the criminal justice system. Instead, it was limited to private lawsuits by those who are assaulted in the making of pornography, who are assaulted by a consumer of pornography, or most controversially, who bring the suit on behalf of women who are subordinated by the pornography. The law was adopted by the city of Indianapolis, but a federal appellate court struck down the law as a violation of the First Amendment, taking issue with the definition of pornography within the statute (*American Booksellers Association, Inc., v. Hudnut*). That definition, which included the depiction of women as subordinate, encompasses both different and a greater range of materials than those defined as obscene within the Supreme Court's jurisprudence. These feminists have objected to obscenity prohibitions as a mechanism for addressing violence favoring the civil cause of action arising from pornography. Obscenity laws, they argue, are aimed at moral sensitivities, reflecting prudishness rather than concern over victims of violence. A cause of action against the makers of pornography, on the other hand, is aimed at sex discrimination, not moral sensitivities. However, the First Amendment jurisprudence in this area permits regulation of only those materials considered obscene, while protecting much of what is considered pornographic, so the feminist distinction does not have much impact on law in the United States. It has, however, influenced legal regulation of sexually explicit materials in neighboring Canada.

The striking exception to the rule that private possession of pornography in the home is not itself a crime is for the possession of child pornography. Through the lens of consent, the reason is obvious: real children are not able to consent to participation in the production of pornography. But the ban on possession of child pornography goes farther; it is constitutionally permissible to, and most states do in fact, ban possession of materials depicting children engaged in sexual activity even where real children are not used as models. This is justified by the belief that such materials will incite consumers to commit real world violence against children. It is an interesting exception to the arguments by some that adult pornography does not lead to violence against adults.

KATHARINE B. SILBAUGH

See also CRIMINALIZATION AND DECRIMINALIZATION; DEVIANCE; FEMINISM: CRIMINOLOGICAL ASPECTS; FEMINISM: LEGAL ASPECTS; POLICE: POLICING COMPLAINANTLESS CRIMES; SEXUAL PREDATORS; SEX OFFENSES: CHILDREN; VICTIMLESS CRIMES.

BIBLIOGRAPHY

AMERICAN LAW INSTITUTE. *Model Penal Code and Commentary.* Philadelphia: ALI, 1980.

ARCHARD, DAVID. *Sexual Consent.* Boulder, Colo.: Westview Press, 1998.

BALDWIN, MARGARET A. "Split at the Root: Prostitution and Feminist Discourses of Law Reform." *Yale Journal of Law and Feminism* 5 (1992): 47.

ESKRIDGE, WILLIAM N. *Gaylaw: Challenging the Apartheid of the Closet.* Cambridge, Mass.: Harvard University Press, 1999.

ESTLUND, DAVID M., and NUSSBAUM, MARTHA CRAVEN. *Laws and Nature: Shaping Sex, Preference, and the Family.* New York: Oxford, 1996.

FRIEDMAN, LAWRENCE M. *A History of American Law,* 2d ed. New York: Simon and Schuster, 1985.

GIBBONS, ANN. "The Risks of Inbreeding Among Humans." *Science* 259 (26 February 1993): 1252.

GORDON, SARAH BARRINGER. "'Our National Hearthstone': Anti-Polygamy Fiction and the Sentimental Campaign against Moral Diversity in Antebellum America." *Yale Journal of Law & the Humanities* 8 (1996): 295.

GRUEN, LORI, and PANICHAS, GEORGE E. *Sex, Morality, and the Law.* New York: Routledge, 1996.

HALLEY, JANET E. *Don't: A Reader's Guide to the Military's Anti-Gay Policy.* Durham, N.C.: Duke University Press, 1999.

HIRSHMAN, LINDA R., and LARSON, JANE E. *Hard Bargains: The Politics of Sex.* New York: Oxford University Press, 1998.

HOBSON, BARBARA MEIL. *Uneasy Virtue: The Politics of Prostitution and the American Reform Tradition.* Rev. ed. Chicago: University of Chicago Press, 1990.

KANDEL, MINOUCHE. "Whores in Court: Judicial Processing of Prostitutes in the Boston Municipal Court in 1990." *Yale Journal of Law and Feminism* 4 (1992): 329.

KOROBKIN, LAURA HANFT. *Criminal Conversations: Sentimentality and Nineteenth-Century Legal Stories of Adultery.* New York: Columbia University Press, 1999.

MACKINNON, CATHERINE. *Only Words.* Cambridge, Mass.: Harvard University Press, 1993.

MACKINNON, CATHERINE, and DWORKIN, ANDREA. *In Harms Way: The Pornography Civil Rights Hearing.* Cambridge, Mass.: Harvard University Press, 1998.

MALAMUTH, NEIL M., and DONNERSTEIN, EDWARD, eds. *Pornography and Sexual Aggression.* Orlando, Fla.: Academic Press, 1984.

MILLER, JOANN L. "Prostitution in Contemporary American Society." In *Sexual Coercion: A Sourcebook on Its Nature, Courses, and Prevention.* Edited by Elizabeth Grauerholz and Mary A. Koralweski. Lexington, Mass.: Lexington and D.C. Heath, 1991. Page 45.

POSNER, RICHARD A. *Sex and Reason.* Cambridge, Mass.: Harvard, 1992.

POSNER, RICHARD A., and SILBAUGH, KATHARINE B. *A Guide to America's Sex Laws.* Chicago: The University of Chicago Press, 1996.

RADIN, MARGARET JANE. *Contested Commodities.* Cambridge, Mass.: Harvard University Press, 1996.

SILBERT, MIMI H., and PINES, AYALE M. "Occupational Hazards of Street Prostitutes." *Criminal Justice and Behavior* 8 (1981): 395.

STROSSEN, NADINE. *Defending Pornography: Free Speech, Sex, and the Fight for Women's Rights.* New York: Anchor Books, 1996.

VAN WAGONER, RICHARD S. *Mormon Polygamy: A History.* 2d ed. Salt Lake City, Utah: Signature Books, 1989.

CASES

American Booksellers Association, Inc. v. Hudnut, 771 F.2d 323 (1986).

Bowers v. Hardwick, 478 U.S. 186 (1986).

Cleveland v. United States, 329 U.S. 14 (1946).

Miller v. California, 413 U.S. 15 (1973).

Osborne v. Ohio, 495 U.S. 103 (1990).

Reynolds v. United States, 98 U.S. 145 (1878).

Roth v. United States, 354 U.S. 476 (1957).

Stanley v. Georgia, 394 U.S. 557 (1969).

United States v. Orito, 413 U.S. 139 (1973).

SEXUAL PREDATORS

This entry addresses laws for the civil commitment of sexually dangerous persons. Beginning in the 1930s, many states expanded the traditional reach of civil commitment to include "sexual psychopaths." By the 1970s these psychopath laws were judged to be a failed experiment. In the 1990s, social forces combined to produce a suite of innovative approaches to sexual violence, including a second generation of sex offender commitment laws. Often born in the white-hot light of public outrage over heinous crime, these laws have been dubbed *sexual predator commitments*.

This entry begins by situating sex offender commitments in the legal landscape governing the deprivation of liberty. It sketches the rise and fall of the sexual psychopath laws, and then discusses the social forces that led to the resurrection of civil commitment as a tool to address sexual violence. The entry also describes the operation of commitment laws. It then addresses the constitutional controversy concerning these laws, and concludes with a discussion of the critiques of these laws as a tool in the fight against sexual violence.

Civil commitment and the criminal law

To understand how sex offender commitment laws are situated in American jurisprudence, one must understand the two sets of intersecting concepts that describe the exercise of governmental power to deprive individuals of their liberty. These concepts describe the sources of the power and the modes in which it is exercised. The sources of governmental power are two: The police power authorizes the state to act to protect the general health, safety, and well-being of the society. The criminal law and public health regulations are two classic examples of police power interventions. The *parens patriae* power authorizes the state to protect individuals who are unable to help themselves. Guardianship laws and some civil commitment laws have parens patriae justifications.

The power is exercised in two modes. The *criminal* mode is exercised with an intent to punish. It is retrospective in the sense that the deprivation of liberty is tied to a past act (*actus reus*) for which the individual is blameworthy (done with *mens rea*, a guilty mind, and not excused by an insane mind). Criminal intervention can have a preventive aspect (incapacitation), but it must be governed by the *principle of desert*, that is, the incarceration must be triggered by a blameworthy act (dangerousness alone is not enough) and the level of intervention may need to be roughly proportional to the blameworthiness of the individual. Criminal interventions require the most stringent procedural standards (e.g., proof beyond a reasonable doubt) and invoke a unique set of rights and immunities (e.g., right against self-incrimination, no ex post facto punishment, no double jeopardy).

Governmental intervention that is *civil*, in contrast, emphasizes a prospective view, seeking to protect against some future harm. Civil intervention, of course, considers past behavior. However, since blame and guilt are hallmarks of punishment, courts emphasize that the past is relevant not to demonstrate guilt or blame, but rather to serve as an evidentiary foundation for diagnosis or prediction. Civil interventions require only moderate procedural protections (e.g., proof by "clear and convincing evidence") and do not trigger the full panoply of rights and protections (e.g., individuals may be forced to testify against themselves, ex post facto, and double jeopardy protections do not apply).

Contemporary sex offender commitment laws are civil interventions that are not based on the parens patriae power because they are not addressed to offenders who are incompetent. Sex offender commitments address conduct that has traditionally been the province of the criminal justice system. They thus raise a difficult question of law and social policy: What are the permissible boundaries of civil commitment where its sole justification is the police power? To what extent, if at all, can civil commitment address behavior that is also subject to criminal justice intervention?

Sexual psychopath laws

In the early twentieth century, the Progressive movement focused on the causes of deviance and emphasized treatment and discretionary responses to individual cases. In the 1930s, newly developed psychiatric explanations of habitual criminality (including sexual deviance) and the influx of psychiatry into the courts laid the groundwork for the sex psychopath statutes, a series of laws that were enacted in about half the states during the late 1930s to the 1960s. These statutes took a variety of forms. Some were civil commitment statutes; some were criminal sentencing statutes; and some were hybrids. All, however, were based on the assumption that criminal sexual conduct, or at least some forms of it, were the product of mental disorder, and that afflicted individuals were too sick to deserve punishment. The sex psychopath laws were thus conceived as alternatives to the criminal justice system. For example, a Minnesota law was initially aimed at relatively harmless individuals for relatively trivial crimes. But the laws were written exceedingly broadly, and their application varied geographically and temporally. The rate of commitment in Minnesota during the period 1939–1969 was approximately 15 percent of those convicted, whereas in California in the 1950s, about 35 percent of apprehended sex offenders were committed as psychopaths. By the 1970s, the focus of the Minnesota law had shifted to violent recidivists, and the rate of commitments had dropped by 90 percent.

In 1977, the Group for the Advancement of Psychiatry ("GAP") issued an influential report entitled *Psychiatry and Sex Psychopath Legislation: The 30s to the 80s*. This report, along with several other influential professional reports, recommended the repeal of the sex offender commitment legislation. The GAP Report characterized sex offender commitment statutes as an "experiment [that] has failed" (p. 942). Professionals lacked adequate clinical skills to predict future behavior and to treat sexual violence effectively. This resulted in a failure to accomplish the treatment goal of the laws, and the unjust incarceration for extended periods of time of people who did not pose a danger. By the 1980s, most of the states with sex offender commitment laws had either repealed them, or had ceased actively using them.

Second generation sex offender commitment laws

Emergence. In the late 1980s and early 1990s, a confluence of factors produced a set of innovations that supplemented the traditionally reactive governmental role in addressing sexual violence. The main tools of the new approach were registration, notification, and civil commitment. Underlying notification and civil commitment is a fourth tool, systematic risk assessment. All of these tools recast the role of government, placing upon it the affirmative task of prevention through the systematic identification and control of individuals who pose a danger of future sexual harm.

The beginnings of the second generation of sex offender commitment laws took root in about 1989. Task forces in the states of Washington and Minnesota proposed a renewed use of civil commitment as a tool for containing sexually violent individuals. Both states were addressing public outrage and intense media coverage of heinous crimes committed by sex offenders recently released from prison. Both states faced the same dual-faceted problem: First, in the early 1980s Washington and Minnesota had replaced indeterminate sentencing with determinate schemes under which incarceration terms were set at sentencing. This change deprived the states of their power to exercise long-term, flexible control over offenders deemed too dangerous to release from prison. Second, both states replaced indeterminate sentences with a system of presumptive sentencing guidelines. By the late 1980s, society's increased attention to sexual assault had produced a change in its perceived seriousness. The sentencing guidelines were seen as inadequate punishment. By the late 1980s and early 1990s, individuals imprisoned under the new sentencing guidelines became eligible for release. This exposed a gap in the states' ability to protect against recidivist sexual violence.

Contemporary Western thought endorses the view that the state has a strong obligation to protect its citizens from violence. This protection imperative manifested itself in the form of a principle of incapacitation—the notion that public protection against violence is best accomplished by locking up criminals. Thus, the need to close the gap in sexual-violence protection produced a strong push to extend the systems for the incapacitation of sex offenders.

Key constitutional constraints prevented the states from addressing this incapacitation imperative by simply increasing criminal punishments for sexual violence. Retroactive increases would have run afoul of prohibitions on ex post facto legislation and double jeopardy prosecutions. Prospectively, the states could—and did—increase sentence lengths for sex offenders. But both Washington and Minnesota rejected a return to long indeterminate sentences for sex offenders, at least in part because such a scheme would be inconsistent with the principle of desert. Finally, the Constitution prohibited the state from imposing criminal punishment simply for the status of being mentally disordered and dangerous, or for the punishment of future predicted crimes (*Robinson v. California*, 370 U.S. 660, 666 (1962); Lafave and Scott).

Searching for an escape from these constraints on the criminal law, both states turned to civil commitment to close the "gap" in social control. Neither state addressed in any careful way the failure of the earlier sex psychopath laws, nor did either state attempt to assess whether commitment was a wise allocation of treatment and prevention resources. Soon, Wisconsin, Kansas, and California followed suit.

The new use of civil commitment differed in one critical respect from the first generation of laws. Instead of being addressed to persons considered "too sick" for punishment, the new laws would aim at those considered "too dangerous" to release from prison. Though the statutory language differed from law to law, the structure of all was similar.

Sex offender commitment laws typically contain four substantive elements and two procedural characteristics. Substantively, the laws aim at individuals who have (1) a history of sexually violent or dangerous conduct and (2) a mental or personality disorder or "abnormality" which (3) "causes" or "predisposes" the individual to (4) likely future dangerous sexual conduct. The statutes provide little guidance for either the type of mental disorder that qualifies or the risk-threshold for dangerousness. Some courts, however, have suggested that a high probability of future harm is constitutionally required. The laws specify procedural protections that are typically higher than standard civil litigation standards, but may fall short of the protections required in a criminal prosecution. The laws generally allow the state to force the respondent to testify, and they abrogate the rules of privilege and confidentiality to allow the admission of relevant treatment records without the consent of the individual. Some, but not all, states require proof beyond a reasonable doubt and allow for a jury trial. Although details vary, committed individuals can expect to remain committed until the conditions giving rise to the commitment—either the presence of a mental disorder or the prediction of future dangerousness—are ameliorated. Commitment statutes generally require the provision of treatment.

Constitutional challenges. The new use of civil commitment inspired swift constitutional challenges. In badly split opinions, the supreme courts of Washington, Minnesota, and Wisconsin held the laws to be constitutional. A federal court in Washington and the Kansas Supreme Court held the laws unconstitutional.

In 1997, reversing the Kansas Supreme Court, the U.S. Supreme Court upheld the constitutionality of the Kansas commitment law in *Kansas v. Hendricks*, 521 U.S. 346 (1997). The court disposed of constitutional challenges on two main fronts. The *substantive due process* challenge argued that the laws extend civil commitment beyond its proper scope. The

"punishment" challenge asserted that the laws had a punitive purpose, and therefore violated the double jeopardy and ex post facto prohibitions of the U.S. Constitution.

Substantive due process imposes limits on state power to restrict the liberty of individuals. In a series of cases, the Supreme Court has defined some of the constitutional limits on civil commitment. In *O'Connor v. Donaldson*, 422 U.S. 563 (1975), the Court suggested that it would be unconstitutional for a state to confine a harmless though mentally ill person. In *Addington v. Texas*, 441 U.S. 418 (1979), the Court said that commitment can rest on both parens patriae and police power, but the Court did not clarify whether both powers are necessary, or either is sufficient, to support civil commitment. Some commentators read *United States v. Salerno*, 481 U.S. 739, 748 (1987), a case upholding a statutory system of limited preventive detention of persons charged with criminal offenses, as approving preventive (noncriminal) detention based on dangerousness alone. This theory was rejected, however, in *Foucha v. Louisiana*, 504 U.S. 71 (1992), where the Court struck down dangerousness-based civil commitment in the absence of mental illness.

These cases provided the context for the constitutional challenges in *Hendricks*. Citing *Foucha*, Hendricks argued that the Kansas law exceeded the state's constitutional powers because it failed to require a "mental illness" as a prerequisite to commitment. Challengers argued that terms defining the commitment class either were not "medically valid" (e.g., "mental abnormality") or, though medically valid, were not "mental illnesses" (e.g., "personality disorder"). The Court rejected these arguments. While acknowledging that commitment requires some "mental disorder" predicate, the Court held there was no particular constitutional significance to the term "mental illness," thus personality disorders were not categorically ineligible to be constitutional predicates for commitment. The Court stated that the mental-disorder predicate for civil commitment is a legal, as opposed to a medical, term. Thus, the use of "medically valid" categories is not constitutionally required.

What, then, is the legal definition of "mental disorder" in the commitment context? In *Addington*, the Court focused on mental illness as a foundation for the assertion of the state's parens patriae power. But the state's parens patriae power was not alluded to in *Hendricks*, no doubt because the subjects of sex offender commitments are not incompetent, and the commitments are justified by reference to the public's interest, rather than the individual's. Thus, the question posed in Hendricks is the role played by mental disorder in commitments that rest solely on the state's police power.

Although *Hendricks* is not entirely clear, the Court's holding suggests that the role of "mental disorder" in this context is to maintain the primacy of the criminal law in the fight against antisocial violence. The constitutional role of the "mental disorder" requirement is to limit civil commitment to a small portion of the social control function of the state, and to provide a justification for the use of preventive confinement as a *supplement* to the criminal law. As the Supreme Court in *Hendricks* has stated, mental disorder limits civil commitment "to a small segment of particularly dangerous individuals," and "adequately distinguishes [persons subject to civil commitment] from other dangerous persons who are perhaps more properly dealt with exclusively through criminal proceedings" (521 U.S. at 360). This interpretation reinforces the Court's statement in *Foucha v. Louisiana* that states must justify their departure from the "ordinary criminal processes . . . the normal means of dealing with persistent criminal conduct" (504 U.S. 71, 83 (1992)).

The Supreme Court in *Hendricks* stated that the Kansas law passed this constitutional test by focusing on the individual's inability to control his dangerous sexual behavior. Several state supreme courts have interpreted this language as imposing a constitutional "volitional dysfunction" test for sex offender commitments.

Lack of volitional control is sometimes associated with the insanity defense. Limiting commitments to criminally excused persons would satisfy the Court's requirement of a distinct and narrow application for civil commitment and would preserve the primacy of the criminal law. But, as noted below, this interpretation is contrary to actual practice, where almost all persons committed have been held responsible for their prior crimes. In light of this, many commentators argue that "volitional dysfunction" is an essentially meaningless concept. They argue that the courts' use of volitional dysfunction simply serves to limit commitments to repeat offenders—those whose past course of criminal conduct indicates a failure to control sexually violent behavior.

Double jeopardy and ex post facto. The double jeopardy clause prevents the state from "punishing twice, or attempting a second time to punish criminally, for the same offense" (*Witte v. United States*, 515 U.S. 389, 396 (1995). The *ex post facto* clause "forbids the application of any new punitive measure to a crime already consummated" (*Lindsey v. Washington*, 301 U.S. 397, 401 (1937). Challengers claimed that sex offender commitment laws are, in actuality, punishment masquerading as civil commitment, whose true purpose is to extend the confinement of sex offenders who have served their prison terms. The Supreme Court in *Hendricks* rejected this argument on the ground that incapacitation of dangerous individuals is a well-accepted purpose of civil commitment.

Challengers also argued that the failure to provide effective treatment to committed individuals is evidence of a punitive intent. Doubts about the efficacy of treatment were central to the critique of the earlier sex offender commitment laws. Studies of sex offender treatment in the 1980s were taken as suggesting that "nothing works." Indeed, the legislative preambles to a number of the statutes acknowledged that treatment of sex offenders was problematic. The sex offender commitment laws were thus attacked on the ground that incarceration, rather than treatment, was the primary goal of the legislation.

One branch of this argument asserted that there is no proven effective treatment for the "condition" of being a sexual predator, and that commitment is thus tantamount to lifetime incapacitation. *Hendricks* stated that the availability of effective treatment is not a constitutional prerequisite for civil commitment, explaining that a contrary holding "would obligate a State to release certain confined individuals who were both mentally ill and dangerous simply because they could not be successfully treated for their afflictions" (521 U.S. at 367). An alternative argument asserted treatment is possible, but that Kansas failed to provide it. Most courts acknowledge, under the influence of *Youngberg v. Romeo*, 457 U.S. 307 (1982), that the Constitution requires states to provide available treatment, at least up to some minimum level. In *Hendricks*, the Supreme Court suggested that Kansas' rather "meager" treatment program was not fatal because of the newness of the commitment law. But the laws have since matured. A federal district court has enjoined as constitutionally inadequate conditions and treatment in Washington State's Special Commitment Center (*Turay v. Seling*, 108 F.Supp.2d 1148 (WD Wash. 2000). In a separate case, the Supreme Court held that such conditions do not entitle an inmate to release on a writ of habeas corpus pursuant to the ex post facto and double jeopardy clauses (*Seling v. Young*, 121 S.Ct. 727 (2001)). The *Seling* case did not decide whether persistent unconstitutional conditions might entitle an inmate to release under other legal theories, such as substantive due process.

Commitment statutes in practice. Prior to the Supreme Court's *Hendricks* decision, five states and the District of Columbia had active sex offender commitment programs. In the years after the *Hendricks* decision approximately ten additional states have enacted laws. About twelve additional states had legislation under consideration as of the year 2000.

The sex offender commitment programs follow a common pattern. Officials are required to assess the risk posed by sex offenders who are about to be released from prison. This assessment process identifies a group for referral to the commitment process. Minnesota and Kansas refer about 10 percent, whereas Arizona referred 25 percent and California about 3 percent. Within the judicial system, prosecutors exercise discretion in deciding whether to file a formal petition, and some cases may be dismissed at a probable cause hearing, or after a full-blown trial on the merits. Though judging net commitment rates is difficult, programs appear to commit at rates ranging from less than 1 percent to about 6 percent of sex offenders about to be released from prison.

The targets of contemporary sex offender commitment laws are most often people whose abilities to reason and perceive are not psychotically impaired, who can care for themselves and are properly held responsible for their behavior. These individuals have mental disorders that are characterized by strong "deviant" sexual desires (paraphilias), or maladaptive, persistent personality patterns (personality disorders). A large proportion also have diagnoses of chemical abuse or dependency. Almost all of the commitments are of individuals who have been held criminally responsible for their conduct.

Commitment under these laws is to secure treatment facilities, mostly operated by departments of human services or mental health. In a few states, the facilities are operated by departments of corrections, or are located within correctional facilities. One state's law (Texas) provides for out-patient commitment.

The annual cost for commitment programs ranged (in 1999) from a low of about $70,000 per person to a high of $164,000. As of the year 2000, almost one thousand persons were under commitment nationwide. Commitments are long-term. Only a handful of individuals have been released from commitment, even in those states with relatively mature programs. Thus, state officials predict continued growth in both the population under commitment and the consequent cost of the programs. A Minnesota study predicted growth in cost of 450 percent between 1998 and 2010, and California projects a growth of about 400 percent over the same time period. Legislators and policymakers in some states are alarmed by the growth, and are seeking ways to reduce the use of civil commitment as a tool to prevent sexual violence.

Evaluating sex offender commitment schemes. As indicated above, sex offender commitment laws are controversial. Most of the debate has centered on the constitutionality and morality of the laws. Though the broad constitutional questions have been resolved, serious questions remain about the actual manner in which these statutes are applied. Many of these questions implicate moral concerns, but others raise social policy issues that can be properly resolved only through empirical research. This section summarizes the critiques and social policy concerns.

The civil liberties critique. The civil liberties critique worries that sex offender commitment laws sweep too broadly and arbitrarily, and therefore exceed their proper role as a narrow exception to the primacy of the criminal justice system. Civil confinement is proper only for those dangerous individuals who are "mentally disordered." But researchers report that a majority of prisoners in general, and of sex offenders in particular, are diagnosable with some form of mental disorder, if that term includes personality disorders. Thus, a broad mental-disorder requirement allows commitments to sweep within their reach most of the criminal population, undercutting the argument that commitment schemes are limited and principled exceptions to the primacy of the criminal justice system.

As indicated above, some courts claim they apply commitment only to persons whose mental disorders render them unable to control their sexual behavior. But courts routinely apply the inability-to-control standard to sex offenders who have been held fully responsible for their behavior. Critics contend this is a contradiction that renders the inability-to-control standard a meaningless legal fiction. In practice, commitment requires nothing more than a history of sexual violence and a diagnosed "mental disorder."

Such a definition, rather than distinguishing civil commitment from criminal confinement, allows commitment virtually to swallow the criminal law.

Critics also contend that prediction is so inaccurate that it renders commitment essentially arbitrary, and therefore unconstitutional. This is a "facial" challenge the courts have rejected, in large measure because prediction is central in a broad range of legal settings—from the death penalty to child custody.

Critics also make an "as applied" argument. At least in their rhetoric, some courts and legislatures assert that commitment statutes target only the "most dangerous" offenders who are "highly likely" to reoffend. Challengers argue that the prediction evidence offered in individual cases does not satisfy these thresholds. However, some scholars report advances in the ability to predict sexual recidivism among released sex offenders. Researchers have developed actuarial instruments that employ factors related to sexual recidivism (such as sexual offense history, age, antisocial personality or psychopathy, physiologically measured sexual deviance, and patterns and persistence of victimization) and statistically derived weights that reflect their relative importance. Researches apply these tools to populations of released sex offenders and measure the correlation between the resultant scores and the population's recidivism. In assessment, the test score for an individual is interpreted to indicate a risk of reoffense equal to the proportion of identically scoring study subjects who committed another sex crime. Some researchers conclude that careful risk assessment of this sort can reliably identify a small group of sex offenders with a risk of sexual reoffense of at least 50 percent, and possibly as high as 70 to 80 percent.

Despite these apparent advances, critics urge caution in the use of these risk assessment tools, especially where the consequence is a deprivation of liberty. Samples may not be representative of the present prison-release group, thus introducing a sampling error. Apparent correlations may shrink when tests are cross-validated on other populations. Human error will introduce an error of measurement into the results. High probabilities of sexual reoffense assume a follow-up period of decades, and so may be of little value in making judgments about risk management in the immediate future. At present, most of the instruments take either no, or minimal, account of dynamic or changeable risk factors, such as treatment completion or level of community supervision. These factors can significantly affect risk levels. Finally, some of the test instruments have not been subject to publication in peer reviewed journals, and may not comport with professional standards for psychological testing.

The resource allocation critique. Sex offender commitment programs consume resources hugely disproportionate to the numbers of individuals confined. For example, in a recent year, Minnesota spent about $17 million per year on the 150 men committed as sex offenders, while spending only about $1.2 million per year on sex offender treatment for the eleven hundred men confined to state prisons, and $1.1 million on community-based treatment for sex offenders. Proponents often point to the incapacitation of committed individuals as proof of the efficacy of commitment laws. But commitments confine only a small percentage of all recidivist sex offenders. Most recidivists will be released from prison at the end of their sentences, and the vast majority of future sex offenders are in the community or in the correctional system. Given a finite pool of resources, critics argue that research is needed to determine whether an expensive commitment program that focuses on a very small number of dangerous individuals is the most effective way to spend prevention and treatment dollars. They argue for careful consideration of alternative programs, such as intensive "containment" approaches in the community, beefed-up treatment and supervision programs for offenders under correctional control, and public-health-style campaigns to change widespread attitudes about sexual violence.

Treatment disincentives. Most commentators are at least mildly optimistic about the efficacy of sex offender treatment. But success depends on full investment by the treatment subject, including disclosure of past sexual misconduct. Commitment laws abrogate confidentiality for precommitment treatment disclosures, and permit prosecutors to base commitment cases on information gleaned from treatment sessions. Thus, critics urge study as to whether the specter of commitment may serve as a treatment disincentive for sex offenders in the correctional or community setting.

Public policy distortion. Critics contend that a "psychological" model for sexual violence is central to civil commitment laws and that adoption of this model can distort public policy. Sex offender commitment laws are based on the theory that the sexual violence is caused by a mental abnormality. This model suggests that sexual violence is aberrational rather than systemic, in that sex offenders are different in kind (they have a "disorder") from "normal" individuals. This model suggests that the greatest danger of sexual assault arises from the deranged predator attacking a stranger-victim. Competing explanations characterize sexual violence as relatively ubiquitous, the manifestation of widespread societal attitudes about women, children, and sex. This competing model suggests that the biggest danger is sexual assault committed by an acquaintance or family member, which constitutes 75 percent of all sexual victimizations. By characterizing sexual violence as aberrational and deranged, the psychological model tends to absolve the larger society of its responsibility to change the conditions that produce this violence.

The civil commitment model also undercuts the individual's responsibility for his own sexual behavior. Most commentators characterize sexual violence as a behavior that is chosen by the individual. They view this choice-model as an important heuristic for changing sexually harmful behavior. The civil commitment laws may undercut and confuse this model by reviving the discredited notion that women can trigger uncontrollable sexual impulses in men.

Conclusion

Sex offender commitment laws are one manifestation of an innovative transformation in the societal stance toward sexual violence. In contrast to the traditional criminal law approach, which is essentially reactive to crime, the contemporary approaches to sexual violence place upon the society an obligation systematically to identify the risk of sexual violence, and to prevent it. Although these goals are salutary, civil commitment is a means that is controversial legally, morally, and practically. The *Hendricks* case resolves many of the questions about the constitutionality of the commitment laws but leaves unresolved serious questions in the application of the laws. Further, critics worry that civil commitment programs will consume an increasingly disproportionate share of the prevention and treatment resources and will distort public policy decisions about this important area.

ERIC S. JANUS

See also CIVIL AND CRIMINAL DIVIDE; MASS MEDIA AND CRIME; MENTALLY DISORDERED OFFENDERS; PREDICTION OF CRIME AND RECIDIVISM; RAPE: BEHAVIORAL ASPECTS; RAPE: LEGAL ASPECTS.

BIBLIOGRAPHY

American Psychiatric Association. *Dangerous Sex Offenders: A Task Force Report of the American Psychiatric Association.* Washington, D.C.: American Psychiatric Association, 1997.

BECKER, JUDITH V., and MURPHY, WILLIAM D. "What We Know and Do Not Know About Assessing and Treating Sex Offenders." *Psychology, Public Policy, and Law* 4 (1998): 116–137.

BOERNER, D. "Confronting Violence: In the Act and in the Word." *University of Puget Sound Law Review* 15 (1992): 525–577.

BRAKEL, SAMUEL J.; PARRY, JOHN; and WEINER, BARBARA A. *The Mentally Disabled and the Law*, 3d ed. Chicago: American Bar Foundation, 1985.

BROOKS, A. D. "The Constitutionality and Morality of Civilly Committing Violent Sexual Predators." In *University of Puget Sound Law Review* 15 (1992): 709–754.

CUNNINGHAM, M. D., and REIDY, T. J. "Antisocial Personality Disorder and Psychopathy: Diagnostic Dilemmas in Classifying Patterns of Antisocial Behavior in Sentencing Evaluations." *Behavioral Science and the Law* 16 (1997): 340.

D'EMILIO, JOHN, and FREEDMAN, ESTELLE. B. *Intimate Matters: A History of Sexuality in America*, 2d ed. Chicago and London: University of Chicago Press, 1997.

DENNO, DEBORAH W. "Life before the Modern Sex Offender Statutes." *Northwestern University School of Law* 92 (1998): 1317–1414.

FREEDMAN, ESTELLE B. "Uncontrolled Desires: The Response to the Sexual Psychopath, 1920–1960." *Journal of American History* 74 (1987): 83–101.

GROSSMAN, L. S.; MARTIN, B.; and FICHTNER, C. G. "Are Sex Offenders Treatable? A Research Overview." *Psychiatric Services* 503 (1999): 349–361.

Group for the Advancement of Psychiatry. *Psychiatry and Sex Psychopath Legislation: The 30s to the 80s.* New York: Group for the Advancement of Psychiatry, 1977.

HANSON, R. KARL. "What Do We Know about Sex Offender Risk Assessment?" *Psychology, Public Policy, and the Law* 4 (1998): 50–72.

HARRIS, GRANT T.; RICE, MARNIE E.; and QUINSEY, VERNON L. "Appraisal and Management of Risk in Sexual Aggressors: Implications for Criminal Justice Policy." *Psychology, Public Policy, and the Law* 4 (1998): 73–115.

JANUS, ERIC S., and MEEHL, PAUL E. "Assessing the Legal Standard for Predictions of Dangerousness in Sex Offender Commitment Proceedings." *Psychology, Public Policy, and the Law* 3 (1997): 33–64.

JANUS, ERIC S., and WALBEK, NANCY H. "Sex Offender Commitments in Minnesota: A Descriptive Study of Second Generation Commitments." *Behavioral Sciences and Law* 18 (2000): 343–374.

LAFAVE, WAYNE R., and SCOTT, AUSTIN W., JR. *Criminal Law*, 2d ed. St. Paul, Minn.: West Publishing Co., 1986.

LAWS, D. R.; BARBAREE, H. R.; and MARSHALL, WILLIAM L., eds. *Handbook of Sexual Assault: Issues, Theories & Treatment of the Offender.* New York, Plenum Press, 1990.

LA FOND, JOHN Q., and WINICK, BRUCE J. "Sex Offenders: Scientific, Legal, and Policy Perspectives." *Psychology, Public Policy, and Law* 4 (1998): 3–24.

LIEB, ROXANNE; QUINSEY, VERNON; and BERLINER, LUCY. "Sexual Predators and Social Policy." *Crime and Justice* 23 (1998): 43–114.

LOGAN, WAYNE A. "A Study In "Actuarial Justice': Sex Offender Classification Practice and Procedure." *Buffalo Criminal Law Review* 3 (2000): 593–637.

MORSE, STEPHEN J. "Culpability and Control." *University of Pennsylvania Law Review* 142 (1994): 1587–1660.

PRATT, J. *Governing the Dangerous: Dangerousness, Law, and Social Change.* Sydney, Australia: Federation Press, 1997.

PRENTKY, ROBERT A. "A Rationale For the Treatment of Sex Offenders: Pro Bono Publico." In *What Works: Reducing Reoffending—Guidelines from Research and Practice.* Edited by James McGuire. New York: J. Wiley, 1995.

RICE, MARNIE E., and HARRIS, GRANT T. "The Treatment of Mentally Disordered Offenders." *Psychology, Public Policy, and Law* 3 (1997): 126–183.

SCHOPP, ROBERT F., and STURGIS, BARBARA J. "Sexual Predators and Legal Mental Illness for Civil Commitment." *Behavioral Sciences and the Law* 13 (1995): 437–458.

SCULL, ANDREW T. *Social Order/Mental Disorder: Anglo-American Psychiatry in Historical Perspective.* Berkeley: University of California Press, 1989.

Symposium. "Throwing Away the Key: Social and Legal Responses to Child Molesters." *Northwestern University Law Review* 92 (1998): 1197–1640.

TJADEN, PATRICIA, and THOENNES, NANCY. "Prevalence, Incidence, and Consequences of Violence against Women: Findings from the National Violence Against Women Survey." *Research in Brief.* Washington, D.C.: U.S. Department of Justice, National Institute of Justice, Centers for Disease Control and Prevention, 1998.

TONRY, MICHAEL, and HATLESTAD, KATHLEEN, eds. *Sentencing Reform in Overcrowded Times: A Comparative Perspective.* New York: Oxford University Press, 1997.

ZIMRING, FRANKLIN E., and HAWKINGS, GORDON. *Incapacitation: Penal Confinement and the Restraint of Crime.* New York: Oxford University Press, 1995.

CASES

Addington v. Texas, 441 U.S. 418 (1979).
Foucha v. Louisiana, 504 U.S. 71 (1992).
Kansas v. Hendricks, 521 U.S. 346 (1997).
Lindsey v. Washington, 301 U.S. 397, 401 (1937).
O'Connor v. Donaldson, 422 U.S. 563 (1975).
Robinson v. California, 370 U.S. 660, 666 (1962).
Seling v. Young, 121 S. Ct. 727 (2001).
United States v. Salerno, 481 U.S. 739 (1987).
Witte v. United States, 515 U.S. 389, 396 (1995).

SHAMING PUNISHMENTS

Convicted of drug distribution, Takeisha Brunson—a twenty year old with a lengthy string of prior convictions—might ordinarily have been sentenced to a significant prison term. But the judge in her case decided to try an alternative sanction: *shame*. As a condition of probation, the judge ordered Brunson to place an advertisement in a local newspaper announcing, "I purchased drugs with my two kids in the car." Brunson objected to the sentence as "hard," yet she readily accepted it over more jail time and the certain loss of her children.

As innovative as it was, the use of shame in Brunson's case was by no means an isolated occurrence. Courts in New York, Texas, and other states now order drunk drivers to display brightly colored "DUI" bumper stickers. In Florida and Oregon, judges order nonviolent sex offenders to post warning signs on their property. In Massachusetts, men who are delinquent in their child support payments find their pictures displayed on subways and buses. A federal judge in Washington, D.C., ordered a lobbyist convicted of illegal campaign contributions to compose a narrative on his crime and to distribute it to some two thousand members of his profession. In all these instances and in many others, judges are relying on the pain of public humiliation to produce the deterrent effect of short prison terms at a fraction of the cost.

The widespread advent of shaming sanctions is one of the most significant developments in American criminal justice since the early 1990s. Before then, sentences that included elements of humiliating publicity were rarely imposed and when noticed at all, were typically reported as amusing spectacles. (In one well known case (*People v. McDowell*, 130 Cal. Rptr. 839 (1976)), a court ordered a man convicted of purse snatching to put taps in his shoes to alert potential victims.) But by the end of the 1990s, such sentences had emerged as a highly visible, if still unorthodox and controversial, alternative to jail for serious, but nonviolent, offenders. No longer dismissed as vulgar curiosities, punishments like Brunson's now command the serious attention of criminal justice experts and have won cautious endorsements from mainstream organs of public opinion such as the *New York Times*.

The movement toward shaming in American criminal justice raises many important questions. What are the precedents for such sanctions? What explains the contemporary interest in them? What forms do those sanctions typically take? What legal issues attend the imposition of them? And most important of all, is shaming criminals a just and sensible policy?

Historical antecedents: corporal punishments and imprisonment

The wave of shaming sanctions since the mid-1990s is not America's first experience with humiliation as a form of punishment. Indeed, the infliction of shame played a central role in the historical development of both corporal punishment and imprisonment.

Colonial Americans relied on a rich variety of corporal punishments, from the pillory to the whipping post to the ducking stool. Publicly inflicted in a highly ceremonial fashion, these sanctions were geared to inflict humiliation as much as physical pain. As Adam Hirsch has noted, "The sting of the lash and the contortions of the stocks were surely no balm, but even worse for community members were the piercing stares of neighbors who witnessed their disgrace and with whom they would continue to live and work" (p. 34).

Such punishments had largely fallen out of favor by the early nineteenth century and were overtaken by imprisonment as the dominant punishment for noncapital crimes. This shift was animated by two changes in social conditions. The first was the loosening of the tight communal bonds that had characterized colonial life. As American communities grew and became more impersonal, the disgrace of corporal punishment receded. Hirsch points out that "[t]he threat of a session on the pillory was less daunting when performed before persons with whom offenders were unacquainted, and with whom they need have no further personal contact" (p. 38).

The second change was the democratizing of American society. The Revolution unleashed a passion for equality that impelled Americans to root out all perceived vestiges of social hierarchy from within their institutions. Corporal punishment was targeted for reform because it was perceived to be distinctive of hierarchical relationships. The infliction of acute physical pain was the way that sovereigns disciplined their subjects, husbands their wives, parents their children, and masters their servants or slaves. As such, it rankled Americans' republican sensibilities for states to use this same mode of discipline to punish citizens, even the errant ones who committed crimes.

The advent of the prison responded to both of these changes. The dissipation of community life in early America was accompanied by growing devotion to individual liberty. Accordingly, the threat of liberty deprivation seemed a natural replacement for the threat of status deprivation formerly associated with corporal punishment. In addition, because imprisonment expressed what citizens of a republic shared—their liberty—rather than any settled social distinctions that set the punisher and the punished apart, imprisonment struck nineteenth-century Americans as more in keeping with the principles of republican self-government.

It would be simplistic, however, to view imprisonment as reflecting the complete dissipation of shame as an element of criminal punishment. Precisely because liberty was so intensely and universally valued, imprisonment was viewed by nineteenth-century Americans as an effective instrument for inducing shame even in a society of strangers. Early prisons were thus structured to maximize the public humiliation of offenders, who were "put . . . on display as if in a zoo" (Hindus, p. 101). It is more accurate, then, to see the shift from corporal punishment to imprisonment not as an unqualified repudiation of shame but rather as an adaptation of it to new social conditions.

Contemporary impetus: the search for an expressively appropriate alternative sanction

The renewed attention to shame as a form of punishment reflects two factors. One is the excessive reliance of American jurisdictions on imprisonment for nonviolent offenses. The other is political resistance to fines and community service, alternatives to imprisonment that many see as insufficiently expressive of moral condemnation. Judges have been drawn to shaming punishments as a potentially cost-effective and expressively appropriate alternative to imprisonment.

The United States has long been thought to rely excessively on imprisonment. Incarceration might be the only option for many violent offenders, including murderers, rapists, and armed robbers. But they make up less than half of the American prison population. The remaining inmates have engaged in nonviolent offenses—from larceny to fraud to drug distribution to drunk driving. Nearly half of those individuals, moreover, are serving terms of less than two years. Criminal justice experts have long advocated alternative sanctions for these offenders on the grounds that they need not be incapacitated for public safety and that the short prison terms they receive deter no more effectively than less expensive fines and community service dispositions.

Notwithstanding this expert consensus, however, the call for alternative sanctions has fallen on deaf ears. Over the past two decades, prison sentences have been dramatically lengthened for many offenses (including minor drug crimes) and extended to others (such as federal white-collar crimes) that had traditionally been punished only with fines and probation. Large fines have also become common—especially in federal criminal law—but almost exclusively as supplements to imprisonment, not as substitutes for it. Similarly, community service is now a common disposition but mainly as an additional punishment for offenders who would otherwise have received straight probation. Thus, neither of the so-called alternative sanctions has succeeded in replacing imprisonment in any significant degree.

Because the argument for alternative sanctions has been a prominent part of crime policy debates for nearly two decades, it is implausible to attribute the unpopularity of fines and community service to public ignorance. A more satisfying explanation is that these conventional alternatives fail to satisfy the public's demand for punishments that effectively express society's moral condemnation of crime.

As the philosopher Joel Feinberg has observed, an imposition must do more than make an individual suffer before we recognize it as a punishment. It must also be understood to express moral disapproval of the individual who bears it. A person can lose just as much liberty, for example, in the military as she can in prison. The reason that only imprisonment and not conscription is regarded as punishment is that against the background of widely shared conventions only imprisonment expresses society's authoritative moral condemnation.

Because the public expects punishments to express condemnation, the political acceptability of various forms of punishment will reflect their expressive power. In American society, imprisonment expresses condemnation with unmistakable clarity. Because liberty is such a powerful symbol of what individuals are due, taking it away leaves no doubt about society's condemnation of a criminal wrongdoer. This has been true of imprisonment, moreover, since its inception in the nineteenth century, when Americans turned to it as a gesture of disapprobation more fitting to a republic than was corporal punishment.

Fines, in contrast, condemn much more ambiguously. When combined with a term of imprisonment, it is clear that they are being imposed for doing what is morally forbidden. But when fines are used as a substitute for imprisonment, they sometimes suggest that society is assigning a price to the regulated behavior. Such a connotation is inconsistent with moral condemnation: while we might believe that charging a high price for a good makes the purchaser suffer, we do not condemn someone for buying what we are willing to sell. The sensibility that fines are morally neutral "price tags" seems to lie at the heart of resistance to fines among legislators, judges, sentencing commissioners, and ordinary citizens.

Community service also fails to express condemnation unambiguously. We do not ordinarily condemn persons who educate the retarded, install smoke detectors in nursing homes, restore dilapidated low-income housing, and the like; we admire them. Accordingly, when judges order offenders to engage in such services, members of the public have difficulty accepting that the law takes the underlying conduct seriously. In addition, by saying that such services are fit punishments for criminals, the law inadvertently insults both those who perform such services voluntarily and those whom the services are supposed to benefit. The dissonant connotations of community service as a punishment explain why it has made so little headway as an alternative to imprisonment.

Shaming punishments, in contrast, appear to be making much more headway. It is not the case that all offenders who receive shaming penalties would otherwise have been incarcerated, but many of them would have been. Among the offenses for which shaming penalties are now used are drunk driving, larceny, embezzlement, minor assaults, burglary, perjury, toxic-waste dumping, and drug distribution. When used for crimes such as these, shaming penalties free up imprisonment resources for offenders who more urgently demand incapacitation.

But shaming penalties are also emerging as a serious rival of imprisonment because they do something that conventional alternative sanctions do not: express appropriate moral condemnation. Such penalties, one court explained, "inflict disgrace and contumely in a dramatic and spectacular manner" (*Goldschmitt v. State*, 490 So. 2d 123, 125 (Fla. Dist. Ct. App. 1986)). Thus, like imprisonment but unlike fines and community service, shaming penalties supply an unambiguous and dramatic sign of the wrongdoer's disgrace. Insofar as shaming penalties do successfully convey condemnation, substituting them for imprisonment does not invariably offend widespread expressive sensibilities.

A taxonomy of contemporary shaming punishments

American courts have fashioned a wide variety of shaming punishments. Although categorizing them risks understating their diversity, these penalties can be grouped into four classes: stigmatizing publicity; literal stigmatization; self-debasement; and contrition.

Stigmatizing publicity is the most straightforward. Penalties in this class attempt to magnify the humiliation inherent in conviction by communicating the offender's status to a wider audience. Some municipalities, for example, publish offenders' names in newspapers or even display them on billboards, a disposition that is especially common for men convicted of soliciting prostitutes. Other jurisdictions broadcast the names of various types of offenders on community-access television channels.

Literal stigmatization is just that–the stamping of an offender with a mark or symbol that invites ridicule. Some judges order petty thieves to wear T-shirts announcing their crimes. Others achieve the same effect with brightly colored bracelets that read "DUI Convict," "I Write Bad Checks," and the like. One judge ordered a woman to wear a sign declaring "I am a convicted child molester."

Less dramatic but even more common are penalties that attach stigmatizing marks to property. Some jurisdictions now require persons guilty of drunk driving to display special license plates or bumper stickers. Courts have also ordered those convicted of sexual assaults and other crimes to post signs at their residences warning others to steer clear.

Self-debasement penalties involve ceremonies or rituals that publicly disgrace the offender. In a contemporary version of the stocks, for example, some communities require offenders simply to stand in public spaces (such as the local courthouse) with signs describing their offenses. More imaginative forms of self-debasement attempt to match the penalty to the character of the offense. A judge in Tennessee orders convicted burglars to permit their victims to enter their homes and remove items of their choosing. In New York, a slumlord was sentenced to house arrest in one of his rat-infested tenements (where tenants greeted him with the banner, "Welcome, You Reptile!"). Hoboken, New Jersey, requires Wall Street brokers (and others) who urinate in public to clean the city's streets. This is only a small sample; self-debasement sanctions are as diverse and particular as the crimes that they are used to punish.

Contrition penalties come in two forms. The first requires offenders to publicize their own convictions, describing their crimes in first-person terms and apologizing for them. These penalties combine stigmatizing publicity with an element of self-debasement; the sincerity of the offenders' remorse seems largely irrelevant.

Another form of contrition is the apology ritual. In Maryland, for example, juvenile offenders must apologize on their hands and knees, and are released from confinement only if their victims and government officials are persuaded that their remorse is sincere. Other jurisdictions use community-based sanctions that include public apologies and appropriate reparations. Because many of these penalties contemplate genuine rapprochement, apology rituals seem to be used primarily in cases in which the offender is connected to the victim by family or close community ties.

Legal issues

Shaming punishments have been subjected to two sorts of legal challenges, one constitutional, the other nonconstitutional. The constitutional challenge asserts that shaming punishments are "cruel and unusual" for purposes of the Eighth Amendment. This is a difficult claim to establish insofar as shaming is typically used as an alternative to a prison sentence, which tends to visit just as much humiliation on an offender as shaming but which adds a variety of other hardships. Unsurprisingly, all the courts that have considered Eighth Amendment challenges to shaming have rejected them (e.g., *People v. Letterlough,* 613 N.Y.S. 2d 687, 688 (1994), reviewed on other grounds, 631 N.Y.S. 2d 105 (1995); *Lindsay v. State,* 606 So. 2d 652, 657 (Fla. Dist. Ct. App. 1992); *Ballenger v. State,* 436 S.E.2d 793, 794–795 (Ga. 1993); *State v. Bateman,* 771 P.2d 314, 318 (Or. 1989); *Goldschmitt,* 490 So. 2d at 125–126.)

The nonconstitutional challenge is that judges lack the statutory authority to impose shaming punishments. This claim has proven relatively more successful. Typically, judges order shaming punishments as a condition of probation. Although sentencing statutes tend to vest judges with wide discretion to determine whether to grant probation and on what terms, they ordinarily require that such a sentence conduce to rehabilitation. Some appellate courts have held that shaming is thus an inappropriate probation condition because it is geared toward "punishing" rather than "rehabilitating" the offender (*People v. Meyer,* 680 N.E.2d 315 (Ill. 1997); *State v. Burdin,* 924 S.W.2d 82 (Tenn. 1996); *People v. Letterlough,* 631 N.Y.S.2d 105 (1995).) Paradoxically, in jurisdictions in which sentencing judges lack the authority to impose shame as a condition of probation, those judges might be more inclined to sentence offenders to prison, an unambiguously punitive disposition that likely impedes rehabilitation more than a shaming sentence does.

In practice, appellate decisions holding shame to be outside the scope of a sentencing judge's authority is not a major obstacle to the use of shaming punishments. Because it is not constitutional in nature, this limitation in judicial authority can be remedied by a statute expressly authorizing judges to shame offenders. More-over, offenders typically prefer shaming punishments to imprisonment. In most jurisdictions, the consent of the offender to a shaming punishment in lieu of imprisonment effectively immunizes his or her sentence from appellate review. Thus, judges have continued to impose shaming sanctions on consenting offenders even in states in which appellate courts have deemed shame to be outside the sentencing judge's statutory authority.

Policy issues

The most important questions posed by the advent of contemporary shaming penalties are normative ones. Criminal justice experts have engaged in a lively debate over whether such punishments are effective and just.

Deterrence.   Not surprisingly, the issue that has provoked the most dispute among policy analysts is whether shaming punishments are likely to be effective in deterring criminality. The best answer is that it is simply too early to say. Shaming punishments are still too new to have been subjected to rigorous empirical study. But at least one such study is well underway. With the cooperation of the Australian government, criminologist John Braithwaite has organized a large-scale experiment involving hundreds of convicted offenders who have received shaming sentences. The results of this study should help to bring the deterrence debate closer to a definitive resolution.

But because judges must decide what punishments to impose in the meantime, other analysts continue to present pragmatic conjectures on the likely effectiveness of shame. Shame proponents argue that shaming penalties are likely to deter for the same reason that other penalties, including imprisonment and fines, deter: because they hurt. Those who lose the respect of their peers can suffer a crippling diminishment of self-esteem. Moreover, criminal offenders are as likely to be shunned in the marketplace as they are in the public square, leading to serious financial hardship.

Shame skeptics question whether the threat of shame can effectively deter misconduct in modern urbanized societies, where social bonds are relatively loose and impersonal. The perceived inefficacy of shaming, they note, played a critical role in the shift from corporal punishment to imprisonment in nineteenth-century America.

Shame proponents acknowledge that shame may no longer be as potent a motivator as it was in colonial times, but assert that it would be a mistake to infer that that modern social conditions have vanquished shame altogether. A corporate executive deciding whether to authorize toxic waste dumping might not care that much what an auto mechanic in a remote part of town will think of him if he is caught and word of his offense is broadcast to the community at large. But he probably cares a lot about what his family, his colleagues, his firm's customers, his neighbors, and even the members of his health club think. Thus, the prospect of being disgraced in their eyes, shame proponents argue, continues to furnish a strong incentive—psychological, economic, and otherwise—to avoid criminality.

Critics also argue that shaming punishments are likely to deter unevenly across offenses. It is plausible to think that shaming will be less effective for offenses typically committed by the poor and disaffected, for example, than for offenses more likely to be committed by middle-class or affluent individuals, for whom the reputational cost of conviction is likely to be the largest.

Proponents respond that the selective efficacy of shame supplies a reason only to be selective about the use of shaming penalties, not to reject them wholesale. Even if many potential drug dealers and muggers are shameless (a proposition that not all shame advocates would concede), it seems unlikely that all potential drunk drivers, embezzlers, statutory rapists, tax evaders, and toxic-waste dumpers are.

Individual dignity.   The critics of shaming punishments also invoke the value of individual dignity. It is inappropriate, they argue, for the law deliberately to humiliate or degrade anyone, even criminal offenders.

In proponents' view, the dignity objection ignores the practical consequences of denying judges the authority to shame. Shaming punishments are an alternative to imprisonment. Imprisonment also humiliates and degrades; indeed, the power of liberty deprivation as a symbol of the offender's sunken status is exactly what explains the public's stubborn preference for imprisonment over less expressive alternatives such as fines and community service. Moreover, as a practical matter, imprisonment imposes a host of indignities that shame cannot hope to rival, from physical confinement to the exposure of private bodily functions to physical violence at the hand of other inmates.

Because shaming penalties are typically imposed as a condition of probation, offenders can opt for imprisonment over shaming if they prefer by declining to accept probation on such terms. Unsurprisingly, offenders rarely if ever choose jail over shame. Critics who object to shame as contrary to individual dignity, the proponents point out, find themselves in the paradoxical position of arguing that society must disregard the individual offender's own preferences in order to treat him or her with respect.

The most sophisticated reply to this defense of shaming treats "dignity" not as an individual good only but as a public one as well. According to this argument (Whitman), shaming punishments—particularly in their most dramatic and ritualistic forms—risk creating a public appetite for degradation that imprisonment, because of its relative low visibility and antiseptic profile, does not risk creating. The result of adding shame to the schedule of criminal punishments, these critics fear, will be a less dignified regime of criminal administration, and ultimately a less civilized tone of public life.

Equality.   The critics and advocates of shaming also disagree about whether this form of punishment is consistent with the value of equality. Like fines and community service, shaming penalties are not suitable for all offenders. Shaming punishments probably will not be nearly as effective for some offenders as they would be for others, including white-collar ones. Even more important, some offenders require incapacitation and not just condemnation. Making what is probably the most compelling objection to shaming, critics argue that it violates equality to punish these offenders with imprisonment while merely shaming white-collar or other nonviolent offenders who commit crimes of equal moral culpability.

Shaming proponents point out that we can assess the equivalence of punishments along multiple dimensions, including their expressive power, their regulatory effect, and their painfulness. To indict a particular alternative sanction on grounds of equality, then, requires showing not only that that sanction differs in one or more of these ways from imprisonment but that the difference is morally relevant.

Expressive significance is one dimension of equivalence that clearly matters from a moral point of view. Fines and community service, for example, do not express condemnation as clearly as imprisonment does; because condemnation is essential to punishment, imprisoning one offender while ordering another equally culpable one to pay a fine or to perform community service creates an objectionable form of inequality.

Corporal punishment has also been understood to express inequality because against the background of historically rooted social norms, this mode of discipline connotes the offender's natural or social inferiority.

Shaming, its advocates contend, does not suffer from either of these defects. It clearly does express condemnation; that is exactly why it is succeeding in replacing imprisonment for certain offenses. Yet shaming does not express hierarchy. The particular sorts of shaming penalties now being enforced by American judges are free of any historical association with slavery or other forms of inequality.

Regulatory effect is another dimension of equivalence that clearly matters. But again, at least according to the shaming advocates, there is little reason to believe that shame will not be roughly as effective in deterring crime as the short terms of imprisonment that nonviolent offenders would otherwise likely receive.

Finally there is the dimension of painfulness. It seems plausible to think that even short terms of imprisonment are more painful than dramatic shaming rituals. But shaming advocates deny that this inequivalence matters from a moral point of view. The idea that the justice of punishment should be measured in the currency of pain is a recognizable form of retributivism, but it is surely the one that has the least to recommend it. Suffering, abstracted from all else, should not be a goal of punishment. If shaming is good enough from expressive and deterrence points of view, shaming advocates conclude, let's just get on with it and not worry about whether we are hurting criminals enough.

DAN M. KAHAN

See also DETERRENCE; RESTORATIVE JUSTICE; RETRIBUTIVISM; SENTENCING: ALTERNATIVES.

BIBLIOGRAPHY

BRAITHWAITE, JOHN. *Crime, Shame, and Reintegration.* Cambridge, U.K.: Cambridge University Press, 1989.
———. "Shame and Modernity." *British Journal of Criminology* 33 (1993): 1–19.
BRAITHWAITE, JOHN, AND MUGFORD, STEPHEN. "Conditions of Successful Reintegration Ceremonies." *British Journal of Criminology* 2 (1994): 139–160.
FEINBERG, JOEL. "The Expressive Function of Punishment." In *Doing and Deserving: Essays in the Theory of Responsibility.* Edited by Joel Feinberg. Princeton, N.J.: Princeton Press, 1970. Pages 95–121.
GARVEY, STEPHEN P. "Can Shaming Punishments Educate?" *University of Chicago Law Review* 65 (1998): 733–794.
HINDUS, MICHAEL S. *Prison and Plantation: Crime, Justice, and Authority in Massachusetts and South Carolina, 1767–1878.* Chapel Hill: University of North Carolina Press, 1980.
HIRSCH, ADAM J. *The Rise of the Penitentiary: Prisons and Punishments in Early America.* New Haven: Yale University Press, 1992.
HOFFMAN, JAN. "Crime and Punishment: Shame Gains Popularity." *New York Times,* 17 January 1997, page A1.
KAHAN, DAN M., and POSNER, ERIC A. "Shaming White-Collar Criminals: A Proposal for Reform of the Federal Sentencing Guidelines." *Journal of Law and Economics* 42 (1999): 365–391.
KAHAN, DAN M. "What Do Alternative Sanctions Mean?" *University of Chicago Law Review* 63 (1997): 591–653.
MASSARO, TONI M. "Shame, Culture, and American Criminal Law." *Michigan Law Review* 89 (June 1991): 1880–1944.
———. "The Meanings of Shame: Implications for Legal Reform." *Psychology, Public Policy, and Law* 3 (1997): 645–704.
New York Times. "Alternative Sentencing." *New York Times,* 20 January 1997, p. A16.
WHITMAN, JAMES Q. "What's Wrong with Inflicting Shame Sanctions?" *Yale Law Journal* 107 (January 1998): 1055–1092.

SHOPLIFTING

Shoplifting is a form of larceny, a taking and carrying away of the property of another with fraudulent intent—traditionally, intent permanently to deprive the true owner thereof. Since the goods taken are items held for sale, the intent to deprive involves an intent to obtain the goods without paying for them or without paying the full price, for example, by changing the marked price. As a form of larceny under traditional American statutes, shoplifting is a misdemeanor or a felony depending on the value of the property taken. In most cases shoplifting will be a misdemeanor, since American statutes make larceny a felony only if property of substantial value is taken. In a few states, all shoplifting offenses are felonies (Note, 1971, p. 866).

Application of the law

The application of the law of larceny to shoplifting requires proof of wrongful taking. In order to prove that the taking was with fraudulent intent, must store personnel wait until the subject has left the store without paying for the goods, or is concealment of the goods or failure to pay at the place where the goods would normally be paid for sufficient? The problems of proof are compounded by the risks to merchants who act on unfounded suspicion. Under the law of many American jurisdictions, even an honest attempt to arrest on reasonable grounds may be wrongful if no misdemeanor was in fact committed by the person arrested. A customer wrongfully accused or unlawfully detained or arrested may have a legal claim to compensation for slander, false arrest, or false imprisonment. Additionally, more and more people are becoming (rightly) concerned about the injustices of "racial profiling" in shoplifting, where store employees use race as a primary heuristic for suspicion (Austin). A substantial judgment against a store that has acted improperly poses great financial risks for the merchant (Keeton and Prosser).

Changes in substantive law

Most states have responded to the substantive and procedural problems by enacting special shoplifting statutes (Comment, 1973a, pp. 312–314). The substantive difficulty of proving fraudulent intent and the wrongfulness of the taking of possession is sometimes resolved by a provision making concealment of merchandise or similar acts criminal. Thus, the New Jersey code of criminal procedure (N.J. Stat. Ann. tit. 2C: 20–11 (1999)) defines shoplifting to include purposely concealing merchandise offered for sale with the intention of depriving the merchant of such merchandise without paying for it. The New Jersey code also defines other essentially preparatory acts as shoplifting when done with the requisite intent: altering or removing any label or price tag, or transferring merchandise from the container in which it is displayed to any other container. Such conduct indicates an intent to deprive and constitutes an exercise of wrongful dominion over the merchant's property even though the taker has not yet left the merchant's premises or the area in which it would be appropriate to pay for the goods. Indeed, the statutes of a number of states recognize a presumption of intent to deprive from concealment of merchandise.

Procedural innovations

Perhaps more significant than the changes in the substantive law of theft are the procedural provisions authorizing merchants and their employees to detain suspected shoplifters. These statutes, such as that in Illinois (720 ILCS 5/16A-5, A-6 (1999)) take the form of specific provisions authorizing detention on reasonable grounds and providing merchants and their employees immunity from civil liability to a person so detained. Some states permit searches of a suspected shoplifter. The Iowa statute requires, however, that unless made with the permission of the suspect, the search be made under the direction of a peace officer (Iowa Code Ann. § 808.12 (1999)).

In addition to authorizing detention of suspected shoplifters, the statutes usually provide immunity from civil liability from a person so detained, either in general terms or with reference to such specific actions as slander, false arrest, false imprisonment, and unlawful detention (Note, 1971, pp. 836–837). The statutory immunity will depend on the existence of reasonable cause to detain the suspect and the reasonableness of the detention under all the circumstances, including time, manner, and place of detention (Comment, 1973b, pp. 162–165). Worthy of specific note is Michigan's statute, which does not provide complete immunity to the merchant even for reasonable detentions (Mich. Compiled Laws Ann. 600.2917 (1999); *Bonkowski v. Arlan's Department Store*, 383 Mich. 90, 174 N.W.2d 765 (1970)). While the merchant will not be liable for damages "resulting from mental anguish" nor for "punitive, exemplary or aggravated damages," compensatory damages may be awarded. Thus, if the person detained can show actual injury or monetary loss resulting from the merchant's action in arresting or detaining him, he will be able to obtain compensation for such injury or loss.

Despite the proliferation of such statutes designed to deter shoplifting and provide protection to merchants, shoplifting continues to increase. The statutes have apparently not been fully effective in motivating merchants and their employees to initiate action against suspected shoplifters.

It seems likely that shoplifting will continue to be a substantial problem for merchants unless the public comes to recognize it as a crime of serious economic consequence. Perhaps the most effective means of dealing with the problem is a combination of approaches designed to make the public more aware of the costs of shoplifting and the likelihood of prosecution and conviction. Under such a multilevel approach the law will have a role to play, but so will efforts at public education and private measures by merchants to deter and detect retail theft.

LIONEL FRANKEL

See also POLICE: PRIVATE POLICE AND INDUSTRIAL SECURITY; THEFT.

BIBLIOGRAPHY

AUSTIN, REGINA. "A Nation of Thieves: Securing Black People's Right to Shop and to Sell in White America." *Utah Law Review* (1994): 147–177.

BLANKENBURG, ERHARD. "The Selectivity of Legal Sanctions: An Empirical Investigation of Shoplifting." *Law and Society Review* 11 (1976): 109–130.

Comment. "Shoplifting Law: Constitutional Ramifications of Merchant Detention Statutes." *Hofstra Law Review* 1 (1973a): 295–314.

Comment. "Shoplifting: Protection for Merchants in Wisconsin." *Marquette Law Review* 57 (1973b): 141–169.

Comment "Stopping and Questioning Suspected Shoplifters without Creating Civil Liability." *Mississippi Law Journal* 47 (1976): 260–277.

HUBER, BARBARA. "The Dilemma of Decriminalisation: Dealing with Shoplifting in West Germany." *Criminal Law Review* (1980): 621–627.

KEETON, W. PAGE, and PROSSER, WILLIAM L. *Prosser and Keeton on Torts,* 5th ed. St. Paul, Minn.: West, 1984.

LUNDMAN, RICHARD. "Shoplifting and Police Referral: A Reexamination." *Journal of Criminal Law and Criminology* 69 (1978): 395–401.

Note. "The Merchant, the Shoplifter, and the Law." *Minnesota Law Review* 55 (1971): 825–869.

Note. "Merchants' Responses to Shoplifting: An Empirical Study." *Stanford Law Review* 28 (1976): 589–612.

SOLICITATION

Introduction

Solicitation, or incitement, is the act of trying to persuade another person to commit a crime that the solicitor desires and intends to have committed. Occasionally this type of criminal activity is defined in terms of a specific substantive offense, making it criminal, for example, to offer a bribe, to suborn perjury, to incite a riot, or to advocate overthrow of the government. Such activity is also dealt with in a general fashion, however, simply by punishing one who invokes another to commit a crime.

Variously known as *advising, commanding, counseling, encouraging, enticing, entreating, hiring, importuning, inciting, instigating, procuring, requesting, stimulating,* and *urging,* or referred to by other terms descriptive of attempting to persuade another (the solicitant) to commit a crime, solicitation traditionally exists only when the crime solicited (the object crime) has not been completed, criminally attempted, or agreed to. If the solicitant agrees to commit the crime, both he and the solicitor are liable for conspiracy; if the solicitant attempts to commit the crime, both are liable for attempt; if the solicitant actually completes the crime, the solicitor is liable, under principles of accomplice liability, for being either an accessory before the fact or a principal in the crime that he solicited. Although under the common law the solicitor could be liable for the crime of solicitation only when the solicitant rejected the request, under some statutory schemes (like in Alabama and Illinois), the solicitor may be found guilty whether or not the solicited crime was ever actually committed.

The rationale for the crime is that deliberate inducement of another to commit a crime posits a danger calling for preventive intervention and manifests sufficient danger in the solicitor to warrant criminal liability. The case against criminalizing such activity is that the uncertainty that the object crime will ever be endeavored or committed—in part because the solicitor has shown an unwillingness to commit that crime himself, placing an independent actor between him and the potential crime—signifies that the unsuccessful solicitation is too far removed from any actual harm to present a genuine social danger and, therefore, to warrant criminal sanction. Its emphasis, like that of other inchoate—or relational or anticipatory—crimes, comes too close to punishing evil thoughts or intentions alone.

These competing arguments have produced considerable tension in the United States and other countries, including England, France, Italy, and Germany, as well as a diversity of substantive and procedural principles that are designed both to promote effective law enforcement and to minimize the dangers of abuse and overextension.

Common law development

Background. The crime of solicitation has its roots in English common law, at which the solicitation of another to comma a felony, an aggravated misdemeanor, or an offense that disturbed the public peace or was detrimental to the public welfare was punishable as a misdemeanor. Although there are suggestions that the crime first appeared in England as early as 1704, it was not until 1801, in the bellwether case of *Rex v. Higgins*, 102 Eng. Rep. 269 (K.B. 1801), that solicitation was adjudged to be a distinct substantive common law offense. Holding that the bare solicitation of a servant to steal his master's goods, although the servant had ignored the request, was an indictable offense, the court rejected the contention that the crime punished a person solely for having criminal intentions: "It is argued, that a mere intent to commit evil is not indictable, without an act done; but is there not an act done, when it is charged that the defendant solicited another to commit a felony? The solicitation is an act" (*Higgins*, 274).

Elements of the crime. Any encouragement, probably including a mere suggestion, was a sufficient actus reus, or guilty act. Even invoking evil spirits to cast a spell or give the evil eye was proscribed. Further, the communication need not be a personal one; solicitation could occur when the inducement was directed to a group of people or to the general public. Nor must the inducement be oral; it could even appear in a newspaper article. But, in the case of a written inducement to commit a crime, there was a split of authority at common law as to whether the communication had to reach the intended party in order to satisfy the necessary actus reus. Those courts that did not find solicitation, however, nevertheless convicted the writer of attempt to solicit, thus criminally punishing the actor for even more distant conduct. In either case, the punishment was justified on the ground that the solicitor's attempt to communicate was sufficient manifestation of his criminal design.

The requisite mens rea, or state of mind, of solicitation was the purpose (sometimes called specific intent) to have the object crime committed. When this mental element concurred in time with the communication, the crime of solicitation was complete. If the solicitor believed, therefore, that the object crime could be consummated, he was liable for solicitation, notwithstanding the impossibility of the crime either at the time of the communication or at some later time.

Defenses. It is unclear whether, at common law, a voluntary and complete renunciation or abandonment of the criminal purpose would serve as a defense to solicitation, for there is no conclusive case law on the point (and as statutory law has now overwhelmed the common law in the area of criminal justice, there is unlikely to be one in the future). The argument in favor of such a defense is that the renunciation demonstrates that the solicitor has negated his prior dangerousness; moreover, the existence of the defense would provide him an incentive to halt his criminal activity before the commission of the crime. On the other hand, to the extent that solicitation aims at one who has indicated his antisocial tendencies, simply because he abandons his criminal intention on one occasion does not necessarily negate his future criminality. He has also planted the seed of criminal conduct in the mind of another.

Statutory development

Background. While the common law has retained much importance, statutory proscriptions against solicitation have increased. For example, by 1961 only nine states had cataloged solicitation as a general substantive crime; by the end of the century the number had risen to more than thirty. This dramatic increase indicates that society, through its legislative voice, has recognized solicitation as a sufficiently significant public harm to require penal sanction, for, where the common law of crimes has been abolished by statute, without appropriate legislation solicitation even to commit a felony might not constitute a crime.

State statutes employ various criteria to define the crime of solicitation indicating fundamental differences in criminal justice policy and practice. Most commonly addressed in the statutes are the following five factors: types of crimes indictable as criminal solicitations, elements of the crime, existence of a corroboration requirement as a limitation on the crime, degree of punishment, and available defenses.

Types of crimes indictable. Unlike the common law, which generally (and vaguely) described the object crimes covered by solicitation as those that breached the public peace, state statutes refer to their own systems of criminal classification—misdemeanors and felonies. In this way, the legislatures are able to control the nature and scope of crime, thereby restricting judicial interpretation and discretion. Many states impose penalties for soliciting the commission of any crime; others apply it only to felonies. The California statute, for example, specifically enumerates the particular object felonies that are subject to solicitation charges, such as murder, felonious assault, kidnapping, and arson. Other states, like Kansas, Louisiana, Colorado, and Michigan, criminalize the solicitation of felonies generally, but not misdemeanors.

Elements of the crime. Since solicitation, like the other inchoate crimes of attempt and conspiracy, is a specific-intent crime, every state solicitation statute requires that the solicitor's menial state be either an intent to cause the solicitant to commit or attempt to commit the object crime, or be sufficient to establish the solicitant's complicity in its commission or attempted commission. Some states have broadened the sting of solicitation by holding the solicitor liable even when the commission of the object crime is contingent on double inchoateness. For example, if A solicits B to solicit C to commit a crime, A could be convicted of solicitation.

Several states expressly include in solicitation the attempt to solicit. Thus, if A writes a letter soliciting B to kill C but is prevented from mailing the letter, A can still be held liable for solicitation; the theory is that he should not escape punishment because of a fortuitous event beyond his control.

An interesting and important feature in many states' definitions of the actus reus of solicitation is the focus on promoting or facilitating the commission or attempted commission of a crime. Such an element incorporates the otherwise separate crime of facilitation—which penalizes the giving of assistance in cases in which the object crime is not committed—into the solicitation statute, in effect extending greater criminal punishment to persons who are even more remotely involved in criminal activity. This vexatious question of line drawing is, of course, common to the many facets of inchoate crime.

Corroboration requirement. Because of this perplexing issue, some states deal with the potential injustice resulting from charges of solicitation by imposing a requirement of corroboration. This limitation essentially mandates that the state substantiate its charge by introducing extrinsic evidence to support the solicitor's intent to promote criminal activity. Several states, like California, Maine, and Colo-

rado, require either the corroboration of two witnesses, or one witness plus corroborating circumstances. Iowa provides that the corroboration must be demonstrated by clear and convincing evidence, rather than by some lesser standard. North Dakota requires that the solicitant commit, in response to the solicitation, an overt act in furtherance of the object crime. Such a condition goes beyond he traditional definition of solicitation, making its elements more closely resemble those of attempt and conspiracy.

Degree of punishment. The severity of punishment for the commission of an offense is a strong indication of the legislature's perception of the crime. Naturally, the more serious the crime is considered to be, the harsher the penalty ought to be. Thus, one might expect that the penalty for solicitation would be less than that for attempt, and certainly less than that for the object crime. Most states conform to this expectation, by providing sanctions that either are less severe than those for attempt or are described as being one grade less than the range of sanctions for the object crime.

Yet several states prescribe the same punishment for solicitation as for attempt, and some have enacted sanctions that are identical to those for the completed crime, making exception only for very serious offenses. The justification for this approach is that the solicitation, as an expression of the solicitor's intent, is sufficiently injurious to the public that it merits punishment without regard to its consequences.

Defenses. The most common statutory defense, offered for instance by Alabama, Colorado, Delaware, Florida, Kansas, Kentucky, and Michigan, is that of renunciation, or abandonment. It is an affirmative defense that is available only if the solicitor voluntarily prevents the commission of the object crime. His voluntariness is measured not by fear that his chances of apprehension have increased but rather by his sense of repentance or change of heart.

Another defense that is sometimes codified provides, as does the common law, that under substantive or accessorial principles, the solicitor could not be held liable for the substantive offense. The rationale for this defense is that, since the legislature chose not to impose punishment for the completed crime (as with a minor who has intercourse with an adult), to sanction a solicitation to commit that crime would be inconsistent and would frustrate the objectives of the substantive criminal law. Other jurisdictions, however, disagree, and explicitly reject such a defense.

Finally, the solicitant's criminal irresponsibility or other legal incapacity or exemption typically is no defense to the solicitor.

Model Penal Code

No discussion of solicitation could be complete without examining the relevant provisions of the American Law Institute's Model Penal Code, after which many state statutes have been and are likely to be patterned, at least in part.

On the threshold question of whether there should exist a separate substantive crime of solicitation, the drafters of the Code concluded emphatically in favor of criminalization: "Purposeful solicitation presents dangers calling for preventive intervention and is sufficiently indicative of a disposition towards criminal activity to call for liability" (§ 5.02).

The Code would impose liability for the solicitation of *any* crime, if the solicitor specifically intends that the object crime be attempted or completed. A conviction for solicitation also would attach to the solicitor if the conduct of the solicitant would establish his guilt under a theory of complicity (§ 5.02(1)). Exemplifying the strict view of the Code toward solicitation is the additional provision that treats attempt to solicit as a criminal offense (§ 5.02(2)). This section makes the actual communication immaterial to prosecution as long as there was an intent to effect such communication, for the actor has demonstrated his need for corrective sanction.

The mental state for solicitation is defined in terms of acting "with the purpose of promoting or facilitating" the commission of a crime (§ 5.02(1)). Moreover, the Code does not require corroboration of the solicitor's intent.

Taken together, these provisions suggest quite clearly that the American Law Institute designed a solicitation statute that would be both immediately applicable to many situations and far-reaching in its impact. This conclusion is confirmed by the defenses that are expressly recognized in the Code—renunciation and the immunity of the solicitor to prosecution for the object crime (§§ 5.02(3), 5.04(2))—as well as by those that are omitted. The mental state of the solicitant is immaterial if the solicitor believed that the solicitant could perform the solicited act (§ 5.04(1)). Coinciding with its position that impossibility is no defense to the crime of attempt, the Code would probably also reject such a defense to a charge of solicitation, although there is no specific provision on this point. The solici-

tor's culpability would be measured by the circumstances as he believes them to be.

The offense grade and degree of punishment for solicitation, attempt, and conspiracy alike under the Code correspond to the most serious offense solicited, attempted, or conspired. Departure from this classification occurs only when the offense is a capital crime or a first-degree felony, in which instances the inchoate offense is one of the second degree (§ 5.05 (1)). The drafters sought to temper the harshness of this grading section by incorporating a mitigation provision, pursuant to which if the court finds that the inchoate crime charged "is so inherently unlikely to result . . . in the commission of a crime," the judge is permitted to reduce the grade of the crime or, in extreme cases, to dismiss the indictment (§ 5.05(2)). Despite this allowance for a modicum of judicial discretion, the overall impact of the Model Penal Code's solicitation provisions is severe.

Conclusion

Both sides of the controversy on solicitation are meritorious, from certain perspectives. Those who instigate criminal activity do represent a threat to law and order and should be held accountable. Law enforcement authorities should be able to stop crime before actual harm, often very serious, occurs. But solicitation, which in essence is an attempt to conspire, has the potential of imposing liability too far back in time, before the object crime is ever even attempted. It can thus be subject to great abuse, with the police incorrectly construing equivocal behavior as part of an endeavor to commit a crime.

If solicitation is to be proscribed, one alternative that can minimize the risk of abuse is to draft statutes precisely, with appropriate regard for the scope and grading of each crime and its punishment and with such precautionary safeguards as a corroboration or overt-act requirement. Attention should also be given to the free-speech implications of solicitation, for legitimate agitation of an extreme nature can easily be misinterpreted as solicitation to commit crime, resulting in either direct or indirect suppression of speech.

Another possible approach to solicitation is to view it not as a distinct crime but rather as a step in the direction of crime, on the continuum of preparatory acts that also includes facilitation, conspiracy, and attempt. Indeed, a major debate in the criminal law is whether to treat all inchoate criminal activity as forms of criminal attempt. To do this intelligently would require a reconsideration of basic principles of the law of attempt—particularly the traditional distinction between acts of preparation and acts of perpetration—as well as of schemes of punishment.

Whatever approach is ultimately adopted, above all it must be recognized that the criminalization of solicitation is an experiment, both in dealing with human behavior and in drawing lines between innocent and culpable conduct at the borders of criminality; it is a balancing of acts and intentions, of predicting and preventing harmful conduct.

IRA P. ROBBINS
DAN M. KAHAN

See also ACCOMPLICES; ATTEMPT; CONSPIRACY.

BIBLIOGRAPHY

American Law Institute. *Model Penal Code and Commentaries: Official Draft and Revised Comments.* Philadelphia: ALI, 1985.
Annotation. "Construction and Effect of Statutes Making Solicitation to Commit Crime a Substantive Offense." *American Law Reports,* vol. 51. 2d series. Rochester, N.Y.: Lawyers Cooperative, 1957, pp. 953–962.
Annotation. "Solicitation to Crime as a Substantive Common-law Offense." *American Law Reports, Annotated* 35 (1925): 961–969.
BLACKBURN, JAMES B. "Solicitation to Crimes." *West Virginia Law Quarterly* 40 (1934): 135–150.
CURRAN, JOHN W. "Solicitations: A Substantive Crime." *Minnesota Law Review* 17 (1933): 499–512.
LAFAVE, WAYNE R., and SCOTT, AUSTIN W., JR. *Handbook on Criminal Law,* 2nd ed. St. Paul, Minn.: West, 1986.
ROBBINS, IRA P. "Double Inchoate Crimes." *Harv. J. Legis* 26 (1989): 1–116.
TORCIA, CHARLES E., ed. *Wharton's Criminal Law,* 15th ed. Deerfield, Ill.: Clark Boardman Callaghan, 1989.
WECHSLER, HERBERT; JONES, WILLIAM KENNETH; and KORN, HAROLD L. "The Treatment of Inchoate Crimes in the Model Penal Code of the American Law Institute: Attempt, Solicitation, and Conspiracy." *Columbia Law Review* 61 (1961): 571–628.

SPEEDY TRIAL

The right to a speedy trial finds expression in the U.S. Constitution, state constitutions, state and federal statutory law, and state and federal case law. The Sixth Amendment to the U.S. Constitution, and the case law surrounding this amendment, provide the best place to start analysis of the basic questions of primary concern: What interests does the right protect? When and why are these interests triggered? And how should these interests be protected, both to prevent their violation whenever possible and to remedy the effects of violations when violations nonetheless occur?

The words of the Sixth Amendment guarantee, among other things, that "In all criminal prosecutions, the accused shall enjoy the right to a speedy . . . trial." Although this right, like everything else in the Bill of Rights, originally applied only against the federal government (*Barron v. Baltimore,* 32 U.S. (7 Pet.) 243 (1833)), it has since been "incorporated" via the Fourteenth Amendment to apply to the states as well (*Klopfer v. North Carolina,* 386 U.S. 213 (1967)). In a nutshell, the Framers designed the right to protect a person from prolonged de facto punishment—extended accusations that limit his liberty and besmirch his good name—before he has had a full and fair chance to defend himself. If government accuses someone, it must give him the right, speedily, to clear himself at trial and regain his good name and full liberty. And if government holds the accused in extended pretrial detention, courts must ensure that the accuracy of the trial itself will not thereby be undermined—as might occur if a defendant's prolonged detention itself causes the loss of key exculpatory evidence.

A series of cases decided by the Supreme Court during the second half of the twentieth century laid down seven general propositions concerning the constitutional right to a speedy trial. (1) The Court has repeatedly identified three major and distinct interests protected by the Sixth Amendment speedy trial clause: an interest in avoiding prolonged pretrial detention, an interest in minimizing the anxiety and loss of reputation accompanying formal public accusation, and an interest in assuring the ultimate fairness of a delayed trial. (2) The Court has made clear that the major evils of pretrial restraints on liberty and loss of reputation occasioned by accusation exist quite apart from the third major evil of possible prejudice to an accused's defense at trial. (3) The Court has held that the clause simply does not apply to the time between the commission of the crime and the time that the defendant is in some way "accused" (usually by arrest or indictment) by the government. In other words, the clause applies only to the formal "accusation period"—the period between governmental accusation and trial. (4) Relatedly, the Court has held that the clause does not apply to any period during which the government drops its initial charges while retaining the right to re-indict later—the defendant is not "accused" during this time, and so the speedy trial clock stops ticking against the government during this period. (5) The Court has held that if preaccusation delay compromises the defendant's ability to defend herself, the main safeguard against injustice comes from the applicable statute of limitations. In cases of substantial prejudice to a fair trial caused by a prosecutor's purely strategic delay in bringing the initial accusation, defendants may also seek relief by appealing to general due process principles. (6) The Court has said that the judicial remedy for speedy trial violations of dismissing the case with prejudice—that is, dismissing with no possibility of refiling charges later—is unsatisfactorily severe because it means that a defendant who may be guilty of a serious crime will go free, without ever having been tried. Such a remedy, the Court has noted, is more severe than the Fourth Amendment exclusionary rule, which limits the introduction of certain evidence, but typically does not altogether bar a trial. (7) Nonetheless, the Court has repeatedly held that dismissal with prejudice is the only possible remedy for speedy trial clause violations. Given the first six propositions, the analytic soundness of proposition seven seems questionable to some scholars, although the law appears quite clear on this point.

It may be seen that the first of the principles set out above suggests that each of the three interests protected by the clause may have a different time limit. Imagine, for simplicity, a case in which the liberty interest would be violated by anything more than a month of pretrial detention: by hypothesis, any detention longer than this would be an unacceptable deprivation of liberty for a man who has yet to receive all the safeguards of a full-blown trial—a man who has not yet been, and may never be, convicted of anything. Now imagine a second defendant, charged with the identical crime but released on her own recognizance pending trial. In this second case, no pretrial detention interest exists, and her distinct anxiety and reputation interest would not necessarily be violated by a similar one-month gap between indictment and trial. For example, a full year might elapse before this distinct consti-

tutional interest—which demands that at some point an accused person must be allowed to answer the government's accusation and thereby clear her good name—would be violated. The fair trial interest may have a different time period still, depending on the particular ways in which the government's accusation threatens to impede a defendant's ability to fully defend himself at trial. For example, some pretrial detentions might severely obstruct the defendant's ability to assemble evidence and witnesses for his trial defense; other detentions might not, depending on the particular conditions of confinement and state of the evidence; and still other indictments will not involve any pretrial detention.

Moreover, it is clear that the clause is violated by overlong detention regardless of what happens later on: an impermissibly lengthy detention violates the clause whether it ends in a trial or in the charges being dropped. So far as the pretrial liberty interest is concerned, it is the detention, and not the trial, that violates the speedy trial clause. This is suggested by the second proposition: the pretrial liberty and reputation interests are independent of the conditions of the trial, as the Court made clear in the 1971 case of *United States v. Marion*, 404 U.S. 307. *Marion* also illustrated the third proposition in upholding, against a Sixth Amendment challenge, an indictment handed down three years after prosecutors supposedly knew about the crime and defendants' involvement in it; the defendants, said the Court, were simply not "accused" during those three years. In accordance with the fifth proposition, the Court ruled that the statute of limitations was the defendants' primary safeguard, and further noted that if defendants could show substantial prejudice to their defense created by a bad-faith prosecutor seeking delay simply to gain tactical advantage, a due process challenge would be appropriate.

Thus, the speedy trial clause is *accusation-based*: it applies only to harms caused when and because one is "accused." (The 1992 case of *Doggett v. United States*, 505 U.S. 647, decided by a 5–4 vote, might be thought inconsistent with this general statement, but on careful analysis it is not. In *Doggett*, which involved an indictment that was allowed to linger for eight years, the accusation itself did indeed cause harm to the defendant, because the indictment tolled the relevant five-year statute of limitations. Perhaps the best way of explaining *Doggett*'s result—if not all its language—is to say that the case involved the interaction of the Sixth Amendment and the statute of limitations; the proper rule to be derived from the case is that if an accusation period is unconstitutionally long under the Sixth Amendment, the indictment should automatically lapse, and thus cease to toll the statute of limitations, whose clock begins to tick again.)

This accusation-based interpretive scheme makes functional and textual sense. If the three major evils of speedy trial clause violations are loss of liberty, loss of reputation, and harm to the defendant's ability to defend herself at trial, then it seems clear that the speedy trial clause is applicable only during the time that a person is in custody or under indictment. After all, it is accusation itself that triggers the threat to the liberty, reputation, and fair trial interests. A person who has not been arrested suffers no loss of liberty; a person not under arrest or indictment suffers no formal government-created loss of reputation; nor does such a person face an upcoming trial. All of the harms, however, become imminent upon arrest or indictment—upon accusation. The accusation-based language of the clause strongly reinforces this analysis; its words come into effect only when a person becomes "the accused"—typically, by arrest or indictment. Elsewhere, the Sixth Amendment speaks of the district in which "the crime shall have been committed." If the speedy trial clock were meant to begin ticking before arrest or indictment, it would have made more sense to speak of the "time at which the crime shall have been committed" in the speedy trial clause. Instead, the use of the word "accused" indicates that it takes effect only after arrest or indictment. Of course, this is not to say that a prosecutor may properly wait as long as he likes to file charges (perhaps in the hopes that key defense evidence will fade away or defense witnesses disappear). As proposition (5) reminds us, statutes of limitations provide the primary defense against this kind of prosecutorial abuse, and due process principles are applicable as well.

Although the Constitution speaks of a speedy trial as the right of the "accused," the Court has recognized that society at large also has its own legitimate interests in the prompt resolution of criminal accusations. Many defendants—especially guilty defendants—might prefer to delay their trials, perhaps in the hopes that prosecutorial evidence will become stale, making it more difficult for the government to carry its ultimate burden of proof beyond reasonable doubt. But the Constitution does not give a de-

fendant a general right to an "unspeedy" trial—unlike, for example, the Sixth Amendment right of counsel, which is accompanied by a general right not to have counsel (see *Farretta v. California*, 422 U.S. 806 (1975)). Nevertheless, at some extreme point, an accusation period could be so short as to violate general due process principles: a defendant must be given sufficient time to arrange his defense, as the Supreme Court recognized in its famous ruling in the so-called Scottsboro case (*Powell v. Alabama*, 287 U.S. 45 (1932)).

In light of this analysis of the nature and the timing of speedy trial clause rights, it remains to ponder how these rights should be legally protected and remedied. Although the Court has said that dismissal with prejudice is the only possible remedy, there are reasons to doubt the analytical soundness of this assertion. Consider the first interest protected by the clause, the bodily liberty interest offended by overlong pretrial detention. Judges can simply refuse to allow this violation to happen by issuing writs of habeas corpus directing the release of prisoners who have served as much pretrial time in jail as the clause will tolerate. Historically, the history of the speedy trial right in England tightly intertwined with the famous English Habeas Corpus Act of 1679. However, habeas is less a remedy than a means of prevention. What should the remedy be when the judge fails to issue a writ? One controversial possibility would be to allow for compensatory and punitive damages directly against the government. Extending its landmark ruling in *Bivens v. Six Unknown Agents of the Federal Bureau of Narcotics*, 403 U.S. 388 (1971), which held that government officials who conducted unreasonable searches could be sued directly under the Fourth Amendment, the Court could find a direct cause of action against the government itself under the Sixth Amendment's speedy trial clause. Indeed, unconstitutionally long detentions would seem to be a subset of unreasonable seizures of persons, and so the Fourth Amendment might seem directly applicable as well. The prospects for such a doctrinal development, however, seem bleak. The most natural damage remedy would lie against the government itself. (Judges who ordered the detention would enjoy judicial immunity; prosecutors who allowed the defendant to languish in jail pretrial would likewise claim that a court had authorized the detention; and the jailer would insist that he was acting in good faith reliance upon a judicial order of confinement.) But principles of sovereign immunity would likely make it difficult to prevail in a damage suit brought directly against the government, even though its executive and judicial agents combined to deprive a defendant of his constitutional rights to bodily liberty.

Similarly, for the second speedy trial interest—reputation—the judge can prevent violations by simply quashing indictments that linger too long, with permission to reindict whenever the prosecutor is ready to proceed immediately to trial. Again, if the judge fails to prevent a violation, civil damages would be a remedial possibility, just as they are in other cases of damaged reputation (e.g., slander and libel): the accused has been charged by the government of having committed an infamous act, but has been denied his right to speedily clear his name in a fair trial. Here, too, however, the problem of sovereign immunity has blocked the development of this analytically attractive remedy.

One of the main virtues of damage remedies is that they seek to vindicate the rights of innocent men and women wrongly detained and accused; dismissal with prejudice is not a true, or tailored, remedy for someone who is clearly innocent, and would have obviously prevailed at trial. (Dismissal with prejudice can also be an unfortunate windfall to the guilty in some cases, as shall become more clear below.) In other words, although dismissal with prejudice might well vindicate whatever fair trial interest might exist—if it exists—it does nothing to redress the analytically distinct wrongs of pretrial loss of bodily liberty and reputation that can occur when a defendant is held too long in pretrial detention, or accused too long without a chance to speedily clear his name at trial. The framers of the Constitution cared a great deal about innocent persons, and designed many provisions of the Fourth, Fifth, and Sixth Amendments to protect these innocent persons from erroneous punishments and impositions. The speedy trial clause is clearly, at its core, designed to give an innocent man wrongly accused a right to a speedy trial so that he can clear his good name and end whatever pretrial deprivations of liberty he may be suffering. These two major interests—in reputation and liberty—are ill served by the current absence of good remedies to make innocent men and women whole when these interests have been violated by government.

Consider finally the fair trial interest, designed to ensure that an overlong accusation itself (which of course may trigger pretrial detention and which may cause an immediate loss of reputation that worsens with every day the indictment lingers) does not compromise the ability of a defendant to put on a full and unimpaired defense at trial. Here, too, the Amendment is centrally designed to protect an innocent defendant from being erroneously imposed upon. A judge could again prevent violations of this interest by ordering the pretrial release of the defendant or ordering the conditions of confinement softened so that the confinement does not cause the loss of key exculpatory evidence. If this fails, however, there are several possible judicial remedies. One is dismissal with prejudice. The idea here is simple: if, because of the government's unconstitutionally long accusation period, a fair trial is simply no longer possible, then the trial itself should be permanently aborted, and the defendant set free. This is a precisely tailored remedy—but only for that subset of cases in which the fair trial interest has been incurably compromised. Another possible option, in cases where it is less than clear that a trial would itself be unfair, is to rely on the due process rule of *In re Winship*, 397 U.S. 358 (1970), requiring the government prove guilt beyond a reasonable doubt in criminal cases. A defense argument to the jury that an unreasonable delay by the prosecutor's office caused key evidence to be lost could certainly be grounds for reasonable doubt.

Under the foregoing remedial analysis, the different speedy trial clause interests—protecting bodily liberty, reputation, and fair trials—call for different and precisely tailored remedies. Dismissal with prejudice is not, contra the Court's pronouncements in *Barker v. Wingo*, 407 U.S. 514 (1972), and *Strunk v. United States*, 412 U.S. 434 (1973), "the only possible remedy" for speedy trial clause violations. It is indeed a precisely apt remedy where a trial itself would be incurably unfair, because of the government's own conduct during the accusation period. But it is inapt in many other cases in which rather different if speedy trial clause interests may have been violated. Thus, dismissal with prejudice, without more, underprotects the innocent defendant who would have won acquittal in any event, but who is not compensated for the loss of his distinct interests in bodily liberty and reputation. Here, dismissal alone is too little. In other cases, it is too much: it overprotects guilty defendants in cases where there is no threat to a fair trial but where there has been a violation of distinct speedy trial interests—for example, an overlong detention that offended the bodily liberty interest, or an overlong accusation that implicated the reputation interest. If dismissal with prejudice is indeed the only possible remedy, the guilty defendant gets a windfall, while the innocent one receives nothing for months or years of detention and/or a ruined reputation. It is submitted here that a more sensible enforcement scheme—one consistent with propositions (1)–(6)—would call for timely judicial orders to either prosecute immediately or drop the charges or release the prisoner (depending on which time period has tolled). Dropping the charges would still permit the prosecutor to reindict later, and proceed immediately to trial. Such an enforcement scheme would also call for compensatory and (in egregious cases) punitive damages against the government for defendants who have either been subjected to unconstitutionally long periods of imprisonment or prolonged attacks on their good names. Note that those defendants ultimately found guilty in fair trials would likely have no case for claiming that the overlong accusation besmirched their good names: had the trial occurred sooner, they would have been found guilty even sooner, with even more (and deserved) discredit heaped on their reputation. As for overlong detentions, to avoid any possible double punishment, the guilty could receive sentencing offsets for time served, as is currently provided for in federal cases by 18 USC section 3585 (b). It is still possible that a guilty defendant would have a case for damages: perhaps his pretrial detention was so long as to be greater than the length of his eventual sentence upon conviction. Here, again, it would seem that he has been unconstitutionally seized in a way that a *Bivens*-type suit should appropriately remedy. But in general, those defendants who won acquittals at trial—innocent defendants—would tend to recover more than those defendants later found guilty at trial. This is as it should be if indeed the speedy trial right is centrally concerned with protecting innocent persons from erroneous governmental deprivations of liberty and reputation.

Because dismissal with prejudice has been held by the Supreme Court to be the only appropriate remedy for speedy trial clause violations, it is possible that judges have gone out of their way to avoid finding violations, in order not to create a severe windfall for guilty defendants. Indeed, the Court has opted for a rather loose, multi-factor test to assess speed. In this test, judges must weigh the length of the pretrial delay; the reason for the delay; whether and when the defendant asserted his speedy trial right; and

whether the delay in fact prejudiced the defendant's trial. There are few fixed guidelines or strict deadlines under this approach.

In 1974, Congress responded to this loose judicial regime with the Speedy Trial Act, 18 USC sections 3161–3174, providing a tighter, fixed schedule regulating the accusation period. For example, the act requires persons arrested to be charged within thirty days and arraigned within ten days of indictment or information; the trial must then commence within sixty days of arraignment. If, after this time, a trial has not commenced, a defendant can move for dismissal of the charges, either with or without prejudice—with the decision turning on factors including the seriousness of the offense, the facts and circumstances leading to dismissal, the impact on the administration of justice, the prejudice to the defendant, the length of the delay, and the defendant's own role in contributing to the delay. The act also provides a rather intricate framework for determining various periods of delay during which the statutory clock stops ticking.

The states have also enacted legislation to ensure the right to a speedy trial. The Interstate Agreement on Detainers is a 1970 compact between forty-eight states, the District of Columbia, and the federal government. Under the terms of this agreement, if a person is serving prison time in one state and charges are pending against him in another state, he has the right to be brought to trial within 180 days of requesting final settlement of the pending charges. The agreement also provides for extradition between states for the purposes of standing trial, and requires that an extradited prisoner be tried within 120 days of his arrival in the receiving state. Finally, if any of these terms are violated, or if officials of the receiving state refuse to accept custody of a prisoner against whom they have an indictment, the indictment will be dismissed with prejudice.

The foregoing discussion has been somewhat abstract and analytical; the contemporary legal reality is more messy, and rather depressing to contemplate. A great many suspects in today's world are subject to considerable pretrial detention, notwithstanding the letter and spirit of the Sixth Amendment and the Eighth Amendment bail clause. Dejected and demoralized, many poor defendants may end up pleading guilty, even to crimes that they may not have committed, so that they can be released on the basis of time already served. (With no damage remedy awaiting them upon acquittal for their overlong pretrial detention, many have little incentive indeed to put the prosecution to its ultimate proof at trial.) The result is a system that in reality falls short of vindicating the noble principles of the Constitution.

AKHIL REED AMAR

See also ARRAIGNMENT; BAIL; CRIMINAL JUSTICE PROCESS; CRIMINAL PROCEDURE: CONSTITUTIONAL ASPECTS; TRIAL, CRIMINAL.

BIBLIOGRAPHY

AMAR, AKHIL REED. "Foreword: Sixth Amendment First Principles." *Georgetown Law Journal* 84 (1996): 641.
AMSTERDAM, ANTHONY G. "Speedy Criminal Trial: Rights and Remedies." *Stanford Law Review* 27 (1975): 525.
ARKIN, MARC M. "Speedy Criminal Appeal: A Right without a Remedy." *Minnesota Law Review* 74 (1990): 437.
GODBOLD, JOHN C. "Speedy Trial: Major Surgery for a National Ill." *Alabama Law Review* 24 (1965): 265.

CASES

Barker v. Wingo, 407 U.S. 514 (1972).
Barron v. Baltimore, 32 U.S. (7 Pet.) 243 (1833).
Bivens v. Six Unknown Agents of the Federal Bureau of Narcotics, 403 U.S. 388 (1971).
Farretta v. California, 422 U.S. 806 (1975).
In re Winship, 397 U.S. 358 (1970).
Klopfer v. North Carolina, 386 U.S. 213 (1967).
Powell v. Alabama, 287 U.S. 45 (1932).
Strunk v. United States, 412 U.S. 434 (1973).
United States v. Marion, 404 U.S. 307 (1971).

STALKING

Beginning in the late 1980s *stalking* became an accepted word in the American vocabulary and a distinct criminal offense under state and federal law. The sensitivity of the mental health and legal communities to this abnormal social behavior was heightened by the notable cases of Prosenjit Poddar (*Tarasoff v. Regents of University of California,* 551 2d 334 (1976); Meloy, 1996) and John Hinckley, Jr. (Caplan). Extensive media coverage of the stalking of some celebrated actors, musicians, and television show hosts raised the consciousness of the American public to this offense in the mid-1990s.

Stalking is the willful and malicious act of following, viewing, harassing, communicating with, or moving threateningly or menacingly toward another person. Stalking behaviors may be expressed by written and verbal communications, unsolicited and unrecognized claims of romantic involvement on the part of victims, obsessive surveillance, harassment, loitering, and following that may produce intense fear and psychological distress to the victim. Stalkers use telephone calls, conventional and electronic mail, and vandalism to communicate their obsessional interests.

Stalking is typically a long-term crime without a traditional crime scene. The stalking occurs at the target's residence, place of employment, shopping mall, school campus, or other public place. There are a number of aborted or obscene phone calls or anonymous letters addressed to the target professing love or knowledge of the target's movements. Written communications or symbolic items are often left on vehicle windows or placed in mailboxes or under doors by the stalker. The tone of communications may progress from protestations of adoration, to love, to annoyance at not being able to make personal contact, to threats of violence and menacing.

Although the actual number of stalking victimizations has yet to be systematically documented, a congressional report of 1998 estimates that approximately 1.5 million victims are subjected to the terror of threatened violence annually (Department of Justice). Remarkably, there are an estimated 200,000 stalkers in the United States. One of every twelve women in the United States has been or will be a victim of a stalker during her lifetime; one out of every forty-five men has suffered or will suffer the same fate. Stalking over the Internet, known as cyberstalking, claims additional victims from an estimated forty thousand offenders (Karczewski).

All states in the United States (including the District of Columbia) have passed antistalking legislation, following California's lead, in an attempt to fill the gaps left by generally ineffective civil restraining orders and criminal statutes prohibiting such activities as "threats of violence," "criminal trespassing," and "harassment" (Geberth). Many of these state statutes are patterned after provisions of a model anti-stalking law jointly drafted by the National Criminal Justice Association (NCJA) and sponsored by the National Institute of Justice (NIJ) (Fein, Vossekuil, and Holden). Federal anti-stalking legislation (the Interstate Stalking Punishment and Prevention Act of 1996) targets perpetrators who travel across state lines to commit crimes.

Victimology and targets of stalkers

Historically, the study of crime began with and focused primarily on the study of offenders (Goring; Goddard; Lindesmith and Dumham; Rennie; Megargee and Bohn; Roebuck). In the late 1960s, social scientists began to theorize that a true understanding of crime required an examination of the role of the victim (Schafer). Consequently, researchers began to address the role of the victim in the victimization process and the acute and long-term effects of violence on both victims and their social network (Kinder; Burgess and Holmstrom; Cook, Smith, and Harrell; Wirtz and Harrell; Lerman).

The study of victims (victimology) has contributed to the way social scientists and practitioners view the role of victims and the dynamics of criminal acts. The victim's account of "what happened" often provides a contrasting view to the offender's account. Offenders may distort or misrepresent the facts of the criminal incident in order to minimize their responsibility, may have "fantasies" about the criminal act, or may simply claim that the victim is lying (Groth; Kestler).

The victim often provides detailed information about the circumstances surrounding the crime, including interactions and conversations with the offender prior to and after the crime; threats and demands that the offender made of the victim; weapons, if any, used by the offender during the crime; the identity and location of the offender; and details about the offender's personality (if the victim knows the offender). It is information from the victim that assists clinicians and investigators in classifying and investigating the crime and eventually questioning the offender (Douglas, Burgess, Burgess, and Ressler; Kestler).

Targets of stalkers often feel trapped in an environment filled with anxiety, stress, and fear that often results in their having to make drastic adjustments in how they live their lives. The terms "target" and "victim" are not necessarily interchangeable. The term "target" is used to describe the primary recipient of the stalker's attention. However, in many cases innocent parties and the target's circle of friends and associates become victims of the stalker's behavior.

From the target's perspective, the stalker is either known or anonymous. With stalking, there is a continuum of no physical contact to a lethal amount of contact and aggression. Until stalking legislation, law enforcement was often unable to arrest an individual unless there was evidence of direct contact in the form of assault.

Early research efforts addressing the crime of stalking come from victims of domestic violence who are often stalked by their offenders. One domestic violence study in Boulder and Denver, Colorado, noted that 48 percent of those who had obtained restraining orders were stalked prior to the issuance of the order and 12 percent were stalked within three months after the issuance of the order (Harrell, Smith, and Cook). Anecdotal accounts of victim assistance service providers support the findings of Harrell and colleagues (Harrell, Smith, and Newmark).

Targets have often crossed paths with the stalker, most likely without notice by the target. They will, therefore, have no knowledge of the stalker's identity. The relationship between the stalker and target is one-way. The target will eventually become aware of the stalker's presence. Other potential victims are spouses, partners, or any who are viewed as an obstacle that comes between the stalker and his or her target.

In a nonrepresentative study of stalking targets, Hall examined questionnaires completed by 145 current and prior stalking victims from twenty states who ranged in age from sixteen to seventy and who had been stalked for varying lengths of time, with some cases beginning or going back to the 1960s. Seventeen percent had been stalked from less than one month to six months; 23 percent from six months to one year; 29 percent from one to three years; and 13 percent for five years or more, with one case having continued for over thirty-one years. Although 57 percent of the victims were stalked by their former intimate partners, only 50 percent of the victims were females stalked by a male intimate partner. Over one-third (35%) of all the stalkers had had prior, nonintimate relationships with their victims (only four of these cases were workplace related) and the remaining 6 percent were strangers with no prior relationship to their victims.

Motivation

Isolated research has reported findings from cases involving the pursuit of public figures (Dietz, Matthews, Martell et al., 1991), of serial homicide (Ressler, Burgess, and Douglas), or describing the personalities and motivations of a small sample of stalkers (Hazelwood and Douglas; Geberth). Newspaper and anecdotal accounts are more prevalent than the academic literature; however, these accounts reveal little about the overall dynamics of the crime beyond the specific incident.

Stalker crimes are primarily motivated by interpersonal aggression rather than by material gain or sex. The purpose of stalking resides in the mind of stalkers, who are compulsive individuals with a misperceived fixation. Stalking is the result of an underlying emotional conflict that propels the offender to stalk and/or harass a target.

Because of the cognitive component to the behavior, stalking can be conceptualized as occurring on a continuum from nondelusional to delusional behavior. Delusional behavior may indicate the presence of a major mental disorder such as a schizophrenia, psychosis, or delusional disorder (American Psychological Association). Nondelusional behavior, while reflecting a gross disturbance in a particular relationship and a personality style or disorder, does not necessarily indicate a detachment from reality. This distinction is significant because of the potential legal implications, that is, pleas of insanity. What most readily distinguishes the behavior on this spectrum is the nature of the relationship an offender has had with his target and the content of the communication.

On the delusional end of this spectrum there is usually no actual relationship, rather such a relationship exists only in the mind of the offender. Communication content includes the presence of bizarre or nonbizarre delusions (American Psychological Association). On the nondelusional end of the spectrum there is most often a historical relationship between the offender and victim. These tend to be multidimensional relationships such as marriage or common law relationships replete with a history of close interpersonal involvement. Communication content includes a one-sided romantic fixation. In between these two poles are relationships of varied dimensions and stalkers who exhibit a mix of behavior. The offender may have dated his target once, twice, or not at all. The target may only have smiled and said "hello" in passing or may in some way be socially or vocationally acquainted.

Relationship to target: nondomestic stalkers

The stalker with no interpersonal relationship with the victim may target an individual from a prior meeting or from nothing more than an observation. In nondomestic or anonymous stalker cases, the target usually cannot identify the stalker when first aware of the behavior. This classification has two types: the organized stalker and the delusional stalker.

The organized stalker's identity is unknown or at some point the individual may make his or her identity known through continuous physical appearances at the victim's residence, place of employment, or other location. It is unlikely that the victim is aware of being stalked prior to the initial communication or contact. Only after the stalker has chosen to make personal or written contact will the target realize the problem.

The stalker may place himself or herself in a position to make casual contact with the target at which time verbal communication may occur. A description of this contact may be used in a later communication to terrorize and/or impress upon the target that the stalker is capable of carrying out any threats.

A delusional stalker or erotomania-related stalking is motivated by an offender-target relationship that is based on the stalker's psychological fixation. This fantasy is commonly expressed in such forms as fusion, where the stalker blends his personality into the target's, or erotomania, where a fantasy is based on idealized romantic love or spiritual union of a person rather than sexual attraction (American Psychological Association). The stalker can also be motivated by religious fantasies or voices directing him to target a particular individual. This preoccupation with the target becomes consuming and ultimately can lead to the target's death. The drive to stalk arises from a variety of motives, ranging from rebuffed advances to internal conflicts stemming from the stalker's fusion of identity with the target. In addition to a person with high media visibility, other victims include superiors at work or even complete strangers. The target almost always is perceived by the stalker as someone of higher status. Targets often include political figures, entertainers, and high media visibility individuals but do not have to be public figures. Sometimes the victim of a stalker's violence is perceived by the stalker as an obstruction.

Although the research on menacing, harassing, and stalking behaviors in persons who have or had a prior relationship is relatively new (Walker), the psychiatric literature has been building a classification scheme on a subgroup of stalkers diagnosed with erotomania in whom the relationship exists only in fantasy and delusion (Seeman, 1978). Mullen and Pathé note that erotomania has long been known to be associated with stalking behaviors of both men and women and has the potential to lead to overt aggression; they provide a historic perspective both on the forensic aspects of stalking and the psychodynamic components. The physician Claude De Clérambault outlined the features of an erotic delusion syndrome in his book *Les Psychoses Passionelles* (1942). De Clérambault observed that *erotomania* began with love and hope but then disintegrated into resentment and anger. The patients, usually female, were described as holding the delusional belief that a man, usually older and of an elevated social rank, was passionately in love with them. This love became the purpose of the patients' existence; they may have sent letters and telephoned the person both at home and at work. Raskin and Sullivan observed that the patients may be dangerous and threaten the life of their victim or his family especially when the patient reaches the stage of resentment or hatred that replaces love. Meloy (1989) has suggested the dynamics of blurring of unrequited love and the wish to kill.

Rekindling an interest in the forensic aspects of erotomania has been credited to Goldstein and Taylor, Mahendra, and Gunn, and has also led to various classifications of stalkers. Zona and colleagues (1993) analyzed police files and classified persons as either erotomanic, love obsessional, or simple obsessional. Stalkers have been classified from a mental health intervention standpoint using short-term crisis intervention to assist survivors (Roberts and Dziegielewski) and a law enforcement perspective (Wright et al.) based on the nature of the relationship, nondomestic or domestic; the content of communication, nondelusional or delusional; level of aggression (low, medium, or high); level of victim risk; motive of stalker; and outcome. Forensic studies of obsessional harassment and erotomania have occurred in criminal court populations (Meloy and Gothard). Meloy and Gothard have suggested the term *obsessional follower* for someone who engages in an abnormal or long-term pattern of threat or harassment directed toward a specific individual. Consequently, stalking patterns in domestic violence are now seen as dangerous and the forensic aspect is being tested (Perez). Erotomania in and of itself is insufficient for explaining stalking behavior. When focusing on relationships involving romantic attachment and domestic activities, empirical investigation demonstrates different characteristics associated with stalking behaviors than those found in erotomania (Meloy, 1996).

As with other classifications of stalking, the activity of the erotomanic stalker is often long-term and includes written and telephonic communications, surveillance, attempts to approach the target, and so on. With the passage of time, the activity becomes more intense. Sometimes the preoccupation with the victim becomes all-consuming and may ultimately lead to the death or injury of another party. John Hinckley, Jr., both an attempted political assassin and a celebrity stalker, is one such example. His erotomanic obsession with the actress Jodie Foster was never destined to be consummated. Celebrity stalkers like Hinckley seek a self-identity through actions or fantasies, and often seek relationships with targets through the media. All actions are ultimately designed to fill the bottomless personality void, and are designed to bring media attention to someone with serious personality and social defects. Stalkers like Hinckley are likely to transfer targets of obsession. Indeed, Hinckley first staked out Jimmy Carter and only settled on Ronald Reagan when access to Carter eluded him. He injured both his target and surrounding victims. In Hinckley's 1998 release petition hearing, a state witness (a commander) testified that Hinckley was stalking her, in that he had gathered information about her personal schedule, recorded love songs for her, and, when ordered not to contact her, disobeyed by sending her a package. A state mental health expert testified that Hinckley's psychotic disorders were in remission but that Hinckley was still dangerous. The expert based his opinion on Hinckley's "relationship" with the commander, stating it was strikingly similar to the "relationship" he had with Jodie Foster (*Hinckley v. U.S.*, 140 F.3d 277, 286 (1998)).

Domestic stalkers

Domestic stalking occurs when a former partner, family member, or household member threatens or harasses another member of the household. This definition includes common law relationships as well as long-term acquaintance relationships. The domestic stalker is initially motivated by a desire to continue or reestablish a relationship, a desire that can evolve into an attitude of "If I can't have her no one can."

A study by Burgess and others (1997) examined data from 120 male and female batterers of varied age, marital, educational, and economic status, who attended group treatment for batterers or who were charged with domestic violence in a district court. One-third of the sample group admitted to stalking, and their behaviors indicated the possibility of continuing violent acts even though separation with the partner had occurred. Researchers determined that both open and clandestine stalking occurred. At this point it is not clear if this sample is representative of a particular pattern. Stalkers feel that they have a right to do what they do. They also did not feel that the victim provoked their stalking behaviors. Such attitudes suggest that the triggering event is less predicated on behavior of the victim and resides more in the fantasy life of the stalker. A potential stalker might be provoked by displacement, for example, being humiliated or disappointed in areas of life outside of the home.

Factor analysis of batterers who stalk compared to nonstalking batterers found three stalking patterns of pursuit. First, stalkers are open in their attempts to contact their former partners; when this fails they begin to contact others and discredit the partner. The second factor is the conversion of positive emotion of love to the negative emotion of hate. Stalkers essentially go underground with the clandestine behavior, including anonymous or hang-up phone calls and entering the residence without permission. Just before they go public again, there is a phase of ambivalence indicating the splitting of love and hate, when, for example, they might send gifts and flowers. The third factor is when they move from the mix of public and secret behavior to a public display of stalking and targeting behavior, and, in the sample just cited, entered the victim's residence and displayed violence.

The stalking behavior reveals far more personal disturbance in the perpetrator than the loss of control and anger arising purely within an interpersonal exchange, for example, the man who has had a bad day at work, comes home and becomes enraged at the wife, feeling she has slighted him or not attended to the house. This is in contrast to a man who is fixed on a partner and pursues her with little or no provocation from the victim.

The stalking behavior represents a self-generating pattern within the individual rather than being linked to the victim. Such intense predatory preoccupation suggests such diagnostic categories as: obsessive-compulsive disorder, psychotic behavior, delusional fixation, or a combination of behaviors.

Cyberstalking

Computer technology has provided the stalker with another means for accessing a target. Some investigators specialize in prosecuting Internet *cyberstalking*. While some cases involve adults as both offenders and victims, many pedophiles exploit children with this technology.

In *U.S. v. Reinhardt*, 975 F. Supp. 834 (W.D. La. 1997), the court granted the government's motion for pretrial detention of an alleged pedophile cyberstalker. The defendant was charged with producing and distributing child pornography. On government's motion for pretrial detention under the Bail Reform Act, the district court held that: (1) the defendant's case involved a crime of violence; (2) there were no conditions of release that could reasonably assure safety of the community; and (3) the defendant also posed a risk of flight.

Reinhardt illustrates how the Internet can be a tool for pedophiles and child pornographers. It demonstrates a pedophile's use of technology to stalk children for sexual purposes, to gain control over the child and his family, to recruit new victims, and to communicate with other pedophiles. *Reinhardt* exemplifies the amount of detail, care, and compulsiveness that is demonstrated in the profile of a career pedophile.

Pedophiles' social networks consists of other pedophiles. They socialize, telephone, write letters, e-mail, network, and share strategies for continuing their deviant relationships with children even when in prison. In Florida, one convicted child pornographer used his prison post office box number to expand his distribution of child pornography until he was discovered.

Pedophiles can move from an isolated position as solo operators into a network of perpetrators; Reinhardt, for example, had a co-defendant. Indeed, an elaborate and organized pedophile network exists on the Internet both nationally and internationally. The *Reinhardt* case illustrates the Internet pedophile as entrepreneur, one who has a product line on his own home page. Reinhardt provided advice to a "chat room" correspondent on how to build a long-term relationship with a young boy, how to manipulate parents in order that they not "cause problems," and taught his victims how to answer questions about the ongoing sexual relationship.

Pedophiles are totally preoccupied with their sexual interest in children. The probation office identified nine jobs Reinhardt held in four states between 1986 and 1997. The defendant's obsession with the Internet was reflected in his owner-ship of several computers. This case reveals the inner workings of pedophiles and child pornog-raphers. The general public can now access all dimensions of child sexual exploitation through the Internet. They can call up a pedophile's home page or talk with him or her in a "chat room."

State and federal anti-stalking laws

The legal history of stalking is a testament to the limitations of applying existing statutory law, and the passage of innovative legislation to ad-dress a newly conceived crime that extends be-yond the boundaries of common law offenses. From the ineffectiveness of civil protection or-ders to the limited utility of a federal antistalking statute, victims are often left with little practical legal recourse. Add to this an often-muted re-sponse from criminal justice agencies and it is no wonder that nearly half of all stalking victims are dissatisfied with the law enforcement response to their victimization (Department of Justice).

Civil protection orders.   The first line of de-fense for victims is a civil protection or restrain-ing order that has the effect of enjoining the stalking behavior. These orders are designed to restrict an offender from making contact with the victim, or from appearing at a particular place, such as a victim's home or work. Sanctions in-clude contempt of court, fines, and jail time or prison sentences. In a number of states, includ-ing California, Colorado, Delaware, Maine, South Carolina, Texas, and West Virginia, anti-stalking legislation has prompted more serious sanctions for violations of protection orders.

Eligibility restrictions for restraining orders in many states, however, severely limit their pro-tective value. For example, some states require a legally recognizable relationship between the vic-tim and offender (e.g., marriage) for a restrain-ing order to be issued. Others will not issue an order unless there is a finding of actual physical abuse (Bradfield). Beyond such restrictions, re-straining orders are far less than a guarantee of protection. Commentators note that: (1) approx-imately four out of every five orders are violated; (2) less than 20 percent of these violations result in an arrest; (3) there is an insufficient law en-forcement commitment to protective orders; and (4) taking out a protective order, at best, does lit-tle to protect against future victimization and, at worst, may incite a stalker to retaliate against his victim (Walker, 1993; Patton).

Extending the application of related stat-utes.   Until recently, the discretionary use of criminal statutes provided a remedy for the defi-ciencies of protective orders, as well as for the ab-sence of carefully drafted antistalking laws. Over time, prosecutors have come to rely on various offenses found in most state penal statutes—statutes prohibiting harassment; terrorist threats; threatening or intimidating behavior; and telephone threats or harassment, letter threats, and threats using electronic technologies such as e-mail or facsimile. Critics have called these statutes inadequate given their failure to: (1) account for the repetitive nature of stalking, which is a primary feature of the offense; (2) con-sider the full range of bizarre behaviors found within stalking activity; and (3) recognize any-thing less than an explicit threat as a crime. Moreover, most of these statutes have narrowly drawn intentionality requirements that further limit their application to stalking cases. Finally, the sanctions associated with these statutes are often insignificant and, when applied, can have the effect of trivializing the serious crime of stalk-ing (Bradfield).

State anti-stalking statutes.   Antistalking statutes, prompted by the brutal murder of ac-tress Rebecca Schaffer in California in 1989, at-tempt to address some of the limitations found with civil protection orders and related statutes. Many are drafted with an explicit consideration of the behavioral idiosyncrasies that characterize stalking offenses; without a requirement that the stalker has committed a violent act; with less sig-nificant mens rea or intentionality provisions; and with increased sanctions. In a majority of ju-risdictions, a first-time offender may be indicted on either felony or misdemeanor charges; repeat stalking is most often prosecuted as a felony.

The requirements of state anti-stalking stat-utes generally require proof of a "course of con-duct" and distinct threats by the offender that cause an actual fear of death or injury on the part of the victim. The former requires that the of-fender must have engaged in a persistent course of purposeful action amounting to a pattern of behavior. This may consist of nonconsensual communication, for example, obsessive surveil-lance, lying in wait, or physical harassment. A majority of states specify the number of incidents required to constitute a pattern of behavior or course of conduct.

Statutes differ with respect to the threat re-quirement. Some states require either a threat or conduct. Others mandate both a threat and conduct for prosecution. Still others impose threat, conduct, and intent requirements. A minority of jurisdictions requires that the stalker's behavior constitute an objectively "credible threat," that is, a threat that would create fear in a reasonable person in like circumstances.

The intent requirements of state statutes vary considerably as well. Most state statutes require that the offender purposefully or willfully intended to instill or cause fear; others require lesser mental states, for example, "knowing" negligent creation of fear. Only a few states omit the intent requirement. For obvious reasons, the more significant the intent requirement, the more difficult it is to obtain the proof necessary to secure a conviction.

Following passage of the first state statute in California in 1990, many legal scholars, advocates, and legislators predicted a series of constitutional challenges. The predictions were accurate. More than twenty state statutes have faced constitutional challenges for being broad and vague (Karbarz). Only a few cases have been successful beyond the trial level (Harmon). The Texas Court of Criminal Appeals is the highest state court to declare an antistalking statute unconstitutional, on the ground that it lacked sufficient clarity with regard to prohibited conduct; provided inadequate notice; and had a "vague" threat requirement (*Long v. State*, 931 S.W. 2nd 285 (1996)).

Model anti-stalking statute. The Model Anti-Stalking Code (Model Code) developed by the National Criminal Justice Association and sponsored by the National Institute of Justice took state legislation one step farther in an effort to address some apparent limitations in state statutes. According to Bradfield "some anti-stalking statutes still require that the stalker overtly threaten his victim, thereby allowing stalkers who communicate their threats through conduct to escape punishment. Likewise, some statutes still require that the stalker intend to cause fear, enabling stalkers who do not possess such intent to continue terrorizing their victims" (p. 245). Many states have amended their statutes in response to the well reasoned and carefully drafted provisions found in the Model Code.

The Model Code's act requirements are generous, allowing for a cause of action where there is:

1. A course of conduct involving repeated physical proximity (following) or threatening behavior or both;

2. the occurrence of incidents at least twice;
3. threatening behavior, including both explicit and implicit threats; and
4. conduct occurring against an individual or family members of the individual.

Satisfaction of the intent requirements is similarly relaxed. Prosecutors need only prove:

1. Intent to engage in a course of conduct involving repeated following or threatening an individual;
2. knowledge that this behavior reasonably causes fear of bodily injury or death;
3. knowledge (or expectation) that the specific victim would have a reasonable fear of bodily injury or death;
4. actual fear of death or bodily injury experienced by the victim; and
5. fear of death or bodily injury felt by members of the victim's immediate family.

Federal anti-stalking statutes. In an effort to "close the gaps" between individual state laws and to bolster their deterrent effect, Congress passed the Interstate Stalking Punishment and Prevention Act of 1996. The act prohibits stalking across state lines, makes restraining orders issued in one state valid in other states, and prohibits stalking on federal property, for example, post offices, national parks, and military bases. Violations of the act result in five years imprisonment, and twenty years in prison for violations that result in an injury or acts where the offender used a dangerous weapon. Life imprisonment is prescribed for stalking that results in the victim's death.

The limits of substantive law. The stark reality of the criminal justice system often places a severe constraint on the value of substantive stalking laws, no matter how carefully statutes are written and in spite of the many legislative advances around the United States since around 1990. Consider the risks to the victim that accompany the arrest of the offender. Pretrial detention for those charged with stalking offenses is rare. Arrests often escalate violence or lead to retaliation, with or without victim notification of release. In the unlikely event of a trial and conviction, a prison sentence does little to address the mental health treatment needs of most stalkers. Mental illness undermines principles of deterrence. In the end, the burden of fashioning a workable, realistic remedy to avoid future stalking often falls on the victim.

ANN W. BURGESS
WILLIAM S. LAUTER

See also ATTEMPT; DOMESTIC VIOLENCE; PREDICTION OF CRIME AND RECIDIVISM.

BIBLIOGRAPHY

American Psychiatric Association. *Diagnostic and Statistical Manual,* 4th ed. Washington, D.C.: American Psychiatric Press, 1994.

BRADFIELD, JENNIFER L. "Anti-Stalking Laws: Do They Adequately Protect Victims?" *Harvard Women's Law Journal* 21, no. 229 (1998): 229–266.

BURGESS, ANN W., and HOLMSTROM, LYNDA L. *Rape: Crisis and Recovery.* West Newton, Mass.: Awab, Inc., 1986.

BURGESS, ANN W.; BAKER, TIMOTHY; GREENING, DEBORAH; HARTMAN, CAROL; DOUGLAS, JOHN; and HALLORAN, RICHARD. "Stalking Behaviors Within Domestic Violence." *Journal of Family Violence* 12 (1997): 389–403.

CAPLAN, LINCOLN. *The Insanity Defense and the Trial of John W. Hinckley, Jr.* New York: Dell, 1987.

COOK, ROGER F.; SMITH, BARBARA E.; and HARRELL, ADELE V. *Helping Crime Victims: Levels of Trauma and the Effectiveness of Services. Report submitted to the National Institute of Justice.* Washington, D.C.: Institute for Social Analysis, 1985.

DE CLERAMBAULT, CLAUDE G. *Les psychoses passionelles. In Oeuvres psychiatrique.* Paris: Presses Universitaires de France, 1942. Pages 315–322.

Department of Justice. *Stalking and Domestic Violence: The Third Annual Report to Congress Under the Violence Against Women Act.* Washington, D.C.: U.S. Department of Justice, 1998.

DIETZ, PARK E.; MATTHEWS, DARREL B.; MARTELL, D. A.; STEWART, T. M.; HROUDA, D. R.; and WARREN, JANET. "Threatening and Otherwise Inappropriate Letters to Members of the United States Congress." *Journal of Forensic Sciences* 36 (1991): 1445–1468.

DOUGLAS, JOHN E.; BURGESS, ANN W.; BURGESS, ALLEN G.; and RESSLER, ROBERT K. *Crime Classification Manual: A Standard System for Investigating and Classifying Violent Crimes.* New York: Lexington Books/Macmillan, 1992.

FEIN, ROBERT A.; VOSSEKUIL, BRYAN; and HOLDEN, G. A. *Threat Assessment: An Approach to Prevent Targeted Violence.* NIJ Research in Action. Washington, D.C.: U.S. Department of Justice, 1995.

GEBERTH, VERN J. "Stalkers." *Law and Order* 10 (1992): 1–6.

GODDARD, HENRY H. *Feeblemindedness: Its Cause and Consequence.* New York: Macmillan, 1914.

GORING, CHARLES. *The English Convict.* London: H.M. Stationery Office, 1913.

GROTH, A. NICHOLAS. *Men Who Rape.* New York: Plenum Press, 1979.

HALL, D. M. "Stalking Often Linked to Sexual Assaults." *Sexual Assault Report* 1 (1997): 6.

HARMON, BRENDA K. "Illinois Newly Amended Stalking Law: Are All the Problems Solved?" *Southern Illinois University Journal* 19 (1994): 165–197.

HARRELL, ADELE V.; SMITH, BARBARA E.; and NEWMARK, LISA. *Orders for Domestic Violence Victims.* Washington, D.C.: The Urban Institute, 1993.

HARRELL, ADELE V.; SMITH, BARBARA E.; and COOK, ROGER F. *The Social Psychological Effects of Victimization. Report submitted to the National Institute of Justice.* Washington, D.C.: Institute for Social Analysis, 1985.

HAZELWOOD, ROBERT R., and DOUGLAS, JOHN E. "The Lust Murderer." *FBI Law Enforcement Bulletin* 49 (1980): 18–22.

KARBARZ, SUZANNE L. "The First Amendment Implications of Antistalking Statutes." *Journal of Legislation* 21 (1995): 331–350.

KARCZEWSKI, LISA A. "Stalking in Cyberspace: The Expansion of California's Current Antistalking Laws in the Age of the Internet." *McGeorge Law Review* 30 (1999): 517.

KESTLER, JEFFREY L. *Questioning Techniques and Tactics.* Colorado Springs, Colo.: Shepards/McGraw-Hill, 1982.

KINDER, GARY *Victim: The Other Side of Murder.* New York: Delacorte Press, 1982.

LERMAN, LISA G. *Prosecution of Spouse Abuse: Innovations in Criminal Justice Responses.* Washington, D.C.: Center for Women's Policy Studies, 1983.

LINDESMITH, ALFRED R., and DUNHAM, H. WARREN. "Some Principles of Criminal Typology." *Social Forces* 19 (1941): 307–314.

MEGARGEE, EDWARD I., and BOHN, MARTIN I. *Classification of Criminal Offenders: A New System Based on the MMPI.* London: Sage Publications, 1979.

MELOY, J. REID. "Unrequited Love and the Wish to Kill." *Bulletin of the Menninger Clinic* 53 (1989): 477–492.

————. "Stalking (Obsessional Following): A Review of Some Preliminary Studies." *Aggression and Violent Behavior* 1 (1996): 147–162.

MELOY, J. REID, and GOTHARD, S. "Demographic and Clinical Comparison of Obsessional Followers and Offenders with Mental Disorders." *American Journal of Psychiatry* 152, no. 2 (1995): 258–263.

MULLEN, P. E., and PATHÉ, M. "Stalking and the Pathology of Love." *Australian and New Zealand Journal of Psychiatry* 28 (1994): 469–477.

PATTON, E. A. "Stalking Laws: In Pursuit of a Remedy." *Rutgers Law Journal* 25 (1994): 465–515.

PEREZ, CHRISTINA. "Stalking: When Does Obsession Become a Crime?" *American Journal of Criminal Law* 20 (1993): 264–290.

RASKIN, D. E., and SULLIVAN, K. E. "Erotomania." *American Journal of Psychiatry* 131 (1974): 1033–1035.

RENNIE, YSABEL. *The Search for Criminal Man: The Dangerous Offender Project.* New York: Lexington Books/Macmillan, 1977.

RESSLER, ROBERT K.; BURGESS, ANN W.; and DOUGLAS, JOHN E. *Sexual Homicide: Patterns and Motives.* New York: Lexington Books/Macmillan, 1988.

ROBERTS, ALBERT R., and DZIEGIELEWSKI, S. F. "Assessment Typology and Intervention with the Survivors of Stalking." *Aggression and Violent Behavior* 1 (1996): 359–368.

ROEBUCK, JULIAN B. *Criminal Typology,* 2d ed. Springfield, Ill.: Charles C. Thomas Co., 1967.

SCHAFER, STEVEN. *The Victim and His Criminal: A Study in Functional Responsibility.* New York: Random House, 1968.

WALKER, J. M. "Anti-Stalking Legislation: Does It Protect the Victim without Violating the Rights of the Accused?" *Drexler University Law Review* 71 (1993): 273–302.

WALKER, LEONORE E. *Battered Women.* New York: Harper and Row, 1979.

WIRTZ, PAUL, and HARRELL, ADELE V. "Police and Victims of Physical Assault." *Journal of Criminal Justice and Behavior* 14 (1987): 81–92.

WRIGHT, JAMES A.; BURGESS, ALLEN G.; BURGESS, ANN W.; LASZLO, ANNA T.; MCCRARY, GREG O.; and DOUGLAS, JOHN E. "A Typology of Interpersonal Stalking." *Journal of Interpersonal Violence* 11 (1996): 487–502.

CASES

Hinckley v. United States, 140 F.3d. 277, 286 (1998).

Long v. State, 931 S.W. 2nd 285 (1996).

Tarasoff v. Regents of the University of California, 551 2nd 334 (1976).

United States v. Reinhold, 975 F. Supp. 834 (W.D. La. 1997).

STATISTICS: COSTS OF CRIME

Estimating the costs of crime serves many purposes. At a very basic level, such estimates indicate the burden of crime for individuals and society. Victims often lose or have their property damaged. Replacing or repairing damaged goods, even in an era of widespread insurance, can result in substantial monetary loss. Victims also often sustain physical injury and suffer considerable psychological trauma. In seeking treatment or counseling, not to mention days lost from work, decreased productivity, and even long-term financial distress, victims of crime often experience a diminished quality of life and substantial financial burden. As the myriad consequences of crime are diverse and varied, estimates of monetary costs provide a common, easily interpretable measure for understanding the impact of crime on individuals and society.

Estimates of monetary costs also have important policy implications. They facilitate comparisons with the costs of other social ills, provide an indication of the relative importance of crime as a social problem, and give guidance for the general allocation of resources. Such estimates also help identify the relative harm for specific types of crime and indicate where policies and resources are best directed. Accurate estimates of the costs of criminal violence are also important for making cost-benefit assessments of different policy options. They facilitate assessments of the savings that might accrue from particular crime-prevention strategies. These can be compared to the costs of implementing particular strategies to assess the overall benefit of different policy options. Ultimately, accurate estimates of the costs of crime are central to understanding crime as a social problem and to the formulation and implementation of crime-related social policy.

While it is difficult enough to enumerate the many *consequences* of crime, it is considerably more difficult to quantify and *monetize* these consequences to estimate costs. While some costs are relatively easy to estimate, others are virtually impossible. Still, an extensive and growing body of research in criminology and economics has attempted to place dollar values on the pain, suffering, and loss that accompany criminal activity. This entry provides a conceptual framework for estimating costs of crime and examines both costs of crime and vulnerability to such costs.

The social cost framework

Typically, costs of crime are considered within a "social cost" framework. Economists refer to social costs as any resource-using activity that reduces aggregate well-being. Such a broad conceptualization considers issues well beyond the monetary costs of crime and includes a variety of resources often nonmonetary and sometimes not readily measurable. There are two broad categories of costs that can be considered when estimating the costs of crime. *Direct costs* are costs imposed by the offender and usually incurred by the victim. *Indirect costs*, on the other hand, stem from society's response to criminal activity. These include costs arising out of the desire to prevent crime, as well as costs arising from society's desire to punish known offenders and deter potential criminals.

Direct costs of crime

Estimates of the direct costs of crime are relatively clear. Criminal activity generates expenses for victims and occupies an offender's time, time that could be spent in other resource-generating activities. Such costs are relatively easy to assess.

Costs borne by victims fall into four categories. First, there are out-of-pocket expenses, such as property damage and loss and costs of medical care. For example, national crime surveys indicate that approximately one-third of all violent crimes result in some property loss or damage, with the average violent crime resulting in a loss of approximately $137. Although insurance often covers partial or full restitution for such costs, victims can still be required to pay insurance deductibles and face higher premiums when renewing their insurance.

Second, victimization often results in physical injury, particularly in the case of violent crimes. Almost one-quarter of all victims of violent crime sustain some physical injury, of which almost 7 percent incur some form of medical expense and almost 5 percent receive hospital care. Injury during property crime is much rarer as much property crime involves no physical contact between victims and offenders. Compounding these expenses, a considerable proportion of victims has no healthcare insurance. At the same time, victims of crime often experience decreased productivity or lost wages due to ab-

sences from work. Time away from work is typically short, between one and five days, yet sometimes extends into weeks and even months.

A third category of costs stems from psychological trauma. Post-traumatic stress disorder (PTSD) and its symptoms are well-recognized consequences of criminal violence. Research on behalf of the National Institute of Justice found that one-quarter of all crime victims experienced a related PTSD, including nervous breakdowns, suicide ideation, and suicide attempts. Not surprisingly, victims of crime often seek assistance from various mental health services. Research indicates that almost half of all victims of sexual assault and approximately 5 percent of victims of assault and robbery incur costs for mental health services.

Finally, there are also less tangible costs, such as those stemming from pain, suffering, and reduced quality of life. As there is no established market value for intangible costs, estimation is more complicated. The most common strategy for estimating intangible costs is to base estimates on jury awards to crime victims and burn victims. Typically, these estimates are based on the portion of the jury verdict designed to compensate the victim for pain, suffering, and diminished quality of life.

Various works summarize the components to estimate the overall personal costs of crime. For example, the 1994 National Academy of Science report *Understanding and Preventing Violence* estimates that the average sexual assault costs victims approximately $68,800, while assault and robbery cost approximately $21,100 and $24,400, respectively. Although estimates of homicide are typically much greater and estimates of property and vice crimes are typically much lower, such work provides clear evidence that the personal costs of crime are substantial.

While less obvious, there are also costs incurred or hypothetically incurred by the offender. For example, both property and personal crime often involves the use of tools and weapons that may have been purchased by the offender. In addition to this, the labor and energy that offenders devote to criminal activity could hypothetically be put to more productive uses. In this regard, offender-related costs stem from the lost productivity of engaging in crime rather than other more normative activities. Finally, offenders often do not emerge unscathed from criminal interactions. Victims may injure offenders in the course of defending themselves. Offenders may be forced to abandon property, tools, and weapons, or have their vehicles damaged when fleeing crime scenes. While such costs may seem just, they still contribute to the overall costs of crime. To date, there have been few attempts to estimate offender-related costs comprehensively.

Indirect costs of crime

When considering and estimating direct costs of crime, the general focus is costs associated with the criminal act itself. In contrast to this, costs are also incurred through individual and societal reactions to crime. These can be considered the indirect costs of crime. As criminal activity is generally regarded as a damaging, undesirable, and antisocial activity, the many costs associated with preventing crime, responding to crime, and punishing offenders are substantial. One means of assessing such costs is to consider the various crime-related expenses associated with state agencies and those associated with private individuals and enterprises.

Public sector costs. A large and increasing proportion of state resources are devoted to responding to crime. In 1993 alone, over $97 billion was spent on criminal justice activity. While attributing all criminal justice expenditure as "crime related" costs is wrong as much criminal justice activity is more about maintaining order and assisting the public, there are still substantial crime costs stemming from state response to criminal activity. One gains a better sense of these costs by considering each specific stage of the criminal justice system.

An initial source of costs arises from police investigation and apprehension. The majority of police activity is reactive in that police are usually alerted or notified of criminal activity by victims or witnesses. The effectiveness of police services requires extensive expenditure on communications equipment, transportation equipment, and safety and apprehension equipment as well as the extensive manpower necessary to investigate crime and apprehend offenders. Determining the specific proportion of these costs that are directly attributable to crime requires assessing the amount of police activity that is explicitly devoted to crime investigation and response. Interestingly, there is considerable evidence that the vast majority of police activity, upward of 80 percent, is *not* directly related to crime.

In addition to policing, there are also costs associated with courts and the judiciary. With the objective of punishing the guilty and protecting the innocent, the courts are the central body of determining the legitimacy of criminal justice sanctions. Court-related costs attributable to crime consist largely of time and energy spent on criminal cases. Estimations of these costs focus on the average salaries of judges, prosecutors, and defense attorneys divided by the amount of time spent on criminal cases. A 1994 report for the National Academy of Science suggests that the average trial costs per case may be as high as $30,000, although only a fraction of all crimes result in a trial.

A final source of costs stems from the sanctioning of convicted offenders. Offenders can be subject to a wide range of sanctions. Some sanctions, including fines and community service, do not explicitly involve public costs, but instead represent a transfer of resources from the individual to the public. Other sanctions, such as probation, jail, and imprisonment, do involve substantial costs to the public. Incarceration, for example, is imposed in almost all murder cases, the majority of rape and robbery cases, and almost half of all aggravated assault convictions. Estimates of the crime-related costs involve estimation of the annual cost of incarceration per individual multiplied by the average length of time served. Probation, on the other hand, has institutional costs associated with the maintenance of probation offices. Combining estimates of the average costs of incarceration and probation, the cost of imposing sanctions per offense may be as high as $75,000 per murder, $5,000 per rape, and just over $3,500 for robbery and aggravated assault.

Private sector costs. In addition to costs associated with the public's desire to apprehend and punish offenders, considerable other indirect costs are borne more directly by private individuals and commercial institutions. Costs associated with preventing criminal victimization are the main source of costs for both these groups.

Private citizens spend vast amounts of money to prevent crime victimization. Some of these costs are largely hidden. For example, houses and cars typically come with locks for doors. Yet, the price of the locks is built into the overall price of the house or car. Other costs are add-ons to purchases. Purchasing a bicycle typically involves the additional purchase of a lock. People often augment existing security precautions. Cars are fitted with alarms or other antitheft devices. Additional locks are added to doors and windows and old, less effective devices are replaced with new, more effective ones. Individuals may purchase dogs for security, thus incurring the costs of care and feeding. In even more extreme cases, people purchase firearms to protect themselves against intruders. National surveys show that almost 10 percent of all households own firearms primarily for protection. Importantly, all such costs are borne by individuals in the effort to protect themselves from criminal victimization.

Businesses and commercial establishments also spend considerable money on crime prevention. Commercial establishments, both large and small, often carry extra staff to guard against crime. Often such staff is specifically employed for crime-prevention purposes. Department stores may employ "floorwalkers" to guard against shoplifting, while bars and nightclubs employ "bouncers" as a means of protecting both patrons and property from harm and damage. Probably most significant, recent decades have seen the proliferation of security guards in both individual establishments and commercial venues such as shopping malls. The growth of private security has been so significant that it has dramatically outpaced the growth of conventional police and law enforcement.

In addition to personnel costs, various crime prevention devices are standard features in commercial establishments. Consistent with efforts to "target harden," such devices make establishments less attractive by increasing risks of apprehension. For example, convenience stores purchase "height tape" to be placed on doors such that employees can estimate the height of a thief or robber fleeing an establishment. They also often have time-release safes to limit the amount of money that can be stolen in any given time. The presence of surveillance cameras has also proliferated in recent years. That both personnel costs and the adoption of various crime prevention technologies are typically factored into the everyday or routine operating expenses of businesses is a significant indicator of the degree to which crime prevention has become "normalized" in society.

Although less intuitive than the direct costs of crime, responses to crime and crime-prevention strategies are important considerations in both understanding and estimating the overall costs of crime. The identification of such costs indicates the myriad ways in which citizens pay for crime. Importantly, a consideration of such factors demonstrates the generalized vulnerability to crime costs that all citizens bear rather than only those borne by those directly victimized by crime.

Distribution of costs

Although our consideration of private expenditure on crime and crime prevention indicates widespread vulnerability to crime costs, it is important to recognize that costs of crime are not borne equally by all members of society. In particular, there are many geographic and social factors that increase vulnerability to criminal victimization and increase vulnerability to the costs of crime.

Geographic aspects. Over the past century, researchers have documented the importance of place for understanding crime. Differences in crime rates exist across countries, regions, counties, states, cities, neighborhoods within cities, and even across individual locations such as houses, restaurants, bars, and stores. Importantly, particular features of environments appear to influence the amount of crime within those environments and consequently influence risks of crime victimization.

Two factors stand out as prominent geographic risk factors for crime victimization. The first of these is resource deprivation. Areas that have high levels of poverty, higher income inequality, high unemployment, and lower average income tend to have significantly higher levels of crime. In addition to resource deprivation, areas with higher geographic mobility, the rapid turnover in population, are also more crime prone. In such transitional areas, residents are less likely to feel any long-term commitment to the community and are less likely to be involved in community activities. This increases the potential for serious crime. In recognizing geographic differences in crime rates, we also draw attention to important differences in exposure to crime. Residents of such resource-deprived and transitional neighborhoods have significantly greater risk of victimization. Likewise, property and businesses in these communities are also more likely to experience crime. Consequently, residents and businesses in deprived and transitional neighborhoods are more likely to bear the costs of crime.

Social aspects. In addition to geographic risk factors, there are also numerous social attributes that increase vulnerability to crime. Age is consistently related to criminal victimization, with teenagers and early adults having comparatively high risk of victimization. Particularly with respect to violent crime, risk of victimization increases sharply into late adolescence and then declines monotonically with increasing age. Adolescents have victimization rates that are typically three to five times greater than older adults do.

Another factor that influences victimization risk is socioeconomic status. In some research, unemployed people are considerably more likely to suffer personal and violent victimization. Other research shows that low occupational status and low personal or family income also increase risk of victimization. Although often closely related to socioeconomic and geographic effects, there is also evidence of racial susceptibility to crime: African Americans have much higher levels of victimization, particularly for serious violent crime. Finally, while gender differences in victimization are complicated and varied, women are overwhelmingly susceptible to sexual victimization that has some of the most significant and long-term costs.

While this entry has discussed the various factors that increase risks of victimization separately, it is important to recognize that these risk factors have compounding effects. That is, young urban males, particularly minority males living in deprived and transitional neighborhoods, have dramatically higher risk of victimization, particularly for serious violent crime. The tremendous costs that can stem from crime are typically borne by those who already lack social and financial resources. Thus, crime and its ensuing costs may play a significant role in the reproduction of social inequalities.

Directions for future research

A potentially important area for future research is the possibility of long-term socioeconomic deficits. Estimates of the costs of crime to victims generally focus on relatively short-term costs. Costs associated with property loss, property damage, physical injury, and psychological distress are all costs that incur during the victimization event itself or during the short period after the crime. Previous estimates have yet to fully consider long-term socioeconomic detriments stemming from violent victimization. Although this possibility is acknowledged, previous work has yet to articulate fully the mechanisms by which criminal victimization has long-term monetary costs and to incorporate such considerations in estimates of the overall costs of criminal violence.

Recent work in life-course sociology and human development provides a framework for estimating such costs. In general, life-course researchers attempt to identify the connections be-

tween disparate life-course events by demonstrating the effects of earlier events on later life-course outcomes. Life-course researchers delineate the complex ways in which life-course experiences influence expectations and aspirations that shape the direction of life-course development. From this perspective, we might anticipate that the crime-related psychological distress, even if short-lived, has the potential to disrupt processes of educational and occupational attainment, particularly when experienced during the early stages of the life course. Crime victimization in adolescence may reduce perceived self-efficacy with the consequence of lower educational attainment, higher unemployment, and poorer occupational status. Ultimately, diminished educational and occupational attainment should result in significantly lower income in later adult life. Through the linking of experiences with crime victimization, their psychological consequences, and life course paths of socioeconomic attainment, further and potentially substantial costs of crime seem likely. Exploring such long-term costs is an important avenue of future work.

Conclusion

Research on the costs of crime is important for understanding crime as a social problem. It also has the potential to influence policymaking on issues of crime and justice. First and foremost, it indicates the significance of crime as a social problem. Without even considering costs associated with individual and societal responses to crime, crime undermines quality of life and has significant personal costs for those most affected. Second, this work suggests an important avenue of social policy: minimizing both the direct and indirect costs of crime. Although prevention is clearly the most potent avenue for minimizing costs, other strategies that attack the various ways in which crime-related costs are incurred are also important. Third, this work provides an important means of evaluating current crime prevention and criminal justice practices. Estimates of the costs of crime can be compared with the costs of particular criminal justice initiatives and policies to assess the overall efficiency of criminal justice responses. With the increased expenditure on police and prisons in the late twentieth century, such comparisons seem both timely and important. Ultimately, estimating the costs of crime should play a key role in the development of effective social policy to reduce crime.

ROSS MACMILLAN

See also CRIMINOLOGY AND CRIMINAL JUSTICE RESEARCH: METHODS; CRIMINOLOGY AND CRIMINAL JUSTICE RESEARCH: ORGANIZATION; STATISTICS: REPORTING SYSTEMS AND METHODS.

BIBLIOGRAPHY

COHEN, MARK. "Pain, Suffering, and Jury Awards: A Study of the Costs of Crime to Victims." *Law and Society Review* 22, no. 3 (1988): 537–555.

COHEN, MARK; MILLER, TED; and ROSSMAN, SHELLI. "The Costs and Consequences of Violent Behavior in the United States." In *Understanding and Preventing Violence*. Edited by Albert Reiss and Jeffrey Roth. Washington, D.C.: National Academy Press, 1994. Pages 67–166.

MILLER, TED; COHEN, MARK; and WIERSEMA, BRIAN. *Victim Costs and Consequences: A New Look*. National Institute of Justice, 1996.

MOORE, MARK; PROTHROW-STITH, DEBRA; GUYER, BERNARD; and SPIVAK, HOWARD. "Violence and Intentional Injuries: Criminal Justice and Public Health Perspectives on an Urgent National Problem." In *Understanding and Preventing Violence*. Edited by Albert Reiss and Jeffrey Roth. Washington D.C.: National Academy Press, 1994. Pages 167–216.

PERKINS, CRAIG; KLAUS, PATSY; BASTIAN, LISA; and COHEN, ROBYN. *Criminal Victimization in the United States, 1993*. Washington, D.C.: Bureau of Justice Statistics, 1994.

SAMPSON, ROBERT, and LAURITSEN, JANET. "Violent Victimization and Offending: Individual Situational, and Community-Level Risk Factors." In *Understanding and Preventing Violence: Social Influences*. Vol. 3. Edited by Albert Reiss and Jeffrey Roth. Washington, D.C.: National Academy Press, 1994.

STATISTICS: HISTORICAL TRENDS IN WESTERN SOCIETY

The extent of crime in Western societies is an issue of grave concern to public officials and criminologists alike. Those who are projecting police budgets and building prisons need to know the levels and kinds of crime to expect in future years, just as those who think more broad-ly about the causes of crime need to know how it has undermined society in years past. Many in the public seek information about crime trends, and many groups develop such information. The problems inherent in determining the distribution of crime in society as well as its historical trends are substantial, and before an estimate of its historical extent in Western society can be provided, the difficulties in gathering such information should be considered.

Problems of measurement

Since the incidence of crime is largely unpredictable—like an earthquake—it can be measured only after it has already taken place. The measurement of crime, therefore, is subject to all the errors that indirect measurements entails. Attempts to measure crime omit some cases, record some that are not criminal, and incorrectly classify others. All attempts to measure crime reflect not simply the underlying incidence of criminal behavior but also any biases inherent in the measurement process itself.

Three common sources of information about crime include governmental organizations (the police, the courts, and correctional departments), individual researchers in contact with offenders (self-report studies), and survey organizations such as the U.S. Census Bureau, which collects victimization data. Most of what is known about crime is derived from at least one of these sources. Each assesses a distinct facet of crime and experiences distinct problems. Crime data issued by the courts and police have been a major source of information regarding criminality, especially before the modern era, but one must be aware of biases in data.

Police departments in particular are subject to many pressures that distort the crime picture they present. Some large departments are more effective in solving criminal cases than others, as a result of professional leadership, high morale, careful recruitment, or strong training programs. At the same time small departments in towns under ten thousand where neighborliness is the rule often have more accurate statistics regarding offenders, whether juveniles or adults; whites or blacks; or males or females, because thanks to cooperative attitudes among local people, they are able to solve a much larger portion of their minor crimes than departments in large cities. In towns with populations under 10,000 for example, 27.6 percent of motor vehicle thefts were cleared by arrests in 1998, but in cities with populations of one million or over, only 8.8 percent of these offenses were cleared.

This differential carries important implications for crime data on such problems as juvenile delinquency. If auto thefts are not cleared by arrests, the police have no basis for knowing what portion was committed by juveniles—normally about 8 percent in cities greater than 1 million. Since motor vehicle thefts are solved in small towns at rates substantially higher than in major cities, demographic data on auto thieves in small towns is more accurate than in large cities. In comparing the delinquency problem in major cities and small towns one must keep this difference in mind.

Inaccurate population estimates and subsequent distortions in crime rates also pose problems. It is very difficult to estimate population levels of cities and towns during serious social turmoil. During the Civil War large numbers of citizens were transplanted, thus making it difficult to gauge population size. For example, the U.S. Census Bureau conducted a census in Massachusetts at the beginning of the 1860s, and the state itself carried out another in 1865. But with a rapid influx of immigrants from Ireland and disturbances accompanying the Civil War, many lower-class people were not counted. Although the arrest figures were apparently accurate, arrests per 10,000 (as computed in those days) were inflated as a result of an under-estimate in the overall count. Crime data must be presented as rates per unit of population to enable comparisons among different sized cities, but if the population is inaccurately counted, crime rates will be skewed and comparisons unwise.

A different kind of problem plagues comparisons of criminality during different periods in the history of a city. It is common knowledge that policing takes several different forms or styles and that these distinctive styles operate at different levels of effectiveness. James Q. Wilson (1968) has identified three common patterns of operation among police departments. The service department tends to be small, close to the community, and informal, with few authority levels and little specialization. The watchman department tends to be larger, serving ethnically diverse cities in a balanced, unaggressive fashion. It seeks to avoid interethnic conflict and attempts above all to maintain stability in the community. The legalistic department puts more emphasis upon careful recruitment, sound training, and careful, dispassionate administration of the law (Wilson, chapters 6–8). This typology, though often criticized, has been widely used in police research. As a police department grows, if often becomes more formal and less approachable (Ferdinand, 1976). And as it evolves from a service to a legalistic or watchman pattern, its overall effectiveness and clearance rate decline. Such changes can have a sharp impact on complaints known to the police and on estimates of delinquency. Changes in city crime rates over several decades may well reflect such organizational changes. Long-term fluctuations in violent crime in Boston and Salem, cited below, probably also reflect such changes, that is, shifts in police style. Citizen cooperation, complaints brought to the police, and clearance rates all gradually decline as the community and its police department mature.

Court data must also be used with an eye to the peculiarities of a changing court system. Different criminal courts normally have jurisdiction over different segments of the criminal spectrum. City, state, and federal courts each despose of a distinctive blend of crime, and no single court can provide an accurate estimate of crime in a city. Each has its own distinctive jurisdiction, but two courts at different levels in the same system provide a more complete picture. Each court nevertheless follows different policies in prosecuting crime, and their jurisdictions do not overlap precisely. It is not always feasible, therefore, to assemble an accurate estimate of crime in the community from the activities of two or more related courts at different levels in the same system.

Pitfalls also await those who would compare the activities of a single court over time. For example, the *same* court may change its name and jurisdiction with the result that historians might inadvertently compare a lower court with a higher court. The Boston Municipal Court was established in 1800, but in 1859 it was renamed the Superior Court of Suffolk County. The Boston Police Court was founded in 1822, and in 1859 it was renamed the Municipal Court of Boston! A comparison of the Municipal Court in 1850 with the Municipal Court in 1870 would be inappropriate, because it would compare a lower court with a higher one. Despite these problems, the courts and the police are very useful sources of information regarding the incidence and distribution of crime, and for historical periods they offer virtually the only systematic data available. It is wise, nevertheless, to be aware of their weaknesses.

Criminality in the premodern era

Since criminal justice agencies did not issue regular reports before the modern era, knowledge of premodern criminality is limited. It is based for the most part on studies of early court records, church documents, or coroners' rolls and requires a painstaking effort to collect and infer useful data from handwritten documents. Studies of medieval European towns generally report very high levels of violent personal crime but lower levels of property crime. Naeshagen discovered that the homicide rate in Bergen, Norway, dropped from 80 per 100,000 in 1550 to 1 per 100,000 in 1800, and a study of coroners' rolls in fourteenth-century London revealed an annual homicide rate of about 44 per 100,000, or 110 times the modern rate of 0.4 per 100,000 in London (Hanawalt, p. 98). Very few infanticide cases were reported in Hanawalt's early study, and only about 2 percent involved intrafamilial violence, suggesting that such homicides were seriously underreported. At the same time, contemporary documents report a heightened alarm among citizens regarding the level of violence. Medieval communities from the Baltic to the Mediterranean were dangerous places. Given estimates, for example, that "every person in England in the thirteenth century, if he did not personally witness a murder, knew or knew of someone who had been killed" (p. 40).

By the end of the sixteenth century judges and others in England regularly lamented the rising tide of lawlessness, although the best evidence indicates that violent crime had not increased significantly since the fourteenth century. In rural areas crime was more typical of yeomen than peasants, though the gentry regularly defied the courts and were rarely punished. Justice was certainly swift in sixteenth-century England, but it was by no means sure (Baker). Those convicted of capital crimes and sentenced to die were, in the absence of reprieve, marched out of the courtroom and promptly hanged. But there were many legal detours on the way to the gallows. Pardons, both special and general, were one way of cheating the hangman; insanity, pregnancy, and childhood were others. The most common loophole was benefit of clergy, which by the sixteenth century had been extended to all who could read but was limited to cases of minor theft.

With the growth of commerce in seventeenth-century England, violent crime seems to have receded. A study of seventeenth-century Surrey and Sussex Counties indicates that the annual rate of homicide indictments for 1663–1694 was about 5.7 per 100,000, but by 1780–1802 this figure had dropped to 2.3 per 100,000. Property crime, however, increased slightly, with 53 indictments in the 1690s to 65 per 100,000 by the 1760s (Beattie, 1974). Indictments for both violent and property crimes were more common in urban areas (see Beattie, 1986, chaps. 3 and 4).

Colonial America experienced an even higher level of recorded criminality. The rate of violent crime in Boston in the early decades of the eighteenth century was about equal to that found for Surrey and Sussex, that is, 37 indictments per 100,000 between 1703 and 1732, but property crime in Boston was roughly twice as common at 123 indictments per 100,000 (Ferdinand, 1980a). This contrast is particularly striking in that Puritan New England had a reputation among the American colonies for sober conventionality and low crime.

Overall, one can place some confidence in these early studies of criminality, particularly those of homicide, since violent death was treated seriously by legal institutions. But medieval definitions of homicide embraced a much broader range of violent deaths than is the case today. They included, for example, many forms of accidental death that would not have found their way into a modern criminal court. While today's deadly weapons can kill from afar without warning (see Lane, 1979, p. 80), three hundred years ago fists, feet, spears, swords, and daggers required a determined effort that involved dangerous confrontations. Very high rates of homicide reported in the medieval period reflect these differences. On the other hand, infanticide was relatively common though prosecuted only haphazardly in earlier times (see Beattie, 1986, pp. 117–124; Lane, 1979, pp. 96–100, 110–111). Today it is systematically prosecuted as homicide. All in all, however, the level of violence was substantially higher in premodern Europe.

The figures for lesser crime are difficult to evaluate since legal institutions generally played a limited role in adjudicating minor offenses in deference to the church or other informal methods for punishing minor misbehavior. A large number of minor property crimes was settled privately by the victim and offender, and any estimate of premodern property crime probably underestimates its actual incidence. Many victims were reluctant to take their complaints to the courts, which had a reputation for uneven justice. Moreover, even short-term prison sentences often meant death, since living conditions in prison were abominable (Beattie, 1986, pp. 302–303). Many offenders went free, and many victims preferred to settle matters themselves. Unless there was a powerful reason for reporting a criminal offense to the court, many victims simply suffered in silence or settled matters individually.

Estimates of crime in the modern era

Early studies of property crime during the late eighteenth and early nineteenth centuries are colored by the role of legal institutions in the community. Where the courts were merely formal instruments for carrying out the informal will of the community—or where, in addition to the courts, the church and other nonlegal institutions played a major part in sanctioning wrongdoers as in medieval Europe and colonial America—the picture of crime provided by studies of court records probably underestimates the actual level of minor property crime. Where the courts had already achieved a high degree of independence and authority in a largely secular society, as in eighteenth-century England, estimates of criminality based upon court records are more accurate.

As the estimates of crime for modern societies are examined, the pattern becomes more interesting. Much more is known about the sociopolitical and legal forces that produced the reported crime patterns. The strains that modernization fostered in these societies are well understood, and the legal institutions themselves were often straining to develop the structures and procedures of a modern court system. The training of lawyers and judges was improved, criminal procedures were sharpened and rationalized, and new forensic methods for coping with a mounting volume of minor crime were invented, so that as the character of criminality changed in response to modernization, the legal institutions for coping with it were simultaneously perfected. Since both processes were occurring simultaneously, it is difficult to know which picture crime studies represent: crime as a changing social phenomenon, or crime as a reflection of evolving criminal institutions. In most cases the picture is a double exposure reflecting both aspect of the crime scene.

Nineteenth-century criminality

A number of studies relying heavily on court records have focused on crime in nineteenth-century cities and nations. Police data became available around the middle of the nineteenth century, and accordingly several investigators utilized this important source as well. Virtually every study reports a steady but substantial decline in crime during the nineteenth century. In France, for example, serious crime fell by nearly 90 percent between 1826 and 1954 (Lodhi and Tilly). In England and Wales indictable offenses declined by 79 percent between 1842 and 1891, and in London they declined by 63 percent between the 1820s and 1870s (Gatrell and Hadden). Much of the decline in London reflects a sharp drop in violent crime of about 68 percent between the 1830s and the 1860s. Larceny indictments also decreased in London, from about 220 per 100,000 in the 1830s and 1840s to about 70 per 100,000 in the 1850s, again by 68 percent. This decline, however, stems at least partially from a revision of the criminal code in 1855, which removed minor larcenies from the indictable category and permitted courts to deal with them summarily. Although this revision treated simple assaults similarly, nearly all the decline in assaults had occurred by 1855. Other property crimes, particularly burglary, fraud, and embezzlement, increased during this period or remained steady. In Stockholm the number of persons accused of theft fell from about 75 per 100,000 in the 1840s to about 22 in 1990, a 71 percent decline, and the number of persons sentenced for assault or breach of the peace dropped from about 400 per 100,000 in the 1840s to about 60 in the 1920s, an 85 percent decrease (Gurr, Grabosky, and Hula, pp. 256–257).

One of the few studies to reveal a different pattern focused on the Black Country, an area around Birmingham, England, that became a major steel-producing region in the late eighteenth and early nineteenth centuries. As the Black Country industrialized, it experienced steady increases in criminality. Larceny committals to trial rose from 91 per 100,000 in 1835 to about 262 in 1860, an increase of 188 percent, and committals to trial for offenses against the person increased from about 6 per 100,000 to about 14, a 133 percent increase (Philips, p. 143). This study suggests that rural areas and small towns exhibited sharply higher levels of criminality as they industrialized, whereas other studies of more heavily urbanized areas such as London and Stockholm found declines in serious criminality as they and their surrounding communities developed.

Studies of criminality in nineteenth-century American cities tend to bear out these data. In Boston the peak of recorded violent crime during the nineteenth century occurred in 1824 and was not exceeded until the 1970s. In 1824, shortly after it was established, the Boston Police Court recorded 1,430.5 prosecutions per 100,000 for crimes against the person, a figure close to four times the comparable arrest figure of 387.8 per 100,000 recorded by the police in 1967. Fluctuations in crime corresponding to wars and economic cycles beset Boston over the years, but the low mark in serious violent crime was recorded during 1928–1930, when the rate was only 28 percent of the 1824 peak. Property crime during the nineteenth century rose slightly from 859.4 per 100,000 in 1824 to 878.2 per 100,000 in 1884–1885 (Ferdinand, 1980a), and similar declines in violent crime occurred during the nineteenth century in Buffalo, New York (Powell), and Salem, Massachusetts (Ferdinand, 1972). On the other hand, a study of crime in Rockford, Illinois, founded in the 1840s, revealed that violent crime rose sharply from 1882–1884 to 1905–1907 (Ferdinand, 1976). After declining in the first half of the twentieth century, it rose sharply again during the 1950s and 1960s. Thus, established cities like Boston, Salem, and Buffalo enjoyed declining violent crime rates as they modernized, whereas relatively new communities and rural areas suffered rising violent crime rates as they industrialized.

The distinctive crime pattern of old cities undergoing industrialization has been explored carefully in a series of historical studies of European communities (Zehr). Older cities, though already high in violent crime, initially experienced even greater increases in violence as they industrialized. Low levels of property crime but high levels of violence were characteristic of premodern villages and rural areas, but industrialization tended to transform them into metropolitan centers with lower levels of violent crime and higher levels of theft. Thus, four distinct patterns of crime can be discerned: High levels of violent crime in old, premodern cities; low levels of property crimes in old, premodern rural areas; and two transitional patterns in which (1) old cities are transformed into urban, industrial centers with rising levels of violence initially but with declining levels ultimately and (2) rural areas transformed into new industrial centers with little theft but growing violence—prompted in each case by industrialization (see Zehr, pp. 122–126).

In the United States, however, this paradigm does not seem to describe the development of Boston, Buffalo, Salem, and New Haven as old cities. Befitting premodern small towns, they all displayed declining violence, along with property crime that at least remained steady—a pattern that was accented by the early courts as they rejected minor violent crimes to minimize caseloads. Had they been old, industrializing cities in the European sense, they would have shown *rising violent crime rates* in the short-run at least. Rockford, Illinois, however, which began as an industrializing village in the 1840s, did show rising violence as it grew into a city (Ferdinand, 1967, 1978). "Old" American cities, which were actually preindustrial small towns, came into the industrial era already experiencing relatively high levels of violent crime. As they industrialized, they attracted poor Irish immigrants and democrats protesting autocratic governments in northwestern Europe. With industrialization and minimal immigration their rates of violence receded from already high levels, but new American cities that industrialized virtually from the beginning showed rising levels of violent crime as rural people from the hinterland streamed in. Clearly, "old" American towns came into the cycle at different points than the medieval cities in Europe, though the cycle may well be similar in Europe and the United States.

At the same time legal institutions also began to play a much broader role in controlling public behavior (Ferdinand, 1992, chaps. 2 and 5). As the criminal courts displaced the church in controlling minor crime, they often recorded increases in the number of criminal cases well beyond those handled by the church because at first they attempted to maintain much the same standard of behavior the church had imposed earlier. Some of this rise reflects the zealousness of the courts, but it also derives from social changes noted above. Since these changes (legal as well as social) do not act in close harmony with one another, the overall crime trends of a wide range of cities usually fail to show a consistent pattern (cf. Zehr).

Criminality in the twentieth century

During the late nineteenth and early twentieth centuries, criminality in Western societies, particularly property crime, fluctuated in response to changing economic conditions. Although wars had an impact on crime rates, reducing them during hostilities and raising them afterward, their effects were not long-lasting in America. Periods of economic distress usually resulted in higher levels of property crime, especially burglaries, whereas prosperity typically produced lower levels. Oddly enough, juvenile delinquency rates followed a very different path during the 1930s and 1940s (Glaser and Rice). They rose during prosperity and fell during depression. Throughout this period juveniles consisted of a small but growing part of the crime problem with the spreading influence of peer groups and youth culture. Overall, the trend in property crime was downward, at least through World War II.

The Western decline in criminality during the late nineteenth and early twentieth centuries has triggered a controversy among historians and criminologists. Some believe that the decline represents a gradual adaptation of nineteenth-century immigrants to urban living (Lane, 1997, p. 186). Others argue that the decline reflects a growing effectiveness of urban police departments (Gatrell). On the whole, however, there are glaring difficulties with the thesis that declining urban crime rates between 1830 and 1950 resulted primarily from growing police efficiency. The earliest police departments were organized during the first half of the nineteenth century. The first was the London Metropolitan Police, in 1829, followed in the United States by police departments in Philadelphia (1833), Boston (1838), New York (1844), and Baltimore (1857). Their primary responsibility was to contain the civil disturbances that swept English and American cities during the early decades of the nineteenth century. During this period the middle class was growing rapidly, and they feared the mobs that gathered in cities during the summer months. Constables had checked crime in American cities during the early nineteenth century, but they were unable to cope with the riots that broke out with increasing frequency. Political support for an effective, centralized police force grew in these cities during the antebellum period.

If the decline in criminality after 1830 was an outgrowth of growing police effectiveness, why was the sharpest drop in violent personal crime and not in property crime? To be sure, property crimes are difficult to police because witnesses are rare, but why would the police concentrate mainly on violent crime? Moreover, why did violent crime continue to fall long after the appearance of well-organized police departments in the cities? In Boston, as reported, violent crime declined from 1824 (long before a modern police

force was even proposed) to a level in 1928–1930 just 28 percent of that prevailing a century earlier. Those who see the police as an important factor in this decline must explain why a decline in violence preceded the establishment of a police force and why the benefits continued long after its introduction. Further, conviction rates improved during the nineteenth century in London, which might suggest greater police effectiveness, but more probably it reflects a tendency by the police to reject minor cases. By the end of the twentieth century, the clearance rates in most Western police departments, including those in London, had gradually declined.

The close relationship between declining crime rates and a growing bureaucratization of the police in the twentieth century also undermines the thesis of greater police effectiveness as a reason for lower crime rates. A sharp decline in arrests followed closely a shift from foot patrols to motorized patrols in Salem, Massachusetts, and in Rockford, Illinois (see Ferdinand, 1972 and 1976). Further, in Boston several officers made more than 1,000 arrests in the 1850s, and in Salem the mean number of arrests per officer per year rarely fell below 30 during the latter half of the nineteenth century (Ferdinand, 1992, p. 45; 1972). But when the Salem police force began to patrol in cars, annual arrests per officer dropped sharply, and throughout the 1920s and 1930s the rate never rose above 21. By the 1950s and early 1960s the rate had slipped below 10 arrests per officer per year. The decline in criminality noted in the last half of the nineteenth century and the first half of the twentieth century probably stems more from broad changes in police organization than improvements in their ability to suppress crime.

Other shifts in police organization may also have contributed to a decline in crime rates between 1830 and 1950. Early police departments in American cities were often headed by men of reputation and integrity. Benjamin Pollard, who became Boston's first city marshal in 1823, was a Harvard graduate, a lawyer, and a man of distinction. His immediate successors, Daniel Parkman and Ezra Weston, served as Boston's police chiefs when the department was formed in 1838, and they were Harvard graduates and lawyers as well. In the beginning the Boston department was served by a cadre of officers who understood the purpose of police in a democratic society. But after the Civil War the department declined under the impact of fierce ethnic rivalries, intense political struggles, and organized vice.

Other urban departments, most notably in New York and Philadelphia, suffered similar burdens, and in general the quality of several major police departments, particularly in the old cities of the Northeast, dipped in the decades after the Civil War. The decline in crime in late nineteenth-century American cities can probably be attributed to a growing ineffectiveness in major urban police departments. Was an increasing efficiency of police departments a major factor in the decline in crime rates in the past 150 years? Probably not.

Another explanation is that urban immigrants, who had recently arrived from rural societies, were becoming better adapted to their communities as they gained experience with urban life (see Lane, 1997, p. 186). After settling into urban occupations and the city's established neighborhoods, they were drawn to a more stable, relatively crime-free life by churches, ethnic clubs, labor unions, political groups, informal social groups, family, and relatives. For the most part it was the rootless poor who fell into crime. As growing numbers of newcomers were absorbed into the mainstream, tramps and hoboes of the nineteenth century began to disappear.

During the 1930s a mobile army of rootless men reappeared, but all through the late nineteenth and early twentieth centuries their ranks had been shrinking in favor of a stable working class that increasingly established itself in neighborhoods throughout the cities of America. It is probably no coincidence that drunkenness and prostitution also declined steadily during the 1920s. As the working classes assumed a settled, stable pattern of life, criminality bespeaking a disorganized lifestyle also shrank.

The post–World War II crime wave

With the end of World War II and the economic recovery in Europe in the 1950s, crime rates and particularly rates of violent crime began to climb once again throughout the West. In England and Wales, murder and assault cases increased from 13 per 100,000 in 1950 to 144.3 per 100,000 in 1975, for an eleven-fold increase (Gurr, p. 363). During the same period the rate of larceny-theft rose from 847 per 100,000 to 3,659 per 100,000 for a more than four-fold increase, and by 1997 this figure came to 4,083 per 100,000. In Scandinavia much the same pattern unfolded. Between 1960 and 1974–1975, assaults and murders in Finland more than doubled from 127.9 to 282.0 per 100,000, and thefts

more than tripled from 886 to 2,850 per 100,000. And in Stockholm between 1950 and 1971 the rates of thefts, assaults, and murders more than quadrupled (Gurr, p. 364).

These increases in Europe were recorded mainly in the cities, and a similar pattern prevailed in the United States. Between 1960 and 1997 violent crimes known to the police in the United States shot up from 160.9 to 610.8 per 100,000, and property complaints rose from 1,726.3 to 4,311.9 per 100,000 (see F.B.I., 1961–1997).

The sources of this wave were certainly varied. They included among others a relative increase in the number of young people, the emergence of well organized juvenile peer groups, and expressionism—a strong belief that one's basic intuitions are accurate and justifiable. Expressionism took root in several hitherto tightly controlled groups—young people, females, blacks, and residents of rural areas. Between 1960 and 1997 the rate of arrests for violent crimes increased 500 percent among youths under 18; in rural counties the arrest rate for violent crimes increased by 251 percent between 1960 and 1980 for the same group (F.B.I., 1960–1997); and for blacks the comparable figure was 215 percent (Uniform Crime Reports, 1961–1997; *Statistical Abstracts*, 1960–1997). Property crime in the United States showed similar increases. From 1960 to 1977 the rate of females arrested for property crimes rose by 401 percent; the arrest rate of youths under 18 increased by 278 percent; and the arrest rate of blacks for property crimes climbed by 276 percent. Rural counties made a smaller contribution to the overall increase in property crime, rising by just 165 percent in the same period (F.B.I., 1961–1997). Such sharp increases are virtually unprecedented and are given careful consideration elsewhere.

Expressionism seems also to have affected the young people of Europe. After World War II several mildly antisocial groups became prominent in postwar European life: the Teddy Boys and Rockers in London, the Provos in Amsterdam, and the Raggare in Stockholm, and in the 1980s and 1990s other more criminal groups, such as football hooligans, skinheads, and, in the United States, youth gangs. In Europe youth crime was concentrated among young adults from eighteen to twenty-five, but in the United States youthful perpetrators were mainly under eighteen.

Among the explanations for sharp increases in youth crime in both the United States and Europe is the rapidly climbing birthrate after World War II. By the 1960s postwar babies had become teenagers and young adults, and as their numbers in comparison with other population segments grew, so did the percentage of those involved in crime. A study of the impact of the growing numbers of adolescents on postwar American crime revealed that 11.6 percent of the rise in serious crime between 1950 and 1965 was due simply to changes in the relative numbers of those 10–24 years old in the population. Auto theft and forcible rape were affected dramatically, up 13.8 and 47.1 percent, respectively; and homicide and aggravated assault were affected least of all—just 5.5 percent and 9.2 percent, respectively (Ferdinand, 1970).

But the young people in the 1960s had an impact on Western society not simply by virtue of their growing numbers. They were becoming increasingly conscious of their social and political position, and in the 1960s the dissenting voices of young people in Berkeley, Paris, and elsewhere were heard demanding change. This aggregation of young people into political, social, and seriously delinquent groups is a relatively modern development and is a major factor in the elevated crime rates of people at all levels of society. Young people learn the attitudes and techniques of delinquency and crime through the dominant youth culture, through their friends and peers, and as these peer networks have expanded, the problems of delinquency and youth crime also climbed sharply. In the United States youth gangs—many of them led by young adults—have supplanted traditional organized crime groups in several American cities, such as Chicago and Los Angeles. The rapid rise in youth crime in the postwar period is to some extent a consequence of an expanding youth culture, the growth of expressionism, and a rejection of traditional bourgeois values.

A critical view of conservative Victorian values was inspired partially by the civil rights struggles during the 1960s and 1970s, though such criticism has roots back at least to the 1920s and to Sinclair Lewis's *Main Street* and *Babbit*. Critical themes were embraced generally by young people after World War II, and the youth of Europe seized on iconoclastic themes as well. By the 1900s "hooligans" and "skinheads" in Europe had also become troublesome with their criminal behavior.

Conclusion

The discussion has identified several patterns in Western criminal behavior. First, evolving social and legal institutions in the West have contributed basically to a long-term, secular decline in violent offenses—a decline in homicide from fourteenth-century London to seventeenth-century Surrey and Sussex; a decline in violent offenses from 1824 to 1928 in Boston; and sizable declines in Bergen, Norway, and nineteenth-century London and Stockholm undoubtedly owe much to the gradual emergence of civic culture and rational legal institutions in the West.

The forerunner of modern legal institutions in England appeared first during the Middle Ages as the "King's Peace"—a domestic peace enforced by the King himself. Serious violations of the law were taken as violations of the King's Peace and were tried and punished by the King's royal courts. It was not possible, however, to institute a system of law everywhere at once by decree. Subduing violence depended upon a maturation of public culture so that individuals were willing to submit their personal quarrels to the king and his officers. Justice had to be legitimate, strong, and widespread to guarantee that those who accepted its authority would not be subsequently plundered by those who did not. As people recognized the fairness and justice of the royal courts, the legitimacy of legal solutions was increasingly accepted, and violence became less common in both public and private life. Under the impact of evolving legal institutions, a civic temper took hold among the English, and as this civic temper gained broader sway, serious crime and particularly violent crime receded. Acceptance of the King's Peace was the beginning of a gradual process growing out of the public's growing awareness of the efficacy of justice.

At the same time other forces were at work undermining the civilizing effects of royal justice and its institutions. As English society evolved from a folk-communal society to an urban-commercial society and later to an urban-industrial one, legal institutions displaced other important institutions in sanctioning deviance. The expanding jurisdiction of the criminal courts at first drove crime rates higher, but as we have seen, when legal institutions took firm root crime rates began to shrink.

A second conclusion focuses on the social bases of criminality. During much of the nineteenth century and the early part of the twentieth century, crime trends and particularly property crimes were closely attuned to improving economic conditions in America. Moreover, criminality as recorded by the courts and police was largely a working-class or lower-class phenomenon; relatively few middle-class individuals were implicated in common law violations. By the turn of the nineteenth century economic crime by the middle classes was drawing keen attention, but it had not yet been addressed comprehensively in the law.

During the 1960s and beyond, however, the close association between poverty and crime weakened. Prosperity was widespread and living standards were improving generally. But criminality rose even more rapidly, especially among the wealthy classes. It is now apparent that the values of broad segments of society changed during the 1960s and that new styles of behavior arose, some of which violated the criminal law. The changing crime patterns of the 1960s challenged economically based explanations of crime that had dominated the thinking of policymakers and criminologists for decades. Organized criminal groups became a major factor in the crime picture of Western nations.

A historical survey of crime patterns provides an excellent perspective against which to interpret modern developments. Present-day crime is relatively slight when compared with earlier times, and this improvement depends as much upon an emergence of civic culture as on instruments of justice. Such a survey also provides a basis for projecting future trends, though caution must prevail. Conditions that were important in the past may well prove insignificant in the future.

Although the levels of crime in the West may decline in the new millennium, the most prominent forms of crime in coming years will continue to be those spawned by youthful expressionism—gangs, illegal drugs, and violence. Crimes of protest will also continue, though probably not with the same intensity as in the recent past. Youth culture is a permanent feature of the modern world, and the implications of this fact for criminality are inescapable. A significant segment of the youth will continue to engage in criminal behavior, but skillful management of a prosperous economy could mean lower overall crime rates among both blacks and youths in the twenty-first century.

The assimilation of blacks in broader society has begun, and a black middle class with significant economic and political impact has emerged

so that crime by blacks may well continue to moderate in coming years. Indeed, the incidence of black crime has already slackened. In 1976 47.5 percent of violent crimes were committed by blacks, but in 1997 the corresponding figure was 41.1 percent (F.B.I., 1976–1997). Since 1976 the increase in violent crime by blacks has not kept pace with that of the society as a whole. In the United States the groups that have been heaviest contributors to criminality since the 1960s—young people and blacks—will lead a gradual decline in the coming decades. Indeed, between 1994 and 1998 violent juvenile crime dropped 19.2 percent (F.B.I., 1998, Table 34, p. 216), and continued declines in the future seemed likely. Violent crime rates could fall 10 to 15 percent from present levels by 2010.

Young women, like blacks, are intensely involved in a male-dominated youth culture, and expressionism among women is not uncommon. The expressionism of young women assumes a distinctive form, one that focuses heavily on sexual liberation and male-female relationships (Carns); mature women, on the other hand, are more independent, less imitative of male culture, less focused on male relationships, and more concerned with asserting their social and economic equality. How these differences evolve, as well as how they translate into crime, remain to be seen. Further increases in minor drug violations and larceny, along with continued instability in family relationships, seem likely for women as a whole. But female crime is only a small part of the overall picture, and increases here, even if in percentage terms, will not alter significantly the prediction of an overall 15 to 20 percent reduction in serious crime.

All the other components contributing to criminality in American cities, such as organized crime, professional crime, and immigration patterns should continue in much the same way as in the 1990s. Thus, declines in criminality projected for blacks and youths should contribute to an overall reduction of criminal activity in the United States by about 15 percent. Cities with heavy Hispanic immigrations, such as Miami, Chicago, and Los Angeles, will show declines smaller than those in cities like Minneapolis or San Jose, which have little Hispanic immigration. Added to these adjustments in the continued long-term integration of the underclass into the urban social fabric, which will also contribute to a slow decline in lower-class crime. Social dislocations such as severe depressions or political divisions will aggravate the crime problem, but the crime pattern of the nineteenth century, in which economic conditions in the lower classes broadly affected the level of crime in society, is being replaced by a pattern more closely affected by the values and morale of distinctive social and political groups. Some of these groups—women, blacks, and youths—are influenced more by their general social prospects than by their immediate economic condition. Accordingly, economic explanations of crime advanced by theorists in the 1970s will be of less value in the 1980s than theories focusing on the existential and social conditions of groups central to the crime problem.

THEODORE N. FERDINAND

See also DEVELOPING COUNTRIES, CRIME IN; ECOLOGY OF CRIME; GENDER AND CRIME; RURAL CRIME; STATISTICS: REPORTING SYSTEMS AND METHODS; URBAN CRIME.

BIBLIOGRAPHY

BAKER, J. H. "Criminal Courts and Procedure at Common Law, 1550–1800." Crime in England, 1550–1800. Edited by J. S. Cockburn. Princeton, N.J.: Princeton University Press, 1977. Pp. 15–48.

BEATTIE, J. M. "The Pattern of Crime in England, 1660–1880." Past and Present 62 (1974): 47–95.

———. Crime and the Courts in England, 1660–1800. Princeton, N.J.: Princeton University Press, 1986.

BELLAMY, JOHN G. Crime and Public Order in England in the Later Middle Ages. London: Routledge & Kegan Paul, 1973.

Bureau of the Census. Statistical Abstracts of the United States. Washington, D.C.: U.S. Department of Commerce, annual, 1960–1967.

CARNS, DONALD E. "Identity, Deviance, and Change in Conventional Settings: The Case of 'Sexual Revolution.'" Our American Sisters: Women in American Life and Thought. 2d ed. Edited by Jean E. Friedman and William G. Shade. Boston: Allyn & Bacon, 1976. Pp. 401–416.

Federal Bureau of Investigation. Crime in the United States. Uniform Crime Reports for the United States. Washington, D.C.: U.S. Department of Justice, annual, 1961–1998.

FERDINAND, THEODORE N. "The Criminal Patterns of Boston since 1849." American Journal of Sociology 73, no. 1, (July) 1967: 84–99.

———. "Research and Methodology: Demographic Shifts and Criminality: An Inquiry." British Journal of Criminology 10 (1970): 169–175.

———. "Politics, the Police, and Arresting Policies in Salem, Massachusetts since the Civil War." Social Problems 19 (1972): 572–588.

———. "From a Service to a Legalistic Style Police Department: A Case Study." Journal of Police Science and Administration 4, no. 3 (1976): 302–319.

———. "Criminal Justice: From Colonial Intimacy to Bureaucratic Formality." Handbook of Contemporary Urban Life. Edited by David Street. San Francisco: Jossey-Bass, 1978. Pp. 261–287.

———. "Criminality, the Courts, and the Constabulary in Boston: 1702–1967." Journal of Research in Crime and Delinquency 17 (1980a): 190–208.

———. "Delinquency in Developing and Developed Societies." Critical Issues in Juvenile Delinquency. Edited by David Shichor and Delos H. Kelly. Lexington, Mass.: Heath, Lexington Books, 1980b.

———. "The Theft-Violence Ratio in Antebellum Boston." Criminal Justice Review 16 (1990): 42–58.

———. The Lower Criminal Courts of Boston: 1814–1850. Newark, Del.: The University of Delaware Press, 1992.

GATRELL, V. A. C. "The Decline of Theft and Violence in Victorian and Edwardian England." Crime and the Law: The Social History of Crime in Western Europe since 1500. Edited by V. A. C. Gatrell, Bruce Lenman, and Geoffrey Parker. London: Europa, 1980. Pp. 238–370.

GATRELL, V. A. C., and HADDEN, T. "Criminal Statistics and Their Interpretation." Nineteenth-Century Society: Essays in the Use of Quantitative Methods for the Study of Social Data. Edited by Edward A. Wrigley. Cambridge, Eng.: Cambridge University Press, 1972. Pp. 336–396.

GIVEN, JAMES B. Society and Homicide in Thirteenth Century England. Stanford, Calif.: Stanford University Press, 1977.

GLASER, DANIEL, and RICE, KENT. "Crime, Age, and Employment." American Sociological Review 24 (1959): 679–686.

GURR, TED ROBERT. "On the History of Violent Crime in Europe and America." Violence in America: Historical and Comparative Perspectives. Rev. ed. Edited by Hugh Davis Graham and Ted Robert Gurr. Beverly Hills, Calif.: Sage, 1979. Pp. 353–374.

GURR, TED ROBERT; GRABOSKY, PETER N.; and HULA, RICHARD C. The Politics of Crime and Conflict: A Comparative History of Four Cities. Beverly Hills, Calif.: Sage, 1977.

HANAWALT, BARBARA A. *Crime and Conflict in English Communities, 1300–1348*. Cambridge, Mass.: Harvard University Press, 1979.

JOHNSON, DAVID R. *Policing the Urban Underworld: The Impact of Crime on the Development of the American Police*. Philadelphia: Temple University Press, 1979.

LANE, ROGER. *Policing the City: Boston 1822–1885*. Cambridge, Mass.: Harvard University Press, 1967.

———. *Violent Death in the City: Suicide, Accident, and Murder in the Nineteenth-Century Philadelphia*. Cambridge, Mass.: Harvard University Press, 1979.

———. *Murder in America*. Columbus, Ohio: Ohio State University Press, 1997.

LODHI, ABDUL QAIYUM, and TILLY, CHARLES. "Urbanization, Crime, and Collective Violence in Nineteenth-Century France." *American Journal of Sociology* 79 (1973): 296–318.

NAESHAGEN, FERDINAND L. "The Drastic Decline in Norwegian Homicide Rates Between 1500 and 1800." Paper presented at the American Society of Criminology meetings in Boston, 1995.

PHILIPS, DAVID. *Crime and Authority in Victorian England: The Black Country, 1835–1860*. London: Croom Helm, 1977.

POWELL, ELWIN H. "Crime as a Function of Anomie." *Journal of Criminal Law, Criminology, and Police Science* 57 (1966): 161–171.

RUGGIERO, GUIDO. *Violence in Early Renaissance Venice*. New Brunswick, N.J.: Rutgers University Press, 1980.

WILSON, JAMES Q. *Varieties of Police Behavior: The Management of Law and Order in Eight Communities*. Cambridge, Mass.: Harvard University Press, 1968.

ZEHR, HOWARD. *Crime and the Development of Modern Society: Patterns of Criminality in Nineteenth-Century Germany and France*. Totowa, N.J: Rowman & Littlefield, 1976.

STATISTICS: REPORTING SYSTEMS AND METHODS

In order to better understand, explain, and control crime, one needs accurate counts of its occurrence. *Crime statistics* represent the counts of criminal behavior and criminals. They are typically uniform data on offenses and offenders and are derived from records of official criminal justice agencies, from other agencies of control, and from unofficial sources such as surveys of victimization or criminal involvement. Particularly in the case of official crime statistics, they may be published annually or periodically in a relatively standard format of data presentation and analysis.

Official crime statistics are generated at different levels of government (municipal, state, and federal) by a variety of criminal justice agencies (police, court, and corrections) and at different stages in the criminal justice process (arrest, prosecution, conviction, imprisonment, and parole). Official statistics are also produced on the violation of laws, codes, and standards of a variety of administrative and regulatory agencies of control, primarily at the federal level. Official crime statistics are based on the records of those agencies that are the official registrars of criminal behavior and criminals.

Unofficial crime statistics are produced independently of the records of official agencies of crime control. The sources of these statistics are the records of private security and investigative agencies and the data collected by social scientists through experiments and observations, as well as through surveys of victimization and of self-reported criminal involvement.

Crime statistics emerged in the early nineteenth century as an adjunct to the administration of justice, the primary purpose being the measurement of the amount of crime, particularly "to know if crime had increased or decreased" in order to inform crime control policy and practice (Sellin and Wolfgang, p. 9). Early researchers pointed out the ultimately more important purpose of measuring the distribution of crime by a variety of social, demographic, and geographic characteristics. Both official and unofficial crime statistics have distinctive problems and sources of error, but a major one they share is the underestimation of the actual amount of crime. However, it is probable that the various measures generate similar distributions of crime, meaning that there is convergence rather than discrepancy in their depictions of the characteristics and correlates of crime. It is also likely that multiple indicators of crime best inform research, theory, policy, and practice.

The major types of official and unofficial crime statistics are discussed here in terms of their history and contemporary sources; their role as measures of crime; methodological and utilization issues and problems; and the general issue of discrepancy or convergence among crime statistics regarding the distribution and correlates of crime.

History of crime statistics

Simultaneously with the emergence of the discipline of statistics in the seventeenth century, the fledgling discipline's luminaries began to call for crime statistics in order to "know the measure of vice and sin in the nation" (Sellin and Wolfgang, p. 7). It was not until the nineteenth century that the measurement of a nation's moral health by means of statistics led to the development of the branch of statistics called "moral statistics." France began systematically collecting national judicial statistics on prosecutions and convictions in 1825. For the first time, comprehensive data on crime were available to the overseers of moral health, as well as to researchers. The French data became the source of the first significant statistical studies of crime, by the Belgian Adolphe Quetelet and the Frenchman Andre Michel Guerry, who have been called the founders of the scientific sociological study of crime. Soon afterward, similar analytical and ecological studies of crime were carried out by other Europeans who were influenced directly by, and made frequent references to, the work of Quetelet and Guerry.

In the United States, the earliest crime statistics were state judicial statistics on prosecutions and convictions in court and on prisoners in state institutions. New York began collecting judicial statistics in 1829, and by the turn of the twentieth century twenty-four other states had instituted systems of court data collection. Prison statistics were first gathered in 1834 in Massachusetts, and twenty-three other states had begun the systematic collection of prison data by 1900 (Robinson). The early state data on imprisonment were augmented by the first national enumeration of persons institutionalized in prisons and jails as part of the 1850 census and by subsequent decennial (taken every ten years) population counts thereafter. These early United States Bureau of the Census statistics are relatively complete and informative, including for each prisoner the year and offense of commitment, sex, birthplace, age, race, occupation, and literacy status.

By the end of the nineteenth century, most European countries and a number of states in the United States were systematically collecting judicial and prison statistics, and concomitantly most of the problems relating to these statistics and the measurement of crime in general had been identified. Numerous critics pointed to the fact that judicial and prison statistics were "incomplete" measures of the actual amount and distribution of crime in the community, primarily because of the "dark figure" of undetected, unreported, unacted upon, or unrecorded crime. It has always been clear that not all crimes committed in the community come to the attention of the police, that only a portion of crimes known to the police eventuate in arrest, that not all offenders who have been arrested are prosecuted or convicted, and that only a small fraction of the cases where there is a conviction lead to imprisonment. This underestimation of the volume of crime is not necessarily problematic if, as Quetelet suggested, we "assume that there is a nearly invariable relationship between offenses known and adjudicated and the total unknown sum of offenses committed" (p. 18). In other words, if there is a constant ratio between the actual amount of crime (including the dark figure of unknown offenses) and officially recorded crime, whether recorded by arrest, prosecution, conviction, or imprisonment, then the latter is "representative" of the former and acceptable as a measure of crime. Later research showed this to be a fallacious assumption, but during the nineteenth century and through the first quarter of the twentieth century, scholars and practitioners alike generally operated under this assumption in using and defending judicial statistics as the true measure of crime in a society. Critics pointed to the fact that judicial statistics were not representative of the actual number of crimes or criminals in their proposals that police statistics, particularly of "offenses known to the police," be used in the measurement of crime.

Beginning in 1857, Great Britain was the first nation to systematically collect police data, including offenses known to the police. The significance of this type of data was appreciated by only a few nineteenth-century scholars, among them Georg Mayr, the leading criminal statistician of the time. In 1867, he published the first statistical study using "crimes known to the police" as the primary data source, proposing that crimes known to the police should be the foundation of moral statistical data on crime (Sellin and Wolfgang, p. 14). A few researchers called for utilization of police statistics, but judicial statistics on prosecution and conviction remained the crime statistic of choice in studies of the amount and distribution of crime.

Although the origin, utilization, and defense of judicial statistics were a European enterprise, the emergence of police statistics as a legitimate and eventually favored index of crime can be characterized as an American endeavor. As a result of a growing dissatisfaction with judicial statistics and of the fact—axiomatic in criminology—that "the value of a crime rate for index purposes decreases as the distance from the crime itself in terms of procedure increases" (Sellin, p. 346), the American criminologist August Vollmer in 1920 proposed a national bureau of criminal records that, among other tasks, would compile data on crimes known to the police. In 1927 the International Association of Chiefs of Police made this suggestion an actuality by developing a plan for a national system of police statistics, including offenses known and arrests, collected from local police departments in each state. The Federal Bureau of Investigation became the clearinghouse for these statistics and published in 1931 the first of its now-annual Uniform Crime Reports (UCR). That same year, "offenses known to the police" was accorded even more legitimacy as a valid crime statistic by the Wickersham Commission, which stated that the "best index of the number and nature of offenses committed is police statistics showing offenses known to the police" (U.S. National Commission on Law Observance and Enforcement, p. 25). Ever since that time, "offenses known to the police" has generally been considered the best source of official crime data. However, most of the European countries that had developed national reporting systems of judicial statistics did not include police statistics, particularly crimes known, until the 1950s, and ironically, Great Britain did not acknowledge that crimes known to the police was a valid measure of crime until the mid-1930s, although these data had been collected since the mid-nineteenth century (Sellin and Wolfgang, pp. 18–21).

According to Thorsten Sellin's axiom, "crimes known to the police" has the most value of all official measures of crime because it is closest procedurally to the actual crime committed, probably as close as an official crime statistic will ever be. Even so, as with each and every measure and crime statistic, there are problems regarding even this best of official crime statistics.

Official crime statistics

Contemporary official crime statistics, proliferating with the growth of crime-control bureaucracies and their need to keep records, are more comprehensive and varied than nineteenth-century judicial statistics and early twentieth-century police statistics. The purposes and functions of crime statistics have also changed.

Whereas the early judicial statistics were utilized to measure a nation's moral health or the social and spatial distribution of crime, many of the more contemporary official statistics are the by-products of criminal justice "administrative bookkeeping and accounting." For example, data are collected on such matters as agency manpower, resources, expenditures, and physical facilities, as well as on warrants filed and death-row populations. Consequently, in the United States there are hundreds of national— and thousands of state and local—sources of official statistics, most of which are best characterized as data on the characteristics and procedures of the administration of criminal justice and crime control.

Given the different histories of judicial and police statistics in Europe and the United States, it is not surprising that in the latter there are relatively good police data compiled on a nationwide annual basis and relatively poor judicial data. In fact, the United States is one of only a few developed countries that publishes no national court statistics. Reflecting the unique history of corrections in the United States, where the state prison and local jail are differentiated by jurisdiction, incapacitative functions, type of inmate, and record-keeping practices, there are relatively comprehensive annual national data on the number and characteristics of adults under correctional supervision in state and federal prisons, but no national statistics on jail populations are published. A review of sources of criminal justice statistics concluded, "the absence of regular annual data on jail inmates is, along with the absence of court statistics, the most glaring gap in American criminal justice statistics" (Doleschal, p. 123).

Official crime statistics measure crime and crime control. Clearly, the historically preferred source of official statistics on the extent and nature of crime is police data, particularly crimes known to the police. Other official data gathered at points in the criminal justice system that are procedurally more distant from the crime committed are less valid and less useful measures of crime. However, these data can serve as measures of the number and social characteristics of those who are arrested, prosecuted, convicted, or imprisoned; of the characteristics, administration, and procedures of criminal justice within and between component agencies; and of the socially produced and recognized amount and distribution of crime. Official statistics, except for data on crimes known to the police are more correctly regarded as measures of crime control because they record a social-control reaction, of the criminal justice system to a known offense or offender. For example, a crime known to the police typically reported to the police by a complainant, and the record of it is evidence of the detection of a crime. If the police clear the offense through arrest, the arrest record is evidence of the sanction of a criminal, a measure of crime control (Black). In other words, a crime known to the police registers acknowledgment of an offense; an arrest, of an offender; a prosecution and conviction of the offender. Arrest, prosecution, conviction, and disposition statistics as well as administrative bookkeeping and accounting data, are best thought of as information of the characteristics, procedures, and processes of crime control. The focus in this entry will be the official statistics of crime, specifically police statistics of offenses known.

A measure of crime: offenses known to the police.   From the beginning, the primary objective of the Uniform Crime Reports was made clear in 1929 by the committee on Uniform Crime Records of the International Association of Chiefs of Police—to show the number and nature of criminal offenses committed. At the time it was argued that among the variety of official data, not only were "offenses known" closest to the crime itself, but a more constant relationship existed between offenses committed and offenses known to the police than between offenses committed and other official data—assumptions shown to be erroneous by victimization surveys many years later. Nevertheless the UCR have always been the most widely consulted source of statistics on crime in the United States.

The UCR are published annually by the F.B.I. and provide statistics on the amount and distribution of crimes known to the police and arrests, with other, less complete data on clearances by arrest, average value stolen in a variety of property offenses, dispositions of offenders charged, number of law enforcement personnel, and officers assaulted or killed. The statistics are based on data submitted monthly by the fifteen thousand municipal, county, and state law enforcement agencies, which have jurisdiction over approximately 98 percent of the U.S. population.

Of crimes known and arrests, data are collected in twenty-nine categories of offenses, using standardized classifications of offenses and reporting procedures. Crimes known and arrests are presented for the eight original "index crimes"—murder, rape, robbery, aggravated assault, burglary, larceny, motor-vehicle theft, and arson—and arrests only, for the remaining (nonindex) crimes. Arson was added as an index crime in 1979. For each index crime, crimes known to the police are presented by number of crimes reported, rate per hundred thousand population, clearances, nature of offense, geographical distribution (by state, region, size, and degree of urbanization), and number of offenders arrested. Arrests are presented by total estimate for each index and nonindex crime, rate per hundred thousand population, age, sex, race, and decade trend.

The index crimes are intended to represent serious and high-volume offenses. The Total Crime Index is the sum of index crimes, and subtotals are provided on violent and property index crimes. The Total Crime Index, and to a lesser extent the violent- and property-crime indexes, are often used to report national trends in the extent and nature of crime.

The statistics presented in the UCR of crimes known to the police are records of "reported" crime, and since reporting and recording procedures and practices are major sources of methodological and utilization problems, they deserve further attention. Crimes known to the police are typically offenses reported to the police by a victim or other person and are recorded as such unless they are "unfounded," or false. For property crimes, one incident is counted as one crime, whereas for violent crimes one victim is counted as one crime. Except for arson, the most serious of more than one index crime committed during an incident is counted; arson is recorded even when other index crimes are committed during the same incident. For example, stealing three items from a store counts as one larceny, but beating up three people during an altercation counts as three assaults.

Larceny and motor-vehicle theft account for the largest proportion of index crimes, for reasons pointed to by critics. Both are the least serious of the index crimes, with larceny of any amount now eligible to be counted, and motor-vehicle theft having one of the highest rates of victim reports to the police because theft must be established to file for insurance claims. On the other hand, many crimes that could be considered more serious because they involve physical injury and bodily harm to a victim are not index crimes. Moreover, completed and attempted crimes are counted equally for more than half of the index crimes. Robbery is counted as a violent crime and accounts for almost one-half of all reported violent index crimes. Most other countries classify robbery as a major larceny, as did the United States before the inception of the UCR. Of course, this difference in classification explains in part the relatively higher rate of violence in the United States. A number of other serious offenses are not counted at all in the reporting program, including a variety of victimless, white-collar, and organizational crimes, as well as political corruption, violations of economic regulations, and the whole array of federal crimes. One might characterize the Total Crime Index as a measure of the extent, nature, and trends of relatively ordinary street crime in the United States.

There are also some problems in the presentation of these data. The Total Crime Index, as a simple sum of index offenses, cannot be sensitive to the differential seriousness of its constituent offense categories and to the relative contributions made by frequency and seriousness of offenses to any index of a community's crime problem (Sellin and Wolfgang). Rudimentary summations of data also mask potentially important variations among offenses and other factors. Comparisons of data from year to year, and even from table to table for the same year, may be hampered in some cases because data may be analyzed in various ways (for example, by aggregating data in different ways for different tables). Comparisons are also made difficult by the use of inappropriate bases (or denominators) in the computation of the rates that are presented both for crimes known to the police and for arrests.

The crime rates given in the UCR, as well as in most criminal justice statistical series, are computed as the number of crimes per year per hundred thousand population. This type of "crude" rate can lead to inappropriate inferences from the data. The use of crude rates can conceal variation in subgroups of the population, so it is desirable to standardize rates for subgroups whose experience is known to be different, for example, by sex, race, and age. These subgroup-specific rates also facilitate comparisons between groups: male-female rates, white-black rates, and juvenile-adult rates.

At times, inappropriate population bases are used in calculating rates. A crime rate represents the ratio of the number of crimes committed to the number of persons available and able to commit those crimes; this ratio is then standardized by one hundred thousand of whoever is included in the base. For some offenses, the total population is an inappropriate base. For example, a forcible-rape crime rate based on the total population is less appropriate than a rate based on the number of males available and able to commit rape. Similarly, the juvenile crime rate should reflect the number of crimes committed by the population of juveniles.

Crime rates can be interpreted as victimization rates, depending on who (or what) are included in the base. If the total population base can be considered potential criminals, they can also be considered potential victims. For crimes where the victim is a person, the calculation of surrogate victimization rates using crime data is relatively straightforward—the number of available victims becomes the base. Again, in the case of forcible rape, the total population and the male population would be inappropriate bases—here the population of available victims is essentially female. Therefore, the surrogate victimization rate would be calculated as the number of forcible rapes known to the police per hundred thousand female population.

For property crimes it is more difficult, but not impossible, to calculate surrogate victimization rates. Here the denominator may have to be reconceptualized not as a population base but as a property base. For example, Boggs, and later Cohen and Felson, included "opportunities" for property theft in the bases of their analyses, including, for example, the number of cars available to steal. They reported that the subsequent opportunity-standardized rates were very different from the traditional population-standardized crime (or victimization) rates. Opportunity-standardized rates may sometimes differ even in direction. For example, rather than showing the rate of motor vehicle–related theft increasing, a corrected rate showed it to be decreasing (Wilkins; Sparks). Ultimately, of course, much more precise victimization rates are available from victimization survey data.

Finally, the total population base may be used incorrectly if the decennial Bureau of the Census counts of the population are not adjusted for projected population estimates on a yearly basis. For example, if the 1990 census data are used in the base to calculate 1999 crime rates, the rates will be artificially inflated simply as a consequence of using too small a population base. Obviously, 1999 population estimates are more appropriate in the calculation of 1999 crime rates.

Overall, the data presented in the UCR are "representative." However, the greatest threat to the validity of these statistics is differential reporting to the F.B.I. by local police, within participating departments, and to local authorities by citizen victims or other complainants. There is underreporting both by and to the police.

The reports of participating law enforcement agencies to the F.B.I. can be affected in a variety of ways, leading to variations in the uniformity, accuracy, and completeness of reporting. In spite of efforts to standardize definitions of eligible offenses, police in different states with different statutory and operational definitions of offense categories may classify crimes differently. There may be internal and external pressures on police agencies to demonstrate reductions in community crime or specific targeted offenses, and these pressures may induce police to alter classification, recording, and reporting procedures. Such changes can have a dramatic impact on the amount and rate of crime. A classic example was the reorganization of the Chicago police department. As part of the reorganization, more efficient reporting and recording procedures were introduced, and reported crime increased dramatically from 57,000 offenses in one year to 130,000 in the next (Rae).

To make the problems with the UCR even more complicated, the reported statistics can vary across time and place as policies change, police technology becomes more sophisticated, laws and statutes are modified, commitment to the program wavers, demands for information change, available resources fluctuate, and so on (Hindelang). Unfortunately, even if all the difficulties of validity, reliability, and comparability were eliminated and the statistics became completely and uniformly accurate, there would remain the more serious problem of differential reporting to the police by victims and other citizens. There is evidence of substantial underreporting and nonreporting to the police by victims of crime; in fact, the majority of crimes committed are not reported to the police.

The assumption of the originators of the UCR that there is a constant ratio between crimes known to the police and crimes committed has been shown to be fallacious by studies using unofficial crime statistics. One may never know the actual volume of crimes committed, and therefore the true base remains indeterminate. But more importantly, underreporting or nonreporting to the police varies by offense type, victim and offender characteristics, perceptions of police efficiency, and the like. In short, the dark figure of undetected and unreported crime limits the adequacy of even the historically preferred crimes-known-to-the-police index of the amount and distribution of crime.

NIBRS. During the 1980s, law enforcement agencies sought to improve official reporting methods, particularly the UCR. In 1985 the Bureau of Justice Statistics (BJS) and the F.B.I. released *Blueprint for the Future of the Uniform Crime Reporting Program* (Reaves, p. 1). This blueprint outlined the next generation of official reporting methods, specifically the National Incidence-Based Reporting System (NIBRS). Starting with 1991 data, the UCR program began to move to this more comprehensive reporting system. While the UCR is essentially offender-based, focusing on summary accounts of case and offender characteristics, the NIBRS is incident-based, seeking to link more expansive data elements to the crime, included in six primary categories: administrative, offense, property, victim, offender, and arrestee (Reaves, p. 2).

The first segment, the administrative, is a linking segment that provides an identifier for each incident. Further, this segment provides the date and time of the original incident as well as any required special clearance for the case. The second segment, the offense, details the nature of the offense(s) reported. Unlike the UCR, which is limited to a relatively small number of F.B.I. index crimes, NIBRS provides details on forty-six offenses. This specificity allows for more accurate reporting of the offense, as well as improved ability to analyze other characteristics of the crime. The offense category also examines conditions surrounding the event, such as drug or alcohol involvement at the time of the incident, what type of weapon, if any, was used, and whether or not the crime was completed. Segment three deals with the property aspects of the incident, such as the nature of the property loss (i.e., burned, seized, stolen), the type of property involved (i.e., cash, car, jewelry), the value of the property, and if the property was recovered and when. The fourth segment, victim, lists the characteristics of the individual victimized in the incident. The victim's sex, age, race, ethnicity, and resident status are presented and, in cases where the victim is not an individual, additional codes for business, government, and religious organizations are provided. Each of the victims is linked to the offender, by the offender number and by the relationship between the victim and the offender. Segment five focuses on the individual attributes of the offender rather than the victim. The final segment, arrestee, gives information on those arrested for the incident—the date/time of the arrest, how the arrest was accomplished, whether or not the arrestee was armed, and age, gender, race, ethnicity, and residence status of the arrestee (Reaves).

Data collection for NIBRS follows a process similar to that of the UCR, with local agencies reporting to the state program, which passes the information along to the F.B.I. However, one major change exists for those states desiring to participate in the NIBRS program—to begin regular submission of NIBRS data a state must be certified by the F.B.I. (Roberts, p. 7). The state must meet the following four criteria before becoming certified: First, the state must have an error-reporting rate of no greater than 4 percent for three consecutive months. Second, the data must be statistically reasonable based on trends, volumes, and monthly fluctuations. Third, the state must show the ability to update and respond to changes within the system. And finally, the state NIBRS program must be systematically compatible with the national program.

Calls for service.   Another method by which crime may be monitored utilizes emergency calls to the police. Some of the criticisms that have been leveled at arrest records (e.g., that they measure reactions to crimes rather than criminal involvement) and at victimization surveys (e.g., there may be systematic bias in the willingness of victims to report certain crimes to interviewers) may be addressed by this method of crime measurement.

It is suggested that the primary advantage of measuring crime through calls-for-service (CFS) is that it places the data closer to the actual incident. This removes additional layers in which bias or data loss can occur. For example, in order for a crime to be recorded as an arrest, the police must respond to the call, investigate the crime, find and arrest a suspect. At any one of these steps the process can be halted and nothing recorded, hiding the occurrence of the crime and contributing to the "dark figure." Similarly, within victimization surveys the respondent may forget events in the past, or the victim may choose not to give accurate information due to the sensitive nature of the crime. By placing the data gathering at the point of actually reporting the event to authorities means that the reports are "virtually unscreened and therefore not susceptible to police biases"(Warner and Pierce, p. 496).

As potentially valuable as these calls for service are, several weaknesses exist that create difficulty in utilizing them as crime measures. The first relates to the coding of a call to the police. Not all calls for police service focus on crime or legal issues—many are calls for medical or physical assistance, general emergencies, information requests, or "crank" calls. Clearly, they do not measure crime. At first glance, these appear easy to filter out of the data. But there are ambiguities; for example, how are medical conditions brought on by illegal activity (an individual consumes an illegal substance and has a negative reaction) coded? The call to 911 requests medical assistance but fails to mention the origin of the medical distress. The code for this event appears to be medical but in fact also represents a crime. Another concern surrounding the coding of a call has to do with the accuracy of what the individual is reporting to the operator. Not only can this lead to problems in the general categorization of a call as a crime (or not), but also in the specific crime being reported. The caller may not understand the nature of the event they are witness to, or the caller may desire a faster response from the police and inflate the severity of the offense. Further, even if citizens have a sound understanding of the legal nature of the event, they may be unable to articulate critical features of the event (e.g., high levels of anxiety, English as a second language).

A second major issue with CFS as a measure of crime is that many crimes come to the attention of the police by methods other than phone calls to the police department. Officers can observe crimes while patrolling or information can be directly presented to officers by citizens while on patrol or at station houses (Reiss). This creates a new aspect of the "dark figure"—reliance on CFS may tend to undercount crimes as police officers discover criminal activity through other means. Data collected by Klinger and Bridges found that officers sent out on calls encountered more crime than reflected in the initial coding of the calls (Klinger and Bridges, p. 719).

A final consideration in using CFS as a crime measure is that calls tend to vary according to the structural characteristics of the neighborhood. Where residents believe police respond slowly to their calls, where residents are more fearful of crime, and where there exists more criminal victimization, there will be systematic variation in the presentation of calls for service (Klinger and Bridges). For example, in high crime rate areas, residents may be sensitized to crime and report all behavior, resulting in many false positives. Thus, differences in CFS across communities may introduce additional sources of error.

Utilization of CFS data is an innovative approach to the measurement of crime. However, until the strengths and weaknesses of these records of initial calls to the police for a variety of services have been scrutinized to the same degree as the more traditional measures, some caution should be exercised with this "new" indicator of crime.

Accessing official reports

One of the most significant changes in using crime data over the past decade reflects the means of access to official crime statistics. Traditionally, in order to gather official crime figures one has either to rely on published documents (e.g., the annual UCR) or to contact the agency (federal, state, or local) that is the repository of the data and request access to the appropriate information. With the expansion of the Internet, many of these same agencies have placed their crime data online.

At the federal level, one example among many is the Bureau of Justice Statistics (www.ojp.usdoj.gov/bjs/). The BJS provides aggregate level data for the United States, in both absolute figures and rates for index and nonindex crimes. The BJS also provides data by region. Thus information, such as the UCR, can be accessed directly and within a format that allows for easy comparison between regions and over time.

Likewise, various state agencies have started to provide crime and criminal justice information on their web sites. For examples, the California Attorney General (www.caag.state.ca.us/) provides information on crimes within the state from 1988 until the present and presents comparative information on other states over the same period of time. The Texas Department of Criminal Justice (www.tdcj.state.tx.us/) not only provides information on crime rates within the state, but also gives statistics on demographic and offense characteristics of prisoners, including those on death row.

Even local agencies, such as city police departments, provide crime statistics. For examples, the San Diego Police Department (www.sannet.gov/police) provides a breakdown of total aggregate crime citywide, the respective rates of each crime, and the geographic distribution of crime citywide and for specific areas with-

in the city. The Dallas Police Department (www.ci.dallas.tx.us/dpd/) presents a map of the city divided into "reporting areas" that allows the viewer to select an area in which they are specifically interested and to gather the relevant crime data.

The expansion of the Internet and its utilization by law enforcement agencies facilitate access to criminal justice data sources and statistics within minutes rather than days or weeks. The information is provided typically within a spreadsheet format or simple tables. This makes the utilization of information on crime much easier, for law enforcement, researchers, and the public.

Applications of official data

A number of computerized information and data management systems have been created to facilitate both the apprehension of offenders and research on crime. They are typically local or regional efforts, providing law enforcement agencies in particular the capacity to store, manage, and utilize individual-level, comprehensive record information on case characteristics, offenders, victims, tips, crime locations, and so on. The goal, in increasing the quantity and quality of information available to law enforcement agencies, is to enhance the effectiveness and efficiency of the criminal justice system. One example of this type of data system is the Homicide Investigation and Tracking System (HITS).

The HITS program was originally funded under a National Institute of Justice (NIJ) grant that sought to examine homicides and their investigations within Washington State (Keppel and Weis). A computerized information system, which included all homicides in the state from 1980 forward, was created to facilitate the examination of solvability factors in homicide investigations, as well as to provide a comprehensive, ongoing database to be used by investigators to inform and enhance their case investigations. This was accomplished by having law enforcement officers fill out a standardized case form, which contains hundreds of pieces of information, on the victim(s), offender(s), locations, time line, motives, cause of death, autopsy results, evidence, and so on. In effect, a digitized version of the most relevant features of a case file were input to the database.

The HITS program contains information from six major sources and is stored in seven different data files: murder, sexual assault, preliminary information, Department of Corrections, gang-related crimes, Violent Criminal Apprehension Program, and timeline. These data files can then be queried by the investigator for a wide range of information, such as victims' gender, race, and lifestyle; date and cause of death; location of body; and other similar characteristics. This allows investigators to make their search as wide or narrow as the case demands, in order to improve their ability to focus on an offender.

HITS also provides an excellent source of information for researchers. The HITS program provides initial official reports of crimes that are generated in close temporal proximity to the crime. Also, because the HITS program maintains separate databases of information provided by public sources (e.g., licensing, corrections, motor vehicles), researchers can link separate sources of information on the same case, improving the analysis of the crime. The query system also allows researchers to create aggregate data sets, adjusting for a range of variables such as time of year or day, location within state, mobility of offenders, and so on. The HITS system, and others like it, then, not only improve the ability of law enforcement to solve crimes but also the ability of researchers to analyze them.

Unofficial crime statistics

Even though most of the fundamental problems with official crime statistics had been identified before the end of the nineteenth century, including the major problem of the dark figure of unknown crime, it was not until the mid-twentieth century that systematic attempts to unravel some of the mysteries of official statistics were initiated. Turning to data sources outside of the official agencies of criminal justice, unofficial crime statistics were generated in order to explore the dark figure of crime that did not become known to the police, to create measures of crime that were independent of the official registrars of crime and crime control, and to address more general validity and reliability issues in the measurement of crime.

There are two categories of unofficial data sources: social-science and private-agency records. The first of these is much more important and useful. Among the social-science sources, there are two major, significant measures, both utilizing survey methods. The first is self-reports of criminal involvement, which were initially used in the 1940s to "expose" the amount of hidden crime. The second is surveys of victimization, the most recent and probably the most important and influential of the unofficial crime statistics. Victimization surveys were initiated in the mid-1960s to "illuminate"—that is, to specify rather than simply to expose—the dark figure and to depict crime from the victim's perspective. There are also two minor, much less significant sources of social-science data: observation studies of crime or criminal justice, and experiments on deviant behavior. Among the sources of private-agency records are those compiled by firms or industries to monitor property losses, injuries, or claims; by private security organizations; and by national trade associations. The focus here will be on the social-science sources of unofficial crime statistics, particularly victimization and self-report surveys.

Victimization surveys. Recognizing the inadequacies of official measures of crime, particularly the apparently substantial volume of crime and victimization that remains unknown to, and therefore unacted upon by, criminal justice authorities, the President's Commission on Law Enforcement and Administration of Justice initiated relatively small-scale pilot victimization surveys in 1966. One was conducted in Washington, D.C. A sample of police precincts with medium and high crime rates was selected, within which interviews were conducted with residents. Respondents were asked whether in the past year they had been a victim of any of the index crimes and of assorted nonindex crimes. Another surveyed business establishments in the same precincts in Washington, D.C., as well as businesses and residents in a sample of high-crime-rate precincts in Boston and Chicago. The instruments and procedures used in the first pilot survey were modified and used to interview residents in the second study. Owners and managers of businesses were asked whether their organization had been victimized by burglary, robbery, or shoplifting during the past year. The third pilot survey was a national poll of a representative sample of ten thousand households. Again, respondents were interviewed and asked whether they or anyone living with them had been a victim of index and nonindex crimes during the past year. They were also asked their opinions regarding the police and the perceived personal risk of being victimized.

The pilot studies verified empirically what criminologists had known intuitively since the early nineteenth century—that official crime statistics, even of crimes known to the police, underestimate the actual amount of crime. However, these victimization studies showed that the dark figure of hidden crime was substantially larger than expected. In the Washington, D.C., study, the ratio of reported total victim incidents to crimes known to the police was more than twenty to one (Biderman). This dramatic ratio of hidden victimizations to reported crimes was replicated among the individual victims in the Boston and Chicago study (Reiss) and in the national pilot survey, which showed that about half of the victimizations were not reported to the police (Ennis). The survey of business establishments discovered the inadequacy of business records as measures of crime, showed higher rates of victimization than police records indicated, and verified the valid reporting of business victimization by respondents (Reiss). These studies also demonstrated that the discrepancy between the number of victimizations and of crimes reported to the police varies importantly by the type of offense and by the victim's belief that reporting a crime will have consequences. In general, the more serious the crime, the more likely a victim is to report it to the police; minor property crimes are reported least frequently. As a result of the startling findings of these pilot victimization surveys and of the subsequent recommendations of the President's Commission, an annual national victimization was initiated in the National Crime Victim Survey (NCVS).

In 1972 the United States became one of the few countries to carry out annual national victimization surveys. The NCVS is sponsored by the Bureau of Justice Statistics (within the United States Department of Justice) and is conducted by the Bureau of the Census. Its primary purpose is to "measure the annual change in crime incidents for a limited set of major crimes and to characterize some of the socioeconomic aspects of both the reported events and their victims" (Penick and Owens, p. 220). In short, the survey is designed to measure the amount, distribution, and trends of victimization and, therefore, of crime.

The survey covers a representative national sample of approximately sixty thousand households, and through 1976 it included a probability sample of some fifteen thousand business establishments. Within each household, all occupants fourteen years of age or older are interviewed, and information on twelve- and thirteen-year-old occupants is gathered from an older occupant. Interviews are conducted every six months for three years, after which a different household is interviewed, in a constant process of sample entry and replacement.

The crimes measured in the NCVS are personal crimes (rape, robbery, assault, and theft), household crimes (burglary, larceny, and motor-vehicle theft), and business crimes (burglary and robbery). These crimes were selected intentionally for their similarity to the index crimes of the UCR in order to permit important comparisons between the two data sets. The only two index crimes missing are murder, for which no victim can report victimization, and arson, the ostensible victim of which is often the perpetrator.

The statistics on victimization generated by the NCVS provide an extremely important additional perspective on crime in the United States. Ever since they were first published, the survey's reports have forced a revision in thinking about crime. For example, a report on victimization in eight American cities, using data from the very first surveys, provided striking confirmation of the magnitude of the underreporting and nonreporting problem identified in the pilot projects. Comparing the rates of victimization and crimes known to the police, the victimization data showed fifteen times as much assault, nine times more robbery, seven times the amount of rape, and, surprisingly, five times more motor-vehicle theft than reported in the UCR for the same period (U.S. Department of Justice).

Some of the discrepancy in the two rates can be accounted for by the practices of the police—not viewing a reported offense as a crime, failing to react, and not counting and recording it. But since the time of the pilot research it has been clear that the major reason for the discrepancy is the reporting practices of victims: the pilot national survey reported that approximately 50 percent of victimizations are not reported to the police (Ennis). An analysis of preliminary data from the first NCVS in 1973 concluded that nonreporting by victims accounted for much more of the difference between victimization and official crime rates than did nonrecording by the police. Almost three-fourths (72 percent) of the crime incidents are not reported to the police, ranging from a nonreporting rate of 32 percent for motor-vehicle theft to a rate of 82 percent for larceny (Skogan).

The primary reasons for citizen hesitancy to report crime to the police are relatively clear—the victim does not believe that reporting will make any difference (35 percent) or that the crime is not serious enough to bring to the attention of authorities (31 percent) (U.S. Bureau of the Census). The less serious crimes, particularly minor property crimes, are less often reported to the police, and the more serious ones are reported more often. Paradoxically, some of the more serious personal crimes, including aggravated assault or rape, are not reported because a personal relationship between victim and perpetrator is being protected or is the source of potential retribution and further harm (Hindelang, Gottfredson, and Garofalo). Another crime, arson, presents the problems of potential overreporting and of distinguishing between victim and perpetrator, since collecting insurance money is often the motive in burning one's own property.

The NCVS does not merely provide another national index of crime, a view of crime from the perspective of the victim, and illumination of the dark figure of hidden crime. It has also contributed to a better understanding of crime in the United States, forcing scholars and criminal justice professionals alike to question many basic assumptions about crime. Perhaps most perplexing are the implications of the victimization trend data. From 1973 to the 1990s, the overall victimization rate remained relatively stable from year to year, whereas the UCR showed a more inconsistent and upward trend. It was not until the observed decline in crime from about 1992 until 2001, that the UCR and NCVS both showed the same trend, due perhaps to refinements in both systems. However, there are a number of possible interpretations for the differences, centering on the relative strengths and weaknesses of official records of crimes known to the police, as compared to unofficial victim reports.

In general, victimization surveys have the same problems and threats to validity and reliability as any other social-science survey, as well as some that are specific to the NCVS. Ironically, there is a "double dark figure" of hidden crime—crime that is not reported to interviewers in victimization surveys designed to uncover crimes not reported to the police! Such incomplete reporting of victimization means that victimization surveys, like official data sources, also underestimate the true amount of crime. Of course, this suggests that the discrepancy between the crime rate estimates of the NCVS and of the UCR is even larger than reports indicate.

A number of factors contribute to this doubly dark figure of unreported victims. One of the most difficult problems in victimization surveys is to anchor the reported crime within the six-month response frame. A respondent not only has to remember the crime incident, but must also specify when it took place during the past six months. Memory may be faulty the longer the period of time between the crime and interview; the more likely is memory to fail a respondent who either forgets an incident completely or does not remember some important details about the victimization. The less serious and more common offenses are less worth remembering because of their more trivial nature and ephemeral consequences. The concern and tolerance levels of victims may also affect their recollection of crime incidents. Moreover, telescoping may take place: the victimization may be moved forward or backward in time, from one period to another. A victim knows that a crime took place but cannot recall precisely when. Another source of inaccurate and inconsistent responses is deceit. Some respondents may simply lie, or at least shade their answers. There are many reasons for deceit, including embarrassment, social desirability (wish to make a socially desirable response), interviewer-respondent mistrust, personal aggrandizement, attempts to protect the perpetrator, disinterest, and lack of motivation. Memory decay and telescoping are neither intentional nor manipulative, and are therefore more random in their effects on responses. They are likely to contribute to the underestimation of victimization. However, deceit is intentional and manipulative, and it is more likely to characterize the responses of those who have a reason to hide or reveal something. The effects on victimization estimates are more unpredictable because deceit may lead to underreporting among respondents but to overreporting among others. One can assess the extent of underreporting through devices such as a "reverse record check," by means of which respondents who have reported crimes to the police are included in the survey sample (Turner; Hindelang, Hirschi, and Weis, 1981). Comparing a respondent's crime incidents reported in the victimization interview with those reported to the police provides a measure of underreporting. A problem, though, is that underreporting can be validated more easily than overreporting. One "underreports" crimes that actually took place. For every official crime known to the police of a particular offense category, one can be relatively certain of underreporting if no victimization is reported for that offense category. If more victimizations are reported for an offense category than are known to the police, one cannot know whether the respondent is overreporting. A person may "overreport" crimes that never took place—they cannot be known, verified, or validated.

One of the strengths of the NCVS, namely, that the crimes included in the questionnaire are F.B.I. index crimes, is also a problem. In addition to the fact that two of the index crimes (murder and arson) are not included, many other important crimes are not measured in the victimization surveys. Obviously, the whole array of crimes without victims are excluded, as well as the nonindex crimes and crimes not included in the UCR program. The result is that the victimization statistics are somewhat limited in their representativeness and generalizability.

An important limitation of the design of the NCVS is a strength of the UCR—its almost complete coverage (98 percent) of the total United States population and the resultant ability to examine the geographic and ecological distribution of crime from the national level to the levels of regions, states, counties, Standard Metropolitan Statistical Areas, cities, and local communities. Historically, data on victimization have been collected from a sample of the population, which has varied around 100,000 respondents, distributed geographically throughout the United States. There are simply not enough data to generate meaningful and useful statistics for each of the geographic and ecological units represented in the UCR. This would require a comprehensive census of households, the cost of which would be prohibitive.

Another design problem is referred to as bounding, or the time frame used as the reference period in interviews, which is established at the first interview on a six-month cycle for "household location." This is done to fix the empirically determined optimum recall period of six months and to avoid double reporting of the same crime incident by respondents. The bounding of household locations rather than of the occupants of the household has also been a problem. If the occupants move, the new occupants are not bounded, and it has been estimated that about 10 to 15 percent of the sample consists of unbounded households. This factor, coupled with the mobility of the sample, creates a related problem: complete data records covering the three-year span of each panel are available for perhaps only 20 percent of the respondents. This restricts general data analysis possibilities, particularly the feasibility and utility of these data for longitudinal analyses of victimization experiences (Fienberg).

Finally, there are the inevitable counting problems: When there is more than one perpetrator involved in a crime, it is particularly difficult for respondents to report the number of victimizers with accuracy. The typical impersonality of a household burglary makes it impossible for a victim to know the number or characteristics of the burglars. Even as personal a crime as aggravated assault often presents the victim with problems in accurately recalling his perceptions when more than one person attempted or did physical injury to his body. The respondent's reports, then, may be less accurate when the perpetrator could be seen or when there was more than one observable perpetrator. If a respondent reports multiple victimizers in a crime incident, whether a property crime or violent crime, it counts as one victimization—the general counting rule is "one victim, one crime." By itself this is not necessarily problematic, but if one compares victimization rates and official crime rates for property offenses (for which the UCR counting rule is "one incident, one crime"), there may be sufficient noncomparability of units to jeopardize the validity of the comparison. For example, a three-victim larceny would yield three reports of victimization but only one crime known to the police. A three-victim assault would yield three of each and present fewer problems of comparability. The perspectives of the victim and the police are different, as are those of the NCVS and the UCR in counting and recording crime incidents with different statistical outcomes and interpretations.

A more serious counting problem involves series victimizations or rapid, repeated similar victimization of an individual. For a victim, it can be very difficult to separate one crime from another if they are very similar and happen within a compressed time period. The consequence is that validity suffers and there is a tendency to "blur" the incidents and to further underestimate the number of victimizations. The questionnaire separates single and series incidents, which are defined as three or more similar crimes that the respondent cannot differentiate in time or place of occurrence. Early publications of the NCVS excluded these series victimizations from the published victimization rates, raising the possibility that the rates are underestimations. Even more of the dark figure of hidden crime might be illuminated. If this and other problems with victimization surveys are resolved, the discrepancy between the amount of crime committed and the amount eventually reported to the police may become more substantial. There is little evidence that victims (except those of forcible rape) are changing their patterns of reporting crimes to the police, but there is mounting and more rigorous evidence that our ability to measure the amount and distribution of the dark figure of unreported crime is improving.

Self-report surveys. Surveys of self-reported criminal involvement are an important part of the improved capacity to illuminate the dark figure, in this case from the perspective of the criminal (or victimizer). The origin of self-report surveys predated victimization surveys by more than twenty years. Preliminary, groundbreaking research on self-reported hidden crime was conducted in the 1940s, but the method of simply asking someone about the nature and extent of his own criminal involvement did not become a recognized standard procedure until the late 1950s, with the work of James Short and Ivan Nye.

Austin Porterfield first used this variation of the survey research method of "self-disclosure" by a respondent in 1946, to compare the self-reports of college students regarding their delinquent activities while they were in high school with self-reports of delinquents processed through the juvenile court. Not only were more offenses admitted than detected, but also more significantly, it appeared that the college students had been involved in delinquency during their adolescence in ways similar to those of the officially defined delinquents. These findings suggested that the distinction between delinquent and nondelinquent was not dichotomous, but rather more continuous, and that crime was perhaps distributed more evenly in the American social structure than official statistics would suggest. Fred Murphy, Mary Shirley, and Helen Witmer reported in 1946 that the admissions of delinquent activities by boys who participated in a delinquency prevention experiment significantly surpassed the number of offenses that came to the attention of juvenile authorities. James Wallerstein and Clement Wyle conducted a study that remains unique in self-report research because it surveyed a sample of adults in 1947. They discovered that more than 90 percent of their sample of about fifteen hundred upper-income "law-abiding" adults admitted having committed at least one of forty-nine crimes included in the questionnaire.

These early self-report survey findings confirm empirically what criminal statisticians, law enforcement authorities, and even the public had known since the time of Quetelet—that a substantial volume of crime never comes to the attention of the criminal justice system. The hint that some of this invisible crime is committed by persons who are not usually considered candidates for official recognition as criminals was even more revelatory and intriguing, but remained dormant for a decade.

Heeding suggestions that criminology needed a "Kinsey Report" on juvenile delinquency, Short and Nye in 1957 developed an anonymous, self-administered questionnaire that contained a checklist of delinquent acts, which was administered to populations of students and incarcerated delinquents. Their research had a more profound and longer-lasting impact because it was tied to theory-testing and construction (Nye) and, more importantly, because it provocatively verified the hint only alluded to in the earlier self report-studies—that crime is not disproportionately a phenomenon of the poor, as suggested by official crime statistics. The self-report data were apparently discrepant with the official data because they showed that self-reported delinquency was more evenly distributed across the socioeconomic status scale than official delinquency. This one provocative finding called into question the correlates and theories of juvenile delinquency and crime because most were based on official crime statistics and that period's depiction of crime and delinquency as a phenomenon of the poor. The controversy set off by the work of Short and Nye still continues.

Literally hundreds of similar studies have been carried out since Short and Nye's pioneering work, most with similar results: there is an enormous amount of self-reported crime that never comes to the attention of the police; a minority of offenders commits a majority of the offenses, including the more serious crimes; the more frequently one commits crimes, the more likely is the commission of serious crimes; and those most frequently and seriously involved in crime are most likely to have official records. Self-report researchers have tended to assume that self-reports are valid and reliable—certainly more so than official measures. Ever since the mid-1960s, work critical of criminal justice agencies and of official crime statistics generated further support for these assumptions. A few theorists, such as Travis Hirschi, even constructed and tested delinquency theories based on self-report measures and their results.

It has been suggested, "confessional data are at least as weak as the official statistics they were supposed to improve upon" (Nettler, p. 107). This criticism is damning to the extent that the statistics produced by the self-report method and official statistics are valid and reliable measures of crime: if one rejects official statistics, then one should also question the adequacy of self-report statistics. Furthermore, as with official records and victimization surveys, there are a number of problems with the self-report method. Some of these are problems shared by victimization surveys and self-report surveys, and others are unique to the latter. The shared problems are the basic threats to the validity and reliability of responses to survey questions, including memory decay, telescoping, deceit, social-desirability response effects, and imprecise bounding of reference periods. The unique problems fall into four categories: inadequate or unrepresentative samples, unrepresentative domains of behavior measured, validity and reliability of the method, and methods effects.

Whereas the national victimization surveys cannot provide refined geographical and ecological data because of the dispersion of the probability samples across the United States, self-report surveys have other problems of representativeness and generalizability because they do not typically use national samples. Practically all self-report research is conducted with small samples of juveniles attending public schools in a community that, characteristically, is relatively small, often suburban or rural, and modally middle-class and white. This, of course, restricts the ability to generalize beyond these kinds of sample characteristics to adults, juveniles who are not in school, those who refuse to participate, urban inner-city juveniles, and poor and nonwhite youngsters. Such "convenience" samples also create analytic problems because data on those variables that are correlated with delinquency are simply unavailable or underrepresented in the sample. In short, most self-report research has somewhat limited generalizability because of typical sample characteristics. On the other hand, unlike the NCVS or UCR, self-report surveys were not intended originally to produce national or even generalizable estimates of the amount of juvenile delinquency crime in the United States.

Self-report surveys were intended, however, to produce data on a variety of delinquent behaviors. Compared to the restricted range of index crimes included in the NCVS, the domain of behavior measured in self-report surveys is expansive, with as many as fifty illegal acts in a questionnaire not being uncommon. Such expansiveness, however, creates other problems. Historically, the juvenile court has had jurisdiction over both crimes and offenses that are illegal only for juveniles, usually referred to as status offenses and including truancy, incorrigibility, curfew violation, smoking, and drinking. Self-report surveys have correctly covered crimes and status offenses alike in studying juvenile delinquency, but in some cases there has been an overemphasis on the less serious offenses. To the extent that there is an overrepresentation of less serious and perhaps trivial offenses, self-report measures are inadequate measures of the kind of serious juvenile crime that is likely to come to the attention of authorities. This is important in describing accurately the characteristics of juvenile offenders and their behavior, as well as in comparing self-report and official data. Such comparison is crucial to validation research, where one needs to compare the same categories of behavior, including both content and seriousness, in order to assess the reciprocal validity of self-report and official measures. In criminology as elsewhere, one should not compare apples with oranges!

Unfortunately, there has been a dearth of this kind of careful validation research, as well as of systematic research on reliability. The accuracy and consistency of self-report surveys have been assumed to be quite acceptable, or, if questions have been posed, they have typically come from validity and reliability research on general social-science survey methods. For example, it has been assumed that anonymous surveys are more valid than signed surveys and that interviews are preferred over self-administered questionnaires. Yet no study had directly compared the validity, and only one had compared the reliability, of two or more self-report methods within the same study until the work of Michael Hindelang, Travis Hirschi, and Joseph Weis in 1981. In those isolated studies where validity and reliability were addressed, external validation criteria such as official record data have been used too infrequently.

Of course, critics have remained skeptical about the accuracy of responses from liars, cheaters, and thieves, as well as from straight and honorable persons. The latter are not motivated by deception or guile, but they may respond incorrectly because a questionnaire item has poor face validity meaning that it does not make sufficiently clear what is being asked and that the respondent is consequently more free to interpret, construe, and attribute whatever is within his experience and imagination. For example, a common self-report item, "Have you ever taken anything from anyone under threat of force?" is intended to tap instances of robbery. However, respondents might answer affirmatively if they had ever appropriated a candy bar from their kid sister. This problem of item meaning and interpretation is chronic in survey research, but it only remains problematic if no validation research is undertaken to establish face validity. Unfortunately, this has been the case in the development of self-report instruments.

There has been a basic inattention to the psychometric properties of self-report surveys and attendant methods effects on measurement. From the psychometric research that went into the development of the NCVS, it is clearer that the bounding practices in self-report research have been inadequate: the reference periods are typically too long and variable from study to study. Most self-report surveys ask whether a respondent has "ever" committed a crime, a few use the past "three years," some use the past "year," but very few use the past "six months" (or less), which was established as the optimum recall period for the national victimization surveys. This poses threats to the accuracy of responses since it is established that the longer the reference period, the more problems with memory decay, telescoping, and misinterpretation of events.

A related problem arises when the self-report researcher wants to find out how often within a specified period a respondent has committed a crime. A favored means of measuring the frequency of involvement has been the "normative" response category. A respondent is asked, "How often in the past year have you hit a teacher?" and is given a set of response categories that includes "Very often," "Often," "Sometimes," "Rarely," and "Never." One respondent can check "Rarely" and mean five times, whereas another can check the same response and mean one time. They each respond according to personal norms, which are tied to their own behavior, as well as to that of their peers. This creates analytic problems because one cannot norm (that is, accurately compare) the answers of each respondent, obviating meaningful comparisons. A great deal of information is thus lost. Simply asking each respondent to record the actual frequency of commission for each offense can solve these problems.

Finally, unlike the NCVS and the UCR, there is very little about self-report surveys—

whether their samples, instruments, or procedures—that is "standardized." This restricts the kinds of comparison across self-report studies that could lead to more improvements in the method and provide a more solid empirical foundation for theory construction and testing, as well as the possibility of nationwide self-report statistics comparable to those of the NCVS and the UCR.

This lack of standardization, inadequacies of samples, and the question of the differential validity and reliability of self-report and official measures of crime have led to two important developments in the research of crime statistics. The first is the initiation of surveys of national representative samples of juveniles for the purpose of estimating the extent and nature of delinquency and of substance abuse in the United States. The second is the conducting of more rigorous and comprehensive research on the differential validity and reliability of official, as compared to self-report, measures of crime and delinquency. In 1967, the National Institute of Mental Health initiated the first of an interrupted but relatively regular series of National Youth Surveys of a representative sample of teenage youths, who were interviewed about a variety of attitudes and behaviors, including delinquent behavior. This survey was repeated in 1972, and in 1976 the National Institute for Juvenile Justice and Delinquency Prevention became a cosponsor of what has become an annual self-report survey of the delinquent behavior of a national probability panel of youths aged from eleven to seventeen years. The two major goals are to measure the amount and distribution of self-reported delinquent behavior and official delinquency and to account for any observed changes in juvenile delinquency.

These periodic national self-report surveys allow more rigorous estimation of the nature and extent of delinquent behavior. It is ironic, however, that the validity, reliability, and viability of the self-report method as an alternative or adjunct to official measures was not assessed rigorously until Hindelang, Hirschi, and Weis began a study of measurement issues in delinquency research, focusing on the comparative utility of self-report and official data.

Within an experimental design, a comprehensive self-report instrument was administered to a random sample of sixteen hundred youths from fourteen to eighteen years of age, stratified by sex, race (white or black), socioeconomic status (high or low), and delinquency status (nondelinquent, police contact, or court record). Officially defined delinquents, boys, blacks, and lower-socioeconomic-status subjects were oversampled in order to facilitate data analysis within those groups that are often underrepresented in self-report studies. Subjects were randomly assigned to one of four test conditions that corresponded to four self-report methods of administration: anonymous questionnaire, signed questionnaire, face-to-face interview, and blind interview. A number of validation criteria were utilized, including the official records of those subjects identified in a reverse record check, a subset of questions administered by the randomized response method, a deep-probe interview for face validity testing a subset of delinquency items, and a follow-tip interview with a psychological-stress evaluator to determine the veracity of responses. The subjects were brought to a field office, where they answered the questions within the method condition to which they were randomly assigned. This experimental design, coupled with a variety of external validation criteria and reliability checks, ensures that the findings and conclusions can be drawn with some confidence—undoubtedly with more confidence than in any prior research on validity and reliability in the measurement of delinquency.

Hindelang, Hirschi, and Weis's study produced a variety of findings on the whole range of previously identified methodological problems and issues. Official crime statistics, it concluded, generate valid indications of the sociodemographic distribution of delinquency. Self-reports, indeed, measure a domain of delinquent behavior that does not overlap significantly with the domain covered by official data, particularly for the more serious crimes. However, self-reports can measure the same type and seriousness of delinquent behaviors as are represented in official records. Within the domain of delinquent behavior that they do measure, self-reports are very reliable, and basically valid. Self-report samples have been inadequate in that they do not include enough officially defined delinquents, nonwhites, and lower-class youths to enable confident conclusions to be drawn regarding the correlates of the more serious delinquent acts for which a juvenile is more likely to acquire an official record. Delinquency, whether measured by official or self-report data, is not equally distributed among all segments of society—there are real differences between those youngsters who engage in crime and those who do not. Methods of administration have no significant effects on the prevalence, incidence, validity, or reliability of self-reports. There is apparently less validity in the self-reports of those respondents with the highest rates of delinquency—male, black, officially defined delinquents. Perhaps the most significant finding of the research is related to this finding of differential validity for a small subpopulation of respondents. As originally proposed by Hindelang, Hirschi, and Weis in 1979, the empirical evidence shows that there is no discrepancy in the major correlates of self-reported or official delinquency, except for race, which may be attributable to the less valid responses of black subjects, particularly males with official records of delinquency.

The finding that self-reports and official measures do not produce discrepant results regarding the distribution and correlates of delinquency, but rather show convergence, is a critical piece of evidence in the controversy that has existed among criminal statisticians since the dark figure was identified at the beginning of the nineteenth century. Does the distribution of crime look the same when those crimes not known to the police are included in the overall distribution and with the distribution of crimes known to the police? Are the different sources of crime statistics producing discrepant or convergent perspectives of crime?

Conclusion: discrepancy or convergence?

Returning to the two primary purposes of crime statistics, to measure the "amount" and "distribution" of crime, it is clear that there has been, and will probably continue to be, discrepancy among the estimates of the amount of crime that are generated by the variety of crime statistics. The dark figure of crime may never be completely illuminated, the reporting practices of victims will probably remain erratic, and the recording of crimes by authorities will continue to be less than uniform.

However, the ultimately more important purpose of crime statistics is the measurement of the distribution of crime by a variety of social, demographic, and geographic characteristics. Fortunately, the major sources of crime data—crimes known to the police, victimization surveys, and self-report surveys—generate similar distributions and correlates of crime, pointing to convergence rather than discrepancy among the measures of the basic characteristics of crime and criminals. The problems associated with each of the data sources remain, but they diminish in significance because these imperfect measures produce similar perspectives of crime. As Gwynn Nettler concluded, "Fortunately, despite the repeatedly discovered fact that more crime is committed than is recorded, when crimes are ranked by the frequency of their occurrence, the ordering is very much the same no matter which measure is used" (p. 97).

Comparisons of data from the UCR and the NCVS program show that they produce similar patterns of crime (Hindelang and Maltz). There is substantial agreement between the two measures in the ordering of the relative frequencies of each of the index crimes. Comparisons of self-reports of delinquency with crimes known to the police show that each provides a complementary rather than a contradictory perspective on juvenile crime (Hindelang, Hirschi, and Weis, 1981; Belson). Self-reports do not generate results on the distribution and correlates of delinquency that are contrary to those generated by police statistics or, for that matter, by victimization surveys. The youngsters who are more likely to appear in official police and court record data—boys, nonwhites, low achievers, youths with friends in trouble, urban residents, and youths with family problems—are also more likely to self-report higher rates of involvement in crime.

This message should be of some comfort to a variety of people interested in crime and delinquency, from researchers and theorists to policymakers, planners, program implementers, and evaluators. The basic facts of crime are more consistent than many scholars and authorities in the past would lead one to believe. In fact, the major sources of official and unofficial crime statistics are not typically inconsistent in their representations of the general features of crime but rather provide a convergent perspective on crime. The characteristics, distribution, and correlates of crime and, therefore, the implications for theory, policy, and programs are not discrepant by crime measure, but convergent. The data generated by a variety of measures are compatible and confirming sources of information on crime. The study and control of crime can best be informed by these complementary sources of crime statistics.

JOSEPH G. WEIS
BRIAN C. WOLD

See also CRIMINOLOGY AND CRIMINAL JUSTICE RESEARCH: METHODS; CRIMINOLOGY AND CRIMINAL JUSTICE RESEARCH: ORGANIZATIONS; STATISTICS: COSTS OF CRIME; STATISTICS: HISTORICAL TRENDS IN WESTERN SOCIETY.

BIBLIOGRAPHY

BELSON, WILLIAM A. *Juvenile Theft: The Causal Factors—A Report of an Investigation of the Tenability of Various Causal Hypotheses about the Development of Stealing by London Boys.* New York: Harper & Row, 1975.

BIDERMAN, ALBERT D. "Surveys of Population Samples for Estimating Crime Incidence." *Annals of the American Academy of Political and Social Science* 374 (1967): 16–33.

BLACK, DONALD J. "Production of Crime Rates." *American Sociological Review* 35 (1970): 733–748.

BOGGS, SARAH L. "Urban Crime Patterns." *American Sociological Review* 30 (1965): 899–908.

COHEN, LAWRENCE E., and FELSON, MARCUS. "Social Change and Crime Rate Trends: A Routine Activity Approach." *American Sociological Review* 44 (1979): 588–608.

DOLESCHAL, EUGENE. "Sources of Basic Criminal Justice Statistics: A Brief Annotated Guide with Commentaries." *Criminal Justice Abstracts* 1 1 (1979): 122–147.

ENNIS, PHILIP H. *Criminal Victimization in the United States: A Report of a National Survey.* Chicago: University of Chicago, National Opinion Research Center, 1967.

Federal Bureau of Investigation. *Crime in the United States.* Uniform Crime Reports for the United States. Washington, D.C.: U.S. Department of Justice, F.B.I., annually.

FIENBERG, STEPHEN E. "Victimization and the National Crime Survey: Problems of Design and Analysis." *Indicators of Crime and Criminal Justice. Quantitative Studies.* Edited by Stephen E. Fienberg and Albert J. Reiss, Jr. Washington, D.C.: U.S. Department of Justice, Bureau of Justice Statistics, 1980. Pages 33–40.

GUERRY, ANDRE MICHEL. *Essai sur la slatistique morale de la France, precede dun Rapport a L Academie des Sciences, par MM. Lacroix, Silvestre, et Girard.* Paris: Crochard, 1833.

HINDELANG, MICHAEL J.; GOTTFREDSON, MICHAEL R.; and GAROFALO, JAMES. *Victims of Personal Crime: An Empirical Foundation for a Theory of Personal Victimization.* Cambridge, Mass.: Ballinger, 1978.

HINDELANG, MICHAEL J. "The Uniform Crime Reports Revisited." *Journal of Criminal Justice* 2 (1974): 1–17.

HINDELANG, MICHAEL J.; HIRSCHI, TRAVIS; and WEIS, JOSEPH G. "Correlates of Delinquency: The Illusion of Discrepancy between Self-

Report and Official Measures." *American Sociological Review* 44 (1979): 995–1014.

———. *Measuring Delinquency*. Beverly Hills, Calif.: Sage, 1981.

HIRSCHI, TRAVIS. *Causes of Delinquency*. Berkeley: University of California Press, 1969.

KEPPEL, ROBERT, and WEIS, JOSEPH G. "Improving the Investigation of Violent Crime: The Homicide Investigation and Tracking System." Washington, D.C.: U.S. Department of Justice, 1993.

KLINGER, DAVID, and BRIDGES, GEORGE. "Measurement Error in Calls-For-Service as an Indicator of Crime." *Criminology* 35 (1997): 705–726.

KULIK, JAMES A.; STEIN, KENNETH B.; and SARBIN, THEODORE R. "Disclosure of Delinquent Behavior under Conditions of Anonymity and Nonanonymity." *Journal of Consulting and Clinical Psychology* 32 (1968): 506–509.

MALTZ, MICHAEL D. "Crime Statistics: A Mathematical Perspective." *Journal of Criminal Justice* 3 (1975): 177–193.

MURPHY, FRED J.; SHIRLEY, MARY M.; and WITMER, HELEN L. "The Incidence of Hidden Delinquency." *American Journal of Orthopsychiatry* 16 (1946): 686–696.

NETTLER, GWYNN. *Explaining Crime*, 2d ed. New York: McGraw-Hill, 1978.

NYE, F. IVAN. *Family Relationships and Delinquent Behavior*. New York: Wiley, 1958.

PENICK, BETTYE K. EIDSON, and OWENS, MAURICE E. B. III, eds. *Surveying Crime*. Washington, D.C.: National Academy of Sciences, National Research Council, Panel for the Evaluation of Crime Surveys, 1976.

PORTERFIELD, AUSTIN L. *Youth in Trouble: Studies in Delinquency and Despair, with Plans for Prevention*. Fort Worth, Tex.: Leo Potishman Foundation, 1946.

President's Commission on Law Enforcement and Administration of Justice. *The Challenge of Crime in a Free Society*. Washington, D.C.: The Commission, 1967.

QUETELET, ADOLPHE. *Recherches sur le penchant au crime aux differens ages*, 2d ed. Brussels: Hayez, 1833.

RAE, RICHARD F. "Crime Statistics, Science or Mythology." *Police Chief* 42 (1975): 72–73.

REAVES, BRIAN A. "Using NIBRS Data to Analyze Violent Crime." *Bureau of Justice Statistics Technical Report*. Washington, D.C.: U.S. Department of Justice, 1993.

REISS, ALBERT J., JR. *Studies in Crime and Law Enforcement in Major Metropolitan Areas*. Field Survey III, vol. 1. President's Commission on Law Enforcement and Administration of Justice. Washington, D.C.: The Commission, 1967.

ROBERTS, DAVID. "Implementing the National Incident-Based Reporting System: A Project Status Report: A Joint Project of the Bureau of Justice Statistics and the Federal Bureau of Investigation [SEARCH, the National Consortium for Justice Information and Statistics]." Washington, D.C.: U.S. Department of Justice, 1997.

ROBINSON, LOUIS N. *History and Organization of Criminal Statistics in the United States* (1911). Reprint. Montclair, N.J.: Patterson Smith, 1969.

SELLIN, THORSTEN. "The Basis of a Crime Index." *Journal of the American Institute of Criminal Law and Criminology* 22 (1931): 335–356.

SELLIN, THORSTEN, and WOLFGANG, MARVIN E. *The Measurement of Delinquency*. New York: Wiley, 1964.

SHORT, JAMES F., JR., and NYE, F. IVAN. "Reported Behavior as a Criterion of Deviant Behavior." *Social Problems* 5 (1957–1958): 207–213.

SKOGAN, WESLEY G. "Dimensions of the Dark Figure of Unreported Grime." *Crime and Delinquency* 23 (1977): 41–50.

SPARKS, RICHARD F. "Criminal Opportunities and Crime Rates." *Indicators of Crime and Criminal Justice: Quantitative Studies*. Edited by Stephen E. Fienberg and Albert J. Reiss, Jr. Washington, D.C.: U.S. Department of Justice, Bureau of Justice Statistics, 1980. Pages 18–32.

TURNER, ANTHONY. *San Jose Methods Test of Known Crime Victims*. Washington, D.C.: U.S. Department of Justice, Law Enforcement Assistance Administration, National Institute of Law Enforcement and Criminal Justice, 1972.

U.S. Bureau of the Census. *Criminal Victimization Surveys in the Nation's Five Largest Cities: National Crime Panel Surveys of Chicago, Detroit, Los Angeles, New York, and Philadelphia*. Washington, D.C.: U.S. Department of Justice, Law Enforcement Assistance Administration, National Criminal Justice Information and Statistics Service, 1975.

U.S. Department of Justice, Law Enforcement Assistance Administration, National Criminal Justice Information and Statistics Service. *Criminal Victimization Surveys in Eight American Cities: A Comparison of 1971/1972 and 1974/1975 Findings*. Washington, D.C.: NCJISS, 1976.

U.S. National Commission on Law Observance and Enforcement [Wickersham Commission]. *Report on Criminal Statistics*. Washington, D.C.: The Commission, 1931.

VOLLMER, AUGUST. "The Bureau of Criminal Records." *Journal of the American Institute of Criminal Law and Criminology* 11 (1920): 171–180.

WALLERSTEIN, JAMES S., and WYLE, CLEMENT J. "Our Law-Abiding Law-Breakers." *Probation* 25 (1947): 107–112.

WARNER, BARBARA D., and PIERCE, GLENN L. "Reexamining Social Disorganization Theory Using Calls to the Police as a Measure of Crime." *Criminology* 31 (1993): 493–517.

WILKINS, LESLIE T. *Social Deviance: Social Policy, Action, and Research.* Englewood Cliffs, N.J.: Prentice-Hall, 1965.

STATUTORY RAPE

See RAPE: LEGAL ASPECTS.

STRICT LIABILITY

Although there is some dispute as to whether Anglo-American criminal law has always required the state to prove that the defendant had a culpable mental state for every element of an offense, there is general consensus that, except for the rule that ignorance of the law is no excuse and the felony murder doctrine, such a mental state has been required for criminal liability over the last few centuries. In the middle of the nineteenth century, however, both American and English courts began interpreting newly coined statutes that did not specify a mens rea as to one or more elements as dispensing with this bedrock requirement (Husak; Sayre; Singer). The practice has been criticized by commentators almost unanimously, and there is some reason to believe it is on the wane. Nevertheless, it is still highly controversial.

The paradigmatic case of strict criminal liability is where a totally innocent actor (Joan) possesses, sells, or transports a white powder that she honestly and reasonably believes to be salt but that turns out to be cocaine. If she is held criminally responsible for possessing cocaine, she is said to be held "strictly liable." Most cases of "strict criminal liability" involve instances where the defendant has made a mistake with regard to an attendant circumstance (fact) of the crime.

Strict criminal liability is often confused with vicarious liability, with which it may overlap. Thus, if A, B's employee, knowingly serves liquor to a minor, and B is held liable, B is vicariously liable, but not strictly liable, since someone for whom he is held responsible acted with mens rea.

If, however, A did not know his customer was a minor, and is nevertheless held liable, A is strictly liable. And if B is held liable as well, he is now vicariously and strictly liable. Many of the early cases understood to impose strict liability actually involved vicarious liability.

Historical reasons for development

The development of strict criminal liability between 1850 and 1950 may be explained in several ways.

Legal positivism. Courts—particularly nineteenth-century courts in democratic societies—were extremely deferential to legislatures, finding little constitutional limitation upon legislative power, because legislatures and not courts were democratically elected. If a statute did not contain a mens rea word, the courts assumed the legislature had affirmatively intended *not* to adopt such a requirement and they upheld the statute. The assumption that legislatures intentionally omit a mens rea word, however, is always problematic and frequently wrong.

Regulatory statutes. As markets grew more widespread, legislatures reached out to control perceived widespread abuses in the manufacturing and sale of products generally. Intending to protect the consumers from ills they could not discover for themselves, legislatures passed, and courts enforced, strict liability statutes that carried relatively mild penalties (usually fines) against the merchants. Thus, a person who sold diluted milk would be guilty of an offense even if, in fact, there was no way for him to detect the dilution, and he had taken every possible precaution against such dilution. These statutory "children of the industrial revolution" were said to be necessary for several reasons: (1) the sheer bulk of cases could overwhelm court systems; (2) the difficulty of proving mens rea would create lengthy and cumbersome trials; (3) the penalties imposed would not stigmatize the defendants, but merely regulate their behavior by making them more cautious. With the growth of the (civil) regulatory state, however, the need for such criminal liability has become increasingly dubious.

Minor penalties. Courts often sustained such offenses by pointing out that in many of these crimes, the penalties were "light"—often, but not invariably, involving only fines and no loss of liberty. Two problems with this approach, however, were ignored: (1) some of these offenses did provide for imprisonment; (2) all criminal convictions are deemed to carry with them the stigmatization of at least grossly careless conduct and character. The assertion that strict liability offense did not carry stigma was totally untested. Moreover, many statutes interpreted as applying strict liability apply rather severe penalties. For example, in *United States v. Balint* (258 U.S. 250 (1922)), the Supreme Court intimated that strict criminal liability could be imposed notwithstanding a possible punishment of five years. In the decision of *Staples v. United States* (114 S. Ct. 1793 (1994)), the Court, while emphasizing that a long prison sentence might well require interpreting a statute to require mens rea, rejected a suggestion that a ten-year prison sentence would automatically exclude strict criminal liability.

Protection of minors.   Many of the statutory schemes read as dispensing with mens rea involved protecting minors. For example, allowing minors to be present in billiard halls, or the serving of alcohol to minors, were held to be strict liability crimes with regard to the age of the person present or served. No matter how carefully defendants acted to assure that the person involved was not a minor, if they were wrong, they were frequently convicted.

Sexual conduct.   Many of the statutes involved sexual conduct—bigamy, adultery, fornication, and so-called statutory rape. Besides the arguable prudishness of the age, these statutes might now have been seen as ways to protect marriage and minors.

Greater legal wrong theory.   Courts would sometimes impose criminal liability upon a defendant who knew, or at least suspected, that he was committing a civil offense, such as a tort or breach of contract. If it also turned out that his act was a crime, the courts held him liable for the greater legal punishment. For example, if defendant contracted with a parent to provide food for a child, he might know that failure to do so would result in a breach of contract suit, but be unaware that the contract might be read as creating a criminal duty upon himself as well.

Greater moral wrong theory.   As suggested above, many statutes read as imposing strict criminal liability regulated sexual activities among nonmarried persons. Since such actions were morally suspect the courts were willing to place upon the actors the risk that they were perpetrating not merely a moral wrong, but a crime as well. The most notorious liability of this kind was so-called statutory rape, by which a defendant who (reasonably) believed the other party was over the age of consent would be held liable if the partner was under a specific statutory age.

Greater crime theory.   As with the felony murder doctrine, defendants engaged in criminality sometimes found that the actual crime they committed was greater than they had planned. Courts held them for the "greater crime," possibly on the theory that one involved in crime could reasonably be required to take the risk of more punishment. Thus John, who stole what he believed to be a watch worth $10, but which turned out to be worth $1,000, was guilty not of the "petty theft" he had intended, but of the "grand theft" he actually perpetrated.

Not surprisingly, the possibility of "easy kills"—of convicting defendants without having to prove mens rea—lured both legislatures and prosecutors into expanding the reach of strict criminal liability. By 1922, the U.S. Supreme Court, in dictum, upheld the possibility of allowing strict criminal liability in the sale of drugs even though the penalty was five years imprisonment (*United States v. Balint*, 258 U.S. 250 (1922)). By the mid 1940s, many legislatures and most courts had embraced that specific doctrine in drug cases, and were including environmental and many white-collar harms as well.

These results were hardly inevitable. Almost none of this legislation, state or federal, explicitly dispensed with mens rea with regard to any element. It would have been relatively easy for courts to have take the position that, even assuming the constitutionality of strict criminal liability, it was so anathema to the historical understanding of the criminal law that legislatures would be required to state unequivocally that no mens rea was required with regard to a specific element before a statute would be so interpreted.

"Halfway houses."   The tension with the heritage requiring culpability proved too strong for most courts in most countries, including all European courts and legislatures. Even if they would not require the prosecution to prove knowledge of a specific element (age, kind of illegal drug, etc.), many courts adopted a "halfway house," either requiring the prosecution to prove negligence, or permitting the defendant to show non-negligent lack of knowledge of that element. Even though this contradicts the general rule that defendants need not prove any defense that goes to mens rea, it can be seen as an ameliorative device to dilute strict criminal liability. Only in the United States have courts continued to apply strict criminal liability, and even here, as discussed below, numerous jurisdictions have substantially reduced the number of statutes interpreted as imposing strict criminal liability.

Sentencing factors v. elements

A recent movement has had the same result as imposing strict liability. In the past several decades, some courts (mostly federal) have characterized certain facts as "sentencing factors" rather than as elements of crimes, and have therefore held that no mens rea need be shown as to these facts. For example, federal courts have consistently held that the amount of drugs possessed by a defendant is not an element of the crime of possession of a controlled substance, but only a sentencing factor. In two recent 5–4 decisions—*United States v. Almendarez-Torres* (118 S.Ct. 1219 (1998)) and *Jones v. United States* (119 S.Ct. 1215 (1999))—the U.S. Supreme Court has taken two different positions on this issue, attempting to deal with it as one of specific statutory interpretation. In *Torres,* the Court held that whether recidivism, which increased the maximum sentence permissible from two years to twenty, was not an element of the offense and could be determined by a judge, whereas in *Jones* the Court held that the presence of serious bodily harm, which increased the maximum sentence from 15 to 25 years, was an element of the crime to be determined by a jury. The larger Sixth Amendment issue of depriving the defendant of a jury determination of a fact critical to his punishment, however, is likely to require the Court to resolve at least some parts of this question in the near future.

Arguments for strict criminal liability

In addition to the pragmatic considerations listed above, there are several normative arguments in favor of strict criminal liability.

Difficulty of proving mens rea, and the likelihood of mens rea. Some voices favoring strict criminal liability argue that defendants really are negligent (at least) but that the use of strict liability avoids the difficulties of proving such negligence, as well as the possibility that some truly culpable defendants will be wrongly exonerated (Simon). Leaving aside the issue of whether negligence—at least civil negligence—can ever be an adequate basis for criminal punishment, such a view would see every citizen as liable for not having altered his character. For example, a bartender who serves a minor who provides eight very persuasive falsified means of identification

would be seen in this view as liable not only because his examination of the eight sources was wrong but because he had not previously spent hours (perhaps years) in training himself to identify false identification. Besides the obvious disutility in such a requirement, the unfairness to the defendant is manifest. Moreover, if mens rea is difficult to prove for these offenses, it is just as difficult to prove in cases such as homicide and rape. Yet few have suggested that this is a reason for dispensing with requiring such proof in the most serious crimes.

On the other hand, many actors, while not "knowing" that a specific circumstance exists, or that a specific result "will" or "may practically certainly" occur, may be culpable—but less culpable than knowing—with regard to such a factor. For example, Joan above may not "know" that the white powder is cocaine, but if she is told to take the glassine envelope to Roger, who will pay her $1,000, and to keep the envelope hidden from view until the sale, a jury might well find her either willfully blind, reckless, or criminally negligent with regard to the circumstance of the powder being cocaine. If "reckless" or "criminally negligent" possession, or transportation, were criminalized (and punished less severely than knowing possession), holding Joan would not necessarily be seen as imposing strict liability upon her.

This useful and legitimate insight has sometimes been expanded, somewhat too broadly, to suggest that anyone who engages in certain activities (banking, manufacturing, transporting) "knows" that there is a risk that a prohibited result will occur as a result of that activity. It is then argued that imposing criminal liability upon them when that result occurs is not unfair because they were aware of that risk before they entered the activity. Aside from relying on a definition of recklessness or negligence that is far too broad, this rationale could encompass virtually all acts (e.g., we all "know" that car accidents occur and, therefore, might be held strictly liable if we "cause" an accident which "causes" death).

Unfair advantage. Another argument in favor of strict criminal liability contends that defendants who act in circumstances where only strict liability can catch them would be "unjustly enriched" if exculpated. Thus, a driver whose gas pedal sticks and accelerates his car to ninety miles per hour has benefited above the honest driver who not only stayed within the speed limit, but who had his gas pedal checked every week. The eighteen year old who has sexual intercourse with a seventeen year old (believing her to be the age of consent) has obtained a benefit over the person who has remained celibate (or dated only persons clearly over forty) rather than risk sex with an underage partner. These benefits, it has been argued, warrant imposing some kind of liability upon the otherwise "lucky" defendant. This view, however, does not explain why *criminal* liability, stigma, and punishment is the proper path to follow *even* if one agrees that there has been some unjust enrichment.

Moral luck. Permeating the discussion of many aspects of criminal liability is the philosophical debate about the status of "moral luck." The question is whether the unintended results of an actor's (intended) actions should be imputed to the actor. The issue is present both for "good" and "bad" moral luck. For example, a defendant who *wants* to kill his victim, but who (luckily for the victim, but unluckily for the defendant) misses, is charged with attempted murder, rather than murder, and is punished less severely. Similarly, one who intends to injure, but who does *not* wish to kill, but unluckily does, may under a moral luck theorem receive a punishment equivalent to that of a person who *did* wish to kill. Many argue that this is anomalous, and that the defendant's liability should be based solely upon his culpability and not upon the fortuity of the results of his actions (Singer). Imposing strict criminal liability obviously raises the same issues. If a defendant who intends to possess only sugar but actually possesses cocaine is held liable for possessing cocaine that defendant is suffering "bad" moral luck. Moral luck raises critical questions for all ascriptions of responsibility, but nowhere are these questions more dramatically raised than in the criminal law, where the defendant's freedom is often at stake.

Criminalizing v. Grading

Professor Kenneth Simons has posited a distinction between at least two kinds of strict criminal liability. What he terms "strict liability in criminalizing" reaches the cases, mentioned above, of the "greater legal and moral wrongs," as well as the simple case where the defendant believes he is possessing sugar. Strict liability in *grading*, however, covers the "greater crime" situation, where the defendant knows he is involved in a low level of criminality, but turns out to have committed a greater harm than he envisioned. The distinction is helpful in several ways, most importantly because it distinguishes be-

tween the person who is not culpable at all and the person who is, in any event, culpable with regard to (part of) the result.

The retreat from strict criminal liability

The legal positivism of the nineteenth century has been at least mitigated by two twentieth-century phenomena: (1) judicial activism; (2) a legal realism about the ways in which legislation is passed. The deference that courts gave legislatures has been substantially reduced in favor of protection of autonomy and privacy. Moreover, the nineteenth-century judicial assumption that an absence of a mens rea word in a statute was intentional has been replaced by a recognition that legislatures are far too busy to sustain such a presumption, and that the long-lived requirement of mens rea should be followed unless the legislature clearly and explicitly rejects it. Such a view, moreover, simply places with the legislature the power—and responsibility—of speaking clearly when imposing criminal sanctions.

The Model Penal Code. The Model Penal Code expressly rejects the general notion of strict criminal liability. In § 2.05, which specifically aims at strict liability, the Code precludes any liability for a "criminal offense" without a showing of mens rea with regard to each element of the crime, although it allows such liability if there is no possibility of incarceration at all. Just as importantly, the Code requires legislatures to articulate the precise mens rea required with regard to every element of every crime, and provides a series of rules of statutory interpretation to cover cases where the legislature fails to do so. Thus, the legal positivism of the nineteenth century, which was generated by statutes that did not include a mens rea word, is avoided. Finally, the Code rejects all of the "greater evil" theories outlined above. Section 2.04 expressly provides that a defendant who, believing that he commits a crime, makes a mistake as to an element is to be punished as though the facts were as he believed them to be. Thus, in the hypothetical above, John is guilty of petty theft—the crime he thought he was committing—rather than grand theft. In addition to repudiating the general doctrine of strict liability with regard to elements of a crime, the Code virtually abolishes the felony murder doctrine, and ameliorates the "ignorance of the law is no excuse" doctrine as well.

Statutory rape and other sex offenses. Perhaps because sexual mores have changed, or merely because of the recognition that articulated sexual mores did not reflect practice, a sizable number of state courts, and some state legislatures, following the lead of the Model Penal Code, have recently rejected the earlier views as to statutory rape, and have allowed a defendant's reasonable mistake as to the age of his consenting partner to be a defense in most cases.

Drug offenses. Another sea change has occurred with regard to illegal drugs. As noted above, the Supreme Court in the 1920s appeared to allow the imposition of strict criminal liability in cases involving illegal drugs. Thus, Joan, who reasonably thought she was transporting salt, could be convicted of transporting heroin, and imprisoned for years. Today, however, every state except Washington requires the prosecution to prove that the defendant knew he was involved with drugs, and even Washington allows the defendant to prove "unwitting possession" as a defense to the charge. Some courts appear to require the prosecution to prove that the defendant knew the exact amount of drugs involved, at least where the amount has a statutorily enhancing effect upon the penalty (*State v. Headley*, 6 Ohio St. 3d 475, 453 N.E. 2d 716 (1983); *Comm v. Myers*, 554 PA. 569, 722 A.2d 645 (1998)).

Supreme Court animosity. Prior to the mid 1980s, the Supreme Court's position on strict criminal liability was, at best, ambiguous. Although there was no direct holding either way, language in some of the leading cases seemed fully to endorse strict criminal liability (for example, *Balint v. United States* (Supr.)), while others spoke in glowing terms of the requirement of mens rea as an immovable part of American criminal and constitutional law (*T.G. Morrisette v. United States*, 342 U.S. 246(1952)). Inside the same opinion one could find language supporting and opposing strict criminal liability. That lack of clarity seems, however, to have dissipated. While it is always dangerous to attempt to read the tea leaves of decisions from any court, it is nevertheless reasonable to note that the Court seems to have moved substantially against strict liability. In a series of opinions beginning in the 1980s, the Court interpreted statutes dealing with regulated activities (such as federal food stamps, gun registration, tax laws and banking transactions) and sexual activities (transportation of pornographic films involving minors) so as to require mens rea as to all elements of the offense, and to require knowledge of the laws involved. Although in two of these cases the Court, in footnotes, left open the possibility of imposing strict criminal liability with regard to some actors, the

general impact of these opinions is to fully embrace, at least as a matter of interpreting federal statutes, the requirement of mens rea with regard to all elements of an offense. Perhaps a paradigm example is *United States vs. X-Citement Video* (115 S.Ct. 464 (1994)), in which the Court interpreted a statute that made illegal the "knowing . . . transportation" . . . of a film involving the use of minors in sexually explicit conduct. All agreed that the government must show that the defendant knew he was transporting (1) a film and (2) a film showing sexual conduct; the issue was whether the government had to prove that the defendant *knew* that the film involved a minor. Given that the case involved both minors and sex—two categories in which strict liability had first been generated—it would not have been surprising if the Court had held that no level of mens rea had to be demonstrated. Instead, the Court read the mens rea word ("knowing") to "run through the entire statute," and proclaimed that any other reading would risk the criminalization of too many innocent persons. Indeed, in each of the cases referred to, the Court has emphasized, as a reason for imposing a mens rea requirement, the possibility of convicting the morally innocent (see Singer and Husak). Combined with recent decisions treating as an element of a crime anything that affects punishment, the Court's full endorsement of mens rea seems inexorable. While these decisions are not binding on state courts, they may nevertheless influence both those courts, and federal courts applying constitutional doctrine.

Empirical studies

Since most of the arguments in favor of strict criminal liability are based on practical considerations, such as the difficulty of proving mens rea and the need to protect the consumer, it is not merely relevant but critical to examine actual prosecutorial practice in these areas. In the area of "industrial revolution" statutes, for example, state enforcing agencies have not prosecuted individuals or entities whom they believe were not aware of the facts that made their acts criminal. Thus, while prosecutors could charge any corporation whose shipments of foodstuffs involve, however inadvertently, contaminated products, only those corporations who have received at least one—and usually many—warnings are prosecuted (see for example, *United States v. Park*, 421 U.S. 658 (1975)). Were prosecutors required to prove mens rea, this evidence would almost surely provide that proof. Although the prosecution may in fact proceed as one of strict liability, the availability of such evidence severely undercuts the contention that prosecutors would be unable to demonstrate mens rea in such circumstances. Moreover, whatever force there might have been in the perceived need to protect consumers has been filled not only by the mechanisms of welfare government, but by civil remedies as such as suits for product liability damages, which often hold the defendant strictly liable in tort. There is virtually no evidence that criminal liability adds significant marginal deterrence to the threat of lawsuits involving potentially millions of dollars in damages.

An argument that "it is invariably the case that the actor could have avoided liability by taking earlier steps which were hardly impossible," including refusing to take responsible managerial positions, fails to note the obvious disutility of such decisions. During the 1990s, it was rumored that some corporate officials joked about having a "vice president in charge of going to jail," a position which, if it truly existed, would hardly have many applicants. That is to say, the more we chill persons from engaging in honest actions because there may be some strict liability aspect to their conduct, the more we deter desirable conduct. In *X-Citement Video*, discussed earlier, the Court noted that transportation of child pornography could be virtually halted by imposing strict liability upon every person, including Federal Express couriers, who delivered such films, but at the prohibitive price of so chilling commercial activity that much desirable transportation of packages might also cease.

Strict criminal liability remains a possibility in the United States, but courts and legislatures appear increasingly inclined to reaffirm that the prosecution must prove mens rea as to every element of a crime before tarnishing a person's name and sending her to prison. In a society that values highly freedom and reputation of character, this is essential.

RICHARD G. SINGER

See also ACTUS REUS; MENS REA; MISTAKE; RAPE: LEGAL ASPECTS; VICARIOUS LIABILITY.

BIBLIOGRAPHY

HUSAK, DOUGLAS. "Varieties of Strict Liability." *Canadian Journal of Law & Jurisprudence* 8 (1995): 189.

KNOLL, MARK, and SINGER, RICHARD. "Searching for the 'Tail of the Dog': Finding Elements of Crimes in the Wake of *McMillan v. Pennsylvania*." *Seattle University Law Review* 22 (1999): 1057.

LEVINSON, LAURIE. "Good Faith Defenses: Reshaping Strict Liability Crimes." *Cornell Law Review* 78, no. 3 (1993): 401.

MICHAELS, ALAN. "Constitutional Innocence." *Harvard Law Review* 112, no. 4 (1999): 828.

PRIESTER, BENJAMIN. "Further Developments on Previous Symposia: Sentence for a 'Crime' the Government Did Not Prove: Jones v. United States and the Constitutional Limitations of Factfinding by Sentencing Factors Rather Than Elements the Offense." *Law & Contemporary Problems* 61 (1998): 249.

SAYRE, FRANCIS. "Public Welfare Offenses." *Columbia Law Review* 33, no. 1 (1933): 55.

SIMONS, KENNETH. "When Is Strict Criminal Liability Just?" *Journal of Criminal Law and Criminology* 87 (1997): 1075.

SINGER, RICHARD. "The Resurgence of Mens Rea: III—The Rise and Fall of Strict Liability." *Boston College Law Review* 30, no. 2 (1989): 327.

SINGER, RICHARD, and HUSAK, DOUGLAS. "Of Innocence and Innocents: The Supreme Court and Mens Rea Since Herbert Packer." *Buffalo Criminal Law Review* 2 (1999): 226.

WASSERSTROM, RICHARD. "Strict Liability in the Criminal Law." *Stanford Law Review* 12 (1960): 731.

WILEY, JOHN. "The New Federal Defense: Not Guilty by Reason of Blamelessness." *Virginia Law Review* 85, no. 5 (1999): 1021.

SUICIDE: LEGAL ASPECTS

The taking of one's own life has raised ethical, religious, and legal issues for centuries. Although the suicide rate in some countries is declining, in the United States it remains high, virtually equaling the homicide rate each year.

At English common law, suicide was a felony punishable by burial in the public highway with a stake driven through the body and forfeiture of all one's goods to the Crown. In the minority of American jurisdictions that continue to recognize common law crimes, suicide is in theory a criminal offense; but in practice no penalty has ever been applied in the United States for a successful suicide. Penalties may, however, be imposed for attempting suicide or for aiding another to attempt or to commit suicide.

Until the 1970s the statutes of a number of states forbade attempts to commit suicide. In codified form a typical example is a former Oklahoma law, Okla. Stat. Ann. tit. 21, § 812 (1958) (repealed 1976):

Any person who, with intent to take his own life, commits upon himself any act dangerous to human life, or which if committed upon or toward another person and followed by death as a consequence would render the perpetrator chargeable with homicide, is guilty of attempting suicide.

In states retaining common law crimes, attempted suicide is a criminal offense, but this is not true in most jurisdictions. In the past there was considerable sentiment for making attempted suicide an offense: the thought persisted that it was contrary to societal interest to attempt to take human life, even one's own life. That policy has been generally rejected today. One who is bent on self-destruction is not likely to be deterred by the possibility of punishment if he fails. Thus, the rationale for punishing attempted suicide is eliminated. Modern American attitudes toward punishing both suicide and attempted suicides are similar to those expressed in England. The English Suicide Act, 1961, 9 & 10 Eliz. 2, c. 60, s. 1, provides that suicide should no longer be deemed criminal.

A different issue arises if an individual, while attempting to take his own life, kills another person. Most commonly, this issue arises when someone who is attempting to prevent another from committing suicide is accidentally killed by the latter. Some lawyers have argued that the sanction for involuntary manslaughter should be imposed upon the person who initially attempted the suicide, for in these cases the death was caused by actions of the defendant that were performed recklessly.

Other lawyers contend that in these cases the defendant should be convicted of murder. Several theories support the argument. First, in jurisdictions in which suicide is a felony, the resulting death could constitute murder under a broadly based felony-murder theory—that is, it is a killing that took place during the commission of a felony. Second, the conviction of murder could be upheld under the theory of transferred intent, where the intent to take one's own life is transferred to the taking of another's life. This rule normally applies when the defendant shoots at the victim, misses him, and kills an innocent bystander. Third, the murder conviction could be sustained in jurisdictions such as Illinois, which define murder as a killing by the defendant with knowledge that his "acts create a strong probability of death or great bodily harm to another" (Ill. Ann. Stat. ch. 38, § 9-1 (a)(2) (1979)).

A more troublesome problem arises when the defendant does not seek to take his own life but aids another to commit suicide. At common law, the person who knowingly aided the suicide victim would be considered a principal in the homicide offense if he was present when the suicide occurred; he would be considered an accessory before the fact if he provided aid but was not at the scene at the time of the death. In modern legislation one rendering such aid may be guilty of either aiding a suicide or of aiding a suicide attempt. The issue is troublesome in situations in which the suicide asks for assistance because he is in great pain as the result of a long terminal illness. Although some courts have indicated that such assistance would not result in criminal responsibility, the question is still very much open in most jurisdictions.

If the defendant causes the victim to take his own life, the answer is clearer. When the victim is so severely injured that he is induced to kill himself, the defendant may be held criminally responsible for murder. The principle here is that the death is the foreseeable and proximate result of the defendant's illegal acts, and the defendant, therefore, may be prosecuted under a homicide charge. Where the defendant's assault on the victim is less severe, however, the subsequent suicide of the victim may not be deemed predictable. In such instances the defendant, although guilty of assault, escapes criminal liability for the suicide.

In the United States today, one may be held criminally responsible for aiding another to commit suicide, whether successful or attempted. It is also quite clear that appropriate criminal penalties should be imposed to deter behavior that lures another into suicide or attempted suicide. The major policy decision, however, does not fall into these two areas. Rather, members of the public and the police must be given adequate power to intervene in order to save life when persons are threatening suicide, except in situations—perhaps including terminal illness—in which society concludes that suicide is not an improper end to life.

PAUL MARCUS

See also EUTHANASIA AND ASSISTED SUICIDE.

BIBLIOGRAPHY

American Law Institute. Commentary on Section 210.5. *Model Penal Code: Tentative Draft No. 10.* Philadelphia: ALI, 1960.

LaFave, Wayne R., and Scott, Austin W., Jr. *Handbook on Criminal Law.* St. Paul, Minn.: West, 1972.

Larremore, Wilbur. "Suicide and the Law." *Harvard Law Review* 17 (1904): 331–341.

Mikell, William E. "Is Suicide Murder?" *Columbia Law Review* 3 (1903): 379–394.

Note. "Criminal Aspects of Suicide in the United States." *North Carolina Central Law Journal* 7 (1975): 156–163.

T

TERRORISM

Although the terrors of war and criminal violence have been known since the dawn of human existence, the concept of terrorism as a form of political violence originated in *le terreur* of the French Revolution. Initially a word for the brutal excesses of a revolutionary government (some forty thousand persons were guillotined), by the late nineteenth century "terrorism" referred almost exclusively to the antigovernment violence of groups such as the Russian Narodnaya Volya ("Will of the People"). Since then, the designation of particular groups and actions as terrorist has varied with political assumptions and aims.

To defenders of government, almost any violence by opponents may be defined as terrorism. To opponents, virtually any governmental effort to restrain or repress opposition may be defined as terrorism. Whether "oppositional" or "state" terrorism, the distinction itself is embedded in a snarl of issues raised by the intersection of ideological and analytical concerns.

Defining terrorism

After noting that more than one hundred definitions have been offered, Laqueur (1999) concludes that the only generally accepted characteristic of terrorism is that it involves violence or the threat of violence. Nonetheless, most observers also include political motivation and some notion of an organization that accepts and fosters violence as a political tactic.

Political motivation may vary from a scarcely articulate resentment of felt obstructions and sensed antagonists to a highly developed consciousness and analysis of political relationships. Mob violence against despised racial or ethnic groups typically has no specific political rationale and goals, despite the tendency of politicians and media commentators to impute responsibility for such violence to agitators and conspirators. At a somewhat higher level of political consciousness are planned attacks by individuals aroused by ideological messages warning them of some threat (e.g., extinction of the white race, loss of national sovereignty, environmental catastrophe, economic ruin) and blaming it on some population (e.g., Jews, Arabs, nonwhites, whites) or institution (e.g., the American "Zionist Occupation Government," the United Nations, the International Monetary Fund). Revolutionary strategists such as Che Guevara and Carlos Marighela, as well as counterrevolutionary strategists such as East Germany's Markus Wolff and Argentina's General Augusto Pinochet, exemplify the application of reason to planning and justifying the systematic use of terrorism and other forms of violence for political ends. Whether in the revolutionists' manuals of guerrilla warfare and bomb-making or the counterrevolutionists' manuals of "low intensity warfare" and antiterrorist operations, the rationales for violence are derived from quite explicit (though sometimes bizarre) understandings of the historical and social dimensions of the conflict situation.

Whether individuals acting on their own initiative may be terrorists depends on how one defines political organization. Wardlaw is one of the few analysts to allow for the possibility of a lone terrorist who uses or threatens violence to coerce a target group, beyond the immediate victims, into acceding to political demands. Theodore Kaczinski (the Unabomber) might be seen as an example. However, the Unabomber acted in awareness that a great many people agreed or sympathized with his views on the environmental threats posed by corporate greed aided and abetted by irresponsible scientific research and governmental corruption. Similarly, the fugitive Eric Robert Rudolph, wanted for abortion clinic bombings as well as for the Atlanta Olympics bombing, acted with at least the tacit (and probably some material) support of antiabortion and antigovernment extremists. That their views were drawn from or coincided with the ideologies of terrorist organizations (ranging from Earth First and the May 19th Communist Organization (M19CO) to Aryan Nations and The Order) indicates that they acted in an organizational context, from which they drew inspiration, orientation, and justification.

The notion of organizational context implies that terrorists may be more or less loosely organized, and that particular organizations may be indirectly as well as directly responsible for terrorist incidents. For instance, while the Saudi Arabian exile Osama bin Ladan cannot possibly be directly responsible for every attack by Islamic fundamentalists, his ideological and financial support for their cause encourages terrorism far beyond the operations of his own organization. Indeed, bin Ladan's organization appears to be more accurately described as a network of quasi-independent militant groups who benefit from his capacity to provide inspirational leadership and logistical support.

So far we have observed that terrorism is politically motivated violence for which organizations are directly or indirectly responsible. What remains to be settled is just how terrorism differs from other political violence. To begin, no definition of terrorism has included rioting, civil war, revolution, or international war, though analysts have agreed that terrorist incidents may occur in conjunction with or as a part of such violence. The consensus is that terrorist violence is more organized and deliberate than rioting, lesser in organization and scale than war. And though guerrillas are often pictured as terrorists by their government opponents (e.g., the Zapatista rebels in Mexico), guerrilla resistance to governmental forces does not necessarily involve terrorist acts.

Differentiating assassination and terrorism is more problematic. Ben-Yehuda argues strongly that terrorism must be distinguished from assassination, but has been unable to pin down the exact nature of the presumed differences. He suggests that terrorism is indiscriminate killing aimed at a general target while assassination tar-

gets specific individuals, but is admittedly unable to maintain the distinction in his own case analyses (pp. 38, 46–47). As the number of victims rises, observers appear to be increasingly likely to describe the incident as terrorism rather than assassination. And insofar as "innocents" such as children, café patrons, and passing motorists are victims, the violence is more likely to be viewed as terrorism. But the difficulty is that deliberate attacks on specific individuals because of their political importance may harm people who just happen to be in the line of fire or nearby when the bomb explodes. Moreover, "innocents" may be victimized by assassins not only accidentally but sometimes deliberately—for example, to eliminate witnesses, distract pursuers, or intimidate bystanders.

Perhaps the best working solution is to accept Ben-Yehuda's general point: that assassination is targeted at specific persons even though others may be harmed, while terrorism is characterized by essentially random targeting. Both aim at maximum political impact, but differ in the rationale for target selection: the assassin believes that killing one or more specific persons will be effective in weakening the will of the opposition; the terrorist believes that the randomness of victimization—especially if casualties are maximized—will be effective, particularly by spreading the perceived risks of victimization.

To summarize, terrorism is defined as politically motivated violence, for which organizations are directly or indirectly responsible, that is intended to weaken the will of the opposition by using random targeting to spread the fear of victimization.

Terrorism and law

There is no established legal definition of terrorism. Internationally, efforts within and outside the United Nations have failed in the face of widely divergent perceptions of what constitutes terrorism and who are terrorists. In 1972 the General Assembly formed an Ad Hoc Committee on Terrorism that met for seven years. There were prolonged debates on whether it is necessary or possible to reach a definition (Higgins). Moreover, it became clear that terrorism cannot be defined in terms of specified acts, targets, purposes, or actors. For instance, the shooting of a high official by an individual may be motivated by personal jealousy or envy; a plane may be destroyed in a plot to collect insurance; a diplomat may be kidnapped to force payment of a ransom.

Beyond the apparent technical impossibility of defining terrorism as a distinct criminal offense, international rivalries make it politically impossible.

Probably the most intractable political issues have been whether a legal definition should or can include (1) violent actions by a state, and (2) violent resistance to internal or foreign oppression. On the question of state terrorism, governments have adamantly rejected any legal definition that might apply to their own acts of violence against external or internal enemies. On the second issue, governments have sharply disagreed on whether the concept of terrorism might extend to violence on behalf of such causes as "national liberation" from colonial rule or imperial domination, "progressive" opposition to capitalism, resistance to "cultural genocide," or impeding "assaults on the environment." The outcome has been a consensus to abandon the quest for a legal definition of terrorism in favor of a piecemeal strategy: the ad hoc prohibition of carefully delimited acts against specified targets such as skyjacking commercial airliners.

Apart from the United Nations, there have been other multinational attempts to establish a legal basis for cooperation against oppositional (including state-sponsored) terrorism. Most such efforts involve operational agreements among states to help one another in such ways as sharing intelligence, apprehending and extraditing suspects, and joint training of special police and military units. The most ambitious such arrangement is the 1992 agreement (the Maastricht "third pillar") institutionalizing cooperation among the twelve members of the European Union in combating "terrorism, drug trafficking, and serious organized crime" (Chalk, p. 3). The treaty commits the members to eliminating internal border controls, while leaving the definition of terrorism to the discretion of the operational executive (the "K4 Committee"). Given the greater freedom of movement and the lack of oversight by either national parliaments or elected EU institutions, there is some concern that Western Europe is becoming more vulnerable to terrorism while at the same time weakening democratic legal controls over antiterrorism policy decisions (Chalk).

Within the United States, the legal status of terrorism is similarly unsettled. Although it is the subject of a growing stream of congressional committee hearings, presidential statements, and reports from the cabinet level down through the complex of intelligence and investigative agencies, terrorism is as much a term of convenience in American legal discourse as it is in international law. A statutory definition is found in the United States Code, Section 2656f(d): "premeditated, politically motivated violence perpetuated against noncombatant targets by subnational groups or clandestine agents, usually intended to influence an audience." However, it is used by the State Department as a guideline for compiling incidence reports, but not by either the Defense Department or the F.B.I., which have their own definitions reflecting the differences in agency priorities and interests (Hoffman, pp. 37–38). Though crimes of violence believed to be politically motivated are given the highest investigative priority, the F.B.I. emphasizes specific criminal conduct in developing evidence on which charges are based. Accused persons are indicted not for terrorism but for "a plethora of traditional and, occasionally, exotic criminal offenses" (Smith, p. 7). Two sets of guidelines have been issued by the Attorney General: domestic terrorism investigations are conducted under explicit public guidelines, "foreign-based" terrorism investigations under classified guidelines allowing greater leeway. Increased federal powers (including controversial restrictions on habeas corpus) to deal with both domestic and foreign terrorism were provided in the Antiterrorism and Effective Death Penalty Act of 1996 (Kappler). It is increasingly clear that although political motivation is typically avoided as an element in the prosecution of terrorists, conviction does result in significantly longer sentences (averaging 167 months) than for comparable conventional offenders (averaging 46 months)—with identification as "terrorist" being the most powerful predictor of sentence severity (Smith and Damphousse).

Because of their openness and commitment to the rule of law, democracies are indeed more likely than dictatorships to suffer terrorist attacks, and tend under attack to increase police discretionary powers. (For the classic review of the issues, see Wilkinson.) It appears highly unlikely that democratic institutions can be protected from oppositional terrorism without sacrificing, at least temporarily, some freedoms. Whether and how far antiterrorism measures can proceed without themselves contributing to the permanent weakening of democracy is the subject of continuing debate.

Explaining terrorism

Research aimed at explaining terrorism has focused on the psychological characteristics of individual terrorists, the nature of terrorist organizations, and the social or cultural environments in which terrorist organizations emerge.

The psychology of terrorists. In a useful summation of the literature, Ross has identified seven psychological approaches that have been used in efforts to understand terrorists: psychoanalytical, learning, frustration-aggression, narcissism-aggression, trait, developmental, and motivational/rational choice. Finding some merit in each, though none is satisfactory in itself, he proposes an integration of their key features in a model consisting of five "etiological features of terrorism listed in increasing order of importance" (p. 182). First: the development of facilitating traits, with the most often reported being fear, hostility, depression, guilt, antiauthoritarianism, perceived lack of manliness, self-centeredness, extreme extroversion, need for high risks or stress, and alienation. Second: frustration or narcissistic rage resulting in aggressive behavior. Third: associational drives arising from social marginality and isolation. Fourth: learning opportunities to which members of terrorist organizations are exposed, through which orientations and behaviors are shaped. Fifth: cost-benefit calculations by which terrorist acts are justified as the only or most effective means to achieve political goals.

To his credit, Ross argues that these psychological factors constitute a process inclining, though not determining, an individual to become a terrorist. Further, he embeds the psychological model in a larger model of historical and structural factors that define the contexts, either facilitating or inhibiting, in which the processes operate. The full model incorporating both psychological and structural factors summarizes numerous hypotheses about causal paths. This is an ambitious and commendable effort to organize all that has been learned about terrorists and terrorism, as the basis for further research. However, the vast body of research on which it is based is extremely uneven in quality, in terms of both conceptual and methodological rigor. In particular, the psychological studies have generally ignored the political and ideological clashes in which terrorists and terrorism are defined. The assumption of psychopathology has dominated the field of terrorist research, and the measurement of psychological variables has been characterized by low reliability and dubious validity.

The potential value of psychological studies of individual terrorists appears to be quite limited at best. Perhaps the most promising line of inquiry is to follow Crenshaw's lead in recognizing that terrorist behavior is a matter of strategic choice. In Hoffman's words, the "terrorist is fundamentally a *violent intellectual*, prepared to use and indeed committed to using force in the attainment of his goals" (p. 43). Whatever one thinks of the content and implications of terrorist reasoning, it is clear that terrorists do base their decisions on what they know, or believe they know, about the realities of the political situations in which they operate. That their knowledge and the conclusions to which it leads may be mistaken or even bizarre in the eyes of outsiders is a function not of psychopathology but instead of the information and analyses to which they have access. Among the most important determinants of what terrorists can know and believe are the organizations to which they belong, or at least from which they receive inspiration and direction.

The nature of terrorist organizations. Terrorist organizations vary from the classic secret "cell" structure to loosely defined networks of persons with essentially the same political ideology who have adopted terrorist tactics. Examples of tightly organized (and extensively researched) groups are the Irish Republican Army, the Italian Red Brigade, the German Baader-Meinhof Group (Red Army Fraction), and the Algerian National Liberation Front (FLN). There are fewer examples of terrorist networks, and less has been written about them, partly because they have proven to be more difficult to locate and study and partly because the shift toward less tightly knit and identifiable organizations is a relatively recent development. (Debates in the 1960s–1980s era over the existence of a worldwide terrorist network dominated by the former USSR were driven by cold war politics rather than any real evidence.) Perhaps the prototypical network internationally is that associated with Osama bin Ladan, widely considered ultimately responsible for the 1993 World Trade Center bombing in New York, the 1996 destruction of an American military housing complex in Dhahran, Saudi Arabia, and the 2000 attack on the *U. S. S. Cole* while berthed for refueling at Aden, Yemen.

Within the United States, there is an emerging network of right-wing terrorists, many of whom are sometime members of an assortment of militias, secessionist communities, white supremacy organizations, and morality movements, most of them adherents to some variant of Christian Identity ideology. The main impetus for shifting to more loosely organized domestic terrorism is the success of the F.B.I. and other law enforcement agencies in obtaining criminal convictions of leaders and members of such organizations as the Ku Klux Klan and Richard Butler's Aryan Nations, which have also been bankrupted by civil suits. To date, the most deadly incident linked to the rightist network is the 1995 bombing of the Murrah federal office building in Oklahoma City (in which 168 people died) by Timothy McVeigh, with help from a few associates and at least tacit approval of many others.

Becoming a terrorist appears to be a "process of radicalization" (Turk) in which politically aware individuals move through blurred and overlapping stages of alienation, searching, recruitment, commitment, and action. Whether a particular individual will in fact become a terrorist cannot be predicted because of the myriad factors affecting the transitions at every point. One of the few safe generalizations is that the many who begin the process become a relative few by its end. And it should be kept in mind that what is known about the radicalization process is based almost entirely on studies of "cell" organizations.

The trajectory begins with a vaguely disturbing sense that "our" kind of people and values are threatened, combined with the assumption that one can "do something about it." This level of political consciousness tends to reflect the individual's perceptions of social divisions and conflicts, with the most common being those associated with class, ethnic, racial, nationalist, and ideological distinctions. Accordingly, it is very likely that a particular group will be seen as the threat which needs to be countered. Conventional political activities such as helping in elections and signing petitions may result in perceived failures to improve the situation. Repeated experiences of political failure lead to frustration with conventional politics: the resentment of threatening others is now heightened by alienation from "the system."

Searching for alternatives may take the alienated individual through a range of ideological and organizational possibilities. Reading, listening to speeches and debates, going to meetings, arguing with others: the search may lead from one version of truth to another, from one group to another, in what some searchers find a confusing odyssey that they wish to end in a clear resolution. They feel the need to believe and do "something." Some of the options will at least raise the issue of whether and when it is right to use violence to further political objectives. And some will offer convincing justifications for violence. Whatever the form of violence advocated or encouraged, eventually the killing of opponents will be the key issue in deciding how serious are one's political concerns. Taking up the gun or bomb is at this point the test of commitment.

The searcher will by now probably have been noticed by those already committed to terrorism. Whether the individual will become a terrorist is problematic, as terrorist organizations screen out the great majority of potential recruits. Regardless of their fervor, individuals seen as lacking the potential for total commitment and disciplined action will not be recruited. Those who are selected will have to "cross the bridge" to be accepted as members of the terrorist organization, which usually means they will be given the assignment of murdering a police officer or committing some other deadly act. The test serves both to confirm the recruit's willingness and ability to carry out an act of illegal violence and to give the organization the power to turn the offender over to the authorities if necessary—for example, in the event of a refusal to obey orders or a future change of heart.

Commitment is ensured by a strict regimen of internal discipline combining isolation, blackmail, coercion, and indoctrination. Physical and social isolation is accomplished by persuading or forcing the individual to cut off ties to family, friends, and anyone else outside the organization. In rare instances, a contact may be authorized, usually in order to obtain funds, supplies, information, target access, or something else of use to the organization. Movements from place to place are tightly controlled. Members are required to turn over all financial and other personal assets to the organization. Blackmail is a constant threat should the member become seriously troublesome. More often, members who are thought to be weakening in their commitment or to be insubordinate, careless about security, or losing their nerve are punished by beatings, confinement, deprivation of food or other amenities, torture, rape, or murder.

While the elements of isolation, blackmail, and coercion place the individual terrorist in a highly vulnerable controlled environment, real commitment is achieved by indoctrination. Access to unauthorized sources of information is prohibited, exposure to authorized sources is required. Increasingly, the terrorist develops a perspective shaped only by the organization's ideology. Factual assertions cannot be checked, explanations cannot be tested, assumptions and implications cannot be debated. Dissensus becomes an impossibility as well as an offense within the organization. Not surprisingly, the world view promoted by indoctrination typically exaggerates the salience and resources of the organization and the effectiveness of its actions. The major themes are that the cause is just, the organization's power is growing, the struggle is the foremost political reality for opponents as it is for the terrorists, the opposition is weakening, and victory is assured.

The end product of the radicalization process is a dedicated terrorist, whose convictions are nonetheless real even though based as much on isolation and lack of knowledge as much as on collegial support and knowledge of political realities. To the terrorist, responsibility for terrorism and its casualties lies with the opposition, whose threats and intransigence have forced adoption of the terrorist option. The struggle is not a "fantasy war" but a real one.

Environments of terrorism. Excepting the most ruthless dictatorships, terrorist organizations have emerged in virtually every kind of society: democratic and authoritarian, developed and developing, ethnically or racially diverse and homogeneous societies. The diversity of social and cultural environments of terrorism has, so far anyway, defeated efforts to explain terrorism by pointing to class, racial, or other social inequalities; economic exploitation or decline; political oppression; demographic imbalances; or other social structural factors. (For exhaustive reviews of general theories of terrorism and other forms of political violence, see Schmid and Jongman, and Zimmermann.) If theories focused on political and economic factors have achieved little, their failure has at a minimum encouraged the questioning of the common assumption that violence is a political abnormality somehow caused by political and/or economic inequities. That violence may well be not just a potential aberration but an ever-present option in political conflicts is suggested by Laqueur's observation that terrorist organizations usually arise from "a split between the moderate and the more extreme wings of an already-existing organization" (p. 104).

A far more promising path to explanation is suggested by the increasing significance of religious elements, and the declining importance of secular materialist notions of class and power struggles, in the ideologies of terrorism. Juergensmeyer has in a monumental study opened up the implications of this historic shift, demonstrating that the meaningfulness of their struggle for most contemporary terrorists derives from religious traditions and innovations (seldom acknowledged as such) that constitute, or are compatible with, "cultures of violence" (pp. 10–12). The thesis is developed through case studies of "social groupings" (encompassing huge and small networks as well as tight organizations) whose ideologies express themes found in five major religious traditions: Christianity, Judaism, Islam, Sikhism, and Buddhism.

In each case it is shown that the terrorist ideology cannot be cavalierly dismissed as simply a distortion or deviation. Christian antiabortionists such as Michael Bray justify the bombing of clinics and the murder of surgeons by complex theological arguments against killing the innocent and for establishing a new moral order. Yoel Lerner's 1995 assassination of Israel's prime minister Yitzhak Rabin was justified by Rabbi Meir Kahane as a religious act to ensure the survival of the state of Israel, which is the essential forerunner of the biblical Israel to be fulfilled through divine redemption (the coming of the Messiah). The World Trade Center bombing and other violence against the United States and its allies is defended by invoking the Koran's prescription of violence to defend the faith against its enemies, including whoever threatens the material and cultural survival of the faithful. Sikh terrorism in India and abroad is similarly justified by such leaders as Simranjit Singh Mann as protecting the faith from the corrosive effects of secularism and Hinduization. And despite Buddhism's pacifist teachings, Shoko Asahara found justification for releasing sarin gas in the Tokyo subway in traditional Buddhist teachings that the rule of nonviolence can be broken when five conditions are satisfied: "something living must have been killed; the killer must have known that it was alive; the killer must have intended to kill it; an actual act of killing must have taken place; and the person or animal attacked must, in fact, have died" (Juergensmeyer, p. 113). Force may be used to defend the faith and to establish a peaceful moral order.

In each case, religious ideas provide an explanation of the believer's sense of loss and threat in this world; define in cosmic terms the need to struggle against those responsible; and give the believer's life a wonderful new significance as a holy warrior in a just cause. Doubt, confusion, and hopelessness are overcome by a transcendent truth that makes sense of what for many have been "real experiences of economic destitution, social oppression, political corruption, and a desperate need for the hope of rising above the limitations of modern life" (Juergensmeyer, p. 242). Increasingly, the religious ideologies driving terrorist movements resonate with widely held feelings that the secularism of the modern world order is threatening the nonmaterial values (family, morality, faith, caring, sharing) on which human societies depend for meaning and survival.

Three conclusions are drawn from reviewing efforts to explain terrorism. First, terrorists are not psychologically much different from the rest of us. Second, their organizations are shifting toward looser networks rather than the tight hierarchies of the past. Third, the environments inspiring terrorism are increasingly cultural, and specifically religious. The implications for the future appear to be grim.

The future of terrorism

Because individual terrorists and their organizations are becoming harder to keep track of, and given the difficulties of identifying terrorists and terrorism in the first place, the policy assumptions of the past are likely to be counterproductive in the future. Containment, in particular, does not seem to be a promising strategy when the ease of travel and communication are helping to make anachronisms of international borders. Similarly, efforts to control investments and limit technology transfers appear to be not only failing but also aggravating the fears of people around the globe who distrust the motives of multinational economic and political entities. The 2000 demonstrations in Seattle and elsewhere against the International Monetary Fund are harbingers of what we can expect as the development-investment programs of the Western power centers sharpen the great differences between those favored by the programs and those disadvantaged by them.

The "new terrorism" of religiously dedicated holy warriors is less vulnerable to being deterred by military and law enforcement threats. Indeed, the use of violence has not only failed to diminish international and domestic terrorism but also provided the ideologists of terrorism with useful ammunition. Rightist domestic terrorism in the United States has been strengthened by such incidents as the Waco assault, as has Islamic terrorism by the attempted assassinations of Osama bin Ladan and other leading figures. Though understandable and perhaps even appropriate in some instances, military tactical responses to terrorist threats and attacks have given credence in the eyes of believers to religious depictions of Western, particularly American, societies as satanic. The new terrorists are convinced of divine approval of their actions and of ultimate victory, even if it is to be a supernatural one. As Laqueur emphasizes, the new terrorists are so dangerous precisely because they "are not primarily interested in gain or glory, but instead want a state or a society in their own image, cleansed of their enemies" (p. 277).

Such warriors can be expected to show little reluctance to use weapons of mass destruction. Although governments have concentrated investigative resources on reducing the threat of major nuclear attacks, most analysts are more concerned with the growing possibility of small-scale yet spectacularly alarming weapons being used. Small nuclear devices are perhaps less likely to be used than chemical or biological weapons, but in any event the casualties of the future will probably be much greater on average than in the past. Meanwhile, conventional weapons continue to be readily available, along with instructions on how to make and use them. The portent is more incidents, more deaths and injuries, and more terrorist challenges to established social orders.

AUSTIN T. TURK

See also CRIME CAUSATION: POLITICAL THEORIES; INTERNATIONAL CRIMINAL LAW; POLITICAL PROCESS AND CRIME; WAR AND VIOLENT CRIME; WAR CRIMES.

BIBLIOGRAPHY

BEN-YEHUDA, NACHMAN. *Political Assassination by Jews.* Albany: State University of New York Press, 1993.

CHALK, PETER. *West European Terrorism and Counter-Terrorism.* New York: St. Martin's Press, 1996.

CRENSHAW, MARTHA. "The Logic of Terrorism: Terrorist Behavior as a Product of Strategic Choice." *Origins of Terrorism.* Edited by Walter Reich. Cambridge, U.K.: Cambridge University Press, 1990.

HIGGINS, ROSALYN. "The General International Law of Terrorism." *Terrorism and International*

Law. Edited by Rosalyn Higgins and Maurice Flory. New York: Routledge, 1997. Pages 13–29.

HOFFMAN, BRUCE. *Inside Terrorism*. New York: Columbia University Press, 1998.

JUERGENSMEYER, MARK. *Terror in the Mind of God: The Global Rise of Religious Violence*. Berkeley: University of California Press, 2000.

KAPPLER, BURKE W. "Small Favors: Chapter 154 of the Antiterrorism and Effective Death Penalty Act, the States, and the Right to Counsel." *Journal of Criminal Law and Criminology* 90, no. 2 (2000): 467–598.

LAQUEUR, WALTER. *Terrorism*. Boston: Little, Brown, 1977.

———. *The New Terrorism: Fanaticism and the Arms of Mass Destruction*. New York: Oxford University Press, 1999.

ROSS, JEFFREY IAN. "Beyond the Conceptualization of Terrorism: A Psychological-Structural Model of the Causes of This Activity." *Collective Violence: Harmful Behavior in Groups and Government*. Edited by Craig Summers and Eric Markusen. New York: Rowman and Littlefield, 1999. Pages 169–192.

SCHMID, ALEX P., and JONGMAN, ALBERT J. *Political Terrorism*. New York: North-Holland Publishing Company, 1988.

SMITH, BRENT L. *Terrorism in America: Pipe Bombs and Pipe Dreams*. Albany: State University of New York Press, 1994.

SMITH, BRENT L., and DAMPHOUSSE, KELLY R. "Punishing Political Offenders: The Effect of Political Motive on Federal Sentencing Decisions." *Criminology* 34, no. 3 (1996): 289–321.

TURK, AUSTIN T. "Political Crime." *Major Forms of Crime*. Edited by Robert F. Meier. Beverly Hills, Calif.: Sage Publications, 1984. Pages 119–135.

WARDLAW, GRANT. *Political Terrorism: Theory, Tactics, and Counter-Measures*, 2d ed. New York: Cambridge University Press, 1990.

WILKINSON, PAUL. *Terrorism and the Liberal State*. London: Macmillan, 1977.

ZIMMERMANN, EKKART. *Political Violence, Crises, and Revolutions: Theories and Revolutions*. Cambridge, Mass.: Schenkman Publishing Company, 1983.

THEFT

Introduction

Theft is a general term embracing a wide variety of misconduct by which a person is improperly deprived of his property. The purpose of theft law is to promote security of property by threatening aggressors with punishment. Property security is valued as part of the individual's enjoyment of his belongings and because the community wishes to encourage saving and economic planning, which would be jeopardized if accumulated property could be plundered with impunity. Another function of the law of theft is to divert the powerful acquisitive instinct from non-productive preying on others to productive activity.

One problem that dogs the law of theft, as will be seen below, is that in a commercial society no clear line can be drawn between greedy anti-social acquisitive behavior on the one hand and, on the other hand, aggressive selling, advertising, and other entrepreneurial activity that is highly regarded or at least commonly tolerated. Here two important principles of constitutional and criminal law come into play to restrict the scope of the law of theft. A criminal law must not be so comprehensive as to jeopardize the ordinary behavior of decent citizens. Nor may a criminal law be so vague that it fails to warn the citizen what is forbidden and leaves to the discretion of enforcement officers or judges whether certain behavior should be punishable. The tension between these principles, and the impulse to penalize all egregious greed, account for the fact that theft law inevitably falls short of penalizing all rascality. At the same time—such are the refractory problems of legislative drafting—it is impossible, even with the most painstaking draftsmanship, to avoid overpenalizing in some cases. For example, obviously trivial peculations such as using an employer's stationery for writing personal notes quite clearly fall within theft law; yet it has proved impossible to articulate exceptions that will exclude this and a myriad of other trivial violations. Such things remain, therefore, within the province of prosecutorial and judicial discretion.

Within the broad category of theft, the law has long made important distinctions according to the particular means employed to appropriate the property, the nature and value of the property, the "criminal intent" or its absence, and other circumstances. These variables are reflected in the number of distinct criminal offenses that the law developed to deal with theft—for example, larceny, embezzlement, false pretense, fraudulent conversion, cheating, robbery, extortion, shoplifting, and receiving stolen goods. Before the emergence of the British Parliament and royal courts as the dominant lawmaking institutions, it may be assumed that all such misbehavior was subject to the rather arbitrary sanctions of local baronial justice.

A uniform central justice would first be invoked in the most serious cases, especially where capital punishment might be imposed. Thus, the great "common law felonies"—treason, murder, arson, rape, robbery, and burglary—became the first concern. Of these, robbery and burglary were typically property crimes, but with distinctive circumstances of aggravation. Robbery with theft accompanied by personal violence was notably an offense of the highway, impairing the security of a communications network that was important to the monarchy and to commercial interests. Burglary involved violent invasion of the home for felonious purpose (not necessarily theft) at night. One may speculate that burglary was an early concern of royal courts because it, like arson, occurred as an incident of warfare among the barons or of peasant revolts. As time passed, the aggravating circumstances sufficing for royal jurisdiction of these felonies were attenuated. By the end of the eighteenth century, a purse-snatching in London would be robbery in view of the "violence" suffered by the owner from the momentary pull of the purse handle. A thief became a burglar if he opened the door of a henhouse on the home lot of a townsman.

Larceny

Larceny, not an original common law felony, must have emerged as the royal courts extended their jurisdiction beyond robbery to reflect increasing central concern for property security generally and to control the imposition of capital punishment, a sanction often employed in the illusory hope of repressing theft. As might be expected, the initial excursion of the royal courts into the law of theft was sharply limited. Larceny was defined as taking and carrying away tangible personal property of another by trespass and without his consent with the purpose of stealing or permanently depriving the owner of possession. Consideration of the technical limits that the courts derived from, or built into, this seemingly simple definition will throw light on the way law evolves and on the process that ultimately made it necessary for Parliament and other legislatures to take up the task of extending the law of theft.

A property offense.   Larceny deals with tangible property. There are many ways of inflicting pecuniary injury on another apart from taking his tangible property. For example, one can cheat another out of services due him, as where a municipal or corporate officer causes underlings to labor for the officer's private benefit on time paid for by the municipality or corporation. One can cause an actor, physician, architect, or other professional to provide valuable service by false promises or representations. One can bypass the electric meter or obtain power service without paying for it. One can plagiarize another's book or music, or "steal" technical information that has been entrusted in confidence. Only much later and by explicit legislation did such frauds become punishable, usually as offenses distinct from larceny.

Personal versus real property.   Only certain forms of property were covered by larceny law, namely, tangible personal property. In legal parlance, personal property means assets other than "real property," that is, real estate. The distinction is underlined by the specification in the definition that the stolen property must be "carried away." Obviously, real estate cannot be carried away. The general distinction made between real and personal property was not all arbitrary. Precisely because real estate cannot be carried off, purloined, or hidden away, there is no danger that it will disappear. Controversies over entitlement to the use and enjoyment of the land will normally be between persons having colorable title, such as co-owners or landlord and tenant. The civil law affords remedies uniquely adapted to restore possession of real estate to the persons entitled and to reimburse for lost profits. But the rationality of the basic distinction does not extend to many of the refinements invented by the courts over the course of centuries in the interpretation of the definition of larceny. (For example, a quite movable document evidencing title to real estate could be excluded from the category of "personal property.") Notably, the exclusion of real estate from larceny extended to crops, turf, mineral deposits, or lumber taken from the land, despite the obvious mobility and concealability of these assets and their susceptibility to stealthy removal. One can see here either the traces of a medieval casuistry whereby the mysterious essence of land is somehow infused into materials that were once a part of the land, or, more functionally in the modern spirit, a desire to avoid imposing the harsh sanctions prescribed by larceny law for minor peculations in the agricultural countryside. Other rationalizations must be found to explain why products of the land were transmuted into personal property if they were assembled in stacks or heaps before removal; it was said, for example, that manure spread upon a field was real estate, but that a manure pile was personal property within the law of larceny.

Tangible property. The requirement that the personal property be "tangible" served to exclude many forms of interpersonal economic claims from the larceny offense, including debts, contract rights, promissory notes, trade secrets, and patents. Controversies over such commercial interests, like controversies over land, were generally between identifiable rivals, not with sneak thieves, the prime target of larceny law, and these controversies could ordinarily be resolved by civil law suits. Perhaps one can see here also the beginnings of that special tolerance for what was later to be identified as white-collar crime, that is, middle-class nonviolent peculation, often by persons of the same social class as the legislators, judges, and prosecutors.

Take and carry away; attempted larceny. The requirement of proof that the property had been "taken and carried away" had to do with the pervasive concern of Anglo-American criminal law to avoid penalizing persons who may be thinking about or tempted to commit crime but who take no unequivocal steps toward committing an offense. Antisocial action, not bad character or evil impulse, is in principle the proper domain of the criminal law. As late as the twentieth century, however, the law of theft as supplemented by the law of vagrancy included a petty offense that consisted of being "a common thief," so identified by repute, by want of an obvious source of legitimate income, and by a tendency to loiter in public places where potential victims congregate (*Levine v. State,* 110 N.J.L. 467, 166 A. 300 (1933)). But latter-day constitutional principles invalidate such vague laws that subject people to police action on the basis of status rather than present misconduct (*Papachristou v. City of Jacksonville,* 405 U.S. 156 (1972)).

What, then, is the quantum of actual misbehavior that will suffice for a larceny conviction? The answer was found in the definition of larceny insofar as it requires proof that the actor did "take and carry away," that is, exercise physical dominion over the property, thus interfering with the possession of the true owner. Such interference constitutes the "trespass" discussed below, but more is required. The actor must move the property, however slightly; that is, begin to move it or carry it away. A culprit, observing a packing case on the loading platform of

a warehouse, might go so far as to tip the case up on one corner without actually committing larceny; only if there was additional movement resulting in the displacement of "every atom" of the object would the offense be complete.

On the other hand, the significance of these intriguing technicalities is diminished by the fact that the suspect may be convicted of *attempted* larceny if he has not gone far enough to "complete" the crime. The law of attempt has its own requirements with regard to how far criminal action must proceed in order to cross the line between "mere preparation," which is not criminal, and criminal attempt. One may therefore be guilty of attempted larceny although the larceny requirement of carrying away is not satisfied. Grave consequences turn on whether there has been a completed larceny or only an attempt. In the eighteenth century, when some larcenies were capital offenses, life or death might depend on whether the suspect had merely tipped the case on end or had moved it entirely. In modern law, criminal codes frequently set lower sentence maxima for attempts than for completed offenses.

Making important differences in potential sentence turn on nice distinctions between attempted larceny and completed larceny is additionally curious when one perceives that many "completed" larcenies prove, on analysis, to be frustrated, rather than successful, efforts to steal—in other words, attempts. Our culprit of the warehouse loading platform, having indeed moved the case a few inches, may desist from his nefarious purpose upon observing the arrival of a policeman. A pickpocket, having the victim's wallet already in his grasp and having partly removed it from the pocket, may find that the alert victim has grasped him firmly by the wrist. Abandoning the tempting wallet, the pickpocket seeks only to escape. The law would hold this to be larceny rather than attempt.

Confusion is further confounded when it is observed that the "aggravated larcenies," robbery and burglary, are analytically attempts, although centuries of treatment as distinct substantive offenses obscure this analytic truth. Assaults *for the purpose* of larceny are robbery. The slightest intrusion into a building *for the purpose* of larceny is burglary, although the burglar has succeeded only in inserting his screwdriver or crowbar under the window. Activity that has not accomplished its purpose falls logically into the category of attempt. There may be good reason to treat these particular inchoate larcenies more severely than the ordinary "completed" larceny, since the culprit manifests special dangerousness by embarking on larceny in especially frightening circumstances. Moreover, since the preliminary steps taken for the purpose of larceny, that is, assault and trespass, are themselves criminal offenses, it is possible to regard the purpose to steal as merely an aggravating circumstance attending the commission of those "completed" offenses. But these explanations leave undisturbed the perception that the mere distinction between attempt and completed larceny hardly suffices to justify special leniency toward culprits who do not fully accomplish their larcenous purposes.

By trespass and without consent. Extraordinary extensions of larceny law were accomplished by daring judicial pronouncements in the eighteenth century with regard to the central concept of larceny—that an owner's possession must be shown to have been disturbed without his consent, a disturbance known in law as "trespass" (*Rex v. Pear*, 168 Eng. Rep. 208 (Crown Cases 1780)). The one thing the old English judges did not want to be involved in as administrators of the criminal law was quarrels between an owner and one to whom the owner had entrusted his property for such purposes as to sell, store, transport, repair, process, or invest. These relationships, known in law as bailments, were perceived as quintessentially civil matters of contract. A merchant must take his chances and could minimize his risks by care in selecting those to whom he entrusted goods. Moreover, if criminality were to depend on the bailee's having done something not authorized by the contract of bailment, there was the difficulty of proving exactly how far that authority went. This would depend on customs of the trade and, frequently, on verbal understandings of ambiguous import. The circumstances, in short, were altogether different from the typical larceny involving a thief without a shadow of claim of right.

There is one situation where a matter that has the appearance of consent by the owner does not bar conviction of larceny. That is where the owner of goods, suspecting that his employees are stealing, purposely exposes the goods to easy taking while concealed law enforcement officers keep the scene under surveillance in order to apprehend the thief. The owner obviously does not consent to be deprived of his goods; indeed, he has taken effective measures to prevent loss of the decoy. Although the case can thus be disposed of under substantive larceny law, it is close-

ly intertwined with an independent problem of law enforcement procedure, that of entrapment. It is lawful for police to "provide an opportunity" to commit crime, but not to "induce" by methods that would overcome the resistance of an ordinary law-abiding citizen, the commission of an offense by one not shown to be predisposed to commit the offense. The police have on occasion conducted large-scale enterprises in which, with appropriate publicity in the underworld, they engage in buying stolen goods, while a secret camera photographs the sellers. The encouragement to theft given by this ready market supplied by law enforcement officers does not constitute illegal entrapment.

"Custody" versus "possession." Consider, then, what is to done with the butler who, while polishing his master's silver, is overcome by the temptation of illicit gain and absconds with the family plate. Is this to be regarded as "bailment"? Has milord, who may reside in distant London, voluntarily transferred "possession" to the trusted butler, so that the butler's misappropriating what is rightfully in his own possession cannot amount to a "trespass" against his master's possession? As early as the sixteenth century, the lordly gentlemen of the bench sought to find their way past such obstacles so as to convict the butler of larceny. They did so by perceiving or inventing a distinction between "possession" and mere "custody." A servant had mere custody; he held the master's belongings only as a proxy for the master. Thus the master retained "possession," and the servant committed trespass against the master's possession when he carried off the plate. A similar extension was easily made in favor of merchants, whose clerks and apprentices in stores, banks, and factories were treated as holding mere custody of goods that remained in possession of the employers.

Trespass by bailee in possession. Economic and social pressures mounted in favor of applying theft sanctions to bailees. With increasing specialization of labor and increasing nationalization of the market, more and more goods were unavoidably entrusted to other participants in the process of production, transportation, and marketing—participants who most certainly were not servants but "independent contractors," that is, bailees. Theft law began to respond as early as the fifteenth century, but fitfully. A hauler entrusted with a case of goods was convicted of larceny when he broke the case open and helped himself to the contents (*The Carrier's Case*, Y. B. Pasch. 13 Edw. IV, f. 9, pl. 5 (Star

Chamber 1473)). The judges could bring themselves to say that the case, but not the contents, had been delivered into the possession of the hauler by consent of the owner. The contents thus remained in the possession of the owner, against which possession the hauler had committed trespass.

Larceny by trick. A famous prosecution in the eighteenth century involved an accused who hired a coach and horses for a specified trip and duration, although his real purpose was to make off with the coach and dispose of it. There could be no question that the transaction began as a bailment. But the court was willing to say that "possession" reverted to the lessor upon breach of the bailment contract, so that the lessee trespassed on the lessor's possession. Moreover, in the court's view, the voluntary aspect of the initial delivery of the car to the bailee was vitiated by the bailee's fraudulent misrepresentation of his intentions. Fraud in inducing a transfer of possession vitiated the apparent "consent" of the bailor to the change of possession. This was the famous "larceny by trick," a far cry from the archetypal covert snatch, and ancestor of the legislation to come that would penalize obtaining property by false pretenses even when the transaction induced was a transfer of money or other property, a change of ownership rather than merely possession as in larceny—in short, a sale.

Lost or abandoned property. If an owner abandons or loses, that is, loses possession of, his property, another's taking of it is not a trespass against the owner's possession; hence no larceny. However, the interests of property losers eventually received some criminal law protection. It had long been recognized that an owner possessed goods, in the sense that he asserted continued dominion over them even if he were far from them and thus in no position to exert immediate physical control. Ingenious judges availed themselves of this idea by drawing a distinction between lost and "mislaid" property. Thus, a cab driver who appropriates a wallet that a passenger has inadvertently left on the seat or dropped to the floor takes "mislaid" rather than "lost" property, trespassing against the owner's continued "possession." Nevertheless, there was reluctance to extend the harsh penalties of larceny to finders, who do not aggressively act against the property security of others. Their misbehavior, if it be such, consists of a failure to take steps to restore property to its true owners. Anglo-American law has traditionally been adverse to penalizing inaction, and in the lost-property situation, to make a thief out of a finder runs counter to the folk wisdom of "finders, keepers." Special legislation has been passed to define the affirmative action required and to penalize only egregious departures from ordinary standards of behavior, as where the property has substantial value, the identity of the owner is manifest, and the property can be restored to the owner without disproportionate effort and expense. Violation of such a duty of affirmative action would not ordinarily be characterized as theft, and the maximum authorized sentence would be much lower.

Larceny within the family. The ideas of trespass and consent played a special role in determining the criminality of theft from a spouse. Before the "separate property" legislation of the nineteenth and twentieth centuries, the husband's plenary power to dispose of his wife's personal property made it technically difficult to regard any action of his as a trespass against her property. Accordingly a husband could not be convicted of larceny of his wife's belongings. The wife had a corresponding immunity against prosecution for stealing from the husband. This immunity would be rationalized on the theory of the "unity" of husband and wife or on the theory that, since her property was in any event subject to his dominion, her "taking" was not a trespassory disturbance of his possession. But behind these fictions lay substantive psychological considerations. In most households the stock of commonly held available belongings is regarded by the spouses as being in their joint possession; presumably they consent to each other's appropriations, at least for the common ménage. Even if such consent is explicitly withdrawn in a particular situation, criminal prosecution of one spouse on the testimony of the other hardly seems an appropriate remedy for the underlying marital discord.

Moreover, it would be perceived by prosecutors, judges, and the public that a "thief" whose disregard of others' ownership is manifested only by taking something belonging to his or her consort is hardly a threat to the general security of property. Police experience has long recognized that prosecution under these circumstances will probably be abortive, for the complaining party frequently repents of hasty invocation of official intervention and refuses further collaboration with the prosecution. If willingness to carry through with prosecution is rare, the cases that do occur are likely to be manifestations of vengefulness or blackmail, in which it is hardly right that officialdom should aid. Such an analysis leads to the conclusion that *neither* wife nor husband is liable to conviction for larceny from the other. In modern times some of the states recognize bispousal immunity, whereas others follow the logic of the separate-property legislation by abolishing all interspousal immunity for theft. Prosecutions remain rare.

A sensitive legislator or judge will see the spouse-theft problem as only one example of a set of situations that seem to call for consistent treatment. What is to be done with couples who live together without being legally married? What about theft by children from parents, or among brothers, sisters, and other members of the family living in a common household? What about non-family-related joint living arrangements? In all these situations there is likely to be considerable tolerance for, if not actual consent to, some appropriation of one another's goods, the miscreant does not show himself as generally thievish merely by taking what seems to him part of a commonly held stock of goods, and a complainant is likely to desert the prosecution once it has been initiated. Nevertheless, the law that declares such peculations to be punishable larceny has been only rarely and marginally changed. It is left to the discretion of prosecutors to decline to bring charges, or to the discretion of judges to impose only lenient sentences upon proof of the mitigating circumstances that the goods were temptingly available as part of a household of which the defendant was a member.

Much is learned about criminal law generally by reflecting on the reasons for a seemingly arbitrary distinction between immunity for interspousal larceny and discretionary leniency for other intrafamily larceny. The basic reason is that it is virtually impossible to draw a defensible line anywhere along the spectrum of increasingly attenuated personal relationships: too many cases would be swept into the immunity category. For example, a son at the culmination of a series of quarrels with his father leaves home with the family car and his mother's life savings. An orphaned youth taken into the family quickly departs with Grandma's jewelry. Moreover, even the most generous immunity rule would exclude some cases that necessarily must be handled by discretionary leniency, for example, the young clerk who, in a moment of personal crisis, appropriates the wallet that a customer has left on the counter. If temptation and availability should be a defense to prosecution for larceny, the law would be sending very ambiguous signals to those whom it would like to deter, and the security of property might be substantially impaired.

It should be remembered that in all these family cases the defendant may have a complete defense that the owner had actually consented to the particular taking. Consent need not be explicit, but may be implied from previous practices. Moreover, once the defendant has introduced some evidence of consent, the prosecution has the burden of disproving consent beyond a reasonable doubt, since nonconsent is an element of the offense.

The larcenous intent. Generally speaking, serious crimes such as larceny cannot be committed unknowingly or innocently. There is a requirement of mens rea (wickedness or evil intent). Three aspects of this psychological component of larceny are worth discussing here: (1) purpose to appropriate; (2) claim of right; and (3) permanence of intended deprivation.

Purpose to appropriate. Purpose to appropriate serves to differentiate acquisitive misbehavior from destructive behavior—that is, larceny from malicious mischief. The classic Latin formulation was *lucri causa* ("for the sake of gain"). Vandalism of property has always been regarded as a less serious offense, although that is by no means a self-evident proposition, considering that stolen goods remain part of the social stock, since they are merely redistributed, whereas destroyed things are irretrievably lost. On the other hand, temptation to acquire illicitly seems to be much more pervasive. Yielding to it leads readily to the adoption of thievery as a way of life. A clever thief can become a professional criminal and make a living without the labor endured by his honest and indignant fellow citizens. Accordingly, if I take my neighbor's vase meaning to make it my own or to sell it, I am guilty of the felony of larceny (or one of the modern composite theft offenses of which larceny becomes a component); but if I merely toss it to the floor, shattering it, that amounts only to the misdemeanor of property destruction or malicious mischief. Interesting variants can occur, as where the culprit first "appropriates"—that is, takes and carries away—and thereafter destroys. He is guilty of both offenses even if the original taking was with purpose to destroy.

Purpose to appropriate means that one cannot be guilty of larceny by taking what he believes, however unreasonably, to be his own, for one does not intend to "appropriate" what is already his own, or to deprive another. There is lacking the thievish state of mind that would identify the taker as a threat to the property of others. In some connections, such as homicide, the law recognizes "recklessness" as a sufficient mens ea; but in the case of larceny even the most careless mistake as to ownership will absolve the accused. In the jargon of the law, larceny is a crime requiring "specific intent," that is, the conscious purpose to trespass against another's right of possession.

Yet there is a class of situations involving "claim of right" where the accused's subjective good faith will not save him from conviction for larceny. If a man appropriates property that he knows to belong to another, he commits larceny even if he takes the property to satisfy a real or supposed obligation that is due from the owner. Thus an employee who believes that the employer has illegally withheld wages may not with impunity help himself to a corresponding amount of the employer's cash or goods. A farmer who thinks or, for that matter, knows that his neighbor has stolen one of his calves violates the larceny law if he helps himself to an equivalent calf belonging to the neighbor. In sum, the defense of claim of right requires a showing of belief that the actor owned (or otherwise had the right to possession of) the specific article, not merely that he was entitled to some form of compensation. It seems doubtful whether creditors' self-help is sufficiently analogous to the basic misbehavior condemned by the law of theft, or sufficiently identifies the actor as an egregious threat to the property interests of others, to warrant social castigation as a thief. Yet in the absence of alternative categories of minor crime into which creditor self-help might be fitted, society has chosen to leave to prosecutorial discretion whether such over-zealous creditors should be prosecuted as thieves.

Intent to deprive permanently. This aspect of the definition of larceny serves to exclude unauthorized borrowing from larceny. In general, temporary takings ought to be excluded from larceny, although it is worth noting by way of anticipation that when the issue is embezzlement rather than larceny, even temporary misappropriation by a trustee, agent, or other fiduciary leads to conviction. The courts have shown no disposition to hear a lawyer or stockbroker say, "I took my client's securities or cash only briefly to meet an urgent need of my own and with full intent to return the property." Larceny borrowings, however, would ordinarily not involve large sums of liquid assets that can readily disappear, nor is there involved the aggravating circum-

stance that the culprit breached a strong duty of fidelity he owed to the owner who had entrusted property to him. The harm done when an ordinary tool, article of clothing, or bicycle is borrowed without permission is minimal if the object is returned promptly in good condition. The possibility of professional thievery based on illicit borrowing is remote.

Criminal borrowing. However, there are many situations in which borrowing without the owner's consent presents a serious enough risk of substantial loss as to warrant excluding a defense that the taking was without intent to deprive permanently. The courts readily convicted of larceny where the taker had only a conditional intent to restore the property, that is, if the owner would pay a reward. So also where the taker, although abjuring any purpose to appropriate permanently and, indeed, professing hope that the property will be regained by the owner, deals with the property in a way that reveals his essential indifference to returning the property. Having "borrowed" a shotgun from his neighbor's barn to go hunting, he abandons it in the woods. Such recklessness regarding restoration of the property was held sufficient mens rea for larceny.

A second category identified by modern reformers as appropriate for larceny conviction despite the alleged intention of the taker to restore the property is where the property is withheld "under such circumstances that a major portion of its economic value or its use and benefit has in fact been appropriated." This formulation was adopted in the Model Penal Code of the American Law Institute (§ 223.0) and in the *Proposed New Federal Criminal Code* of the United States National Commission on Reform of Federal Criminal Laws (§ 1741 (b)). Thus, the draftsmen sought to extend larceny to cases such as the prolonged "borrowing" of an art treasure or the surreptitious "borrowing" of a mowing machine precisely for the season in which the owner would need it.

"Joyride" statutes. A third category of criminal borrowing, of great practical importance, is dealt with by the so-called joyride statutes. These laws penalize unauthorized borrowing of automobiles or other vehicles. One of the commonest offenses committed by youths in an automobile civilization is to take an available car for a fast (and risky) drive, without any intention of keeping the vehicle. When abandoned, it will soon be restored to the owner by the police. The great risk presented by this activity—not only to valuable property but also to the lives of those encountered on the highway—led to penal legislation against it, sometimes by way of expanding larceny, and sometimes under a nonthievery designation. How far should the principle be extended? To boats, motorcycles, and airplanes, clearly. But should it also be extended to other motor-propelled vehicles, including snowmobiles, motor scooters, parachutes, and hang gliders? Should special laws be enacted to penalize unauthorized borrowing of dangerous machines, nuclear materials, or guns? Does the number of exceptions from the principle of penalizing only permanent deprivations multiply so uncontrollably that the principle itself should be abandoned except for the most trivial borrowing of personal belongings, thus leaving it to the discretion of prosecutors and judges which illegal borrowings should be prosecuted and punished?

Statutory dilution of intent requirement.   It is not uncommon for legislatures to push the concept of larceny beyond its traditional boundaries, including the boundary of larcenous "intent." A notable example was the statute involved in *Morissette v. United States,* 342 U.S. 246 (1952). Here Congress, not content with providing up to ten years' imprisonment for "stealing" anything of value belonging to the United States, added that anyone who "knowingly converts" federal property should be dealt with similarly. The defendant, a junk dealer, had picked up spent air force bombing cases on an air force bombing range, believing, he claimed, that the air force had abandoned them. Such a defense would undoubtedly be valid against a charge of stealing or larceny. The prosecutor relied on the "knowing conversion," a term taken from civil law, where it refers to the owner's right to be reimbursed for property appropriated, whether or not with intent to steal. It could be argued plausibly that Congress must have intended to go beyond the traditional larceny intent when it explicitly added conversion to the theft statute. Nevertheless, the Supreme Court rejected the argument, pointing to the infamy of a conviction for theft, the long tradition of requiring specific intent in this offense, and the less-than-perfect clarity of Congress's will to weaken the traditional requirement.

Embezzlement

In the eighteenth and nineteenth centuries the pressures to extend theft law beyond the "trespass" limits of common larceny became irresistible. An offense had to be created to penalize the defalcations of bailees, trustees, and the like who clearly did *not* wrongfully infringe on the possession of others, since they had themselves been put in possession either by the owners or by authority of law, as where an executor, administrator, or trustee took property under a will subject to a fiduciary obligation to administer for the benefit of heirs. Embezzlement is, then, misappropriation of the property of another when that property is already in possession of the embezzler. The law expanded cautiously, as might be expected, since the objections to an expansive theft law, which had been felt in connection with larceny, did not evaporate. Initially only a few of the numerous classes of potential embezzlers, such as fiduciaries and haulers, were named in the statutes. Eventually the coverage of the embezzlement statutes was enlarged to cover anyone who had property of another in his own possession.

One of the objections to expanding theft law—the harshness of larceny penalties—was met by providing milder although still heavy sanctions for embezzlement, thus introducing the somewhat surprising phenomenon that different forms of theft would be treated with varying degrees of severity depending on the historic moment when a particular expansion of theft law was effectuated. A major peculation by a trustee or bank official might carry a lesser penalty than a minor trespassory larceny, although many would consider that the former was the more heinous and harmful behavior. Over a period of time the severity of larceny penalties gradually moderated; and ultimately, when various forms of theft were consolidated into a single offense, the same statutory maximum would become applicable to both larceny and embezzlement.

Misappropriation.   "Misappropriation" is the criminal act that characterizes embezzlement, just as "taking" characterizes larceny. It is generally more difficult to decide whether misappropriation occurred than to decide whether property was unlawfully taken. A real estate broker or a lawyer, for example, may receive the proceeds of a sale or property or money recovered in a lawsuit. It is easy to say that such monies are misappropriated if the broker or lawyer pockets the whole fund and spends it for his personal needs. But what if the broker deposits the buyer's check in the broker's personal bank account, meaning to write a check later payable to the client for the amount of the proceeds less commission? That way of handling the transaction may violate standards of professional behavior which explicitly require clients' funds to be deposited and held in separate accounts; but it would be a harsh rule that transformed every violation of prophylactic professional regulations into a severely punishable theft. Ethical codes of the professions generally provide lesser sanctions, such as reprimand or suspension from practice, and no ethics committee of a professional association should have the power to redefine crime by changing its rules of ethics. On the other hand, the mere fact that an act violates professional standards should not immunize professional misbehavior from criminal sanctions that apply to identical conduct engaged in by nonprofessionals.

Perhaps the resolution of this dilemma lies in the proposition that identical acts have different significance in different circumstances. If I give my friend $1,000 with which to pay my bills while I am on a long journey, and he deposits the money in his own account to avoid the inconvenience of opening a separate account, it would be unreasonable to conclude that he is misappropriating my property. However, if I give money to my lawyer to pay a judgment against me and the lawyer deposits it in his own account, quite different implications may arise. For the lawyer, having a separate account for clients' funds is no temporary or occasional need but part of the normal way of doing business, explicitly mandated by codes of professional ethics. Accordingly, the commingling of client funds with personal funds ordinarily represents not merely a lazy avoidance of minor inconvenience, but rather a significant and, for the professional, unusual choice among available accounts. In short, the lawyer appears to have taken the first step toward applying the client's money to his own private use. One could call that preparation or attempt to misappropriate the money, the offense becoming complete later when the lawyer draws checks on the account to pay his personal bills. However, the law chooses to treat the initial deposit in the lawyer's account as already an exercise of hostile dominion over the entrusted fund. Just as has been seen above in the case of larceny, the logical distinction between attempted and completed theft is not always maintained.

The ambiguity of "misappropriation" is further illustrated by cases where an agent has been convicted of misappropriating a check made out to his principal *even though he deposits that check in his principal's account.* This result has been reached in situations where the agent, owing the principal money on account of earlier transactions, covers up the shortage by depositing current checks with vouchers falsely attributing them to the earlier transactions. Because of the false accounting, the agent is seen as having applied the current checks *to his own purposes,* squaring himself with the company, and thus misappropriating.

An extreme and dubious extension of the concept of misappropriation is expressed in some statutes that make any shortage in the accounts of a public official a basis for convicting him of embezzlement. The reasoning goes as follows. There is proof that the official received X amount, as tax collector. He has on hand only X minus Y. Thus he must have misappropriated Y, or at least failed to exercise proper care in collecting, conserving, or disbursing tax monies. Such reasoning and legislation confound theft with negligence, or, even more at variance with Anglo-American traditions, seeks to facilitate convicting an official of a presumed embezzlement by eliminating the necessity of proving misappropriation.

Property of another. The embezzlement statutes transcended the difficulties experienced in larceny law over the kinds of property covered. One can embezzle real as well as personal property, negotiable instruments and securities as well as tangible physical goods. But limiting embezzlement to "property" plays an important role in one class of situations, namely, where it may be necessary to decide whether a defendant exerted control over property belonging to another or whether instead he merely failed to pay a contracted debt owed to the other. The distinction is of constitutional importance where imprisonment for debt is constitutionally forbidden. It is, in any event, important from a policy viewpoint because putting the force of the criminal law behind fulfillment of contracts would have immense social and economic implications. Department stores, banks, credit card agencies, and other creditors would then be able to call upon prosecuting attorneys to aid in collections, the threat of jail for defaulting debtors would be legitimated, and creditors, especially of the poor, would be partially relieved of the necessity of carefully screening their extensions of credit.

Distinguishing property from contract obligations is not always easy. One tends to think of "having" money in a bank, whereas the true relationship is that depositing money "in" one's bank account, unlike stashing it in a safe-deposit box, is in effect a transfer of ownership to the bank. Thereafter the bank merely owes money to the depositor. That means that the banker may, the moment he has the depositor's cash in hand, use that cash as he will. He does not misappropriate it even though he proceeds forthwith to the race-track, where he loses it all at the betting windows. That may violate certain banking laws; it is not theft.

The niceties to which the distinctions between property and contract can give rise are illustrated by *Commonwealth v. Mitchneck,* 130 Pa. Super. 433, 198 A. 463 (1938). Mitchneck operated a small coal mine during the Depression of the 1930s. He had an arrangement with the miners whereby they could obtain groceries from a storekeeper on credit. Mitchneck would pay the grocer and deduct the amount from the miners' paychecks. At some point, Mitchneck found himself unable to pay the grocer, although he had deducted the grocery bills from the wage payments. That is to say, the cash withheld from wages had gone either into Mitchneck's pocket or to pay some of Mitchneck's more pressing bills. The theory of the prosecution was that the defendant had misappropriated money belonging to the miners. The prosecution failed because Mitchneck never had any of the miners' money; he had merely paid them less than was owed in wages, and continued to owe the balance. He had only broken his contract with his employees to pay their grocery bills. So also vis-à-vis the grocer: Mitchneck had merely violated his agreement to pay the grocer if the grocer extended credit to the miners. By reflecting on the different result that would have been reached if there were a slight change in the facts, one can see how close this decision was to the line.

If the arrangement at the office of Mitchneck's paymaster had been that the employees filed past two windows, receiving full wages at the first and paying their grocery bills at the second, an embezzlement conviction would have been possible because payments at the second window would have put money belonging to the miners in Mitchneck's hands. Whether an embezzlement conviction would actually have been sustained would depend on analysis of the transaction at the second window. If the understanding was that Mitchneck would hold these monies in a special drawer or account reserved for the grocer, his dipping into that drawer or account would have been embezzlement. But if the understanding went no farther than Mitchneck's

undertaking a contractual obligation to pay the grocer, the miners' payments to him would have given rise only to an indebtedness by Mitchneck. Failure to pay a debt is not embezzlement.

Intention and motives. The statutory definitions of embezzlement include no express requirement that the culprit means to deprive the owner permanently. Accordingly, unauthorized "borrowing" of trust funds by a trustee or of a customer's securities by his broker is embezzlement. It will be observed, however, that these examples involve valuable liquid assets that are jeopardized by deviation from propriety in handling them. The cases thus resemble larceny cases where, despite a professional intention to deprive the owner only temporarily, the borrower disposes of the property in a way that creates a high risk that it will not be restored. Moreover, cash or fungible securities "temporarily" borrowed are unlikely to be literally returned; the borrower intends to return *equivalent* money or securities, which is to say that the intent is to pay at some time in the future for what is presently taken. The kind of trivial borrowing that escapes punishment as larceny might also be excluded from embezzlement by finding that no "appropriation" had occurred. The executor of an estate who lets his daughter take a ride on a bicycle that is part of the estate is not only unlikely to be indicted, as a matter of the prosecutor's discretion, but also is probably immune under the law of embezzlement.

Beneficent motives. Beneficent motives do not bar prosecution for theft, whether by larceny or embezzlement. Such ameliorating circumstances are considered only by the prosecutor in determining whether to lodge charges, or by the sentencing judge. Thus, stealing for charity or out of necessity is as criminal as stealing out of greed. A mother who "steals" narcotics from an errant son in the hope of saving him from addiction is theoretically guilty of larceny. A trustee holding property subject to restrictions in a will that forbid investment in anything but first mortgages of government bonds is guilty of embezzlement if he invests instead in gold or oil, hoping thus to multiply the return for the benefit of the charity named in the will or the testator's grandchildren. Some embezzlement laws expressly state that appropriation is covered whether the appropriation is for the use and benefit of the trustee or "for the use of another." Even without such explicit provision, the courts would hold that improper disposition of property by a fiduciary, however kindly intended, was an unlawful assertion of dominion by the fiduciary and an appropriation for his own psychic satisfaction.

We have come a long way from the core concept of thievery to a kind of penal sanction against violation of codes of good behavior for fiduciaries. Perhaps a completely rational—that is, ahistorical—theft law would be cut back to the old common law notion of *lucri causa*. That is, theft would be limited to acquisitive behavior for the sake of gain. But doing this would entail creating additional penal offenses, outside of or auxiliary to the theft legislation, to deal with specific property offenses not for the purpose of gain: compare the traditional "malicious mischief" law.

False pretenses and fraud

Larceny and embezzlement deal with takings and appropriations without the consent of the true owner. It is necessary now to confront the question of how far the penal law should go where the owner is not merely deprived of possession or enjoyment of his property, but voluntarily transfers his title to the property, as where he is induced to sell the property or to part with money as a result of trickery or misrepresentation by the other party to the transaction. The expansion of common law larceny to include "larceny by trick" in cases where the theft obtained possession by deception has already been noted. But this covered a small fraction of the domain of fraud because it was limited to transfers of *possession*. If the swindler induced the owner to part with title, that is, to sell or otherwise transfer ownership, the transaction was seen as falling within the realm of contract or commerce.

A number of reasons conjoined to delay the advance of penal regulation in this area. With regard to controversies between merchants, there was a long history or special tribunals and guild regulation that must have seemed to them preferable to the heavy-handed intrusion of national law and officials. With regard to protection of the ordinary citizen and consumer, the ancient common law misdemeanor of "cheating" might have been cited as filling most of the need. That reached the use of false weights and measures or other devices by which *the public generally* was mulcted. It did not, in principle, inquire into single transactions, where bargainers were supposed to protect themselves ("Let the buyer beware!"). To a cautious eighteenth-century legislator or judge, it would have seemed dangerous, paternalist, and a nuisance to involve the

high courts in such trivial, nonviolent controversies. Dangerous, because conviction would so often depend on appraisal of the complaining victim's credibility and that of the defendant, who in the early days at least could not testify in his own defense and enjoyed limited or no assistance of counsel. Moreover, it would have been evident to opponents of penalizing "private" fraud that there would be serious difficulties in distinguishing substantial deception from sellers' exaggeration of value and other conventional puffing of wares (*Rex v. Wheatley*, 96 Eng. Rep. 151 (K.B. 1761)). Such concerns would manifest themselves during the eighteenth and nineteenth centuries in the first penal laws against private fraud by the very narrow limits placed on the kind of misrepresentation that would be criminal. To this day, under the Penal Code of France mere lying by one party to bargaining is not criminal. To prove criminal fraud the prosecution must also show a "mise-en-scène," that is, a stage setting for the lie such as would inveigle even skeptics.

False representation. The first false-pretense statutes were couched in terms of obtaining money or other property by means of a knowingly false and fraudulent misrepresentation of fact. We may pass without further comment the conventional restriction of this new theft law to theft of "property," and defer for a moment discussion of "knowingly false and fraudulent." What would constitute a sufficient "misrepresentation of fact"? That question may be best be answered by specifying what was not included.

Misleading omissions. The false-pretense laws did not create an affirmative obligation to tell the other party to a bargain everything that he might like to know. Silence is not misrepresentation, even when it is obvious that the other party labors under a misunderstanding. The antiques dealer may acquire Grandma's rocking chair for one-tenth of its market value, she being manifestly ignorant of the fact that it is a rare piece of seventeenth-century Americana. The oil company may send its disguised agent to buy Farmer Brown's land cheap without telling him that oil has been discovered on adjoining land. Not until the enactment of the twentieth-century "blue sky laws" and the federal Securities Act of 1933 did affirmative disclosure become an obligation enforced by penal law, and then the obligation was particularized by specific questions that the promoter was obliged to answer in the registration forms drafted by the enforcement agency. The principle has been extended to other kinds of promotions, such as land sales and franchising.

Opinions and promises.   Opinions, including most certainly the seller's expressed opinion of the value of his goods, were not treated as punishable misrepresentations of fact under the typical false-pretense statute, however clear the proof might be that the seller did not hold that opinion. Promises, predictions, and statements of intention were not covered, however clear the proof that the promisor did not intend to perform or did not believe his prediction. Although modern courts are willing to regard such deception as factual misrepresentation of the state of mind of the swindler, the earlier attitude was that the true state of mind of the accused with respect to promises and intentions incident to a bargain seemed too chancy an issue for a criminal trial. Moreover, penalizing false promises would seem as dangerously close to using criminal law to enforce debts and other contracts. True, such a law would reach only promisors who did not *at the time of promising* mean to abide by the promise, so that honest promisors would, theoretically, not be imperiled. But again, who could judge reliably the subjective good faith of a promisor? Every user of a credit card, every borrower from a small-loan company, every purchaser on deferred payment, would be in jeopardy if at the time of the transaction his financial condition and prospects were so unfavorable as to give rise to an inference that he knew he would be unable to pay the obligation when it came due.

Misrepresentation of law.   Nothing would have seemed more self-evident to lawyers and judges than the dichotomy of law and fact; and a statute penalizing misrepresentation of fact must, especially in view of the libertarian principle that penal statutes are to be "strictly construed," not be extended to misrepresentation of law. Misrepresentation of law was not covered. This result was facilitated by a mechanical misapplication of the adage that everyone is presumed to know the law. That adage properly applies only to exclude the defense, in any criminal prosecution, that the accused did not know that his behavior was prohibited. Of course, a misrepresentation of law might under some circumstances escape the false-pretense statute by being couched as an expression of opinion. But it seems clearly arbitrary to give categorical immunity to such knowingly false representations as "This transaction is tax-exempt," "This insecticide may be lawfully used in this state," or "This insurance policy cannot be legally terminated for any reason."

Materiality of misrepresentation.   Since the false-pretense statute speaks in terms of obtaining property "by means of" misrepresentation, a causal relation between the swindler's deception and the victim's loss must be shown. For example, if the victim knew the true facts, it could not be said that he parted with his money as a result of the misrepresentation, although the swindler might in such situations be guilty of attempt to obtain by false pretense. It was not necessary that the false pretense be the sole cause of the harm to the victim: deception by others, false rumor, or the victim's greed or self-deception might be contributory causes without immunizing the swindler's fraud.

The idea that the misrepresentation must be material is linked to the causation element of the offense. A salesman may feign a joviality or enthusiasm he does not feel. He may assume a name other than his own, pretend to be rich or pious, or falsely claim membership in a lodge or a veterans' association. Except where such identifications are relevant to an extension of credit to him, they would be held immaterial to the transaction, that is, presumptively not causative. This would be the case even if it could be proved conclusively that the victim would not have entered into the transaction but for a deception of this sort, as where the victim was intensely prejudiced against the race or religion of the salesman, who consequently misrepresented himself in that respect while avoiding all deception as to the mercantile aspects of the deal.

It is thus apparent that the requirement of materiality goes beyond the question of actual causation, and enables the courts to disregard some effective deception for reasons of policy. In effect, it is held that some methods of advertising and "hard sell," although possibly reprehensible, are so pervasive and so uncertainly separable from laudable business activities as to call for repression by less drastic methods than the penal law, for example, by affirmative administrative regulation of competitive practices.

Transcending the limitations of the early false-pretense statutes.   Beginning in the nineteenth century, mounting social pressures to penalize all sorts of swindling led to judicial evasion of the limits fixed by the false-pretense statutes and to supplementary legislation, culminating in the federal Mail Fraud Act, which reaches every trick, artifice, or scheme to defraud (18 U.S.C. §§ 1341–1342 (2000)). Judicial expansion of the concept of criminal false pretenses often rested on the incontrovertible proposition that misrepresentations need not be express but can be implied. Thus, granting that omission is not to be penalized, the stock salesman who garnishes his expressed rosy view of the company's profitability (mere "opinion" and "puffery") with the reassuring statistic that the stock has earned an *average* profit of 20 percent for the last ten years might nevertheless be convicted on a showing that he omitted to state that all the earnings had been in the first year, with steady losses thereafter. Notwithstanding the literal truth of the "average" figure, there would be a finding of an "implicit" misrepresentation that 20 percent was typical of recent earnings.

In the same way, opinions might give rise to implied representations of underlying fact. For example, if a stock salesman assured the customer that the share were nonassessable, when he knew that in fact the necessary steps had not been taken to qualify for nonassessability, he implicitly misrepresented those facts. Opinions were, in any event, not ruled out as a basis of liability if given by one who spoke with purported professional expertise, such as a lawyer, doctor, or disinterested appraiser. Even promises might be brought within the literal scope of "misrepresentation of present fact" when some courts began to view the promisor's state of mind as a "fact like the state of his digestion." The promise could be said to imply that the promisor then had in mind a good faith purpose to perform.

Mail fraud. The Mail Fraud Act incorporates the broadest definition of criminal fraud. Any "trick, scheme, or device" suffices for conviction, and false promises are explicitly included. Opinion, value, or law may be the subject of material deception. Materiality does not totally disappear as a criterion, but a misrepresentation that, standing alone, would have been held immaterial under a false-pretense statute may figure as one element of a "scheme to defraud." The Mail Fraud Act is not confined to obtaining property; a "scheme to defraud" obviously may be directed at defrauding others of valuable services. Indeed, it has been held that the government is defrauded where its normal administrative processes are vitiated through the exercise of improper influences upon officials.

Even the criminal-intent requirement has been somewhat diluted so as to come very close to penalizing reckless as well as knowingly false representations. This result was reached by holding that a promisor's state of mind is a fact that may be misrepresented. Thus, a promoter who makes confident predictions of profit in order to sell securities may be convicted of mail fraud if he is far less confident than he represents himself to be and omits to disclose circumstances that impugn that confidence. Being sanguine himself, he actually believes what he asserts, so that he acts in good faith and without intent to deceive. The prediction is honest but reckless. Or, stated more cautiously, the promoter, aware of his own secret doubts, knowingly misrepresents the extent of his confidence (*Knickerbocker Merchandising Co. v. United States,* 13 F. 2d 544 (2d. Cir. 1926)).

Mail fraud is a peculiarly American phenomenon that deserves a word of explanation. In principle, under American federalism ordinary crime is the concern of the states rather than of the federal government. The federal government would naturally promulgate penal law relating to treason against the United States, to enforcement of federal tax and customs laws, and to perjury committed before the federal courts and agencies. Theft law, under this concept, would fall within the domain of the states, as do murder, rape, arson, burglary, and assault. But the line begins to blur. Theft of *federal* property seems to demand uniform national law and enforcement, and appropriate legislation is enacted. As the interstate rail and highway system developed, protection of this national network similarly evoked federal penal legislation against train robbery, stealing of goods moving in interstate commerce, transportation of stolen goods across state lines, and even transportation of women "for immoral purposes." Thus arose a dual jurisdiction whereby a great many local crimes could be prosecuted either by the state or by the national government if some federal "peg" could be proved.

In the case of mail fraud, the federal peg was use of the mails to carry out the scheme to defraud. This was more than a technicality. The mails were extensively employed to conduct fraudulent public promotions extending far beyond the bounds of the state or foreign country where the enterprise was operated. The federal government, by making the subsidized facilities of the postal service available to swindlers, would be perceived as aiding in the exploitation of the victims. State officials where the victims resided would be hampered in investigating operations thousands of miles away, and there would be overlapping and wasteful enforcement effort when numerous state investigations were initiated. Within the postal service, enforcement officers called postal inspectors were employed to determine when the mails were being used for noxious purposes (including not only fraud but extortion, dissemination of pornography, and the like) and to assemble evidence for prosecuting those who thus exploited the federal facilities. Unfortunately, once this enforcement apparatus was created, it followed the tradition of bureaucratic expansionism and involved itself in a great deal of petty local misconduct where, for example, the culprit used the mail, however peripherally, in writing to the victim in the same city or state.

Continuing limits on criminality of fraud. Notwithstanding the breadth of the mail fraud statute and some comparable state laws, much chicanery remains beyond the scope of theft law. If businessmen combine to raise prices above the competitive level that would prevail but for their conspiracy, their illegal behavior must be explicitly penalized by antitrust laws. If a merchant takes advantage of the buyer's ignorance or need for credit to overcharge him outrageously, no crime is committed. If the officers of a corporation vote themselves unconscionable salaries and bonuses, only civil suits present a slim possibility of recovery. Immune from theft law also are manufacturers who cut costs and increase profit by substituting inferior ingredients, and manufacturers who purposely build rapid obsolescence into their automobiles so as to sell more high-profit replacement parts. The taxpayer who defrauds the government of taxes by understating his income and the importer who evades customs duties by smuggling face prosecution under specific statutes, but not for theft. The advertisers who secure our patronage by manipulating our emotions rather than by misrepresentation—for example, by baselessly associating health, virility, sexual attraction, or worldly success with their cereals, skin creams, and cigarettes—are not guilty of theft if, without representations, they merely suggest the association by depicting virile men and lovely women availing themselves of these products.

Perhaps the most interesting noncriminal frauds are found in the fields of religion, politics, and love. Here the problem is not so much that the theft statutes do not apply as that proof is exceedingly difficult and prosecution would run head-on into widespread complacency about prevarication on these subjects, as if deception were, to some extent, part of the game.

As to religion, even the Constitution comes into play to provide a special preserve for fraud, as shown in the famous case of *United States v. Ballard,* 322 U.S. 78 (1944). The Ballards, husband and wife, were indicted under the Mail Fraud Act for mulcting the members of a religious sect organized and presided over by themselves. Among the knowingly false representations charged to have been made were assertions that the defendants had communications with various saints and that they had the power of healing, which generally manifested itself in transactions transferring wealth to the Ballards. The defense objected to any attempt to prove that the religious assertions were false, arguing that this would amount to a heresy trial contrary to the guaranty of freedom of religion in the First Amendment. The trial court accepted this argument and limited proof to a showing that the Ballards did not believe their assertions; that is, the fact knowingly misrepresented was their own state of mind, not the actuality of communication with the saints. On this theory they were convicted by the jury, and that theory was ultimately upheld by the United States Supreme Court.

However, in a notable and witty dissent, Justice Robert Jackson argued that the First Amendment difficulty was not solved by limiting the proof to the defendants' subjective disbelief of their own statements, since the normal way of demonstrating such disbelief would be to show that the statements were incredible and would not be believed by a reasonable person. Justice Jackson could not see how a governmental effort to establish the incredibility of a religious assertion could be squared with the First Amendment. But going beyond that, he inclined to the view that it was too dangerous to permit criminal prosecution of a preacher based on his subjective reservations as to this or that tenet of his faith. Moreover, Justice Jackson viewed pecuniary support of church and faith as quite distinct from commerce. The contributor is not seeking his money's worth but rather expresses his faith through giving.

In politics, there is a significant paucity of prosecutions instigated by disappointed contributors against candidates who upon election promptly abandon elements of the party platform, giving rise to an inference that the platform was never meant to be carried out. Political contributions, too, must be treated as expressions of faith rather than purchases of commitments. The grounds of politics are too shifting to subject a change of position to potential prosecution. The inhibitions on electioneering generated by potential prosecutions under such circumstances would raise free-speech issues. Political bias, real or suspected, in a trial where the issue was the good faith of a "promising" candidate would evoke public cynicism, and suggests the imprudence of treating false political promises as a crime.

As for love, whether or not "all's fair in love and war," who is to tell whether the fateful declaration "I love you" was true of false? Does the declaration mean "I lust for you" or "I would die for you"? Does it mean "tonight" or "forever"? To what extent was the victim deceived? To what extent are passionate declarations conventional expressions shaped by literature, movies, or television broadcasts, rather than representations or promises? Would the quality of courtship, sexual relations, or communal life be enhanced by authorizing criminal prosecution in this area, prosecutions that would be as exceptional as were prosecutions for adultery when that was pervasively penalized?

Seduction, that is, obtaining sexual intercourse by deception, seems a fairly straightforward fraudulent obtaining of services, and was once widely punishable not as theft but as part of the regulation of sexual behavior. It no longer is. Notably, even civil suits for "breach of promise" or seduction have been widely discountenanced by law as facilitating blackmail. It remains paradoxical that a villain who obtains one dollar from a trusting woman by falsely representing his credentials commits the serious offense of theft, whereas securing her sexual compliance by the same deception remains unpunishable.

Would-be participants in the "religious racket," attracted by the thought that constitutional protection of religious freedom somewhat obstructs prosecution for fraudulent religious pretenses, should bear in mind that there is no constitutional barrier to prosecution for misrepresenting the purpose to which religious contributions are to be applied. Thus, pretending that the contribution is sought to build a church when in fact the swindler intends to pocket the funds is punishable fraud. Similarly, embezzling funds over which the swindler was given control for a specified religious use is punishable theft.

Receiving stolen goods

The law generally penalizes an accessory to a crime only if he conspired or aided in its commission or if, after the commission, he harbors or conceals the offender, that is, obstructs law enforcement. The objective encouragement that a "fence," of professional receiver, gives to theft does not amount to conspiring or aiding in the theft, although a receiver can easily cross the line and become a conspirator, for example, by entering into a continuing relationship with the thief, promising to buy regularly, or suggesting what would be best stolen and where. Merely buying the loot does not amount to harboring the thief. These limits of accessorial liability gave rise to special legislation penalizing those who buy stolen goods or otherwise aid the thief in disposing of them.

In principle, the receiving, like other theft offenses, should be confined to situations where the offender knows he is dealing with property that does not belong to the person bringing it to him. The difficulty of proving such knowledge led to broadening the statutes to cover recklessness or negligence with respect to true ownership. Sometimes the statutes created a presumption of knowledge where the receiver bought at far less than the market value of the goods, although such a presumption appears to contradict the constitutional requirement that conviction of infamous crime be based of proof beyond a reasonable doubt. An alternative approach to the problem of the professional receiver is to license and regulate pawnshops, junk dealers, and secondhand stores. The regulations may require the dealer to keep record of the identity of the sellers, to report certain purchases to the police, to submit to police inspections, and the like. Violations lead to suspension or revocation of license and of the right to do business, or to misdemeanor penalties for breach of regulations.

Grading of theft offenses

The function of a penal code is not only to specify what is punishable but also to set legislative limits on the discretion of judges in imposing sentences and to express a legislative judgment on the relative heinousness of different offenses. The question then is, What do legislatures provide, and what should they provide, in the way of maximum sentences for various forms of theft? One might initially expect that if "theft" is a rational category of behavior, the legislature would content itself with providing a maximum sentence of, say, ten years' imprisonment for theft of the greatest scale under the most aggravating circumstances. Within the ten-year legislative maximum, the sentencing judge would have discretion to impose individual sentences that reflect the infinite variety of circumstances and offenders. Actual duration of imprisonment under an indeterminate sentence imposed by the judge would be determined at the discretion of a parole board, which may judge that the prisoner has been sufficiently reoriented by his prison experience to be safely returned to the community.

Sentence limits expressed in categories as gross as larceny or theft are unacceptable. Already in the eighteenth century, the extreme penalty authorized for larceny led to statutes barring capital punishment where only petty values were involved. By the twentieth century, the grading of theft offenses by value had become more complex. There would be not only "grand" and "petty" larceny, but ladders of value with three or more rungs, for example, at $100, $500, $5,000, and $100,000. Petty-value grading might be denied in the case of particular classes of property, the misappropriation of which was especially to be discouraged. Examples are guns, drugs, public records, vehicles, mail, and keys. Similarly, legislative downgrading based on low value might be denied because of aggravating circumstances, such as theft of public property by a civil servant, theft by means of certain threats, or theft of property by one to whom it was entrusted in a fiduciary capacity. Of special interest is the development of statutes dealing uniquely with shoplifting, or stealing merchandise from stores, carrying very low maximum sentences. It seems strange that merchants would seek legislation reducing the penalties for stealing their goods. They recognized, however, that lower penalties, which can be imposed in less formal proceedings before magistrates, would be a more effective deterrent than cumbersome prosecution for conventional larceny.

Apart from different maxima corresponding to amounts stolen, there were differences depending on the manner in which the theft was effectuated. The historic evolution of theft legislation had the consequence that every time a legislature added a new category of theft, such as embezzlement or false pretense, it made a contemporary judgment of the appropriate maximum for that "new" offense without aligning that maximum with older, more rigorous sanctions applicable to larceny. After the consolidation of theft offenses, discussed below, these differences tended to disappear, leaving only traces in the value-grading where certain betrayals of trust, such as embezzlement, may carry higher legislative maxima than a corresponding larceny.

Consolidation of theft offenses. Penalizing thievish rascality by means of a variety of distinguishable offenses entailed a number of technical legal problems that led twentieth-century legislators to attempt to consolidate the historic array of theft offenses into a single comprehensive offense called theft or stealing. One of these problems was legislative, having to do with the propriety of prescribing different penalties for different forms of theft. More pressing was the prosecutor's problem of choosing the right offense to charge. From information provided by the police, he might reasonably conclude that a case was larceny by trick, only to have that charge defeated by evidence that the culprit secured not merely possession but title; this would make the offense an obtaining by false pretenses rather than a larceny. If the prosecutor were foresighted enough, he might have charged both offenses, leaving it to the jury to select the proper one. But the vagaries of juries and the subtlety of the distinction might result in conviction on the wrong count and acquittal on the other. Upon appeal, the conviction on the wrong count would be reversed, and the reprosecution on the right count would be barred by constitutional prohibition against retrying an accused on a charge upon which he has once been acquitted. In one case, a woman obtained money from a prominent actor upon her representation that she had had intercourse with him and had borne his child. The actor denied having had intercourse with her. She was convicted of obtaining by false pretense, but the conviction was set aside on appeal on the ground that the actor, knowing that he had not had relations with her, could not have been deceived; the offense was extortion by threat rather than obtaining by deception (*Norton v. United States*, 92 F. 2d 753 (9th Cir. 1937)).

The frustration felt by prosecutors, victims, the press, and the public at the spectacle of swindlers thus eluding punishment is understandable. The consolidation statutes were not, however, an unqualified success. The accused was still entitled, as a matter of fair procedure, to be given notice in advance of the trial regarding particulars of the charge. The particulars given would tend to show one or another of the traditional categories of theft, and the prosecutor would be required to prove the case so outlined and no other, lest the defense be unfairly "surprised."

What was really needed here to prevent frustration of the law was a more flexible and realistic view of "harmless surprise." The legislators might even have retained the older, multiple-category theft if they also had enacted a rule that conviction for any category of theft should be valid if the evidence proved guilt under any other category in the absence of demonstrated prejudicial surprise. It would be a rare case in which a defendant and his lawyer would not be fully aware of the nature of the transaction charged as criminal, and the choice of the proper penal label ought not to matter. The argument is tempting, but it encounters formidable objections. Sometimes it does matter, for example, if the legislature has prescribed different penalties. Where trial by jury is a fundamental right, it matters that the jury, not a judge, determine what offense has been committed. On the other hand, as a practical matter courts do indeed implement a casual version of the doctrine of "harmless surprise." They will not throw out a conviction because of variances between the indictment and the prosecutor's case unless the variance is "material," and the defendant suffered "prejudice" as a result of the surprise. (See, for example, *Thompson v. Nagle*, 188 F.3d 1442 (11th Cir. 1997); *United States v. Mills*, 366 F.2d 512 (6th Cir. 1966)).

Under the consolidation statutes the old distinctions still retain importance because the outer boundaries of the consolidated theft offense are an amalgamation of the boundaries of the constituent offenses. The line between what is criminal and what is noncriminal continues to derive from the older law. Thus, a misrepresentation that is noncriminal under classic false-pretense law might suffice for larceny-by-trick. It becomes crucial, then, to know whether the case involves a transfer of *title* (false pretense) or a tricky taking and carrying away from the *possession* of another (larceny). Moreover a consolidation statute is likely to need and to incorporate sentencing distinctions that parallel the categories of the older theft law. For example, leniency for petty larcenies may be inappropriate for small embezzlements by fiduciaries or public officials.

The consolidation reform may have assumed an importance for prosecutors, judges, and academic lawyers that is disproportionate to its practical significance. However striking and provocative the cases of individual swindlers who "get off" may be, it must be remembered that these make up the tiniest fraction of theft prosecutions, which in turn represent a small fraction of thefts committed. The security of our belongings is not measurably impaired by these rare, though spectacular, acquittals, although politicians and press may play up these incidents in such a way that we all feel less secure. Important increments in property security can come only from more effective policing, improved technology, greater economic justice, and a lessening of the alienation of segments of the population from the general community and its standards of behavior.

LOUIS B. SCHWARTZ
DAN M. KAHAN

See also BURGLARY; COMPUTER CRIME; EMPLOYEE THEFT: BEHAVIORAL ASPECTS; EMPLOYEE THEFT: LEGAL ASPECTS; ROBBERY; SHOPLIFTING.

BIBLIOGRAPHY

American Law Institute. *Model Penal Code and Commentaries: Official Draft and Revised Comments.* 3 vols. Philadephia: ALI, 1985.
BEALE, JOSEPH H., JR. "The Borderland of Larceny." *Harvard Law Review* 6 (1892): 244–256.
CLARK, WILLIAM L., and MARSHALL, WILLIAM L. *A Treatise on the Law of Crimes.* 7th ed. Marian Quinn Barnes, revising ed. Mundelein, Ill.: Callaghan, 1967.
HALL, JEROME. *Theft, Law, and Society.* 2d ed. Indianapolis: Bobbs-Merrill, 1952.
HASEN, RICHARD L., and MCADAMS, RICHARD H. "The Surprisingly Complex Case Against Theft." *International Review of Law and Economics* 17 (1997): 367–378.
HERLING, JOHN. *The Great Price Conspiracy: The Story of the Antitrust Violations in the Electrical Industry.* Washington, D.C.: Luce, 1962.
LAFAVE, WAYNE R., and SCOTT, AUSTIN W., JR. *Handbook on Criminal Law.* 2d ed. St. Paul, Minn.: West, 1976.
Note. "A Rationale of the Law of Aggravated Theft." *Columbia Law Review* 54 (1954): 84–110.
PEARCE, ARTHUR R. "Theft by False Promises." *University of Pennsylvania Law Review* 101 (1953): 967–1011.
PERKINS, ROLLIN M., and BOYCE, RONALD M. *Criminal Law.* 8th ed. Mineola, N.Y.: Foundation Press, 1939.
RADZINOWICZ, LEON. *A History of English Criminal Law and Its Administration from 1750.* Foreword by Lord MacMillan. London: Stevens, 1948.

RIESMAN, DAVID. "Possession and the Law of Finders." *Harvard Law Review* 52 (1939): 1105–1134.

STEPHEN, JAMES FITZJAMES. *A History of the Criminal Law of England.* 3 vols. London: Macmillan, 1883.

SUTHERLAND, EDWIN H. *White Collar Crime.* New York: Dryden Press, 1979.

TIGAR, MICHAEL E. "The Right of Property and the Law of Theft." *Texas Law Review* 62 (1984): 1443–1475.

U.S. National Commission on Reform of Federal Criminal Laws. *Final Report: A Proposed New Federal Criminal Code (Title 18, United States Code).* Washington, D.C.: The Commission, 1971.

TREASON

Article III, Section 3 of the Constitution of the United States provides:

Treason against the United States, shall consist only in levying War against them, or in adhering to their Enemies, giving them Aid and Comfort. No Person shall be convicted of Treason unless on the Testimony of two Witnesses to the same overt Act, or on Confession in open Court.

The Congress shall have Power to declare the Punishment of Treason, but no Attainder of Treason shall work Corruption of Blood, or Forfeiture except during the Life of the Person attainted.

State constitutions today contain similar limiting definitions of treason against a state. Since national independence there has been almost no action or doctrinal development under the state provisions; the law of treason in the United States has been almost wholly the product of the national Constitution and decisions of federal courts.

Treason is the only crime defined in the Constitution, and basic to the treatment of this offense has been a mingling of values protective of government and of individuals. The crime of treason strikes at the foundations of the legal order and deals with the most serious threats to the existence of the state. Congress has reflected this judgment in prescribing penalties that may mount to death or life imprisonment. Where charges have fallen plainly within the bounds of the constitutional definition, judges have firmly applied the law. On the other hand, the limiting language of the Constitution (treason shall consist "only" in the two named forms of the offense), constitutional history, and the responses

of judges bear witness to a restrictive approach in marking the outer boundaries of the crime. Thus the treason clause not only protects the security of the legal order but is functionally analogous to the Bill of Rights, protecting the civil liberties of individuals.

The restrictive dimension departs from the main directions of the statute and case law in England and in this country before 1789, which gave clear primacy to the security of government, often to serve the interests of those holding official power at a given time. Into the late eighteenth century, English political history was marked by aggressive resort to charges of treason as weapons of partisan conflict, with much vindictive prosecution and loose use of evidence. Security in the most elemental sense was at stake for the English colonies in North America under the threat of the French and Indian Wars, and in the new states torn through the Revolution by bitter divisions between those loyal to the Crown and those asserting independence. Thus the legislation of the colonies and of the new states in the Revolutionary years was studded with broad and sometimes vague definitions of subversion, in sharp contrast to the limited definition written into the national Constitution.

Records from the framing and ratification of the Constitution contain little information about the treason clause. But what is there shows sensitivity to lessons drawn from English experience of the dangers that loose resort to treason prosecutions might present to individual and political liberty. Two fears were prominent: that holders of official power would misuse the treason charge to suppress peaceful political opposition and destroy those who were out of official favor, and that under the dread charge popular fear and emotion might be stirred to produce convictions without proper evidence. Subsequently, federal judges recognized this restrictive background in decisions limiting extension of the offense. In *Cramer v. United States*, 325 U.S. 1, 47 (1945), the first treason case to reach the United States Supreme Court, the Court reaffirmed the restrictive construction of the scope of treason.

Elements of the offense

Three key elements are necessary for an offense to constitute treason: an obligation of allegiance to the legal order, and intent and action to violate that obligation. Treason is a breach of allegiance and of the faithful support a citizen owes to the sovereignty within which he lives. A citizen of the United States who is subject to the law of a foreign state may owe allegiance to that state at the same time he owes fealty to the United States. But this dual nationality does not relieve him of obligation to refrain from volunteering aid or comfort to the foreign nation if it is at war with the United States. Although the matter has not been presented to a court in this country, an individual present here and enjoying the nation's protection owes it his obedience while he is resident, and thus may be guilty of treason if he commits what would be the offense when done by a citizen.

Wrongful intent.   Wrongful intent is a necessary element of the crime of treason, varying in character according to which of the two forms of the offense is in issue. To be guilty of levying war against the United States, the individual must intend to use organized force to overthrow the government. Under older, broad doctrines of treason in English law, intent by group force to prevent or overcome enforcement of a particular statute or other lawful order or to obtain any particular group benefit contrary to law was treason. A similar tendency was shown in two early American instances involving violent group resistance: the first, to a federal excise on whiskey (the Whiskey Rebellion of 1794), and the second, to a property excise (Fries's Rebellion of 1799); in both, federal courts found treason. However, the later interpretation is that no intent short of intent to overthrow the government suffices to constitute the offense. After the Homestead Riot of 1892 several labor leaders were indicted for levying war against the Commonwealth of Pennsylvania. But the indictments were later quietly dropped, and use of the treason charge met with prompt and unanimous criticism from conservative jurists. Violent group actions short of challenge to the existence of the government are now treated as riot or unlawful assembly.

Adhering to an enemy requires intent to render the enemy tangible support ("aid and comfort"). Long-established doctrine has defined *enemies* as only those against whom a legally declared state of war exists. However, in the twentieth century the reality of such undeclared shooting hostilities as the Korean War raises questions about the older limitation. That the accused may have acted with mixed purposes, such as to make money by selling goods to the enemy, does not rebut existence of the requisite intent for treason, if one of his purposes was in fact to render performance useful to the enemy. In many crimes the law holds an individual responsible as intending the foreseeable consequences of his conduct, even though he pleads that he did not mean to bring about the particular outcome for which he is charged. In treason cases, however, the prosecution must prove that the accused had a specific intent to levy war or aid enemies. This requirement does not necessitate proof by explicit statement or direct admission of guilty purpose; the prosecution may prove the guilty intent by strong inference from the context of the accused's behavior.

Overt act.   The commission of some overt act to effect a treasonable purpose is a distinct element of the crime that the government must prove in addition to proving wrongful intent. The most striking, restrictive feature of the Constitution's definition of treason was the omission of any analogue of that branch of old English law that punished one who would "compass or imagine the death of our lord the King" (Treason Act, 1351, 25 Edw. 3, stat. 5, c. 2 (England)). The Crown had used this charge to suppress not only action likely to lead to the king's death, but also the mere speaking or writing of views critical of exercise of royal authority. Pursuing that line, the government obtained convictions of individuals because the "natural" consequences of their speaking or writing might endanger the state.

The calculated omission of this feature in the definition of the crime emphasized the need to show specific intent to prove treason as defined in the United States. Moreover, the omission underlines the need to prove substantial action by the accused. The function of the overt act element, said the Supreme Court in *Cramer*, is to ensure "that mere mental attitudes or expressions should not be treason"; the prosecution must show that the accused moved from the realm of thought, plan, or opinions into the world of action. However, the Supreme Court's treatment of the act element has clouded this requirement. In *Cramer* the Court seemed to say that the act must itself be evidence of the treasonable intent, a position apparently contrary to the general insistence that the intent and act elements are distinct. In *Haupt v. United States*, 330 U.S. 631 (1947), the Court clarified the matter somewhat: behavior proved by the required testimony of two witnesses need not indicate wrongful intent. But where the charge was aiding the enemy, if the proven overt act can be demonstrated to have given aid to the enemy only when appraised in light of evidence of other conduct of the accused, then that other conduct—as well as the particular overt act—must be proved by two witnesses. On the other hand, to prove the offense, it is not necessary to show that the accused succeeded in delivering aid to the enemy; it is enough that he took overt action to attempt delivery. More than mere planning must be shown. To establish treason by levying war, the government must prove an armed assembly; conspiracy alone does not prove the crime.

Application of the law in the United States

Since national independence, fewer than fifty cases involving the application of the law of treason as defined in the national or state constitutions have been brought to court in the United States. A tally of the thirty-eight major instances indicates that the cautious moderation sought by those who wrote the Constitution has been fulfilled in practice. Only eight cases show what critics might call broad interpretations of the offense; sixteen cases fall within explicit dimensions of the crime as set forth in the Constitution; in fourteen instances judges have taken a restrictive approach, refusing to enlarge the reach of the offense. This record suggests regard for the restrictive aspects of the constitutional history and probably indicates that by and large the country has enjoyed substantial political stability. In any event, the record shows little vindictive resort to the charge of treason, and few cases carrying politically controversial tones.

During the American Revolution most actions taken against British Loyalists were to confiscate property. Treason cases arising out of the Whiskey Rebellion, Fries's Rebellion, the Burr conspiracy, Jefferson's Embargo Act, and resistance to enforcement of the Fugitive Slave Law grew out of differences over domestic political issues. Decisions in these cases were rendered in 1795, 1800, 1807, 1808, and 1851, respectively, but were of limited practical impact. Treason prosecutions by state authorities incident to the Dorr Rebellion in Rhode Island (1842) and John Brown's raid (1859) were exceptional because of their broad political repercussions. Because of the scale of the Civil War there was no resort to prosecution for treason, although clearly supporters of the seceded states levied war against the United States. Some cases had tones of domestic ideological conflict over the country's entry into World War I. In *United States v. Werner*, 247 F. 708, 710–711 (E.D. Pa. 1918), the defendant was indicted for treason by giving aid to the enemy through publication of newspaper stories unfavorable to the cause of the United States. The trial court ruled for the government on the demurrer. On appeal, the Supreme Court disposed of the case on other grounds, but its opinion made clear that the prosecution carried a strong ideological tone (*Schaefer v. United States*, 251 U.S. 466 (1920)). But this cast was notably absent from treason prosecutions incident to World War II.

In the practice of Congress and in decisions of the courts, the constitutional definition of treason has never barred creation of other statutory offenses involving subversion of the legal order. Thus, *United States v. Rosenberg*, 195 F. 2d 583 (2d Cir. 1952) held that the defendants were validly convicted of conspiracy to violate the federal Espionage Act, 18 U.S.C. § 794 (1976) by communicating protected information to the USSR. However, established doctrine forbids Congress to enlarge beyond the constitutional definition the kinds of conduct that may be punished as treason, and assures the protection of the two-witness requirement where the charged conduct amounts to levy of war or adherence to enemies. Nonetheless, legislators might seek to punish it under another name. Loose use of the epithet *treason* amid the Cold War emotions of the 1950s showed that there was still potential power in the dread cry as a weapon of partisan or ideological combat. But the limits set by the constitutional definition have curbed resort to treason prosecutions to suppress or harass peaceful, legitimate political competition.

JAMES WILLARD HURST
DAN M. KAHAN

See also CONSPIRACY; FEDERAL BUREAU OF INVESTIGATION: HISTORY; FEDERAL CRIMINAL JURISDICTION; SEDITION AND DOMESTIC TERRORISM.

BIBLIOGRAPHY

ABRAMS, STUART E. "Threats to the President and the Constitutionality of Constructive Treason." *Columbia Journal of Law and Social Problems* 12, no. 3 (1976): 351–392.
CHAPIN, BRADLEY. *The American Law of Treason: Revolutionary and Early National Origins.* Seattle: University of Washington Press, 1964.
HILL, L. M. "The Two-Witness Rule in English Treason Trials: Some Comments on the Emergence of Procedural Law." *American Journal of Legal History* 12 (1968): 95–111.

HURST, JAMES WILLARD. *The Law of Treason in the United States: Collected Essays.* Westport, Conn.: Greenwood Press, 1971.

REHNQUIST, WILLIAM H. *All the Laws but One: Civil Liberties in Wartime.* New York: Alfred A. Knopf, 1998.

———. "Civil Liberty and the Civil War: The Indianapolis Treason Trials." *Indiana Law Journal* 72 (1997): 927–937.

SIMON, WALTER G. "The Evolution of Treason." *Tulane Law Review* 35, no. 4 (1961): 667–704.

STILLMAN, ARTHUR M., and ARNER, FREDERICK R. *Federal Case Law concerning the Security of the United States.* 83d Cong., 2d sess. Printed for use of the Special Subcommittee on Security Affairs. Washington, D.C.: Government Printing Office, 1954.

WIENER, FREDERICK BERNAYS. "Uses and Abuses of Legal History: A Practitioner's View." *Law Society's Gazette* 59, no. 6 (1962): 311–315.

TRESPASS, CRIMINAL

Introduction

The common law crime of criminal trespass generally consists of two basic elements. The first is trespass, which can be broadly defined as interference with another's actual and peaceable possession of property. Examples of such interference are entry onto or refusal to leave premises against the expressed wishes of the possessor. The second is breach of the peace, which generally involves force, violence, or some threat thereof. Where force is involved, issues concerning the title of ownership of property or the right to possession are irrelevant on the policy ground that such issues should be settled peacefully through the legal process rather than by potentially violent private action. Because of this concern with the use of force, the crime is sometimes referred to as *forcible trespass.*

Many statutes have abandoned the requirement of a breach of the peace, however, and prohibit any unauthorized intrusion. This can be accomplished by a general statutory prohibition of such intrusions (Model Penal Code, § 206.53) or by statutes aimed at particular conduct. Examples of the latter are specific prohibitions against entering upon land that has notices posted indicating that entry is forbidden; and against entering or refusing to leave despite a request to stay out or to leave by the person in possession of the premises. Where intrusion, rather than breach of the peace, is the focus of the prohibition, issues

concerning ownership or some other right to be on the premises could become relevant. Thus, for example, a person cannot be convicted of entering land against the wishes of the person in possession if the former has a right to be on the premises.

Related crimes

Criminal trespass often overlaps with, or is similar to, other crimes. Three types of such related crimes are relevant here.

The use or threat of force. Since criminal trespass may involve the use or threat of physical force, it overlaps with crimes prohibiting such use or threat. In particular, a criminal trespass may also involve the following distinct crimes:

1. *Breach of the peace.* This crime includes not only unlawful force but also such offenses as language or other conduct that is abusive, insulting, loud, or disturbing.
2. *Battery.* This crime prohibits any unlawful touching of another's person.
3. *Assault.* This crime prohibits attempted battery or conduct that threatens another with battery.

Criminal forcible entry and detainer. Criminal trespass overlaps to a considerable degree with the crime of forcible entry and detainer. Forcible entry is the entry onto another's land accompanied by force, threat, violence, or other breach of the peace. Forcible detainer covers cases of forceful refusal to leave, rather than cases of entry. The crime of forcible entry and detainer, like criminal trespass, is designed to prohibit the use of potentially violent private action in disputes over the rights to possession of property. Thus, both crimes focus on possession rather than on the ownership of the property involved.

The exact relationship between trespass and forcible entry and detainer is often unclear. Some authorities indicate that trespass prohibits interference with the possession of chattels (tangible personal property), whereas forcible entry concerns the possession of real property. However, such a distinction is not followed universally, and there are virtually no modern decisions involving criminal trespass in relation to chattels.

Entry with specific intent and under specific circumstances. Criminal trespass also overlaps with a class of crimes prohibiting certain types of entry with a specific intent. For example, the common law crime of burglary involves a type of entry with a specific intent—breaking and entering a dwelling at night with intent to commit a felony. Many codes have expanded this type of crime and include prohibitions on entry upon land or into buildings with a specific intent, for example, entry upon land with intent to steal livestock.

Historical background

Trespass originated in England in the thirteenth century as a general concept indicating that the defendant had done a wrong and should, therefore, pay damages and be fined. Although there was no clear distinction between crime and tort (wrongs for which a civil remedy exists) at this time, the main emphasis was on providing civil remedies such as payment of damages or return of possession. The allegation of breach of the peace or some use of force apparently served more as a device to justify judicial action than as an indication of the criminal nature of the defendant's conduct. In the late fourteenth century, Parliament adopted criminal statutes prohibiting forcible entry on real property. This legislative scheme was further developed in the next two and a half centuries, primarily to provide for return of possession and to prohibit forcible detainers (refusals to leave).

In the first half of the eighteenth century a series of English cases explicitly recognized for the first time the existence of the common law crime of criminal trespass. The lateness of this development is apparently explainable by a variety of factors: the existence of civil remedies for the tort of trespass; the availability of the legislation concerning forcible entry and detainer, which provided both a civil remedy and criminal sanctions; and the failure to remedy certain conditions—such as the general weakness of the executive branch of government and thus of the means for prosecuting he crime—until the sixteenth century.

The recognition of the crime of criminal trespass was complete by the time of the American Revolution, and the individual states adopted the common law crime of criminal trespass. They also adopted the prohibition of forcible entry and detainer, either as a part of a broadly defined common law or in statutory provisions.

F. Patrick Hubbard
Dan M. Kahan

See also Burglary.

BIBLIOGRAPHY

American Law Institute. *Model Penal Code and Commentaries: Official Draft and Revised Commentaries.* Philadelphia: ALI, 1985.

Deiser, George F. "The Development of Principle in Trespass." *Yale Law Journal* 27 (1917): 220–241.

Holdsworth, William Searle. *A History of English Law,* vol. 3. London: Methuen, 1965.

Sharpe, David J. "Forcible Trespass to Real Property." *North Carolina Law Review* 39 (1961): 121–153.

Woodbine, George E. "The Origins of the Action of Trespass." *Yale Law Journal* 33 (1924): 799–816; 34 (1925): 343–370.

TRIAL, CRIMINAL

Criminal trials have always held a special fascination for Americans and have furnished the plots for numerous books, plays, films, and television shows. Although civil trials can occasionally be of broad general interest, violations of criminal law frequently arouse strong popular emotions. Not surprisingly, horrific crimes are frequently front-page features in the newspapers. Trials that retell those crimes are often likely to be of interest to the public. To the extent that such trials deal with basic human weaknesses such as greed, anger, or jealousy, they frequently recount a fascinating tale.

In recent years, through changes in trial rules in some states, the American public has been able to get beyond newspaper coverage of criminal trials and actually watch selected criminal trials on television. Some of these trials have proven very controversial and have sparked considerable interest in our criminal trial system.

Civil versus criminal trends

Criminal trials differ from civil trials in several important respects. For one, criminal trials are always prosecuted on behalf of the state, not on behalf of victims or individual citizens. Thus a prosecutor in deciding whether or not to prosecute a possible crime or whether to offer a defendant a plea bargain has to make decisions in the public interest. For this reason, the head of each prosecuting agency is typically an elected public official who must answer to the voters for the decisions of the office.

Another important difference between criminal cases and civil cases is that criminal cases are regulated by the Constitution to a much greater extent than civil cases. Many provisions of the Bill of Rights, such as the right to indictment by grand jury, the right to counsel, the protection against compulsory self-incrimination, the right to confront witnesses, and the right to a speedy trial are directed only to criminal cases. This concern in the Constitution reflects the fact that, unlike civil cases which are usually concerned with money damages, what hangs in the balance in a criminal case is usually the freedom of the defendant and, sometimes, even the life of the defendant. For this reason, the Constitution provides defendants with guarantees aimed at ensuring that their treatment at the hands of the state is proper and that the trials they receive will be fair.

Burden of proof. The most important procedural difference between civil trials and criminal trials is the difference in the burden of proof. In civil trials where, for example, driver Smith claims that driver Jones was at fault in causing an accident and thus was responsible for Smith's damages, Smith must prove Jones's negligence by a preponderance of the evidence. This simply means that the jury must find Smith's evidence on the issue more convincing, even if only slightly so, than any evidence Jones offers. The scale must tip at least a bit in Smith's favor for Smith to prevail.

In a criminal trial the situation is quite different: the prosecution must prove the defendant's guilt *beyond a reasonable doubt*. This is obviously a very heavy burden of proof. To explain its meaning a standard jury instruction tells jurors that in order to find the defendant guilty they must be convinced by "proof of such convincing character that a reasonable person would not hesitate to rely and act upon it in the most important of his or her own affairs" (Devitt, Blackmar, and Wolff, p. 354). If, after hearing all the evidence, a jury has a reasonable doubt, then it must return a verdict of not guilty.

The reasonable-doubt standard in criminal cases is constitutionally required, and it has long been viewed as a central safeguard against erroneous conviction and the resulting loss of the wrongly convicted defendant's liberty and good name. Because a defendant in a criminal trial has at stake interests of immense importance, the U.S. Supreme Court has made it clear that due process demands that the margin of error in criminal cases be reduced in the defendant's favor by placing on the prosecution the burden of proving the defendant guilty beyond a reasonable doubt (*In re Winship*, 397 U.S. 358 (1970)).

Implications of proof beyond a reasonable doubt. The most obvious implication of proof beyond a reasonable doubt is that criminal cases are almost always close cases. The prosecution may have a strong case against a defendant, and yet, given the heavy burden of proof, it may still not be able to obtain a conviction from a jury. The jury may return a verdict of not guilty, even in a strong case, because the prosecution was not able to prove the defendant guilty beyond a reasonable doubt.

A second implication of the heavy burden of proof placed on the prosecution by the Anglo-American system of criminal procedure has to do with the meaning of a *not guilty* verdict. News accounts sometimes report that a jury in a criminal case "found the defendant innocent," and this seems to imply that the jury was convinced that the defendant was innocent or that it perhaps found the defendant's evidence more likely to be true than the prosecution's evidence. But a jury that has been properly instructed on the burden of proof and the meaning of proof beyond a reasonable doubt will often find the prosecution's evidence to be far stronger than the defendant's and yet feel compelled to acquit the defendant. Even if the defendant's explanation is rather implausible, it may leave the jury with a reasonable doubt and thus entitle the defendant to an acquittal. In short, the task of the defense in a criminal trial is not to convince the jury of the defendant's innocence, but rather to convince the jury that a reasonable doubt remains as to the defendant's guilt and that the defendant must thus be acquitted.

Adversarial versus inquisitorial trial systems. It is often suggested that Western trial systems can be divided neatly into those that are *adversarial* and those that are *inquisitorial*. In adversarial systems responsibility for the production of evidence is placed on the opposing attorneys with the judge acting as a neutral referee between the parties. By contrast, in inquisitorial trial systems responsibility for the production of evidence at trial is the job of the trial judge and it is the trial judge who decides which witnesses will be called at trial and who does most of the questioning of witnesses.

According to this claimed division among Western trial systems, the trial systems in the United States and England are considered adversarial in nature while those on the Continent in countries such as France or Germany are supposed to be inquisitorial.

But this distinction is not clear today. One reason for this is that European trial systems have all incorporated some adversarial features into their systems. Thus, for example, lawyers in Europe today have the right to question witnesses and they can also demand that certain witnesses be called to testify. By the same token, in the American criminal trial system trial judges are not always passive. They have the right to ask questions of witnesses and even to call witnesses not called by either party. Particularly, when a jury has been waived by the defendant, trial judges can be quite active in questioning witnesses.

But even if there is no litmus test that sharply distinguishes adversarial trial systems from those that are inquisitorial, it certainly remains accurate that the adversarial elements are much more emphasized in the American trial system. American lawyers have much more responsibility for the production and presentation of evidence than do lawyers in other Western trial systems, and trial judges in the United States tend to be much more passive at trial than judges in other Western trial systems. A trial in the United States is conceptualized as a battle in which the trial judge is a neutral and passive referee between the two combatants with the ultimate decision to be made by a jury.

Discovery in civil versus criminal cases. Another important difference between civil and criminal cases that affects what takes place in the courtroom is the difference in the amount of discovery that is permitted in preparing for trial. *Discovery* is the process by which each side preparing for trial learns about the witnesses and other evidence that the other side intends to introduce at trial.

In civil cases there is very broad discovery. For example, in civil cases both parties have the right prior to trial to take depositions of persons with information about the issues at stake in the lawsuit. A *deposition* provides an opportunity for lawyers on both sides of the case to question a person under oath in the presence of a court reporter who makes a record of what is said. As a result of this face-to-face questioning, the lawyers will not only learn all the information that the person being deposed may later present at trial, but they may also develop a good idea of how the witness will be perceived by a jury and thus will be able to plan for the examination or cross-examination accordingly.

Although there is considerable variation in criminal discovery from one jurisdiction to an-

other, many jurisdictions do not require the prosecution even to disclose the names of the witnesses whom it intends to call at trial, let alone allow the defense to take wide-ranging depositions from them.

In short, in criminal cases the amount of information available to the prosecution and the defense will usually be much less than would be available to opposing sides in a civil lawsuit. As a result of this limited discovery, prosecutors and defense attorneys often question witnesses for the opposing side to whom they have not talked before the trial. Indeed, there may be witnesses of whose existence they were not even aware prior to the trial. This adds an element of uncertainty and surprise that further distinguishes criminal from civil trials.

The atmosphere surrounding the trial

Due process demands that the trial a defendant receives be a fair one. It is obvious that even if a trial is technically correct in terms of evidentiary rulings, jury instructions, and other rulings during the trial itself, a trial can still be unfair because it takes place in an atmosphere that is prejudicial to the defendant.

In *Sheppard v. Maxwell*, 384 U.S. 333 (1966), the Supreme Court reversed a murder conviction because the trial had violated due process in a case that, one hopes, represents a high-water mark in terms of a prejudicial trial atmosphere. In that case the publicity for a local murder trial was pervasive and, more important, it was very prejudicial; numerous editorials insisted on the defendant's guilt, and even news accounts were sometimes slanted against the defendant. In addition, the newspapers reported sensational rumors or "evidence" that was in fact never disclosed at the trial. Not only were the jurors not protected from this barrage of prejudicial publicity, but reporters themselves were disruptive even during trial proceedings as they moved in and around the courtroom, creating so much noise that it was difficult for witnesses or lawyers to be heard. In the Court's words, the trial was conducted in a "carnival atmosphere."

Controlling the courtroom. Many occurrences in a courtroom or courthouse can prove distracting to a jury or otherwise threaten a fair trial. Examples include reporters who move around the courtroom and even attempt to handle or photograph exhibits during recesses; spectators who are noisy or who try to intimidate particular witnesses by comments in the courtroom or threatening gestures in the hall outside it, and overcrowding, which interferes with the entry or exit of witnesses and may precipitate disputes between spectators over the right to a seat.

Although there is no one solution to all these problems, a trial judge has the right to control the courtroom and the courthouse premises to help ensure that the defendant receives a fair trial. Given the limited size of most courtrooms, a judge may have to restrict the number of spectators or media representatives who can attend the trial, and may find it necessary in certain highly publicized cases to require the use of a ticket system to prevent corridors from being thronged with would-be spectators. It may also be necessary to bar spectators or media representatives from entering or leaving a crowded courtroom except during recesses.

The problem of pretrial publicity. One problem that has gotten worse for trial judges in recent years is the problem of how best to guarantee a defendant a fair trial in a high-publicity case. In such cases there can be pervasive and highly prejudicial publicity about the offense or the suspect in the period leading up to trial and this may continue even during the trial.

At one time, one weapon for countering prejudical pretrial publicity was for the trial judge to order a change of venue so that the trial would take place at a distant location from the county or city in which the crime occurred (*Rideau v. Louisiana*, 373 U.S. (1963)). But this is far less an effective antidote today. The concentration of new sources, the rise of cable and satellite television systems, and the ability of newspapers to publish immediately on the Internet make it harder to insulate jurors from possibly prejudicial trial publicity.

The steps in a criminal trial

Jury selection. While technically a trial begins when the jury is sworn in at the end of the jury selection process, jury selection is considered so important by trial lawyers that it is appropriate to consider jury selection as the first step in a criminal trial.

During jury selection either the lawyers or the trial judge will question potential jurors to make sure that they can be fair in deciding the case. As a result of such questioning, if the prosecutor or the defense attorney believes a certain juror cannot be fair and impartial either lawyer can challenge that juror *for cause*. If the trial judge agrees, the potential juror will be removed from the panel of jurors.

A second way a prosecutor or defense attorney can remove a potential juror is through a *peremptory challenge*. A peremptory challenge permits a lawyer to remove a possible juror without the necessity of showing a reason. Each jurisdiction allots a certain number of peremptory challenges to each side in a criminal case, and the number usually varies depending on factors such as the size of the jury or the seriousness of the crime. While the number varies from jurisdiction to jurisdiction, in a routine criminal case, such as a burglary or a theft case, the prosecutor and the defense attorney will often have five or six peremptory challenges at their disposal.

Opening statements. Because a trial can last days or even weeks, obviously it will be easier for jurors to understand how the bits and pieces of evidence that come to their attention fit together if they can be given an overview of the issues and evidence that will be central to the trial. This overview is provided by the opening statements that are delivered by the lawyers at the start of the trial.

The prosecution's opening takes place after the jury has been selected and sworn, but before the first witness has been called to testify. Although the opening does not supply the jury with any evidence (the evidence comes only from the witness stand and whatever exhibits are admitted at trial), nonetheless the prosecution's opening statement is very important. First, it provides an opportunity to explain the nature of the charge, or charges, for which the defendant is on trial. Some charges are easily understood by a jury, and in such instances it may be sufficient for the prosecutor simply to read the charging document as part of the opening. But other trials involving more complex charges, such as conspiracy or fraud, may require a more careful explanation of the elements involved.

A second function of the prosecutor's opening is to explain the evidence that will be produced in an attempt to prove the defendant's guilt beyond a reasonable doubt. This preliminary overview of the case is especially important if the trial will be protracted. But even in a trial lasting a relatively short time, an explanation of the prosecution's case can be important because witnesses may not always be able to testify in the order that a logical presentation of the evidence might suggest. For example, a fingerprint expert may have to testify early in the case, if other obligations make it impossible for the expert to appear later in the trial. But it may only be later in the trial that the gun which the fingerprint expert examined is connected to the defendant. An opening statement can help the jury understand how all the evidence fits together.

An opening statement is also important in a case that is based on a number of pieces of circumstantial evidence. In such a case, there may be no one witness who can tie the whole case together. A jury may grow bored or even frustrated as the prosecutor questions a witness at length about some apparently minor detail whose importance will be apparent only later in the trial. An opening statement helps the jury understand the significance of such pieces of evidence. It is easier for the jury to be patient while the prosecutor elicits testimony about a particular piece of evidence if the jury understands how that evidence fits into the mosaic.

Finally, opening statements are also exercises in persuasion. The opening and closing statements are the only opportunities the lawyers have to speak directly to the jury, and trial lawyers recognize the lasting impression that a clear, forceful, and logical opening statement can make on the jury.

Although the prosecutor always delivers his opening statement at the start of the trial, in many jurisdictions the defense attorney has a choice. The defense can present its opening after that of the prosecutor, or can reserve it until the prosecution has finished presenting its case and the defense is about to begin its own case.

Calling witnesses.   The U.S. system of criminal trials is a part of the Anglo-American adversary system, under which trials are controlled to a large extent by the opposing sides. Each side presents its case and vigorously argues the merits of its evidence while attacking, as energetically as is proper, the evidence supporting the opposing side. The selection and questioning of witnesses is thus primarily the obligation of the opposing lawyers. Although a judge in a criminal case may occasionally call a witness and is permitted to ask questions of witnesses, by tradition the role of the judge is that of a neutral referee between the prosecution and the defense.

Both the prosecutor and the defendant have the power to subpoena witnesses who have relevant testimony to offer at trial. In fact, the Sixth Amendment specifically guarantees that a defendant have "compulsory process for obtaining witnesses in his favor." This subpoena power is necessary because many witnesses would prefer not to testify at trial, especially if there is likely to be a rigorous cross-examination.

Although subpoena power in criminal cases is broad, there are privileges that restrict the ability to call to the stand certain witnesses. For example, the Fifth Amendment privilege against self-incrimination bars the prosecution from calling the defendant as a witness as part of its case. Some states also have enacted laws providing for a marital privilege, which bars the prosecution from calling as a witness the spouse of the defendant if the defendant objects to having the spouse testify.

Even if there is no bar to calling certain witnesses to the stand, privileges may still protect certain matters from being revealed at trial. Thus, a witness for either the prosecution or the defense may refuse to answer certain questions out of fear that his answers will incriminate him. (Sometimes the prosecution will avoid this problem by granting the witness immunity.) Or a witness may invoke a number of other privileges, for example, the doctor-patient privilege or the priest-penitent privilege. Such privileges are designed to protect confidential communications arising out of these relationships from subsequent disclosure, even at a trial.

Exclusion of witnesses from the courtroom.   The prosecution has the burden of proving the defendant guilty beyond a reasonable doubt and always presents its case first. But before any witnesses are called to the stand, it is frequently moved by either the prosecution or the defense that all witnesses be sequestered. This means that all witnesses who will be called at the trial are ordered to remain outside the courtroom until it is time for a particular witness to take the stand. Thus, a witness who is called late in the trial will not have heard the testimony of earlier witnesses. It is believed that sequestration helps discourage fabrication or collusion and also helps expose any inaccuracies in testimony.

Motions for sequestration of witnesses are usually routinely granted, and in most jurisdictions there is a right to sequestration by either side. There are, however, some exceptions. Usually a person whose presence in the courtroom is essential to the presentation of the case, such as the police officer who investigated the case, will be permitted to remain in the courtroom. The defendant, of course, has a constitutional right to be present and thus must also be permitted to remain in the courtroom even if he or she intends to testify. Finally, some states have exempted crime victims from sequestration rules and permit the victim to remain in the courtroom throughout the trial.

Examination of witnesses. The general sequence of the witnesses at a trial is as follows. First, the prosecution presents its direct case, aimed at proving that the defendant committed the crime in question. When the prosecution has finished with the presentation of its case against the defendant, the defendant has an opportunity to call witnesses and put on a defense. If the defendant chooses to put on a defense, the prosecution is then permitted to call additional witnesses to rebut the defense witnesses.

For example, the prosecution may present a series of witnesses in an effort to show that the defendant robbed a certain bank on a certain date. The defense may then call witnesses with the aim of establishing that at the time of the robbery the defendant was bowling at a certain bowling alley and thus could not have robbed the bank. Finally, the prosecution may call employees of the bowling alley in question to try to prove that the defendant was not at that bowling alley at the time of the robbery.

Each witness called to testify is questioned first by the side that called the witness. This is known as the *direct examination* of the witness. When the direct examination is over, the lawyer for the opposing side is permitted to question the witness in what is called *cross-examination*. After cross-examination is completed, the side that originally called the witness may question him in what is called *redirect examination*. This is usually limited to explaining or developing matters that were raised during the cross-examination. In some instances, if new matter has come out in redirect examination, a judge has permission to permit *recross-examination*.

The main difference between direct examination and cross-examination is the manner of questioning. In cross-examination an attorney is permitted to ask leading questions, which suggest the desired answer and usually call for a yes or no response. But in direct examination the questions should not be leading. Thus, in direct examination of a witness to a robbery, it would be improper for the prosecutor to ask a series of questions such as "And the man you saw robbing the bank was six feet tall, wasn't he?" or "And he was dressed in jeans and a green sweater, wasn't he?" On the other hand, questions of the same form would be permitted in cross-examination, for example, "It's true, isn't it, that you only saw the robber for fifteen seconds?" and "Isn't it a fact that you were very frightened at that time?"

The distinction between the form of questions permitted in direct examination and the form permitted in cross-examination reflects the fact that the witness's testimony usually is favorable to the side calling the witness, and unfavorable to the other side. In examining a witness called by the other side whose testimony is damaging, leading questions are needed in order to make an effective challenge to the witness's perception, memory, or credibility.

In addition, since each side usually calls witnesses who are generally cooperative and whose testimony is helpful to it, leading questions are not needed in direct examination. The attorney for that side has generally gone over the questions with the witness outside the courtroom, and sometimes there have been several rehearsals of the trial testimony in the days before trial. Given the reality of extensive witness preparation that takes place prior to important trials, there is less need for leading questions in direct examination and more need for leeway in attacking testimony that is not as spontaneous as it may appear to a jury.

Of course, witnesses do not always cooperate with the side that called them, and the leeway permitted in both the scope of examination and the manner of questioning the witness is always a matter for the discretion of the trial judge.

Admissible evidence

The judge's screening function. To understand criminal trials, it is necessary to understand the role of the trial judge in the admission of evidence. In the Anglo-American trial system the judge performs a screening function for the jury, making sure that the evidence brought before it is relevant and that it is not prejudicial to the defendant or to the state. Many items of evidence that are relevant in a broad sense are kept from the jury because the trial judge has decided that the danger of prejudice to the defendant outweighs the probative value of the piece of evidence in showing that the defendant committed the crime in question. Thus in a murder case, evidence offered by the prosecution showing past arrests of the defendant for assault will not be admitted, nor will evidence of the defendant's reputation as a violent person be admitted as part of the prosecution's direct case. Even gruesome pictures of the body of a murder victim that show the wounds may not be admitted for the jury's inspection if a trial judge feels that the pictures may inflame the jury and distract it from its job of carefully evaluating the evidence in the case. Of course, most evidentiary rulings can only be understood in context, taking into account the other evidence in the case and the legal and factual issues being contested. But it should be apparent that many major battles at a trial may take place outside the hearing of the jury because of the judge's obligation to rule on the admissibility of evidence. Thus one who observes a trial frequently sees the lawyers and the judge conferring at the side of the judge's bench in whispers discussing the admissibility of a piece of evidence or the propriety of a line of questions. Normally, judges try to resolve these questions quickly so they do not have to remove the jury from the courtroom and the trial can continue without a long interruption. Hence the convenience of arguing some evidentiary issues at the side of the judge's bench (so-called *sidebar conferences*). But sometimes the issue is too complicated or too important to be argued in that abbreviated way and the judge will order the jury to return to the jury assembly room so that a full discussion of the issue can take place in the courtroom. Often a substantial part of a trial is consumed by arguments on evidentiary and other legal issues outside of the hearing of the jury.

Hearsay evidence. Besides the general screening function performed by the trial judge in making sure that the probative value of an item of physical evidence or a line of questioning outweighs any prejudice to the defendant, there are many specific rules of evidence designed to enhance the reliability of trial verdicts. One rule that is central to the Anglo-American system of trials—both civil and criminal—is the rule that bars hearsay testimony.

A hearsay statement is defined as an out-of-court statement offered for the truth of the matter asserted. This rule is perhaps best understood by considering an example. Imagine a bank robbery trial in a case investigated by Federal Bureau of Investigation agent Mary Smith. At the trial of John Doe, the government calls Smith, who proceeds to tell the whole story of the robbery as she learned it from the witnesses. She explains that a bank teller, Johnson, described the robber and picked out Doe in a lineup; she testifies that a bank customer, King, said that the robber wore a green plaid suit and a red bow tie with white polka dots. Finally, Agent Smith testifies that she interviewed Doe's ex-girlfriend and that the girlfriend said Doe owned a green plaid suit and a red bow tie with white polka dots.

All of this evidence as testified to by Agent Smith would be hearsay evidence—it is a series of statements that were made out of court to Agent Smith, and they are being offered for their truth. The problem with such hearsay is that the jury hears only Agent Smith, when the crucial witnesses who should be examined in the jury's presence are the bank teller, the bank customer, and the ex-girlfriend. Because hearsay testimony is inadmissible unless it fits within a recognized exception, the government in this example cannot present its case through secondhand reports of what others said. Instead the prosecution must call the actual witnesses to testify to exactly what they observed and what they each know personally. The jury will then be in a better position to assess the credibility of the witnesses, especially when it is considered that the defense will have an opportunity to cross-examine each of the witnesses and to expose any weaknesses in their testimony.

The ban on the use of hearsay testimony is not absolute. There are many exceptions that would allow it, and, like rules of evidence in general, these exceptions vary from jurisdiction to jurisdiction. One common exception is the rule that permits the admission of a witness's prior testimony if he or she is unavailable. Thus, where a witness testified at the first trial of defendant Doe and there was a *hung jury* necessitating a second trial, the testimony of this witness could be introduced at the second trial under the hearsay exception if the witness had died before the second trial.

The trial ends

Closing arguments.   At the conclusion of the presentation of all the evidence there remain two very important steps: *closing arguments* and the judge's instructions to the jury. In a majority of jurisdictions the closing arguments, or *summations*, precede the judge's instructions to the jury but in some jurisdictions the judge first instructs the jury and then closing arguments are made.

Closing arguments are vital because a good one can have a strong impact on the jury's deliberations, which begin shortly after the closings take place. For both prosecutor and defense counsel, the closing argument affords an important chance to review the testimony and exhibits that have been admitted during the trial, as well as to argue for any inferences that they may wish the jury to draw from the evidence. Closing arguments are supposed to be argumentative, and appeals to common sense, attacks on the motives and credibility of unfavorable witnesses, and rather emotional pleas for a certain result are common. Closings also provide the opportunity to remind the jury of how the evidence intertwines with the law, and a good closing argument will weave together favorable evidence and the jury instructions that the lawyer giving the closing believes will support a favorable verdict.

There are some important limitations on the scope of closing arguments. Although a lawyer may argue vigorously for a certain conclusion, it is unethical for a lawyer to assert the lawyer's personal opinion as to the guilt or innocence of an accused (American Bar Association, p. 325). Thus, a defense lawyer may not state in closing that he or she has a reasonable doubt of the client's guilt, but an argument that the evidence at trial clearly raises a reasonable doubt would be proper.

Another, perhaps obvious, restriction on final arguments is that the arguments in closing must be tied to the evidence developed at trial. Inferences and conclusions from the evidence at trial can be argued quite freely, but to mention evidence that was never presented (and perhaps even ruled inadmissible by the trial judge) would be improper.

Still another limitation on closings is related to the defendant's decision whether or not to testify. This decision is often a very important tactical one. For example, if a testifying defendant has been convicted of other serious crimes, the prosecution will often be permitted to attack the defendant's credibility by asking about these convictions and showing that the defendant has indeed been previously convicted. In such a situation a defendant thus must balance the importance of his or her testimony against the fact that the jury will learn of other convictions if he or she testifies.

If the defendant decides not to testify, a prosecutor may not comment in the closing argument on the fact that the defendant did not choose to testify. In *Griffin v. California*, 380 U.S. 609 (1965), the Supreme Court indicated that comment by the prosecution on the defendant's failure to testify would violate the Fifth Amendment privilege against compelled self-incrimination. Thus in the closing argument the prosecutor may not argue that an adverse inference should be drawn from the defendant's silence at the trial. To back up this prohibition, if requested by the defendant, the trial judge will specifically instruct the jury that no adverse inference should be drawn from the defendant's decision not to testify.

Instructions to the jury. In speaking of instructions to the jury, it is natural to think first of the instructions at the end of the trial. But although these instructions are of crucial importance, there are often other occasions during the trial when the jury is instructed by the judge. Some judges choose to give a brief instruction on the law controlling the case at the beginning of the trial. Even during the trial, a judge may stop the taking of testimony to instruct the jury about the law surrounding an item of evidence. Thus, to continue the example above, when a defendant is impeached with a prior conviction, a judge should immediately instruct the jury that the conviction can be considered only as it bears on the defendant's credibility and not as evidence of his guilt.

However, it is at the end of trial that the judge gives the complete body of instructions to the jury. The instructions, of course, go into careful detail on the meaning of each of the elements of the crime, but they also cover many other general matters. A jury is usually instructed on such varied matters as the prosecution's burden of proof and the presumption of innocence, the meaning of reasonable doubt, the use of circumstantial evidence, the credibility of witnesses, the jury's role as fact finder, any defenses that have been raised, and the procedures to be followed in the jury room.

Before the judge instructs the jury, the prosecution and the defense will have an opportunity to submit instructions they wish the judge to give the jury. There will also usually be a conference between the judge and the lawyers outside of the hearing of the jury at which the judge hears argument from the lawyers about the instructions to be given.

If, during its deliberations, the jury feels that it needs more guidance, it so informs the judge, and the judge may repeat or further clarify any of the earlier instructions. In addition, if the jury is having difficulty in reaching a verdict, the judge often gives a supplemental instruction asking members of the jury to listen carefully to the arguments of other jurors and encouraging them not to hesitate to reexamine their own views (*Lowenfeld v. Phelps*, 484 U.S. 231, 235 (1988)).

The verdict. In civil trials a jury may be instructed to return either a general verdict (in which the jury simply indicates that it has determined the case for one of the sides) or a special verdict (which can be a rather lengthy list of specific questions on which the jury must reach agreement). As a practical matter in criminal cases, however, juries are always asked to return a general verdict of guilty or not guilty. Indeed, it has even been suggested that a special verdict may be an unconstitutional interference with the right to a jury trial (*United States v. Spock*, 416 F.2d 165 (1st Cir. 1969)).

In federal courts and in the courts of most states, the verdict of the jury must be unanimous. This is not a constitutional requirement because the Supreme Court in *Apodaca v. Oregon*, 406 U.S. 404 (1972), upheld an Oregon constitutional provision that permitted ten members of a twelve-person jury to render a guilty verdict in a noncapital case. But only Oregon and Louisiana permit nonunanimous jury verdicts in criminal cases.

Of course, not all juries are able to reach a verdict. When a jury indicates that it is deadlocked, the judge usually asks it to continue deliberations until the judge is convinced that further deliberations would be futile. If no verdict can be reached despite continued deliberations, the judge will order the jury discharged. In the event that the first trial ended in a deadlocked ("hung") jury, there is no *double jeopardy* bar to trying the defendant again.

WILLIAM T. PIZZI

See also ADVERSARY SYSTEM; BURDEN OF PROOF; CIVIL AND CRIMINAL DIVIDE; CONFESSIONS; COUNSEL: ROLE OF COUNSEL; CRIMINAL JUSTICE PROCESS; CRIMINAL PROCEDURE: CONSTITUTIONAL ASPECTS; CRIMINAL PROCEDURE: COMPARATIVE ASPECTS; CROSS-EXAMINATION; DISCOVERY; EXCLUSIONARY RULE; JURY: BEHAVIORAL ASPECTS; JURY: LEGAL ASPECTS; PUBLICITY IN CRIMINAL CASES; VENUE.

BIBLIOGRAPHY

American Bar Association, Center for Professional Responsibility. *Annotated Model Rules of Professional Responsibility.* 3d ed. Chicago: ABA, 1996.

DEVITT, EDWARD J.; BLACKMAR, CHARLES B.; and WOLFF, MICHAEL A. *Federal Jury Practice and Instructions*, vol. 1. 4th ed. St. Paul, Minn.: West, 1987.

FRANK, JEROME. *Courts on Trial: Myth and Reality in American Justice.* Princeton, N.J.: Princeton University Press, 1949.

FRANKEL, MARVIN E. *Partisan Justice.* New York: Hill & Wang, 1980.

MAUET, THOMAS A. *Fundamentals of Trial Techniques.* 4th ed. Boston: Little, Brown, 1996.

PIZZI, WILLIAM T. *Trials without Truth: Why Our Criminal Justice System Has Become an Expensive Failure and What We Need to Do to Rebuild It.* New York: NYU Press, 1999.

STRIER, FRANKLIN. *Reconstructing Justice: An Agenda for Trial Reform.* Chicago: University of Chicago Press, 1994.

STRONG, JOHN WILLIAM, ed. *McCormick on Evidence.* 4th ed. St. Paul, Minn.: West, 1992. With periodic supplements.

CASES

Apodaca v. Oregon, 406 U.S. 404 (1972).
Griffin v. California, 380 U.S. 609 (1965).
In re Winship, 397 U.S. 358 (1970).
Lowenfeld v. Phelps, 484 U.S. 231, 235 (1988).
Rideau v. Louisiana, 373 U.S. (1963).
Sheppard v. Maxwell, 384 U.S. 333 (1966).
United States v. Spock, 416 F.2d 165 (1st Cir. 1969).

TYPOLOGIES OF CRIMINAL BEHAVIOR

Sorting people into types according to distinguishing traits or forms of behavior that are presumed to characterize them is a common social process. For example, high school students often label their classmates as "hoods," "jocks," "Goths," or "brains." These slang terms identify certain students as delinquents, as overly interested in school athletic programs, as disaffected persons who dress in black and affect various deviant styles, or as particularly interested in good grades. Closer to criminology, police officers sometimes speak of "car clouters" (persons who steal packages and other items from cars) or "hubcap thieves." Similarly, prison inmates sometimes single out fellow convicts as "right guys," "outlaws," "wolves," or other types.

Such *existential types* refer to categories of people or of behavior that arise as persons go about trying to simplify and make sense of people and events they encounter in everyday social interactions. By contrast, *constructed types* are delineated by sociological theorists. For example, Edwin Lemert drew attention to offenders he labeled as naïve check forgers, but the persons so labeled did not use that label nor did those with whom they associated. Although constructed types are sometimes more precise and explicit than existential types, in many typological classifications the identifying features of specific types are unclear, with the result that researchers have difficulty in assigning persons to them. The following discussion reviews the construction and application of classificatory schemes in criminology.

Typologies in criminology

In the scientific study of crime, investigators have long noted enormous variety among criminals and criminal acts in complex societies. One of the first observers to address this diversity was Cesare Lombroso (1835–1909). He claimed that about one-third of all offenders were born criminals, that is, throwbacks to a more primitive human; more than half were criminaloids, people who were neither biologically nor psychologically abnormal; and the remainder were insane. Although this scheme—and in particular the notion of born criminals—has few advocates today, criminologists have argued that more accurate typologies would facilitate causal analysis. Investigators have sought explanations of criminal behavior by sorting different forms of criminality into homogeneous types because they have been skeptical that a single theory can account for the entire array of crimes or criminals. For example, the criminality of some offenders may be due mainly to psychological problems, whereas other lawbreakers may be responding principally to economic pressures. Although different types of criminal activity may share some causal factors, the weighting of these and other influences would probably differ from one offender type to another.

Typologies may also facilitate crime prevention or correctional efforts, whose success depends on accurately identifying and addressing the specific problems underlying different kinds of lawbreaking behavior (Gibbons, 1965). This argument is similar to a medical one, in which it is assumed that the probability of successful prevention or treatment at certain physical illnesses is greatly enhanced when corrective efforts are tailored to a precise diagnosis of the ailment being attacked.

Crime-centered versus person-centered typologies

Criminologists have developed both crime-centered and person-centered typologies. The former sort out criminal activities into homogeneous groupings, such as residential burglary, car clouting, white-collar crime, and forcible rape. Criminologists base such types on offend-er-victim relations, techniques employed in the crime, and spatial or temporal features of the lawbreaking activity. By contrast, person-centered typologies assign individuals to role careers, syndromes, criminal roles, and other social and behavioral categories on the basis of similarities on their part in criminal involvement, attitudes, personality patterns, and other presumably relevant characteristics. In short, crime-centered classifications seek to identify distinct forms of crime, while criminal-centered endeavors search for relatively distinct patterns or types into which real-life offenders can be sorted.

Perhaps criminologists will ultimately identify a number of distinct crime forms and a collection of offender types as well. Or it may turn out that distinct patterns of lawbreaking can be identified, but persons who specialize in them may rarely be encountered. For example, while residential burglaries may follow a common pattern (occurring most often during daylight hours, etc.), few if any "burglars" who specialize in that form of crime may exist. Finally, it is possible that there are no distinct forms of crime or types of offenders.

Criteria for criminal typologies

Classification systems (taxonomies) identify the set of categories into which instances of a given phenomenon can be placed. The Stanford-Binet intelligence test is a familiar single-variable classification system: it permits the assignment of any human population to intelligence groups ranged along a scale. Populations of offenders have often been sorted into intelligence levels on the basis of this or other intelligence tests by correctional officials. A multivariate classification might sort individuals according to income, educational attainment, and intelligence; the classification scheme would include all the logically possible combinations of these three variables. In similar fashion, a multivariate system could assign lawbreakers to types defined by age, intelligence score, and current charged offense. In both of these illustrations, some of the groupings might be unpopulated, that is, no actual cases would fall within them—there may be no child molesters who are under twenty-five years of age or who have relatively high intelligence scores, even though the classification included such a pattern.

Typologies are a special kind of taxonomy in that they involve truth claims. Typologies identify groupings assumed to exist in the real world;

thus, the category of youthful and intelligent child molesters noted above might be excluded from a typology constructed by a criminologist because he or she considered this pattern to be rare or nonexistent among actual offenders.

In order to be useful in causal inquiry or correctional intervention, typologies must meet several requirements. First, a typology must be sufficiently detailed and clear so that offenders can be reliably assigned to its categories. A second requirement is that the typology identify mutually exclusive types, so that actual offenders fall into only one slot. A third criterion is parsimony, that is, a relative limit in the number of types. Finally, typologies must be empirically congruent; that is, the typological description should closely fit the individuals in a given type, and the population under scrutiny should largely fall within the typology without a residual category of unclassified cases.

Typological schemes in criminology often fail to meet these four criteria, as the following review of person-centered classifications demonstrates.

Offender typologies

Criminologists have developed typologies of both adult and juvenile offenders. Some schemes rest on psychological criteria, whereas others use patterns of behavior common in correctional institutions to establish criminal types; sociological approaches emphasize individual criminal activities, personal attitudes, self-concepts, group relations, and similar variables. Examples of these approaches follow.

Psychological typologies. Psychiatrist Richard Jenkins and sociologist Lester Hewitt put forth an influential psychological typology of juvenile offenders many years ago. They examined youths in a child guidance clinic and concluded that delinquents fall into two groups: pseudosocial boys and unsocialized aggressive youths. The former were psychologically normal youngsters who were responding to antisocial conditions in their local communities, while the latter were asocial, violent juveniles who had suffered severe parental rejection.

A more recent and well-known psychological typology of offenders is Marguerite Warren's Interpersonal Maturity Levels (I-Levels) description of delinquents. Warren hypothesized that children become well-adjusted social beings by passing successfully through seven stages, from infantile dependence to adult maturity and inter-

personal competence. Some individuals fail to attain the highest levels of personal development: their development stops at an intermediate stage, and they consequently behave in relatively immature ways. According to Warren, juvenile delinquents are usually found in three of the lowest levels of maturity. For example, some are easily led by peers into misbehavior, whereas others have great difficulty conforming to reasonable demands of authority figures.

The I-Levels model is faulty in some respects (Gibbons, 1970). For example, Warren did not adequately compare nondelinquents with offenders in terms of interpersonal competence. Moreover, the validity of the scheme is suspect. Investigators have tried to assign delinquents to Warren's typology through the use of personality tests or inventories, but have generally failed to obtain results consistent with I-Levels diagnoses based on clinical judgment.

Another psychological typology rests on felons' Minnesota Multiphasic Personality Inventory scores (Megargee et al.). This typology can be useful in correctional programs, but many nonoffenders would probably exhibit psychological profiles similar to those that have been found among prisoners.

Finally, a number of psychiatrists have drawn upon their clinical experiences with offenders to create less formal typologies of lawbreakers. These descriptive typologies of murderers, sex offenders, and other kinds of criminals usually emphasize forms of psychological maladjustment that are said to differentiate criminal types.

Inmate social role typologies. Existential types noted among inmates of both juvenile correctional institutions and adult facilities have sometimes served as the basis of offender typologies. Proponents of this approach argue that these types parallel behavior patterns among lawbreakers at large.

In this tradition, Clarence Schrag reported that male prisoners are labeled in inmate argot as "square Johns," "right guys," "outlaws," or "politicians," according to the nature of their relationships with fellow prisoners (pp. 346–356). Loyalty to other inmates is the decisive variable: thus, the "right guy" is faithful to his peers and hostile toward guards and other authority figures, whereas the "square John" is an alien in the convict social system. Schrag also contended that the criminal records and other characteristics of prisoners vary predictably with their position in the inmate role system.

In fact, however, there is only a relatively loose fit between this inmate typology and the real world. Peter Garabedian conducted research in the same prison from which Schrag's conclusions were derived. Garabedian assigned inmates to role types on the basis of their responses to an attitude questionnaire containing statements designed to reflect social roles. Significantly, he found that about one-third of the sample was unclassifiable through this procedure and that the correlations between offender characteristics and social roles were relatively weak.

Robert Leger studied inmate social categories as well. Using Garabedian's attitude questionnaire to identify inmate role types, Leger asked prisoners to indicate their own type. Additionally, he queried guards concerning prisoner roles, and included social background information on inmates as another measure of role. These techniques did not consistently assign particular individuals to a single type, nor did they agree on the total number of prisoners within each role.

Sociological typologies.   The state and federal criminal codes represent a typology into which lawbreakers might be placed. For example, offenders could be classified on the basis of the crime with which they are currently charged. However, criminal codes do not meet the parsimony criterion; in addition, offenders violate different laws over time, which challenges the requirement of mutual exclusivity.

Sociological criminologists have attempted to overcome such problems with legal codes by developing offender typologies that assign persons who engage in similar collections of offenses to particular criminal behavior systems, role careers, or criminal behavior patterns. Typological efforts have also sought to discover offender groupings whose members share social background factors and causal experiences. In short, criminologists have tried to identify sociologically meaningful types.

One of these sociological typologies was constructed by Marshall Clinard and Richard Quinney, who used both offense- and person-centered criteria to define nine criminal behavior systems, including those involving violent personal criminal behavior, public-order criminal behavior, and occasional property criminal behavior (pp. 14–21). They also discussed the criminal careers of offenders who fell into these groupings, implying that individuals in fact specialize to some degree.

Daniel Glaser has also offered a typological description of offenders. He identified ten offender patterns delimited by "offense descriptive variables" and "career commitment variables." Among his types, the "adolescent recapitulator" engages in an assortment of offenses; his criminality reflects a failure to assume a stable adult role. Glaser's "vocational predators" pursue crime as a livelihood. In this typology, drug addicts constitute another category, that of "addicted performers" (pp. 27–66).

Glaser's scheme exhibits a number of flaws. First, it omits certain offenders, such as political criminals involved in political protest, and perpetrators of relatively petty offenses that are sometimes termed folk crimes—for example, traffic violations or fish and game law violations. Second, the adolescent recapitulator and certain other types are based on causal processes separating these offenders, rather than on their offense patterns and criminal careers. Third, although his descriptions of the types provide considerable detail consistent with much research on lawbreakers, Glaser's typology does not spell out the identifying characteristics of the offender categories with sufficient precision; one would be hard put to assign a population of actual offenders to these types.

Don Gibbons developed detailed and comprehensive typologies for both juvenile delinquents and adult offenders (1965, pp. 75–125; 1979, pp. 85–92). These typologies establish offender categories on the basis of the offenses in which the person is currently involved, his or her criminal career or prior criminal record, and the self-concept and role-related attitudes of the lawbreaker. For instance, one adult offender type, the "naïve check forger," writes bad checks on his or her own bank account, shows little criminal skill, views himself or herself as a noncriminal, and expresses such views as "you can't kill anyone with a fountain pen." Some of Gibbons's types rest on research findings reported by criminologists: Edwin Lemert's study of naïve check forgers provided some of the information on which Gibbons based this type description. Other types are grounded in criminological theory. In all, Gibbons established nine delinquent and fifteen adult offender categories.

What portion of the offender population falls within these types? Although no research has directly investigated the juvenile typology, the available data seem inconsistent with Gibbons's type descriptions (Gibbons and Krohn). The most striking evidence on delinquent behavior emphasizes its transitory or episodic character. Self-reported or so-called hidden delinquents most commonly indicate that they have been involved in infrequent and petty acts of lawbreaking, while juvenile offenders who turn up in the juvenile justice system often engage in numerous illegal acts rather than a few forms of lawbreaking. Researchers have been able to identify some of the latter as "serious and/or violent offenders" or as "chronic delinquents," but have not been able to make finer distinctions among them (Loeber, Farrington, and Waschbusch). In short, the delinquency typology posits more patterning of behavior among juvenile offenders than actually exists.

Gibbons's adult offender typology has been directly examined, and, as will be presently shown, other studies of offenders that bear on the question of empirical congruence are also relevant to this analysis.

Clayton Hartjen and Gibbons asked county probation officers to sort probationers into Gibbons's typology categories. The raters used abridged typological profiles of offenders; moreover, groups of three officers acted as independent judges who read the probationers' case files in order to determine to which types, if any, these persons belonged. Slightly less than half of the probationers were assigned to a type, although Hartjen subsequently placed most of the unassigned cases into seven ad hoc groups.

James McKenna also studied Gibbons's adult offender typology. Having examined their arrest records, he classified inmates in a state correctional institution into twelve offender types. McKenna then sought to determine whether the combinations of characteristics said to differentiate types actually existed among offenders. In only one of the twelve types did the hypothesized pattern of behavior and social-psychological characteristics emerge; that is, the vast majority of prisoners assigned to a particular type did not consistently exhibit similar attitudes and other differentiating features. These findings indicate that many real-life offenders cannot be assigned with precision in existing criminal typologies.

Other research studies as well have raised doubts about the accuracy of offender typologies. Joan Petersilia, Peter Greenwood, and Marvin Lavin studied forty-nine individuals serving prison terms for armed robbery. Their average age was thirty-nine, and thus most had been criminally active for some years. When these offenders were asked the number of times they had committed any of nine specific crimes since becoming involved in lawbreaking, they confessed to more than 10,000 offenses, or an average of 214 per person. Even more striking was the diversity of offenses: 3,620 drug sales, 2,331 burglaries, 1,492 automobile thefts, 995 forgeries, 993 major thefts, and 855 robberies. This finding undermines the assumption of offense specialization among lawbreakers and seriously challenges most offender typologies.

Another study by Mark Peterson, Harriet Braker, and Suzanne Polich involved over six hundred prison inmates who were asked to indicate the number and kinds of crimes they had committed during the three years prior to their present incarceration. For each type of crime, most of those who reported doing it said they did so infrequently, but a few of them confessed to engaging in the crime repeatedly. The researchers concluded that there are two major kinds of offenders: occasional criminals and broadly active ones. Few prisoners claimed to have committed a single crime at a high rate; thus there were few crime specialists in prison.

In still another investigation, Jan and Marcia Chaiken studied 2,200 jail and prison inmates in three states who were given a lengthy questionnaire that included self-report crime items. They were then asked to report the number of times they had committed robberies, assaults, burglaries, forgeries, frauds and thefts, and drug deals. About 13 percent of them said they had committed none of the offenses in the previous two years, while the rest reported involvement in one or more of the offenses, but most commonly, at relatively low rates. Also, while a sizable minority of the prisoners admitted having frequently committed one or more crimes prior to incarceration, most of them reported having been involved in crime-switching, rather than crime specialization.

Female offenders. Until relatively recently, criminologists paid relatively little attention to types of juvenile or adult female offenders. An implicit assumption has been that most female delinquents come to the attention of the police or the juvenile court, either because of minor misbehavior or sexual promiscuity. Similarly, a common presumption has been that many adult women offenders are petty thieves such as shoplifters while others have been involved in domestic violence, often directed at their common law or legal spouses.

However, in recent years, investigators have begun to examine female lawbreaking in more detail. In particular, considerable attention has focused on the different routes or pathways through which women enter into lawbreaking. One case in point is Eleanor Miller's research on women who have been involved in "street hustling," that is, a pattern of property crimes, drug use, and prostitution. She reported that there are four pathways that lead to street hustling. Mary Gilfus has provided parallel findings regarding women who have been involved in street crime. Similarly, Kathleen Daly has sorted female felons into several types, based on the kinds of offenses they have committed and their relationships' with spouses, boyfriends, and other associates. Then, too, investigators have directed attention at females who have been involved in homicides. Taken together, these studies indicate that there are a number of patterns or types that are involved in female criminality.

The future of typologies in criminological investigation

Criminologists will probably continue to endeavor to classify and categorize forms of crime and kinds of offenders despite the numerous problems identified above. Classification systems that sort offenders or crimes into relatively homogeneous categories alert observers to broad groupings of lawbreakers or offenses. These typological characterizations constitute benchmarks against which actual offenders or criminal incidents can be compared. In addition, typologies are useful in developing principles of correctional intervention in that they indicate the need for differential treatment, that is, intervention matched to the offender.

The population of offenders includes a large number of persons who do not fit existing typologies. Behavioral diversity among lawbreakers, rather than offense specialization, suggests that a loose fit will continue to exist between typological categories and actual offenders, with many of the latter falling outside of the classificatory scheme. Accordingly, future efforts will probably focus on patterns of crimes.

Several important steps have been taken in this direction. For example, Thomas Reppetto's study of burglary indicated that particular cases of burglary tend to resemble one another closely in terms of crime techniques employed, objects stolen in the burglaries, and so on. More generally, Weisburd, Wheeler, Waring, and Bode examined a number of federal offenders who had been convicted variously of antitrust violations, securities fraud, mail fraud, false claims, bribery,

tax fraud, credit fraud, and bank embezzlement. They indicated that these offenses could be combined into three relatively distinct types in terms of offense complexity and the degree of harm to victims. Finally, Farr and Gibbons have developed a comprehensive typology of crime forms: organizational crime, organized crime, workplace crime, "street crime," social protest crime, violent crime, and folk/mundane crime. While a number of these crime patterns have been noted by others in the criminological literature, Farr and Gibbons have provided detailed and explicit accounts of the distinguishing features of each of these crime forms. More work of this kind is in order.

DON C. GIBBONS

See also CRIME: DEFINITION; CRIMINAL CAREERS; ORGANIZED CRIME; PREDICTION OF CRIME AND RECIDIVISM; SEXUAL PREDATORS; VICTIMLESS CRIME; VIOLENCE.

BIBLIOGRAPHY

CHAIKEN, JAN, and CHAIKEN, MARCIA B. *Varieties of Criminal Behavior*. Santa Monica, Calif.: Rand, 1982.

CLINARD, MARSHALL B., and QUINNEY, RICHARD. *Criminal Behavior Systems: A Typology*. 2d ed. New York: Holt, 1973.

DALY, KATHLEEN. "Women's Pathways to Felony Court: Feminist Theories of Lawbreaking and Problems of Representation." *Southern California Review of Law and Women's Studies* 2 (December 1992): 11–52.

FARR, KATHRYN ANN, and GIBBONS, DON C. "Observations on the Development of Crime Categories." *International Journal of Offender Therapy and Comparative Criminology* 34 (1990): 223–237.

GARABEDIAN, PETER G. "Social Roles in a Correctional Community." *Journal of Criminal Law, Criminology, and Police Science* 55 (September 1964): 338–347.

GIBBONS, DON C. *Changing the Lawbreaker*. Englewood Cliffs. N.J.: Prentice-Hall, 1965.

———. "Differential Treatment of Delinquents and Interpersonal Maturity Levels Theory: A Critique." *Social Service Review* 44 (March 1970): 22–33.

———. *The Criminological Enterprise*. Englewood Cliffs, N.J.: Prentice-Hall, 1979.

GIBBONS, DON C., and KROHN, MARVIN D. *Delinquent Behavior*. 5th ed. Englewood Cliffs, N.J.: Prentice Hall, 1991.

GILFUS, MARY S. "From Victims to Survivors to Offenders: Women's Routes of Entry and Immersion Into Street Crimes." *Women and Criminal Justice* 4 (1992): 63–89.

GLASER, DANIEL. *Adult Crime and Social Policy*. Englewood Cliffs, N.J.: Prentice-Hall, 1972.

HARTJEN, CLAYTON A., and GIBBONS, DON C. "An Empirical Investigation of a Criminal Typology." *Sociology and Social Research* 54 (October 1969): 56–62.

JENKINS, RICHARD L., and HEWITT, LESTER E. "Types of Personality Structure Encountered in Child Guidance Clinics." *American Journal of Orthopsychiatry* 14 (January 1944): 84–94.

LEGER, ROBERT G. "Research Findings and Theory as a Function of Operationalization of Variables: A Comparison of Four Identification Techniques for the Construct, 'Inmate Social Type.'" *Sociology and Social Research* 63 (January 1979): 346–363.

LEMERT, EDWIN M. "An Isolation and Closure Theory of Naïve Check Forgery." *Journal of Criminal Law, Criminology, and Police Science* 44 (September–October 1953): 296–307

LOEBER, ROLF; FARRINGTON, DAVID P.; and WASCHBUSCH, DANIEL A. "Serious and Violent Juvenile Offenders." In *Serious and Violent Juvenile Offenders*. Edited by Rolf Loeber and David P. Farrington. Thousand Oaks, Calif.: Sage, 1998. Pages 13–29.

MCKENNA, JAMES J. *An Empirical Testing of a Typology of Adult Criminal Behavior*. Ph.D. dissertation, University of Notre Dame, 1972.

MEGARGEE, EDWIN I.; BOHN, MARTIN J., JR.; MERCER, JAMES E., JR.; and SINK, FRANCES. *Classifying Criminal Offenders*. Beverly Hills, Calif.: Sage, 1979.

MILLER, ELEANOR M. *Street Woman*. Philadelphia, Pa.: Temple University Press, 1986.

PETERSILIA, JOAN; GREENWOOD, PETER W; and LAVIN, MARVIN L. *Criminal Careers of Habitual Felons*. Washington, D.C.: U.S. Department of Justice, Law Enforcement Assistance Administration, 1978.

PETERSON, MARK A.; BRAKER, HARRIET B.; and POLICH, SUZANNE M. *Doing Crime*. Santa Monica, Calif.: Rand, 1980.

REPPETTO, THOMAS A. *Residential Crime*. Cambridge, Mass.: Ballinger, 1974.

SCHRAG, CLARENCE. "Some Foundations for a Theory of Correction." In *The Prison*. Edited by Donald R. Cressey. New York: Holt, 1961. Pages 309–357.

WARREN, MARGUERITE Q. "Intervention with Juvenile Delinquents." In *Pursuing Justice for the Child*. Edited by Margaret K. Rosenheim. Chicago: University of Chicago Press, 1976. Pages 176–204.

WEISBURD, DAVID; WHEELER, STANTON; WARING, ELM; and BODE, NANCY. *Crimes of the Middle-Class*. New Haven, Conn.: Yale University Press, 1991.

U

UNEMPLOYMENT AND CRIME

Because criminal sources of income, such as theft and fraud, are alternatives to legitimate earnings, they tend to be associated with unemployment. This linkage, however, is far from clear and consistent.

Dependence on labor force attributes

One variable that greatly affects crime and employment relationships is the age of persons who are unemployed. Government statistics regularly indicate that juveniles and young adults greatly exceed older persons in rates of arrest for burglary, robbery, and other crimes of taking property belonging to others. A 1959 pioneer study found that this inverse relationship of such crimes to unemployment was most pronounced for young persons, and less evident for older persons out of work (Glaser and Rice). In 1968 a British study yielded similar findings, showing that the relations between crime and unemployment are most intense for youths who were out of school as well as work (Farrington et al.). The old adage that "idle hands are the devil's workshop" seemed to be confirmed.

These findings also appear to support the 1999 assertion by Bruce Western and Katherine Beckett that the U.S. penal system is "a labor market regulating institution." They justified this statement by pointing out that confinement institutions remove able-bodied but idle young men from the workforce, and that once these men have a record of imprisonment, their subsequent job prospects are greatly diminished (imprisoned women are not sufficiently numerous to affect the total female labor force significantly).

Unfortunatly, any statistical generalizations on the linkage of crime to unemployment, as well as to age or other personal attributes of offenders and nonoffenders, can only be tested with imperfect data. The completeness of our knowledge on lawbreakers necessarily varies with the extent to which they are caught, and with the use of imprisonment rather than alternative penalties for those convicted. Data on employment, age, and various other attributes of persons committing crimes is usually reported for those offenders who are arrested, but their total number, and information on them is somewhat diminished (although presumably made more accurate) if one studies only those arrestees who are subsequently convicted of the crimes for which they were arrested. Furthermore, data on the personal attributes of those convicted are often not compiled in as much detail for those fined or released on probation as for those who are imprisoned.

In 1939 two European scholars, Georg Rusche and Otto Kirchheimer, refugees from Hitler's Germany, published what proved to be a classic volume of historical scholarship, *Punishment and Social Structure*. In it they treated the variations in reaction to crime from ancient to contemporary periods, and generalized that the types of penalties used—such as executions, transportation to distant colonies, torture, mutilation, confinement in idleness, of forced labor—depended greatly on economic conditions, particularly on the current value of labor. The cruelest penalties became most frequent, they asserted, when unemployment was extensive, making labor cheap.

These rather vague assertions were subsequently formalized and tested statistically by others, with diverse data, as can be illustrated by summarizing a few of the most methodologically sophisticated studies. Mathematician David Greenberg concluded from multivariate analysis in the 1970s, that "oscillations in the rate of admissions to prison in Canada in recent years have been governed almost entirely by changes in the unemployment rate. The same relationships appear to hold in the United States as well" (p. 651). Sociologists Andrew Hochstetler and Neal Shover, however, found in the 1990s that the intensity of this relationship in the United States varied greatly in different historical periods, and in various regions.

Hochstetler and Shover note that the incarceration rate in the United States, defined as the number of imprisoned adults per 100,000 population, was 462 for the southern states in 1994, but only 291 for the northeastern states. From a regression analysis of 1990 data for a sample of 269 U.S. counties that they showed were highly representative of all counties, they conclude that R-square (the variance explained) was only 0.14. But regressing 1990 imprisonment data for these counties with the 1980 unemployment rates of the same counties yielded an R-square of 0.74. They interpret this finding of a lag in the impact of unemployment on crime rates by pointing to the fact that the highest rates of known offenses, particularly unspecialized street crimes, occurs among teenagers, and in those whose childhood was spent in the most poverty-stricken urban areas, the slums. Their main conclusion is:

Change in violent street crime, in the proportionate size of the young male population, and in labor surplus, contribute to change in the use of imprisonment, while changing levels of property crime do not. These relationships persist even when street-crime rates and other presumed correlates of imprisonment are controlled. . . . The criminal justice system grows increasingly punitive as labor surplus increases. The fact that our findings were achieved using both a unit of analysis more appropriate theoretically than measures employed by most investigators, and a longitudinal design, only strengthens confidence in them.

Other factors in crime-unemployment relationships

Of course, unemployment rates, age, and offense do not operate alone in determining sentences of imprisonment. In 1966 David Jacobs and Ronald E. Helms showed, in their multivariate analysis of historical and geographical fluctuations of incarceration rates in the United States, that unemployment's impact on crime seemed to have a close linkage with other conditions not noted in prior studies. They point out that rates of state plus federal imprisonment of adults per 100,000 population in the United States changed only from 43.4 to 50.9 from 1918 to 1965, dropped to 35.9 by 1968, then nearly doubled in 13 years to 69.7 in 1981, and rose by 84 percent to 127.9 in 1989. There was no such large movement in rates of crime known to the police, which increased only 12.1 percent in 1975–1991. They found that because of this small range in reported crime rates for this long time span, a multivariate regression only yielded very strong results if crime rates were squared. Also, in their regression analysis, out-of-wedlock births—an index of the rate of breakdown in family relations—was one of the best predictors of imprisonment rates, especially when using birthrate data for five years before the prison figures, to allow for the time before such family conditions could promote higher imprisonment rates. Furthermore, rather than unemployment rates, income inequality, and votes for the Republican Party—an index of conservative political trends—were among the strongest predictors of crime rates.

In 1999 Michalowski and Carlson ascribed the diversity of findings in tests of "the Rusche-Kirchheimer hypothesis" to variations in the historical periods covered by these studies. Their analysis is based on theories about stages in what they call "social structures of accumulation," or "SSAs." The first stage is "Exploration," which occurs when new institutional arrangements emerge to cope with high levels of unemployment and with the displacement of both farm and industrial populations. The second is "Consolidation," an effort to maintain whatever new arrangements seem to help capital to preserve its profit margins. The third stage is "Decay," when conditions develop that impede consolidation policies, thus increasing unemployment and preventing children of workers from achieving upward status mobility.

The Michalowski and Carlson analysis of unemployment and imprisonment for crime focuses on what they and some others call the "Fordist" SSA of 1933–1992, for which they differentiate the three phases indicated. During Exploration, from 1933 to 1947, new types of "capital-labor accords" and welfare policies "socialized the costs of labor force displacement." Thus, unemployment insurance and old-age pensions, both adjusted for changes in the cost of living, shifted burdens of dealing with economic distress in this period from businesses to governments, and helped to maintain social order. In Consolidation, from 1948 to 1966, periods of unemployment were shortened by the bargaining strength of organized labor and its central position in the Democratic Party, which transferred government tax income to the poor, the disabled, and the elderly. These "profit-eroding" developments "made it difficult for capital to protect profit margins in the face of growing foreign competition," these authors claim, so that Decay occurred in 1967–1979, during which unemployment and inflation rose while profits declined and the United States lost the Vietnam War despite sending 3 million workers there.

These authors identify a new Exploration phase from 1980 until 1992, in which "cybertechnology" accelerates labor displacement, and also increases earning inequality between workers in digital information systems and those at "hamburger jobs." The latter were disproportionately from minority groups, and in this period there was a "shift away from placative social welfare strategies . . . toward repressive control strategies based on increased use of imprisonment" (p. 226). Consequentially, even with rates of arrest and of unemployment in the 1990s usually below those of prior decades, the rate of imprisonment nearly tripled, confining predominantly young men who had dropped out of school and work. The latter were disproportionately African Americans, whose rates of unemployment exceeded what one would predict for white workers of similar education and work experience. Although their higher rates of joblessness are doubtless due in large part to prejudice against them, it is also because they are below the growing number of Latinos in the labor market in their "reservation wage"—the lowest pay rate for which they would be willing to work (Moss and Tilly, p. 9). Another major factor in their unemployment rates is that they exceed other racial and nationality groups in the proportion who have entered military service, or are enrolled full-time in schools, which probably removes those with the highest earning potential from the labor market (Mare and Winship). But still another influence was their ready opportunity, in the segregated slum areas in which most of the housing available to them was located, to gain much greater income from drug dealing than from the jobs available to them.

In summary, evidence and analysis indicate that unemployment is predictive of crime, but disproportionately for youth, the least educated, those in broken or disorganized families, and those segregated in poor minority residential areas. Also, these relationships of unemployment to crime are likely to continue unless unsegregated housing, special education, family unity, work experience, and appealing career jobs become more readily available to those who are unemployed.

DANIEL GLASER

See also CLASS AND CRIME; CRIME CAUSATION: ECONOMIC THEORIES.

BIBLIOGRAPHY

CHIRICOS, THEODORE G., and DELONE, MIRIAM A. "Labor Surplus and Punishment: A Review and Assessment of Theory and Evidence." *Social Problems* 39, no. 4 (1992): 421–446.

D'ALESSIO, STEWART J., and STOLZENBERG, LIZA. "Unemployment and the Incarceration of Pretrial Defendants." *American Sociological Review* 60, no. 3 (1995): 350–359.

FARRINGTON, DAVID P.; GALLAGHER, BERNARD; MORLEY, LYNDA; ST. LEDGER, RAYMOND J.; and WEST, DONALD J. "Unemployment, School-leaving, and Crime." *British Journal of Criminology* 26, no. 4 (1986): 335–356.

GLASER, DANIEL, and RICE, KENT. "Crime, Age and Employment." *American Sociological Review* 24, no. 5 (1959): 679–686.

GREENBERG, DAVID F. "The Dynamics of Oscillatory Punishment Processes." *Journal of Criminal Law and Criminology* 68, no. 4 (1977): 643–651.

HOCHSTETLER, ANDREW L., and SHOVER, NEAL. "Street Crime, Labor Surplus, and Criminal Punishment, 1980–1990." *Social Problems* 44, no. 3 (1977): 358–367.

JACOBS, DAVID, and HELMS, RONALD E. "Towards a Political Model of Incarceration: A Time-Series Examination of Multiple Explanations for Prison Admission Rates." *American Journal of Sociology* 102, no. 2 (1996): 323–357.

MARE, ROBERT D., and WINSHIP, CHRISTOPHER. "The Paradox of Lessening Racial Inequality and Joblessness Among Black Youth: Enrollment, Enlistment, and Employment, 1964–1981." *American Sociological Review* 49, no. 1 (1984): 39–55.

MICHALOWSKI, RAYMOND J., and CARLSON, SUSAN M. "Unemployment, Imprisonment, and Social Structures of Accumulation: Historical Contingency in the Rusche-Kirchheimer Hypothesis." *Criminology* 37, no. 2 (1999): 217–250.

MOSS, PHILLIP, and TILLY, CHRIS. "Hiring in Urban Labor Markets: Shifting Labor Demands, Persistent Racial Differences." In Ivar Berg and Arne Kalleberg, eds. *Sourcebook on Labor Markets: Evolving Structures and Processes.* New York: Plenum, 2000.

RUSCHE, GEORG, and KIRCHHEIMER, OTTO. *Punishment and Social Structure.* New York: Columbia University Press, 1929. Reprint, New York: Russell and Russell, 1967.

WESTERN, BRUCE, and BECKETT, KATHERINE. "How Unregulated Is the U.S. Labor Market? The U.S. Penal System as a Labor-Market Regulating Institution." *American Journal of Sociology* 104, no. 4 (1999): 1030–1060.

URBAN CRIME

Early twentieth century criminology might reasonably be considered the criminology of urban places. During the 1920s and 1930s much of the attention of criminologists focused on the "criminogenic city," however, by the close of the century researchers had moved away from the notion that the city is itself criminogenic. Instead research on urban crime has become concerned mainly with explaining why urban crime rates vary, why some social, economic, and spatial characteristics are correlated with variations in urban crime rates, and how certain crime characteristics of urban places affect individual criminality.

Concern that the city might have a crime-causing effect did not begin with American criminologists. Émile Durkheim (1897), Max Weber (1958), Ferdinand Toennies (1887), and other European sociologists wrote about the changes that occurred as a result of the transition of societies from agrarian and village-based forms to industrial and urban-based ones. They proposed that during rapid social change, growing and expanding cities would be hotbeds of crime (and experience a number of other problems). One can safely assume that most eighteenth- and nineteenth-century philosophers and social scientists believed that even without rapid change, city life itself would be criminogenic. That is, they believed that in circumstances of slow change or even social stability that negative influences of cities themselves would lead to higher levels of crime than would occur in nonurban populations. This belief was not without reason. London and other major European cities were difficult places to live. To go out at night before the advent of gaslights meant moving about with a large group of men carrying weapons and torches. To do otherwise was to invite nearly certain mayhem and robbery (Stark).

American sociologists shared similar beliefs. Social Darwinists at the turn of the century saw pathology in urban life itself (Wirth; Davis). Early social workers, taking their intellectual justification from the Social Darwinists, created the juvenile court and other social service agencies (for example, Hull House founded by Jane Addams in Chicago) to try to control crime and delinquency among wayward urbanites, many of whom were thought to be negatively influenced by life in the city.

In the period between 1920 and World War II, sociologists associated with the University of Chicago began to construct explanations concerning why cities might have higher crime rates than the hinterland. But more importantly, they were interested in documenting and explaining variations in crime levels within cities (Park, Burgess, and McKenzie; Shaw and McKay). At the time, many believed that crime in the city, and especially in particular sections of the city, was caused by the influx of immigrants, and especially those from "crime prone" ethnic groups. However, researchers from the Chicago School observed in their studies that some sections of cities consistently had higher crime rates than others, regardless of who populated those areas. They argued and demonstrated with data that crime rates can be explained more accurately by focusing on the ecology of areas in the city, rather than on the ethnic composition of the population inhabiting those areas. They described a process whereby immigrants, upon arrival into the United States, typically moved into the poor, blighted neighborhoods because that is where they could afford to live. Crime in these areas was high and reflected poor living conditions, as these neighborhoods experienced great levels of poverty, racial heterogeneity, transience, and family disruption. However, as succeeding generations of these immigrant families improved their lot they moved to better neighborhoods, and as a result, their ethnic groups' crime rate declined. Meanwhile, new immigrants from different ethnic groups repopulated the neighborhoods that the earlier arrivals had vacated. Despite the near complete change in population composition, crime levels in these transitory areas remained high. Chicago School criminologists thus concluded that it was not criminogenic characteristics of ethnic groups that led to elevated rates of crime, but the nature of the urban ecology in which they lived.

Nearly seven decades later, theories that address urban crime rely on the earlier findings from the Chicago School studies and continue to adopt an approach that emphasizes the importance of urban ecology. Thus, the roots of modern criminology's examination of urban crime can be traced to the theories of the Chicago School and their contemporaries. At the dawn of the twenty-first century, while criminologists use new analytic techniques, new research tools, and modified explanations, even the casual reader of the current literature cannot help but be impressed by the debt that modern researchers owe to their predecessors in the effort to understand and explain crime in urban areas.

Are crime rates higher in urban areas?

Before continuing, we should examine the latest evidence about urban crime. Although most often assumed to be the case, an important question is whether crime levels are higher in urban versus rural areas. According to crime statistics, community size does make a difference, as crime rates are higher in urban than in rural areas. Violent and property crime rates in our largest cities (Metropolitan Statistical Areas, or MSAs) are three to four times as high as the rates in rural communities (Barkan). These statistics hold for nearly all types of crime. For example, according to 1995 statistics from the Uniform Crime Reports, in U.S. metropolitan areas, homicide claims 11 victims per 100,000 inhabitants and more than 25 per 100,000 in some of the largest cities. In small cities and in rural counties, homicide claims only 5 victims per 100,000, and fewer than 2 per 100,000 in our most rural states (Federal Bureau of Investigation). This pattern also occurs for robbery and assault; they are much more common in large urban areas than elsewhere. Like violent crime, property crime is lowest in rural areas (Barkan). Further, this urban-rural difference has been found in Canada, England, Australia, and the Netherlands (Shover). These statistics present criminologists with the challenge of explaining why crime levels are much higher in urban than rural areas.

Explaining urban crime

The research literature on urban crime is generally of two types. There are studies that compare cities, seeking to understand why some have higher crime rates than others. And there are studies that focus on explaining variations in crime levels within cities. However, both types of studies use similar theories and focus on the same social forces to understand their observations. The primary theories used to study urban crime are social disorganization, subculture, and conflict theories.

Social disorganization theory (discussed earlier) is concerned with the way in which characteristics of cities and neighborhoods influence crime rates. The roots of this perspective can be traced back to the work of researchers at the University of Chicago around the 1930s. These researchers were concerned with neighborhood structure and its relationship to levels of crime. Classical Chicago School theorists, and Shaw and McKay in particular, were most concerned with the deleterious effects of racial and ethnic heterogeneity, residential mobility, and low socioeconomic status on an area's ability to prevent crime. However, since the work of Shaw and McKay and others, researchers who adopt the macrosocial approach to the study of urban crime have identified a number of additional "disorganizing" factors including family disruption (Sampson and Groves), relative poverty (Messner, 1982), and racial segregation (Peterson and Krivo).

Researchers in this area believe that characteristics such as these are likely to lead to high levels of social disorganization, which in turn increases the likelihood of crime and criminal violence. In general terms, social disorganization refers to the inability of a community structure to mobilize the common values of its residents to maintain effective social controls (Kornhauser). Empirically, the intervening dimensions of community social organization can be measured in terms of the prevalence and interdependence of social networks in a community (both formal and informal) and in the span of collective supervision that the community directs toward local problems (Thomas and Znaniecki; Shaw and McKay; Kornhauser). Given this, neighborhoods characterized by high levels of poverty or economic deprivation, residential mobility, ethnic heterogeneity, family disruption, poor housing conditions, and low levels of education are most likely to be disorganized and have higher levels of crime and violence. Disorganization, a lack of solidarity and cohesion, and the absence of a shared sense of community and mutual commitment between residents allows crime to flourish because the community's capacity for informal social control (that which does not depend on the less efficient formal criminal justice institutions) is inhibited. Social disorganization theory has been criticized for failing to appreciate the diversity of values that exist within urban areas (Matza), for not recognizing that communities in urban areas indeed may be organized, but around unconventional values, and for failing to define clearly its main concept, social disorganization, thereby making the identification and operationalization of variables difficult (Liska).

Subcultural theories to explain urban crime are of two types—subculture of violence and subculture of poverty. Common to both types is the belief that certain groups carry sets of norms and values that make them more likely to engage in crime. The subculture of violence thesis holds that high rates of violence result from a culture where criminality in general, and violence in particular, are more acceptable forms of behavior. Carriers of a subculture of violence are quicker to resort to violence than others. Situations that normally might simply anger others could provoke violence by those carrying subculture of violence values. In the formulation of these ideas, subcultural theorists claim that social institutions themselves contribute to the development and persistence of a subculture conducive to criminality and violence. For example, the disintegration of particular institutions (i.e., churches, families, and schools) denies certain populations (and in particular, minorities) the opportunity to learn conventional norms and values. The result of such processes is that certain groups are more likely to use violence in their day-to-day encounters, and violence is seen as an acceptable means to solving disputes. The classic statement on the subculture of violence is Wolfgang and Ferracuti's *The Subculture of Violence: Towards an Integrated Theory in Criminology* (1967), although others have contributed as well (Elkins; Curtis, 1975). According to critics, the main drawbacks with this perspective are that it tends to overlook the interrelation of normative processes and institutional deterioration with more structural features of a given community, and that it is difficult to operationalize it in a testable fashion (how is the presence of subcultural values measured in individuals other than by the behavior that is being predicted?).

Subculture of poverty explanations have focused more on urban crime than have subculture of violence explanations. Subculture of violence explanations have been used to explain crime in urban and nonurban settings, but those who have written about the subculture of poverty have been concerned primarily with the criminal behavior in the ghettos and barrios of central cities (Banfield). The central thesis here is that values and norms that discourage work and investment of money or energies are likely to develop in poor communities. Because carriers of this subculture are disinclined to strive to achieve, have limited patience, and are less likely to defer gratification, they act impulsively. Too often these impulses lead to crime. Critics of this theory cite a biased, middle-class perspective that seems to neither understand the plight of the poor—the effects of social structures and institutions on their behavior—nor accurately describe their lives, options, or behavior.

The most notable expression of conflict theories as an explanation of urban crime has focused on income inequality (Blau and Blau). Here scholars have argued that frustration is a by-product of income gaps that are viewed as unjust by those in subordinate positions. Social structural cleavages based on race have also been used to explain why poor urban blacks and Latinos have higher crime rates than the general population (Blau and Blau). Marxist scholars (Chambliss; Quinney; Lynch and Groves) describe how the contradictions inherent in advanced capitalism make crime—particularly where populations are concentrated, such as in the city—more likely. Most of their critics assert that conflict theorists are inaccurate (e.g., it is not income inequality that predicts crime, but absolute poverty), or too political.

Explaining variation in urban crime

Although there is general consensus among criminologists that urban areas have higher rates of crime than rural areas, of less certainty is why certain urban settings have higher crime rates than other urban settings. That is, not all cities or neighborhoods experience similar levels of crime and violence; there is widespread variation in crime levels across urban spaces. Thus, the question of interest for criminologists is what is the source of this variation? What causes certain cities or neighborhoods to experience high levels of crime while other cities or neighborhoods enjoy relatively low levels of crime?

Criminologists address these questions by attempting to uncover the correlates of urban crime rates. In line with social disorganization theory mentioned earlier, most research of this type focuses on city or neighborhood characteristics associated with high crime levels in an area. Although the range of correlates studied is quite extensive, the most common characteristics include socioeconomic and demographic characteristics of the area, such as the poverty level, racial composition, residential mobility, labor force characteristics, age structure, and divorce rate. These correlates appear again and again in studies of urban crime rates. Here we will focus on three important correlates that have received continued attention among criminologists—poverty and other economic characteristics, racial composition, and labor force characteristics.

Poverty, inequality, and urban crime. Within the extensive body of literature on the relationship between social class and crime exists a smaller but nonetheless important group of studies that examine the effects of poverty on crime. Interestingly enough, this smaller group of studies mirrors the larger body of literature from which it extends; essentially, there seems to be as much controversy and disagreement over whether poverty is related to crime.

The significance of urban socioeconomic conditions for the incidence of crime was early recognized in ecological studies at the University of Chicago. In the most famous of these, Shaw and McKay compared delinquency rates in various areas within twenty-one cities and concluded that three urban conditions promote high delinquency rates: poverty, racial heterogeneity, and mobility, with poverty surfacing as the most important factor.

Over the decades, numerous aggregate studies have empirically supported the poverty and crime relationship. Many of these studies have observed the highest crime rates within the poorest urban slums (Curtis, 1974). A linkage between crime and economic conditions has also been found at higher levels of aggregation, such as cities and states (Loftin and Hill; Smith and Parker). Many leading criminologists believe that the poverty-crime relationship is clear and direct.

This positive relationship between poverty and crime, for the most part, went uncontested until Blau and Blau put forth the hypothesis that racial economic inequality, more than poverty, spells the potential for violence. Socioeconomic inequalities associated with ascribed positions (i.e., being a minority), they argue, engender pervasive conflict in a democracy. While great economic inequalities generally foster conflict and violence, ascriptive inequalities do so partic-

ularly. Pronounced ascriptive inequalities transform the experience of poverty for many into the hereditary permanent state of being one of the poor. Blau and Blau also argue that ascriptive socioeconomic inequalities undermine the social integration of a community by creating social differences and conflict that widen the separations between ethnic groups and social classes. The Blaus tested these ideas using data collected on the 125 largest Standard Metropolitan Statistical Areas (SMSAs). Their findings show that once economic inequality is controlled, the positive relationship between poverty and criminal violence disappears. That is, poverty no longer plays a role in explaining crime. The authors conclude their study by pointing out that in a society founded on the principle that "all men are created equal," economic inequalities rooted in ascribed positions violate the spirit of democracy and are likely to create alienation, despair, and conflict—all of which are associated with higher crime rates.

At the same time, a 1982 study by Messner examined the relationship between poverty, inequality, and violent crime for a sample of 204 SMSAs. Messner tested whether relative poverty (poor relative to those in one's community) is more important than absolute poverty (poor with reference to a fixed set of human needs) for explaining crime. What Messner discovers is quite surprising. While his economic measure of family income inequality proves to be insignificant, his second economic measure, size of the poverty population, exhibits a significant negative correlation with the homicide rate. That is, the size of the impoverished population is inversely related to the homicide rate.

Together, the work of Messner and Blau and Blau challenged common conceptions concerning the relationship between poverty and crime and pointed out that areas with high populations of people in poverty do not necessarily have corresponding higher rates of violent crime, as previously theorized. More recent studies on the poverty-crime relationship continue to report conflicting results. Thus, many argue that it is too premature to make a confident conclusion about the role that poverty plays in the production of criminal violence. A promising line of inquiry focuses on underclass neighborhoods that are characterized by the isolation and concentration of people in poverty. It may be that in the context of these "concentration effects" urban poverty may be related to higher crime rates (Sampson and Wilson).

Racial composition and urban crime.
Unlike poverty, studies that analyze racial composition and crime clearly find that there is a strong positive relationship between criminal violence and an area's racial composition. This has been shown to be true across all levels of aggregation, including states (Huff-Corzine et al.), SMSAs (Balkwell), cities (Sampson), and neighborhoods (Warner and Rountree), as well as for all types of crime, including both violent (Messner, 1982) and property (Kubrin). In many of these studies, racial composition is defined in terms of the percentage of the population that is black. More recently, however, there have been attempts to incorporate additional racial groups outside of blacks and whites into measures of racial composition. These measures more accurately represent racial heterogeneity or levels of racial diversity within an area. Interestingly, race effects have been documented in both studies that use percent black and white heterogeneity as their measure of racial composition. Given consistent findings, researchers interested in the race-crime relationship have moved away from the question of whether race effects exist to a more difficult question: Why do race effects exist?

To a great extent, the answer to this question is linked to the type of racial composition measure used in the study. For example, studies that use percent black as a proxy for racial composition, and find that it is a significant predictor of the crime rate, often propose subcultural explanations to explain the race effect (Messner, 1982, 1983). These researchers argue that if the subcultural explanations are correct, there should be an effect of racial composition on the crime rate that is independent of socioeconomic and demographic factors. When such an effect appears, it is frequently interpreted as support for the subculture of violence thesis. At the same time, studies that document race effects using a measure of racial heterogeneity have very different explanations for why race and crime are correlated at the city and neighborhood levels. These studies are usually more concerned with racial diversity and its relationship to crime, highlighting the "disorganizing" effects of racial heterogeneity on social control or interpersonal interactions at the neighborhood level (Warner and Rountree). Regardless of the measure, studies that examine the relationship between racial composition and crime find evidence of strong race effects.

Significant race effects have also been documented in criminological literature that focuses on changes in an area's racial composition and its relation to changes in violent and property crime rates. One of the most important findings of the classic Shaw and McKay delinquency research is that the spatial distribution of delinquency in a city was the product of "larger economic and social processes characterizing the history and growth of the city and of the local communities which comprise it" (p. 14). Further, in a 1982 study by Bursik and Webb using neighborhoods in Chicago, the authors find that changes within the ecological structures of localities had an appreciable impact on changes in community delinquency levels during the 1950s and 1960s. They interpret these findings in terms of the disruptive influence that community reorganization (processes of invasion and succession) has on the maintenance of social institutions, social networks, and informal social controls. In light of their findings, Bursik and Webb remind researchers of the crucial differences between static and dynamic spatial approaches to crime and delinquency. Since their work, recent studies that examine the relationship between changes in racial composition and changes in urban crime levels continue to find a strong positive relationship between the two (Miethe, Hughes, and McDowall; Kubrin).

Labor market conditions and crime. One possible line of inquiry that bridges debates about economics and crime and race and crime in the city is the research that focuses on how the labor market is related to crime. Historically criminologists have tried to sort out the relationship between unemployment and crime, but the literature is inconclusive. Some studies find that unemployment is positively associated with crime while others do not find a significant relationship. Examinations that go beyond the simple consideration of employed versus unemployed persons have found that areas with unstable unemployment circumstances for relatively large portions of adults have higher crime rates (Crutchfield; Crutchfield, Glusker, and Bridges). Labor market segmentation research seeks to explain how job allocation perpetuates systems of stratification, which regulate the poor and some minority populations to economic disadvantage across generations. The line of research may help to explain why underclass urban neighborhoods, composed heavily of African American and Latino residents, have higher crime rates.

Conclusions

What do we know about urban crime? We know that cities are generally more crime prone than the hinterland. We also know that crime rates vary within cities. We are not quite sure why this variation exists nor why variations in crime rates vary dramatically across cities. The major theoretical perspectives that are used to explain these observed variations include social disorganization theory, subculture theory, and conflict theories. We believe that the current evidence favors the two social structural alternatives—disorganization and conflict—but acknowledge that the social structure of the city affects urban culture, which, too, influences criminality. It appears that social inequality, in varied forms, is an important social force affecting many facets of urban life, including crime.

ROBERT D. CRUTCHFIELD
CHARIS E. KUBRIN

See also CRIME CAUSATION: SOCIOLOGICAL THEORIES; DELINQUENT AND CRIMINAL SUBCULTURES; ECOLOGY OF CRIME; FEAR OF CRIME; JUVENILE AND YOUTH GANGS; RACE AND CRIME; RIOTS: BEHAVIORAL ASPECTS; STATISTICS: HISTORICAL TRENDS IN WESTERN SOCIETY; URBAN POLICE.

BIBLIOGRAPHY

BALKWELL, JAMES W. "Ethnic Inequality and the Rate of Homicide." *Social Forces* 69, no. 1 (1990): 53–70.

BANFIELD, EDWARD. *The Unheavenly City.* 2d ed. Boston: Little, Brown, 1970.

BARKAN, STEVEN E. *Criminology: A Sociological Understanding.* Englewood Cliffs, N.J.: Prentice Hall, 1997.

BLAU, JUDITH R., and BLAU, PETER M. "The Cost of Inequality: Metropolitan Structure and Violent Crime." *American Sociological Review* 14 (1982): 114–129.

BURSIK, ROBERT J., and WEBB, JIM. "Community Change and Patterns of Delinquency." *American Journal of Sociology* 88, no. 1 (1982): 24–42.

CHAMBLISS, WILLIAM. "Toward a Political Economy of Crime." *Theory and Society* 2, no. 2 (1975): 149–170.

CRUTCHFIELD, ROBERT D. "Labor Stratification and Violent Crime." *Social Forces* 68, no. 2 (1989): 489–512.

CRUTCHFIELD, ROBERT D.; GLUSKER, A.; and BRIDGES, G. S. "A Tale of Three Cities: Labor Markets and Homicide." *Sociological Focus* 32, no. 1 (1999): 65–83.

CURTIS, LYNN. *Criminal Violence: National Patterns and Behavior.* Lexington, Mass.: D. C. Heath, 1974.

———. *Violence, Race, and Culture.* Lexington, Mass.: D. C. Heath, 1975.

DAVIS, NANETTE J. *Sociological Constructions of Deviance: Perspectives and Issues in the Field.* 2d ed. Dubuque, Iowa: Brown, 1980.

DURKHEIM, ÉMILE. *Suicide.* 1897. Reprint, New York: The Free Press, 1966.

ELKINS, STANLEY. *Slavery.* New York: Grosset and Dunlap, 1959.

Federal Bureau of Investigation. *Crime in the United States, 1995.* Washington, D.C.: U.S. Government Printing Office, 1995.

HUFF-CORZINE, LIN; CORZINE, JAY; and MOORE, DAVID C. "Southern Exposure: Deciphering the South's Influence on Homicide Rates." *Social Forces* 64 (1986): 906–924.

KORNHAUSER, RUTH R. *Social Sources of Delinquency: An Appraisal of Analytic Models.* Chicago: University of Chicago Press, 1978.

KUBRIN, CHARIS E. "Racial Heterogeneity and Crime: Measuring Static and Dynamic Effects." In *Research in Community Sociology,* vol. 10. Edited by D. A. Chekki. Greenwich, Conn.: JAI Press, 2000.

LISKA, ALLEN E. "A Critical Examination of Macro Perspectives on Crime Control." *Annual Review of Sociology* 13 (1987): 67–88.

LOFTIN, COLIN, and HILL, ROBERT H. "Regional Subculture and Homicide: An Examination of the Gastil-Hackney Thesis." *American Sociological Review* 39, no. 5 (1974): 714–724.

LYNCH, MICHAEL J., and GROVES, BYRON. "Causes of Crime: A Radical View." In *A Primer in Radical Criminology,* 2d ed. New York: Harrow and Heston, 1989. Pages 51–71.

MATZA, DAVID. *Becoming Deviant.* Englewood Cliffs, N.J.: Prentice-Hall, 1969.

MESSNER, STEVEN F. "Poverty, Inequality, and the Urban Homicide Rate: Some Unexpected Findings." *Criminology* 20 (1982): 103–114.

———. "Regional and Racial Effects on the Urban Homicide Rate: The Subculture of Violence Revisited." *American Journal of Sociology* 88 (1983): 997–1007.

MIETHE, TERRANCE D.; HUGHES, MICHAEL; and McDOWALL, DAVID. "Social Change and Crime Rates: An Evaluation of Alternative Theoretical Approaches." *Social Forces* 70, no. 1 (1991): 165–185.

PARK, ROBERT; BURGESS, ERNEST; and McKENZIE, RODERICK. *The City.* Chicago: University of Chicago Press, 1925.

PETERSON, RUTH D., and KRIVO, LAUREN J. "Racial Segregation and Black Urban Homicide." *Social Forces* 71 (1993): 1001–1026.

QUINNEY, RICHARD. "The Social Reality of Crime." In *Criminology*. Edited by Richard Quinney. Boston: Little, Brown, 1975. Pages 37–41.

SAMPSON, ROBERT J. "Race and Criminal Violence: A Demographically Disaggregated Analysis of Urban Homicide." In *Crime and Delinquency* 31, no. 1 (1985): 47–82.

SAMPSON, ROBERT J., and GROVES, WILLIAM B. "Community Structure and Crime: Testing Social Disorganization Theory." *American Journal of Sociology* 94 (1989): 774–802.

SAMPSON, ROBERT J., and WILSON, WILLIAM J. "Toward a Theory of Race, Crime, and Urban Inequality." *Crime and Inequality*. Edited by John Hagan and Ruth D. Peterson. Stanford, Calif.: Stanford University Press, 1995. Pages 37–54.

SHAW, CLIFFORD R., and MCKAY, HENRY. *Juvenile Delinquency and Urban Areas*. Chicago: University of Chicago Press, 1942.

SHOVER, NEIL. "Burglary." In *Crime and Justice: A Review of Research*, vol. 14. Edited by M. Tonry. Chicago: University of Chicago Press, 1991. Pages 73–113.

SMITH, M. DWAYNE, and PARKER, ROBERT N. "Type of Homicide and Variation in Regional Rates." *Social Forces* 59, no. 1 (1980): 136–147.

STARK, RODNEY. *Sociology*. 7th ed. New York: Wadsworth, 1998.

THOMAS, WILLIAM I., and ZNANIECKI, FLORIAW. *The Polish Peasant in Europe and America: Monograph of an Immigrant Group*. Boston: Richard G. Badger, 1920.

TOENNIES, FERDINAND. *Community and Society*. 1887. Reprint, New York: Harper and Row, 1963.

WARNER, BARBARA D., and ROUNTREE, PAMELA W. "Local Social Ties in a Community and Crime Model: Questioning the Systemic Nature of Informal Social Control." *Social Problems* 44, no. 4 (1997): 520–536.

WEBER, MAX. *The City*. New York: The Free Press, 1958.

WIRTH, LEWIS. "Urbanism as a Way of Life." *American Journal of Sociology* 44 (1938): 1–24.

WOLFGANG, MARVIN E., and FERRACUTI, F. *The Subculture of Violence: Towards an Integrated Theory in Criminology*. London: Tavistock, 1967.

URBAN POLICE

In the 1970s, changes in the nature of economic development and growth left many northern industrial cities stagnating with declining populations. During this time period, many urbanites moved to the suburbs to escape the congestion and rising crime rates of inner cities. Described as "white flight," middle- and upper-class, predominantly white Americans moved to the suburbs, further eroding the tax base in inner city areas. Poverty and crime increased in these areas, where remaining residents were primarily lower-income minorities. Massey and Denton argue that African Americans and Puerto Ricans are the only groups who have "*simultaneously* experienced high levels of residential segregation and sharp increases in poverty," which created underclass communities, characterized by "poverty, family instability, welfare dependency, crime, housing abandonment, and low educational achievement" (pp. 146, 130).

Policing these underclass communities is a distinctly urban phenomenon that is particularly challenging for police. Egon Bittner has described "skid row" as a distinct geographic area within inner cities where people "lack the capacities and commitments to live normal lives," (1967b, p. 705). This limited capacity may be due to drug or alcohol addiction, mental illness, or poverty. Skid row areas are often characterized by high crime rates and poverty, and in America's "throw away society," the people living in these areas are treated as expendable. They reside in areas where "the overall air is not so much one of active distrust as it is irrelevance of trust" (1967b, p. 705). Dealing with situations where suspects and victims often have "nothing to lose" requires special handling by police. Most police tactics involve "containing" these areas.

Previous studies have shown that the majority of service calls in urban areas are concentrated within a few addresses. For example, Sherman, Gartin, and Buerger reported that 50 percent of the calls for service in Minneapolis during a three-year period came from only 3 percent of the addresses within the city. This entry examines some of the issues involved with special populations and types of crimes that present policing problems in these "hot spots." Special populations considered in this entry include minorities, juveniles, mentally ill citizens, the homeless, and crowds. In addition, special types of situations described include narcotics enforcement, gun violence, minor offenses and incivilities, and domestic violence. For each of these topics, the role, strategies, and changes in the policies of urban police will be described.

Policing minority citizens

Historically, cooperation and communication between police and minorities has been troubled. Williams and Murphy described a history of policing shaped by the enforcement of laws that have discriminated against minority groups, particularly African Americans. Slavery, segregation, and discrimination are historical realities that shaped the current distrustful, strained, and often hostile relationship between police and minority citizens. This poor relationship reached its pinnacle during the police-citizen crisis of the 1960s. The civil rights movement had gained momentum and become more militant. Protesters gathered to demonstrate against race discrimination and injustice within the criminal justice system. Police officers responded to protesters with physical brutality, which increased the tension between minorities and the police. This tension exploded in the form of riots and civil disobedience, often sparked by incidents involving the police (Walker, 1999).

As a result of several crime commission reports and research findings questioning the effectiveness of "professional" police organizations, police organizational strategies evolved to focus on strengthening relationships and creating partnerships between the police and citizens. Police departments attempted to improve community relations through the creation of police-community relations units, race relations training for officers, and the hiring of more minorities and women. Some of these techniques were relatively successful. As reported by Walker (1999), African American officers represented a majority of the force in departments such as Detroit, Washington, and Atlanta in 1993. In addition, African Americans were selected as police chiefs in several large departments, including New York City, Los Angeles, Atlanta, Chicago, Houston, and others. Furthermore, by the mid-1990s, women represented 13 percent of all officers in large police departments.

Despite these advances, police still struggle with minority community relations. In 1993, the acquittal of four officers accused of beating Rodney King, an African American motorist in Los Angeles, sparked race riots across the country. Other major cases of police abuse of force in the 1990s (e.g., the Louima and Diallo cases in New York City) further increased tension between the police and minorities. In 1996, 26 percent of African American citizens surveyed reported they had very little or no confidence in the police, compared to only 9 percent of white respondents (Bureau of Justice Statistics, 1996). Furthermore, when asked about attitudes toward use of force, 60 percent of whites had favorable attitudes compared to 33 percent of African Americans and 42 percent of Hispanics (Huang and Vaughn).

Serious questions regarding police discrimination remain. Studies routinely show that minorities are overrepresented as suspects who have force used against them, and who are shot and killed by officers. Worden's analysis of 1977 data showed that police were more likely to use both reasonable and unreasonable force against black male suspects. This is also true of the use of deadly force. However, changes in police departments' administrative policies led to decreases in the use of deadly force by officers. In a study of the New York City Police Department, Fyfe found that changes in the department's formal policies governing police shootings in 1972 reduced the average numbers of shots fired by officers by 30 percent. The total number of uses of deadly force decreased by nearly 50 percent from 1970 to 1984. In that same time period, the ratio of African Americans to whites who had deadly force used against them decreased from six-to-one to three-to-one (Walker, 1999). Reductions in police use of deadly force toward minorities were also noted after the fleeing-felon standard guiding police use of deadly force was ruled unconstitutional by the Supreme Court in *Tennessee v. Garner*, 105 S. Ct. 1694 (1985).

African Americans are also disproportionately arrested more often than whites. It is unclear whether these disparities in arrest statistics represent actual discrimination (i.e., disparity based on extra legal factors, such as race). When other factors are taken into consideration (e.g., seriousness of the offense, the evidence available, demeanor of the suspect, etc.), it appears that arrest decisions are influenced more by situational and legal factors than strictly race (Riksheim and Chermak). However, police are more likely to police inner-city neighborhoods, which are predominantly minority areas. In this sense, police may be showing a form of contextual discrimination by heavily policing particular neighborhoods or particular types of crimes.

A concern is that police officers are profiling citizens based on race and ethnicity. The term

DWB or *driving while black* is a vivid descriptor of this phenomenon. Minority groups claim that police are more likely to pull over motorists simply because of their race. In fact, studies of New Jersey State Police have shown that minorities are pulled over disproportionately. This same argument is made in urban areas, where minorities believe they have become the targets of police harassment through tactics of aggressive enforcement of minor crimes. Studies of police have shown that African Americans and Hispanics are disproportionately stopped, questioned, and frisked by police (Browning et al.). Surveys of citizens also indicated that African Americans and Hispanics are more likely to be stopped and interrogated by police. One survey of African American high school students revealed that 80 percent had been stopped by police and 62 percent of those stopped said the police treated them disrespectfully (Walker, Spohn, and De-Lone).

At the same time, however, minority citizens complain that police are not responding to their needs in these areas. Citizens allege that police are not providing adequate protection or attention in their neighborhoods. According to Walker, this apparent contradiction can be explained by "the diversity *within* racial and ethnic minority communities . . . . Complaints about police harassment generally come from young males who have a high level of contact with the police. Most members of racial minority communities, however, are law-abiding adults with jobs and families. Like their white counterparts, they want more not less police protection" (1999, p. 222).

In the 1980s, new strategies of community-oriented policing have encouraged the partnership between citizens and the police. Research has shown, however, that strategies of community policing tend to have the strongest impact on neighborhoods where they are least needed. Satisfaction with community policing techniques is highest in homogeneous, higher socioeconomic status communities, and lowest in heterogeneous, lower socioeconomic status communities (Bayley, 1988). It is clear that new approaches to improve police-minority relations are needed.

Policing juveniles

Walker (1999) notes that policing juveniles represents a special problem for police in urban areas for a number of reasons. First, officers are more likely to come into contact with juveniles because they often "hang-out" in groups on the streets that officers patrol. Second, juveniles have less favorable attitudes toward police, although it is unknown if juveniles are more likely to act disrespectfully based on these attitudes. Finally, juveniles "represent a large proportion of the crime problem: 16 percent of all arrests, 29 percent of all Index crime arrests, and 33 percent of all property crime arrests" (p. 114).

Although handling juvenile incidents is believed to be a special problem for police, researchers know very little about actual street interactions between police and juveniles. Research conducted in the 1960s suggests that officers are more likely to initiate contact with juveniles than with adults and that officers have a large amount of discretion during these encounters. This research also shows that taking no official action is the most likely outcome of encounters with juveniles. When arrest is used, it is more likely in situations that are more serious, when victims request arrest, and the juvenile suspect acts in a hostile manner toward police (Piliavin and Briar; Black and Reiss).

Historically, police have taken a patriarchal role toward juveniles. In the late 1800s and early 1900s, police departments housed wayward youths. In the early to mid 1990s, larger police departments became specialized and juvenile units were created. Police organizations recognized the need to treat juveniles as a distinct group, and police working in these units emphasized the goals of prevention, education, and treatment. A survey of large police departments in 1993 revealed that 88 percent of departments had special juvenile units and 76 percent had special gang units (Bureau of Justice Statistics, 1995).

As late as the 1980s, police departments were still emphasizing crime prevention and education programs for juveniles. However, in the 1990s, with the exception of the DARE program (Drug Abuse Resistance Education), crime prevention and education in many departments were virtually abandoned in favor of aggressive enforcement policies. Most citizens perceive that juvenile crime is on the rise. Police departments and juvenile courts systems across the country have been barraged with "get tough" attitudes emphasized by politicians and the media, and have changed their policies as a result. Yet, in his examination of juvenile crime rates, Thomas Bernard notes that with the exception of homicide, juvenile crime has actually declined "by about one-third over the last twenty years" (p. 337).

Relative to homicide, Bernard notes that the number of juvenile arrests between 1984 and 1993 nearly tripled. While the rate declined by 31 percent from 1993 to 1996, the rate in 1996 was still twice as high as it was in 1984. The increase in homicide rates is often attributed to changes in drug markets and the organization of juvenile gangs. Gangs are represented in over one hundred cities across the United States. Juvenile street gangs in Los Angeles and Detroit are believed to control about 60 percent of the crack cocaine drug trade in those areas (Gaines et al.). Estimates of juvenile gang membership are as high as 150,000 in Los Angeles alone.

Gaines and his colleagues describe four misconceptions related to youth gangs, the drug trade, and law enforcement. First, they note that although law enforcement officials portray gangs as highly organized and structured, they are in reality loosely defined and have high turnover. Second, they note that their violence is based mostly on disputes over turf and respect, rather than the drug trade itself. Third, police often incorrectly label youths as gang members (particularly minorities). And finally, they note that youth gangs are street-level retailers that do not control the drug supply. Due to these misconceptions, Gaines and his colleagues argue that unnecessary panic and media attention guide policymaking regarding juvenile gangs.

Traditional law enforcement responses to gang-related problems involved prevention. Police gang units tried to prevent intra-gang violence by collecting information and interceding when possible. These strategies are largely ineffective. Alternative strategies involve aggressive law enforcement, including enforcement of anti-gang legislation. However, some of this legislation has been struck down by the courts as unconstitutional. For example, in 1999, the U.S. Supreme Court in *City of Chicago v. Morales*, 119 S. Ct. 1849 (1999) struck down Chicago's anti-loitering law aimed at gang members, which initiated 42,000 arrests in its three years of enforcement (Hornblower). Furthermore, the aggressive tactics of antigang police units have come under intense scrutiny. Officers in the infamous CRASH (Community Resources Against Street Hoodlums) unit of the Los Angeles Police Department have been accused of falsifying and planting evidence on suspects, perjury, and extreme abuses of force. In what is being described as the largest police misconduct scandal in recent history, as of August 2000, ninety-eight criminal cases have been reversed, five officers are facing felony criminal charges, and twenty-five officers have been suspended, fired, or resigned (Feldman).

Policing mentally disordered citizens

Police have long been recognized as a community mental health resource, a role that has expanded in recent years as a result of *deinstitutionalization*. Policies of deinstitutionalization implemented in the United States have reduced the state and county hospital psychiatric patient populations from a total of 560,000 in 1955 to 125,000 in 1981, a decline of 75 percent (Wacholz and Mullaly). As a result, individuals with mental disorders currently reside in communities where psychiatric care is provided by community-based mental health facilities or the criminal justice system. Within this context, police serve as gatekeepers responsible for choosing which type of facility, mental health or criminal justice, that citizens with mental disorders will enter.

As a result of deinstitutionalization, police calls to incidents involving citizens with mental disorders have increased significantly, leading to increases in criminal justice processing of these citizens (Bonovitz and Bonovitz). The notion that the criminal justice system is increasingly relied upon to handle persons with mental disorders—particularly those engaging in minor offenses—is often referred to as the *criminalization* of the mentally disordered. The criminalization hypothesis rests on the belief that mentally disordered citizens are more likely to be arrested than non-mentally disordered citizens, and that the population of mentally disordered people in prison has risen dramatically (Lamb and Weinberger). Only two studies have examined the relative probabilities of arrest for mentally disordered versus non-mentally disordered suspects. Teplin's 1984 study of police discretion toward mentally disordered citizens in Chicago in 1981 found the probability of being arrested was approximately 20 percent higher for mentally disordered suspects compared to non-mentally disordered suspects. However, another study of police discretion in multiple sites in 1977 and 1996–1997 has found that police are significantly less likely to arrest mentally disordered suspects (Engel and Silver). Therefore, the debate over the criminalization hypothesis continues.

Police have a large amount of discretion available to them when deciding what course to take regarding mentally disordered suspects.

Observations of the police suggest that they are more likely to use informal means to handle situations involving mentally disordered citizens. For example, officers often use "psychiatric first aid" as an alternative to hospitalization or arrest (Teplin and Pruett). This may be due to the strong standards generally attached to hospitalization. For example, in the state of Florida, the Baker Act requires that citizens who pose a danger to themselves or others be involuntary hospitalized. Other states have similar legislation. Officers are also reluctant to hospitalize mentally disordered citizens because hospitals often refuse to admit them because they do not have enough beds, cannot handle dangerous or violent persons, or impose higher admissions criteria than required by the law.

In an effort to better handle situations involving mentally disordered citizens, 45 percent of large departments surveyed in 1998 indicated that they use some type of specialized response (Deane et al.). This research group reported that three models of specialized police response were the most common: (1) police-based specialized police response (sworn officers trained to provide mental health crisis intervention, also act as liaisons to mental health system); (2) police-based specialized mental health response (mental health consultants hired by police department provide telephone consultations to officers in the field); and (3) mental health–based specialized mental health response (use of mobile mental health crisis teams). Nonetheless, more than half of the large departments surveyed did not have any type of specialized response developed for handling mentally disordered citizens, and officers often consider handling "mentals" as social work that should not be the responsibility of the police (Bittner, 1967).

Policing the homeless

Historically, the police role included providing shelter to homeless persons. During the late 1800s, the Boston Police Department was responsible for lodging homeless, and the Philadelphia police department offered lodging to 100,000 citizens a year (Monkkonen). After 1900, care for the homeless became the responsibility of social service agencies; however, the problem of homelessness still influences the activities of patrol officers. Police routinely handle calls from business owners and residents requesting that homeless persons be removed from the neighborhood. Furthermore, homeless persons are often crime victims.

During the 1970s and 1980s, the homeless population increased significantly. Although reports vary greatly, a median estimate of the number of homeless in the late 1980s was 400,000 (Jencks). It has also been suggested that deinstitutionalization policies have led to larger numbers of mentally ill persons in the community, some of whom inevitably become homeless. In addition to increases in the number of homeless, changes in the character of this population have occurred. Previously, the homeless population was largely male substance abusers and alcoholics. During the 1980s, larger numbers of families, including women and children, were forced into a life on the streets. Changes in the character of the homeless population has been described as the "new homeless problem" (Walker, 1999).

The image of the homeless has changed from "harmless bums" to those committing predatory crimes. For example, the Santa Monica (California) Police Department reported that the homeless accounted for 25 percent of burglary and 19 percent of robbery arrests in 1985; these figures jumped to 53 percent and 49 percent in 1990 (Melekian). Other research has found, however, that homeless men are more likely to be arrested for minor crimes such as public intoxication, shoplifting, and violations of city ordinances, concluding that the depiction of homeless men as serious predatory criminals is faulty (Snow et al.).

Most departments do not have a specialized plan for handling these problems. One survey of police departments in 1991 showed that 40 percent of departments did not keep records regarding contact with the homeless, and 50 percent provide no specialized training to officers dealing with this population (Plotkin and Narr). As a result, police response to the "new homeless problem" varies greatly. For example, in the early 1990s, Los Angeles designated a fifty-square-block area where homeless persons are allowed to sleep on the streets. Community policing officers in Seattle distribute blankets and make referrals to homeless shelters and drug abuse treatment centers (Walker, 1999). In comparison, aggressive order maintenance tactics used in New York City encourage the use of arrest for minor offenses, including vagrancy, loitering, and public intoxication.

Policing crowds

Crowd control is a specialized function of urban police forces. Officers must maintain security during public gatherings that are both planned and unplanned. Planned public gatherings include permitted rallies, protests, demonstrations, vigils, parades, holiday celebrations, and other specialized events. McCarthy and McPhail have noted changes in the nature of public gatherings and police response over the past forty years. During the 1960s, police responded to public gatherings with suspicion and aggressive enforcement. Police often tried to prevent demonstrations and protests. If public gatherings did occur, police tactics often included the use of force and arrest, which escalated disorder and violence.

Over the next three decades, McCarthy and McPhail argue that protest events have become institutionalized, or governed by formal rules and regulations as well as by informal norms. Since the 1980s, public order policing reflects communication and negotiation between police departments and citizens. Most groups file requests and receive permits, allowing them to legally gather in specific areas at specific times. Police departments negotiate with these groups and informally work out what activities and behaviors will be allowed during these gatherings. As described by McCarthy and McPhail, "under negotiated management policing, an 'acceptable level of disruption' is seen by police as an inevitable byproduct of demonstrator efforts to produce social change. Police do not try to prevent demonstrations, but attempt to limit the amount of disruption they cause" (p. 97).

Urban police must control unplanned public gatherings as well. Unplanned public gatherings include events that exist without a permit, along with gatherings resulting from natural disasters and riots. Policing unplanned public gatherings is difficult for police departments. Several examples of public gathering and riot situations occurred during the 1990s, where police were criticized for being unprepared, too lenient, or too aggressive (e.g., the LAPD during the Rodney King riots in 1993; St. Petersburg, Florida, police during race riots in 1996; Seattle Police Department during the World Trade Organization protests in 1999, etc.). Again, the response by police during these and other situations was believed to escalate, rather than control, the situation.

Most large departments provide officers with some form of crowd control or riot training. Much of the training includes documented rules and regulations resulting from *crisis management*. Police policies are often made as a result of an inadequate response to an immediate crisis and are unsystematic (Manning). Departments' procedural guidelines are often situation-specific or, alternatively, terribly vague. In fact, many departments learn better ways to handle crowd situations through documentation of poorly handled initial situations.

Narcotics enforcement

Samuel Walker has suggested that the drug problem in the United States is both directly and indirectly responsible for "the dramatic rise in the murder rate in the 1980s, gang violence, the soaring prison population, the worsening crisis in race relations, and the steady erosion of individual rights in the Supreme Court" (1998, p. 243). While drug use has declined since the late 1970s, it has significantly increased among members of the underclass. As the political climate changed in the 1980s, a "war on drugs" was declared. Enforcement of drug-related offenses increased dramatically, as did the severity of the sentences for these crimes. Critics of these policies have suggested that "racial minorities are the primary victims of the war on drugs" (1998, p. 249). Although African Americans made up only 12 percent of the U.S. population and 13 percent of monthly drug users in 1993, they accounted for 35 percent of drug arrests and 74 percent of prison sentences for drug convictions (Mauer and Huling).

According to David Bayley, there are six major strategies to control the use of illegal drugs in the United States; however, urban police departments focus primarily on two: suppressing the sale of drugs between suppliers and consumers and educating people about the perils of illegal drug use. Numerous tactics have been used to advance these strategies, although most have not been effective (Walker, 1998). The most common police strategy is a *crackdown*, where additional manpower and resources are used for aggressive enforcement in targeted areas. Most crackdown efforts reduce crime in the short term; however, they do not have lasting long-term effects. Crackdowns also pose the risk of *displacement effects*, where criminal activity is simply moved to another location not targeted by police, or *replacement effects*, where dealers who are arrested are immediately replaced with other dealers. Furthermore, research on the impact of

DARE, the best known and most widely used police education tactic, has consistently shown that it does not reduce later drug use (Emmett et al.).

Recent studies of police drug enforcement tactics utilizing the techniques of *problem-oriented policing* have shown more positive results (Goldstein). Studies of the SMART (Specialized Multi-Agency Response Team) program in Oakland, California, have shown a reduction in drug-related crime without any evidence of displacement effects (Greene). Likewise, an evaluation of the Drug Market Analysis (DMA) program in Jersey City, New Jersey, found strong effects on the number of disorder-related calls for service and little evidence of a displacement effect (Weisburd and Green). Perhaps these types of police strategies are more effective than traditional crackdowns because they "take a more specific approach to crime and disorder" while also targeting "specific problems or places." Weisburd and Green conclude that although their study "does not directly test problem-oriented policing, it provides evidence that tailor-made responses to problems are essential if police are to deal more effectively with crime and crime-related problems" (p. 732).

Gun violence

Gun violence has also become a major concern for police in urban areas. The dramatic rise in the murder rate during the 1980s is generally attributed to changes in the drug market. Furthermore, while the murder rate among offenders over age twenty-five dropped 25 percent between 1990 and 1994, the murder rate among for those age fourteen to seventeen increased 22 percent (Walker). In 1992, the number of handgun crimes increased by about 40 percent compared to the prior five-year period, and handguns were used in about 60 percent of all murders (Bureau of Justice Statistics, 1994).

Confiscating illegal guns through aggressive enforcement was attempted in Kansas City with some positive results. Using methods of *directed patrol*, an alternative to random patrol where officers are given specific directions to follow regarding enforcement of particular types of persons or crimes, officers focused on confiscating weapons in *hot spot* areas. The Kansas City Gun Experiment first identified hot spots through computer analyses of calls for service and arrest statistics (Sherman and Rogan). For twenty-nine weeks, four officers focused exclusively on gun detection in the target areas, while other officers were

told to focus on this activity when not responding to calls for service. Gun detection was conducted by making traffic and pedestrian stops. During this period, there was a 65 percent increase in gun seizures. In addition, Sherman and Rogan reported a 49 percent decrease in gun-related crime with little or no observable displacement. Citizens in the target areas reported being less fearful and more satisfied with police. Once the experiment ended, however, gun-related crime returned to previous levels. Again, many of the police crackdown techniques showed similar results—effects in the short-term but not in the long-term (Sherman).

Minor offenses and incivilities

In the 1990s, citizens, politicians, and police administrators began to focus their attention on minor offenses and quality-of-life issues. In a seminal article, James Q. Wilson and George Kelling proposed the *broken windows* thesis. They argued that a broken window symbolizes a lack of care about a property, making it ripe for criminal activity. Wilson and Kelling stressed the importance of controlling minor crimes and disorders in an effort to curb more serious crime. They argue that making citizens feel safer and improving their quality of life should be the goal of police. Research has documented the spiraling decline of neighborhoods, where fearful citizens retreat into their homes, community ties break down, disorder increases, and more serious forms of crime develop (Skogan). In many departments across the country, minor disorders and incivilities have become the focus of aggressive law enforcement tactics.

Often referred to as *zero-tolerance policies*, departments are using tactics of aggressive enforcement of minor crimes to clean up the streets and make citizens feel safer. There are two distinct but related concepts underlying zero-tolerance policies. First, these policies send a clear message to citizens that illegal conduct will not be tolerated. Second, proponents argue that by focusing on minor crimes, more serious crimes will decrease. For example, people arrested for minor crimes might be carrying an illegal weapon or be wanted on arrest warrants for other crimes. The highest profile example of the use of this policing strategy is in New York City's police department. The NYPD adopted the zero-tolerance policy in 1993 after abandoning CPOP (Community Patrol Officer Program), a community policing strategy. Officers began making arrests and issuing citations for such minor crimes as fare beating (jumping the turnstiles in subways), urinating in public, jaywalking, and loitering. In addition, police and media attention focused on "squeegee" people (people who clean car windows at intersections for money).

Kelling and Coles argue that tougher enforcement of these minor crimes contributed to a higher quality of life for residents and visitors in New York, along with a lower crime rate for more serious crimes. The crime rate in New York dropped significantly during the 1990s. The murder rate in 1997 was the lowest it had been in thirty years. Similar trends in the lowering of the crime rate, however, are being experienced by other cities not using zero-tolerance policies. Therefore, it is unclear whether zero-tolerance policies are the actual stimulus behind the decline in crime rates.

Domestic violence

A 1985 national survey indicated that 11.3 percent of wives experience some form of domestic violence, while 3 percent experience severe violence. This same study showed that 4.4 percent of husbands surveyed also experienced severe violence at the hands of their spouse (Gelles and Straus). Indeed, there is accumulating evidence that males and females experience similar rates of domestic violence (Straus).

However, it is also clear that police calls for service overwhelmingly represent situations with women victims. Brookoff (1997) found that 78 percent of police calls for service regarding domestic disputes involved female victims. A larger proportion of incidents involving female injury and a male's reluctance to admit that he was assaulted may explain this disproportionate level of calls for service (Straus). Research has also found that domestic violence calls for service are concentrated in particular areas. For example, Sherman, Gartin, and Buerger reported that the majority of calls for domestic disturbances occurred in only 9 percent of the total number of street addresses in Minneapolis. Lower-income female victims are more likely to call the police, compared to middle and upper class women who use private sources of help. Therefore, although officers policing rural and suburban areas also handle calls for domestic violence, officers in urban areas handle these types of situations on a routine basis.

Prior to the mid-1980s, officers had much discretion in handling domestic dispute inci-

dents. In the early 1980s, researchers conducted the Minneapolis Domestic Violence Experiment. When responding to calls for service for misdemeanor domestic violence, officers were told to randomly assign one of three treatments: arrest, separation, or mediation. The researchers reported that offenders who were arrested were significantly less likely to have repeated incidents of violence compared to suspects who separated or mediated (Sherman and Berk). *Mandatory arrest policies* were adopted by departments across the country as a result of this study, the influence of feminist groups calling for law enforcement in domestic violence situations, and several successful lawsuits against departments by victims of domestic violence. Mandatory arrest policies are one of the first attempts to control police officer discretion through the use of administrative rulemaking. A survey of large departments in 1993 reported that 95 percent had written policies guiding police discretion in domestic dispute situations. Furthermore, 53 percent of the departments surveyed had a specialized domestic violence unit (Bureau of Justice Statistics, 1995; Walker, 1999).

The Minneapolis Domestic Violence Experiment has been heavily criticized (Lempert), and follow-up studies have not produced the same results. More recent research suggests that the employment status of the offender is important to consider when determining the successful use of arrest. Unemployed offenders who are arrested are more likely to commit future violence, while employed offenders are less likely (Sherman et al., 1992). It appears that the effects of arrest are situation-specific. Officers, however, are not likely to be able to predict the future violence of those suspects they encounter. They must decide what course of action to take based on the specifics of the situation itself. Police officers are more likely to arrest when there is evidence of an injury, evidence of drug or alcohol use, the suspect is disrespectful, or the victim requests an arrest (Worden and Pollitz).

Conclusion

Urban policing represents a challenge to police departments. For the most part, the majority of crimes are located in a few concentrated areas within inner cities. This entry has presented a number of different types of citizens and situations that urban police encounter on a routine basis. For each of these groups of citizens or situations, the historical and current role of police has been described, along with the tactics and strategies guiding police discretion. Over time, policies have been enacted to meet the challenges of urban policing. Some have been more effective than others, however few have been clear successes. Perhaps as additional research is focused on these areas, police organizations will develop policies to more effectively meet the challenges of policing urban areas.

ROBIN SHEPARD ENGEL

See also FEDERAL BUREAU OF INVESTIGATION: HISTORY; POLICE: HISTORY; POLICE: COMMUNITY POLICING; POLICE: CRIMINAL INVESTIGATIONS; POLICE: HANDLING OF JUVENILES; POLICE: ORGANIZATION AND MANAGEMENT; POLICE: POLICE OFFICER BEHAVIOR; POLICE: POLICING COMPLAINANTLESS CRIMES; POLICE: PRIVATE POLICE AND INDUSTRIAL SECURITY; POLICE: SPECIAL WEAPONS AND TACTICS (SWAT) TEAMS; SCIENTIFIC EVIDENCE; URBAN CRIME; VAGRANCY AND DISORDERLY CONDUCT.

BIBLIOGRAPHY

BAYLEY, DAVID H. "Community Policing: A Report from the Devil's Advocate." In *Community Policing: Rhetoric or Reality.* Edited by J. Greene and S. Mastrofski. New York: Praeger, 1988.
————. *What Works in Policing.* New York: Oxford University Press, 1988.
BERNARD, THOMAS J. "Juvenile Crime and the Transformation of Juvenile Justice: Is There a Juvenile Crime Wave?" *Justice Quarterly* 16, no. 2 (1999): 337–356.
BITTNER, EGON. "Police Discretion in Emergency Apprehension of Mentally Ill Persons." *Social Problems* 14 (1967a): 278–292.
————. "The Police on Skid Row." *American Sociological Review* 32 (1967b): 699–715.
BLACK, DONALD, and REISS, ALBERT J., JR. "Police Control of Juveniles." *American Sociological Review* 35, no. 1 (1970): 63–77.
BONOVITZ, J., and BONOVITZ, J. "Diversion of the Mentally Ill into the Criminal Justice System: The Police Intervention Perspective." *American Journal of Psychiatry* 138 (1981): 973–976.
BROOKOFF, D. *Drugs, Alcohol, and Domestic Violence in Memphis.* Washington, D.C.: U.S. Department of Justice, 1997.
BROWNING, SANDRA L; CULLEN, FRANCIS T.; CAO, LIQUN; KOPACHE, RENEE; and STEVENSON, THOMAS J. "Race and Getting Hassled by the Police: A Research Note." *Police Studies* 17, no. 1 (1994): 1–11.
Bureau of Justice Statistics. *Guns and Crime.* Washington, D.C.: Government Printing Office, 1994.
————. *Law Enforcement Management and Administrative Statistics, 1993.* Washington, D.C.: Government Printing Office, 1995.
————. *Sourcebook of Criminal Justice Statistics 1995.* Washington, D.C.: Government Printing Office, 1996.
DEANE, MARTHA WILLIAMS; STEADMAN, HENRY J.; BORUM, RANDY; VEYSEY, BONITA A.; and MORRISSEY, JOSEPH P. "Emerging Partnerships between Mental Health and Law Enforcement." *Psychiatric Services* 50, no. 1 (1999): 99–101.
EMMETT, SUSAN T.; TOBLER, NANCY; RINGWALT, CHRISTOPHER; and FLEWELLING, ROBERT L. "How Effective Is Drug Abuse Resistance Education? A Meta-Analysis of Project DARE Outcome Evaluations." *American Journal of Public Health* 84 (1994): 1394–1401.
ENGEL, ROBIN SHEPARD, and SILVER, ERIC. "Policing Mentally Disordered Suspects: A Reexamination of the Criminalization Hypothesis." Unpublished manuscript under review. 2000.
FELDMAN, CHARLES. "Los Angeles Police Scandal May Be Helping the Guilty." http://cnn.com/2000/US/02/09/lapd.effects/.
FYFE, JAMES J. "Administrative Interventions on Police Shooting Discretion: An Empirical Assessment." *Journal of Criminal Justice* 7 (1979): 309–323.
GAINES, LARRY K.; KAPPELER, VICTOR E.; and VAUGHN, JOSEPH B. *Policing in America.* Cincinnati, Ohio: Anderson Publishing, 1999.
GELLES, RICHARD J., and STRAUS, MURRAY A. *Intimate Violence.* New York: Simon & Schuster, 1988.
GOLDSTEIN, HERMAN. *Problem-Oriented Policing.* New York: McGraw-Hill, 1990.
GREENE, LORRAINE. *Policing Places with Drug Problems.* Thousand Oaks, Calif.: Sage, 1996.
HUANG, W. S. WILSON, and VAUGHN, MICHAEL S. "Support and Confidence: Public Attitudes toward the Police." In *Americans View Crime and Justice: A National Public Opinion Survey.* Edited by T. J. Flanigan and D. R. Longmire. Newbury Park, Calif.: Sage, 1996. Pages 31–45.
JENCKS, CHRISTOPHER. *The Homeless.* Cambridge, Mass.: Harvard University Press, 1994.
KALINICH, D. B., and SENESE, J. D. "Police Discretion and the Mentally Ill in Chicago: A Reconsideration." *Police Studies* 10 (1987): 185–191.
KELLING, GEORGE L., and COLES, CATHERINE. *Fixing Broken Windows.* New York: Free Press, 1996.
LAMB, H. B., and WEINBERGER, L. E. "Persons with Severe Mental Illness in Jails and Prisons: A Review." *Psychiatric Services* 49 (1998): 483–492.

LEMPERT, RICHARD E. "Humility Is a Virtue: On the Publicization of Policy-Relevant Research." *Law and Society Review* 23 (1989): 145–161.

MANNING, PETER K. *Police Work.* Cambridge, Mass.: MIT Press, 1977.

MASSEY, DOUGLAS S., and DENTON, NANCY A. *American Apartheid: Segregation and the Making of the Underclass.* Cambridge, Mass.: Harvard University Press, 1993.

MAUER, MARC, and HULING, TRACY. *Young Black Americans and the Criminal Justice System: Five Years Later.* Washington, D.C.: The Sentencing Project, 1995.

MCCARTHY, JOHN D., and MCPHAIL, CLARK. "The Institutionalization of Protest in the United States." In *The Social Movement Society: Contentious Politics for a New Century.* Edited by David Meyer and Sidney Tarrow. New York: Rowman & Littlefield Publishers, 1998. Pages 83–110.

MELEKIAN, BARNEY. "Police and the Homeless." *FBI Law Enforcement Bulletin* 59 (11): 1–6.

MONKKONEN, ERIC H. *Police in Urban America, 1860–1920.* Cambridge, Mass.: Cambridge University Press, 1981.

PILIAVIN, I., and BRIAR, S. "Police Encounters with Juveniles." *American Journal of Sociology* 70 (1964): 206–214.

PLOTKIN, MARTHA R., and NARR, ORTON A. *The Police Response to Homelessness: A Status Report.* Washington, D.C.: Police Executive Research Forum, 1993.

RIKSHEIM, ERIC, and CHERMACK, STEVEN M. "Causes of Police Behavior Revisited." *Journal of Criminal Justice* 21 (1993): 353–382.

SHERMAN, LAWRENCE W. "Police Crackdowns: Initial and Residual Deterrence." In *Crime and Justice: A Review of Research.* Edited by M. Tonry and N. Morris. Chicago: University of Chicago Press, 1990.

SHERMAN, LAWRENCE W., and BERK, RICHARD A. "The Specific Deterrent Effects of Arrest for Domestic Assault." *American Sociological Review* 49 (1984): 261–272.

SHERMAN, LAWRENCE W.; GARTIN, PATRICK R.; and BUERGER, MICHAEL E. "Hot Spots of Predatory Crime: Routine Activities and the Criminology of Place." *Criminology* 27, no. 1 (1989): 27–55.

SHERMAN, LAWRENCE W.; SCHMIDT, J.; ROGAN, D.; SMITH, D.; GARTIN, P.; COHN, E.; COLLINS, D.; and BACICH, A. "The Variable Effects of Arrest on Criminal Careers: The Milwaukee Domestic Violence Experiment." *The Journal of Criminal Law and Criminology* 88, no. 1 (1992): 137–169.

SHERMAN, LAWRENCE W., and ROGAN, DENNIS R. "Effects of Gun Seizures on Gun Violence: 'Hot Spots' Patrol in Kansas City." *Justice Quarterly* 12, no. 4 (1995): 673–694.

SKOGAN, WESLEY G. *Disorder and Decline: Crime and the Spiral of Decay in American Neighborhoods.* New York: Free Press, 1990.

SNOW, DAVID A.; BAKER, SUSAN G.; and ANDERSON, LEON. "Criminality and Homeless Men: An Empirical Assessment." *Social Problems* 36, no. 5 (1989): 532–549.

STRAUS, MURRAY A. "The Controversy over Domestic Violence by Women: A Methodological, Theoretical, and Sociology of Science Analysis." In *Violence in Intimate Relationships.* Edited by X. B. Arriaga and S. Oskamp. Thousand Oaks, Calif.: Sage, 1999. Pages 17–44.

TEPLIN, LINDA A. "Criminalizing Mental Disorder: The Comparative Arrest Rates of the Mentally Ill." *American Psychologist* 39 (1984): 794–803.

TEPLIN, LINDA A., and PRUETT, NANCY S. "Police as Streetcorner Psychiatrist: Managing the Mentally Ill." *International Journal of Law and Psychiatry* 15 (1992): 139–156.

WACHOLZ, S., and MULLALY, R. "Policing the Deinstitutionalized Mentally Ill: Toward an Understanding of its Function." *Crime, Law, and Social Change* 19 (1993): 281–300.

WALKER, SAMUEL. *Sense and Nonsense about Crime and Drugs: A Policy Guide.* 4th ed. Belmont, Calif.: West / Wadsworth, 1989.

———. *The Police in America.* 3d ed. Boston, Mass.: McGraw-Hill College, 1999.

WALKER, SAMUEL; SPOHN, CASSIA; and DELONE, MIRIAM. *The Color of Justice: Race Ethnicity and Crime in America.* 2d ed. Belmont, Calif.: Wadsworth, Thomson Learning, 2000.

WEISBURD, DAVID, and GREEN, LORRAINE. "Policing Hot Spots: The Jersey City Drug Market Analysis Experiment." *Justice Quarterly* 12, no. 4 (1995): 771–736.

WILLIAMS, HUBERT, and MURPHY, PATRICK V. "The Evolving Strategy of Police: A Minority Perspective." *Perspectives on Policing* 13. Washington, D.C.: National Institute of Justice, 1990.

WILSON, JAMES Q., and KELLING, GEORGE L. "Broken Windows: The Police and Neighborhood Safety." *The Atlantic Monthly* (no. 249, 1982), pp. 29–38.

WORDEN, ROBERT E. "The Causes of Police Brutality: Theory and Evidence on Police Use of Force." In *Police Violence: Understanding and Controlling Police Abuse of Force.* Edited by William A. Geller and Hans Toch. New Haven,

Conn.: Yale University Press, 1996. Pages 25–51.

WORDEN, ROBERT E., and POLLITZ, ALISSA A. "Police Arrests in Domestic Disturbances: A Further Look." *Law & Society Review* 18 (1984): 105–119.

CASES

City of Chicago v. Morales.
Tennessee v. Garner, 105 S. Ct. 1694 (1985).

V

VAGRANCY AND DISORDERLY CONDUCT

Vagrancy and disorderly conduct are examples of a category of legal prohibitions commonly referred to as *public order offenses*. Such offenses share a number of general characteristics. They usually prohibit relatively trivial types of public misconduct such as, for example, aggressive panhandling, public drinking, or loitering in the vicinity of an automated teller machine. In the main, they provide for comparatively low-level punishments. In addition, police commonly exercise a considerable degree of discretion in the enforcement of public order laws. This is partly because such laws are often not formally enforced even when they are clearly violated. Instead, these laws are frequently invoked by police informally, to require offenders to put an end to behaviors seen to threaten the public peace. Public order offenses thus provide police with the legal authority to discharge their "order maintenance" or "peacekeeping" responsibilities, meaning those responsibilities associated with helping to maintain order in public places, as opposed to enforcing the criminal law.

It is impossible to provide a precise definition of either vagrancy or disorderly conduct. These offenses have been described differently at different times and the laws treating them have varied considerably from state to state. Historically, however, state legislatures and municipal authorities in the United States tended to define vagrancy and disorderly conduct very broadly so that these offenses operated, in effect, as catch-all provisions that subjected a wide variety of public behaviors and conditions to police authority. Vagrancy laws were often drafted not to prohibit particular acts of public misconduct, but instead to criminalize statuses—such as being a rogue, a known criminal, a vagabond, a loiterer, a habitual loafer, or a common thief. Thirty categories of vagrancy were identified in 1962 as then existing in laws to be found throughout the United States (Note). Similarly, disorderly conduct at around this time was in some places defined simply as being a vagrant. Even when disorderly conduct laws prohibited behaviors, rather than statuses, moreover, these behaviors were often defined very generally to include any conduct that tended to disturb the safety, health, or morals of others.

During the period from the 1950s into the 1970s, public order laws of this type were increasingly seen to pose significant problems. They imposed criminal sanctions on conditions or behaviors—like poverty or alcohol abuse—that were viewed by many as social or medical problems not properly within the ambit of criminal law. In addition, the breadth and vagueness of such laws conferred considerable discretion on police as to how they should be enforced—discretion that was frequently exercised in ways that discriminated against racial or ethnic minorities, as well as the poor. Because the penalties for public order offenses were often relatively trivial, moreover, the real punishment for such infractions was often simply the inconvenience and embarrassment of an arrest—a punishment that could be meted out solely at the hands of police. The criminal courts charged with handling prosecutions involving these low-level offenses were also poorly run and often failed to afford defendants even the basic essentials of a fair adjudication. Philadelphia magistrates' courts in the early 1950s, for example, routinely handled fifty or more cases in fifteen minutes or less. Mostly un-counseled defendants were rarely even informed of the charges, nor was there even a pretense of proving these charges by competent evidence.

The concerns of this period produced calls for legislative reform and some movement in this direction. Moreover, a rise in crime in the 1960s coupled with other factors, including a growing emphasis among police on criminal investigation, led many police departments in the 1960s and 1970s to de-emphasize order maintenance and to focus resources on the enforcement of laws against serious crime. Perhaps the most significant change in the area of public order law and its administration during this period, however, came as a result of federal constitutional decisions. Supreme Court cases extended the right to counsel and jury trial in the prosecution of many petty offenses. The Court rejected status as a basis for the imposition of criminal sanctions. Most significantly, many public order laws were invalidated as unconstitutionally vague or overboard.

This entry briefly describes the history of the broad "vagrancy-style" public order offenses invalidated during the 1960s and 1970s. It also discusses the Supreme Court cases that dramatically changed public order law and its administration during this period. Finally, the entry recounts how a growing emphasis on community policing and the quality of life in public spaces in the 1980s and 1990s sparked renewed interest in order maintenance by police. It describes how state legislatures and municipalities in the 1990s attempted to enact constitutionally acceptable public order laws to address the concerns with this class of offenses while at the same time affording police legitimate authority to be used in the amelioration of problems of crime and disorder.

History

The roots of laws against vagrancy and disorderly conduct in the United States can be traced to England. The breakup of feudal estates in fourteenth-century England, combined with severe regional labor shortages caused by the Black Death, resulted in the enactment of the Statute of Labourers in England (23 Edw. 3, New Statute, c. 1 (1349) (repealed) and 25 Edw. 3, Stat. 1, c. 1 (1350) (repealed)). The Statute of Labourers attempted to control the wandering of former serfs by requiring able-bodied persons without means of support to work for fixed wages and to

refrain from traveling about the country to find better wages or to avoid offers of work. Originally aimed at enforcing labor, the English vagrancy laws came to be seen as serving other interests in the sixteenth and seventeenth centuries. Various conditions in England during this period, including the destruction of the monasteries during the reign of Henry VIII and the enactment of the enclosure acts (see *Ledwith v. Roberts*, (1936) 3 All E.R. 570, 585, 594 (C.A.)), which converted agricultural land into pasture for sheep, gave rise to a mass of people who wandered the country without means of livelihood. The vagrancy laws at this time were seen to protect local residents from the perceived potential criminality of vagrants and to safeguard parishes and municipalities from the financial burden of caring for nonresidents.

These policies underlying the English vagrancy laws were transplanted to colonial America. Under the Articles of Confederation, "paupers" and "vagabonds" were excepted from the guarantee of free movement between the states (art. 4). At the time of the founding, state and local governments customarily criminalized various forms of vagrancy, including loitering in public places. During the nineteenth century, the Supreme Court observed that it is "as competent and as necessary for a State to provide precautionary measures against the moral pestilence of paupers, vagabonds, and possibly convicts, as it is to guard against the physical pestilence. . . ." (*Mayor of City of New York v. Miln*, 36 U.S. (11 Pet.) 102, 143 (1837)). Until the mid-1960s, most states had broad vagrancy, loitering, and disorderly conduct laws. Vagrancy-style laws were employed at various times and in varying ways throughout American history to control the migration of the unemployed. They were also used after the Civil War to keep former slaves in conditions of servitude. During the Jim Crow era, vagrancy laws criminalizing the status of being unemployed were sometimes invoked to pressure African Americans to enter into unfavorable labor contracts.

Public order laws were rarely challenged in the courts until the 1960s, when attorneys became more widely available to the indigent following the Supreme Court's decision in *Gideon v. Wainwright*, 372 U.S. 335 (1963), which held that felony defendants unable to afford an attorney must be provided with one at state expense. A Jacksonville, Florida, ordinance reviewed by the Supreme Court in *Papachristou v. Jacksonville*, 405 U.S. 156 (1972), was characteristic of the vagrancy laws to be found in many localities during the period leading into the mid-1960s:

Rogues and vagabonds, or dissolute persons who go about begging, common gamblers, persons who use juggling or unlawful games or plays, common drunkards, common night walkers, thieves, pilferers or pickpockets, traders in stolen property, lewd, wanton and lascivious persons, keepers of gambling places, common railers and brawlers, persons wandering or strolling around from place to place without any lawful purpose or object, habitual loafers, disorderly persons, persons neglecting all lawful business and habitually spending their time by frequenting houses of ill fame, gaming houses, or places where alcoholic beverages are sold or served, persons able to work but habitually living upon the earnings of their wives or minor children shall be deemed vagrants. . . . (156 n.1)

Typical disorderly conduct laws of the period often contained general provisions prohibiting acts likely "to unreasonably disturb or alarm the public" (*Garner v. Louisiana*, 368 U.S. 157, 165 (1961)), as well as provisions aimed at "breach[es] of the peace,. . .riotous or disorderly conduct, open obscenity, public drunkenness or any other conduct grossly indecent or dangerous to. . .citizens" (*Barr v. City of Columbia*, 378 U.S. 146, 148 n.2 (1964)).

Such laws were sometimes said to assist in crime prevention by authorizing police to intervene early in suspicious circumstances, before people had the opportunity to engage in serious criminal activity. Because these laws were vague in terminology and often did not predicate arrest on the commission of any specific act, however, they were also said to invite arbitrary and discriminatory enforcement. Critics charged that public order laws were sometimes used for purposes like breaking strikes or "rounding up" ostensible suspects (for whom there was no individualized suspicion) when a crime had been committed. Caleb Foote documented how these laws were employed by Philadelphia police in the 1950s to "clean up" city neighborhoods by summarily removing prostitutes, drunks, and other "undesirables" from public places (Foote). In addition, public order laws were sometimes improperly invoked by police during civil rights struggles in the South. Indeed, the immediate impetus for the Supreme Court's consideration of cases involving public order laws during the 1960s was often the use of such laws against participants in peaceful sit-ins and civil rights demonstrations.

Constitutional considerations

A number of Supreme Court cases decided in the 1960s and 1970s have affected the scope and administration of public order laws. *Argersinger v. Hamlin*, 407 U.S. 25 (1972), for instance, held that absent a waiver, no person may be imprisoned for an offense, even if it is classified as a misdemeanor or petty offense, unless represented by counsel. The Court held in *Baldwin v. New York*, 399 U.S. 66 (1970), that the right to jury trial applies to any offense for which imprisonment for more than six months is authorized. Though these cases by no means resolved all problems of fairness in the administration of public order laws, they did dramatically transform and improve procedure in the lower criminal courts, where public order offenses are generally prosecuted.

In 1962, the Court decided a case that had far-reaching implications for the scope of vagrancy-style laws. In *Robinson v. California*, 370 U.S. 660 (1962), the Court invalidated a state law that made it a crime to be a narcotics addict, stating that it violated the Eighth Amendment's prohibition against cruel and unusual punishment. In a later case, a plurality of the Court interpreted *Robinson* to mean that the punishment of "mere status" is unconstitutional: "[C]riminal penalties may be inflicted only if the accused has committed some act . . . which society has an interest in preventing" (*Powell v. Texas*, 392 U.S. 514, 533 (1968)). Though *Robinson* did not arise under a vagrancy or disorderly conduct law, its holding cast serious doubt on the constitutional validity of any public order law that provided for punishment of one's status as a common drunkard, loiterer, or the like, without proof of the commission of some criminal act.

In cases like *Gooding v. Wilson*, 405 U.S. 518 (1972), the Court next drew into question those public order laws with potential application to protected First Amendment activity. In *Gooding*, the Court invoked its overbreadth doctrine to invalidate a statute providing for the punishment of anyone "who shall, without provocation, use to or of another, and in his presence . . . opprobrious words or abusive language, tending to cause a breach of the peace" (405 U.S. at 519). In its traditional and most common form, the overbreadth doctrine permits individuals in certain circumstances to challenge a law, even when their own conduct might validly be prohibited under it, when the law could potentially reach activity that falls within the protections afforded to freedom of speech. The theory underlying this doctrine is that "overbroad" laws—laws reaching conduct legitimately prohibited by legislatures, but also constitutionally protected activity—should not be permitted to stand, lest they chill conduct that is deserving of constitutional protection. This doctrine led to the invalidation of a number of broadly worded laws prohibiting breaches of the peace in the 1960s and 1970s.

The Court did not directly address the constitutional status of a vagrancy law until 1972. In *Papachristou*, the Court invalidated Jacksonville's vagrancy ordinance as "void for vagueness." The Court held that the law violated the Constitution's due process guarantee by failing to give ordinary persons fair notice that contemplated conduct was forbidden and by encouraging arbitrary and erratic arrests and convictions. Writing for a unanimous Court, Justice William O. Douglas placed particular stress on the argument that an "all-inclusive and generalized" list of crimes that included such things as wandering or strolling about from place to place without lawful purpose encouraged discriminatory law enforcement (405 U.S. 166). In the Court's words:

The implicit presumption in these generalized vagrancy standards—that crime is being nipped in the bud—is too extravagant to deserve extended treatment. Of course, vagrancy statutes are useful to the police. Of course, they are nets making easy the roundup of so-called undesirables. But the rule of law implies equality and justice in its application. Vagrancy laws of the Jacksonville type teach that the scales of justice are so tipped that even-handed administration of the law is not possible. (405 U.S. 171)

Though it was not a basis for the Court's holding, the *Papachristou* opinion also observed that the Florida ordinance's classifications, which originated in the early English poor laws, were archaic: "The Jacksonville ordinance makes criminal activities which by modern standards are normally innocent" (405 U.S. 163).

The void-for-vagueness doctrine invoked by the Court in *Papachristou* was the basis for many lower federal and state court decisions invalidating vagrancy and disorderly conduct laws, both immediately before and after the Court's decision in that case. After the ruling in *Papachristou*, many states repealed their vagrancy laws, often replacing such elements of vagrancy as being a common prostitute or a habitual drunkard with separate, conduct-based offenses dealing with prostitution, public intoxication, and the like. Disorderly conduct laws remained common, but

in many places were substantially revised, often along the lines suggested in the American Law Institute's Model Penal Code. The revisions aimed to make disorderly conduct laws more precise and to hinge punishment on the commission of specific acts, rather than on statuses.

Papachristou and related cases were extremely important to the legal authority of police to maintain order in public places. Collectively, these cases established that police could no longer enforce public order laws so vague that they in effect empowered police to devise their own standards of public decorum. Public order laws were required not only to deal with prohibited acts, rather than statuses, but to do so in language of adequate definiteness—in language clear enough to constrain the opportunity for arbitrariness on the part of local law enforcement.

Significantly, however, *Papachristou* did not articulate how far courts should go in demanding specificity in public order laws. Within months of the *Papachristou* decision, the Court noted in *Grayned v. City of Rockford*, 408 U.S. 104, 108 (1972), that courts could not require mathematical certainty in the language of such laws and that the exercise of some degree of police judgment in the employment of public order laws is necessary. Defining limits on the circumstances in which courts would entertain wholesale challenges to laws regulating trivial forms of public misconduct, however, was not of pressing concern by the time *Papachristou* was decided. Police had already shifted their attention away from order maintenance to focus on serious crime. Patrol by automobile, rapid response to calls for service, and the retrospective investigation of serious offenses—none of which involves police in the routine employment of public order laws—had become the principal operating strategies of police departments. It was not until the 1980s and 1990s that changes in policing philosophy caused many police departments to afford order maintenance a higher priority. Accordingly, it was at this time that the *Papachristou* reforms came up for closer reexamination.

Community policing and public order law

The emergence of community policing in the 1980s produced renewed interest in order maintenance by police. Community policing is a policing philosophy that grew out of perceived inadequacies in earlier approaches to local law enforcement. Broadly, community policing holds that police can more effectively address crime and disorder when they develop working relationships with people in the communities they police. It draws upon the idea of community-police reciprocity "to redefine the overall purposes of policing, to alter the principal operating programs and technologies on which the police have relied, and to found the legitimacy and popularity of policing on new grounds" (Moore). Among other characteristics, police in a community policing regime focus more attention on crime prevention and the quality of life in local neighborhoods. They may place emphasis on foot patrols and community organizing. They are more open to community-nominated problems and priorities.

Hundreds of police departments across the country began experimenting with community policing in the 1980s and 1990s. This provoked new interest in order maintenance in part because police learned from consultation with community members that people were extremely concerned with "low-level" matters like chronic vandalism, loitering gang members, and unsafe parks. Perhaps the most important ingredient in the revival of interest in order maintenance, however, was a 1982 essay by James Q. Wilson and George Kelling entitled "Broken Windows."

"Broken Windows" argued that the narrow focus of many police departments on the investigation of serious crime had resulted in the atrophy of a vital police role in promoting the quality of life in local neighborhoods. The fear endemic in many big-city neighborhoods in the early 1980s, Wilson and Kelling argued, stemmed as much from fear of disorderly conditions as from a realistic appraisal of residents' likelihood of being victimized by serious crime. Residents' fear of disorder should nevertheless be addressed, they contended, because such fear weakens a neighborhood's informal social control mechanisms by causing fearful residents to retreat from public places and from intervention in the matters occurring there. This abandonment of public spaces, Wilson and Kelling argued, damages residents' quality of life and even renders neighborhoods more vulnerable to criminal invasion. Wilson and Kelling urged that patrol officers should be deployed on foot, at least in those neighborhoods where they might help strengthen informal social ties, that they should be significantly neighborhood-oriented, and, in particular, that patrol officers should attend to matters like abandoned property, accumulating litter, inebriates slumped on neighborhood side-

walks, and teenagers loitering or fighting in front of stores.

"Broken Windows" 's critique of dominant trends in American policing that had de-emphasized the order maintenance function was extraordinarily influential. It helped to stimulate the community policing movement and to revive interest in many localities in addressing minor disorder. Beginning in the early 1990s, municipalities across the country began to enact ordinances or take other legal steps to ameliorate public order problems. Juvenile curfews, for instance, became the norm in major American cities (Ruefle and Reynolds). Anti-drug and prostitution loitering ordinances were enacted in many places, as were laws directed at aggressive panhandling, loitering in the vicinity of automatic teller machines, automobile cruising, and the like. These new laws were generally much more specific than the broad public order laws invalidated during the 1960s and 1970s. Significantly, they also received critical support in several places from African Americans who historically had been principal targets of repressive order maintenance policing but who now supported the measured use of public order laws by politically accountable police to address serious problems of crime and disorder (Kahan and Meares).

These developments raised the question of how courts would treat this new generation of public order laws. Several federal appellate courts rejected vagueness and other constitutional challenges to juvenile curfews in the 1990s, though in some places courts did invalidate such laws. Ordinances prohibiting automobile cruising and aggressive panhandling were generally upheld in the face of constitutional attack. Courts split, however, on the constitutionality of drug and prostitution loitering ordinances, with a number of judges viewing such laws as overly vague or overbroad.

The Supreme Court addressed the constitutionality of one of these new public order laws in *Chicago v. Morales*, 527 U.S. 41 (1999). The case involved a Chicago, Illinois, ordinance that authorized police to order any group of two or more people found loitering in public places to move along on pain of arrest, so long as at least one of the group was reasonably believed to be a member of a criminal street gang. The ordinance was enacted in 1992, during a period of extraordinary gang violence in Chicago. The Chicago City Council issued findings that were included in the text of the law to explain the reasons for its enactment. These findings asserted, among other things, that street gangs had "taken over" entire neighborhoods in Chicago by intimidating residents from using public places. The gang loitering law was directed at regaining control of these public areas.

Morales produced six different opinions. The lead opinion, by Justice John Paul Stevens, was joined in full by only two Justices and in part by three others. The *Morales* majority concluded, in an extremely narrow holding, that the Chicago ordinance's definition of loitering ("to remain in any one place with no apparent purpose") was unconstitutionally vague in that it failed to set sufficiently specific limitations on the enforcement discretion of Chicago police (527 U.S. at 60–65). A plurality composed of Justices Stevens, Ruth Bader Ginsburg, and David Souter went further to opine that the freedom to loiter for innocent purposes is an attribute of personal liberty protected by the Constitution's due process clause. These three Justices in effect concluded that loitering is a constitutionally protected activity and that there are thus limits on the ability of localities to regulate it.

On the whole, however, the *Morales* opinions suggested a willingness on the part of the Court to uphold many laws regulating the use of public spaces, including laws directed at activities like loitering. Three Justices dissented in *Morales* and concluded that Chicago's gang loitering law was plainly constitutional. Significantly, even the majority opinion concluded that loitering by gang members could be regulated. Indeed, this opinion asserted that an ordinance limited to loitering by gang members that had an apparently harmful purpose would satisfy the vagueness doctrine. In an opinion concurring in part and concurring in the judgment, Justice Sandra Day O'Connor, joined by Justice Stephen Breyer, suggested several additional ways in which Chicago might constitutionally prohibit gang members from loitering in public places so as to intimidate others from using them.

Morales thus offered municipalities room in which to continue to experiment with affording police new authority to address public order concerns. Indeed, in the wake of the *Morales* decision, the Chicago City Council enacted a new gang loitering ordinance on the lines suggested by the majority opinion.

This is not to conclude, however, that all problems in the administration of public order laws evaporated once state and local legislatures narrowed the scope of such laws. In fact, the new public order laws of the 1990s raised many of the same concerns associated with earlier vagrancy and disorderly conduct laws. These concerns sometimes centered on whether the criminal law was the most effective mechanism for dealing with specific public order problems. Many communities during this period successfully addressed some such problems with programs that involved noncriminal sanctions or that combined law enforcement with various forms of social service.

Perhaps the most consistent area of concern, however, involved the ways in which police exercise discretion in order maintenance. In many places, a new emphasis on public order in the 1990s did help renew public confidence in the ability of police to contribute to the well-being of the neighborhoods they serve. Elsewhere, however, police initiatives directed at crime and disorder provoked legitimate anxiety about police intrusiveness, particularly as directed at minorities and the homeless.

At the same time, it became increasingly evident during this decade that the judicial invalidation of reasonably specific public order laws was not the answer to police misuse of such laws. Because police decide when, where, and whether to enforce public order laws, they exercise considerable discretion in this area even when public order laws prohibit narrowly defined behaviors, and even when such laws are very precise. The proper exercise of this discretion, however, can be very beneficial to communities and need not lead to police abuse.

In the late 1990s, increased attention came to be paid to ways in which communities might exercise better political and administrative control over the performance of police order maintenance responsibilities. There was experimentation with civilian complaint review boards and early warning systems, both designed in part to alert police administrators to problem officers who might be misusing their authority. Attention was paid to guidelines that might inform police in the exercise of their discretion, as well as to the role elected officials might play in overseeing police departments. Mechanisms for the political and administrative constraint of police were still developing at the end of the decade. Commentators argued, however, that changes in political conditions since the 1960s related to the growing political power of minority communities rendered such mechanisms viable and, further, that such mechanisms constituted more reliable controls on police discretion than the search by judges for textural precision in public order laws (Kahan and Meares).

DEBRA LIVINGSTON

See also CRIME: DEFINITION; CRIMINALIZATION AND DECRIMINALIZATION; DRUGS AND CRIME: LEGAL ASPECTS; JUVENILE AND YOUTH GANGS; POLICE: POLICING COMPLAINANTLESS CRIMES; RIOTS: BEHAVIORAL ASPECTS; RIOTS: LEGAL ASPECTS; VICTIMLESS CRIMES.

BIBLIOGRAPHY

ALSCHULER, ALBERT W., and SCHULHOFER, STEPHEN J. "Antiquated Procedures or Bedrock Rights? A Response to Professors Meares and Kahan." *University of Chicago Legal Forum* (1998): 215–244.

American Law Institute. *Model Penal Code and Commentaries: Official Draft and Revised Comments.* 3 vols. Philadelphia: ALI, 1980.

FEELEY, MALCOLM M. *Court Reform on Trial.* New York: Basic Books, 1983.

FOOTE, CALEB. "Vagrancy-Type Law and Its Administration." *University of Pennsylvania Law Review* 104 (1956): 603–650.

FORCE, ROBERT. "Decriminalization of Breach of the Peace Statutes: A Nonpenal Approach to Order Maintenance." *Tulane Law Review* 46 (1972): 367–435.

HASCOURT, BERNARD E. "Reflecting on the Subject: A Critique of the Social Influence Conception of Deterrence, the Broken Window Theory, and Order-Maintenance Policy New York Style."*Michigan Law Review* 97 (1998): 291–389.

JEFFRIES, JOHN CALVIN, JR. "Legality, Vagueness, and the Construction of Penal Statutes" *Virginia Law Review* 71 (1985): 189–245.

KAHAN, DAN M., and MEARES, TRACEY L. "Foreword: The Coming Crisis of Criminal Procedure." *Georgetown Law Journal* 86 (1998): 1153–1184.

KELLING, GEORGE L., and MOORE, MARK H. "From Political to Reform to Community: The Evolving Strategy of Police." In *Community Policing: Rhetoric or Reality.* Edited by Jack R. Greene and Stephen D. Mastrofski. New York: Praeger, 1988. Pages 3–25.

KENNEDY, RANDALL. *Race, Crime, and the Law.* New York: Pantheon Books, 1997.

LACEY, FORREST W. "Vagrancy and Other Crimes of Personal Condition." *Harvard Law Review* 66 (1953): 1203–1226.

LIVINGSTON, DEBRA. "Police Discretion and the Quality of Life in Public Places: Courts, Communities, and the New Policing." *Columbia Law Review* 97 (1997): 551–672.

———. "Gang Loitering, the Court, and Some Realism about Police Patrol." *Supreme Court Review* (1999): 141–202.

MEARES, TRACEY L., and KAHAN, DAN M. "The Wages of Antiquated Procedural Thinking: A Critique of *Chicago v. Morales*." *University of Chicago Legal Forum* (1998): 197–214.

———. "Black, White, and Gray: A Reply to Alschuler and Schulhofer." *University of Chicago Legal Forum* (1998): 245–259.

MOORE, MARK HARRISON. "Problem-solving and Community Policing." In *Modern Policing.* Edited by Michael Tonry and Norval Morris. Chicago: University of Chicago Press, 1992. Pages 99–158.

Note. "The Vagrancy Concept Reconsidered: Problems and Abuses of Status Criminality." *New York University Law Review* 37 (1962): 102–136.

PERKINS, ROLLIN M. "The Vagrancy Concept." *Hastings Law Journal* 9 (1958): 237–261.

RUEFLE, WILLIAM, and REYNOLDS, KENNETH MIKE. "Curfews and Delinquency in Major American Cities." *Crime and Delinquency* 41 (1995): 347–363.

SHERRY, ARTHUR H. "Vagrants, Rogues, and Vagabonds: Old Concepts in Need of Revision." *California Law Review* 48 (1960): 557–573.

WILSON, JAMES Q., and KELLING, GEORGE L. "Broken Windows." In *Critical Issues in Policing.* Edited by Roger G. Dunham and Geoffrey P. Alpert. Prospect Heights, Ill.: Waveland Press, 1993. A reprint of the original article that appeared in the March 1982 issue of *Atlantic Monthly*.

CASES

Argersinger v. Hamlin, 407 U.S. 25 (1972).
Barr v. City of Columbia, 378 U.S. 146 (1964).
Chicago v. Morales, 527 U.S. 41 (1999).
Garner v. Louisiana, 368 U.S. 157 (1961).
Gideon v. Wainwright, 372 U.S. 335 (1963).
Gooding v. Wilson, 405 U.S. 518 (1972).
Grayned v. City of Rockford, 408 U.S. 104 (1972).
Mayor of City of New York v. Miln, 36 U.S. (11 Pet.) 102 (1837).
Papachristou v. Jacksonville, 405 U.S. 156 (1972).
Powell v. Texas, 392 U.S. 514 (1968).
Robinson v. California, 370 U.S. 660 (1962).

VENUE

Venue is the appropriate place of trial, as between different geographical subdivisions of a state or between different federal districts It is determined by constitutional, statutory, and administrative provisions. Venue should be distinguished from the related concepts of jurisdiction, vicinage, and cross-sectional representation.

Subject matter jurisdiction, which includes territorial jurisdiction, is a court's power to try cases based on a state's sovereign power to make laws for acts that occur in or have an effect in its territory. Lack of venue in one situs can result in the transfer of a prosecution to another county or district, while lack of jurisdiction terminates the prosecution by other courts of the same sovereign. Although venue can be waived or conferred by consent, jurisdiction cannot.

Vicinage is the right to be tried by a jury drawn from the vicinity in which the crime occurred. Although a defendant may claim it, the vicinage requirement protects the right of the offended community to pass judgment in criminal matters. Venue and vicinage are usually the same, but a jury of the vicinage may decide a case in which venue has been moved to another district.

The right to cross-sectional representation is a demographic requirement, which assures a criminal defendant a trial by a jury selected without systematic or intentional exclusion of cognizable economic, social, religious, racial, political, and geographical groups. In recent times, decisions regarding change of venue have raised questions concerning cross-sectional representation, leading some commentators to suggest that changes of venue be made to a district or county with a similar racial composition as the original venue.

The U.S. Constitution guarantees trial by jury and venue ". . . in the State where the said Crimes shall have been committed; but when not committed in any State, the Trial shall be at such Place or Places as the Congress may by Law have directed" (Article III, section 2, clause 3). The Framers' concern for the locality of criminal prosecutions was generated by the threat of the Crown to try American revolutionaries in England or other colonies. This was condemned in the Declaration of Independence, charging the King for "transporting us beyond Seas to be tried for pretended offenses." The Sixth Amendment includes a vicinage right, often treated as a venue provision, that draws vicinage more tightly than Article III venue: "In all criminal prosecutions the accused shall enjoy the right to a speedy and public trial, by an impartial jury of the State and district wherein the crime shall have been committed, which district shall have been previously ascertained by law."

The Framers' belief that venue is an important safeguard to liberty has been borne out in political trials. There is strong historical evidence that President Thomas Jefferson sought a venue favorable to the prosecution of Aaron Burr for treason in 1807. An account of a more recent trial of political dissidents suggests that federal prosecutors virtually constructed a group of conspirators in the 1968 trial of Dr. Benjamin Spock for antidraft activity during the Vietnam War in order to find a more favorable venue (Boston) than New York or Washington, where prominent antiwar activity occurred.

The Supreme Court has not coherently articulated underlying venue policy. Although it has, at times, suggested that fairness and convenience to defendants should be the underlying policy, it has more often ruled that the basic requirement of placing venue in the district wherein the crime has been committed must be determined from the nature of the crime alleged and the location of the act or acts constituting it. The Court has said that questions of venue in criminal cases "are not merely matters of formal legal procedure. They raise deep issues of public policy in the light of which legislation must be construed" (*United States v. Johnson*). The Federal Rules of Criminal Procedure adhere to the basic rule that the prosecution shall be had in a district in which the offense was committed, but allow the courts to consider such factors as the convenience of defendants and witnesses and the prompt administration of justice in setting venue and considering motions for the change of venue.

There is no single defined policy or mechanical test to determine constitutional venue. In determining proper venue federal courts have created a number of tests. These tests may be complementary, overlapping, or contradictory in their effects, thus creating confusion in properly laying venue. Where the crime is unambiguously committed in one district, the venue lies there. At common law there was a single situs test that was modified by statute when that rule proved too restrictive. Where the acts constituting the crime and the nature of the crime charged implicate more than one location, the constitution does not command a single venue. A variation of the single situs test is that for some crimes venue lays in the district in which the effects of the act occur. Thus, in a homicide prosecution, where the act or omission is inflicted in one venue and the victim dies in another, English statutes placed venue in the place where death occurred, but the federal statute lays venue in the district where the injury was inflicted. Advances in communications and transportation and the expansion of federal criminal law have made it increasingly difficult to determine where, for the purpose of laying venue, a crime is committed.

Congress usually appends a venue provision to criminal statutes, which provides a method of fixing the place of prosecution. Congress is free to establish venue in any district that has a minimal contact with the crime. To this end, Congress has provided that "any offense against the United States begun in one district and completed in another, or committed in more than one district, may be inquired of and prosecuted in any district in which such offense was begun, continued, or completed." As a general rule, then, venue in "continuing crimes" may be laid in any district in which the crime occurred. Venue in conspiracy cases, for example, is proper in any district where the agreement was formed or where an overt act in furtherance of the conspiracy was performed. On the other hand, federal courts have held that venue for the prosecution of a substantive crime that arises out of a conspiracy lies only in the district where the substantive crime occurred. To lay venue in any district in which the conspiracy occurred would in effect engraft a forum shopping option as to the substantive offense on the already broad venue rule for conspiracy.

When a statute contains no venue provision, the situs of the crime must be determined from the nature of the crime alleged and the location of the act constituting it (*United States v. Anderson*). To this end federal courts have had recourse to a "key verbs" or "essential verbs" test. This has led to formalistic decisions. For example, the Court held that in a prosecution for failure to file a required statement regarding the harboring of an alien, venue was improperly laid in the defendant's home district in the state of Washington because filing does not occur until the document is delivered and received. Since the culpable omission was "committed" where the duty should have been performed, venue lay only in the District of Columbia and not where the required statement would normally be prepared and mailed (*United States v. Lombardo*).

The limitations of the key verbs test is seen in the current division among federal circuits over where to lay venue in prosecutions for obstruction of justice when the defendant allegedly acted in one judicial district to obstruct a proceeding that was pending in another. The obstruction of justice statute is complex and includes verbs that point to venue where the acts occurred ("injures") or in the affected or "focus" district ("influences"). It is apparent that in some instances, the key verbs test is no test at all.

The examination of verbs, as the Supreme Court has made clear, is not an exclusive method of determining the proper venue. Another, somewhat broader, test used by some courts is the "elements of the crime" test, said to be more true to the overriding principle that venue depends on the nature of the crime. Courts have also examined legislative intent. A test supported by many commentators may be called the "ease of fact finding" test. The source of this test is an opinion by Justice John Marshall Harlan, dissenting in a case where a union officer was charged with making and filing false affidavits with the National Labor Relations Board (NLRB). The majority held that venue lay only in Washington, D.C., where the documents were sent, and not in the district (Colorado) where the affidavits were made (*Travis v. United States*). The fact-finding test examines the nature of the crime alleged and the location of the act or acts constituting it. This test views the basic policy of the Sixth Amendment as providing for trial in the vicinity of the crime as a safeguard against the unfairness and hardship involved when an accused is prosecuted in a remote place. Thus, where a minimal contact exists, venue lies where the witnesses and relevant circumstances surrounding the contested issues more probably will be found.

An even broader "substantial contacts" rule incorporates several of the previously noted tests and takes them all into account—the site of defendants' acts, the elements and nature of the crime, the locus of the effect of the criminal conduct, and the suitability of each district for accurate fact-finding. This approach is taken by the Second Circuit and results in the greater likelihood that venue will be found to exist in the district of the trial (*United States v. Reed*).

After a hiatus of two decades, the Supreme Court has begun to resolve conflicts regarding venue, holding in *United States v. Cabrales* (1998) that venue for a prosecution for money laundering is the district where the money laundering took place and not the district of the anterior criminal conduct that yielded the funds allegedly laundered. The *Cabrales* case, holding the government to a strict account of venue, appears to express a different policy concern than the decision in *United States v. Rodriguez-Moreno* (1999), which held that the venue for a prosecution of the crime of using a firearm during a crime of violence may be laid in any district where the predicate crime of violence occurred, even if no weapon was used in that district. The Court, in deprecating the verb test, expressed a concern that a close adherence to that test "creates a danger that certain conduct prohibited by statute will be missed." Thus, the Court's recent venue rulings again fail to provide a consistent policy.

Venue is a fact that the prosecution must prove. Beyond this, rules as to the proof of venue vary among jurisdictions. Some states have a statutory presumption that venue is proper in the absence of contrary evidence. The federal rule is that venue may be proven by a preponderance of the evidence. This is followed by a majority of states ruling on the question, based on the idea that venue is neither an essential element of a crime nor of the same nature as defenses that relate to guilt or innocence. The Model Penal Code and a few states have ruled that venue must be proven beyond a reasonable doubt. This rule is based upon the view that venue is a material fact or issue in a criminal prosecution that the prosecution is required to prove.

Under the Federal Rules of Criminal Procedure a defendant can move for a change of venue because of prejudice in the district depriving the defendant of a fair trial, for the convenience of parties and witnesses, and in the interest of justice. A motion for change of venue is addressed to the sound discretion of the trial judge. The Supreme Court noted nine factors to be considered in making a change of venue determination for the convenience of the parties: (1) location of the defendant; (2) location of witnesses; (3) location of events likely to be in issue; (4) location of documents and records; (5) disruption of the defendant's business; (6) expense to the parties; (7) location of counsel; (8) relative accessibility of place of trial; and (9) docket conditions in each district (*Platt v. Minnesota Mining & Mfg. Co.*). A district court can transfer the prosecution to any district, including a district in which no part of the offense was committed.

State venue and change of venue provisions parallel federal venue rules. Some state laws provide that venue for offenses committed near the boundary between counties is proper in either county. When a crime is committed on a train or other public conveyance, the "common carrier exception" allows venue to be laid in any county through which the vehicle passed, even if it is clear that all of the elements of the crime occurred in one county. The states are split on whether a prosecutor may seek a change of venue, and some states restrict the number of times that a change of venue is permitted. Some states allow a change of venue on the grounds of the bias or prejudice of the judge, as well as on such factors as pretrial publicity and the convenience of the parties.

MARVIN ZALMAN

See also FEDERAL CRIMINAL JURISDICTION; JURISDICTION; JURY: LEGAL ASPECTS; PUBLICITY IN CRIMINAL CASES.

BIBLIOGRAPHY

CASES

Platt v. Minnesota Mining & Mfg. Co., 376 U.S. 240 (1964).
Travis v. United States, 364 U.S. 631 (1961).
United States v. Anderson, 328 U.S. 699 (1946).
United States v. Cabrales, 524 U.S. 1 (1998).
United States v. Johnson, 323 U.S. 273 (1944).
United States v. Lombardo, 241 U.S. 73 (1916).
United States v. Reed, 773 F.2d 477 (2nd Cir. 1985).
United States v. Rodriguez-Moreno, 526 U.S. 275 (1999).

VICARIOUS LIABILITY

Vicarious liability, which is common in some areas of the law, refers to legal responsibility for the actions of another. If a law holds X responsible for Y's actions, then X's liability is said to be vicarious. In the criminal law, however, courts and commentators use the term in several different ways. Sometimes the term vicarious liability may be intended to refer only to cases that hold X criminally responsible for Y's conduct based on the relationship between X and Y. Sometimes the term may be used to describe X having liability for Y's conduct even though X was not at fault. The term may also be used to refer to all situations in which X is held criminally liable for Y's conduct.

Under any definition, the criminal law disfavors vicarious liability. The general rule is that one is liable only for one's own actions and not for the actions of others. Although this general rule against vicarious liability has some exceptions, the principle that one is criminally responsible only for one's own actions has considerable force, influencing both legislation and judicial decisions.

Laws that punish a defendant's own act or omission that allows another person to do something unlawful impose direct liability, not vicarious liability, although such laws are sometimes mislabeled. Parents, for example, sometimes face criminal liability for allowing their minor children to use guns or automobiles or to skip school. These crimes are examples of direct liability, not vicarious liability, because the statutes explicitly hold the parent liable for the parent's own act (e.g., negligently storing a weapon) or omission (e.g., culpably failing to see that a child attended school) that caused the harm, rather than for the child's conduct.

Vicarious liability and strict liability distinguished

Vicarious liability should also be distinguished from the closely related concept of strict liability. Under strict liability, the defendant must engage in prohibited conduct, but the separate requirement that the defendant have a culpable mens rea—some degree of fault—is removed. Vicarious liability, in contrast, dispenses with the requirement that the defendant engage in the prohibited conduct, instead holding the defendant liable for the conduct of another. For example, a law holding X liable for selling alcohol to Y, a minor, even though X reasonably believed Y was over twenty-one, imposes strict liability. A law holding W, X's employer, liable for X's sale to Y imposes vicarious liability. Laws can (and sometimes do) impose strict and vicarious liability simultaneously—for example, a law that held W liable for X's sale to a minor even though W and X had taken reasonable precautions to avoid such sales. However, laws can also impose either kind of liability separately.

Why vicarious liability is disfavored

In many applications, vicarious criminal liability would violate either or both of two basic principles of the criminal law. According to the first principle, the actus reus requirement, a person cannot be guilty of a crime unless the person's guilty conduct includes a voluntary act or omission. One feature of the actus reus requirement is the protection of personal security it affords by forcing criminal statutes to provide a

bright line that a person can choose not to cross and thereby avoid criminal liability. By holding a person liable for the conduct of another, vicarious liability undermines this control principle of the actus reus requirement, because a person cannot control the conduct of others in the same way that she can control her own. Just as importantly, vicarious liability may violate a second principle, that criminal liability must be based on personal fault. Both retributive and utilitarian justifications for criminal penalties demand that fault accompany the moral condemnation and harsher punishments associated with criminal conviction. By punishing the parent for theft if a child steals, for example, vicarious liability could violate this basic rule. Although neither of these principles is absolute, they do cabin (confine to a small space) the use of vicarious liability. As explained below, vicarious liability becomes more controversial as it does greater offense to these principles.

Vicarious liability for accomplices and coconspirators

Criminal responsibility for a person who intended the commission of some crime and did something to advance its commission presents the least controversial use of vicarious liability. Accomplices and coconspirators face such liability. If X assists Y in a burglary by serving as the lookout while Y enters the building and steals, X is guilty of burglary, even though the burglary was committed by Y's conduct, not X's. This sort of vicarious liability is not controversial, however, because the accomplice both engaged in some prohibited conduct—such as aiding or encouraging a criminal act—and acted culpably with regard to the criminal act—usually with the purpose of assisting it. The basic principles of the criminal law are satisfied, and some prefer not to categorize such liability as vicarious at all.

A more controversial application of vicarious liability occurs when an accomplice purposely aids the commission of crime A, but the person aided also commits crime B. In many jurisdictions, the accomplice is guilty not only of crime A, which the accomplice intentionally aided, but also of crime B, provided that crime B was a reasonably foreseeable consequence of the conduct the accomplice aided. Thus, the accomplice may be held liable for conduct that the accomplice did *not* intend to aid. This form of liability intrudes upon the principle that ties criminal liability to fault. Indeed, for this reason, the Model Penal

Code (§ 2.06(4)) and some jurisdictions that follow it limit the liability of the accomplice for unintended crimes to the accomplice's level of culpability for those crimes. Many jurisdictions, however, relying on the fact that the defendant did commit an act of aiding, and had some culpability regarding the unintended crime (because it was foreseeable) allow vicarious liability in this circumstance.

The felony murder rule presents the most controversial application of vicarious liability in the accomplice context, at least among commentators. Under this rule, a death that results from a felony is murder, even if the death was caused accidentally. The felony murder rule extends liability to accomplices, so an accomplice in a felony is liable for murder if a death occurs during the felony, even if the accomplice neither caused, intended, nor foresaw the death. The special controversy surrounding the felony murder rule, however, derives not so much from the presence of vicarious liability as from the use of strict liability. The heart of the controversy lies in holding the conduct of the principal—which extends vicariously to the accomplice—sufficient for murder without culpability regarding the death.

In the many jurisdictions that follow the so-called *Pinkerton* rule, members of a conspiracy are subject to even broader vicarious liability than accomplices (see *Pinkerton v. United States,* 328 U.S. 640 (1946)). *Pinkerton* liability makes all members of a conspiracy liable for the crimes committed by their coconspirators that are within the scope of the conspiracy and reasonably foreseeable consequences of it. Such liability is particularly controversial because the coconspirator may not only lack culpability with regard to the crime, but also may not even have committed an act to aid it. The two criminal law principles are satisfied only to the limited extent that the coconspirator voluntarily and culpably acted by agreeing to commit a crime that foreseeably led to the vicarious crime. Not surprisingly, a number of jurisdictions have followed the Model Penal Code's example (Model Penal Code § 2.06 cmt. at 307–310) and the urging of many commentators and rejected application of vicarious liability to coconspirators who would not be liable as accomplices.

Corporate criminal liability

At common law, the general rule that criminal liability had to be personal rather than vicarious prevented corporations from being held criminally liable, since a corporation could not itself engage in a physical act. Beginning in the latter half of the nineteenth century, however, such limitations were gradually eliminated. Under modern statutes, corporations face vicarious liability for the criminal conduct of certain employees, although the wisdom, fairness and scope of such liability remain controversial. Relying on the fiction that the acts of the employee are the acts of the corporation, some defend such liability as direct rather than vicarious. More persuasively, some consider vicarious liability for corporations a justifiable departure from the basic principles because the penalties involve only fines rather than imprisonment and send less of a message of moral condemnation. Furthermore, it is argued, the corporation is not a true person, and the people most directly affected, the shareholders, suffer losses more akin to civil than criminal penalties.

Vicarious liability based on the relationship between the parties

In vicarious liability's most controversial form, the law convicts one person for the conduct of another based *solely* on their relationship. With the exceptions of the crimes of nuisance and libel, such liability was unknown at common law. In the twentieth century, however, this type of vicarious criminal liability, almost always in the form of an employer being held liable for the acts of an employee, became more common, particularly in the context of so-called regulatory crimes, which are designed to regulate businesses and usually entail misdemeanor punishments only. Examples include liability for employers based on the conduct of employees who mislabel drugs, sell alcohol to minors, or hire underage workers, even when such conduct runs against the employer's orders. In this context, vicarious liability is often imposed in conjunction with strict liability—the employee may be convicted for mislabeling the drugs without a showing of mental fault (strict liability) *and* the employer may be convicted for the mislabeling by the employee solely on the basis of the employer-employee relationship (vicarious liability).

Advocates of this kind of vicarious liability make arguments similar to those used to support strict liability. They contend that it makes employers more careful in choosing and managing their employees. They argue further that without such liability employers who encourage wrongful conduct will escape punishment because their authorization will be difficult to prove. Another argument is that the broad societal harm avoided by such regulatory crimes outweighs any injustice to the "innocent" employer held vicariously liable for the employee's conduct, particularly because the penalties imposed are usually light and often involve only fines (although in many jurisdictions employers face at least the theoretical possibility of imprisonment).

Opponents of vicarious liability, however, insist on the two basic principles set out earlier: individuals should be criminally responsible only for their own actions, and there should be no criminal liability without fault. This form of vicarious liability, they argue, directly contradicts such principles and should be precluded. The Model Penal Code adopts this view (see Model Penal Code § 2.06 cmt. at 305–306), prohibiting vicarious liability outside of the complicity and corporate liability contexts.

Constitutionality of vicarious liability

Vicarious liability based on complicity and conspiracy, even in its most extreme forms (such as felony murder and *Pinkerton* liability), almost always passes constitutional muster. Similarly, the Supreme Court has upheld the constitutionality of vicarious liability for corporations (see *New York Central & Hudson River v. United States*, 212 U.S. 481 (1909)). Courts are less uniform, however, in their judgments about the constitutionality of vicarious liability based solely on the relationship between two people. Much of the difference in case outcomes can be explained, however, by consideration of the degree to which the particular use of vicarious liability violates one of the basic criminal law principles.

With regard to the actus reus principle, courts approving vicarious liability often contend that defendants voluntarily "assumed the responsibilities" the statutes imposed or had it within their power to prevent the crimes in question (see *Morisette v. United States*, 342 U.S. 246, 256 (1952)). On this basis, most (though not all) courts agree that vicarious liability is constitutional in the employer-employee context (see *United States v. Park*, 421 U.S. 658 (1975)) and in statutes imposing liability on vehicle owners for traffic offenses committed by those the owner permitted to use the car (see *City of Chicage v. Hertz Commercial Leasing Corp.*, 395 N.E. 2d 1285, 1290–1291 (1978)). In defense of these rulings, defendants do have some limited control to avoid such criminal responsibility by declining to work

in the particular business or to lend out their cars. On the other hand, courts usually hold vicarious liability unconstitutional when liability is hinged on a relationship that the law cannot expect an individual to avoid. On such grounds, courts have considered unconstitutional statutes that would make parents guilty of their children's crimes or find car owners guilty of traffic infractions committed with their stolen cars (see *State v. Ahers*, 400 A. 2d 38, 40 (1979); LaFave and Scott at 254). In such situations it is very hard to say that defendants have "voluntarily" risked criminal liability.

Even when vicarious liability sufficiently satisfies the control principle of the actus reus requirement, the principle of personal fault can affect its constitutionality. Although defendants may be said to have "assumed the responsibilities" that led to their liability, their level of "fault" with regard to the crimes may simply be too low to permit the penalties the statutes authorize. Thus, some courts state that imprisonment for vicarious liability in the context of regulatory offenses would be unconstitutional—only a fine may be imposed (see *Commonwealth v. Koczwara*, 155 A. 2d 825 (Pa. 1959)). Similarly, the U.S. Supreme Court has indicated that capital punishment for felony murder is unconstitutional when based on vicarious liability, unless the defendant played a major role in the underlying felony and either intended the death or was recklessly indifferent to human life (see *Tison v. Arizona*, 481 U.S. 137, 159 (1987)).

Conclusion

As a general rule, the criminal law does not employ vicarious liability. Such liability would often run afoul of basic precepts that require an actus reus and fault for criminal responsibility. Although vicarious liability is employed in limited circumstances, its wisdom and constitutionality are open to question when its use creates too extreme an affront to these principles.

ALAN C. MICHAELS

See also ACCOMPLICES; ACTUS REUS; CONSPIRACY; CORPORATE CRIMINAL RESPONSIBILITY; STRICT LIABILITY.

BIBLIOGRAPHY

American Law Institute. *Model Penal Code and Commentaries*. Philadelphia: ALI, 1985.
DRESSLER, JOSHUA. *Understanding Criminal Law*, 2d. ed. New York: Matthew Bender, 1995.

———. *Cases and Materials on Criminal Law,* 2d ed. St. Paul, Minn.: West Group, 1999.

EICHELBERGER, EUNICE A. "Criminal Responsibility of Parent for Act of Child." *American Law Reports, 4th Series* 12 (1981): 673–700.

FLETCHER, GEORGE P. *Rethinking Criminal Law.* Boston: Little Brown, 1978.

HALL, JEROME. *General Principles of Criminal Law.* Indianapolis: Bobbs-Merrill, 1947.

HUSAK, DOUGLAS N. *Philosophy of Criminal Law.* Totowa, N.J.: Rowman & Littlefield, 1987.

IHRIE, A. DALE, III. "Comment, Parental Delinquency: Should Parents Be Criminally Liable for Failing to Supervise Their Children?" *University of Detroit Mercy Law Review* 74 (1996): 93–112.

LAFAVE, WAYNE R., and SCOTT, AUSTIN W., JR. *Criminal Law,* 2d ed. St. Paul, Minn.: West Publishing Co., 1986.

MICHAELS, ALAN C. "Constitutional Innocence." *Harvard Law Review* 112 (February 1999): 828–902.

PACKER, HERBERT L. *The Limits of the Criminal Sanction.* Stanford, Calif.: Stanford University Press, 1968.

ROBINSON, PAUL H. *Criminal Law.* New York: Aspen Law and Business, 1997.

SAYRE, FRANCIS BOWES. "Criminal Responsibility for the Acts of Another." *Harvard Law Review* 43 (March 1930): 689–723.

WILLIAMS, GLANVILLE L. *Criminal Law: The General Part.* London: Stevens and Sons, 1953.

VICTIMLESS CRIME

In the continuing debate over the proper scope of the criminal law, it has frequently been suggested that certain crimes are in reality "victimless" and that all statutes defining such offenses should be repealed or at least substantially restricted (Schur; Packer; Morris and Hawkins). Although all authors do not use the term in the same way, the following offenses have been included in the victimless crime category: public drunkenness; vagrancy; various sexual acts usually involving consenting adults (fornication, adultery, bigamy, incest, sodomy, homosexuality, and prostitution); obscenity; pornography; drug offenses; abortion; gambling; and juvenile status offenses (offenses that would not be criminal if the actor were an adult).

Rationale

The arguments for the repeal of laws against victimless crimes fall into two categories. Some proponents of the victimless crime concept argue that, as a matter of principle, society may not legitimately prohibit conduct that harms only the actor or actors (Morris and Hawkins). However, most proponents of the criterion go on to argue that even if it might be legitimate to punish victimless crimes, there are certain practical reasons why it is unwise to do so (Schur and Bedau). The practical arguments against victimless crimes appear to derive from three attributes of these offenses: (1) most involve no complaining parties other than police officers; (2) many involve the exchange of prohibited goods or services that are strongly desired by the participants; and (3) all seek to prevent individual or social harms that are widely believed to be less serious and/or less likely to occur than the harms involved in crimes with victims.

Victimless crimes tend to have no complaining parties other than the police because the immediate participants in these crimes do not see themselves as victims, have no desire to complain to the police, and would fear criminal liability if they did complain. Moreover, since such illegal acts usually take place in private and do not directly victimize any third party, other citizens are unlikely to observe the acts or to have sufficient incentive to complain to the police. As a result, it is argued, victimless crimes are harder to detect and prosecute than crimes with victims, and the police are therefore forced to engage in a number of practices that are subject to serious abuse. These include surveillance and entrapment by undercover agents; the use of unreliable informants from the criminal milieu; various forms of intrusive electronic and physical surveillance (wiretapping, bugging, peering through holes in the ceilings of public washrooms, and the like); and widespread searches of the person, motor vehicles, houses, and other nonpublic places for contraband and evidence. Such techniques tend to bring law enforcement into disrepute, causing lowered public respect for the law and for criminal penalties in general.

The fact that victimless crimes frequently take place without being observed by other citizens also means that certain forms of official misconduct are much more likely to occur: discriminatory enforcement of the law against unpopular groups or individuals; attempts to bribe law enforcement officers; and attempts by law enforcement officers to extort money or other favors from suspects in return for nonenforcement. Such misbehavior further reduces public respect for, and cooperation with, the institutions of criminal justice, particularly among social groups already alienated from society—the poor, ethnic minorities, and the young (Schur and Bedau).

Many victimless crimes involve goods and services that are in great demand, the most extreme example being the drugs craved by addicts. Criminal penalties thus tend to limit the supply more than the demand, driving up the black-market price and creating monopoly profits for those criminals who remain in business. This "crime tariff" reduces consumption possibilities for legal goods and encourages the growth of sophisticated and well-organized criminal groups. Organized crime in turn tends to diversify into other areas of crime. Large profits provide ample funds for bribery of public officials, as well as capital for diversification. Although higher prices tend to discourage some would-be participants in victimless crimes, the fact that these goods and services are greatly desired (and are not seen as truly immoral) ensures a strong demand that, combined with a restricted supply, maintains both high prices and high crime rates. In extreme cases, such as heroin or cocaine addiction, high prices force participants to commit other crimes, for example, drug sales and theft, to pay for the illegal goods. Finally, because of the strong demand, a large number of otherwise law-abiding citizens are driven into association with the criminal elements who supply these goods and services. There is a danger that such citizens will come to view themselves as criminals, since society has labeled them as such; they will thus cooperate less with law enforcement generally, and are more likely to be drawn into other forms of crime.

Victimless crimes are also seen as being measurably less serious than most offenses with victims—the prohibited behavior causes individual or social harms that are either less serious, less likely to occur, or the result of prohibition itself (for example, the adverse health effects caused by ingestion of impure or unexpectedly potent drugs). It is argued that the lack of complaining witnesses to some of these crimes (e.g., illegal gambling) is, in part, a reflection of a societal consensus that the behavior is less serious. The high demand for many of these illegal goods and services, noted above, is further evidence of widespread tolerance of the behavior. Under such conditions, prohibition only serves to reduce respect for law on the part of citizens who believe that their prohibited acts are not wrong. Moreover, the prosecution of these less serious offenses is seen as a waste of scarce criminal justice resources and an unjustifiable burden on the criminal justice system. The amount of police effort required to detect these hard-to-enforce laws might be better spent on more serious offenses, which are easier to detect. It is also argued that the courts are so overburdened with trivial offenses that there are insufficient resources to process more serious offenses adequately. In addition, the enforcement of victimless crime puts great stress on overcrowded pretrial detention and correctional facilities, and increases the cost of replacement facilities.

Critique

Although often agreeing that specific crimes should be repealed, critics of the victimless crime criterion have pointed out that the concept lacks a clear definition, fails to cover some of the offenses to which it has been applied, and applies equally well to other offenses that have not been proposed for repeal. Thus, critics argue, the term is only a cover for subjective value judgments about the wisdom of specific criminal statutes, and fails to provide an objective criminalization standard that could be easily applied and would be deserving of broad acceptance.

Beginning with the term itself, it has been argued that there is no such thing as a victimless crime, because most so-called victimless crimes have victims, or at least potential victims, such as the taxpayers who must eventually pay the cost of rehabilitating the drug addict and supporting his dependents (Oaks). It has also been argued that prostitution and antifemale pornography harm all women, and that "hate speech" harms all members of the target group, by increasing the risk of future violence, causing fear and anxiety of such harms, and reinforcing entrenched social inequalities (Roach). If it is conceded that the criminal law may properly prohibit conduct that involves a risk of harm to the protected interests of others, one is faced with a continuum—a range of behaviors involving varying degrees of actual or potential victimization—with no clear answers about where to draw the line between criminal and noncriminal behavior (Dripps; Packer).

In response to the problems noted above, it might be argued that victimless crimes should be defined as those that lack direct, identifiable victims. However, there are several problems with this formulation. First, some of the offenses on the list of victimless crimes do have direct victims, such as citizens offended or harassed by public drunks or disorderly persons; the spouse of the adulterer, bigamist, or prostitution client; or the spouse, parent, or child of a drug addict. Refusal to recognize the latter forms of victimization requires problematic distinction (for instance, between mere mental distress and physical harm) (Wertheimer). Moreover, in many cases it is quite reasonable to argue that one or more of the participants in a victimless crime is, or will in the future become, a victim of serious harm, such as the sporadic heroin user who becomes addicted (Schur and Bedau), or the young person who becomes a prostitute; moreover, the victims of these harms, who are often members of socially disadvantaged groups, may not freely "consent" to either the prohibited acts or the ensuing harms. Finally, a "no direct victim" definition might include many offenses not proposed to be repealed—for example, inchoate offenses such as possession of burglary tools, drunk driving, and counterfeiting.

It has also been argued that victimless crimes "lack victims in the sense of complainants asking for the protection of the criminal law" (Morris and Hawkins, p. 6). Of course, people can be victimized, or at least put at risk of harm, without knowing it, and much of the absence of complainants is due to the secretive nature of these crimes (Wertheimer). Moreover, the "complaintless" criterion excludes some supposedly victimless crimes, such as pornography, and includes many offenses never proposed for repeal. For example, in bribery, receiving stolen property, possession of unregistered weapons, most traffic law violations, and innumerable health, safety, environmental, and regulatory offenses, the complainant is generally a police officer or paid informant, not a crime victim seeking protection. To argue that the latter offenses are significantly different from the victimless (or complaintless) crimes which should be repealed is to admit that the proposed criterion does not, by itself, make the crucial distinction between what should be criminal and what should not.

Victimless crimes have also been defined as those involving "the willing exchange, among adults, of strongly demanded but legally proscribed goods and services" (Schur, p. 169). The consensual nature of such transactions, and the fact that they are strongly desired, create many of the problems of detection and enforcement previously noted (Schur and Bedau). This definition is still inadequate, however, because it clear-ly does not apply to some victimless crimes, such as public drunkenness, and applies in only the broadest sense to others, such as incest. On the other hand, it does include weapons and stolen property offenses, which are not usually proposed for repeal.

Finally, proponents of the victimless crime criterion argue that even if this concept is not a definitive test of what should be criminal, it is still useful because it identifies a group of statutes most of which should be repealed because "they produce more social harm than good" (Schur and Bedau, p. 112). This sort of cost-benefit approach does provide a useful set of objective criteria for defining the scope of the criminal law. However, such an approach is inevitably very complex, and the victimless crime criterion contributes little to the resolution of these complexities. For example, offenses involving the possession or carrying of weapons are victimless in almost every sense in which drug offenses are, and impose very similar costs of enforcement (Wertheimer; Kessler), yet most proponents of the victimless crime criterion do not apply the criterion to current and proposed gun laws. In addition, the victimless crime concept says very little about the difficult choices between alternatives to current criminal laws: partial decriminalization, regulation by various civil or administrative processes, or total deregulation.

Ultimately, the victimless crime criterion—or any other simple formula—is mostly rhetoric that obscures, rather than contributes to, analysis. The relative victimlessness of an offense is closely related to several important practical issues in the criminalization decision, but labeling a crime as victimless only begins what is, in most cases, a very difficult process of assessing complex empirical facts and fundamental value choices.

RICHARD S. FRASE

See also ABORTION; ALCOHOL AND CRIME: THE PROHIBITION EXPERIMENT; CIVIL AND CRIMINAL DIVIDE; CRIMINAL LAW REFORM: CURRENT ISSUES IN THE UNITED STATES; CRIMINALIZATION AND DECRIMINALIZATION; DRUGS AND CRIME: LEGAL ASPECTS; ENTRAPMENT; GAMBLING; HOMOSEXUALITY AND CRIME; JUVENILE STATUS OFFENDERS; OBSCENITY AND PORNOGRAPHY: BEHAVIORAL ASPECTS; POLICE: POLICING COMPLAINANTLESS CRIMES; PROSTITUTION; SEX OFFENSES: CONSENSUAL; VAGRANCY AND DISORDERLY CONDUCT.

BIBLIOGRAPHY

DRIPPS, DONALD A. "The Liberal Critique of the Harm Principle." *Criminal Justice Ethics* 17 (summer/fall 1998): 3–18.

FEINBERG, JOEL. *The Moral Limits of the Criminal Law.* 4 vols. Vol. 1, *Harm to Others* (1984); Vol. 2, *Offense to Others* (1985); Vol. 3, *Harm to Self* (1986); Vol. 4, *Harmless Wrongdoing* (1988). New York: Oxford University Press, 1984–1988.

KESSLER, RAYMOND G. "Enforcement Problems of Gun Control: A Victimless Crimes Analysis." *Criminal Law Bulletin* 16 (1980): 131–149.

MORRIS, NORVAL, and HAWKINS, GORDON J. *The Honest Politician's Guide to Crime Control.* Chicago: University of Chicago Press, 1970.

OAKS, DALLIN H. "The Popular Myth of the Victimless Crime." *University of Chicago Law Alumni Journal* (1975): 3–14.

PACKER, HERBERT L. *The Limits of the Criminal Sanction.* Stanford, Calif.: Stanford University Press, 1968.

ROACH, KENT. "Four Models of the Criminal Process." *Journal of Criminal Law and Criminology* 89 (1999): 671–716.

SCHUR, EDWIN M. *Crimes without Victims: Deviant Behavior and Public Policy—Abortion, Homosexuality, Drug Addiction.* Englewood Cliffs, N.J.: Prentice-Hall, 1965.

SCHUR, EDWIN M., and BEDAU, HUGO ADAM. *Victimless Crimes: Two Sides of a Controversy.* Englewood Cliffs, N.J.: Prentice-Hall, 1974.

SMITH, WENDY SERBIN. *Victimless Crime: A Selected Bibliography.* Washington, D.C.: U.S. Department of Justice, 1977.

WERTHEIMER, ALAN. "Victimless Crimes." *Ethics* 87 (1977): 302–318.

VICTIMS

The striking increase in attention to victims by the world's criminal justice systems may well have been the most significant development in those systems during the second half of the twentieth century. In earlier times, crime victims were consigned to a peripheral position, necessary as background players but of no true importance. Once their crime report and their testimony had been recorded, they typically were ignored.

Victims were raped, mugged, their homes invaded, their handbags or wallets stolen on the street. Then they were often "double victimized," the second insult being inflicted by the authorities. Law enforcement personnel, hardened from having dealt with so many crimes for so long, failed to understand that for most people victimization is rare, often a unique and novel experience. Further frustrated by their inability to stem offenses such as burglary and car theft—crimes in which the perpetrator usually cannot be described—law enforcement agents tended to be abrupt and dismissive in the face of victims' despair.

If the perpetrator was apprehended, very often the attorney for the accused and the prosecutor bargained the case, trading a guilty plea by the offender for a lesser sentence. Typically, nobody would inform the victim of the plea agreement or of other details regarding a settlement. In those rare instances when a case went to trial, the victim would have to miss work (and often forfeit pay), suffer through any number of postponements, and endure a grilling by the defense attorney that was meant to humiliate. Often victims found themselves alone in a hallway or waiting room with the perpetrator and his friends. In the end, crime victims usually received little satisfaction—beyond a story to tell friends and neighbors, though often a story saturated with irritation and anger.

In the United States, neglect of crime victims changed dramatically from about 1960 onward. The change had two major components. The first was the establishment of programs for victim compensation and victim and witness assistance to ease the physical, financial, and emotional burdens that can accompany criminal victimization. Efforts were made to bring victims more comprehensively into the conduct of criminal justice and to deal directly with their anxieties and outrage. Concern about an apparent growing unwillingness of victims to report offenses and cooperate with law enforcement agencies provided a further impetus for the establishment of assistance programs. Now victim cooperation is required before he or she could be compensated.

The second approach involved efforts to assess more accurately the level of criminal activity by conducting interviews with representative samples of the American population. The surveys also sought to measure correlates of the victimization experience, such as fear of crime, curtailed activities, and the respondents' confidence in the law enforcement machinery.

There also emerged a comprehensive academic and agency research enterprise that dealt with the subject of crime victims. There now exists considerable scholarly literature on the likelihood and consequences of being a victim of particular kinds of crimes. Researchers have learned, for instance, that rape victims tend to be more traumatized if the offender is an acquaintance rather than a stranger. Burglary victims, for their part, often see the crime as an invasion of their private space and feel dirtied.

Numerous self-defense strategies, some of them controversial, have been advanced for victims to use in protecting themselves. An intense debate concerns whether carrying a gun safeguards a person against a predator or instead escalates violence and endangers the carrier by encouraging risky responses. Rape victims confront a similar dilemma: will forceful resistance cause a sexual aggressor to desist, or will it result in greater injury or in death? Other advice is less arguable. To protect against theft, potential victims (all of us) have been advised that the best place to secrete valuables is in a child's room: experienced burglars will get in and out of a house very quickly, usually searching only the bedroom, perhaps a desk, and the kitchen, seeking primarily cash, weapons, and jewelry (Wright and Decker).

Professionals involved with crime victims formed an organization, now called the World Society of Victimology, which cooperates with the United Nations and the Council of Europe on issues related to crime victims. The society directory notes that "its members from around the world brought together by their mutual concern for victims, include victim assistance practitioners, scientists, social workers, physicians, lawyers, university professors, and students." The group first met in Jerusalem in 1973 and ushered in the new century with its tenth meeting, held in Montreal in August 2000.

Distinguishing Victims and Offenders

An obvious but important difference between offenders and victims is that the former have done something against the law. In an effort to understand the roots of their behavior we can look at offenders' upbringing, values, school performance, and associates. We can have them undergo psychological tests to seek to determine how they might differ from nonoffenders and how those who committed one type of offense might be distinguished from those who engaged in another kind of lawbreaking.

Victims of crime, on the other hand, typically do not engage in particular behavior that might result in their victimization. Some, however, may have been involved in actions correlated with

criminal outcomes: drunkenness and aggressive verbal behavior in a bar is one of innumerable examples. But a large percentage of crime victims show no qualities or behavior that might allow them to anticipate their fate. They might be passengers on an airplane that is hijacked, or customers in a grocery store who are shot during a holdup because the perpetrator wants to avoid being identified. Or they may be window-shopping pedestrians who are run over by a drunk driver who loses control of his vehicle. Anyone might readily be a crime victim, but most people will never engage in the heinous criminal offenses that occupy the study of criminal behavior.

Nonetheless, despite the fact that a considerable percentage of victims are virtually random recipients of injury and loss, there exists a coterie of *chronic victims*, persons who suffer multiple victimizations, well beyond the number that would be presumed to be their lot if victimization were a chance occurrence. A review of the four British Crime Surveys—those of 1982, 1984, 1988, and 1992—found that between 1.1 and 2.2 percent of victims of property crimes had been afflicted at least five times in the course of slightly more than one year. For crimes of violence the figure ran from 0.7 to 1.0 percent of the victim totals. In addition, between 24 and 38 percent of personal and property offenses were inflicted on people who experienced five or more such offenses during the same time period.

The British survey found that 63 percent of all property crime victims had suffered at least one other such victimization during the fifteen-month study period. For personal crimes the figure rose to 77 percent. The researchers noted that massive crime reductions are available simply by the reduction of repeat victimization (Ellingsworth, Farrell, and Pease). The precise explanation for the multiple victimization phenomenon is still largely unclear. The first victimization is said to become an important factor in predicting future victimization and that multiple victimizations are related in a complex way to both household and area characteristics (Osborn, Ellingsworth, Hope, and Tickett).

When there are crimes almost invariably there will be criminals, even if they sometimes are anthropomorphized institutions, such as corporations, that commit offenses such as antitrust violations. But there are many crimes in which there are hordes of unknowing victims or no victims at all. What theater patrons who have several dollars in change in the coat that they check in the cloakroom will be aware that the attendant has helped himself or herself to a few quarters? Who counts the number of rubber bands in a package that says, incorrectly, that it has one hundred, or who knows whether a gas station tank reading has been altered illegally?

Drunken driving offers an example of an offense in which there is a criminal offense but not necessarily a victim. For some offenses, the state, under the presumption that its interests have been harmed or that it must protect its citizens from hypothetical outcomes, adopts the role of victim for some so-called victimless offenses, such as the sale of proscribed drugs or prostitution.

Distinctions between actions that produce criminals and those that produce crime victims have contributed significantly to the standing and the tactics that make up the study of victims—or *victimology*, to use the rather awkward term coined by Beniamin Mendelsohn in the early 1940s. Unable to "explain" victimization, those who specialize in its study tend to focus on its dimensions, its consequences, and the way that the social and political system deals with it.

There is some sparse theoretical work bearing on the process of victimization. In a 1958 study, sociologist Marvin Wolfgang noted that for about a quarter of homicides "the victim may be one of the major precipitating causes of his own demise" (p. 245). Wolfgang coined the phrase *victim-precipitation* to identify such situations: "The victim-precipitated cases are those in which the victim was the first to show and use a deadly weapon, to strike a blow in an altercation—in short, the first to commence the interplay of recourse to physical violence" (p. 252).

Almost forty years later, Kenneth Polk in a study of homicides in Melbourne, Australia, found essentially the same pattern and percentage of victim-precipitation that Wolfgang had documented in Philadelphia. William E. Foote, after a comprehensive review of studies using the concept, suggests that in the future attempts ought to be made to divide victim-precipitation into relevant types. Among the more interesting separate forms are incidents that Foote calls *intentional* victim-precipitated deaths, instances in which persons deliberately engage in episodes that they desire to have lethal consequences. Shooting at a police car would be an example of what Foote calls *suicide by cop*.

But when Israeli criminologist Menachem Amir sought to apply the concept of victim-precipitation to rape victims, scholars insisted, correctly, that it did not necessarily travel well from one kind of offense to another, that factors such as wearing "provocative" clothing differ significantly from starting a barroom brawl. William Ryan's classic *Blaming the Victim* satirizes the tendency to denigrate victims with a story of a U.S. senator fulminating in front of colleagues who are debating the origins of the Second World War. "What was Pearl Harbor doing there?" he asks, apropos the 1941 Japanese bombing of the Hawaiian naval base (pp. 153–154).

The emergence of victim concerns

It is not an easy task to disentangle the diverse elements that energized the movement toward greater recognition of the role and importance of victims in criminal justice affairs. For centuries their condition aroused little comment or interest. Then they were "discovered," and afterward it was unclear how their neglect could have gone without remedy for so long.

In the United States, national politics first moved the subject of crime victims onto center stage. In 1964, Barry Goldwater, the Republican candidate for president, thrust the issue of crime into his campaign. It was a false issue, in the sense that the federal government does not have jurisdiction over most kinds of criminal activity that concern the average citizen. A president can do little, except perhaps symbolically, to make a notable impact on criminal behavior; such behavior is almost exclusively the concern of state, county, and municipal governments.

Goldwater, nonetheless, had touched a sensitive public nerve. Citizens responded to his allegations that the Democrats were soft on crime, an accusation seemingly supported by the party's opposition to capital punishment, their considerable concern with the rights of defendants, and their unwillingness to endorse tougher punishment policies.

President Lyndon Johnson, who defeated Goldwater, chose a time-tested political strategy to defuse the crime issue. He appointed the President's Commission on Law Enforcement and Administration of Justice, with a sweeping mandate to examine and make recommendations about virtually all aspects of the crime problem (the death penalty was one of the exceptions). The commission endorsed the fledgling victim compensation programs and launched a pioneering project to better measure the extent of traditional crime by means of a series of surveys of the population. These probes sought to shed some light on what is known as the *dark figure* in crime, offenses that fail to come to the attention of the authorities.

National crime victimization survey (NCVS)

In a variety of sizes and shapes, victimization surveys are conducted today in many of the major countries of the world. Since 1989, under the leadership of the Netherlands, a group of countries have collaborated on a standard survey technique that allows some comparative conclusions to be drawn. In 1989 the lowest European crime rates were found in Northern Ireland, Switzerland, and England, and the highest in Spain and the Netherlands (Dijk, Mayhew, and Killias). Three years later the results were essentially the same, though the English rate had escalated somewhat (Dijk and Mayhew).

In the United States, the National Crime Victimization Survey (NCVS) was begun in 1972 by the Law Enforcement Assistance Administration. A thoroughgoing revision of the survey instrument in 1992 makes it impossible to compare earlier results with those obtained since that date. The new screening procedures introduced in 1992 included detailed cues to help respondents recall crime incidents; they produced a higher reported level of victimization, especially for assaults. The updated approach also focuses more heavily on offenses committed by family members against each other and by acquaintances. These are subjects that respondents often are reluctant to discuss without considerable prompting.

The victimization survey now is conducted by the Bureau of the Census under the auspices of the Bureau of Justice Statistics, housed in the U.S. Department of Justice. NCVS interviews are held every six months, using a national panel of approximately 49,000 households with a total of about 101,000 residents. Ninety-five percent of the persons asked to participate in the survey agree to do so. A single household respondent details crime victimizations for all members of the household over the age of twelve in interviews that take about half an hour. Each household is contacted for information seven times. The first and the fifth interviews are done face-to-face; the other five are conducted by telephone. If a household changes location its members remain in the survey pool for the full period before being replaced on the panel. The approach minimizes *telescoping*, that is, the tendency of persons to report victimizations that occurred before the time period of concern. To keep the data as time-bound as possible, the results of the initial interview with a household are not included in the NCVS.

The victim survey inevitably reports a good deal more criminal activity—more than twice as much—than does the annual Uniform Crime Reports issued by the Federal Bureau of Investigation, which takes into account only offenses reported to the police.

Problems with the victimization survey

A shortcoming of the NCVS is that respondents may be inclined to report events that are not criminal, though they believe them to be. This has been particularly true in regard to minor assaults, which rarely capture the attention of law enforcement. Also, *series incidents*, matters such as spouse abuse, that often have no clearcut beginning or end, frustrate the NCVS since the survey focuses only on discrete events. There also is the matter of bias inherent in the interview format. Persons may desist reporting if what they have to say involves too much of their time and becomes tedious, or they may feel compelled to play into what they interpret as an interviewer's desire to hear about a lot of criminal episodes, real or imagined. Besides, the respondent may not recall or be aware of all of the victimization experiences of other people living in the household. In addition, the NCVS fails to include the experiences of persons not anchored in fixed households, such as the homeless and transients.

Bias that intrudes into victim surveys is shown by the finding that persons with college degrees typically report more assaults than do persons with only an elementary school education (Gove, Hughes, and Geerken). Since it is likely that members of the latter group actually have been victimized by assaults at least as much and probably much more often than the college-educated group, it is reasonable to believe that behaviors that are regarded as routine and inconsequential by persons in the less well-educated group are taken much more seriously by those with more schooling.

Finally, *reverse record checks* have discovered that persons who reported to the police a crime committed against them by an acquaintance often failed to inform a victimization interviewer of the event. The reverse record checks found that two-thirds of such offenses were not mentioned in crime victim surveys, while three-quarters of the crimes reported to the police and committed by strangers were disclosed.

The Bureau of Justice Statistics supplemented the NCVS survey by conducting a city-level telephone survey in 1999. A total of some eight hundred households were contacted in twelve cities, using a method called random digital dialing. The survey found that from 20 to 48 percent of the respondents noted that they were "fearful" of crime, though in no city did more than 10 percent say that they were "very fearful." The highest levels of expressed fear were in Chicago and Washington, D.C. (48%) and the lowest in Madison, Wisconsin (20%) (Smith, Steadman, Minton, and Townsend).

The incidence of victimization

The NCVS shows that Americans experience more than thirty million victimizations each year. In any one year, a person has about a 3 percent chance of being a victim of a crime of violence. That figure is more than double for property offenses.

Teenage black males are the most likely victims of crimes of violence, followed by teenage black females. The next four highest victimization rates, in descending order, are for teenage white males, young adult black males, young adult black females, and teenage white females. The elderly—be they male, female, black, or white—have the lowest victimization rates from violence.

Persons most victimized by property crimes are teenage white males and adult black males. Least victimized are elderly black males and elderly black females. This somewhat counterintuitive finding may result from property offenders targeting affluent neighborhoods where the haul is more likely to be worth the risk.

The surveys pinpoint the considerable toll that crimes of violence take upon young black youths. The strikingly lower rate of victization of elderly persons by both crimes of violence and property offenses in one respect challenges the rationality of the commonly reported high level of fear of crime found among the elderly. An explanation offered is that older persons often have the most to lose if they are victimized: They are less likely to be able to recover (or to survive) a violent crime and they often have no way to recoup the financial loss inflicted by a burglary or other property offenses. In that regard, their fears can be seen as perfectly reasonable.

This finding of higher rates of fear of crime among the elderly, however, has been disputed by Kenneth Ferraro, who argues that too much has been made of answers to a single question on the NCVS survey and that failure to inquire about particular crimes rather than crime in general undercuts the adequacy of the responses to support the usual conclusion of a high level of fear of crime among the elderly. Ferraro's own work indicates that the only particular offense that the elderly fear more than persons in other age groups is panhandling, and that this fear is confined to older women.

Urban metropolitan areas, expectedly, show higher crime victimization rates than suburbs and rural areas. One victimization study found that about 31 percent of the robberies in which suburbanites were victims occurred while they were in a central city and only 6.2 percent outside that city's boundaries (Dodge, p. 2).

White-collar crime victimization

The NCVS's focus on victimization by so-called *street crimes* to the neglect of white-collar or *suite crimes* reinforces the greater public attention accorded offenses generally committed by persons in the lower socioeconomic strata. Fraud and other white-collar crimes can visit severe economic and psychological hardships on their victims. Some white-collar crimes, such as medical malpractice and pollution, kill and maim large numbers of people. While the tally of street crimes dropped significantly during the last decade of the twentieth century, the number of white-collar crimes, enforcement officials believe, has increased greatly. Victim complaints to the Securities and Exchange Commission, for instance, jumped by 20 percent between 1996 and 1998.

Fraud has been labeled *assault with a fiscal weapon*. A newspaper report tells of a bogus scheme in which persons were persuaded to invest in supposedly ultra-safe securities backed by banks and real estate. In the end, the victims of the scam were bilked of at least $20 million. Some lost their homes, many marriages were bruised, and retirements postponed.

The National White-Collar Crime Center reported in mid-1999 that almost 40 percent of the persons in a nationwide sample said that they were defrauded in some way during the previous year. Most complained of consumer rip-offs such as unnecessary auto repairs. Others of the 1,169 respondents said that they had lost money through Internet schemes, credit card fraud, and investment swindles. Victim help groups note that many people who have been cheated prefer to suffer in silence rather than to seek aid because they are embarrassed about their gullibility.

Senior citizens appear to be the most common victims of telemarketing schemes, while people in their thirties and forties, often well-educated, tend most often to fall prey to Internet swindles. A study of female victims of a telemarketing oilwell scam found that the older women were likely to blame themselves, but those who were younger tended to take a more resigned and hard-boiled attitude in shrugging off the loss (Sechrest et al.).

The costs of crime victimization

Researchers have estimated that in the United States the annual cost to victims of crimes against the person to be $105 billion (Miller, Cohen, and Wiersema). This figure includes medical costs, lost earnings, and the outlay for programs that provide victim assistance. Kennedy and Sacco raise the loss figure to $426 billion for violent crimes and $24 billion for property crimes by adding in the price of pain and suffering, but they emphasize that these victim cost estimates are far from being totally reliable figures.

Hate crimes and kindred laws

Distinctions in the law based on the social position of the victim have long existed. Typically, criminal statutes offered greater protection for those with greater social status. In early English jurisprudence, for example, more stringent penalties were attached to the poisoning of husbands by their wives, while wife-poisoning was regarded as but another form of murder. The former called for burning at the stake; the latter for the more common punishment of hanging.

In the past two decades in the United States there has been a proliferation of laws to further protect potential crime victims who are deemed more in need of or more deserving of such protection. The mechanism purported to ensure additional victim security is tougher penalties. Most notable in this category are *hate crimes*, proscribed acts that are judicially determined to be motivated by prejudice against a member of a specified group. Beating a homosexual because of his sexual orientation or torching the house of a rabbi because of his faith or ethnicity will likely get the offender(s) a heavier penalty than if the same crimes had been committed, respectively, against

a nonhomosexual or a non-Jew (Jacobs and Potter; Jenness and Broad).

This kind of special victim protection is extended to the elderly in some states, and during the summer of 1999 witnesses testifying before the U.S. House of Representatives Committee on the Judiciary pled for inclusion of women as a group under hate crime statutes. The witnesses argued that women are less able to protect themselves against male predatory behavior and are an especially vulnerable crime victim group with regard to sexual assault.

This vulnerability of women was underlined by a report in May 1999 of a national survey showing that 17.6 percent of American women have been rape victims at least once during their lifetime, with an additional 14.8 percent being victimized by an attempted rape. Forty-three percent said that they had been slapped or hit at least once in their life, 21.2 percent had been hit with an object, 6.2 percent had been threatened with a gun, and 8.1 percent had been the victim of a stalking. In all, more than half of the women surveyed had been victimized by rape, physical assault, and/or stalking.

Critics of hate crime legislation see such efforts as an alliance between some politicians and segments of the electorate and more of a symbolic gesture than a practical measure. Critics argue that the law should inquire only into behavior, not into subjective motives, and point to existing penalties for non-hate crimes as sufficient to deter, or at least adequately punish, those who commit such acts. What good, some insist, is it to add the legal designation of hate crime to the murder of a black man by bigoted youths when there already exists an adequate penalty for murder? Cynics add that the lesson conveyed by the laws is that if you are going to be a sensible criminal your least dangerous course of action is to victimize someone who shares your own background and beliefs.

Crime victim compensation

Victim compensation programs were the earliest manifestations of what was to become a comprehensive and very powerful victims' movement. The first programs were established in New Zealand in 1963 and in England in 1964; then victim compensation was adopted by California in 1965 and thereafter duplicated in other American states and throughout the world. A 1999 count showed that twenty-nine countries had programs to compensate crime victims. All but three offer benefits for crime-inflicted injuries suffered by foreign citizens on their soil. By law the American programs must provide assistance to U.S. residents or their survivors who are injured or killed in a terrorist attack while visiting a foreign country. The state programs are partially supported by the federally subsidized Crime Victims Fund. By 1999, state programs assisted more than two million crime victims and survivors annually.

Crime victim compensation programs have been bothered from their beginning by attempts to locate a sensible rationale for their existence. If they serve a legitimate government function, then why are there not also programs to compensate persons who suffer losses from illness or from any other problems not of their own creation? One answer has been that prudent people ought to buy insurance to protect themselves from such exigencies; but the same might be said of crime victims. Aiding crime victims has a strong political component—sponsors could score points with the electorate—which explains why this particular issue has been singled out for legislative attention.

Programs providing compensation to crime victims owe their origin to the pioneering efforts of Merger Fry, an Englishwoman and a Quaker, who devoted her life to the cause of correctional reform. Fry ridiculed the inadequacy of restitution as a court-ordered method to allay the deprivation suffered by crime victims. For one thing, she pointed out, in many instances the offender is not apprehended or, if caught, is not convicted. Even if there is a conviction, most offenders are too impoverished to pay the cost of the victim's crime-associated expenses. For those offenders who can contribute something, such monies often have to be diverted from support of their families, who then might have to be subsidized by welfare.

Problems with restitution and with tort remedies were highlighted in the sensational O. J. Simpson case. Survivors of the victims—Simpson's former wife's parents and the family of Ronald Goldman, her ill-starred friend—together received a judgment of $8.5 million and were awarded punitive damages of $25 million. But they have obtained very little of that money, though Simpson lives lavishly on the $25,000 per month he receives from a judgment-proof $4.1 million pension fund.

Compassion joins compensation

After victim compensation efforts were established, an understanding soon developed that crime victims often suffer from difficulties beyond those that can be remedied by money. In a study of victim compensation in an eastern American state, for instance, Robert Elias found that applicants to the program felt more discontented than they would have been had the program not existed. The programs led victims to anticipate that they would be helped in an expeditious and kindly manner. When they encountered delays and bureaucratic barriers to getting the money they had come to expect, they became alienated from the system and hostile to it.

When the burgeoning women's movement turned its attention to the subject of crime, it too acknowledged that victims may need more than money to render them whole. Feminist leaders took up the cause of prostitutes, seeing them as exploited victims of a patriarchal society. Difficulties arose when many prostitutes rejected this definition, insisting that they preferred what they were doing to the menial and low-paying office or sales jobs they might otherwise be able to obtain. They saw themselves as entrepreneurs rather than as victims, and they viewed feminist concern for their plight as condescension by middle-class women.

The women's movement, after abandoning the issue of prostitution, turned its attention to victims of rape. The offense fit particularly well with the feminist ideology of victimization by men. Overwhelmingly rape offenders are men: only two hundred or so cases each year involve arrests of women for rape, most usually as accomplices who, for instance, hold a gun on another woman while a male co-offender sexually assaults her.

Many rape victims were found to suffer profound mental anguish that could only be relieved, if at all, by participation in treatment programs. Rape victims, like victims of other offenses, also had a tendency to assume blame for what had happened to them. They would ask themselves why they had trusted the acquaintance who assaulted them, or why they had not attended to the obvious clues about their assailant's true character. Why had they gone out that night?—and to that particular neighborhood? Why had they not fought back more forcefully or been able to talk their way out of the offense? Why had the man picked on them and not somebody else? Which attributes made them vulnerable and "victimizable"?

The pioneering victim-support programs, often devoted exclusively to rape victims, stumbled along, generally understaffed (and usually depending largely on volunteers), until the passage by Congress in 1984 of the Victims of Crime Act (VOCA). VOCA provided subsidies not only to state victim-compensation programs (35 percent of their costs) but to victim-assistance efforts as well. In 1988, VOCA-supported programs were further authorized to claim subsidies to aid victims of domestic violence and of drunken driving.

The embrace of victim-assistance programs primarily extends to victims of sexual and spousal abuse (including marital rape, a criminal offense newly defined in the 1960s) and child abuse, again offenses largely committed by men against women and children. Somewhat cynical onlookers point out that these offenses have always existed and that the intense limelight suddenly focused on them is based primarily on political and ideological maneuvering rather than on an increase in their number or seriousness. Some claim that deep concern with child abuse is the result of efforts by medical doctors to aggrandize their own position (and increase their income) by creating the issue of *battered-child syndrome* and defining a social problem as a medical matter, one calling for greater recourse to X rays and physician intervention. Attorneys are said to have prospered by filing suits against real and alleged child abusers (Costin, Karger, and Stoesz). The movement against child abuse also gave rise to a number of well-publicized cases in which adults claimed to have recovered long-repressed memories of abuse, usually by their father. Similarly, there have been numerous cases accusing child-care workers of sexual abuse of their young charges. In many of these situations strong evidence emerged that the child had been induced to give damning testimony by leading and suggestive questioning tactics (Ceci and Bruck).

Services to victims and witnesses customarily include crisis counseling (that is, short-term help with emotional difficulties), practical assistance, such as help in locating a new place to live, obtaining pregnancy tests and tests for sexually transmitted diseases, changing locks and repairing windows, and/or filing a criminal complaint. Referrals might be made to other social service agencies, such as welfare offices, and for psychiatric treatment. In addition, there has been a proliferation of shelters where women who are victims of abuse may find refuge and support. Some programs will transport a victim to the courtroom where the assailant's hearing or trial will be held, thus allowing the victim to become familiar with the setting beforehand. That defense witnesses do not usually have the advantage of this strategy is deplored by some, but usually is regarded by those aiding victims as a justified attempt to counterbalance the procedural advantages said to be enjoyed by defendants.

A survey published in 1999 found that nearly eight out of ten persons in the United States reported that they were very or somewhat satisfied with the services they received from victim-assistance programs. The major complaints involved slipshod operating methods and poor follow-through. A typical criticism was this: "They had me fill out forms and I never received any feedback. When I contacted them again they had me fill out the same old forms and nothing happened" (Davis, Lurigio, and Skogan (1999), p. 112).

In 1997, Congress passed a law permitting money in the federal Crime Victims Fund to be allocated to pilot programs that can help those injured by white-collar crimes, although the victims themselves cannot receive direct financial aid. Ironically, most of the money that goes into the fund is derived from fines paid by white-collar criminals.

Coordination of the network of victim service agencies is done by the National Organization of Victim Assistance, headquartered in Washington, D.C. A federal agency, the National Center for Victims of Crime, provides a web site detailing developments in the field and a computerized list of some twenty thousand federal and state victim-related statutes. The center also has created a database of approximately ten thousand court decisions dealing with crime victims and a roster of attorneys who handle civil cases for victims.

Victims of rape

The professional literature came to label the consequences of being a rape victim in medical terms, as *rape trauma syndrome*. Diagnosis of such a condition—later extended to other forms of victimization and formalized in medical annals as *post-traumatic stress disorder*, or PTSD—would come to play a significant role in some court cases. Defense attorneys might argue, for instance, that a person suffering from such a syndrome was no longer able to think rationally and therefore should not be held fully, if at all, responsible for, say, the murder or maiming of the perpetrator, even if the retaliatory act came a considerable time after the original offense. A severely battered woman would stand a decent chance of avoiding charges or being declared not guilty even though she had killed her husband while he was asleep and many hours after she had been mercilessly beaten, as she often was. Opponents of such outcomes complained that however abhorrent, wife-battering is not a death penalty offense.

Victim responsibility

The victim movement has given rise to a complicated issue that fundamentally rests upon an irresolvable question: Do human beings have free will or are their actions determined by immutable forces? Mental health counselors understandably work to relieve victims—especially victims of sexual assaults—of their common belief that in some way they were responsible for what happened to them. Tension exists between the insistence that the perpetrator alone bears full responsibility for his behavior and the victim's indulgence in self-blame. The difficulty becomes manifest when the offender adopts the same posture as the victim. He is not responsible either: it was an abusive father, faulty schooling, a slum upbringing, a brain malfunction, or some other predisposing factor beyond his control that led him to do what he did. A 1999 New Yorker cartoon epitomized the situation, showing a woman testifying in court: "I know he cheated on me because of his childhood abuse," she says, "but I shot him because of mine."

The most public manifestation of this issue surfaced when Hillary Rodham Clinton tried to explain the matter of her husband's infidelity. Her husband had to learn to take responsibility for his sexual waywardness, she declared in an interview, but at the same time she said that his behavior was the result of "abuse" as a child, apparently "abuse" growing out of "terrible conflict" between his mother and grandmother. "He was so young, barely four, when he was scarred by abuse," Mrs. Clinton said, adding that a psychiatrist had told her that being placed in the midst of conflict between two women "is the worst possible situation" for a boy because of his desire to please them both. Her husband's behavior, Mrs. Clinton said, was a "sin of weakness" rather than one of "malice."

Criticism of Mrs. Clinton's statement was widespread, indicating, perhaps, public saturation with the tendency to excuse so much current waywardness by labeling it as an outcome of earlier victimization or deprivation. A New York Times columnist pointed out that Mrs. Clinton had blamed her husband's sexual adventures on two women who adored him and, now deceased, could no longer defend themselves. The columnist also noted that the president's wife had done precisely what she deplored, placed her husband in the middle of a conflict between defending her position and defending his mother and grandmother. The president agreed publicly with what his wife said and at the same time exonerated his mother and grandmother for any role in his sexual waywardness.

Criminological theory and crime victims

Two major criminological theories often are used to interpret crime victimization. Lifestyle theories postulate that certain work and leisure patterns are more highly associated with crime victimization than others. Lifestyles are said to be influenced by three major considerations: the social roles that people play; their position in the social structure; and decisions about desirable behaviors (Hindelang, Gottfredson, and Garofalo). Thus, a woman working a job that ends in the early hours of the day may feel constrained financially to use public transportation and to walk several lonely blocks to her apartment because she cannot afford a taxi; she is more likely to become a crime victim than the woman riding in a taxi.

Routine activities concepts state that criminal offenses are related to the nature of everyday patterns of social existence. When most adults in a neighborhood are working, for instance, there is a greater likelihood that youngsters with increased freedom from adult supervision will get into trouble. So, too, houses unoccupied during the day make much more inviting targets than those with people at home or with neighbors who make it their business to be aware of what is occurring on the street (Cohen and Felson).

Rescuing victims: Good Samaritans

The blatant failure of persons to provide help for victims of crime when they might readily do so occasionally thrusts the issue of Good Samaritan laws into the headlines. Such laws, present in virtually all European countries (except England) but found in fewer than a handful of American states, mandate punishment for persons who, when they safely can, do not take action to assist a person being victimized. It would not be a crime in any but a few American states if an Olympic swimmer, sunning himself on the beach, felt too lazy to rescue a drowning infant a few feet away. Nor does anyone need to warn a blind man if he walks by and unknowingly heads toward a steep cliff a few yards away (Geis).

Particular attention focused in 1997 on the paparazzi who snapped pictures after the car-crash death of Princess Diana. Under French law the photographers could be accused of a criminal offense for failing to provide assistance to a person in need. Good Samaritan laws, such as those in France, take their name from the biblical parable of the Samaritan (Luke 10:29–36).

An early New York appellate court decision, *Zelenko v. Gimbel Bros.* (158 Misc. 904), captures the nature of the American approach to aiding victims in distress. A woman had collapsed in Gimbel's department store and was carried to the store infirmary and left there unattended for several hours. When she died her heirs sued the store and recovered. The court noted that the store and its employees owed the woman "no duty at all" and "could have let her be and die." Had they done so they would have avoided liability. Responsibility came into play only because of the store's "meddling in matters in which legally it had no concern."

The absence in the United States of Good Samaritan statutes is traced to the nation's philosophy of individualism, that nobody should be responsible for anybody but themselves. But there are those who believe that such laws underline the fact that citizens are intertwined and should be compelled to help crime victims if for no other reason than their own future need of such assistance.

Conclusion

At a reunion held in 1997 in the nation's capital to commemorate the thirtieth anniversary of the work of the President's Commission on Law Enforcement and Administration of Justice, James Vorenberg, the commission's director, said that the development that the group had most failed to anticipate was the subsequent surge of concern with crime victims.

Considerations that led to the striking increase in emphasis on crime victims include the broad campaign to empower those who were not being dealt with satisfactorily, among them minorities, women, gays, and the disabled. In addition, support of victim initiatives carried a great number of political pluses: few could oppose aiding victims, except in terms of cost, and those who did would appear cold-blooded and uncaring.

Once launched, the victim's movement inevitably built up a constituency that developed a strong personal vested interest in seeing its expansion: Crisis center workers, victimology scholars, and, of course, victims and potential crime victims. The movement has provided benefits for a great number of people who otherwise might have gone neglected. It has influenced the operation of the criminal justice system, sometimes for better, sometimes for the worse, with that judgment depending on the observer's political preferences. Most importantly, the renewed focus on crime victims has tilted the balance of the scales of justice more toward equity and fairness to all those who participate in and are effected by Western systems of criminal justice.

GILBERT GEIS

See also DISPUTE RESOLUTION PROGRAMS; HATE CRIMES; VICTIMLESS CRIMES; VICTIMS' RIGHTS.

BIBLIOGRAPHY

AMIR, MENACHEM. *Patterns of Forcible Rape*. Chicago: University of Chicago Press, 1971.

CECI, STEPHEN J., and BRUCK, MAGGIE. *Jeopardy in the Courtroom: A Scientific Analysis of Children's Testimony*. Washington, D.C.: American Psychological Association, 1995.

COHEN, LAWRENCE E., and FELSON, MARCUS. "A General Theory of Expropriate Crime: An Evolutionary Ecological Approach." *American Journal of Sociology* 94 (1979): 465–501.

COSTIN, LELA B.; KARGER, HOWARD J.; and STOESZ, DAVID. *The Politics of Child Abuse in America*. New York: Oxford University Press, 1996.

DAVIS, ROBERT C.; LURIGIO, ARTHUR J.; and SKOGAN, WESLEY G. *Victims of Crime*. 2d ed. Thousand Oaks, Calif.: Sage, 1997.

———. "Services for Victims: Market Research Study." *International Review of Victimology* 6 (1999): 101–115.

DIJK, JAN J. M. VAN, and MAYHEW, PAT. *Crime Victimization in the Industrial World*. The Hague: Ministry of Justice, 1992.

DIJK, JAN J. M. VAN; MAYHEW, PAT; and KILLIAS, MARTIN. *Experiences of Crime Across the World: Key Findings of the 1989 International Crime Survey.* Boston: Kluwer, 1991.

DODGE, RICHARD. *Locating City, Suburban, and Rural Crime.* Washington, D.C.: Bureau of Justice Statistics, U.S. Department of Justice, 1985.

ELIAS, ROBERT. *Victims of the System: Victims and the System in American Politics and Criminal Justice.* New Brunswick, N.J.: Transaction, 1983.

ELLINGSWORTH, DAN; FARRELL, GRAHAM; and PEASE, KEN. "A Victim Is a Victim Is a Victim? Chronic Victimization in Four Sweeps of the British Crime Survey." *British Journal of Criminology* 35 (1995): 360–365.

FERRARO, KENNETH F. *Fear of Crime: Interpreting Victimization Risk.* Albany: State University of New York Press, 1995.

FOOTE, WILLIAM E. "Victim-Precipitated Homicide." In *Lethal Violence: A Sourcebook on Fatal Domestic, Acquaintance and Stranger Violence.* Edited by Harold V. Hall. Baton Rouge, La.: CRC Press, 1999. Pages 174–202.

GEIS, GILBERT. "Should I (Legally) Be My Brother's Keeper?" In *Legal Philosophy: Selected Readings.* Edited by Timothy Shiell. Orlando, Fla.: Harcourt Brace Jovanovich, 1993.

GOVE, WALTER R.; HUGHES, MICHAEL; and GEERKEN, MICHAEL. "Are Uniform Crime Reports a Valid Indicator of the Index Crimes? An Affirmative Answer with Minor Qualifications." *Criminology* 23 (1985): 451–50l.

HINDELANG, MICHAEL J.; GOTTFREDSON, MICHAEL; and GAROFALO, JAMES. *Victims of Personal Crime: An Empirical Foundation for a Theory of Personal Victimization.* Cambridge, Mass.: Ballinger, 1978.

JACOBS, JAMES B., and POTTER, KIMBERLY. *Hate Crimes: Criminal Law and Identity Politics.* New York: Oxford University Press, 1998.

JENNESS, VALERIE, and BROAD, KENDAL. *Hate Crimes: New Social Movements and the Politics of Violence.* New York: Aldine de Gruyter, 1997.

KARMEN, ANDREW. *Crime Victims: An Introduction to Victimology.* 3d ed. Belmont, Calif.: Wadsworth, 1996.

KENNEDY, LESLIE W., and SACCO, VINCENT F. *Crime Victims in Context.* Los Angeles: Roxbury, 1998.

MAWBY, ROB I., and WALKLATE, SANDRA. *Critical Victimology: International Perspectives.* London: Sage, 1994.

MILLER, TED R.; COHEN, MARK A.; and WIERSEMA, BRIAN. *Victim Costs and Consequences: A New Look.* Washington, D.C.: National Institute of Justice, 1996.

OSBORN, DENISE R.; ELLINGSWORTH, DAN; HOPE, TIM; and TICKETT, ALAN. "Are Reportedly Victimized Households Different?" *Journal of Quantitative Criminology* 12 (1996): 223–245.

POLK, KENNETH. "A Reexamination of the Concept of Victim-Precipitated Homicide." *Homicide Studies* 1 (1997): 141–168.

ROBERTS, ALBERT R., ed. *Helping Crime Victims: Research, Policy, and Practice.* Newbury Park, Calif.: Sage, 1990.

RYAN, WILLIAM. *Blaming the Victim.* Rev. ed. New York: Vintage Books, 1976.

SEBBA, LESLIE. *Third Parties: Victims and the Criminal Justice System.* Columbus: Ohio State University Press, 1996.

SECHREST, DALE K.; SHICHOR, DAVID; DOOCY, JEFFREY H.; and GEIS, GILBERT. "Women's Responses to a Telemarketing Scam." *Women and Criminal Justice* 10 (1998): 75–89.

SMITH, STEVEN K.; STEADMAN, GREG W.; MINTON, TODD D.; and TOWNSEND, MEG. *Criminal Victimization and Perceptions of Community Safety in 12 Cities 1998.* Washington, D.C.: Bureau of Justice Statistics, U.S. Department of Justice, 1999.

WOLFGANG, MARVIN E. *Patterns in Criminal Homicide.* Philadelphia: University of Pennsylvania Press, 1958.

WRIGHT, RICHARD T., and DECKER, SCOTT H. *Burglars on the Job: Streetlife and Residential Break-ins.* Boston: Northeastern University Press, 1944.

VICTIMS' RIGHTS

At the end of the twentieth century, a broad movement supporting the rights of victims of crime prospered in the United States. This victims' rights movement has many facets, including both liberal and conservative components. Sometimes it conflicts with the prosecution, and sometimes it serves as the prosecution's ally.

Nature of victims' rights movement

The victims' rights movement includes three major elements. The first is an interest in guaranteeing victim participation in criminal proceedings. This dimension includes notice of proceedings and the right to be present and to be heard at them. This element also champions opportunities for victims to consult with prosecutors regarding whether to charge or to plea bargain with defendants. This set of interests may be called the participatory rights dimension of the movement. A second broad goal of the movement is to secure financial benefits and services for crime victims. This effort has led to restitution orders from perpetrators, which are required in many jurisdictions, and victim compensation programs funded from governmental resources. This focus also seeks to secure other services, such as shelters and support services for domestic violence victims, for certain identifiable groups of victims. A third element consists of efforts to secure more certain and harsher punishment for perpetrators, including restricting pretrial release, free admission of evidence against the accused, and tougher sentencing practices. In these efforts, victims frequently become the allies of prosecutorial and political forces that support a law-and-order agenda.

Sometimes these three aspects overlap as they do with evidence about the crime's impact on the victim or victim's family. Such victim impact evidence permits victims to have a direct voice in the sentencing process, often through in-person statements at sentencing that show the degree of injury suffered, and may aid the sentencer in determining the proper scope of restitution. The general, though not inevitable, outcome of victim impact statements is an increase in sentence severity.

Origins of the movement

The motivating force behind a movement that centers on the interests of victims in the criminal justice system has both liberal and conservative roots. Beginning in the 1960s, women's groups and feminists focused on the plight of rape victims. They brought attention to outmoded laws and attitudes toward rape and to the insensitivity of police, prosecutors, and the court system to rape victims. Their target also included lenient treatment of defendants. Later some of these same groups focused on battered women generally as victims, but sometimes as defendants when they responded to battering with self-help violence. Related efforts addressed systemic insensitivity to child abuse, particularly to sexual abuse of children. The leaders of this agenda were predominantly progressive, and they principally attacked conservative attitudes and laws.

A second component of the modern victims' rights movement sprang from conservative roots. In the 1960s the U.S. Supreme Court, under the leadership of Chief Justice Earl Warren, articulated procedural protections for defendants that were grounded in the Bill of Rights. This emphasis on the rights of defendants created resentment in many parts of American society, particularly with some crime victims. The rising crime rate over most of the next thirty years, together with the general rejection of much of liberal thinking regarding the treatment of criminals, such as the declining faith in rehabilitation, deepened those resentments. Victims took for themselves the language of rights that the Warren Court had championed for defendants and argued that such rights were needed to counterbalance the Court's mistakes and excesses and its resulting failures to curb the crime epidemic. Critics were reacting to the perceived failures of liberal treatment of crime and often sought the correction of a perceived imbalance in the criminal justice system that was seen as favoring criminals.

With these roots, the current formulation of much of the victims' rights movement began to take shape in the late 1970s and early 1980s with the founding of several important grassroots victim organizations, such as Parents of Murdered Children and Mothers Against Drunk Driving (MADD). Although having goals similar to those of the broadly focused women's groups that spearheaded the efforts to change rape laws, these organizations were more narrowly concerned with the impact of crime and the criminal justice system.

The movement was given critical shape and a conservative political focus when President Ronald Reagan and Attorney General Edwin Meese convened the President's Task Force on Victims of Crime in 1982. Many beneficial programs and services for victims ultimately flowed from that organizing effort, but an important consequence was to bring victims prominently into the criminal justice debate both as allies and as symbols for law-and-order practices. The effort to amend the U.S. Constitution to grant rights to victims of crime began with the report of the task force.

Goals and successes

The victims' rights movement cannot be understood without noting the reactions of individual victims, whose specific stories are a powerful part of the movement's message. These stories involve insensitivity and mistreatment—"a second victimization"—by the criminal justice system and a complaint that the system is designed to protect the perpetrator rather than the innocent victim. The leaders of the movement and those who fill its ranks are generally individuals who have suffered incredible tragedies through crime victimization. They demand respect and dignity from the criminal justice system. They want full participation in, and sometime control over, its processes. They often need financial support and other services. Many of them seek an outcome for perpetrators that is harsh, but there are elements of the movement that advance the goal of restorative justice. Frequently, victims appear to join the movement in hopes of bringing systemic change from their personal tragedy and thereby giving some meaning to that tragedy.

The successes of the movement are impressive. The one that is the most pervasive, and perhaps the most difficult to document fully, is the increased level of respect and dignity given to victims in the criminal justice system. Until the rise of the victims' movement, victims were relatively ignored in most court systems by the professionals who process criminal cases. Victims were sometimes important witnesses, but little more, and the demands of victims were often seen as an inconvenience. The movement has changed much of that picture. As the century ends, prosecutors' offices in most jurisdictions spend far greater time than they did twenty years earlier giving notice to victims and consulting with them about decisions in their case. Victim/witness coordinators and advocates are a part of the staff of many prosecutors' offices and court systems. They are charged with the general responsibility of shepherding victims through the intricacies of the criminal justice system. For example, they provide notice of proceedings, explain the system's operation, and help secure protection for threatened victims and services and compensation for those who have suffered harm. Laws have been changed to allow victims to be present throughout trials in a number of jurisdictions. Victims' information or their direct voices are heard in court, particularly at sentencing, and frequently at the time guilty pleas are received. In sum, both in giving greater respect and dignity to victims and in honoring their participatory interests, great strides were made during the 1980s and 1990s.

Success has occurred in terms of achieving the basic rights to restitution from defendants and to compensation from governmental funds. Beginning in the 1980s, most jurisdictions enacted laws that provide these benefits. Despite the creation of programs that provide benefits, the issue of restitution remains problematic. Most

defendants have few financial resources to provide in restitution, and many governmental compensation programs, which are often tied to revenues from the criminal justice system, are inadequately funded.

The impact of victims' groups can be seen in many of the other changes in the criminal justice system in the 1980s and 1990s. Rape shield laws, which restrict access to and use of the sexual history of rape victims, have been broadly enacted to encourage victims to come forward. Similarly, young victims of crime are often able to testify outside the presence of the accused. Community notification laws regarding the release of sex offenders, called Megan's law in memory of a child-victim of predatory violence, have been enacted under federal encouragement across the nation. Mandatory arrest and prosecution laws have been implemented in many jurisdictions for domestic violence cases because of the belief that such policies reduce such violence. These are just a few of the laws relating directly to the treatment of victims or potential victims that have been enacted through the advocacy of particular victims' groups. Somewhat related is the broad acceptance of "battered woman syndrome" evidence to support the defense of abused women who resort to self-help violence.

Changes in criminal law enforcement have made conviction more likely and punishment harsher, but some question whether such changes properly relate to victims' rights and whether they are wise. Many of these changes have been labeled by their supporters as part of victims' rights, and victims' groups have often been important to their passage. Tougher drunk driving laws represent one of the clearest example of the impact of victims' groups. Other changes less directly related to the interests of any particular victims' group include preventive detention laws, mandatory sentencing provisions (e.g., mandatory minimum sentences and three-strikes laws), and the abolition of parole. One significant feature associated with the rise of the conservative political component of the victims' rights movement is the role of victims, particularly victims of notorious crimes, in giving tragedy a human face for the public and spearheading a push for tougher law-and-order enactments.

The successes of the movement have been substantial across all three of the interests identified at the outset of this entry, although providing the financial and other services for victims remains problematic. Some argue that a conflict exists between the emphasis on tough crime control goals that focus on punishing defendants and success in securing resources for victims.

The new concentration on victims has been a contributing factor to a growing interest in exploring alternative ways of settling criminal cases. Viewing victims' interests as central to the criminal case means that mediation efforts are sometimes seen as reasonable alternatives to governmental prosecutions, particularly for minor crimes and crimes involving victims and perpetrators from the same community. Mediation efforts are controversial with some victim advocates because of the required contact between victims and those who did them harm, and the pressure placed on victims to compromise. Some victims' groups have pushed even beyond mediation for understanding and healing between victims and perpetrators in a movement called restorative justice, which presents an interesting alternative to traditional prosecution and dovetails with some communitarian justice movements. Here, too, the greatest likelihood of success exists in minor criminal cases, and perhaps juvenile delinquency matters.

Victim impact statements

A major interest of the victims' rights movement has been to have the opportunity to describe at sentencing the harm caused by the crime. Victim impact evidence was quickly accepted in non-death penalty cases. The interests of victims in participating in the process and in providing information to calculate appropriate restitution are generally acknowledged as providing adequate justification for receiving such information. Victim impact statements may be received in written form directly from victims or survivors, may be transmitted through presentence reports, or may be delivered in person at the time of sentencing.

The major area of controversy involved victim impact evidence in death penalty cases. In *Booth v. Maryland*, the U.S. Supreme Court decided in 1987 that the Eighth Amendment's prohibition on cruel and unusual punishment barred the presentation of such information because it created a substantial risk that the decision would be rendered arbitrarily. However, four years later in *Payne v. Tennessee*, the Court reversed its position and concluded that the Eighth Amendment imposed no restriction on this evidence. While it cautioned that victim impact statements could still be excluded if excessively prejudicial, the Court's majority made clear that it had heard

and accepted the voices of the victims' rights movement with respect to the theoretical and practical importance of impact information. The decision in *Payne* represents one of the movement's most impressive victories.

U.S. Constitutional protection for victims

The first serious effort to amend the U.S. Constitution on behalf of crime victims emerged from the efforts of the President's Task Force on Victims of Crime in 1982. The group's report, which is often cited as the watershed event for the victims' rights movement, inspired Congress to create an Office of Victims of Crime in the Justice Department. The Task Force also proposed adding a victims' rights provision to the Sixth Amendment, which otherwise guarantees the rights to the accused in criminal cases, such as the rights to a speedy and public trial and to counsel. It proposed an additional sentence: "Likewise, the victim, in every criminal prosecution shall have the right to be present and to be heard at all critical stages of judicial proceedings." The task force argued that only an amendment would secure the treatment and respect victims deserve.

Direct efforts to amend the federal Constitution were not begun immediately. Instead, supporters worked to build political momentum through victims' rights amendments in the states. Beginning slowly, these efforts have proved very successful. Between 1982 and 1989, five states approved victims' rights amendments. By the end of 1994, the number was twenty, and by the end of the decade, over thirty states had successfully adopted such amendments.

In September 1995, given the successes in amending state constitutions, the National Victims' Constitutional Amendment Network (NVCAN), an umbrella group representing the major victims' rights organizations, adopted specific language that it proposed be added to the Sixth Amendment. This marked the beginning of a serious effort to amend the U.S. Constitution on behalf of crime victims.

The amendment NVCAN proposed was much more complicated and far-reaching than the task force's simple sentence. Although subsequently modified, it provided a general outline for the serious consideration of an amendment. Beginning in 1996, Senators Jon Kyl of Arizona and Dianne Feinstein of California, two leading congressional proponents, introduced a proposed amendment in Congress, and its proponents pressed it forward in subsequent sessions.

In July 1998, it was approved by the Senate Judiciary Committee.

Drafted as a separate amendment, Senate Joint Resolution 3 (1999) would guarantee the following rights to victims of violent crime in federal and state criminal and juvenile proceedings:

- to reasonable notice of, and not to be excluded from, any public proceedings relating to the crime;
- to be heard, if present, and to submit a statement at all such proceedings to determine a conditional release from custody, an acceptance of a negotiated plea, or a sentence;
- to the foregoing rights at a parole proceeding that is not public, to the extent those rights are afforded to the convicted offender;
- to reasonable notice of and an opportunity to submit a statement concerning any proposed pardon or commutation of a sentence;
- to reasonable notice of a release or escape from custody relating to the crime;
- to consideration of the interest of the victim that any trial be free from unreasonable delay;
- to an order of restitution from the convicted offender;
- to consideration for the safety of the victim in determining any conditional release from custody relating to the crime;
- and to reasonable notice of the rights established by the amendment.

The amendment would give victims standing to enforce its provisions but would not authorize a suit for damages against any governmental unit. Congress would have power to enact enforcement legislation, and exceptions could be created only when necessary to achieve a "compelling interest."

The proposed amendment is controversial on a number of dimensions. The proponents argue that it is warranted because only a federal constitutional amendment can assure uniformity. Also, they believe an amendment is required to prevent the rights of victims from being overridden by rights of the defendants and excessive judicial deference to those rights. Moreover, they argue that the participatory rights guaranteed in the amendment are appropriate subjects for federal constitutional protection, similar to right of the press to access to judicial proceedings under the First Amendment. Finally, proponents believe that enshrining the rights in the Constitution is the only way to give victims full rights in the criminal process and thereby bring the system, which they contend currently favors the criminal defendants, into essential balance.

Opponents counter each of these arguments. They contend that uniformity is neither necessary nor appropriate given the youthful state of victims' rights and the traditional interests of the states in criminal law enforcement, which means the amendment would both inhibit experimentation and infringe upon traditional federalism concerns. Critics argue that reported cases show no tendency for courts to defer to defendants' rights by overruling victims' rights in statutes and state constitutional provisions. They believe that participatory rights, to the extent they do not conflict with the rights of the accused guaranteed by the Bill of Rights, can be fully protected by statutes and state constitutional provisions. They contend that to the extent that victims' rights conflict with defendants' rights, they are not the appropriate subject of a constitutional amendment, which should be reserved for protecting those unable to secure protection through democratic action, such as racial minorities and despised groups like those accused of crime, not to further the interests of politically popular victim groups who exercise power successfully through traditional methods.

One area in which the conflict between the traditional values of the criminal justice system and those supported by the amendment can be most clearly seen is in the amendment's constitutional guarantee of a right of victims to be present during all public proceedings. The conflict is most pronounced when several apparent victims are also the only witnesses to an alleged crime. Under longstanding sequestration rules in most U.S. jurisdictions, witnesses may be excluded upon request until it is time for them to testify to prevent the conscious or unconscious tailoring of their testimony to fit that of those who testify earlier. Under the proposed amendment, alleged victims cannot be excluded even though guilt has not yet been determined and their status as true victims therefore not decided. Such difficult cases include self-defense cases and those where charges of assault upon a police officer are countered with claims by the defendant that instead the crime involved is excessive force by the police. Opponents of the amendment argue that the constitutional right of such witnesses to remain in the courtroom undermines justice. Proponents counter that such cases are rare and that traditional truth-seeking tools such as cross-examination and jury argument and the existence of independent evidence in many cases eliminates or reduces the potential problem.

The major objection of opponents to the amendment, however, is conceptual. They argue that to the extent the amendment would affect outcomes in criminal cases it begs the essential questions of who is a true victim and whether the particular defendant is the responsible party. While the identity of the accused is clear at trial, the question of whether the apparent victim should have rights against the accused cannot be known until the verdict. Accordingly, in contrast to rights at sentencing, victims' rights that affect the outcome of the case are illegitimate. Aspects of the amendment that may have such effect include the right of victims to be present throughout the trial, noted above, and the right to affect pretrial release decisions and the decision whether proceedings should be delayed. However, the most significant impact would occur if the amendment was seen as changing the fundamental concept of criminal trials—from one in which the Constitution gives procedural rights to the defendants to protect them against erroneous convictions and to guard against abuses of governmental power, to one that involves a contest between a victim and a defendant both protected by constitutional rights. Rather than error in favor of acquittal of the accused citizen being accepted as the price of limiting governmental over-reaching, any errors in result might now constitute a violation of the government's constitutional duty to one of its citizens who stand on both sides of the case. Moreover, the rights of victims might been seen as added to the prosecution side of the litigation.

Amendment proponents label these last set of arguments as both overblown and misguided liberalism. The amendment's supporters nevertheless have the political attractiveness of the victims' rights concept on their side, which makes the enactment of the proposed constitutional amendment a real possibility.

Conclusion

The victims' rights movement, although a politically powerful force, remains in its infancy. In little over two decades of active life, it has changed the perception and status of victims in many American courtrooms. A respect and dignity is given to them that was absent a generation earlier. Victim services, compensation, and restitution are increasingly available. Another unde-

niable consequence of the movement has been tougher criminal sanctions.

Given its relative youth, the ultimate impact of the victims' rights movement cannot be easily foreseen. As it matures, that impact will no doubt become both more pervasive and more nuanced. The movement, regardless of its ultimate shape, is certain to be a major force in determining the development of the criminal justice system in the early decades of the new century.

ROBERT P. MOSTELLER

See also CAPITAL PUNISHMENT: LEGAL ASPECTS; CAPITAL PUNISHMENT: MORALITY, POLITICS, AND POLICY; CRIMINAL JUSTICE PROCESS; DISPUTE RESOLUTION PROGRAMS; DOMESTIC VIOLENCE; INFORMAL DISPOSITION; POLICE: COMMUNITY POLICING; PROSECUTION: HISTORY OF THE PUBLIC PROSECUTOR; PROSECUTION: PROSECUTORIAL DISCRETION; RESTORATIVE JUSTICE; SHAMING PUNISHMENTS; VICTIMS.

BIBLIOGRAPHY

BANDES, SUSAN. "Empathy, Narrative, and Victim Impact Statements." *University of Chicago Law Review* 63 (1996): 361–412.
———. "Victim Standing." *Utah Law Review* no. 2 (1999): 331–348.
BELOOF, DOUGLAS EVAN. "The Third Model of Criminal Process: The Victim Participation Model." *Utah Law Review* no. 2 (1999): 289–330.
———. *Victims in Criminal Procedure.* Durham, N.C.: Carolina Academic Press, 1999.
BROWN, JENNIFER GERARDA. "The Use of Mediation to Resolve Criminal Cases: A Procedural Critique." *Emory Law Journal* 43 (1994): 1247–1309.
CASSELL, PAUL G. "Balancing the Scales of Justice: The Case for and the Effects of Utah's Victims' Rights Amendment." *Utah Law Review* no. 4 (1994): 1373–1457.
———. "Barbarians at the Gates? A Reply to the Critics of the Victims' Rights Amendments." *Utah Law Review* no. 2 (1999): 479–544.
FLETCHER, GEORGE P. *With Justice for Some: Victims' Rights in Criminal Trials.* New York: Addison-Wesley, 1994.
GERWIRTZ, PAUL. "Victims and Voyeurs at the Criminal Trial." *Northwestern University Law Review* 90 (1996): 863–897.
HENDERSON, LYNNE N. "The Wrongs of Victim's Rights." *Stanford Law Review* 37 (1985): 937–1021.
———. "Revisiting Victim's Rights." *Utah Law Review* no. 2 (1999): 383–442.

KARMEN, ANDREW J. "Who's Against Victims' Rights? The Nature of the Opposition to Pro-Victim Initiatives in Criminal Justice." *Saint John's Journal of Legal Commentary* 8 (1992): 157–175.

LAMBORN, LEROY L. "Victim Participation in the Criminal Justice Process: The Proposals for a Constitutional Amendment." *Wayne Law Review* 34 (1987): 125–220.

MOSTELLER, ROBERT P. "Victims' Rights and the United States Constitution: An Effort to Re-cast the Battle in Criminal Litigation." *Georgetown Law Journal* 85 (1997): 1691–1715.

———. "Victims' Rights and the Constitution: Moving from Guaranteeing Participatory Rights to Benefiting the Prosecution." *St. Mary's Law Journal* 29 (1998): 1053–1065.

———. "The Unnecessary Victims' Rights Amendment." *Utah Law Review* no. 2 (1999): 443–479.

MOSTELLER, ROBERT P., and POWELL, H. JEFFERSON. "With Disdain for the Constitutional Craft: The Proposed Victims' Rights Amendment." *University of North Carolina Law Review* 78 (2000): 371–397.

PIZZI, WILLIAM T., AND PERRON, WALTER. "Crime Victims in German Courtrooms: A Comparative Perspective on American Problems." *Stanford Journal of International Law* 32 (1996): 37–64.

President's Task Force on Victims of Crime. Final Report. 1982.

SENDOR, BENJAMIN B. "Restorative Retributism." *Journal of Contemporary Legal Issues* 5 (1994): 323–363.

SHAPIRO, BRUCE. "Victims and Vengeance: Why the Victims' Rights Amendment Is a Bad Idea." *The Nation* 10 February 1997, pp. 11–19.

ZIMRING, FRANK E. "Populism, Democratic Government, and the Decline of Expert Authority: Some Reflections on 'Three Strikes' in California." *Pacific Law Journal* 28 (1996): 243–256.

CASES

Booth v. Maryland, 482 U.S. 496 (1987).
Payne v. Tennessee, 501 U.S. 808 (1991).

VIGILANTISM

The term *vigilante*, of Spanish origin, means "watchman" or "guard." Its Latin root is *vigil*, for "awake" or "observant." Vigilantes have also been known as "slickers," "stranglers," "mobs," and "committees of safety."

Origins

American vigilantism originally arose as a frontier response to the threat and reality of crime. The first settlers who moved to the Deep South and the Old West were not protected by a criminal justice system. There were no law enforcement agencies, no regularly scheduled court sessions, no nearby jails or prisons, and vast open spaces to which offenders could escape from their victims. In the absence of any legal system, correctional facilities, or institutional mechanisms for redress of grievances, victims and their allies felt compelled periodically to track down and round up outlaws and "take the law into their own hands" (see Madison; Brown).

Vigilance committees were voluntary associations of men (rarely including women) who worked together to combat genuine, exaggerated, or imagined dangers to their communities, families, property, power, or privileges. These short-lived organizations usually had formal hierarchies, strictly defined chains of command, written bylaws, and paramilitary rituals. Their leadership typically was drawn from the elite of frontier society, including local businessmen, plantation owners, ranchers, merchants, and professionals. The members were recruited from the middle strata. The targets of their wrath generally were singled out from the lower classes and marginal groups. Vigilantes blacklisted, harassed, banished, flogged, tarred and feathered, tortured, mutilated, and killed their victims (Madison; Brown).

Lynchings originally were public whippings carried out in Virginia in the late 1700s by a vigilance committee led by a Colonel Lynch. As the years passed, and the violent punishments meted out by vigilante bands escalated, the expression came to mean a summary execution, usually by hanging. *Lynch mobs* were more spontaneous and less organized than vigilance committees. Vigilantes who acted as part of a committee or mob were able to conceal their identities, especially when shrouded by darkness or disguised by hoods, masks, or uniforms. Acting in concert also bolstered their courage, diminished their sense of individual responsibility for the suffering they inflicted, and virtually eliminated their risk of getting caught and punished for their illegal deeds (Burrows).

Vigilantism has been a label placed on so many different situations over the centuries that no precise definition can capture all its elements, and arguments inevitably arise over the appropriateness of categorizing some group or event as an example of vigilantism. The essential defining elements of vigilantism are that it embodies the following: a social reaction to crime; actions taken by civilians (whether as individuals, or as members of clandestine groups, large crowds, or mass movements) as opposed to government officials; a response that involves violence that exceeds the legitimate use of force in self-defense; an intent to inflict punishment and pain in order to avenge a previous wrong or to deter future misconduct or to incapacitate dangerous persons; a belief that the resort to force is necessary and justifiable because government agents cannot or will not provide protection or enforce the law; and a recognition that the remedies undertaken are illegal, since governments claim a monopoly over the legitimate use of force in the form of police and military action (Sederberg; Culberson; Johnston; and Moses).

Examples

American history is peppered with outbreaks of vigilantism. The first recorded series of incidents took place in the backwoods of South Carolina in 1767. To counter a reign of terror imposed by roving gangs of desperadoes and plunderers, isolated frontiersmen banded together and called themselves the Regulators because they viewed their efforts as restoring balance to a situation that had slipped out of control. They carried out a bloody two-year campaign to suppress banditry that successfully reestablished law and order within their immediate territory, but their excesses provoked the mobilization of an opposition movement, the Moderators.

The largest vigilance committee arose in San Francisco when it was a Gold Rush boomtown. As many as eight thousand members joined to retake the streets from criminals who were terrorizing the townspeople in 1856. Four alleged murderers were hanged and many suspected thieves and gamblers were driven away by mob action. But the committee also had a political agenda, and used its power to wrest control of the municipal political machinery from recently arrived Irish Catholics.

The nation's bloodiest vigilante movements swept across Montana from 1863 to 1865, and again in 1884. Thirty people were put to death during the first wave of violent vigilantism, including a corrupt Rocky Mountain sheriff said to be in league with highwaymen and horse thieves.

During the second wave, thirty-five people branded as outlaws were slain by mob action.

Between 1767 and 1909, at least 326 vigilante movements arose across the country. The typical committee had between one hundred and several hundred members, and lasted up to one year. Fewer than half of the known movements claimed any lives. Of the 141 movements responsible for carrying out 729 unauthorized executions, the largest committees tended to be the most deadly. Most of the violence erupted in the West, especially in Texas, Montana, and California, from the time of the Civil War up to the end of the nineteenth century (see Brown).

A much larger death toll mounted because of the rampages of unorganized lynch mobs, primarily in the Deep South. Between 1882 and 1951, angry crowds lynched about 4,730 victims. During the last decades of the nineteenth century, the number of people killed by lynch mobs exceeded the number of court-ordered executions. Even if they formed spontaneously, lynch mobs after Reconstruction also served as a vehicle for white supremacists to intimidate local black residents from exercising their constitutional and civil rights. Black men were the primary but not the only victims of angry crowds. In New Orleans in 1891, a huge mob mobilized by a local vigilance committee stormed the city jail and lynched eleven Italian immigrants alleged to be Mafia leaders responsible for the assassination of a high-ranking police official. After World War I, mob attacks grew more vicious; an estimated 10 percent of the victims were burned alive, and yet Congress failed to respond to an antilynching movement's outcry that federal legislation should compel law enforcement authorities to investigate, arrest, and prosecute ringleaders. Lynchings tapered off by the 1920s and were rare by the 1940s (Hofstadter and Wallace; Moses).

Ideologies of vigilante groups

Vigilante violence is the opposite of revolutionary violence. Revolutionaries resort to force in order to overthrow the established order and create new arrangements, whereas vigilantes unleash violence to restore order and maintain the status quo. In their manifestos, vigilance committees proclaimed that their coercive campaigns were meant to halt destabilizing trends, shore up faltering structures, revive fading traditions, and buttress existing relationships. Their actions were intended to quash challenges to local elites from either below or outside.

To legitimize their lawless deeds, vigilantes argued that their ends justified their means. In order to preserve sacred traditions, enforce conventional moral codes, and further respect for authority, "honorable red-blooded, law-abiding" citizens sometimes were compelled to impose "retaliatory justice." They portrayed themselves as acting in self-defense as they lashed out in righteous indignation against "idlers," "parasites," "intruders," "corrupters," and "predators." They filled their manifestos with appeals to natural law, patriotism, and religion. Claiming that the basic law of nature is survival, vigilante committee spokesmen asserted that a right to self-preservation took precedence over written legislation and procedural guidelines in life-and-death, kill-or-be-killed struggles. In their speeches and writings, leaders and supporters reaffirmed their faith in God and country and in the ultimate sanctity of the law. But they interpreted the democratic ideals of popular sovereignty and the right to revolution as calls to action when government officials seemed inept, corrupt, or overly tolerant of criminal behavior. In their appeals to others to join their mobilization, vigilantes invoked the cherished frontier ethics of self-reliance and of male responsibility for the well-being of women and children. Leading elected officials, judges, lawyers, and legal scholars accepted and defended the vigilante credo during the late 1800s and early 1900s. More concerned with suppressing disruptive behavior than with respecting due process, they granted qualified approval to vigilantism's simple, direct, swift, certain, and severe punishments as a rational response to the inadequacies, delays, and uncertainties of an allegedly "ineffectual" criminal justice process (Hofstadter and Wallace; Madison; and Brown).

The Ku Klux Klan and other "night rider" groups have been the most explicitly ideological of all vigilante groups. Since the period of Reconstruction that followed the Civil War, Klansmen have attacked "troublemakers" that they believed threatened their way of life: rebellious members of minority groups who did not accept their place in the local social order, civil rights activists, labor union organizers, recently arrived immigrants, outside agitators, and alleged subversives. Most of the victims of Klan terror have been African Americans, Catholics, and Jews.

Contemporary vigilantism

Although the frontier disappeared from the American scene long ago, outbreaks of vigilantism persist and even can be considered common if broadly defined. For example, a strain of vigilantism underlies criminal verses criminal revenge killings: drive-by shootings among feuding street gangs, turf battles between rival drug-selling crews, and mob hits among warring syndicates. People engaged in illegal activities cannot present their grievances to the authorities without incriminating themselves, so they feel compelled to take the law into their own hands to retaliate against those who wronged them.

Teenagers act as vigilantes when they attack homeless vagrants and drive them away or set them on fire. Overzealous self-appointed protectors of the neighborhood commit illegal acts of "do-it-oneself justice" when they burn down drug dens like crack houses, or firebomb the homes of former child molesters or rapists whose whereabouts were made public by community notification requirements. Vigilante impulses to inflict on-the-spot punishments surface whenever angry crowds quickly gather, chase after, and mete out "curbstone justice" or "street justice" to known or suspected purse snatchers, prowlers, burglars, robbers, and rapists before the police arrive. Officers themselves can engage in police vigilantism if they beat a suspect on the street, during the ride to the police station, or in its basement, to make sure the perpetrator is punished before being released with a mere "slap on the wrist" by the "revolving door" of an overly lenient justice system (Marx and Archer; Shotland; and Kotecha and Walker).

Highly politicized expressions of vigilantism also marred life in the United States at the end of the twentieth century. Angry citizens frustrated by what they perceived to be an invasion of illegal aliens from Mexico organized their own heavily armed patrols to supplement Immigration and Naturalization Service (INS) efforts to stop border crossings. Certain acts of domestic terrorism embodied vigilantism, as when rogue elements within the right-to-life movement—convinced that abortion constitutes murder—assassinated doctors who legally terminated pregnancies or bombed the clinics where these medical procedures are performed. Some bias crimes that expressed the offender's hatred of the victim's "kind" of person were motivated by an impulse comparable to Klan-type vigilantism to rid society of "undesirables," as when volatile members of white supremacist neo-Nazi groups randomly attacked complete strangers solely because of their race or religion. Survivalists, imbued with the frontier spirit of self-reliance and self-preservation, stockpiled weapons and ammunition and warned that they would resort to vigilantism in the event of a breakdown of law and order in the aftermath of a natural disaster, financial collapse, chemical or biological attack, nuclear war, or political turmoil. Militia groups, motivated by their interpretation of the meaning of patriotism, denounced what they perceived to be treachery at the highest levels of government and proclaimed their willingness to fight local, state, and federal authorities to preserve the first ten amendments of the Constitution. They set up their own "common law courts," in which "sovereign citizens" or "freemen" could exercise their "God-given rights" to avoid taxes, and to indict, put on trial, convict, and call for punishments of troublemakers as well as treasonous public officials (Dees and Corcoran; and Stern).

The theme of victims inflicting severe physical punishments on offenders who were not caught by the police, or not convicted in court, or not sufficiently punished by the court-imposed sentence, has been a popular element in the plots of many books and movies. However, in real life, few former victims have launched anticrime crusades in which they lashed out ferociously against those who would dare to try to harm them; and those that did were not hailed as heroes, and did not inspire copycat crimes. Fears that neighborhood-based civilian anticrime patrols, which serve as the eyes and ears of the police, would evolve into Latin American–type "death squads" whose targets "disappear" turned out to be unfounded as the twentieth century ended.

Tendencies toward vigilantism are held in check by countervailing forces and ideologies. Police and prosecutors press charges against those who exceed the legal limits of the legitimate use of force in self-defense. The tenets of professionalism espoused by law enforcement officials proclaim that the criminal justice process must be controlled by experts, not laymen who want to break rules and impose their own notions of just deserts. Civil rights and civil liberties organizations advance the argument that due process safeguards and constitutional guarantees must be followed in order to protect innocent persons from being falsely accused, mistakenly convicted, and unjustly punished. Vigilante "justice" imposed by lynch mobs has been exposed as too swift and too sure, with its kangaroo courts and railroading of suspects, and too severe, with vicious beatings and brutal on-the-spot executions as punishments that do not fit the crime. Vigilantism turns victims into victimizers. Formerly accepted with pride, the label *vigilante* remains a derogatory term.

ANDREW KARMEN

See also CRIME CAUSATION: POLITICAL THEORIES; JUSTIFICATION: LAW ENFORCEMENT; JUSTIFICATION: NECESSITY; JUSTIFICATION: SELF-DEFENSE; VICTIMS; VIOLENCE.

BIBLIOGRAPHY

BROWN, RICHARD M. "Strain of Violence: Historical Studies of American Violence and Vigilantism." New York: Oxford University Press, 1975.
BURROWS, WILLIAM E. *Vigilante!* New York: Harcourt Brace Jovanovich, 1976.
CULBERSON, WILLIAM C. *Vigilantism: Political History of Private Power in America.* Westport, Conn.: Praeger, 1990.
DEES, MORRIS, and CORCORAN, JAMES. *Gathering Storm: America's Militia Network.* New York: HarperCollins, 1996.
HOFSTADTER, RICHARD, and WALLACE, MICHAEL, eds. *American Violence: A Documentary History.* New York: Knopf, 1970.
JOHNSTON, LAWRENCE. "What is Vigilantism?" *British Journal of Criminology* 36, no. 2 (1996): 220–236.
KOTECHA, KANTI C., and WALKER, JAMES L. "Vigilantism and the American Police." In *Vigilante Politics.* Edited by H. Jon Rosenbaum and Peter C. Sederberg. Philadelphia: University of Pennsylvania Press, 1976. Pages 158–172.
MADISON, ARNOLD. *Vigilantism in America.* New York: Seabury Press, 1973.
MARX, GARY T., and ARCHER, DANE. "Community Police Patrols and Vigilantism." In *Vigilante Politics.* Edited by H. Jon Rosenbaum and Peter C. Sederberg. Philadelphia: University of Pennsylvania Press, 1976. Pages 129–157.
MOSES, NORTON. *Lynching and Vigilantism in the United States: An Annotated Bibliography.* Guilford, Conn.: Greenwood Press, 1997.
SEDERBERG, PETER C. "Phenomenology of Vigilantism in Contemporary America—An Interpretation." *Terrorism* 1, no. 3 (1978): Pages 287–305.
SHOTLAND, R. LANCE. "Spontaneous Vigilantism: A Bystander Response to Criminal Behavior." In *Vigilante Politics.* Edited by H. Jon Rosen-

baum and Peter C. Sederberg. Philadelphia: University of Pennsylvania Press, 1976. Pages 30–44.

STERN, KENNETH S. *A Force Upon the Plain: The American Militia Movement and the Politics of Hate.* New York: Simon & Schuster, 1996.

VIOLENCE

The term *violence* is used to describe animal and human behavior that threatens to cause or causes severe harm to a target. Most animal studies emphasize variations in *aggression* and use the concept of extreme aggression (rather than violence) to denote the most serious and injurious behavior. In studying human behavior, violence and aggression are frequently used as synonyms, with violence marked by an extra degree of excessiveness. In some cases, the choice of the term "aggression" or "violence" is a matter or preference or convention. For example, aggression is most commonly used to describe young children's behavior while such behavior in adolescents is called youth violence. Violence tends to be the preferred term for describing classes of behavior or phenomenon (e.g., domestic violence, media violence, sports violence) without specific reference to the degree of severity involved.

Different authorities have been extremely variable in their willingness to include a range of actions under the heading of violence. Indeed, there has been much controversy about the term and just what actions should be covered. Some have offered more limited definitions based on constraints such as intentionality, legality, and nature of targets. Each limitation provides a more specific definition with associated advantages and disadvantages. For instance, many definitions of both aggression and violence specify that harm be intentional. Accidentally causing serious injury generally is not considered an act of violence in both common discourse and legal proceedings. However, specifying intentionality poses measurement challenges because violence can no longer be judged by merely observing a behavior; rather, the mental state of the person must be assessed or inferred.

Limiting the definition of violence to "illegal behaviors" that cause harm or injury is consistent with legal guidelines. Such a definition is useful from a policy and control perspective because it covers actions generally considered as violent, including forcible rape, armed robbery, aggravat-ed assault, gang violence, and homicide. A problem with this definition is that the same behavior may be judged illegal or legitimate depending on specific cultural and historical conditions. From this perspective, a behavior would only be considered violent if there were official sanctions against it.

Some definitions of violence include only behavior that is designed to harm others (or animate beings). This focus emphasizes the antisocial and immoral nature of violence as an act against others and society. It is consistent with most contemporary criminal definitions of violence. However, it excludes the self as a target of harm and injury, which is inconsistent with public health definitions of violence that generally include harm to self. Other definitions construe the target even more broadly, extending it to include inanimate objects (e.g., destruction of property).

Classification

Violence is not one behavioral pattern but several. The multifaceted and complex nature of violence has led to a number of proposed guidelines and classification schemes for studying its component parts. Behavioral scientists have worked to develop classifications by grouping together meaningful categories of violence that share common characteristics related to etiology and function. One approach has been to classify violence according to the underlying motivation of the aggressor. A frequently used distinction is between *hostile* and *instrumental* motivation. In hostile violence, the major goal is to inflict harm or injury. In other words, hurting is an end in itself. In instrumental violence, actions may cause harm but are not motivated by the desire to cause harm per se. Rather, they are motivated by goals such as taking resources from others. In both cases, this distinction depends on the individual's intent, not on the act itself.

Although not conceptually clean, this distinction has proved useful. Certain types of violence such as armed robbery, murder-for-hire, and terrorism generally are well planned, goal-directed, instrumental actions. Offenders are acting to maximize their benefits and minimize their costs. Many prominent models of criminal behavior emphasize the rational choice component of crime (e.g., Cornish and Clarke). This type of planned behavior is distinguished from more impulsive and hostile violent actions often characterized by loss of control, irrationality, and rage. Such impulsive violent behaviors are frequently labeled emotional violence and are linked with emotions such as anger and fear. Biological models of violence have identified distinct neural patterns that characterize each type of violence. For example, the "low-arousal" aggressor more likely to commit instrumental violence is underreactive and responds sluggishly to stressors. In contrast, the "high-arousal" aggressor who is more prone to hostile violence tends to be hypervigiliant and easily frustrated (Niehoff).

Another distinction between classes of violence that bears some similarity to the hostile/instrumental classification is the difference between defensive and offensive violence. This distinction has been fundamental to animal studies of aggression, with defensive and offensive aggression linked to stimulation of different areas of the brain. In humans, instrumental aggression is roughly analogous to predatory aggression although it is limited to intraspecies behavior. In other words, when humans kill animals for food it is generally not considered offensive violence in the same sense as killing a rival gang member. Similarly, emotional or hostile aggression in humans could be considered the analogue of defensive aggression in response to a threat or perceived threat. Studies of children have found differences in propensity for *proactive* aggression and *reactive* aggression, although some children score high on both types of aggression (Dodge and Coie). This work provides some empirical support for distinguishing between offensive violence that is unprovoked and defensive violence that is a reaction to another's provocation.

Clearly, different classification schemes serve different purposes. In everyday usage, violence is often divided into distinct classes based on criteria useful for description, dialogue, and public policy. Violence can be grouped into categories based on variables such as the agents of violence (e.g., gangs, youth, collective groups), the victims of violence (e.g., women, children, minority groups), the relationship between aggressor and victim (e.g., interpersonal, nonrelated), perceived causality (e.g., psychopathological, situational, learned), and type of harm (e.g., physical, psychological, sexual). These criteria are frequently combined to examine particular forms of violence, such as psychological abuse of women in intimate relationships, youth sexual violence, instrumental collective violence, and so on.

Some efforts have focused on developing classification systems that can guide prevention, intervention, and control efforts. Tolan and Guerra describe four types of youth violence: *situational, relationship, predatory,* and *psychopathological.* This is not an exclusive classification proposed to cover all types of violence, but rather provides some conceptual organization for structuring efforts to prevent or reduce violence. Each distinct type of violence is associated with different causal mechanisms and warrants a different type of intervention. For example, relationship violence is influenced more by anger and conflict than predatory acts of violence such as armed robbery of a stranger. Consequently, biochemical interventions that block anger arousal or conflict-resolution training programs that teach anger management skills may have some influence on relationship violence but much less influence on predatory violence.

The causes of violence

As historical and cross-cultural records demonstrate, our evolutionary history is laced with examples of violence. Indeed, paleontological data reveal a rather continuous stream of human violence dating back thousands of years. It is clear that violence is not restricted to early historical periods or particular cultural groups. Despite recent concerns in the United States and elsewhere over spiraling violence rates, available data suggest that there is actually less violence now than in ancient times. From an evolutionary perspective, human violence may represent a context-sensitive solution to particular problems of social living that may ebb and flow in accordance with changing conditions. In reviewing these adaptive functions, Buss and Shackelford describe seven problems for which violence may have evolved as a solution: (1) co-opting the resources of others; (2) defending against attack; (3) inflicting costs on same-sex rivals; (4) negotiating status and power hierarchies; (5) deterring rivals from future aggression; (6) deterring males from sexual infidelity; and (7) reducing resources expended on genetically unrelated children.

Against a backdrop of adaptive violence, there are still many other factors that play a role in the ontogeny of violence and help explain variations in violence across individuals and social groups. In most cases, a number of different factors converge to increase the likelihood of violent behavior. These factors can be divided into roughly three groups: (1) innate factors; (2) socialization factors; and (3) situational factors.

Innate factors. Early efforts to unveil differences between violent and nonviolent individuals began with attempts to assign precise neural locations to a range of behaviors including violence. Known as *phrenology*, this approach assigned high priority to the innate and presumably defective aspects of individual makeup. The idea that behaviors are linked to physical characteristics also drove some of the first criminological efforts to understand the etiology of violence. Perhaps the most well-known work is that of nineteenth-century Italian criminal anthropologist Cesare Lombroso, who popularized the notion that violent individuals possessed distinct physical features indicative of primitive or inferior development, known as *atavisms*.

A concern over physical features gave way to the far more powerful influence of genetics. Although there was much resistance toward biology-as-destiny approaches, more and more geneticists were taking over the reigns of biology. However, much of the early writing on the genetic underpinnings of violence failed to pinpoint the precise causal mechanisms. The lack of a genetic road map did not unravel efforts to search for the innate determinants of aggression. Support for the idea that aggression was hardwired from birth came from a number of different encampments.

Beginning in the early part of the twentieth century, ethologists saw aggression and violence as a response to the call of internal mechanisms or *instincts*. This emphasis found good company in the Freudian psychoanalysts. They saw aggression as derived from an inborn tendency to destroy. Like all instincts, it builds up over time and must ultimately be discharged in either acceptable or unacceptable ways. This pressure is made worse by frustration. The idea that aggression and violence are linked to frustration had a significant impact on the field and was followed by models emphasizing the frustration-aggression connection (Dollard et al.). Although still grounded in a drive model of behavior, this work also provided evidence that violence can be learned. Still, innate drive theories persisted and were later popularized by the writings of Konrad Lorenz. According to Lorenz, aggression was not simply a response to an instinct but was itself an innate driving force, notable for both its spontaneity and centrality to species preservation.

But drive theories found themselves caught up in an empty vessel. There was little evidence to indicate that aggressive energy builds up until it is released. Further, while the notion of drive or instinct may have some descriptive utility, it offered little in the way of specifying the precise internal mechanisms that underlie violence and ran the risk of engendering a pessimistic attitude about prevention. Fortunately, scientific advances in understanding neuranatomy, brain chemistry, and genetic transmission allowed for increasingly greater precision in understanding the biology of violence, leading us farther from the notion of violence as inevitable instinct. The role of key areas of the brain in regulating emotion and behavior is now well established. Violence has also been associated with some kinds of brain damage from birth trauma, tumors, or head injury. However, rather than acting alone, the biological and social environments seem to exert reciprocal influences.

For example, threat perceptions involve neurotransmitters that partially determine an individual's sensitivity to environmental stimuli—some more reactive, others less so. But environmental exposure to violence, danger, or abuse during the early years can quickly overload the brain's alarm system, creating adolescents who are hypervigilant to stress and overreact to environmental cues (Pynoos, Steinberg, and Ornitz). Hypervigilance to threats may also explain some of the inconclusive findings linking testosterone and aggression. It appears that testosterone is linked to specific types of aggression, notably the tendency to "fight back" in a more defensive or reactive fashion related to heightened threat perception rather than the tendency to start fights or engage in offensive aggression (Olweus, Mattson, and Low).

Socialization factors. Not only does the social environment serve as a trigger for biological development, it also provides a context for learning appropriate behaviors. Whatever propensity for violence is written on an individual's biological birth certificate, it is clearly molded and shaped through interactions with others. There is a sizable body of evidence showing that early socialization across multiple contexts accounts for much of the individual differences in later violent behavior.

Different mechanisms have been implicated in the learning of violence. Early theories stressed the importance of reinforcement. A young child wants a toy, but his playmate will not relinquish it. The boy pushes and grabs the toy and the playmate relents. Aggression works. If followed by reinforcement, both mild aggression and serious violence are likely to increase. Such reinforcement is not limited to tangible objects;

it can include outcomes such as attention, status, and advantageous positioning in the peer status hierarchy, similar to some of the adaptive functions of aggression discussed previously.

In addition to the role of reinforcement, early formulations of social learning theory emphasized the role of observational learning (Bandura). Individuals who see others use and obtain rewards for violence, especially others whom they admire, are more likely to imitate them and behave violently under similar circumstances. As a psychological mechanism, modeling can also explain variation in violence levels across different social groups and cultures. As violence becomes more legitimate in a social group, it is more likely that members will conform to these emerging group norms. Some observers have described a "code of violence" that characterizes the behavior of many inner-city males. Status is associated with willingness to use violence, and children emulate the toughness and violence of older male role models.

Much of the concern about the links between exposure to media to violence and aggression derives from social learning theory. Research with children has clearly demonstrated a correlation with exposure to media violence and aggressive behavior. Children who watch more violent movies and television are more likely to engage in similar behaviors both as children and adults. Long-term exposure to media violence fosters later violence through several mechanisms. In addition to teaching aggressive attitudes and behaviors, it also seems to desensitize viewers to violence, making it more acceptable. People who watch a lot of televised violence also show exaggerated fears of violence, perhaps making them more hypervigilant and susceptible to reactive outbursts.

The media is but one socialization context that can promote the learning of violence. Research has shown that both parents and peers can be a powerful force in shaping children's behavior. Lack of attention to children's behavior and inconsistent parental discipline and monitoring of activities have been consistently related to the development of aggressive and violent behavior patterns. Extremely harsh and abusive parenting has also been linked to later aggression. Stated simply, "violence begets violence." Equally important is the failure of positive encouragement for prosocial and nonviolent behaviors. Many parents ignore children's efforts at solving conflicts peacefully or managing frustration. Oversights such as these may inadvertently teach children that aggressive acts alone are worthy of notice.

Peers also exert an influence from an early age, but seem to become most important during adolescence. Perhaps one of the most robust findings in the delinquency literature is that antisocial and violent peers tend to gravitate toward one another. Delinquents associate with each other and this association stimulates greater delinquency. Nowhere is this more apparent than in the actions of gangs. Not only is violent behavior accepted, it is required. Members must be "jumped in" via violent victimization; the same procedure is followed for those who want to leave the gang.

The environment also operates to influence the learning of violence. Some studies of environmental influences have focused on the effects of poverty and disadvantage. Poverty itself does not cause violence. Rather, being poor affects one's life experiences in several ways conducive to violence. Individuals living in poor neighborhoods have few resources and supports for healthy development and are more likely to experience multiple stressors. In some neighborhoods, there are few legitimate routes to financial success and social status, which may also engender feelings of relative deprivation in contrast to middle-class society. Those who have little also have little to lose. Thus, low social and economic status may contribute to heightened risk-taking behavior, an idea that finds some support in psychological studies showing that artificially lowering an individual's self-esteem gives rise to higher levels of risky or rule-breaking behavior.

In urban settings, poverty often produces situational factors, such as overcrowding, that are linked to violence. Indeed, the highest rates of violence typically are found among the urban poor (Dahlberg). Drive-by shootings and random violence have come to characterize some of the most distressed, inner-city communities. As violence increases and neighborhoods become more dangerous, the use of force may be seen as normal and even necessary for self-protection. A *subculture of violence* can emerge wherein violence is legitimized as an acceptable behavior within certain groups. The idea that degree of violence is related to the prevailing social norms about its acceptability can also shed light on cross-cultural differences. Countries where violence is considered non-normative such as Japan have low homicide rates; countries where violence has become almost a way of life such as El Salvador and Guatemala have homicide rates over one hundred times higher (Buvinic, Morrison, and Shifter).

These different contextual factors can serve as a training ground for violence via their influence on children's learning. However, beyond a focus on how individuals learn violent behavior through socialization, recent efforts have highlighted the importance of cognitive processes that help shape and control behavior—what might be called the software of the brain. Studies have shown that more aggressive and violent individuals have different ways of processing information and thinking about social situations. They tend to interpret ambiguous cues as hostile, think of fewer nonviolent options, and believe that aggression is more acceptable (Crick and Dodge). Once these cognitions crystallize during socialization, they are more resistant to change.

Situational factors. Both innate factors and socialization experiences mold an individual's propensity to violence. But this is not the whole story. It appears that situational catalysts can also lead to violence and increase the seriousness of such behavior. Almost any aversive situation can provoke violence. Frustrating situations are linked to heightened aggression, although frustration does not always produce aggression and is certainly not the only instigating mechanism. Other aversive experiences such as pain, foul odors, smoke, loud noises, crowding, and heat portend heightened aggressiveness, even when such behavior cannot reduce or eliminate the aversive stimulation (Berkowitz).

The influence of pain on violent behavior has been widely studied. Pain-instigated aggression is often cited as one of the clearest examples of aversively generated aggression. Further, the likelihood of overt aggression increases as the pain becomes greater and the ability to avoid it decreases. However, it is not necessarily the pain, per se, that causes aggression. Indeed, investigations of people suffering from intense pain have documented higher levels of anger and hostility and speculate that subsequent aggression may be due to the agitated negative affect that accompanies pain rather than the pain itself. Along these lines, any type of aversive experience that results in heightened negative affect should increase the likelihood of subsequent aggression.

Alcohol has also been shown to promote violence. In studies of alcohol and domestic violence, alcohol use typically is implicated in more than half of all incidents. Similarly, both homicide victims and perpetrators are likely to have elevated blood alcohol levels. Although a relation

has been established, the precise mechanisms by which alcohol increases violence are unclear. It is likely that these effects are related to its impact on how an individual evaluates social situations and decides on an appropriate response. For example, some alcohol-violence studies suggest that ingestion of alcohol makes normal social interactions extremely difficult, heightening the likelihood of a range of inappropriate responses including violence.

Situational cues that suggest violence are also likely to increase violence by priming violence-related thoughts, feelings, and behaviors. Street fights engender more violence because they cue violent responses in observers. The presence of guns can also make violence more likely to occur when they are associated with an aggressive meaning and positive outcomes. For instance, the presence of a hunting rifle will not promote hostile and violent behavior in those who disapprove of aggression toward others. It is not just the weapon but the meaning and anticipated consequences of its use that promote violence. Even the picture of a gun or weapon in a room can increase the chance of an aggressive act. This effect is of particular concern because guns make violence more deadly. For example, the rise in murders of juveniles in the United States during the late 1980s and early 1990s was entirely firearm-related. Firearms are now the leading cause of death among children and youth in many places (Snyder and Sickmund).

Even nonviolent individuals can turn violent when they are part of a violent crowd. Group violence seems to make individuals feel less personally responsible for their behavior, acting in ways they would never do alone. Violence becomes an act of the group with no one person being held responsible. In some groups, violence emerges as a necessary strategy for defense against enemies—as seen in gang warfare, terrorist organizations, and political violence. At the other end of the spectrum, isolation also breeds violence. Different mechanisms to account for the influence of isolation have been proposed. These range from psychological changes akin to delusions of grandeur to disturbances in the balance of neurochemical pathways critical to the control of emotional and stressful responses.

Prevention and control of violence

Although history attests to the ubiquitousness of violence, it is also true that individuals have available and use a wide array of inhibitory or alternate behavioral strategies. Although aggression and violence may be ever present, they are not inevitable. The longevity of a social group, society, or nation hinges, in part, on the peaceful resolution of conflicts and other social problems. Escalating or unacceptably high rates of violence can serve as a call to action to mobilize the forces of prevention and control.

Just as there is no single cause of violence, there is no single solution. Rather, different types of violence are associated with different causal processes and warrant different responses. A reasoned approach to prevention and control hinges on sorting out these multiple influences as they impact the developing individual over time and across contexts. The control of violence requires a confluence of synchronized efforts that address innate, socialization, and situational contributions to violence, for all individuals as well as for those who display more extreme problems.

New research on the biology of violence provides a credible starting point that looks at individual development as it both influences and is influenced by the environment. If this development proceeds on a course that minimizes violent behavior, it results in a nervous system that is in tune with the demands of the outside world, is able to integrate emotional and representational data, and is not hypersensitive to perceived threat. Environmental factors that compromise this development, such as exposure to lead, head trauma, and abuse provide a viable beginning for prevention. The fact that brain development occurs at a rapid pace during the first years of life suggests that these factors must be addressed at an early age. Not only should efforts focus on prevention of trauma, but healthy developmental supports are needed. Healthy Start and Nurse–Home Visitation programs are examples of programs that can address these issues.

To the extent that violent actions are learned, a range of prevention and control responses can interrupt this learning process. First in line are strategies to reduce the perceived or actual positive consequences of violence. These may involve changing peer group and parent norms, providing nonviolent and positive means to achieve desired goals such as status and money, and training parents and other socialization agents to reward cooperative and prosocial behaviors. Under some conditions, punishment can also reduce aggression. A child who is sent to his room after hitting his brother should be less likely to hit his brother the next day. A child who is severely spanked for hitting his brother may

suppress his aggression in the days to come while also learning that violence is a good way to solve problems. Prison is unfortunately one of the best schools for violence known to society. Inmates are held in isolation, under crowded conditions, socializing only with other violent or antisocial peers, with treatment for accompanying mental health or addiction problems the exception rather than the rule. Prisons also come into play far too late in the game, when brain patterns and cognitions are well formed.

Another prevention prescription would focus on reducing the myriad of opportunities to model violent acts as a result of a continuous exposure to glorified violence in television, movies, and video games, as well as "sports" activities such as extreme fighting. Observing violence can increase individual attitudes and beliefs that such behavior is acceptable. In addition to reducing such modeling opportunities, research suggests that cognitive-behavioral interventions can also shift thinking patterns toward more reflective and less automatically aggressive thoughts.

The notion that human violence is innate or inevitable precludes effective prevention and control. In contrast, if we understand violence as an optional strategy that can be increased or decreased through a variety of mechanisms, opportunities for prevention and control abound. Individuals are biologically and socially capable of peaceful coexistence—a clear and powerful antidote to violence.

NANCY G. GUERRA
LYNDEE KNOX

See also CRIME CAUSATION: BIOLOGICAL THEORIES; CRIME CAUSATION: PSYCHOLOGICAL THEORIES; CRIME CAUSATION: SOCIOLOGICAL THEORIES; DELINQUENT AND CRIMINAL SUBCULTURES; DOMESTIC VIOLENCE; GUNS, REGULATION OF; HOMICIDE: BEHAVIORAL ASPECTS; MASS MEDIA AND CRIME; PREDICTION OF CRIME AND RECIDIVISM; PRISONS: PROBLEMS AND PROSPECTS; STALKING; TERRORISM; WAR AND VIOLENT CRIME.

BIBLIOGRAPHY

BANDURA, A. *Aggression: A Social Learning Approach.* Englewood Cliffs, N.J.: Prentice-Hall, 1973.

BERKOWITZ, L. "On the Determinants and Regulation of Impulsive Aggression." In *Aggression: Biological, Developmental, and Social Perspectives.* Edited by S. Feshbach and J. Zagrodzka. New York: Plenum Press, 1997. Pages 187–211.

Buss, D. M., and Shackelford, T. K. "Human Aggression in Evolutionary Psychological Perspective." *Clinical Psychology Review* 17 (1997): 605–619.

Buvinic, M.; Morrison, A.; and Shifter, M. *Violence in Latin America and the Caribbean: A Framework for Action*. Technical report. New York: Inter-American Development Bank, 1999.

Cornish, D. B., and Clarke, R. V. *The Reasoning Criminal: Rational Choice Perspective on Offending*. New York: Springer-Verlag, 1986.

Crick, N. R., and Dodge, K. A. "A Review and Reformulation of Social Information-processing Mechanisms in Children's Social Adjustment." *Psychological Bulletin* 115 (1994): 74–101.

Dahlberg, L. "Youth Violence in the United States: Major Trends, Risk Factors, and Prevention Approaches." *American Journal of Preventive Medicine* 14 (1998): 259–272.

Dodge, K. A., and Coie, J. D. "Social-Information Processing Factors in Reactive and Proactive Aggression in Children's Peer Groups." *Journal of Personality and Social Psychology* 53 (1987): 1146–1158.

Dollard, J.; Doob, L. W.; Miller, N. E.; Mowrer, O. H.; and Sears, R. R. *Frustration and Aggression*. New Haven, Conn.: Yale University Press, 1939.

Lorenz, K. *On Aggression*. New York: MJF Books, 1963.

Niehoff, D. *The Biology of Violence*. New York: Free Press, 1999.

Olweus, D.; Mattson, A.; and Low, H. "Circulating Testosterone Levels and Aggression in Adolescent Males: A Causal Analysis." *Psychosomatic Medicine* 50 (1988): 261–272.

Pynoos, R.; Steinberg, A. M.; and Ornitz, E. M. "Issues in the Developmental Neuro-Biology of Traumatic Stress." *Annals of the New York Academy of Sciences* 821 (1997): 176–193.

Snyder, H., and Sickmund, M. *Juvenile Offenders and Victims: 1999 National Report*. Washington, D.C.: U.S. Department of Justice, 1999.

Tolan, P. H., and Guerra, N. G. *What Works in Reducing Adolescent Violence*. Boulder, Colo.: Center for the Study and Prevention of Violence, 1994.

WAR AND VIOLENT CRIME

In its pure form, war is violence organized by one sovereign state against another in an attempt to influence it. War affects crime in two ways. There are rules for war, and they are often violated by those who wage it. In addition, the sudden shifts in demographic, economic, and social structure, as well as in the law and its administration that are typically associated with war, affect official rates of civilian crime and juvenile delinquency. This entry examines the relationship between war and illegality at both of these levels.

The persistence of war

In the heady optimism of the 1960s, many futurists and students of conflict declared that war had become obsolete as a mechanism of dispute settlement. Skepticism about the use of war as an extension of diplomacy actually emerged much earlier, following World War I. It settled nothing and cost millions of lives and billions of dollars on both sides. World War II was in some ways a continuation of the conflagration, but eventually produced a definite outcome. However, the use of new weapons made possible the total destruction of populations, rather than just active combatants. This frightened political leaders as well as the public and cast even greater doubt on the utility of war as an institution for settling international arguments. Yet wars continued, but without nuclear fallout. In spite of General Douglas MacArthur's efforts to persuade the U.S. Congress to use atomic bombs against North Korea, President Harry Truman, who had already used two nuclear devices against Japan, accepted another stalemate rather

than risk retaliation in kind from the Soviet Union. Further, even when facing the fall of Saigon and total defeat, South Vietnam and its nuclear allies also refrained from using weapons of mass destruction. Thus, as Secretary of State Henry Kissinger had predicted, the threat of mutual annihilation deterred nuclear powers from using their ultimate weapon, and wars continued, using more circumscribed weaponry. As Mark Twain might have written, reports of the death of war have been greatly exaggerated.

War crimes

War was never a no-holds-barred fight between opposing states. War is somewhat like boxing, with rules of conduct extending well back into antiquity. For example, when Odysseus counseled the Greek leaders to blockade shipments of food to Troy in an effort to end what had become a protracted siege, his idea was rejected. At that time, it was widely regarded as improper to extend war to noncombatants in the general population by starving them into submission (this may have been based less on humanitarianism than on the value of the enemy's women and children as slaves). It is noteworthy, too, that Odysseus' successful strategy—celebrated "gift" of a horse that ended the Trojan siege and won the war for the Greeks—which brought victory was regarded as somewhat ignoble, since it was obtained through deceit. In fact, had the Trojans managed to win the war despite the Greeks' ploy, Odysseus might have been vilified as the first war criminal rather than celebrated as one of antiquity's heroes. The Nazi defendant Hermann Göring went further, claiming at his trial following World War II that the most important factor in being charged as a war criminal is to be on the losing side. Although there is certainly a much greater chance of this happening to someone on the losing than the winning side, there is far more to being charged with war crimes than simply losing the contest.

War crimes *mala prohibita*

As noted earlier, there have always been rules for war, and they were often codified in treaties. (In 1785 Benjamin Franklin, John Adams, and Thomas Jefferson drafted one of the first of such treaties, between the United States and Prussia, to protect prisoners of war.) There have also always been violators. Psychological as well as structural factors play a major part. War is terrifying, and soldiers are often quite young, sometimes only a few years past adolescence. They are less likely to run amok in combat than they are to turn tail and run (see Keegan). When either happens, it is likely to be the result of a combination of youthful spontaneity, fear, and extraordinary situations that produce an intense "flight or fight" response. As with policing within states, both represent a serious breakdown in bureaucratic control, which can jeopardize organizational goals. Given the time, resources, and expertise, armed forces try to provide careful selection, extensive training, strong leadership, and an emphasis on group loyalty to counter breakdowns in organizational goals and morale. This is reflected in the military personality and the emphasis on hierarchy in the armed forces.

On another level, apart from xenophobia or ethnic hatred, cultural differences between nation states may affect how closely their soldiers follow rules for war. As with crimes *mala prohibita* within states, there is no widespread agreement across cultures on the illegality of some offenses, which would only be considered wrong because they are defined as such by a law within a nation state (see Nettler, p. 17). For example, in World War II the samurai tradition and the *Bushido* code inclined Japanese military personnel to choose death over capitulation. Such a tradition does not easily coexist with the compassionate treatment of enemy prisoners or of populations who have surrendered. Thus, from the viewpoint of the Western Allies, where collective duty (*makido*) is underdeveloped and individualism high, Japanese occupying armies and prisoner of war camps seemed inordinately disdainful.

In an effort to standardize international conduct concerning the treatment of prisoners and civilian populations, the Geneva Convention for the protection of war victims was drawn up in 1949. These four international agreements were signed by the representatives of sixty-one states. Göring and the other twenty high-ranking Nazis who survived for trial at Nuremberg in 1946, before the advent of the Geneva Convention, were accused of committing "crimes against humanity," misdeeds so heinous that they are generally regarded as crimes *mala in se*, and held to be illegal, whether explicitly codified or not. Although the criminal charges at Nuremberg involved acts that were committed before any laws prohibiting them were written, the illegality of the systematic mass destruction of people by those in charge of a state was regarded as self-evident. Thus, the war crime trials at Nuremberg were not seen by the Allies to have been the *post factum* application of international law. Further, viewing serious war crimes as *mala in se* negates the "just following orders" defense, since their illegality is held to be obvious (Robertson).

War crimes *mala in se*

As noted earlier, in the West the rules of war traditionally precluded attacks on nonparticipants in the enemy population. It was viewed as dishonorable to wage war on women, children, the elderly, and the helpless, even if they were the enemy. However, by World War II conditions had changed. Many nation-states were in fact multination states, often containing and sometimes restraining more than one tribal, ethnic, religious, or racial group. Even in the best of times the coexistence of different groups within the political boundaries of one state is not without some conflict, and war can exacerbate ethnic hatred and xenophobia. When states are at war, civil liberties are often suspended or greatly curtailed in the interests of national security. Fear can produce paranoia, and innocent citizens can be deprived of their land and liberty solely on the basis of shared ethnicity with the enemy. One need look no farther for an example than the U.S. government's treatment of Japanese Americans during World War II. However, in other instances, attacks by governments on their own citizens have been based more on interethnic antagonism than on real or imagined fears about state security.

Historically, conquest has placed the power of the state at the disposal of one cultural or racial category while denying access to another. This has often been problematic. For example, in the case of the British conquest of French territory in eastern North America, it led to the 1755 expulsion from their homeland of Acadians who refused to swear allegiance to England. Although their descendants flourished as the Cajuns of Louisiana, this eighteenth-century version of "ethnic cleansing" by England was decried almost a century later by Longfellow in his epic poem *Evangeline*. At the end of World War I, the Treaty of Versailles ceded what had been German territory to other nation-states. From the German standpoint, this was tantamount to having part of the nation occupied, a bitter pill for any nation to swallow, made worse by the cultural and status differences between victor and vanquished. Twenty years later, World War II was triggered by Germany's invasions of Czech Sudetenland and Poland, actions justified by Adolf Hitler as rescue missions to protect ethnic Germans from their non-German compatriots.

Although it is pertinent, the German invasions were not the source of the war crimes tried at Nuremberg. The Nazi version of pan-Germanism was based on race and ethnicity rather than citizenship. As a consequence, the problem impairing the campaign for German unification was the presence of non-Aryans within the boundaries of the nation-state. The result of this drive for ethnic purification was the expulsion, incarceration, and destruction of its own citizens by the state and the ensuing horror of the Holocaust. This was the basis of the Nuremberg trials and has become the root of most charges for contemporary war crimes as well.

The East-West alliance dissolved after Nuremberg, replaced by a Cold War between the Communist East and the capitalist West. Although wars continued, and East and West accused each other of crimes against humanity, each side blocked any effective United Nations action, and war crimes prosecutions ceased. All this changed with the collapse of the Iron Curtain in 1989, and war criminals are once again pursued by the United Nations (see Chandler).

In contemporary Rwanda, centuries of intertribal hostility erupted into wholesale genocide in 1994, with the state in the hands of one tribe bent on slaughtering another. The collapse of highly centralized states in Eastern Europe and the Soviet Union unleashed centrifugal forces of separatism and interethnic violence. For example, in Yugoslavia, the unraveling of the state ended the precarious peace between Croatians, Serbs, Slovenians, and Albanian Moslems fashioned by that nation's Serbian founder

Josip Broz (Marshal Tito), and ethnic cleansing began in Bosnia and Kosovo. As of early 2001, the U.N.'s International War Crimes Tribunal in the Netherlands was trying to bring the offenders to trial. Another U.N. tribunal may soon be set up in Asia to try officials from Pol Pot's Khmer Rouge government who decimated the urban professional population of Cambodia in death camps during the 1970s (Chandler).

In the end, those in power may use the state to embark on genocidal violence or commit other crimes against humanity, as did the Nazis in Germany. On the other hand, strong, centralized, Communist governments may use the state to prevent sub-populations from committing ethnic violence, as in Tito's Yugoslavia. Like most social inventions, the state can be used either to provoke or prevent violence, including crimes against humanity.

At present, the most publicized war crimes are extreme forms of collective ethnic or class violence, committed by high-ranking officers of the state. These offenses have not been extensively studied by criminologists. However, there are signs that this is beginning to change, especially since the actions taken by the U.N. International War Crimes Tribunal concerning Rwanda and Bosnia (see Hagan). The scope of social scientific interest is also expanding to include crimes against humanity committed by states whether they are at war or not, as in Pol Pot's Cambodia (see Robertson). Even specific acts of violence such as aggressive policing, unwarranted incarceration, or capital punishment committed by states against citizens are increasingly decried as uncivilized. This is somewhat ironic inasmuch as those who were found guilty at Nuremberg were sentenced to hang, a particularly barbaric method of execution. (Göring committed suicide when his request for a firing squad was denied.)

War and rates of adult crime

In theory, war can directly or indirectly affect crime within states in a variety of ways. Some effects are immediate, some long term, and others may cancel each other out. Many of these explanations are indirect and tie into more general social scientific arguments, but some are specific to war.

For example, as noted above, wartime footing typically increases states' emphasis on security at the cost of civil rights. This jeopardizes the freedom of foreign nationals or ethnic groups sharing cultural connections with opponents. International hostilities may also legitimize ethnic violence, and perhaps violence in general, within countries, especially when a nation is occupied by foreign soldiers and a resistance movement is trying to discourage collaboration. War may also increase the number of offenses among nationals inasmuch as there are more rules to break and greater surveillance by the state. On the other hand, from a deterrence perspective, the increased centralization of state power, surveillance, and severity of sanctions should reduce illegal behavior, eventually lowering crime rates.

From an economic standpoint, wartime shortages and rationing can create conditions for crime in two ways. One is through increasing the proportion of the population without resources while at the same time intensifying the desperation of those who were already disadvantaged. The other is through the creation of black market economies. As with organized crime in peacetime, criminal violence may be required to enforce the illegal contracts of black marketeers, who, lacking police protection, may themselves be targets for robbery. On the other side, because of the external conflict, social solidarity and cooperation may be higher during war, with black market activity and associated crime rates minimal.

Immediate and long-term effects

On a demographic level, the removal of young males from the general population and placing them into the armed services or sending them abroad should lower the general crime rate, since this age-sex category is typically responsible for an inordinate number of offenses. Engaging in hostilities may even be cathartic. On the other hand, war may beget violence, even among those who are not directly involved in it. During the Vietnam conflict, for example, F.B.I. reports show that in the United States, rates of homicide increased among all age groups (Archer and Gartner). However, as a lost cause on the other side of the world, the Vietnam conflict was unusual. It generated extraordinary levels of dissension and conflict, not only between political parties at home, but between generations and within families, which continue to reverberate almost a half century later. In fact, one of the founders of modern sociology, Émile Durkheim, observed that in his native France rates of property crime dropped during the Franco-Prussian War in 1870, only to rise after the war to a level greater than they had been before hostilities began. Although the wartime plunge was less pronounced, rates of serious crimes of violence followed a similar postwar pattern.

Like the Vietnam conflict, the Franco-Prussian War can also be considered unusual. It was followed immediately by the state's destruction of the Paris Commune, leaving thousands dead and a host of *communards* charged with serious offenses. This was not a typical postwar phenomenon, and undoubtedly had an impact on official rates of crime. Thus, generalizing from Durkheim's observations of the effects of the Franco-Prussian War on crime even to other wars in France is risky, never mind wars in other times and places. However, the most sophisticated contemporary treatment of the relationship between war and rates of violent crime shows that the pattern observed by Durkheim was by no means unique to the Franco-Prussian War. In their analysis of fifty "nation-wars," Archer and Gartner report that postwar increases in homicide are indeed typical in combatant countries and atypical in nations at peace. Moreover, this pattern holds whether wars are large or small, won or lost, produce low or high unemployment, and, curiously, is as evident among female as well as male offenders. They conclude that "sanctioned killing during war has a residual effect on the level of homicide in peacetime society" (p. 96).

This might be true, but research on total populations is difficult at the best of times, and as Charles Dickens noted, war is also the worst of times. This is especially so for statisticians. Calculating meaningful rates of anything is difficult because the denominator includes young males who are serving in the armed forces, but may be doing so outside the country. As a consequence, during hostilities, the activities of military personnel, criminal and otherwise, may go undetected or be ignored in the context of wartime violence, processed in the host nation or by military courts, and not be recorded at home. The result of any of this would be a decline in rates of activities reported for the population as a whole during war.

An examination of rates of various activities during and following the Franco-Prussian War, on which Durkheim's conclusions were based, sheds interesting light on the crime statistics. Basically, rates of almost everything were stable or dropped during the war, and then increased sharply afterward. This may mean that French soldiers were too busy with the Prussians to file for bankruptcy, get divorced, have fatal accidents, or engage in criminal acts until after the war was over, which they then did with a vengeance. Oddly, this pattern also held for the women of France, most of whom were not directly involved in trying to repulse the Prussians. In view of this, it seems more likely that the part of the apparatus of the state responsible for seeing, detecting, and recording such events was either put on hold or operating at a reduced capacity until after the war was over. This was certainly the case for the judiciary. The gendarmerie was administered as a regiment in the French army, and their primary duty was transferred from patrolling the highways, small towns, and rural areas of France to defending France when war broke out in 1870. This sudden shift in the attention and availability of police would have produced a decline in charges and officially recorded crimes. However, when hostilities ceased, the return of the gendarmes to policing would have inflated the number of charges, surpassing the prewar rate if there were backlogs of complaints. (See Gillis, on the contemporaneous and long-term impact of policing on crime in nineteenth-century France.)

The great gift of the research done by Archer and Gartner is substantiating that the pattern discovered by Durkheim is not specific to the Franco-Prussian War. As noted earlier, this conflict and its aftermath were in many ways unique, and other wars involving other nations may not have affected crime in the same way. In any case, it is clear that war affects official rates of crime. What is less clear is how.

Juvenile delinquency

It is noteworthy that juvenile delinquency may be affected by war in a different way than is adult crime. During World War II studies in England and in the United States found that rates of delinquency increased rather than decreased in the early years of the conflict. The legitimacy of violence produced by war, combined with the absence of fathers who were away in the services, household and school disruptions through evacuation, blackouts, and economic disruptions may have had a different impact on juveniles than on young adults who were integrated into the war effort through their membership in the armed forces or in some other capacity. However, as with the patterns of adult crime, whether these or any other mechanisms actually link war to delinquent behavior is uncertain. In the end, like adult crime, fluctuations in official rates of wartime delinquency may reflect changes in the nature and enforcement of law, or the collection and tabulation of official data, rather than changes in the behavior of juveniles.

In the end, we know that wars affect rates of crime and delinquency, albeit in different ways, and insofar as they are indicated by official records. We also know that when wars occur, so too do war crimes. When viewed more broadly, as crimes against humanity, however, wars are not necessary to generate such offenses, which typically arise from ethnic or class conflict, and the complicity of the state in perpetrating extreme violence on behalf of one category against another. Neither the concentration of power nor the political orientation of the state by itself determines whether such crimes will occur. After a hiatus of almost half a century the United Nations is once again pursuing those who commit crimes against humanity, and this is generating renewed attention from social scientists. Thus, the conditions giving rise to crimes against humanity may yet be more precisely specified.

A. R. GILLIS

See also HOMICIDE: BEHAVIORAL ASPECTS; INTERNATIONAL CRIMINAL COURTS; INTERNATIONAL CRIMINAL LAW; POLITICAL PROCESS AND CRIME; VIOLENCE; WAR CRIMES.

BIBLIOGRAPHY

ARCHER, DANE, and GARTNER, ROSEMARY. *Violence and Crime in Cross National Perspective*. New Haven, Conn.: Yale University Press, 1984.

CHANDLER, DAVID. *Voices From S-21: Terror and History in Pol Pot's Secret Prison*. Berkeley: University of California Press, 2000.

DUKHEIM, ÉMILE. *Professional Ethics and Civil Morals*. Translated by C. Brookfield. London: Routledge and Keegan Paul, 1957.

GILLIS, A. R. "Crime and State Surveillance in 19th-Century France." *The American Journal of Sociology* 95, no. 2 (1989): 307–341.

HAGAN, JOHN. "Making War Criminal." Presented to the Annual Meetings of Law and Society. Miami, Fla., May 26, 2000.

KEEGAN, JOHN. *The Face of Battle: A Study of Agincourt, Waterloo, and the Somme*. New York: Vintage, 1977.

NETTLER, GWYNN. *Explaining Crime*, 3d ed. New York: McGraw-Hill, 1984.

ROBERTSON, GEOFFREY. *Crimes Against Humanity: The Struggle for Global Justice*. London: Allen Lane, 1999.

WAR CRIMES

The most authoritative definition of *war crimes* was formulated in the London Charter of 8 August 1945, which established the International Military Tribunal at Nuremberg. It was adopted in 1946 by the General Assembly of the United Nations in a unanimous resolution approving of the work of the Nuremberg Tribunal:

War Crimes: Violations of the laws or customs of law which include, but are not limited to, murder, ill treatment, or deportation to slave labour or for any other purpose of civilian population of or in occupied territory, murder or ill treatment of prisoners of war or persons on the seas, killing of hostages, plunder of public or private property, wanton destruction of cities, towns, or villages or devastation not justified by military necessity. (*Trial of the Major War Criminals,* vol. 1, p. 11)

War crimes under this definition, which follows the traditional doctrine under international law, have the following elements: (1) they are acts of violence against civilian populations, prisoners of war, or in some cases enemy soldiers in the field; (2) they are committed primarily by military personnel; (3) they are in violation of the laws and customs of war; (4) they are not justified by military necessity; and (5) they often involve weapons or military methods of unusual cruelty or devastation.

In the broadest sense, a war crime is any act of violence by military personnel (or by informal semi-military militia) that exceeds the rules of war. War is by its very nature violent, and military acts in wartime—killing, capture, and destruction—would otherwise be considered criminal under the laws of all civilized societies. But every society suspends the application of its criminal law when dealing with military acts in time of war.

However, whatever immunity is accorded these military acts in war extends only to conduct that conforms to the rules of war (Taylor, pp. 19–20). Thus, the incidental killing of civilians in a bombing raid as part of a military operation is not murder because it is justified by military necessity. But the deliberate killing of defenseless civilians by infantrymen, as in Son My (otherwise known as My Lai) in Vietnam or by militia groups in Bosnia or Kosovo, remains what it always was: murder, because the immunity ordinarily accorded military operations did not apply since the acts violated the rules of war. In fact, Lieutenant William Calley, Jr., was tried and convicted by an American military court-martial of various acts of premeditated murder as a result of the killings at Son My, under the section of the Uniform Code of Military Justice dealing with murder and manslaughter (*United States v. Calley,* 22 U.S.C.M.A. 534, 48 C.M.R. 19 (1973)). He was not charged with a "war crime" as such or tried by a special international tribunal. Rather, he was tried for committing murder by an army court-martial in the same way that a soldier who killed a fellow soldier or a civilian would have been treated for nonmilitary acts committed in that theater of operations.

The narrow definition of war crimes quoted above (excesses by military personnel in the field or atrocities against civilians generally) has been expanded to cover two additional broad categories: (1) crimes against peace, or the "planning, preparation, initiation or waging of a war of aggression or a war in violation of international treaties"; and (2) crimes against humanity, or "murder, extermination, enslavement, deportation or other inhuman acts done against any civilian population" (*Trial of the Major War Criminals,* vol. 1, p. 11).

A more comprehensive definition of war crimes that includes all elements of these offenses is contained in the charter for the International Criminal Court adopted in Rome in the summer of 1998 by the United Nations Diplomatic Conference (U.N. Doc. A/Conf. 183/9, 17 July 1998). The purpose of the Rome conference was to create the International Criminal Court (ICC) as a permanent international judicial body to try war crimes and other international crimes as an alternate to the ad hoc tribunals set up to deal with specific violations of the rules of war in local areas such as Yugoslavia and Rwanda. In the process, the Rome treaty had to define the jurisdiction of the ICC and the defined circumstances under which it would be empowered to act. The definitions of the crimes under its jurisdiction largely follow the Nuremberg model: (a) the crime of genocide; (b) crimes against humanity; (c) war crimes; (d) the crime of aggression (Part 2, Article 5 (1)). However, as noted below, the definitions of these concepts was broadened considerably in the ICC charter.

By the end of 2000, 139 states had signed the Rome treaty containing the broader definitions, although only twenty-seven states had formally ratified it (the treaty needs sixty formal ratifications before it comes into effect). On 31 December 2000, President Bill Clinton signed the treaty on behalf of the United States over objections of both his own Department of Defense and leading members of the U.S. Senate. The senators were concerned that the treaty would apply to nations that did not ratify it and that American soldiers or political leaders might be brought before an international court (without all of the constitutional protections) for actions taken in foreign wars or even for actions taken in their own states (such as a governor who sanctioned the death penalty against minors, mentally retarded prisoners, or against a disproportionate number of a racial or ethnic group).

The broader definition of war crimes generally accepted by the international community includes the following offenses:

Crimes against peace. The concept of "crimes against peace" or "aggression" relate only to the initiation of war and not to its later conduct. Such offenses are primarily crimes of the politically responsible leaders of a country. The theory is of comparatively recent origin, although it is related to the notion of the "just war," described below. The Nuremberg Tribunal had considerable difficulty in determining the origin of the concept of "crimes against peace" in international law. It relied chiefly on the Kellogg-Briand Pact of 1928, which had condemned a "recourse to war for the solution of international controversies" (Article I).

Crimes against humanity. The concept of crimes against humanity does not always or necessarily mean a crime committed during a war. If a nation engages in the systematic slaughter of its own inhabitants (such as the systematic oppression by the Nazis of German Jews and Gypsies before war began in 1939, or the Turkish massacre of Armenians in 1915), those responsible would be guilty of "crimes against humanity" even if there were no international hostilities at the same time. The concept of genocide—killing or causing serious injury to members of a distinct national, ethnic, or racial group or inflicting on the group conditions of life calculated to bring about its physical destruction—grew out of the Nuremberg Tribunal's application of the concept of crimes against humanity. It may be the most typical form of a crime against humanity since a government or state committing such crimes will generally do so against distinct nationalities or ethnic groups, rather than against its own people or against humanity in general. However, crimes against humanity is a broader concept since it covers murder, enslavement, deportation, imprisonment, torture, rape, or other persecution of any identifiable group (political,

cultural, gender), and not merely a national or ethnic group covered by the crime of genocide. Thus the ICC charter contains a very broad definition of crimes against humanity, including any "widespread or systematic attack directed against any civilian population" (Article 7(1)). The ICC definition would cover the destruction of the Cambodian population by the Pol Pot regime in the 1970s, for example, and the mass disappearances of political opponents of military governments in Argentina and Chile in the same period, even though such crimes might not fit within the definition of genocide.

The United Nations General Assembly passed a resolution condemning genocide, and the Genocide Convention was drafted and acceded to by many nations, although not by the United States (Article II). If crimes against humanity take place in the midst of a war and are directed against civilian populations of another country, these acts may constitute both war crimes and crimes against humanity. In fact, the Nuremberg Tribunal frequently combined its discussion of "war crimes and crimes against humanity" under a single heading and found various persons guilty of both counts under a single discussion of the evidence.

War crimes without a formal war

Part of the problem in defining "war crimes" is that formal declarations of war, which generally preceded hostilities between states in earlier times, no longer occur. Thus there may be some doubt when a "war" as defined by international law is present. In addition, the "wars" of the latter part of the twentieth century were often civil wars (Rwanda, Sudan, Lebanon), guerrilla wars (Colombia, Peru, Nicaragua), and political conflicts (Cambodia, Argentina, Chile), with assistance sometimes given to one group from an outside power (Vietnam, Yugoslavia). The formal treaties and protocols drafted by the major powers were often one step behind in defining the circumstances under which war crimes took place. Thus, the Geneva Conventions of 1949 dealt primarily with conduct during an "international armed conflict." The conventions contained a Common Article 3, which applied to all four treaties and covered "an armed conflict not of an international character" to which certain, but not all, of the prohibitions applied.

Later efforts to take account of the new types of armed conflicts often left significant gaps. Protocol II to the Geneva Convention proposed in

1977 would extend the protections of the 1949 conventions to victims of "internal wars," a broader concept than "an armed conflict not of an international character" (Protocols Additional to the Geneva Convention of August 12, 1949 and Relating to the Protection of Victims of International Non-International Armed Conflicts, June 10, 1977, 1125 U.N.T.S 609 (hereinafter Protocol II)). The definition of "internal wars" was as follows: "It shall apply to all armed conflicts which are not international and which take place in a territory of a high contracting party between its armed forces and dissident armed forces or other organized armed groups, which under responsible command exercise such control over a part of its territory as to enable them to carry out sustained and concerted military operations." Therefore, there must be "dissident armed forces" or "organized armed forces" occupying territories in order to satisfy the definition of "internal war" under Protocol II. (The United States has not ratified Protocol II although over 120 states have acceded to it.)

The International Criminal Tribunal for Yugoslavia (ICTY) broadened the predicate for punishing war crimes in its decision in *Prosecutor v. Tadic* (No. IT-94-1-T (Yugoslavia Tribunal Trial Chamber, August 10, 1995, affd No. IT-94-1-AR 72)). (Yugoslavia Tribunal, Appeals Chamber, 2 October, 1995, Tadic Appeal on Jurisdiction, reprinted at 35 I.L.M. 32 (1996) and appeal on the merits, 15 July 1999, reprinted in 38 I.L.M. 1518 (1999).) The Appeals Chamber held in the jurisdictional appeal that an armed conflict exists (and therefore the four Geneva Conventions apply) "when there is resort to armed force between states or protracted armed violence between governmental authorities and organized armed groups or between such groups within a state" (par. 70). Broadening the definition found in the Geneva Conventions and Protocol II, the Appeals Chamber of ICTY held that the technical requirements of an international armed conflict need not be present before the rules contained in those provisions can be applied. The court held that persons engaged in organized armed conflicts either of an international or local nature are bound by "Customary Rules of International Human Rights," which can be applied by both local, ad hoc, and international courts in dealing with excesses against civilian groups or enemy soldiers.

In its second decision on the merits, the Appeals Chamber held that the Bosnian Serb militias were acting on behalf of the goals "and shared strategic objects" of the Serbian government in Belgrade (par. 153), even if they were not directly under the control of the Serbian military, thus bringing their actions within the prohibitions of the Geneva Conventions relating to "international armed conflicts."

The Rome Charter of the ICC also broadens the definition of crimes against humanity by encompassing any attack upon a civilian population under the following circumstances: "a course of conduct involving the multiple commission of acts referred to in paragraph 1 [murder, enslavement, deportation, torture, rape, apartheid, disappearances, or other inhumane acts] against any civil population, pursuant to or in furtherance of a State or organizational policy to commit such attack" (Article 7(2)(a)).

There are slight differences between crimes against humanity as defined in the Rome Charter and the statutes creating the international criminal tribunals for Yugoslavia (ICTY) (U.N. Doc. S/PV. 3217 (1993)) and Rwanda (ICTR) (U.N. Doc. S/RES/955 (1994)). The Rome Charter requires "a multiple commission of acts" against civilians, but it contains no requirement that the acts be committed in the context of an armed conflict. Nor does the ICTR statute require any such conflict. The ICTY statute does require an armed conflict before it can exercise jurisdiction, and also demands some kind of discriminatory motive on the part of the perpetrator, a requirement that is not found in the Rome Charter. But all three enactments greatly expand the defined circumstances under which international law against crimes of war can be applied.

In February 2001, a panel of the ICTY found that rape in and by itself could constitute a crime against humanity and found three Bosnian Serb soldiers guilty of enslaving and abusing hundreds of Muslim women from the town of Foca, near Sarajevo, during the Bosnian conflict. They were sentenced to twenty-eight, twenty, and twelve years' imprisonment, respectively (*Prosecutor v. Kunarac*).

Historical development

Although the notions of crimes against humanity and genocide may be comparatively recent, the concept of war crimes as a restraint on the military is of much older origin. Virtually every recorded civilization placed some limitations on the conduct of its own warfare, and violations of such rules could therefore be considered war crimes. In the Egyptian and Sumerian wars of the second millennium B.C.E., there were rules defining the circumstances under which war might be initiated. In ancient China it was forbidden in wartime to kill wounded enemies or to strike elderly armed opponents. The Chinese philosopher Sun Tzu wrote in *The Art of War* (400 B.C.E.): "Treat the captives well and care for them. All the soldiers taken must be cared for with magnanimity and sincerity so that they may be used by us" (Friedman, p. 3). Similar restrictions on killing the wounded, ordinary citizens, women, children, or prisoners were expressed in Hindu literature of the fourth century B.C.E., in Babylonian texts, and in the Bible (Deut. 20).

The Greeks and Romans introduced further notions of humane and civilized treatment of noncombatants in war. Plato wrote in his *Republic* that war among the Hellenes should have as its end "friendly correction," and not destruction of the enemy. The Romans developed the concept of the "just war" that alone warranted resort to force. Truces, safe-conduct passes, and armistices were respected, and cease-fires were agreed upon so that the dead might be buried. Poisoned weapons were prohibited. This is not to say that the Greeks or Romans did not engage in barbarous acts in time of war. But the development of rules of restraint, although frequently violated, established the principle that limits had to be placed on acts of war—a notion that Christianity was to carry forward over the coming centuries.

In the early Christian era, observance of the Christian principles of pacifism and nonresistance eventually gave way to ferocious efforts to defend Christendom and expand its boundaries. St. Augustine (354–430) and St. Thomas Aquinas (1225–1274) developed the just-war doctrine, arguing that wars by a Christian sovereign to spread and protect the true faith against attack by outside enemies were justified. The early church fathers had insisted that soldiers who killed even in a just war should do penance, and they warned against pillaging and slaughter. Later, ecumenical councils of the church passed various decrees establishing a "Truce of God," when all fighting was to cease, and tried to arrange cease-fires between Christian princes during the Crusades.

Beginning in the fifteenth century, two other developments contributed to the establishment of rules of war on an international basis: (1) the chivalric code of honor took shape, limiting the weapons and methods that could be used in combat; and (2) merchants insisted that unlimited

pillaging and destruction in wartime ought to be restrained. The chivalric code applied across national borders and was founded on natural law, limiting even princes in their capacity as knights and soldiers (Keen, p. 50).

Scholastic teachers, jurists, and theologians reexamined and systematized the laws of war as derived from classical Greek and Roman practice, Christian doctrine, contemporary practice, and chivalric codes. Francisco de Vittoria (1485–1546), a Spanish professor who lectured on Thomist philosophy in Paris and Salamanca, examined the moral and legal problems of the Spanish conquests against the Native Americans in the New World in his work on the law of war. He concluded that "it is never right to slay the guiltless, even as an indirect and unintended result, except where there is no other means of carrying on the operations of a just war" (p. 179). Other important sixteenth- and seventeenth-century writers on the laws of war were Balthazar Ayola, judge advocate of the Spanish armies in the Netherlands; Francisco Suarez; and Alberico Gentili.

The most systematic and comprehensive work on the laws of war was that of the Netherlander Hugo Grotius (1583–1645), who served in many important positions in the Dutch government, including a term as attorney general. In 1625 he published a three-volume work titled *The Law of War and Peace*, which brought together classical and medieval thought on the restraints on war and sought to reconcile Christian dogma and the actual practice of contemporary states in wartime. Grotius attempted to discover what the rules of international law were, using the acts of generals and soldiers as the basis for his search. Writing at the beginning of one of the most ferocious and bitter wars of European history, the Thirty Years' War (1618–1648), Grotius proceeded on the assumption that the experiences and actions of armies in war were not improper deviations from a theological norm. Rather, they were the expressions of a natural order, whose principles he could determine.

Grotius sought to explain what that natural law was. If war does have rules that all states obey (or should obey), then deviation from those rules should become a crime—a war crime, as the twentieth century would call it. Some seventeenth-century Christian princes took Grotius's rules seriously. Gustavus II Adolphus of Sweden carried a copy of Grotius's book with him everywhere, established strict rules against attacking hospitals, churches, schools, or the civilians connected with them, and severely punished those of his own soldiers who disobeyed the rules (Wedgwood, pp. 261, 265). Other generals either did not or could not control their men, and mass destructions and pillage took place frequently. In the rare cases when soldiers were punished for such deeds, it was not because they had committed a war crime—which had no meaning at the time—but because they had committed murder or rape under circumstances that the commander could not overlook.

The rise of the nation-state in the eighteenth and nineteenth centuries and the decline of the church's moral authority led to more concrete efforts to define and codify the laws of war whose violation would constitute a war crime.

The Lieber Code and the development of international treaties

In the nineteenth century, the effort to systematize the laws of war and restrain excesses by the military against civilians and prisoners received a major impetus from an American law professor, Francis Lieber (1800–1872), a German-born veteran of the Napoleonic Wars. In the middle of the American Civil War, Lieber suggested that a code of the law and usages of war be prepared that would be used as a guide by military commanders in their treatment of prisoners of war, irregular guerrilla forces, and captured enemy property. In April 1863, Lieber's code was issued by the Union government under the title "Instructions for the Government of Armies of the United States in the Field." Many European nations, including Prussia, quickly adopted instructions based on the code.

The European nations had meanwhile begun the process of codifying the laws of war by international treaties binding on signatories in all future conflicts. The first step had been the Declaration of Paris (1856), signed by seven European nations, dealing with the seizure of neutral ships carrying enemy goods. The Red Cross Convention (1864), which specifically covered the treatment of the wounded in armies in the field, was signed by twelve European nations. (The United States acceded to it in 1882.) In 1868, eighteen nations signed and ratified another agreement, the Declaration of St. Petersburg, concerned with "projectiles . . . charged with fulminating or inflammable substances."

A more comprehensive treaty, dealing with all aspects of the conduct of war and based largely on the Lieber Code, was prepared by delegates of fifteen nations who met in Brussels in 1874. However, some European powers that had begun to develop new weapons and that faced the prospect of new wars became cool to the idea, and the Brussels Declaration was never officially adopted. Twenty-five years later (1899), on the initiative of Russia, a new conference was called at The Hague that led to the first of a series of international conventions broadly treating the conduct of war. The conference adopted a series of treaties dealing with treatment of prisoners of war and military authority over hostile territory, and prohibiting (for a period of five years) the use of poison gas, expanding bullets ("dumdums"), and bombs dropped from balloons.

In 1907, another conference was held at The Hague, from which emerged fourteen separate treaties, eight of them concerned with maritime matters. Agreement was also reached on a convention dealing with the wounded and prisoners of war, and containing detailed regulations for conduct toward civilians in land warfare. The earlier ban against bombing from balloons was extended.

A new conference at The Hague was planned for 1915. By that time World War I had broken out, and the Hague conventions were being given their first practical application. After the war ended, an Allied commission was appointed to determine whether any enemy soldiers should be tried for violating the laws and customs of war. The commission recommended that an international court be established, composed of representatives of the major powers (a plan later followed in the creation of the Nuremberg Tribunal after World War II), which would apply the principles of the Hague conventions. But the peace commissioners decided to have existing military tribunals from the victorious armies act as the trial courts. The German government strenuously objected, insisting that its own courts should conduct the trials. The Allies agreed to let the Reich Supreme Court at Leipzig handle the charges. A group of German soldiers who had mistreated Allied prisoners were found guilty by the Leipzig court, but were given minor sentences. Two U-boat officers were also tried, for taking part in the torpedoing of a troop ship and the shelling of the survivors (the *Llandovery Castle* case). But five defendants accused of the atrocities against Belgian civilians that had so outraged the world were acquitted.

After World War I, the European nations also returned to the process of codifying the laws of war. In 1925 they prepared a treaty prohibiting the use of bacteriological methods of warfare. In 1929 two detailed conventions were prepared at Geneva dealing with conduct toward the sick and wounded as well as prisoners of war. Both conventions were to be in force during World War II.

The modern industrial powers continued the effort to define war crimes by treaty in Geneva in 1949, after World War II and the Nuremberg trials. Once again, detailed conventions were laid down, in the following four separate agreements.

1. Convention for the Amelioration of the Condition of the Wounded and Sick in Armed Forces in the Field.
2. Convention for the Amelioration of the Condition of Wounded, Sick, and Shipwrecked Members of Armed Forces at Sea.
3. Convention Relative to the Treatment of Prisoners of War.
4. Convention Relative to the Protection of Civilian Persons in Time of War.

After World War II, the United Nations had taken over the major effort to codify the rules of war. It passed the Genocide Convention in 1948; a resolution against nuclear weapons in 1961; and a resolution on human rights, calling for protection of civilian populations in time of war, in 1968. In the early 1970s the United Nations also urged the International Committee of the Red Cross (ICRC) to develop new agreements on rules of war that would take account of colonial and guerrilla wars, as well as new methods of warfare not covered by earlier conventions. The ICRC brought together a group of experts, who in 1977 produced two protocols to the 1949 Geneva Conventions, dealing with colonial wars of liberation, prisoner-of-war status, and protection of civilian populations (Protocols Additional to the Geneva Convention of August 12, 1949 and Relating to the Protection of Victims of International and Non-international Armed Conflicts, June 10, 1977, 1125 U.N.T.S 609). The United States did not ratify the 1977 protocols.

Another conference was held in Geneva in 1980, to consider restrictions on the use of certain conventional weapons. Three additional protocols were prepared in 1981, covering weapons that introduce nondetectable fragments into the human body; mines, booby traps and other devices; and incendiary weapons (United Nations Conference on Prohibitions or Restrictions on Use of Certain Conventional Weapons: Final Act, U.N. Doc., A/CONF. 95/15 of October 27, 1980 reprinted in 19 I.L.M. 1523, 1530).

In December 1997, 122 countries signed the Landmine Treaty (the Oslo Treaty), which grew out of the 1980 Geneva Conference, banning the use, sale, and production of antipersonnel mines, which ravaged many parts of Asia and Africa (Convention on the Prohibition of the Use, Stockpiling, Production and Transfer of Antipersonnel Mines and on their Destruction, 36 I.L.M. 1507). The treaty came into force on 1 March 1999, although the United States refused to sign because of objections made by the Department of Defense, which was concerned that it would inhibit its ability to respond to rogue nations who refused to obey or follow the restrictions contained in the treaty.

Efforts to declare the use of nuclear weapons a violation of international law and therefore a war crime have continued for many years. Proponents of such a declaration argue that nuclear weapons by their nature inflict excessive and unnecessary suffering on civilian populations, in violation of the 1907 Hague Convention and the 1949 Geneva conventions (Falk, Meyrowitz, and Sanderson). In fact, in December 1963 a Japanese court did reach such a decision in the famed *Shimoda* case, in which victims of Hiroshima and Nagasaki sued the Japanese government for damages caused by the dropping of the atomic bombs on those cities. (The Japanese government had waived any claims by its citizens against the United States in the peace treaty of 1951, and thus was sued as a surrogate for the actual perpetrators.)

The Hague and Geneva conventions are a reflection, but not necessarily the source, of the laws of war. International law has evolved out of the customs and practices prevailing among civilized nations, and the rules of war as laid down in the conventions are but one expression of this common heritage. The conventions declare that all nations are bound by basic rules of warfare, whether or not they are signatories to the treaties and whether or not they attempt to withdraw their ratification. Article 63 of the first Geneva Convention of 1949 (relating to wounded and sick in the field) allowed any party to denounce the treaty, but the "denunciation shall have effect only in respect of the denouncing Power. It shall in no way impair the obligations which the Parties to the conflict shall remain bound to fulfill by virtue of the principles of the law of nations, as they result from the usages established among civilized peoples, from the laws of humanity and the dictates of the public conscience." The appeals decision in *Tadic* also recognized that all nations are bound by "Customary Rules of International Human Rights," regardless of the technical application of a particular treaty or protocol and regardless of whether a nation adhered to their legal provisions.

Those common principles have not varied in their basic outlines for thousands of years: defenseless civilians should not be attacked, prisoners should not be killed, the wounded should be cared for, and weapons of unnecessary destructiveness should not be used.

War crimes trials

As noted above, trials of soldiers who raped civilians, tortured prisoners, or killed the wounded have been rare events until modern times. Victorious armies seldom punished their own men. In the days when payment to soldiers was haphazard, commanders found that permitting excesses and the pillaging of the enemy served as a useful escape valve, and clear rules on what was prohibited in war were not definitively laid down.

With the rise of permanent, professional armies, the necessity for imposing discipline upon soldiers was perceived, and the first international treaties on the rules of war were signed. Punishment for violations of these rules began to be imposed. One of the earliest complete records of a war crimes trial as such involved Major Henry Wirz, the Swiss doctor who was in charge of the Confederate army's infamous Andersonville prison camp during the Civil War. A Union court-martial headed by Major General Lew Wallace (the author of *Ben-Hur*) tried and convicted Wirz of murder and mistreatment of prisoners "in violation of the laws and customs of war," which had just been defined in the Lieber Code, discussed above. Wirz raised the defense of superior orders, but the court rejected the claim, and he was hanged for his crimes.

The British army tried some of its soldiers for killing prisoners and civilians during the Boer War (commemorated in the 1980 Australian film *Breaker Morant*), and the American army held trials in the Philippines to punish atrocities committed by its soldiers during the insurrection of 1899–1902. A limited effort was made to try war criminals after World War 1. But it was left to German courts to try their own soldiers, and the defendants were treated quite leniently or were acquitted, as described above.

The most important group of war crimes trials took place after World War II. The Allied powers issued the "Moscow Declaration" in October 1943, announcing that those accused of war crimes would be "brought back to the scene of their crimes and judged on the spot by the peoples whom they have outraged." The declaration also specified that the Allies would take action against the "major criminals whose offenses have no particular geographical localization."

The United Nations War Crimes Commission was established in 1943 to gather evidence of war crimes for later use. It was chiefly concerned with the committing by lower-level officials or soldiers of such crimes as mistreatment of prisoners of war, atrocities against civilians, or execution of hostages.

The Allied powers engaged in considerable debate about what to do about the higher-echelon leaders. As late as April 1945 the British cabinet voted to shoot the chief Nazi leaders on sight, even if they surrendered, rather than hold elaborate trials. But the Americans and Soviets insisted on an international military tribunal, and the British eventually acceded. The procedures for trying the cases were worked out in London in July and August 1945. An international military tribunal made up of representatives of the four major powers (the United States, Great Britain, the Soviet Union, and France) would try the major political and military leaders of the German government. The charges determined by the London Conference included (1) crimes against peace; (2) war crimes; and (3) crimes against humanity, as defined above.

Twenty-two leading members of the German government were tried at Nuremberg between November 1945 and August 1946. Nineteen were found guilty, and twelve were sentenced to death by hanging, including Hermann Göring, Joachim von Ribbentrop, Hans Frank, Wilhelm Frick, Alfred Jodl, and Martin Bormann, the last tried in absentia.

The specific war crimes of which the Nazi leaders were found guilty included the killing of captured Allied soldiers and prisoners of war, the massacre of hostages in occupied territories, the murder and ill treatment of civilian populations, the deportation of civilians for use as slave labor, and, of course, the systematic killing of the Jewish population of occupied Europe. The tribunal found the defendants guilty of these war crimes not only on the basis of violations of the Hague and Geneva conventions, but also because they violated the customary rules of war between nations. The terms of the Hague and Geneva conventions applied only if all belligerents were parties to them, whereas they had not been explicitly ratified by the Soviet Union and some other countries involved in the war.

The rules of land warfare expressed in the (Hague) convention undoubtedly represented an advance over existing international law at the time of their adoption. But the convention expressly stated that it was an attempt "to revise the general laws and customs of war" which it thus recognized to be then existing; but by 1939 these rules laid down in the convention were recognized by all civilized nations and were regarded as being declaratory of the laws and customs of war. (*Trial of the Major War Criminals,* vol. 1, pp. 253–254)

The formation of the International Military Tribunal was an important step in the punishment of war crimes. First, it showed that the Hague and Geneva conventions were an embodiment of international law that could be enforced on an international level. Prior war crimes trials had been held by individual nations applying their own law to their own soldiers or those of the enemy.

Second, persons were put on trial for violating international law even though their own domestic law permitted those acts. As explained by Telford Taylor, chief counsel for the prosecution at Nuremberg, "individuals may be held criminally liable under international law, even though their conduct was valid under, or even required by, domestic law" (Taylor, p. 82).

Third, the Nuremberg trials expanded individual liability for war crimes far beyond the acts of individual soldiers committing atrocities. Contrary to popular belief, the Nuremberg tribunal was not the first court to declare that superior orders was not a defense to a war crime: that defense had been rejected in the trial of Major Wirz and in the *Llandovery Castle* case decided by the Leipzig court in 1921. Indeed, the domestic law of Great Britain, the United States, and Prussia had long since held that a person does not escape liability for a crime by insisting that he was following orders. What the Nuremberg tribunal did do was to apply the converse of the superior-orders rule: namely, that the persons giving the orders, up to and including the political leaders of the nations, could also be guilty of war crimes. Thus, among those found guilty were German generals who had ordered the killing of prisoners of war, the civil administrators of occupied territories, and the economic ministers who had

exploited slave labor. In addition to the trial of the major criminals, the Allies decided that lower-level German officials should be tried by national or occupation courts of each occupying power.

After the major trials in Nuremberg, American military tribunals held 809 trials in both Germany and Japan, involving 1,600 defendants; the British held 524 trials involving 937; and the French tried 2,107 individuals (*Trials of War Criminals*; United Nations, War Crimes Commission). It is estimated that ten thousand persons were tried for war crimes in Europe and the Far East between 1945 and 1950.

In Europe, the individuals tried included soldiers who killed prisoners, civilians, and hostages, officers who did not properly restrain their subordinates, doctors who conducted illegal medical experiments on prisoners, judges who enforced racial laws against Jews and other nationalities, industrialists who exploited slave labor, and even the manufacturers of the Zyklon B gas that was used to kill Jews and Allied nationals in concentration camps.

Similar trials took place in the Far East. An international military tribunal for the Far East tried the leading Japanese political leaders and generals on the same charges as those heard in Nuremberg. A number of the defendants—particularly some of the generals—were found guilty of committing atrocities against civilians in China, Borneo, and the Philippines, of mistreating and starving prisoners of war, or of disregarding their duty to protect civilians and prisoners under their jurisdiction.

Other trials were held by military commissions in occupied territories. The most famous was the trial of General Tomoyuki Yamashita, the Japanese commander of the Philippines in 1944 and 1945. Yamashita was found guilty of "unlawfully disregard[ing] and fail[ing] to discharge his duty as commander in chief to control the operations of the members of his command, permitting them to commit brutal atrocities" (*In re Yamashita*, 327 U.S. 1, 13–14 (1946)). It appeared that Yamashita had poor communication with his troops and little opportunity to control them after the American invasion of Luzon. Nevertheless, he was found guilty of war crimes based on the atrocities committed by his troops. His lawyers appealed to the U.S. Supreme Court, which refused to intervene, over famous dissents by Justices Frank Murphy and Wiley Rutledge.

One of the most significant war crimes trial after the 1940s was that of Adolf Eichmann, kidnapped from Argentina by Israeli agents and tried in Jerusalem in 1961. There was no question that Eichmann was personally involved in—and therefore responsible for—the killing of millions of Jews from occupied countries. The only legal issue of any significance was whether Israel had jurisdiction to try him. Since he was charged with crimes against the Jewish people, the Israeli court had no difficulty in finding that it could act. "The connection between the State of Israel and the Jewish people needs no explanation" (Friedman, p. 1633).

The issue of war crimes became more significant for Americans during the Vietnam War. The best-known episode occurred when an American military company invaded the small hamlet of Son My (My Lai) in South Vietnam in March 1968 and killed virtually every inhabitant, including women, children, and old men, a total of about four hundred persons. The victims were defenseless, made no effort to fight the Americans, and were not hostile. According to testimony at the court-martial of Lieutenant William Calley, Jr., held in March 1971, Calley had ordered his men to kill everyone and had personally killed a number of the inhabitants, including a two-year-old child. He was found guilty of the premeditated murder of twenty-two Vietnamese civilians and sentenced to life imprisonment. The sentence was reduced to twenty years' imprisonment by the commanding general of Fort Benning, and was further reduced to ten years by the secretary of the army. Calley was paroled after serving one-third of the sentence (*Calley v. Callaway*, 519 F. 2d 184 (5th Cir. 1975)).

Three other persons were tried for their involvement in the Son My episode, but all were acquitted of the charges: Captain Ernest Medina, the company commander who denied having given Calley orders to kill, and two sergeants, Charles Hutto and David Mitchell. Thus, only Calley was found guilty of any charges. One other American soldier, marine private Michael Schwartz, was found guilty of killing twelve Vietnamese villagers in a separate incident at Danang.

There was considerable debate about the legality under international law of American bombing of North Vietnamese cities, but most experts believed that it was no different or worse than Allied bombings during World War II. American treatment of Vietcong prisoners raised more serious problems, and one American lieutenant, James Duffy, admitted during his court-martial that he had ordered a prisoner to be killed. He was acquitted after other officers testified that they too had been ordered to take no prisoners in combat.

In the 1990s, war crimes trials were held in both Yugoslavia and Rwanda, following widespread atrocities against civilian populations in both counties. The U.N. Security Counsel established special tribunals with defined jurisdiction to try those responsible for mass killings and other offenses, including deportation and rape. The tribunals were known as the International Criminal Tribunal for Yugoslavia (ICTY) (U.N. Doc. S/PV. 3217 (1993)) and the International Criminal Tribunal for Rwanda (ICTR) (U.N. Doc. S/RES/955 (1994)). Over one hundred individuals were indicted by the ICTY, including the former president of Serbia, Slobodan Milosevic, for his actions in ordering the persecution of Albanian civilians in Kosovo, including the murder and forced removal of many Kosovo Albanian citizens. The trials produced important new rulings on international crimes, including the decision that rape is a crime against humanity (*Prosecutor v. Kunaric*) and that a crime against humanity can be committed in purely internal conflicts by local militias who are acting for the goals of a foreign power, even if not under their direction (*Prosecutor v. Tadic*).

By the end of 2000, the ICTR had indicted close to fifty individuals for genocide and crimes against humanity following the massacre of hundreds of thousands of Tutsis by the Hutu-dominated government in 1994. Half of the Rwanda cabinet in power at the time, including the former Prime Minister, Jean Kambanda, were indicted for genocide. (A much smaller number of Hutu noncombatants were killed by avenging Tutsis, and Louise Arbour, the former chief prosecutor of the ICTR urged that evenhanded justice required their indictment as well.)

Defining and punishing war crimes has remained an anomalous undertaking. Nations encourage soldiers to kill in war, but try to limit their methods and targets. We allow depersonalized mass bombings of cities, which can kill thousands of defenseless civilians, but we punish individual acts of soldiers who actually confront their victims, and we stockpile weapons far worse than the poisoned arrows prohibited in Roman times. With the increase of ferocious wars of liberation, having no distinct battle lines, and with the growing number of guerrilla armies who fight without uniforms or insignia, the formal rules of the Hague and Geneva conventions may seem outdated. But the need for effective and principled control over atrocities and excesses in armed conflicts of any kind continues.

LEON FRIEDMAN

See also EXCUSE; DURESS; INTERNATIONAL CRIMINAL COURTS; INTERNATIONAL CRIMINAL JUSTICE STANDARDS; INTERNATIONAL CRIMINAL LAW; JUSTIFICATION: NECESSITY; JUSTIFICATION: SELF-DEFENSE; TERRORISM; WAR AND VIOLENT CRIME.

BIBLIOGRAPHY

FALK, RICHARD A.; KOLKO, GABRIEL; and LIFTON, ROBERT JAY, eds. *Crimes of War: A Legal, Political, Documentary, and Psychological Inquiry into the Responsibility of Leaders, Citizens, and Soldiers for Criminal Acts in Wars.* New York: Random House, 1971.

FALK, RICHARD A.; MEYROWITZ, LEE; and SANDERSON, JACK. "Nuclear Weapons and International Law." Occasional Paper No. 10. Princeton, N.J.: Princeton University, Center of International Studies, 1981.

FRIEDMAN, LEON, ed. *The Law of War: A Documentary History.* 2 vols. Foreword by Telford Taylor. New York: Random House, 1972.

FRIEDMAN, LEON, and TIEFENBRUN, SUSAN, eds. *War Crimes and War Crimes Tribunals: Past, Present and Future.* Vol. 3 of *Hofstra Law and Policy Symposium.* Hempstead, N.Y.: Hofstra University School of Law, 1999.

GROTIUS, HUGO. *The Law of War and Peace* (1625). 3 vols. Translated by Francis W. Kelsey, with the collaboration of Arthur E. R. Boak, Henry A. Sanders, Jesse S. Reeves, and Herbert F. Wright. Introduction by James Brown Scott. Oxford, U.K.: Oxford University Press, Clarendon Press, 1925. Photographic reprint. Indianapolis: Bobbs-Merrill, 1962.

HAMMER, RICHARD. *One Morning in the War: The Tragedy at Son My.* New York: Coward-McCann, 1970.

KEEN, MAURICE H. *The Laws of War in the Late Middle Ages.* London: Routledge & Kegan Paul, 1965.

LIEBER, FRANCIS. "Instructions for the Government of Armies of the United States in the Field" [The Lieber Code] (1863). *International Law Discussions, 1903: The United States Naval War Code of 1900.* U.S. Naval War College. Washington, D.C.: Government Printing Office, 1904. Pages 115–139.

MARRIN, ALBERT, ed. *War and the Christian Conscience: From Augustine to Martin Luther King, Jr.* Chicago: Regnery, 1971.

MINEAR, RICHARD H. *Victor's Justice: The Tokyo War Crimes Trial.* Princeton, N.J.: Princeton University Press, 1971.

Red Cross, International Committee. *Conference of Government Experts on the Reaffirmation and Development of International Humanitarian Law Applicable in Armed Conflicts: Report on the Work of the Conference.* Geneva: The Committee, 1977.

"Respect for Human Rights in Armed Conflicts." G.A. Res. 2444. *Resolutions Adopted by the General Assembly during Its Twenty-Third Session, September 24–December 21, 1968.* U.N. Doc. A/72 18. New York: UN, 1969. Pages 50–51.

TAYLOR, TELFORD. *Nuremberg and Vietnam: An American Tragedy.* New York: Quadrangle, 1970.

Trial of the Major War Criminals before the International Military Tribunal, Nuremberg, Nov. 14, 1945–Oct. 1, 1946. 42 vols. Nuremberg: The Tribunal, 1947–1949. Reprint. New York: AMS Press, 1971.

Trials of War Criminals before the Nurenberg Military Tribunals under Control Council Law No. 10, October 1946–April 1949. 15 vols. Washington, D.C.: Government Printing Office, 1949–1953.

United Nations, General Assembly. "Declaration on the Prohibition of the Use of Nuclear and Thermonuclear Weapons." G.A. Res. 1653. *Resolutions Adopted by the General Assembly during Its Sixteenth Session, September 19, 1961–February 23, 1962,* vol. 1. U.N. Doc. A/5100. New York: UN, 1962. Pages 4–5.

United Nations, War Crimes Commission. *Law Reports of Trials of War Criminals, Selected and Prepared by the UN War of Crimes Commission.* 15 vols. London: His Majesty's Stationery Office, 1947–1949.

VITTORIA, FRANCISCO DE. "The Second Relectio of the Reverend Father, Brother Franciscus de Victoria on the Indians [and] on the Law of War Made by the Spaniards on the Barbarians." Translated by John Pawley Bate. Edited by Ernest Nys. Preface by James Brown Scott. In *The Classics of International Law,* vol. 7. Washington, D.C.: Carnegie Institution, 1917. Pages 163–187.

WALZER, MICHAEL. *Just and Unjust Wars: A Moral Argument with Historical Illustrations.* New York: Basic Books, 1977.

WEDGWOOD, CICELY V. *The Thirty Years War.* New Haven, Conn.: Yale University Press, 1939.

INTERNATIONAL AGREEMENTS (IN ORDER OF
SIGNING)

General Treaty for the Renunciation of War as
an Instrument of National Policy [Kellogg-
Briand Pact], Aug. 27, 1928, 94 L.N.T.S. 57.

Agreement for the Prosecution and Punishment
of the Major War Criminals of the European
Axis [London Charter], Aug. 8, 1945, 59 Stat.
1544, 82 U.N.T.S. 279.

Convention on the Prevention and Punishment
of the Crime of Genocide, Dec. 9, 1948, 78
U.N.T.S. 277.

Geneva Convention for the Amelioration of the
Condition of the Wounded and Sick in Armed
Forces in the Field, Aug. 12, 1949, 6 U.S.T,
3114, T.I.A.S. No. 3362, 75 U.N.T.S. 31.

Geneva Convention for the Amelioration of the
Condition of Wounded, Sick, and Shipwrecked Members of Armed Forces at Sea,
Aug. 12, 1949, 6 U.S.T. 3217, T.I.A.S. No.
3363, 75 U.N.T.S. 85.

Geneva Convention Relative to the Treatment of
Prisoners of War, Aug. 12, 1949, 6 U.S.T. 33
16, T.I.A.S. No. 3364, 75 U.N.T.S. 135.

Geneva Convention Relative to the Protection of
Civilian Persons in Time of War, Aug. 12,
1949, 6 U.S.T. 35 16, T.I.A.S. No. 3365, 75
U.N.T.S. 287.

Protocols Additional to the Geneva Conventions
of August 12, 1949, and Relating to the Protection of Victims of International and Non-
international Armed Conflicts, June 10, 1977,
International Legal Materials 16 (1977): 1391–
1449; 1125 U.N.T.S. 609.

Convention on the Prohibition of the Use, Stockpiling, Production and Transfer of Antipersonnel Mines and on their Destruction, 36
I.L.M. 1507 (December, 1997).

Charter for the International Criminal Tribunal,
U.N. Doc. A/Conf. 183/9, 17 July 1998.

WHITE-COLLAR CRIME: HISTORY OF AN IDEA

Crimes committed by persons of respectability have drawn the attention of societies throughout history. In the United States, interest in such
phenomena far antedates the first public use of
the concept of white-collar crime by Edwin Sutherland. The muckraking tradition at the turn of
the century produced many persons who condemned abuse of position for private gain. Sociologist E. A. Ross, in *Sin and Society,* drew
attention to "the man who picks pockets with a
railway rebate, murders with an adulterant instead of a bludgeon, burglarizes with a "rake-off"
instead of a jimmy, cheats with a company pro-
spectus instead of a deck of cards, or scuttles his
town instead of his ship" (p. 7).

The varied misdeeds denoted by Ross give
an early hint of both the value of the concept and
the difficulties that have plagued its use. The
value is essentially social and evocative. It connotes not a particular type of crime or a statutory
violation, but a concern for some combination of
abuse of trust, authority, status, or position. In a
society whose criminal justice system deals mainly with common crimes and common offenders,
it bespeaks a concern for the misdeeds of the
haves rather than the have-nots, and it raises the
specter of class bias in law enforcement. However, its signifying power is precisely its weakness
as an analytical tool, for its meaning shifts with
changes in the character of society and in the underlying values and interests of the varied scholars and policymakers who invoke it. It is thus a
distinctively social, rather than legal, concept,
one suffused with vagueness and ambiguity.

The evolution of white-collar crime

The legacy of Sutherland. Sutherland's interest in the topic dates at least to the 1920s, although the research resulting in his *White Collar
Crime* was initiated during the depression years
of the 1930s. The first public treatment of the
subject occurred when Sutherland titled his presidential address to the American Sociological Society in 1939 "The White Collar Criminal." He
was apparently drawn to the topic in his search
for a general theory of crime. The usual explanations in his day (and often today) stressed poverty
and other pathological social conditions, but, argued Sutherland, these factors could not be a
general cause of crime if crimes were also committed by persons of respectability and high social status. In the book-length version of the
speech, which appeared a decade later, Sutherland aimed simultaneously to weaken theories
depending on the behavior of the deprived and
the depraved, and to provide support for his
own social-learning approach to crime causation—the theory of differential association.

Sutherland was rather casual in his conceptualization of white-collar crime, at times stressing social status, at times behavior carried out in
an occupational role, and at times crime committed by organizations or by individuals acting in
organizational capacities. The confusion is reflected in his most frequently cited definition:

"White collar crime may be defined approximately as a crime committed by a person of respectability and high social status in the course of his occupation" (p. 9). His book was devoted, however, to the crimes of organizations, not of persons: seventy large corporations and fifteen public utilities. Thus, a firm basis for ambiguity had been laid. Those following Sutherland sometimes focused on persons of high status, sometimes on occupations, and sometimes on corporate bodies.

Sutherland's book described the illegalities committed by those corporations, arguing that the corporations share most of the characteristics of professional thieves: their offenses are deliberate and organized, they are often recidivists, and they show disdain for law. Needless to say, with these conclusions the book had a controversial reception. Many in the social sciences hailed it as a landmark, whereas many in law and business attacked it as misleading and distorted. The principal basis for disagreement concerned the underlying concept of crime. The "crimes" of the corporations Sutherland examined were rarely prosecuted in criminal court: they were violations of administrative rules or simply contract cases to be processed, if at all, in civil court. Many in the legal community insisted these were not crimes at all. Sutherland's answer was that businessmen were more able to influence the course of legislation; it was only their greater power (relative to the lower-class criminal) that kept their offenses out of the traditional criminal law.

The battle over definition aside, Sutherland's pioneering work stirred few fires in the two decades after its publication. Detailed studies of particular offenses, such as Donald Cressey's examination of the violation of financial trust, were the exception rather than the rule. Of the triumvirate of status, occupation, and organization that underlay Sutherland's conception, interest tended to turn away from the status dimension itself, and toward those crimes made possible because of the defendant's occupational role (Newman). Some analysts spoke not of white-collar crime but of occupational crime. Offenders studied in these terms were not exclusively of high status. They included retail pharmacists, meat inspectors, and bank tellers. Although a much-publicized case of price-fixing in the electrical industry in 1961 (Geis and Meier) helped sustain an interest in the topic of crimes committed through, and on behalf of, organizations, sustained study of organizational crime did not flower until the next decade. Criminological research and theory continued to concentrate on juvenile delinquency and violent crime.

It is unclear why Sutherland's work generated so little new research or theory, although several reasons are plausible. The massiveness of Sutherland's undertaking, as well as confusion regarding the concept itself, may have played a part. The 1950s and 1960s were not depression decades, and the problems of a younger generation occupied public and governmental attention. It had also provided more convenient, historically, for social scientists to study the weak and deprived, rather than those in more powerful positions. The symbolic and evocative nature of the concept remained, however, awaiting changing conditions for new meaning to be infused into it.

From offender to offense. Societal interest in white-collar crime grew rapidly in the 1970s, rivaling the attention street crime had received in the preceding decade. Prosecutors gave it higher priority than in the past. Targets of investigation included individual businessmen, corrupt politicians, and such corporate activities as international business bribery, the manufacture of dangerous products, and environmental pollution. The renewed interest was motivated at least in part by the discovery of corruption and other illegal practices at the highest levels of government, and by a growing sensitivity to dangerous corporate practices. The growth in interest was great enough that it could be fairly labeled a social movement (Katz, 1980).

When the pace of scholarship on white-collar crime also revived, it became evident that the wide range of phenomena suggested by the concept had to be broken down into components. Attention had focused so much on the nature of the offender that actual criminal behavior had gone unexamined. It seemed to make little sense to include under a single rubric as diverse a set of activities as bank embezzlement, land swindles, price-fixing, fraudulent loan applications, and bribery. The first important shift away from the legacy of Sutherland was accomplished by taking the offense itself as the principal object of inquiry. In the first such effort, Herbert Edelhertz proposed to define white-collar crime as "an illegal act or series of illegal acts committed by nonphysical means and by concealment and guile, to obtain money or property, to avoid payment or loss of money or property, or to obtain business or personal advantage" (p. 3). A related shift is to search for behavioral patterns that characterize different *types* of white-collar crime. Susan Shapiro, for example, distinguishes fraud, self-dealing, and regulatory offenses (pp. 20–24), and Mitchell Rothman separates frauds, takings, and collusion.

The impulse that gives rise to typological efforts is the felt need to put order into the enormous range of behaviors at issue. The statutes that define white-collar crime, passed by legislatures for various purposes at various times, are a patchwork. Important as they may be for prosecution, the legal categories are of limited value for analytic purposes. A given statutory offense may include a wide array of actual behaviors; bank embezzlement, for example, may range from a simple theft by a bank teller to a complex fraudulent loan arranged by a trust officer. Essentially the same behavior may be punished under statutes as different as those governing mail and wire fraud, securities fraud, and false claims and statements. Typologies allow one to see some of the similarities between crimes as different as bribery and price-fixing, which share the element of collusive activity.

The underlying assumption of this type of analysis—still to be proved—is that parallels in behavior may suggest parallels in either the causal processes producing such behavior or in the methods of detection and enforcement brought to bear upon them. Such work is likely to be only partially successful until there is greater agreement on the core properties of white-collar crime. To the extent that the legal categories themselves are a function of concerns not reflected in the underlying conduct—a concern, for example, that the conduct be reachable by federal authorities, or that regulatory agencies can police it—typologies that concentrate on underlying conduct may be prematurely dismissive of the important role played by legal categorization itself.

From offense to organization and consequence. A second trend is to emphasize not behavior but its consequences. This trend rediscovers issues that occupied reformers at the turn of the twentieth century—a concern for the power of organizationsand the harms they commit. From the late nineteenth century on, harms caused by the production and sale of adulterated goods and similar activities were recognized as "strict liability" offenses—criminal acts not requiring proof of a guilty mind. Throughout the twentieth century these activities, and many others later recognized to pose a similar threat, came increasingly to be the subject of administrative

regulation, which was seen as a wiser and more effective device for protecting the public interest. Regulation expanded as new dangers to health and to life itself were recognized—dangers to individuals posed by the air they breathed, the water they drank, the food and drugs they consumed, the automobiles and other products they used, and the places at which they worked.

Rediscovery of the power of organizations to inflict physical damage as well as economic injury has led some scholars to direct their attention to specifically organizational offenses. The central concern here is those actions taken by the officials or other agents of legitimate organizations that have a serious physical or economic impact on employees, consumers, or the general public (Schrager and Short). A growing number of analysts thus speak of organizations as offenders of "organizational deviance," and of illegalities committed through the organizational form. This is a response to a society in which organizations increasingly are major actors, and although it reflects experience in the United States, both the concept of white-collar crime and a concern with corporate and governmental offenses are found throughout the world.

The focus on organizational offenses brings with it enduring issues of law and policy. One is the question of the standard by which individual conduct is to be judged. Should organizations' executives be sanctioned for failure to supervise middle-level officials engaged in wrongdoing? Should strict liability be employed, as in some of the earlier public-welfare offenses? How should sanctions be distributed between organization and employees? When the focus is on the corporate body itself, there is the question of how best to protect against harmful corporate practices without stifling organizational innovation and creativity. For example, should unwanted conduct be deterred through increased penalties against the corporation? Or is it more effective to control wrongdoing by reaching inside the organization, either through rules governing production processes and information flow, or rules regarding the composition of the board of directors? The treatment of the offenses of organizations remains fraught with complex policy choices (Coffee; Kadish; Stone).

Finally, there is the issue that sparked the original debate over the concept of white-collar crime: Are these offenses administrative rule violations or "real" crimes? The most complete follow-up study to *White Collar Crime* defines its subject as any act, committed by a corporation, that is punishable by the state, whether through criminal, administrative, or civil law. The title of this study, *Corporate Crime*, while reflecting the shift to the corporate form as a primary focus of inquiry, maintains the view that such conduct be labeled criminal (Clinard and Yeager, p. 16). The corporate sanctions examined, however, are overwhelmingly civil or administrative. Thus, the matter of definition remains controversial some forty years after Sutherland's initial exploration of white-collar crime.

White-collar crime from the enforcement perspective

White-collar crime, in either its individual or organizational form, often involves complex paper manipulations and sophisticated cover-up activities. When these traits are combined with the embeddedness of illegalities in organizations, the problems of gathering evidence with respect to motive, intent, and act are compounded. It is often extremely difficult to know who engaged in or authorized the conduct in question, what specific illegality has been committed, or whether there is a crime at all. For these reasons, crucial differences between white-collar crime and common crime appear when one examines how each is detected and prosecuted.

For common crimes, prosecution and defense are typically brought into play only after a crime has occurred and an arrest has been made; but in the case of white-collar crimes, the investigative work of prosecutors and the protective efforts of defense counsel characteristically precede, rather than follow, formal action. Indeed, from an enforcement perspective, white-collar crimes are those detected and investigated by white-collar workers, in contrast to the men in blue who respond to common crimes (Katz, 1979). The first officials to be brought into the case are not police but, more likely, tax agents or employees of a regulatory agency. Defense counsel will be hired when the defendant first becomes aware that he is a target of an investigation—typically, long before an indictment is forthcoming. This means that white-collar crime prosecution and defense often more closely approximate complex civil litigation, with its various strategic moves to gain or shield information from the opposing side, than they do the typical common-crime case. The effect of these differences is to make prosecution of white-collar cases vastly more expensive and time-consuming than that of typical common crimes. With limited resources, prosecutors may find it difficult to justify heavy expenditures for a problematic white-collar investigation when the same resources might be devoted to a number of common-crime cases.

Sentencing of white-collar offenders is also complicated. As in common crime, most cases will be settled by a guilty plea. But sentencing is problematic because the white-collar defendant, although frequently having committed offenses of long duration and great economic magnitude, is more likely to have an exemplary prior record. Judges are torn between the desire to show such offenders leniency because of their past good citizenship, and the desire to show severity because the white-collar offender has abused a position of trust.

With the advent of determinate sentencing, sanctions for white-collar offenders have become more severe. The Federal Sentencing Commission, for example, substantially raised the sentences for white-collar offenders in order to guarantee short terms of imprisonment for offenders whom judges had previously been fining and placing on probation (Federal Sentencing Guidelines § 1A4(d) (Nov. 1998). In no other offense category did the Commission raise sentencing severity relative to pre-Guidelines averages; the appropriateness of its doing so for white-collar offenders remains a matter of intense political and academic controversy.

Thus, at each stage of the criminal justice system, white-collar offenses present a distinctive set of problems for law enforcement officials. For the legal philosopher as well as the policymaker, these differences raise questions of equality of treatment between common-crime and white-collar crime defendants, as well as questions of fundamental fairness in the operation of the criminal justice system. For the researcher, they point to the need to devote detailed attention to the comparative study of the administration of justice in white-collar-crime and common-crime cases.

Conclusion

As this review suggests, the concept of white-collar crime is in a state of disarray. Its evolution has been marked by changes in meaning that often preserve, rather than reduce, fundamental ambiguities. The term still denotes crimes of high status to some, while to others it refers to either occupational or organizational illegality. Some concentrate on the nature of the offense;

others, on its consequences. The offending conduct appears in a different guise when the enforcement perspective is examined, and analysts still cannot agree whether it should be regarded as criminal.

Given this confusion, the logical solution is to abandon the concept of white-collar crime and develop separate, more neatly bounded areas of inquiry. One body of researchers might devote their attention to the relation of social status to criminality and to sentence disparity; another group, to the use of occupation in the commission of crimes. Still other investigators might study the various layers of formal organizations so as to examine how corporate offenses are conducted, and yet others might focus on regulatory agencies and their enforcement activities.

As neat as this solution might seem, it misses a fundamental point. Ambiguous since its outset, the concept of white-collar crime nevertheless appears to have enormous staying power. Why is it still in use, given its frailties? The suggestion is that the concept reflects deeply felt concerns that make psychological and social sense, even if they present logical ambiguities. The overall crime problem is commonly perceived to center on the lower echelons of society. It is the down-and-out, the unemployed, and the victims of stratification and race prejudice who constitute the bulk of those processed by the criminal justice system. White-collar crime, on the other hand, stands for all the wrongs committed by those in more advantaged positions. The source of the advantage may differ, sometimes reflecting individual status, sometimes occupational role, and sometimes organizational position. The animus that nourishes the concept is often an expression of frustration or outrage at the great imbalance of power between large organizations and their victims. Often, however, it reflects a concern for the weakening of the social fabric created when people in privileged positions destroy trust by committing crimes. Their offenses eat into the life of the community just as surely, if not as visibly, as physical assault. It is this combination of evocative features that keeps the concept of white-collar crime alive despite its flawed logical status.

When the original arguments over the meaning of the concept were at their height, the sociologist Vilhelm Aubert cautioned against efforts to decide on the concept's true meaning. White-collar crime struck him as a phenomenon highly reflective of more pervasive features of the social order. Theoretical interest lies precisely in the varying attitudes regarding such conduct held by persons from different stations in life. This view remains relevant and may well help explain the longevity of the concept. Many middle- and upper-class citizens engage in some forms of white-collar illegality while condemning others. Rather than abandoning the concept because of its logical flaws, there is a need to examine its social meaning, as well as the conditions under which the various offenses that are grouped under the "white-collar" rubric are committed, detected, and sanctioned.

STANTON WHEELER
DAN M. KAHAN

See also CLASS AND CRIME; CORPORATE CRIMINAL RESPONSIBILITY; CRIME CAUSATION: ECONOMIC THEORIES; CRIMINAL JUSTICE SYSTEM; ECONOMIC CRIME: ANTITRUST OFFENSES; ECONOMIC CRIME: TAX OFFENSES; FEDERAL CRIMINAL LAW ENFORCEMENT.

BIBLIOGRAPHY

ALBONETTI, CELESTA A. "Avoidance of Punishment: A Legal-Bureaucratic Model of Suspended Sentences in Federal White-Collar Cases Prior to the Federal Sentencing Guidelines." *Social Forces* 78 (1999): 303–329.
AUBERT, VILHELM. "White-Collar Crime and Social Structure." *American Journal of Sociology* 58 (1952): 263–271.
CLINARD, MARSHALL B., and QUINNEY, RICHARD. *Criminal Behavior Systems*. 2d ed. New York: Holt, Rinehart & Winston, 1973.
———, and YEAGER, PETER C. *Corporate Crime*. With the collaboration of Ruth B. Clinard. New York: Free Press, 1980.
COFFEE, JOHN C., JR. "Beyond the Shut-eyed Sentry: Toward a Theoretical View of Corporate Misconduct and an Effective Legal Response." *Virginia Law Review* 63 (1977): 1099–1278.
COHEN, ALBERT K.; LINDESMITH, ALFRED; and SCHUESSLER, KARL, eds. *The Sutherland Papers*. Bloomington: Indiana University Press, 1956.
CRESSEY, DONALD R. *Other People's Money: A Study in the Social Psychology of Embezzlement*. New York: Free Press, 1953.
EDELHERTZ, HERBERT. *The Nature, Impact, and Prosecution of White Collar Crime*. Washington, D.C.: U.S. Department of Justice, Law Enforcement Assistance Administration, National Institute of Law Enforcement and Criminal Justice, 1970.
ERMANN, DAVID M., and LUNDMAN, RICHARD J. *Corporate and Governmental Deviance: Problems*

of Organizational Behavior in Contemporary Society. 2d ed. New York: Oxford University Press, 1982.

GEIS, GILBERT, and MEIER, ROBERT F., eds. *White-collar Crime: Offenses in Business, Politics, and the Professions.* Rev. ed. New York: Free Press, 1977.

KADISH, SANFORD H. "Some Observations on the Use of Criminal Sanctions in Enforcing Economic Regulations." *University of Chicago Law Review* 30 (1963): 423–449.

KATZ, JACK. "Legality and Equality: Plea Bargaining in the Prosecution of White-Collar and Common Crime." *Law and Society Review* 13, no. 2 (1979): 431–459.

———. "The Social Movement against White-Collar Crime." *Criminology Review Yearbook,* vol. 2. Edited by Egon Bittner and Sheldon L. Messinger. Beverly Hills, Calif.: Sage, 1980, pp. 161–184.

LOTT, JOHN R., JR. "Do We Punish High Income Criminals Too Heavily?" *Econ. Inq.* 30 (1992): 583–608.

NEWMAN, DONALD J. "White-collar Crime." *Law and Contemporary Problems* 23 (1958): 735–753.

ROSS, EDWARD ALSWORTH. *Sin and Society: An Analysis of Latter-day Iniquity* (1907). With a letter from President Roosevelt. Reprint. Gloucester, Mass.: Peter Smith, 1965.

ROTHMAN, MITCHELL LEWIS. "The Criminaloid Revisited." Ph.D. dissertation, Yale University, 1982.

SCHRAGER, LAURA SHILL, and SHORT, JAMES F., JR. "Toward a Sociology of Organizational Crime." *Social Problems* 25 (1978): 407–419.

SHAPIRO, SUSAN P. *Thinking about White-Collar Crime: Matters of Conceptualization and Research.* Washington, D.C.: U.S. Department of Justice, National Institute of Justice, 1980.

STONE, CHRISTOPHER D. "The Place of Enterprise Liability in the Control of Corporate Conduct." *Yale Law Journal* 90 (1980): 1–77.

SUTHERLAND, EDWIN H. *White Collar Crime* (1949). Foreword by Donald R. Cressey. New York: Holt, 1961.

WEISBURD, DAVID; WHEELER, STANTON; WARING, ELIN; and BODE, NANCY. *Crimes of the Middle Classes: White-Collar Offenders in the Federal Courts.* New Haven, Conn.: Yale University Press, 1991.

WHEELER, STANTON; MANN, KENNETH; and SARAT, AUSTIN. *Sitting in Judgment: The Sentencing of White-Collar Criminals.* New Haven, Conn.: Yale University Press, 1988.

WIRETAPPING AND EAVESDROPPING

Wiretapping and electronic eavesdropping are two types of electronic surveillance that play vital roles in criminal investigations. Wiretapping involves the use of covert means to intercept, monitor, and record telephone conversations of individuals. Electronic eavesdropping may involve the placement of a "bug" inside private premises to secretly record conversations, or the use of a "wired" government informant to record conversations that occur within the informant's earshot. Both wiretapping and electronic eavesdropping enable the government to monitor and record conversations and activities without revealing the presence of government listening devices.

Law enforcement officials have utilized these surreptitious techniques for various investigative purposes, particularly in the contexts of organized crime and counterespionage. Electronic surveillance can reveal, for example, the scope of a criminal conspiracy or organization, the nature of its activities, and the identities of its participants. Electronic surveillance also allows investigators to covertly obtain evidence of a particular conversation, series of conversations, or meetings, for use in prosecuting an identified suspect in a known crime.

The impact of electronic surveillance on personal privacy

While electronic surveillance undoubtedly enhances the government's ability to investigate crime, inherent in the nature of these techniques is the potential for grave invasions of individual privacy. Indeed, as one scholar of the topic has noted, "electronic surveillance has long posed a classic confrontation between privacy interests and the need for effective law enforcement" (Goldsmith). Wiretapping obviously invades the privacy interests of people who speak on the telephone. Eavesdropping allows the government to overhear and record all conversations occurring within the range of the bug or wired informant. Further, because electronic bugs and informants can gain access to private areas like homes and offices, eavesdropping can reveal information that is extremely private in nature. Consequently, clandestine electronic surveillance has the potential to eliminate personal privacy if left to the unfettered discretion of police officials. Because of this threat, wiretapping and eavesdropping have been subject to numerous constitutional challenges under the Fourth Amendment, which guarantees all persons the right to be free from unreasonable governmental searches and seizures.

Early restrictions on electronic surveillance

The Supreme Court first considered the constitutionality of wiretapping in the 1928 case of *Olmstead v. United States,* 277 U.S. 438 (1928). The Court ruled that governmental wiretapping of telephone conversations fell outside the protection of the Fourth Amendment. The Court based its conclusion upon a narrow, textual reading of the amendment. First, the Court found that words spoken into a telephone were not tangible things and thus could not be subjected to a search or seizure. Second, it reasoned that because wiretapping could be accomplished without a trespass, there was no physical invasion of property to justify invoking the Fourth Amendment. Finally, the Court assumed that one who uses the telephone "intends to project his voice to those quite outside."

The ruling in *Olmstead* was controversial. The Court split five to four, and there were strong reactions from Congress and the public opposing the ruling. Although *Olmstead* permitted police officials to employ wiretapping without constitutional restraints, *Olmstead* did not address the constitutionality of informant spying. The Court would tackle that issue in the 1952 case of *On Lee v. United States,* 343 U.S. 747 (1952). In *On Lee,* the defendant challenged the constitutionality of the government's use of a wired informant to record his statements. Chin Poy, a friend and former employee of On Lee, went to On Lee's laundry shop secretly wired for sound with a small microphone inside his coat pocket. A federal officer stationed outside the laundry intercepted the conversation between On Lee and Chin Poy. Several days later, the same officer monitored another conversation between On Lee and Chin Poy. During both conversations, On Lee made incriminating statements.

The Court ruled that the government's conduct did not violate On Lee's Fourth Amendment rights. No constitutional trespass had occurred because On Lee consented to Chin Poy's entry into the laundry shop. The Court also rejected On Lee's companion claim that the officer committed a trespass because the electronic equipment allowed him to overhear secretly what transpired inside the shop. The Court called this argument "frivolous." The Court explained that only a "physical entry," such as one associated with force, submission to legal coercion, or without any sign of consent, would trigger constitutional protection against clandestine surveillance. Finally, the Court dismissed the contention that it should treat informant surveillance on an equal footing with police wiretapping. To the Court, the use of a radio wire in these circumstances suggested only "the most attenuated analogy to wiretapping."

By the 1960s, the Court, which was then led by Chief Justice Earl Warren, had reexamined and overturned many constitutional rulings affecting the rights of criminal suspects. But the Warren Court's willingness to limit the search and seizure powers of the police did not extend to informant spying. In a trio of cases in the mid-1960s, the Court refused to impose constitutional restrictions on the government's power to employ informants to monitor and record private conversations. In *Lopez v. United States,* 373 U.S. 427 (1963), the defendant appealed his conviction for the attempted bribery of an Internal Revenue agent who had visited Lopez's business to inquire about the payment of excise taxes. During this visit, Lopez offered the agent a bribe. Several days later, the agent returned to the office secretly equipped with a pocket tape recorder. Pretending to go along with the bribery scheme, the agent recorded his conversation with Lopez, who again made incriminating statements. At trial, the agent's testimony about the bribery conversation and the tape recording of the second conversation were both admitted into evidence.

The Court ruled that Lopez's Fourth Amendment rights were not violated. Critical to the Court's conclusion was the fact that Lopez had consented to the agent's presence. The only evidence seized by the agent was evidence that Lopez had voluntarily given to the agent. While the *Lopez* majority upheld Lopez's conviction, four dissenting Justices not only argued that Lopez's Fourth Amendment rights had been violated, but insisted that both *Olmstead* and *On Lee* were wrongly decided. Notwithstanding the views of the dissenters in *Lopez,* the Court would issue two additional decisions in 1966 that reaffirmed the government's unfettered discretion to plant informants within private places.

In *Lewis v. United States,* 385 U.S. 206 (1966), an undercover police officer misrepresented his identity during a telephone conversation and obtained an invitation to visit Lewis's home to purchase narcotics. The officer visited Lewis's home twice, both times purchasing narcotics. Unlike the government agent in *Lopez*, the officer in *Lewis* was not wired for sound. At trial, both the narcotics and the officer's testimony regarding his conversations with Lewis were admitted into evidence. Upholding Lewis's conviction, the Court implied that Lewis had assumed the risk that his statements would be overheard and used against him by inviting the undercover agent into his home to conduct illegal business. While recognizing that a person's home is normally accorded heightened Fourth Amendment protections, the Court ruled that those protections are waived when, as here, the individual uses his home as a commercial center and invites outsiders in to conduct illegal business.

Hoffa v. United States, 385 U.S. 293 (1966), also rested upon an assumption of risk rationale. A government informant, who was also a member of union leader Jimmy Hoffa's entourage, reported to the F.B.I. incriminating conversations made by Hoffa in his hotel suite and other places. Hoffa argued that the informant's actions infringed his Fourth Amendment rights. The Court upheld Hoffa's conviction, ruling that Hoffa had effectively forfeited his right to rely on the security of his hotel suite by allowing the informant to enter it and to hear and participate in the incriminating conversations. The Court explained that no interest protected by the Fourth Amendment was infringed in *Hoffa*. All that could be said about Hoffa's constitutional interest was that "he was relying upon his misplaced confidence" that the informant would not reveal his wrongdoing. That interest, however, was not protected by the Fourth Amendment.

The contemporary legal status of wiretapping and eavesdropping

Although the Warren Court's rulings on informants were distinctly pro-government in tone and result, one year after *Lewis* and *Hoffa* were decided the Court appeared to adopt a new way of looking at the Fourth Amendment. This new approach was less deferential to the claims of government. In two cases decided in 1967, the Court rejected arguments that law enforcement officials are free to conduct electronic surveillance without satisfying the procedural safeguards required by the Fourth Amendment.

A new judicial framework. In 1967 two rulings by the Court intimated a new doctrinal approach for electronic surveillance cases. The first case, *Berger v. New York*, 388 U.S. 41 (1967), addressed a constitutional challenge to a New York statute allowing court-authorized electronic surveillance. The defendants were convicted of conspiracy to corrupt the New York State Liquor Authority. The incriminating evidence against some of the defendants was obtained pursuant to several court-ordered bugs authorized by the New York statute. A majority of the *Berger* Court concluded that the New York statute was facially unconstitutional for essentially two reasons: the statute did not require that a judge find probable cause before issuing an electronic surveillance warrant, and the statue failed to limit the nature, scope, or duration of the electronic surveillance.

The second decision—*Katz v. United States*, 389 U.S. 347 (1967)—signaled that the old ways of analyzing search and seizure issues were no longer acceptable. In *Katz*, the defendant argued that F.B.I. agents violated his Fourth Amendment rights by attaching an electronic listening and recording device to the outside of a public telephone to monitor his conversations. The Court agreed and reversed Katz's conviction.

The ruling in *Katz*, however, was not based on traditional search and seizure norms that had controlled earlier electronic surveillance cases. The Court began by asserting that the Fourth Amendment did not grant a "general right of privacy." The amendment "protects individual privacy against certain kinds of governmental intrusion, but its protections go further, and often have nothing to do with privacy at all." The Court explained that "the Fourth Amendment protects people, not places. What a person knowingly exposes to the public, even in his own home or office, is not a subject of Fourth Amendment protection. But what he seeks to preserve as private, even in an area accessible to the public, may be constitutionally protected." While Katz chose to make his illegal calls in public, the Court emphasized that public telephones play a vital role in private communications. Consequently, Katz retained the right to assume the words he spoke while on the telephone would not be broadcast to the world.

Katz also extinguished the lingering notion that a physical trespass was necessary to trigger constitutional review of governmental searches and seizures. While recognizing that the rationale of *Olmstead* had not been formally overruled, the Court declared that the reach of the amendment "cannot turn upon the presence or absence of a physical intrusion into any given enclosure." Employing this new framework, the Court concluded that wiretapping without judicial authorization violated the Fourth Amendment.

While *Katz* initiated a new way of thinking about electronic surveillance, a subsequent case demonstrated that this new perspective would not automatically render the previous eavesdropping cases obsolete. In 1971 the Court decided *United States v. White*, 401 U.S. 745 (1971), whose facts closely mirrored those of *On Lee*. At issue in *White* was whether the testimony of federal officers about conversations between the defendant and a government informant, which were overheard by the officers monitoring the frequency of a radio transmitter carried by the informant, implicated the Fourth Amendment. The Court ruled this form of surreptitious electronic eavesdropping was still permissible.

The *White* Court concluded that nothing in *Katz* undermined the reasoning of *On Lee, Lopez, Lewis,* or *Hoffa*. It reasoned that if an individual assumes the risk that a secret informant, acting without electronic equipment, might later reveal the contents of a conversation, the risk is the same when the informant simultaneously records and transmits the conversation to a third party. In either situation, "the risk is his," and the Fourth Amendment offers no protection against police efforts to obtain information in this manner.

Title III: the statutory response. Prior to the 1960s, many persons contended that if Congress or the Court sanctioned electronic wiretapping or bugging by the police, society would rapidly move toward an oppressive police state. Opponents of electronic surveillance argued that the Fourth Amendment compelled an absolute bar on clandestine surveillance. Justice William Douglas contended that electronic surveillance devices "lay down a dragnet which indiscriminately sweeps in all conversations within its scope, without regard to the nature of the conversations, or the participants. A warrant authorizing such devices is no different from the general warrant the Fourth Amendment was intended to prohibit." Notwithstanding Justice Douglas's misgivings, the rulings in *Berger* and *Katz* indicated that the Court would accept some form of regulated electronic surveillance.

Although *Berger* and *Katz* had no impact on electronic eavesdropping practices, these rulings did mandate change in the way law enforcement officers employed wiretapping surveillance.

These cases also provided a constitutional "blueprint" that was utilized by Congress, which was in the process of crafting legislation designed to regulate electronic surveillance techniques. Within several months of the issuance of *Katz*, Title III of the Omnibus Crime Control and Safe Streets Act of 1968 was enacted into law. Title III is a comprehensive law that authorizes wiretapping and electronic eavesdropping so long as enumerated constitutional and statutory limitations are followed. Title III also sanctioned informant spying provided the informant is a party to the communication or one of the parties to the communication has given consent to the spying. Title III does not cover national security electronic surveillance, which is addressed in the Foreign Intelligence Surveillance Act of 1978.

Title III prohibits all electronic surveillance except as specifically provided by the statute and punishes violators with criminal and civil penalties. Another remedy available under the statute is a broad exclusionary rule that prohibits the disclosure of unlawfully obtained evidence in governmental judicial, quasi-judicial, and administrative proceedings. As Professor Michael Goldsmith has explained in his article on Title III, the statute imposes three categories of requirements that were designed to limit the use of electronic surveillance techniques: jurisdictional, documentary, and executional.

Jurisdictional requirements. Title III permits an application for a wiretapping or electronic eavesdropping order only for crimes specifically designated by the statute. Those designated crimes are generally felonies that are either intrinsically serious or characteristic of organized crime. The application must be initially approved by a designated government official. Goldsmith has explained that this requirement ensures that a politically accountable executive branch official exercises a high level of discretion before the application even reaches a court. Finally, the application must be filed before a judge with competent jurisdiction, namely federal district and appellate judges and/or their state counterparts.

Documentary requirements. Title III mandates that electronic surveillance orders only be issued on the basis of a properly authorized application, except in emergency situations described in the statute. As Goldsmith has noted, the statute mandates several safeguards. First, an application must be made in writing and under oath. Second, the application must establish probable cause for the person, crime, conversation, communication facility, and time period. In order to curtail the potential for abuse and harassment, the application must also demonstrate that investigators have exhausted all reasonable alternative forms of investigation. Finally, the application must reveal all previous surveillance requests involving persons or facilities named in the instant application.

Assuming these requirements are satisfied, a qualified judge may properly issue an electronic surveillance order. As Goldsmith has detailed, each judicial order must satisfy specific statutory criteria: first, the order must specify the officials authorized to conduct the surveillance; second, it must identify both the place and, if known, the person or persons targeted for interception; third, it must state the particular crime to which the surveillance relates; fourth, the order must specify the period of surveillance; finally, each order must mandate prompt execution, minimal interception of irrelevant conversations, and termination of surveillance when the evidence sought is obtained or when thirty days have passed, whichever occurs first. Title III allows applications for extensions and authorizes judges to issue extension orders in compliance with all statutory requirements.

Executional requirements.

Finally, as Goldsmith has described, Title III has various "executional" rules. An investigator armed with a valid electronic surveillance order must also obey Title III's executional requirements when performing the surveillance. These rules mandate that only authorized personnel conduct the surveillance. Further, as previously noted, surveillance must be conducted in a manner that minimizes the interception of irrelevant conversations. All monitored conversations should be recorded to ensure that the "most reliable evidence" of the conversations is presented at trial. The statute also imposes several precautionary executional requirements. The recording must be made in a manner that reduces the risk of alteration and, following the authorized period of surveillance, all tape recordings are to be sealed under judicial supervision. Title III also requires investigators to notify all persons named in the application that they were subjected to electronic surveillance. The judge, however, has discretion to decide whether other parties whose conversations were recorded should receive this notification. The practical effect of these notification provisions is to encourage victims of unlawful surveillance to file civil suits. Finally, Title III mandates that a comprehensive report on each surveillance

case must be provided to the Administrative Office of the United States Courts, which in turn will present a compilation of these reports annually to Congress. This final requirement ensures that the public has an opportunity to monitor and evaluate the system.

Judicial interpretation of Title III.

The Supreme Court first considered the scope of Title III in *United States v. United States District Court*, 407 U.S. 297 (1972), a ruling that addressed the president's power to authorize electronic surveillance in internal security matters without prior judicial approval. The Court ruled that Title III did not authorize the president to order warrantless electronic surveillance of American citizens. The Court emphasized that Title III should be interpreted as a broad grant of protection against electronic surveillance, subject to a few narrow exceptions that permits such surveillance.

Several days after the *U.S. District Court* decision, the Court considered the scope of Title III's exclusionary rule provision. In *Gelbard v. United States*, 408 U.S. 41 (1972), the petitioners, grand jury witnesses who had been granted immunity from prosecution, refused to answer questions that were allegedly derived from illegal electronic surveillance. Consequently, they were held in contempt. By a narrow majority, the Court ruled in favor of the petitioners and held that Title III's suppression provision provides a "just cause" defense to contempt charges. This ruling was controversial, however, because it assumed that the electronic surveillance was illegal, when the issue of illegality had not been formally adjudicated by the lower courts that had initially heard the petitioners' claims.

The 1974 cases of *United States v. Giordano*, 416 U.S. 505, and *United States v. Chavez*, 416 U.S. 562, gave the Court an opportunity to issue substantive guidance to lower courts regarding the scope of Title III's exclusionary rule. Each case involved the issue of whether all Title III violations, regardless of their severity, mandate suppression of the evidence obtained from the electronic surveillance. In both cases, the defense challenged the legality of the surveillance on the basis of the improper authorization of the surveillance applications. As noted above, Title III requires surveillance applications to be signed by an approved executive branch official.

In *Giordano*, the attorney general's signature had routinely been affixed by his executive assistant, who was not statutorily authorized to make such approvals, without the review or approval of the attorney general. In *Chavez*, while the attorney general had apparently approved the surveillance request, the defense argued that the surveillance was illegal because the application had misrepresented the authorizing official to be the attorney general's specially designated assistant attorney general.

The *Giordano* Court ruled that because authorization by the proper official is a key requirement to the statutory framework, suppression was mandated. The Court employed this same rationale in *Chavez* as well, but ruled in favor of the government. It concluded that while the misrepresentation violated Title III's identification requirement, suppression was inappropriate because the identification provision was not "central" to the statutory scheme. This "centrality" rationale sparked a negative response from critics who argued that the standard represented an exceedingly narrow interpretation of Title III and that lower courts would have difficulty applying it. The Court would revisit this issue three years later in *United States v. Donovan*, 429 U.S. 413 (1977).

In the meantime, however, the Court stated significant constitutional dicta in *United States v. Kahn*, 415 U.S. 143 (1974), a ruling that would guide the *Donovan* decision. In *Kahn*, the surveillance application and order listed the targets of surveillance as "Irving Kahn and others as yet unknown." Investigators intercepted various calls in which Mrs. Kahn participated and incriminated herself in a gambling scheme. The defense argued that Mrs. Kahn was "known" to the agents; thus, Mrs. Kahn was not "unknown" under the statute or the surveillance order. The Court rejected this contention and, in a strict reading of the statute, ruled that Mrs. Kahn was legally "unknown" because the agents lacked probable cause that Mrs. Kahn was engaged in criminality via the telephone.

Beyond this holding, the *Kahn* Court also intimated that Title III's identification requirement was not constitutionally mandated. As Goldsmith has noted, the Court offered this assertion despite the language in *Berger v. New York* suggesting the opposite, the holding in *Katz* that the Fourth Amendment protects people and not just places, and the legislative history of Title III indicating that surveillance techniques should be used only under limited circumstances that comply with the particularity requirement of the Fourth Amendment.

The significance of *Kahn*'s dicta was demonstrated in *United States v. Donovan*, a decision in which multiple defendants were prosecuted for gambling-related offenses based largely upon evidence obtained by a series of wiretaps. The Court found two separate Title III violations. One violation occurred because the surveillance application and omitted three of the defendants targeted for wiretapping, despite probable cause they would conduct illegal gambling on the telephone. Another violation occurred when two of the defendants failed to receive an inventory notice because the government failed to inform the supervising judge that they were the subjects of surveillance.

The next question for the *Donovan* Court was whether these violations warranted suppression of the evidence obtained from the surveillance. In determining whether the violation of the target identification rule triggered a suppression remedy, the Court reaffirmed *Kahn*'s principle that this requirement was not constitutionally mandated. The Court then applied the *Giordano-Chavez* centrality test and concluded that the identification rule was not crucial under the statute; as a result, suppression was denied.

When conducting electronic surveillance, Title III also requires federal agents to minimize the interception of communications not relevant to the investigation. This provision is called the "minimization requirement." The meaning and scope of this rule remained controversial until *Scott v. United States*, 436 U.S. 128 (1978), was decided by the Court. In *Scott*, agents purposely and knowingly failed to minimize any of the 384 conversations they intercepted over a month-long surveillance period. The Court ruled that the agents' subjective intent was irrelevant in determining whether a violation occurred. The Court looked to the Fourth Amendment's "reasonableness" standard to define Title III's minimization rule. The Court explained that the objectivity test used to decide whether a constitutional violation has occurred should also be used to decide whether a statutory violation has occurred. The Court concluded that the failure to minimize in the *Scott* case was not objectively unreasonable and, as a result, no statutory violation had occurred.

In the 1979 case of *Dalia v. United States*, 441 U.S. 238, the Court addressed whether Title III authorized covert entries into private premises to install surveillance equipment. Emphasizing that electronic surveillance not authorized by the statute was deemed impermissible, the defendant argued that because Title III did not specifically authorize covert entry to install bugging equipment, the judicial order authorizing the surveillance of his office was illegal. The Court disagreed, however, and ruled that the language, structure, and history of Title III demonstrated that Congress intended to authorize covert entries. Testimony presented to Congress demonstrated congressional knowledge that most forms of electronic bugging required covert entries to install surveillance devices. A contrary holding, according to the Court, would contravene Title III's purpose of providing new investigatory methods to curtail organized crime.

Critical perspectives

Americans appear to have a "love-hate" attitude toward governmental electronic surveillance and covert spying. On the one hand, an overwhelming majority of the population supports police efforts to identify and prosecute persons who commit serious and violent crimes. In many contexts, such as political corruption and organized crime cases, informants and wiretaps are critical crime-fighting tools for government investigators. On the other hand, Americans treasure their freedom and resist unsolicited governmental intrusion into their lives. Security and privacy are jeopardized when individuals learn that the government has recruited and planted informants in their lives to gather information. While many concede that informants and spies are essential for effective law enforcement, few cherish the thought that a coworker or girlfriend may actually be a police spy. Put simply, many Americans adopt the view that surreptitious electronic surveillance is fine, but "not in my backyard."

When these strong and sometimes conflicting attitudes toward covert surveillance are combined with a well-documented history of government overreaching, both at the federal and state levels by spying on its citizens, Americans are often surprised to learn that the Court has imposed few restraints on the government's authority to plant or send covert informants and spies into our lives. If one accepts the fundamental historical claim that the Fourth Amendment reflected the Framers' distrust of police power and was designed to limit the discretionary power of the police to invade one's home, it becomes paradoxical for the Court to allow police officials unchecked discretion to plant spies and informants into one's privacy.

Consider, for example, the result in *Lewis v. United States*, the least controversial of the Court's secret spy cases. Many see no constitutional harm where a covert agent enters a home to purchase narcotics from someone like Lewis. On the surface, *Lewis* does appear to be an easy case. But on further study, *Lewis* is troubling. First, the facts reveal a police entry of Lewis's home that was neither authorized by a judicial warrant nor an exigency. Normally, the absence of a warrant or an emergency would preclude police entry into a person's home. Second, the waiver theory utilized by the *Lewis* Court proves too much. Imagine that the police are strongly convinced that a house is filled with illegal weapons. Imagine further that the police also have solid evidence that the owner willingly sells the weapons to anyone who can produce sufficient cash. Can the police enter the premises without a warrant because the owner obviously does not use it as a home and thus, for constitutional purposes, has waived his Fourth Amendment rights by converting the building into an unlawful weapons storage facility? The legal answer is no. Despite the suspect's illegal conduct, there is no "waiver" of his Fourth Amendment rights. Therefore, the fact that Lewis sold drugs from his home should be irrelevant.

If one of the values protected by the Fourth Amendment is freedom from discretionary police intrusion of the home or office, that norm is doubly offended in cases like *Hoffa* because the target chosen for scrutiny by the police is unaware of the government's presence and monitoring of his private activities. The Court found Hoffa's privacy interests illegitimate because the Constitution does not protect "a wrongdoer's misplaced belief that a person to whom he voluntarily confides his wrongdoing will not reveal it." It is submitted here that this statement is specious because the informant in *Hoffa* was not a friend who subsequently decided to betray Jimmy Hoffa, but a government spy right from the start. More importantly, the Court's description of the constitutional interest at stake in *Hoffa* turns upside down the value system inherent in the Fourth Amendment. When positive proof that an individual has committed a crime exists in the traditional search and seizure context, the burden is still on the government to justify and to limit the intrusion.

In the secret spy cases, however, Fourth Amendment values are reversed. After *Hoffa*, the government need not first assemble objective evidence of wrongdoing to covertly invade the homes and offices of its citizens. After *Hoffa*, the government may bypass neutral judicial authorization for the intrusion sought by its undercover agents. After *Hoffa*, secret spying missions need not particularize the person, place, and nature of the conversations subject to surveillance and recording. Whatever the informant sees and hears, regardless of the nexus to criminal behavior, is information known to the police. After *Hoffa*, such wide-ranging surveillance is without time limit and need not be supervised by a judge.

The Court's assumption of risk analysis—utilized in *On Lee, Lopez,* and *White*—also poses constitutional problems. First, the Court does not and cannot reconcile risk theory with the origins of the Fourth Amendment. True, the use of secret informants has deep historical roots. Moreover, the Framers of the Constitution left no specific clues regarding their intent as to whether the Fourth Amendment would regulate or forbid secret informants. The Framers also said nothing about eavesdropping, but that omission did not justify leaving eavesdropping and its modern equivalent, wiretapping, to the whims of the police.

The Framers opposed governmental intrusions that permitted discretionary invasions of the home. In light of this history, is it fair to surmise that the Framers would have favored an interpretation of the Fourth Amendment that grants the police absolute authority to send informants and secret spies into a person's home? Or, is it more likely that the Framers, who despised general warrants because they allowed government agents to search and seize at will, would have also opposed giving those same agents absolute discretion to use secret informants to search and seize at will?

Even if the history of the Fourth Amendment is ignored, there are other flaws in the Court's risk theory. There is no substantive distinction between the modern Court's risk analysis and the Court's prior conclusion in *Olmstead* that an individual who uses the telephone intends to project his voice to those outside. Why is the former conclusion constitutionally reasonable but not the latter? There is no more empirical support for the modern Court's conclusion that citizens assume certain risks whenever they speak to a third party than there was for the now discredited assumption in *Olmstead*.

In 1971 the *White* Court insisted that wiretapping involves "no revelation to the Government by a party to the conversations with the defendant." This assertion is true, but the factual characterization of the mechanics of wiretapping neither justifies nor explains the Court's legal conclusion about the risks associated with informant spying. The *White* Court's risk theory is applicable in contexts beside informant spying. If people assume the risk that their companions are police agents, then why don't people also assume the risk that the government may be wiretapping their calls or reading their mail?

Americans assume the police lack the discretion to covertly monitor their telephone conversations or peruse their mail because the Court has interpreted the Constitution in a manner that requires the police to satisfy certain legal safeguards before such intrusions may occur. If the Fourth Amendment restrains the discretion of the police to wiretap or bug private conversations, it is not apparent why that same provision is inapplicable when the police monitor and record private conversation through the use of a secret informant deliberately positioned to hear those conversations. After all, a secret informant acts as a "human bug" for the government. If there is a constitutional difference between unrestrained wiretap surveillance and unrestrained informant spying, the Court has not yet identified the difference.

If the preceding critique is correct, the Court and Congress alike have erred in exempting informant spying from the constitutional limitations imposed on other forms of electronic surveillance. The use of informants should be regulated in a manner similar to the way in which Title III regulates wiretapping and electronic bugging. For example, the Fourth Amendment's probable cause rule should apply to informant spying the same way it applies to electronic surveillance. Further, a particularity requirement like the one in Title III would limit the unbridled and open-ended intrusions that often occur with informant spying.

Yet Title III, as interpreted by the Court, is not without its own drawbacks. The statute was initially enacted to prohibit most forms of electronic surveillance. In fact, all forms of wiretapping and electronic surveillance were prohibited unless specifically authorized by the statute. As the above discussion illustrates, however, the Court's Title III decisions have departed dramatically from this approach. Many of the safeguards of Title III have been undercut by the Court's failure to strictly enforce the statute.

It is an open question whether the current status of the law governing electronic surveillance will survive as new technological advances continue to emerge that threaten the privacy of individuals. Perhaps, as new methods of investigating crime are developed, the Supreme Court and Congress alike will be forced to clarify, revise, or replace the current legal framework that governs wiretapping and electronic eavesdropping.

TRACEY MACLIN

See also CRIMINAL PROCEDURE: CONSTITUTIONAL ASPECTS; DRUGS AND CRIME: LEGAL ASPECTS; EXCLUSIONARY RULE; FEDERAL CRIMINAL LAW ENFORCEMENT; ORGANIZED CRIME; POLICE: CRIMINAL INVESTIGATIONS; SEARCH AND SEIZURE.

BIBLIOGRAPHY

CARR, JAMES G. *The Law of Electronic Surveillance.* 2 vols. Deerfield, Ill.: Clark, Boardman, and Callaghan, 1998.

FISHMAN, CLIFFORD S. *Wiretapping and Eavesdropping.* Rochester, N.Y.: Lawyers Cooperative Pub. Co., 1978.

———. "Interception of Communications in Exigent Circumstances: The Fourth Amendment, Federal Legislation, and the United States Department of Justice." *Georgia Law Review* 22 (1987): 10.

GOLDSMITH, MICHAEL. "The Supreme Court and Title III: Rewriting the Law of Electronic Surveillance." *Journal of Criminal Law and Criminology* 74 (1983): 1.

KAMISAR, YALE; LAFAVE, WAYNE R.; ISRAEL, JEROLD H.; and KING, NANCY. *Modern Criminal Procedure,* 9th ed. St. Paul, Minn.: West Group, 1999.

MACLIN, TRACEY. "Informants and the Fourth Amendment: A Reconsideration." *Washington University Law Quarterly* 74 (1996): 573.

WESTIN, ALAN F. *Privacy and Freedom.* New York: Atheneum, 1967.

CASES

Berger v. New York, 388 U.S. 41 (1967).
Dalia v. United States, 441 U.S. 238 (1979).
Gelbard v. United States, 408 U.S. 41 (1972).
Goldman v. United States, 316 U.S. 129 (1942).
Goldstein v. United States, 316 U.S. 114 (1942).
Hoffa v. United States, 385 U.S. 293 (1966).
Irvine v. California, 347 U.S. 128 (1954).
Katz v. United States, 389 U.S. 347 (1967).
Lewis v. United States, 385 U.S. 206 (1966).
Lopez v. United States, 373 U.S. 427 (1963).
Nardone v. United States, 302 U.S. 379 (1937).
Nardone v. United States, 308 U.S. 338 (1939).
Olmstead v. United States, 277 U.S. 438 (1928).
On Lee v. United States, 343 U.S. 747 (1952).
Schwartz v. Texas, 344 U.S. 199 (1952).
Scott v. United States, 436 U.S. 128 (1978).
Silverman v. United States, 365 U.S. 505 (1961).
United States v. Chavez, 416 U.S. 562 (1974).
United States v. Donovan, 429 U.S. 413 (1977).
United States v. Giordano, 416 U.S. 505 (1974).
United States v. Kahn, 415 U.S. 143 (1974).
United States v. United States District Court, 407 U.S. 297 (1972).
United States v. White, 401 U.S. 745 (1971).

GLOSSARY

abandonment The act of deserting a pregnant or dependent wife or dependent children without providing proper support; also, the relinquishment of a legal claim, privilege, or right; also, the discontinuation of a planned and intended crime before its actual commission.

abduction The common law crime of taking another person through the use of persuasion, fraud, or violence. In particular, the term refers to a non-custodial parent who illegally takes a child from the parent who has custody of that child. *See also* KIDNAPPING.

abet To knowingly facilitate the commission or attempted commission of a crime. *See also* ACCESSORY; AID AND ABET; CONSPIRACY.

ab initio ("from the beginning") Null and void because of fatal defects at the time an agreement was made (as, in criminal law, an illegal plea bargain).

abrogate To abolish or nullify; to set aside.

abscond To flee or conceal oneself in order to avoid legal proceedings (as to jump bail); also, to flee with the property of another, as when a bank teller absconds with the funds entrusted to him or her.

absolve To free from an accusation or from guilt.

accessory A person, not present at the crime, who has helped the criminal before (accessory before the fact) or after (accessory after the fact) perpetration of the criminal act.

accomplice liability Someone whom the law interchangeably calls an accomplice, accessory, aider and abettor, secondary party, or helper in the crime or crimes of the principal (who is also called a do-er or perpetrator), and is derivatively liable for whatever crime or crimes the principal commits. Punishment for accomplice liability is shared equally among principals and their helpers. *See also* ACCESSORY, AID AND ABET.

accountability The state of being responsible and punishable for a criminal act; this responsibility is reduced or abolished in certain instances because of age, mental defect, or other reason. *See also* EXCUSE.

accusation A formal or informal statement charging a person, persons, or entity, such as a corporation, with having committed a crime. The formal accusation can be made as an information or an indictment.

accusatorial system *See* ADVERSARY SYSTEM.

accuse To charge with the commission of a crime.

accused One or more persons or entities charged with the commission of a crime.

acquit To find not guilty.

acquittal A verdict of not guilty in a criminal trial.

actus reus The conduct constituting the offense, as well as any required circumstances or results of the conduct. The criminal act, as contrasted with mens rea, the criminal intent.

adjudicated The term used when the juvenile court has taken jurisdiction over a juvenile; the juvenile is said to have been adjudicated.

adjudication The process of judicial decision-making or settlement.

adjudication hearing In the juvenile court, the formal hearing comparable to trial in a criminal court, at which evidence is presented about the juvenile's behavior and a decision is reached about whether the juvenile court will take jurisdiction over that juvenile. *See also* DISPOSITION HEARING.

admission An acknowledgment by either prosecution or defense that a statement of fact made by the opposing side is true.

admission against interest An admission of a fact which, though short of confession, tends to suggest possible guilt (for example, that the subject had a motive or the opportunity to commit the crime).

adultery Sexual intercourse between two persons, at least one of whom is married but not to the other.

adversary The opponent; the opposing party in a civil or criminal action.

adversary system A system for resolving both civil and criminal disputes. It is characterized by a contest between the initiating party, called the plaintiff in civil proceedings and the prosecutor (representing the state) in criminal proceedings, and the responding party, called the defendant, and presided over by a judge, who adjudicates and renders final judgment for one party or the other, sometimes with the aid of a jury for finding disputed facts, on the basis of the evidence presented by the parties in open court, and in light of the applicable law. The systems found in England, the United States, and other common law countries all follow the adversary model, but some of them, such as the English system, permit judges to play a more active role. *See also* INQUISITORIAL SYSTEM; PARTY-DOMINATED PROCESS.

affidavit A written statement made under oath.

agent provocateur An undercover police officer or a person acting on behalf of the police, who surreptitiously seeks to incite others to criminal behavior so that the police may intervene and the offenders may be prosecuted.

age of consent The chronological age of a female, usually sixteen or eighteen, after which it is no longer felonious for another to have voluntary sexual relations with her.

aggressive patrol Police saturation of an area that has a high incidence of crime. The patrol officers often employ stop-and-frisk techniques; their object is to arrest absconders, confiscate weapons, and create difficulties for potential offenders.

aid and abet To assist in the commission of a crime by words, act, encouragement, or support. *See also* ABET.

alibi A contention of a defendant that he was in another place at the time of the commission of the criminal act of which he is accused, and hence could not have done what he is charged with doing; also, a lay term for excuse.

alibi, notice of Information that the defense is required to give to the prosecution before a trial if a defense of alibi will be made, that is, if the defense will contend that the accused was elsewhere at the time of the crime. Such a notice is necessary so that the prosecution may investigate before the trial and be prepared for cross-examination and rebuttal.

alibi witness *See* WITNESS, ALIBI.

alien, illegal One who has illegally entered a country of which he or she is not a citizen, or who, having entered legally, violates the terms of his or her visa, as by overstaying or by engaging in prohibited activities.

alienation A sense of estrangement or separation of persons from community or society; a lack of cohesion with the surrounding environment, people, and social institutions. In law, a transfer of property or of a right to another.

allegation An assertion of the facts which a party to an action expects to prove; in a criminal trial, the charge or indictment.

allege To make an accusation.

alleged Used to describe someone who has been accused of or is under suspicion for a crime but who has been neither convicted nor exonerated by a trial.

amenable Suitable, a term used in juvenile court proceedings to determine whether jurisdiction over a juvenile should be waived and that juvenile transferred to criminal court for trial. The question is whether a particular juvenile is amenable to treatment in the juvenile court.

amnesty A form of executive clemency, usually extended to a class or group of offenders (for example, draft evaders); common in many countries to celebrate independence, a coronation or election, or the birth of an heir to the throne.

anomie A state of normlessness, or relative normlessness, in which there is a breakdown of the rules governing social behavior. It was used by Emile Durkheim in the late nineteenth and early twentieth century to explain some suicides, and later by Robert Merton to describe the conflict between culturally instilled goals and socially approved means of attaining those goals.

appeal Review of the trial record by a higher court to determine whether errors of law or procedure justify reversal of conviction.

appearance The coming into court of the parties to an action.

arraignment The formal reading of charges against a defendant and the entry of his plea; presided over by an arraignment judge.

arrest The act of taking a person into custody for the purpose of answering a criminal charge.

arrest, citizen's The arrest, without a warrant, of an alleged offender by a person who is not a law enforcement officer, for a felony or a breach of the peace committed in the latter's presence.

arrest, false (false imprisonment) Unlawful physical restraint of an individual; detention under false or assumed authority.

arrest, house Restriction of an individual to a specific residence and limitation on visitors who may enter it. House arrest is seldom employed in the United States. *See also* HOME DETENTION.

arrest rate The number of arrests as a percentage of the crimes known to police; also, the number of arrests as a percentage of the entire population or a cohort thereof. Examples are the arrest rate for males or for youths under the age of sixteen.

arrest record A list of a person's arrests and of charges that have been made against him, usually including those that have been dropped and those of which he was found not guilty. The arrest record also contains information on dispositions and sentences, where there was adjudication of guilt.

arrest warrant A written order from a court authorizing or directing the arrest of the person named therein.

arson Any willful or malicious burning of a structure or other defined property belonging to another. Also, the burning of one's own property with intent to defraud.

assault The act or threat of physical force against another person; often limited to an attempt. *See also* BATTERY.

assault, aggravated An attack of one person upon another for the purpose or with the consequence of inflicting severe bodily injury. Aggravated assault is usually accompanied by the use of a weapon or by means likely to produce great bodily harm. *See also* BATTERY.

assault, felonious An assault with intent to kill or do grievous bodily harm; assault with a deadly weapon.

assault, indecent Sexual assault not amounting to rape, sodomy, or carnal abuse; uninvited sex-related touching of another.

assault, sexual Touching the body of another with a sexual intent and without the consent of the person being touched. Also used to substitute for the term "rape" in some modern rape statutes. *See also* RAPE.

asset forfeiture Seizure of personal assets that are the product of illegal enterprise. Used particularly with respect to the seizure of the products of illegal drug trafficking.

assisted suicide When one person gives another person the instructions, means, or capability to bring about their own demise. Assisted suicide is not considered to be the same as suicide per se because suicide is an individual act whereas assisted suicide involves a joint enterprise between the suicidal person and a helper to bring about death. *See also* EUTHANASIA.

atavism A theory of criminal behavior, developed by Cesare Lombroso and other evolutionists in the post-Darwinian era. It postulates that criminality diminishes in the evolutionary development of humanity, and that its appearance as a biological predilection in some persons is a hereditary throwback on the evolutionary scale.

attempt An act done with intent to commit a crime but falling short of its actual commission. For example, one who aims and fires a malfunctioning revolver might be charged with attempted homicide.

attorney general The chief legal officer of the United States, head of the Department of Justice, and member of the President's cabinet; also, the chief legal officer in a state.

autopsy A postmortem medical examination, usually mandatory if death results from other than natural causes.

aversive therapy A form of therapy in which painful effects (such as electric shock or induce nausea) are produced so that they may be associated with a form of addictive, criminal, or otherwise undesirable behavior; the intention is to produce an aversion to that type of activity. Aversive therapy has been used in cases of homosexuality, child molestation, substance abuse (alcohol or narcotics), and forcible rape. *See also* BEHAVIOR MODIFICATION.

backlog The untried cases pending on a court calendar.

bail Security (money, property, or a deed on property) posted with authorities by the accused after arrest and before trial, as guarantee that he or she will appear for trial, sentencing, or incarceration. If the accused fails to appear, the money or property is forfeited to the court.

bail, excessive A sum of money set as bail that is in excess of the amount which would reasonably assure the defendant's appearance at subsequent proceedings involving him or her. Excessive bail is prohibited by the Eighth Amendment to the United States Constitution. Determination of whether bail is excessive is sometimes made by a higher court, which may decrease, confirm, or increase the bail or allow the accused to be released on his or her own recognizance (vacating the bail). *See also* DETENTION, PREVENTIVE.

bail bond Security posted by an insurer (bail bondsman) who is paid a fee to guarantee the appearance of a defendant in a criminal proceeding.

bail bondsman One who posts bail for others for a fee, generally 10 percent of the value of the bond. The term is applied to those who post such bonds regularly for a livelihood.

bailiff A court officer who performs a variety of duties. He or she may, for example, maintain order in the courtroom, guard prisoners, run errands for the judge, pass papers and exhibits to authorized persons, and guard the jury room.

barratry The initiating of groundless lawsuits that become either persecutory or a nuisance. Although barratry is a crime in most jurisdictions, persons are seldom charged with this offense.

barrister In the United Kingdom and in certain British Commonwealth countries, a lawyer who is authorized to represent a party in court, in contrast to a solicitor, who is primarily an office lawyer. Most judges are former barristers. *See also* COUNSEL.

baton A "night stick" carried by police officers as a defensive weapon.

battered woman syndrome Evidence that a woman may introduce in court demonstrating the decedent's repeated psychological and/or physical abuse of her in order to support her claim of self-defense. The syndrome depicts a cyclical battering relationship that starts with relatively minor instances of abuse that escalate to the "acute battering incident," followed by a period of time in which the abuser is contrite and loving, only to start the abusing cycle all over again. While being a battered woman by itself is no defense to homicide, the syndrome may assist a jury in understanding two elements of a self-defense claim: (1) the woman's subjective fear of serious injury or death, and (2) the reasonableness of that belief. *See also* DOMESTIC VIOLENCE; SELF-DEFENSE AND DEFENSE OF OTHERS.

battery The application of physical force against another person, resulting in offensive or injurious touching. *See also* ASSAULT.

behavior modification A therapeutic intervention in which conforming behavior is rewarded and unacceptable behavior is punished. *See also* AVERSIVE THERAPY.

bench warrant A written order authorizing the arrest of a defendant or subpoenaed witness who failed to appear on the date scheduled for appearance in court.

bifurcated trial   In capital (i.e., death penalty) cases, the procedure by which the factfinder (usually a jury) first decides whether the defendant is guilty. If guilty, then there is a second and separate proceeding at which time the factfinder decides whether the defendant receives the death penalty.

bill of attainder   Originally, the complete loss of rights and privileges on being condemned (attained) of treason or another felony; now, a legislative conviction without a criminal trial. The United States Constitution specifically forbids a bill of attainder.

bill of particulars   A detailed statement of the allegations at issue in a legal proceeding.

Bill of Rights   The first ten amendments to the United States Constitution. Several of them govern criminal trial procedures and rights of the accused, and were applied to state criminal trials in a series of Supreme Court decisions beginning in the 1930s and continuing through the term of the Warren Court (1953–1969). Some state constitutions contain provisions similar to those in the Bill of Rights.

binding over   At a preliminary hearing, the decision of a magistrate or other judicial officer that sufficient probable cause exists to bring the defendant to trial on some or all of the pending charges. Binding over is generally accompanied by release on recognizance, granting of bail, or, in some instances, holding of the defendant without bail.   *See also* HEARING, PRELIMINARY.

biological factors   Possible influences on behavior consisting of physiological, biochemical, neurological, and genetic sources.   *See also* GENETIC FACTORS; SOCIAL FACTORS.

blackmail   Extortion of money or other desired commodity or favor by threatening to make embarrassing disclosures about another unless payments, goods, or services are given.

blood alcohol level (BAL)   The amount of alcohol in the bloodstream that legally is defined as intoxication. This can be measured by blood, urine, or breath tests. The results of these tests are presented as percentages, where the most common legal standard for intoxication is one-tenth of 1 percent (.10%).

blood feud   A long-time, violent quarrel between clans or families, such as the famous Hatfield-McCoy feud.

blue laws   Regulations that criminalize or restrict certain activities, such as sports contests, movie or theater productions, or shopping in retail stores, on Sundays and religious holidays.

book   To record (log) the arrest of a person in the police station's sequential records of arrests, with particulars of his identity, details of the offense, and the name of the arresting officer. Booking usually takes place at a police station immediately after arrest, and generally includes fingerprinting and photographing the arrestee.

boot camp   An institutional setting which uses physical training and discipline, similar to military boot camps, as a technique for rehabilitating offenders.

Generally, these are used for juvenile or young adult offenders and provide shorter institutional stays than standard imprisonment.   *See also* SHOCK PROBATION.

breach of (the) peace   An act that violates the public order and the tranquility of the community, such as a riot, an unlawful assembly, or an illegal demonstration.   *See also* DISORDERLY CONDUCT.

breaking and entering   Illegal and forcible entry of a premises, as by breaking a lock or window, removing a door, or cutting through a roof or wall. When the entry is for the purpose of committing a felony (often but not necessarily theft), such an act is charged as burglary.

"broken windows" approach   A theory of policing that asserts that immediately dealing with minor symptoms of community disorder (the image is of immediately fixing broken windows in a building) tends to create a sense that order is maintained in a community and therefore tends to reduce serious crime in the long run. For example, in New York City, a policy of arresting "fare beaters" who jump the turnstiles in the subway was said to lead to a marked reduction of serious crime in the subways.

burden of proof   The requirement that one side in an adversary hearing establish with affirmative proof its position on a point of contention. In criminal cases, the prosecution must establish guilt beyond a reasonable doubt.

burglary   Illegal or forcible breaking or entering into any building or enclosure for the purpose of committing any felony, often theft, therein.

bystander   A person, other than the perpetrator, police, or victim, in the vicinity of a crime. The bystander may witness the crime, suffer an injury, or intervene as a Good Samaritan.

calendar   A listing of pending cases and the date and place of the next step in their processing; a listing of all cases in any one court for a given day.

Camorra   *See* MAFIA.

canon law   A body of law governing the organization and administration of the Catholic Church (and other Christian churches) and the conduct of its communicants in matters of concern to the church.

capital crime (capital offense)   Any felony for which capital punishment is permitted.

capital punishment   The death penalty; execution as punishment for crime.

career criminal   One whose principal activity or occupation is criminal; a person who makes his living by burglary, robbery, blackmail, or some other type of crime.   *See also* RECIDIVIST.

carnal abuse (knowledge) of a minor   Intercourse, sodomy, or other sexual relationship with a child under a legally stated age, with or without the consent of the child-victim.   *See also* CHILD MOLESTATION; IMPAIRING THE MORALS OF A MINOR; RAPE, STATUTORY.

case   A legal action, controversy, or trial; any legal proceeding, civil or criminal. Also, an individual in his relation to a court or an official (such as a police, parole, or probation officer).

case load   The total number of cases assigned to one court, judge, or other agency or personnel; for example, the case load of a detective, a unit of the police department, or a parole officer.

causation   The relationship that must be established to hold a person responsible for a consequence of his action.

celerity   Speed or swiftness in the apprehension, trial, and punishment of an offender. The framers of the concept of deterrence regard it as a major factor in the effectiveness of punishment.

censorship   The act of attempting to limit or prevent the distribution of speech or materials deemed offensive or harmful. *See also* OBSCENITY.

certification   A term used in some states to refer to a procedure in which a juvenile court judge waives jurisdiction over a juvenile, who then is transferred to criminal court for trial. *See also* WAIVER OF JURISDICTION, JUVENILE.

certiorari   The transference of an action from an inferior to a superior court for review; the process is initiated by a writ of certiorari.

chain of custody   The transmission of evidence from one person or organization to another. At trial, the chain of custody for the evidence must be completely documented or the evidence itself is considered less reliable.

challenge   An objection, usually regarding a specific prospective juror, made to the judge by a party to a case, requesting that the person in question not be allowed to serve on the jury. A challenge may be for cause or peremptory. The defendant in a court-martial may challenge a member of the court for cause.

challenge, peremptory   A challenge to a prospective juror made without stating a reason or cause. A limited number of such challenges may be made by both defense and prosecution.

challenge for cause   A challenge to a prospective juror for a specific reason or cause.

Chancery Court   In England, an administrative court originating in the 1500s that had jurisdiction over a variety of family and other matters, including children whose parents had died leaving an estate. In such cases, the court used the legal doctrine of "parens patriae" (the state as ultimate parent of all children) to manage the estate "in the best interest of the child" until that child reached the age of majority. Reformers in Chicago used this legal framework in 1899 to establish the modern juvenile court. *See also* PARENS PATRIAE.

charge   Facts or allegations pertaining to an accused in a complaint or indictment; also, the instructions given by the judge when he charges the jury—that is, when he informs it regarding the law and the alternative verdicts it may reach.

Chicago school (of sociology)   The major school of sociological thought in the United States between the two world wars. It had a strong impact on criminological theory and research, stressing particularly the need to study criminals, delinquents, vagrants, prostitutes, and other social outcasts in their natural environment and to perceive the world from their vantage point.

child abuse   Physical assault inflicted on a young child, often by parents, endangering the child's life, health, and welfare. Excessive psychological mistreatment can also be considered child abuse.

child molestation   Any sexual solicitation, contact, or intercourse of an adult with a child; usually refers to children below the age of puberty. Child molestation can be heterosexual or homosexual.

Children in Need of Supervision (CHINS)   A term used in several states to refer to juveniles who commit status offenses (i.e., actions that would not be crimes if committed by an adult), such as truancy, incorrigibility, and running away. *See also* STATUS OFFENSE.

citation   An order issued by a court or the police, commanding that the named person appear before the court on a certain date, usually to answer charges for a minor violation. *See also* SUBPOENA; SUMMONS.

citizen's arrest   *See* ARREST, CITIZEN'S.

civil death   The loss of numerous rights and privileges as a result of a sentence of death or life imprisonment. Such losses may include nullification of a marriage, distribution of an estate, or denial of the right to sue or be sued.

civil disabilities   Rights or privileges denied a person as a result of conviction or a guilty plea, in addition to or other than the imposed legal penalty.

civil disobedience   Deliberate, overt, and nonviolent lawbreaking in which the perpetrators justify their actions on the ground that a particular law is immoral, for example, activities conducted in violation of the segregation laws. Those engaged in civil disobedience seek, by focusing attention on the law, to force concessions from the government.

civil law   The legal system used by most European countries and their former colonies, in which legal rules are based primarily on statutes or codes rather than on judicial decisions. However, judges in most modern civil law systems have some authority to make law by interpreting the governing legislation. *See also* COMMON LAW.

classical school (of criminology)   A dominant trend in the history of political and philosophical thought on crime that flourished for about a century beginning in the 1760s. It was initiated by the publication of Cesare Beccaria's *On Crimes and Punishments* (1764). The classical school assumed the existence of free will, imputed responsibility and accountability to all perpetrators, and stressed the necessity of meting out punishment sufficiently severe to deter would-be criminals—but not so severe as to be cruel, unjust, or unnecessary. *See also* NEOCLASSICISM.

classification   Procedure during which a new inmate of a penal institution is assigned a security status, an educational, work, or therapeutic program, and appropriate institutional housing. Also, a method of classifying fingerprints for easier location and comparison.

classification center   *See* DIAGNOSTIC CENTER.

clear and present danger   The rule that permits curtailment of otherwise constitutionally protected speech when the words used in a specific context threaten imminent and grave harm that the government has the right and duty to prevent.

clemency (executive clemency)   The sovereign prerogative to extend mercy, exercised in the United States by the President (for federal or military offenses) and within individual states by the governor (for violations of the state penal law). Examples of clemency include amnesty, commutation of sentence, pardon, and reprieve.

codefendant   One of the accused in a trial in which two or more persons are charged with the same criminal act or acts and are tried at the same time. A defendant in such an instance may request a separate trial, or severance.

Cointelpro   An F.B.I. counterintelligence program (1956–1971) that emphasized harassment of suspected subversives.

collateral consequence   Any harm that may result from a guilty plea or a conviction, in addition to the preordered punishment. Examples include deportation, disenfranchisement, disbarment, or loss of license to practice certain professions.

commit   To order into custody, either to a correctional facility or a mental institution.

commitment   A judicial order mandating or authorizing confinement in a penal or mental institution.

common law   The legal system that originated in England and spread to the United States and other former British colonies, in which legal rules were based on prior judicial decisions (precedent) rather than on statutes enacted by the legislature. Modern common law systems include many areas of law which are governed by statutes. In the United States, all crimes are at least partially defined by statute. However, judges still have considerable authority to "make law" by interpreting the governing statutes. *See also* CIVIL LAW.

community corrections   *See* CORRECTIONS, COMMUNITY.

community policing   A term used to refer to a wide variety of police practices that emphasize good relationships with the community. The argument is that police primarily respond to initiatives by the public (e.g., calls to the police) and necessarily rely on information from the public (e.g., informants, witnesses). Therefore, maintaining good relationships with the public is essential to accomplishing police goals. For example, a police officer may be assigned to a particular community for a long period of time in order to establish personal relationships with residents of that community.

community restitution   *See* RESTITUTION, COMMUNITY.

community service (compensatory service)   *See* RESTITUTION, COMMUNITY.

competency to stand trial   The concept that a defendant should be tried only if he or she has sufficient ability at the time of trial to understand the proceedings against him or her, to consult with his or her lawyer with a reasonable degree of understanding, and to assist in his or her own defense.

complainant   The victim of a crime, or someone acting for the victim (as a parent or guardian) who initiates the criminal justice process.

complaint   The allegation that a crime or violation of the law has been committed.

compounding a felony   *See* FELONY, COMPOUNDING A.

compulsory process   The right provided for in the Sixth Amendment to the Constitution that a defendant may invoke the subpoena power of the court to compel the appearance of witnesses for the defense at a criminal trial.

compurgation   A process, used at the time of the origin of the jury system, in which the alleged offender attempted to establish his innocence by presenting witnesses who testified under oath as to their belief in his innocence.   *See also* WITNESS, CHARACTER.

computer crime   An illegal act for whose perpetration knowledge of computer technology is required. The crime may be carried out with the aid of a computer (as fraud), or it may consist of the theft of computer time, services, data, or programs. It may also consist of the sabotage or destruction of a computer, its data, or its programs.

concurrent jurisdiction   A situation in which an offender is subject to the jurisdiction of two or more courts for the same offense. With respect to juveniles, in some states, juveniles who commit particular offenses may be subject to the jurisdiction of both the juvenile and the criminal courts, in which case the prosecutor has the discretion of selecting the court in which to initiate legal proceedings. Thus, concurrent jurisdiction is one method of transferring juveniles to criminal court and is sometimes referred to as "prosecutorial waiver."

conduct unbecoming an officer   In police and military disciplinary proceedings, a charge involving violation of the rules and regulations or professional and ethical standards of the department or service.

confession   A voluntary admission by a suspect of his involvement in one or more crimes. A coerced admission, when repudiated and retracted, would not qualify technically as a confession.

confession, coerced   An admission of guilt secured by threat or the use of force.

confidence game   Term for a variety of frauds in which a "con man" obtains the confidence of his victim in order to defraud him or her of money or other valuables.

confidentiality   Restriction of the dissemination of information meant to be kept secret.

confrontation   The right of the defendant to confront his or her accuser and to cross-examine witnesses called by the prosecution.

consensual crime   *See* VICTIMLESS CRIME.

consent decree In juvenile court, a formal agreement signed by a juvenile, the parents, and the juvenile probation officer, in which the juvenile agrees to abide by a set of conditions, much like conditions of probation, for a period of time. If the agreement is kept, then the charges against the juvenile generally are dropped.

conspiracy A plan or agreement by two or more persons to commit an unlawful act, or to commit by criminal means an otherwise lawful act. *See also* ACCESSORY; AID AND ABET.

Constitution of the United States The basic law of the United States, with which all other federal and state laws must not conflict, lest they be declared null and void on the ground of being unconstitutional.

containment theory A theory of criminality, and particularly of juvenile delinquency, set forth in the 1950s by Walter Reckless, Simon Dinitz, and others. It postulates that delinquency and crime occur to the extent that there is a breakdown in "inner" and "outer" containing or restraining forces of society. The inner restraints consist of moral, religious, and superego forces; the outer restraints, of family, educators, and other potentially disapproving forces.

continental system *See* INQUISITORIAL SYSTEM.

continuance *See* CONTINUE.

continue To adjourn a trial or other proceedings until a later time and date. Such an adjournment is called a continuance.

contributing to the delinquency of a minor Any act or behavior by one or more adults involving a minor (or committed in the presence of a minor) that might reasonably result in delinquent conduct. Examples include encouraging a minor to steal, to give false testimony, or to commit vandalism.

control theory An explanation of delinquency and crime which postulates that criminal and delinquent acts occur when the bonds that tie people to the law-abiding society are weakened. These bonds include attachment to others, commitment to conventional lines of action, involvement in conventional activity, and belief in the laws governing forbidden behavior.

convict To find a person guilty of a crime. A convict is one who has been convicted of a crime; the term is seldom used except as a synonym for a prison inmate.

conviction The finding of guilt by a judge or jury.

conviction rate The number of convictions (including guilty pleas) as a percentage of the total number of prosecutions in a given area or for a given crime.

convict lease system The nineteenth-century practice of selling the labor of prisoners to private employers, who paid the state a certain fee for each of the prisoners and then took on the responsibility of guarding and feeding them. In exchange, the employer received the profits of the convicts' labor.

corporate crime An illegal act or acts committed by a corporate body or by executives and managers acting on behalf of a corporation. Such acts include consumer fraud, price-fixing, and restraint of trade. *See also* WHITE-COLLAR CRIME.

corpus delicti ("the body of the crime") The elements of a charge that must be proved to establish that the crime has occurred.

correctional officer A government employee having supervision over alleged or adjudicated offenders in custody. The term is usually not applied to persons supervising juveniles in detention.

correctional reform (prison reform) A movement to bring about changes in the correctional system, usually involving less punitive and more humane treatment of prisoners, shorter sentences, and the introduction of rehabilitative programs.

corrections All rules and regulations, agencies, facilities, programs, procedures, and techniques, and their underlying philosophical foundation, concerned with the supervision and treatment of alleged or adjudicated offenders and delinquents.

corrections, community Any type of supervision over persons convicted of delinquent or criminal activity, in which the supervision takes place outside an institution of confinement. Examples of community corrections include probation and parole.

Cosa Nostra *See* MAFIA.

counsel Attorney representing one side in an adversary proceeding.

counsel, assigned Defense attorneys appointed or assigned by the trial judge for indigent defendants who are not represented by retained counsel, a public defender, or a legal-aid society.

counsel, defense Attorney representing the defendant in a trial.

counsel, right to *See* RIGHT TO COUNSEL.

count Each separate offense charged against one or more persons, as listed in a complaint, indictment, or information.

counterfeiting Unauthorized reproduction of currency, medals, stamps, documents, or artwork, with the intention of fraudulently passing these to others as genuine. *See also* FORGERY.

court A judicial body authorized to adjudicate controversies between persons or prosecutions of criminal defendants.

court, appellate Any court that reviews a trial court's actions, or the decisions of another (but lower-level) appellate court, to determine whether errors have been made and to decide whether to uphold or overturn a verdict.

court, contempt of Behavior that impugns the authority of a court or obstructs the execution of court orders.

court, trial The court before which a case is tried, in contrast to an appellate court.

court-martial A military court for the trial of members of the armed forces and certain civilians said to be "accompanying the armies in the field."

court of appeals *See* COURT, APPELLATE.

court of original jurisdiction *See* COURT, TRIAL.

crime An act of commission or omission prohibited and punishable by law.

crime family An alleged association of people, related to each other by blood or marriage or having common ties of cultural-ethnic heritage, close bonds, and networks, engaged in ongoing criminal activities. *See also* MAFIA; MOB; ORGANIZED CRIME.

crime of passion Unpremeditated murder or assault committed under circumstances of great anger, jealousy, or other emotional stress.

crime of violence Murder, rape, assault, armed robbery, or any other criminal act involving injury or threat of injury to the victim. *See also* CRIMES AGAINST PERSONS.

crime rate The number of crimes (or of a specific crime or type of crime) known to the police, as a proportion of the population in the nation or in an area. A crime rate of 105.3 usually means that 105.3 crimes were known to have been committed for every 100,000 persons; a murder rate of 9.5 refers to 9.5 murders for every 100,000 in the population.

crimes against persons (crimes against the person) A category of crime in which force or the threat of force is used by the perpetrator. Of the index crimes, those against persons include murder and nonnegligent manslaughter, forcible rape, aggravated assault, and robbery. Arson is classified as a crime against property, although it may result in death or injury to persons.

crimes against property (property crime) A category of crime in which force or violence is neither used nor threatened, and where the perpetrator seeks to make unlawful gain from, or do damage to, the property of another. Of the index crimes, those against property include burglary, larceny-theft, automobile theft, and arson.

crimes cleared by arrest A category in the Uniform Crime Reports that discloses the number and percentage of crimes of a distinct type or in a given area for which an arrest is made and for which the police are satisfied that the crime has been solved.

crimes known to police All illegal acts that have been observed by or reported to police, or about which the police otherwise become aware. Such crimes include, but are not limited to, those for which an arrest has been made.

crime statistics Tabulations of crimes by time period, geography, characteristics of perpetrators and victims, modus operandi, effectiveness of police response, convictions, sentences, and other data.

crime wave An unusual perceived increase in the total amount of crime committed, or in any single offense or type of crime. It may be caused by increased media attention or by changes in enforcement or reporting policies; or it may reflect an actual rise in the crime rate.

criminal One who has been convicted of an act contrary to law. *See also* OFFENDER.

criminal insanity *See* INSANITY.

criminal intelligence The surreptitious investigation of crime and the gathering of evidence concerning plans and activities in a criminal subculture or underworld, generally obtained through informants, infiltration, electronic eavesdropping, and other methods.

criminalistics The science of crime detection, which involves the gathering of physical evidence to assist in determining guilt or innocence. Criminalistics includes ballistics, blood-stain analysis, and other tests.

criminalization The passing of legislation imposing criminal sanctions for commission or omission of an act that had formerly been legal or had been an infraction rather than a crime. Also refers to a process or influence that affects the development of a criminal. *See also* DECRIMINALIZATION.

criminal justice The entire system of crime prevention and detection, apprehension of suspects, arrest, trial, adjudication of guilt or innocence, and handling of the guilty by correctional agencies, together with the executive, legislative, and judicial rules governing these procedures and processes.

criminal law The body of legislation and judicial interpretations defining criminal acts (substantive criminal law), in contrast to laws specifying procedures for investigation of crime and determination of guilt or innocence (procedural criminal law).

criminal libel *See* LIBEL.

criminal possession Having on one's person or under one's effective control objects or substances illegally possessed, as guns or drugs. Criminal possession applies also to objects legally possessed when there is the intention of using them to commit a crime, as picks used in burglary.

criminal procedure *See* CRIMINAL LAW.

criminology The systematic, scientific study of crime and the treatment of offenders.

cross-examination The questioning of a witness by adversary counsel after the conclusion of the direct examination.

culpability Blameworthiness and guilt; a determination that a responsible person, acting with the required mental state of intention, recklessness, or negligence, has commited acts constituting a crime. *See also* MENS REA.

custody Legal control over a person or property. Custody of a child consists of legal guardianship and the right of physical control of the child's whereabouts. Custody of a juvenile or adult consists of such restraint and/or physical control as is needed to ensure his presence at any legal proceedings, or of responsibility for his detention or imprisonment resulting from a criminal charge or conviction. Custody of property consists of immediate personal care of property not owned by the custodian, who is responsible for guarding and preserving it.

damages Compensation awarded for injuries (physical, mental, or other types) sustained. Damages are usually demanded in civil actions. They may also be granted for injury at the hands of law enforcement officers, as in unauthorized search and seizure; to bystanders inadvertently injured by a police officer; or to victims who sue the perpetrator of a crime.

dangerousness The degree to which a person or an act is regarded as a threat to others, particularly with reference to physical harm.

dark figure of crime Criminal acts that are not observed, reported, or recorded in crime statistics, either because they are unknown except to the perpetrator or because of reluctance by victims or witnesses to make complaints. Efforts to estimate the extent of this dark figure have been made, particularly through criminal victimization studies.

day fine A fine for which the amount is determined both by the seriousness of the crime and the offender's financial resources. (Traditional, "flat" fines sometimes take the latter factor into account, but are based primarily on the former.) Crime seriousness determines the number of day fine "units" (day fines) imposed by the court. The value of each fine unit is then calculated by a formula which is usually based on the offender's daily net income after taxes, other deductions, and an allowance for living expenses for the offender and his or her dependents. Thus, for example, 50 "day fines" is designed to deprive the offender of fifty days' worth of disposable income; the financial impact of such penalty is assumed to be roughly equivalent for offenders with very different levels of income. Day fines are frequently used for a wide variety of crimes in several European countries. *See also* FINE.

deadly force Any force involving a deadly weapon (gun, knife, or blunt instrument) or physical attack (such as strangling or smothering) likely to inflict death or grievous bodily harm.

death penalty Capital punishment; execution as a punishment for crime.

deceit Fraud or misrepresentation, particularly in the concealment of relevant information.

decriminalization The removing of criminal sanctions from formerly criminal behavior. Decriminalization may reduce the behavior to an infraction or a violation of a local ordinance, as some states have done with regard to the possession of marijuana; or it may consist of legalization of the behavior, in which case it is no longer subject to penalties, as the repeal of Prohibition. *See also* CRIMINALIZATION.

defendant The party in a legal action against whom the proceedings are initiated; in a criminal trial, the party charged with a criminal offense.

defense attorney The counsel for the defendant in a criminal proceeding.

deinstitutionalization In general, the removal of persons from institutions. In particular, the deinstitutionalization of status offenders was a movement to remove from juvenile institutions juveniles who had committed offenses that would not be crimes if committed by adults (e.g., truancy, runaway, incorrigibility).

delict A crime, offense, wrong, or injury. *See also* CORPUS DELICTI.

delinquency, juvenile *See* DELINQUENT; DELINQUENT OFFENSES; JUVENILE DELINQUENT.

delinquent Originally, the term referred to a failure to meet financial obligations. The term was adopted around the year 1800 to refer to juveniles who were in trouble with the law. The term is also a legal status conferred on a juvenile at an adjudication hearing in juvenile court: the juvenile is adjudicated a delinquent.

delinquent offenses This term usually refers to offenses committed by juveniles that would be crimes if committed by adults (e.g., burglary, auto theft, assault). Sometimes the term also refers to status offenses, which are offenses that would not be crimes if committed by adults (e.g., truancy, runaway, incorrigibility).

demeanor The way a person acts toward another. In policing, there is an issue whether the demeanor of the suspect, especially whether the person is hostile and disrespectful, influences the police officer's decision about arresting the person.

demurrer Plea for dismissal on the ground that the alleged crime has no sufficient basis in law, despite the truth of the facts as charged.

denial In juvenile courts, the juvenile does not plead guilty or not guilty. Rather, the juvenile either admits or denies the offense. Thus, a denial in juvenile court is comparable to a plea of not guilty in criminal court.

denial hearing An adjudication hearing in juvenile court. In most juvenile courts, adjudication hearings are held only when the juvenile denies the offense, so that the hearings are sometimes referred to as denial hearings.

de novo To start over again, as from the beginning; used to describe a case that is to be retried as if no previous trial had been held, or to describe the approach of an appellate court to legal issues when no deference is due to the determination of a lower court.

dependent child A child without a proper parent or guardian. In some states, the legal term "dependent child" sometimes includes juveniles who commit status offenses (e.g., truancy, runaway, incorrigibility) and also sometimes includes neglected children (children who have parents but those parents do not provide proper care and guardianship).

deponent One who gives sworn testimony in the form of a deposition.

deportation The act of sending an alien out of a country, and usually banning him or her from reentry. Deportation of a criminal alien can take place before a trial, after conviction, or after a sentence has been served.

deposition The sworn testimony of a witness, taken elsewhere than in open court. Such testimony is legal and binding only when so authorized.

detached workers People assigned to youth gangs in major cities. They seek to transform gang values and organization through individual counseling, influencing interaction within the gang, and developing alternative activities for gang members. *See also* JUVENILE DELINQUENT.

detain   To hold a person (the detainee) in confinement, pending action by a grand jury, trial, transfer to another jurisdiction, or other disposition.

detention   The legally authorized holding of a person subject to criminal or juvenile court proceedings while awaiting a hearing, trial, sentence, or other court action; or such holding of a person as a material witness.

detention, preliminary   The holding of an accused in confinement pending arraignment. If the accused has been arraigned, the term refers to holding him or her in confinement pending trial because bail has been denied or cannot be met. *See also* RELEASE ON OWN RECOGNIZANCE.

detention, pretrial   Detention of one who is ineligible for bail (or is unable to raise or post the bail ordered by the arraigning judge) until final disposition of his case.

detention, preventive   Holding of a person in custody without bail before his or her conviction, on the ground that such custody keeps a high-risk criminal from committing further crimes while the charges are pending.

detention center   A government facility that holds a person in confinement pending court disposition. *See also* JAIL; SHELTER.

detention center, juvenile   A secure and locked facility to temporarily hold juveniles who are awaiting adjudication or disposition in the juvenile court. *See also* INSTITUTION, JUVENILE; SHELTER CARE FACILITY.

detention hearing   A proceeding, presided over by a judicial officer of a juvenile court, to determine whether or not a juvenile is to be detained pending adjudication of his or her case.

deterrence   The discouragement of crime by the threat of punishment of offenders.

deterrence, general   The concept that the example of the punishment of offenders prevents criminality by others.

deterrence, special (individual or specific deterrence)   The concept that future crimes by a specific offender can be prevented by imposing a penalty so severe that it outweighs the pleasure or profit derived from the crime and convinces the offender that he or she should not pursue further criminality.

deviance   Conduct, activity, or condition that is disapproved of, stigmatized, and subject to formal or informal punishment. *See also* LABELING; STIGMA.

diagnostic center (classification center)   A unit within a correctional institution, or a separate facility for persons held in custody, in which an entering convict will be assigned to a specific correctional facility or program. Also, a special place of detention for sex offenders or seriously mentally disturbed convicts.

differential association theory   A major theory in American criminology, set forth by Edwin Sutherland in the 1930s and elaborated upon later by Donald Cressey and others. It postulates that criminal behavior, like normative behavior, is learned, that this learning takes place in association with others already committed to criminality, and that one learns in such association both criminal values and the mechanisms for committing crimes.

diminished capacity (diminished responsibility)   Decreased or less-than-normal ability, temporary or permanent, to distinguish right from wrong or to fully appreciate the consequences of one's act. It is a plea used by the defendant for conviction of a lesser degree of a crime, for a lenient sentence, or for mercy or clemency.

direct examination   Testimony elicited during the interrogation of a witness by the counsel for the side that has called him or her and in whose behalf he or she is testifying. *See also* CROSS-EXAMINATION.

discovery   A motion, usually made by the defense, calling for disclosure to counsel for the accused of all information about a case known to the police and prosecution, or of certain specified information.

discretion   The power given to or assumed by officers of the criminal justice system to make decisions, such as whether or not to arrest (police discretion), prosecute and negotiate a plea (prosecutorial discretion), or impose a severe sentence (sentencing discretion).

dismissal   The terminating of a case against an accused, without determination of guilt or innocence. If the dismissal is with prejudice, no further action can be taken against the accused for the same offense; if without prejudice, the case against the accused may be reopened.

dismissal, delayed   A dismissal of a criminal charge obtained by the defense but which the prosecution withholds for several weeks or months, as a means of warning the defendant, placating the victim, or allowing public and media interest to wane.

disorderly conduct   Behavior that tends to disturb the peace or decorum of the community, or that scandalizes the population or shocks the moral sense of the public.

disposition   The final decision of a trial court in the processing of a case, such as a decision to accept a guilty plea, to render a verdict of guilt or innocence, or not to prosecute.

disposition hearing   A hearing in juvenile court which results in a decision on what to do with the case, where the most frequent outcomes are placing the juvenile on probation or sending the juvenile to a residential treatment facility.

district attorney   The prosecutor in a state criminal case; sometimes called the state's attorney, county attorney, prosecutor, or the attorney general.

diversion   Any decision or program whereby an offender is not brought to trial in a criminal proceeding but is handled in a potentially less punitive and less stigmatizing manner.

DNA (deoxyribonucleic acid)   A chemical messenger of genetic information, a code that gives both common and individual characteristics to people. Except for identical twins, no two individuals share the same DNA pattern. DNA evidence, in one form or another, is admissible in every state and federal circuit.

docket The formal record maintained by the court clerk, listing all cases heard and containing for each case the defendant's name, an identifying number, the date of arrest, and the disposition of the case.

domestic violence Any physical, sexual, or psychological abuse that people use against a former or current intimate partner. Domestic violence refers to a number of criminal behaviors: assault and battery, sexual assault, stalking, harassment, violation of a civil restraining order, homicide, and other offenses that occur in the course of a domestic violence incident.

dossier A record, case file, or personnel file containing biographical information as well as materials relating to a crime or a criminal career; also used for intelligence and espionage records.

double celling The placement of two inmates in a jail or prison cell originally constructed for the custody of only one.

double jeopardy A practice, forbidden in the United States and many other countries, by which a defendant is tried a second time for an offense of which he has previously been acquitted, or for which he has been found guilty and punished. The rule against double jeopardy also forbids the trial of a defendant who has earlier been placed in jeopardy for the same offense.

driving while impaired The offense of driving a motor vehicle while in an impaired mental or physical condition, usually resulting from consumption of alcohol or other drugs; not as serious as drunken driving.

drunken driving (driving under the influence) The crime of driving a motor vehicle on public streets or highways while under the influence of alcohol or other drugs.

due process A principle enunciated in the Fifth and Fourteenth Amendments to the United States Constitution, interpreted as referring to all legal procedures that must be made available in any criminal action which can result in a person's life, freedom, or property being placed in jeopardy.

DUI (driving under the influence) See DRUNKEN DRIVING.

duress The condition prevailing when a threat of imminent death or serious bodily injury causes one to commit a crime. See also EXCUSE; VOLUNTARINESS.

DWI (driving while intoxicated) See DRUNKEN DRIVING.

eavesdropping Interception of oral communications in a surreptitious effort to hear what is being said, without knowledge of at least one of the persons speaking. When hidden electronic equipment is used the process is called bugging, the equipment is a bug, and the premises are said to be bugged.

effective representation An aspect of the right to counsel requiring that counsel provide a competent defense.

electronic monitoring A system for enforcing home detention requirements by means of automated telephone communications between a central computer and a secure (tamper-resistant, non-removable) arm or leg bracelet worn by the offender. Some systems verify the offender's presence by computer dialing of his home telephone at random times; other systems maintain continuous electronic contact with the bracelet, and signal a potential violation if the suspect moves more than a certain distance away from his phone. The latter system can also be used to enforce an order for the offender to avoid certain places, such as the victim's home; improved satellite-based technology may permit monitoring of an offender's location at all times and places. See also HOME DETENTION.

elements of the crime The acts, mental states, results, and attendant circumstances that constitute a criminal offense.

embargo An order forbidding entry or exit of specified or any merchandise, or of vessels, to or from one or many jurisdictions. Violation of an embargo order is a federal crime in the United States.

embezzlement The theft of money or property that is lawfully in one's possession (as by a bank teller, a company treasurer, or a custodian of funds) but that one does not own.

embracery Attempting to bribe, coerce, or corrupt a juror or jury, grand or petit.

entrapment An arrangement made by police, or persons acting on behalf of the police, to induce, encourage, or instigate the commission of a crime that would not have been committed if it were not for the active intervention of the governmental agent and the desire to make an arrest. In defined circumstances it constitutes a defense. See also SCAM; SOLICITATION; STING.

Espionage Act (1917) Federal legislation that defines acts of spying against the United States and provides penalties for such acts.

euthanasia Mercy killing, such as assisting in or hastening the death of a very old or terminally ill person, with or without his consent, or killing a malformed or mentally defective infant. See also ASSISTED SUICIDE.

evidence Proofs, or probative matter including oral testimony, presented at a trial for the purpose of convincing judge or jury of the truth or falsity of charges.

evidence, admissible Oral, written, photographic, or material evidence deemed by the trial judge to be acceptable under the laws of evidence.

evidence, circumstantial Physical or other evidence from which judge and jury may infer facts not directly observed by an eyewitness. For example, a fingerprint on a gun is circumstantial evidence that the gun was handled by the suspect.

evidence, corroborating Evidence that confirms testimony previously admitted.

evidence, exculpatory Evidence that tends to eliminate or diminish the blame or guilt of the accused. When such evidence is known to the prosecutor, it must be divulged to the court or to the defense.

evidence, physical   Items admitted into evidence by prosecution or defense for the purpose of incriminating or exculpating the accused. Examples include fibers from clothing, objects left at the scene of the crime, and samples of handwriting. *See also* CRIMINALISTICS.

examination   Questioning of witnesses for the prosecution and the defense. *See also* CROSS-EXAMINATION; DIRECT EXAMINATION.

examination in chief   Questioning of prosecution witnesses by the prosecutor, and of defense witnesses by counsel for the defense.

exception   A statement made by counsel in a trial, objecting to a ruling by a judge. The statement is made for the trial record, so as to permit appeal on the ground that the ruling was incorrect.

exclusionary rule   A rule that generally operates to exclude from admission at a criminal trial certain evidence, such as physical evidence, the defendant's confession, or identification by a witness, because it was obtained as a result of unlawful activities by law enforcement officers.

excuse   A defense to a criminal charge, based on the abnormality of the defendant or the exigencies in which he acted, that precludes his moral blameworthiness and guilt; examples are infancy, insanity, and duress. *See also* JUSTIFICATION.

ex post facto law   A law passed or coming into effect after an act was committed, which is then applied to the already committed act. The new law may illegalize what was formerly legal, or it may increase the penalty for a crime. Ex post facto law is prohibited by the United States Constitution.

expunge   To delete records from official sources. In some jurisdictions, juvenile records are automatically expunged when the juvenile reaches adulthood. In other jurisdictions, a person may petition the court to expunge juvenile records.

extenuating circumstances   Particular characteristics of an offender or offense that partially or entirely excuse the offender or serve to reduce the gravity of his act.

extortion   The unlawful taking of money or anything of value by a public officer under color of his office. Also, the taking of anything of value from an initially unwilling person by instilling in him or her fear of the consequences of noncompliance; examples include blackmail and racketeering.

extradition   The legal removal of a person from one jurisdiction to another, where he or she is wanted to stand trial or from which he or she is a fugitive. Extradition within the United States can be from one state to another, and a state can refuse to extradite. A person may voluntarily consent to be taken to the jurisdiction seeking him or her, in which case he or she is said to waive extradition. *See also* RENDITION.

eyewitness   One who has been present at a crime while it was being committed, or shortly before or after. The eyewitness testifies to what he or she has seen or heard, usually with the purpose of identifying the defendant.

eyewitness identification   The identifying of a defendant in a police lineup or in court as the perpetrator of a criminal act by its victim or someone else who has witnessed the act.

fact finder (trier of fact)   The individual or group with the obligation and authority to determine the facts (as distinct from the law) in a case. In a jury trial, the jury is the fact finder and is charged with accepting and applying the law as given to it by the judge.

fact-finding hearing   Sometimes used to refer to adjudication hearings in juvenile court. In adjudication hearings, the juvenile court makes a finding about whether the facts alleged in the petition are true. This "finding of fact" is comparable to the verdict (guilty or not guilty) in criminal court. On the basis of this finding of fact, the court decides whether to take jurisdiction over the juvenile.

family court   Courts with original jurisdiction to handle a variety of family matters, including delinquency, adoption, divorce, and child custody. *See also* JUVENILE COURT.

fault   An improper act for which the perpetrator is blameworthy in the sense of having been responsible for it.

Federal Bureau of Investigation   The general enforcement agency for federal criminal laws whose enforcement is not assigned to another federal agency, such as the Internal Revenue Service or the Secret Service. The F.B.I. is also charged with domestic security responsibilities. It publishes annual statistics on crime in its series Uniform Crime Reports.

felon   One who has been convicted of a felony.

felony   A crime of a type more serious in terms of authorized sanctions than a misdemeanor; usually a crime punishable by more than a year in prison. In the federal system, crimes that are felonies must be prosecuted by way of a grand jury's indictment rather than a prosecutor's information.

felony, compounding a   The act, performed by the victim or by someone acting in his or her behalf, of demanding or accepting a payment not to prosecute a felony; making a bargain to allow a criminal to escape prosecution.

felony murder   An unlawful killing of a person while committing or attempting to commit a felony, such as rape or robbery. In felony murder, specific intent to kill need not be proved, since it is implied from the intent to commit the felony. *See also* HOMICIDE; INTENT.

fence   A receiver and seller of stolen goods.

fencing   The act of receiving stolen goods; the receipt, handling, and sale of stolen goods as a business and occupation.

finding   A conclusion reached by a court on a matter of fact, for example, that the defendant is or is not competent to stand trial

fine   A penalty requiring a convicted offender to pay a sum of money to a court. The fine may be the full penalty, it may be imposed in addition to a jail or prison sentence, or it may be in the form of a choice between payment and a jail term. *See also* DAY FINE.

folk crime   A term applied by some criminologists to illegal activity that society generally does not stigmatize; an offense that does not incite a sense of outrage and that is generally thought of as less than criminal, regardless of the penalties involved (for example, a traffic-law violation). *See also* INFRACTION; MALUM PROHIBITUM; VICTIMLESS CRIME; VIOLATION.

foot patrol   Programs in which police officers walk a beat instead of drive in patrol cars. *See also* COMMUNITY POLICING.

forcible entry and detainer   The use of threat, force, or arms to gain possession of the real property of another and to retain it after surrender has been lawfully demanded. *See also* BREAKING AND ENTERING; TRESPASS.

forensic   Relating to law, courts, or the judiciary. For example, forensic science is the application of chemistry, physics, or other sciences to the identification of physical evidence. *See also* CRIMINALISTICS.

forensic psychiatry   The application of psychiatric procedures in a legal setting to determine criminal responsibility, legal sanity or insanity, competency to stand trial, commitment to a mental facility, or related issues. Forensic psychiatry is concerned with psychiatric advice or opinion on a crime, a defendant, or a convicted offender.

forfeiture proceeding   A court action aimed at depriving a defendant of money or property, such as something obtained by police in a search and seizure.

forgery   The creation or alteration of a writing, signature, document, or work of art in such a way as to produce a false impression concerning its provenance or authenticity, for the purpose of deceiving or defrauding others. *See also* COUNTERFEITING.

fornication   Sexual intercourse between a man and a woman outside the bonds of marriage. *See also* ADULTERY.

foster home   A private family that agrees to care for an additional child. Delinquent children sometimes are placed in foster homes. *See also* GROUP HOME.

fratricide   The killing of a sibling.

fraud   Taking advantage of a person by illegal means through concealment or deception, such as misleading him or her as to the value or authenticity of goods offered for sale.

fresh pursuit   *See* HOT PURSUIT.

frisk   To search the outer clothing and property in the immediate possession of a suspect. A frisk is usually less intrusive than a full search of the kind permitted incident to a lawful arrest.

fruit (of the poisonous tree)   Evidence obtained as the result of unlawful governmental action that will be subject to exclusion under constitutional exclusionary rules; for example, physical or testimonial evidence obtained as the result of an unlawful search or coercive interrogation tactics.

fugitive   One who has escaped confinement or absconded from bail, probation, or parole; a deserter; a draft evader; one who flees a jurisdiction or goes into hiding to avoid arrest, indictment, or trial.

gang   A group of alleged offenders or marginal persons suspected of violence or crime. They are in continuing interaction with one another, sometimes acting in concert in their lawbreaking and antisocial activities. The word is often but not exclusively applied to delinquent juvenile groups.

gangster   A member of a criminal gang, a dangerous criminal, or a person reputed to be associated with criminals; usually applied only to adults suspected of being part of organized crime.

genetic factors   Possible influences on behavior consisting of heritable biological factors. *See also* BIOLOGICAL FACTORS; SOCIAL FACTORS.

good behavior   Conduct during incarceration, while in custody, or under supervision, that meets the standards or propriety set by the authorities. In jail or prison, it entitles the convict to credit for good time.

good faith exception   An exception to the Fourth Amendment exclusionary rule that permits the admission of evidence seized by law enforcement personnel relying in good faith on the apparent validity of a judicial warrant that turns out to be constitutionally defective; more generally, any exception to a rule based on the honest and objectively reasonable belief of the rule-breaker that he or she was acting lawfully and properly.

Good Samaritan   A person other than a police officer who is not directly involved in a crime but who steps in to prevent injury, aid a victim, or apprehend the criminal. The Good Samaritan is usually a bystander or passerby.

good time   The portion of a prison term that is deducted from the total term because of the convict's good behavior during incarceration.

graft   Coerced or voluntary payments made to influence public officials in their official conduct; for example, payments made to police to overlook an illegal activity such as prostitution.

grand jury   A body of citizens (usually twenty-three) of a county (or, for federal crimes, of a federal judicial district) which evaluates the prosecution's evidence to ascertain that a crime has been committed and that there is a case against the accused which, if not answered by the defense, would justify conviction. The grand jury serves as an investigative tool of the prosecution and is thought to protect citizens from frivolous or malicious prosecutions. In many jurisdictions it also has the power to investigate corruption, inefficiency, and threats to the welfare of the community, or to study any problem in the operation of a county government. *See also* INDICTMENT; NO BILL; PRESENTMENT; TRUE BILL.

grand jury, runaway   A grand jury that asserts its independence of the prosecutor and, often assisted by a special prosecutor, presses investigations over the regular prosecutor's opposition.

group home   A home-like environment in which a number of juveniles or adults (e.g., six or eight) live in a community setting, managed by "house parents" who are employees. *See also* FOSTER HOME.

guidelines Nonbinding standards to direct the exercise of discretion by an official. *See also* SENTENCING GUIDELINES.

guilt The fact of having committed a wrongful or criminal act.

habeas corpus ("you have the body") A writ or court order mandating that a warden, jailer, or other official holding a person in custody produce that person in court so that the legality of the confinement can be determined. Also resorted to in noncriminal actions, as in the determination of child custody, or a hearing on a patient's demand for release from a mental institution.

halfway house A community-located correctional institution in which offenders are supervised under minimum security and which provides therapy, vocational support, and other services. It is often used to bridge the gap between prison and nonconfining community corrections or unconditional release.

Hammurabi, Code of Babylonian laws of the twenty-second century B.C., generally regarded by historians as a moderate and humanitarian code for its period; one of the oldest codes of law.

harboring a felon The crime of hiding or otherwise aiding an escaped or wanted felon for whom the police are searching. *See also* ACCESSORY.

hearing In criminal procedure, appearance of an alleged offender before a court prior to his or her appearance for trial, as for arraignment or a preliminary hearing.

hearing, preliminary A hearing before a judge or magistrate to determine whether there is sufficient reason for submitting a case to the grand jury or directly to a trial court.

hearsay Inadmissible testimony by a witness as to what he or she heard or was told outside of court. Under special conditions, such hearsay as a dying declaration or a statement by an expert witness is admissible.

hold order A notation on an inmate's file that another jurisdiction which has charges pending against him or her or in which he or she is due to serve time must be informed of his or her impending release.

home detention A court order requiring an offender to remain in his or her dwelling except when authorized to leave for specified purposes, at specified times of the day, such as to go to work or to attend school or a treatment program. These limitations may be enforced by unexpected visits or phone calls from a probation officer or other supervisor, as well as by electronic monitoring. Home detention can be used as a penalty for convicted offenders, and also as a means of preventing flight and criminal conduct by defendants awaiting trial or recently released from jail or prison. *See also* ELECTRONIC MONITORING.

Home Office A British cabinet office that exercises limited jurisdiction over the police, operates the pris-

on and aftercare systems, and organizes research and statistics on crime.

homicide The killing of one human being by another.

homicide, criminal The killing of a human being under circumstances that make the act punishable.

homicide, excusable The killing of a human being by one who is legally insane or who suffers from another internal or external condition that renders the actor morally blameless for the killing. *See also* EXCUSE.

homicide, justifiable The intentional killing of a human being, which although ordinarily criminal, is noncriminal because of circumstances that render the homicide proper, tolerable, or permissible, such as because the killing was done in self-defense or defense of another, or in enforcement of the law. *See also* JUSTIFICATION.

homicide, vehicular The unintentional killing of one or more persons as a result of driving a motor vehicle while drunk, recklessly, or otherwise in violation of the law.

hot pursuit (fresh pursuit) Immediate, in-sight pursuit of an escaping felon that permits a police officer to depart from his or her jurisdiction or to intrude on private premises without a judicial warrant.

"hot spots" A theory by Lawrence Sherman and others that a very large portion of police calls originate from a very few specific addresses, even within high crime areas.

ignorantia legis non excusat ("ignorance of the law is no excuse") The principle that an accused is not freed from criminal responsibility because he or she was unaware that his or her act was in violation of the law.

Illinois Juvenile Court Act (1899) Legislation establishing the first juvenile court. This legislation embodied a philosophy of handling juveniles which later spread through the United States and much of the rest of the world. *See also* CHANCERY COURT.

immunity Exemption from a duty or penalty contrary to the general rule, for example, immunity from prosecution of one who turns state's evidence, or immunity of public officials for their official acts.

immunity, waiver of Voluntary or mandated relinquishment of immunity.

impairing the morals of a minor Engaging in sex-related acts (except intercourse) with a minor, for example, caressing him or her, taking obscene photographs, or exposing the minor to lewd and pornographic materials. *See also* CARNAL ABUSE (KNOWLEDGE) OF A MINOR; CHILD MOLESTATION; RAPE, STATUTORY.

impeach To discredit, particularly by challenging the truthfulness of a witness; also, to charge an official (as president, governor, or judge) with misconduct and seek to remove him or her from office.

impersonating an officer Pretending to be a police officer, an officer of the armed services, or an official of a federal, state, or local law enforcement agency, usually be wearing a uniform, showing an identification card or badge, or falsely identifying oneself as an officer.

imprisonment, periodic (or intermittent) A sentence served discontinuously, for example, only on weekends.

impunity Exemption from penalty or punishment. *See also* IMMUNITY.

in camera ("in a chamber") Criminal proceedings from which press and the general public are barred, as in family and juvenile courts; also, judicial review of confidential materials without making those materials fully available to all parties to litigation.

incapacitation Keeping offenders in prison as a means of preventing them from committing further crimes.

incendiary (arsonist; firebug) A person who ignites an unlawful fire; also, a chemical agent employed to cause combustion; also, a bullet or bomb designed to cause fire on contact with the object struck, or upon detonation.

incest Illegal sexual activity between two persons closely related by blood or marriage. Various societies have indicated the specific relationships forbidden as incestuous. These almost invariably include parent-child and sibling relationships, and sometimes uncle-niece, aunt-nephew, and grandparent-grandchild relationships, as well as those with a brother-in-law, sister-in-law, mother-in-law, or father-in-law.

inchoate crime Conduct made criminal even though it has not yet produced the ultimate harm that the law seeks to prevent. *See also* ATTEMPT; CONSPIRACY; SOLICITATION.

incidence of crime Criminality measured in a given population over a definite time span, as during a single day or in a single year. *See also* PREVALENCE OF CRIME.

incompetent Not qualified; descriptive of a person unable to handle his or her property or affairs because of age, insanity, mental defect, or addiction; also, a person declared ineligible to give testimony or serve on a jury. Used also to characterize testimony that is inadmissible.

incorrigible Unmanageable; refers to juveniles who habitually refuse to obey lawful authority, including the authority of teachers and parents. *See also* STATUS OFFENSE.

indemnity A right that a person subjected to loss or damage is entitled to claim from another at whose request or for whose benefit he or she was acting.

index crimes *See* PART I OFFENSES.

indictment The formal written accusation made by a grand jury and filed in court, alleging that there is probable cause to believe that one or more persons have committed one or several crimes, usually felonies. Each charge in an indictment is called a count. *See also* INFORMATION; NO BILL; PRESENTMENT; TRUE BILL.

indigent Poor; unable to afford effective legal counsel.

industrial school Reform school; institution for delinquent or neglected children.

informant One from whom information about a crime or criminal activity is obtained, usually not for reward (as, for example, from a public-spirited citizen or an opponent of vice). Also, a person who supplies information to a researcher about activity in which he or she is involved or which he or she has an opportunity to observe. *See also* INFORMER.

in forma pauperis ("in the form of a pauper") Request for the waiving of legal fees by an indigent defendant.

information A formal written accusation of a crime; it differs from an indictment in that it is issued by a prosecutor rather than by a grand jury.

information, confidential Information protected by statute, for example, information on national security or income-tax returns. Also refers to information protected against disclosure in evidence, such as information revealed in a patient-physician or penitent-priest relationship. *See also* PRIVILEGED COMMUNICATION.

informer A participant in delinquent or criminal activities or in a criminal subculture, or one who has knowledge of the criminal activities of relatives, friends, and acquaintances, and who passes on information concerning crime to police and other government agencies in return for monetary payment, drugs, or partial or complete immunity from arrest and prosecution. *See also* INFORMANT.

infraction A minor offense, as littering.

injunction A court order requiring a party to refrain from or stop doing a particular act, thus temporarily or permanently guarding against putative future injury to the individual, group, or other party seeking the injunction; more recently used to describe any judicial order commanding a party either to do or to refrain from doing a particular act.

"in loco parentis" A Latin phrase meaning "in the place of parents." The juvenile court is often said to operate "in loco parentis."

inmate code The code of the inmate subculture; the basis for prisonization (as in the admonition not to inform and not to cooperate with guards).

inmate self-government Involvement of an inmate population in decision-making, usually at the lowest levels (as in planning athletic and recreational programs and other entertainment).

inmate subculture The folkways, traditions, and customs of an inmate population.

inquisitorial system A system of criminal prosecution in which a judicial officer has the responsibility to investigate and examine, and adjudication is not limited to the facts adduced by the parties. The civil law systems of continental Europe were originally based on this model, but all of them now give the parties substantial powers, and thus represent varying hybrid forms of the inquisitorial and adversary models. *See also* ADVERSARY SYSTEM.

insanity (legal insanity) A defense based on the defendant's lack of responsibility at the time of the act owing to mental disease or defect.   *See also* CULPABILI-TY; DIMINISHED CAPACITY; EXCUSE; MENS REA; M'NAGHTEN RULE; RESPONSIBILITY.

insanity, temporary   Legal insanity which existed only at the time of the act.

institution, juvenile   A residential correctional facility for juveniles, either secure or non-secure. At disposition hearings, juvenile court judges commit juveniles to these facilities for treatment, rehabilitation, punishment, or social protection. These facilities sometimes are called training schools or reformatories.

intake hearing   An initial and fairly informal hearing in a juvenile court, after juveniles have been arrested or are otherwise referred to a juvenile court. Generally present at the hearing are the intake officer, the juvenile, the juvenile's parents, and the juvenile's lawyer, but not the prosecuting attorney. The intake officer asks whether the juvenile admits or denies the alleged offense. If the juvenile denies the offense, an adjudication hearing usually is scheduled at which the truth of the allegations will be determined by a judge. If the juvenile admits the offense, the intake officer may make any of a variety of decisions about what to do next, including release the juvenile to the parents, detain the juvenile, enter a consent decree, or schedule a disposition hearing before a judge.

intent   The state of mind of a perpetrator who either desires the consequences of his or her actions or knows with substantial certainty that they will occur.   *See also* KNOWINGLY; MENS REA; PURPOSELY.

intent, criminal (mens rea)   The harboring of a plan, hope, or state of mind favorable to the commission of a crime.

intent, general   A term of various meanings. Sometimes, it is the state of mind characterized by recklessness or negligence rather than the specific criminal intent to do what is prohibited; other times, it means any non-specific morally culpable state of mind in regard to the perpetrator's actions. Contrasted to "specific intent."   *See also* INTENT, SPECIFIC.

intent, specific   The state of mind in which the perpetrator intends to commit acts prohibited by law or accomplish a specific purpose, or the state of mind of acting with a specific unlawful motive. Contrasted to "general intent."   *See also* INTENT, GENERAL.

intent, transferred   Intent that is legally transferred from one act to another. For example, if a defendant kills one person while intending to kill another, his intent to kill is transferred to the person killed.

internal affairs   A unit within police departments that investigates charges of police misconduct.

international law   A body of law derived from treaties, decisions of supranational courts (as the Permanent Court for International Justice), and the charters of the League of Nations and United Nations; in a limited sense it governs the conduct of a sovereign nation in matters not entirely internal. Also, legal precedents and procedures governing multinational corporations, the import-export trade, and disputes between nations.   *See also* TRANSNATIONAL CRIME.

Interpol (International Criminal Police Commission)   A body composed of police representatives of many nations, which maintains central communications and records at its Paris headquarters. It processes requests for information about transnational criminals, advises member agencies as to the movements of known criminals, seeks missing persons, identifies unknown dead persons, and publishes the *International Criminal Police Review*.   *See also* TRANSNATIONAL CRIME.

investigatory system   *See* INQUISITORIAL SYSTEM.

irresistible impulse   A compulsion to commit a criminal act that cannot be overcome because disease or defect of reason prevents the accused from conforming to the requirements of the law.   *See also* INSANITY; RESPONSIBILITY.

jail   A short-term confinement facility, usually under the jurisdiction of county, city, or local police. It is used to hold persons awaiting arraignment or trial when no bail has been set or bail cannot be met. It also holds convicted misdemeanants and others sentenced to less than one year, as well as prisoners in transit and occasionally material witnesses.

jail delivery   An obsolete procedure wherein all inmates at a given jail are tried for the offenses for which they are being held.

jeopardy   The point at which a trial has commenced sufficiently so that the defendant has a constitutional right not to have the trial terminated without his consent or some necessity for doing so. In a bench trial this point is when the first witness is sworn; in a jury trial it is when the jury is sworn.   *See also* DOUBLE JEOPARDY.

judge   A judicial officer, appointed or elected, who presides over a court of law, either to try cases or to hear and rule on appeals from a lower-court decision.   *See also* JUSTICE; MAGISTRATE.

judge, trial   The presiding judge at a trial, as distinct from an arraignment judge, appellate judge, and other judicial officers.

judgment   The determination by a court in a controversy that is submitted to it.

judicial notice   The right of the court to take note, without an offer of proof by either party, of facts known to a veritable certainty and available in sources of indisputable accuracy.

judicial officer   A judge, referee, or other court officer with power to hear cases and reach determinations.

jurisdiction   The authority of nations or states to create or prescribe penal or regulatory norms and laws and to enforce them through administrative and judicial action. Jurisdiction can be *in personam* (over a person) or *in rem* (over property).

juror, alternate   A person added to a jury panel; he or she is substituted for a juror who, during the trial, dies, becomes ill, or is excused or disqualified by the trial judge. There may be more than one alternate juror in a trial.   *See also* TALESMAN.

jury, blue-ribbon (or key-man)   A special jury panel selected from the upper or upper middle socioeconomic strata, or from persons with some special expertise. Such selection was used to form grand juries, and occasionally petit juries as well. Blue-ribbon juries are no longer legal.

jury, death-qualified A jury in a capital case from which potential jurors whose scruples about the death penalty would prevent them from imposing it have been excluded.

jury, hung A trial jury which, after exhaustive deliberation, cannot agree on a unanimous verdict, necessitating a mistrial and a subsequent retrial. In cases and jurisdictions where unanimity is not required, a hung jury results when the necessary votes for acquittal or conviction cannot be obtained.

jury, trial The petit jury that hears the evidence in a criminal case, is the trier of the facts, and renders a verdict.

jury nullification The act of a jury of acquitting a defendant on the ground that it would be unfair or unjust to convict rather than because he or she had not committed the crime.

jury of (one's) peers A concept requiring juries to be selected from the general population, without special selection or systematic exclusion of any class, except those legally exempted or excluded from service or incompetent to serve. *See also* JURY, BLUE-RIBBON (OR KEY-MAN).

just deserts (deserts) The punishment that one properly deserves for having committed a crime; its severity depends on the seriousness of the offense and the offender's degree of culpability. *See also* RETRIBUTION.

justice An adjudicative process in which the guilt or innocence of a defendant is established or the legal rights of adversarial litigants vindicated. Also a synonym for judge, usually applied to judicial officers of higher courts.

justification Any defense to an otherwise illegal act that renders the perpetrator's conduct not only criminal by morally proper, permissible, or nonwrongful, such as use of force in self-defense, to defend others, to prevent a crime, or to prevent a greater harm. *See also* EXCUSE.

Justinian, Code of The codification of Roman law by Justinian I in the sixth century A.D. in the form of a body of civil law (*corpus juris civilis*).

juvenile A person who has not reached an age prescribed by law (generally eighteen). A juvenile is not routinely tried by a criminal court if accused of a crime, and is ineligible for voting, military service, marriage, and the making of a binding contract until the prescribed age is reached.

juvenile court A court with original jurisdiction over persons statutorily defined by age as juveniles and alleged to be delinquents, status offenders, or persons in need of supervision.

juvenile delinquent A person under an age prescribed by law who commits an act that would be a misdemeanor or a felony if committed by an adult, or who

commits an offense that is specifically prohibited because of age status, for example, running away or being a habitual truant.

Juvenile in Need of Supervision (JINS) One of several terms used to refer to juveniles who commit status offenses that would not be crimes if committed by adults, such as truancy, runaway, and incorrigibility.

juvenile justice The system of agencies, courts, and custodial facilities established to handle juveniles deemed delinquent, status offenders, or other youths believed to be in need of supervision.

kidnapping The unlawful taking, holding, or carrying away of a person against his or her will, sometimes designated as aggravated kidnapping when a ransom is demanded. *See also* ABDUCTION.

knowingly (or, with knowledge) The state of mind that exists when a person is aware of an attendant circumstance, such that a substance in possession is an illegal drug, or when the person is practically certain that conduct will cause a specific result. The second highest level of culpability under the Model Penal Code. *See also* CULPABILITY; MENS REA; MODEL PENAL CODE; NEGLIGENTLY; PURPOSELY; RECKLESSLY.

labeling A sociological perspective concerned with the negative impact that public identification of an offender as a deviant may have on his or her self-image, future behavior, and prospects in society, and with the stigma and suspicion that fall on him or her. *See also* DEVIANCE.

landmark case A case of great importance in the development of the law.

larceny Unlawfully taking the property of another with intent to deprive him or her of it permanently.

latency theory A psychological concept, developed in particular by the Freudians, that postulates the existence of urges, needs, and potential behavior not manifested in overt conduct but existing on an unconscious level and likely to emerge unless redirected by outside (therapeutic) intervention.

Law Enforcement Assistance Administration (LEAA) A major federal agency (1969–1982) that thrived for many years as part of the United States Department of Justice and that sponsored research into numerous aspects of criminal justice. It has been replaced by the National Institute of Justice, the National Institute of Corrections, and other agencies.

law enforcement officer *See* POLICE OFFICER.

lawyer, jailhouse A prisoner who advises other inmates on grounds for appeal and on other legal matters, not always with good or correct advice.

learning theory An explanation of crime and delinquency which postulates that criminal behavior, like legal and normative behavior, is learned. Such learning may be acquired from those already committed to lawbreaking, as in differential association theory; it may be reinforced through rewards and punishments.

legal aid A system of providing counsel and other legal assistance to indigent defendants through a private or semipublic agency supported by governmental, philanthropic, or other funds. *See also* COUNSEL, RIGHT TO; PUBLIC DEFENDER.

legalization   The rescinding of a statute that made an act illegal or criminal, such as the repeal of Prohibition. Legalization makes the formerly prohibited act completely legal; decriminalization removes criminal sanctions, but the act might still be subject to penalties under local ordinances or civil or administrative laws.

legislative exclusion   One of three legal mechanisms by which juveniles can be transferred to criminal courts to be tried as adults. In legislative exclusion, the legislature enacts a law that excludes certain offenses from juvenile court jurisdiction. The law may specify that the offense is excluded only if the offender has reached a certain age or has a certain type of prior record. This mechanism sometimes is referred to as "legislative waiver." *See also* CONCURRENT JURISDICTION; WAIVER OF JURISDICTION, JUVENILE.

leniency   Punishing an offender less than is deserved or authorized.

lesser included offense   A crime less grave than the one charged but not requiring a separate charge for a guilty verdict, because the less serious offense is automatically implied by the more serious one. For example, one charged with murder may also be found guilty of inflicting bodily harm.

lewd and lascivious conduct   A statutory term describing criminalized sexual behavior that has been denoted as depraved and perverse.

lex talionis   ("law of the claw")   Harsh retaliation for criminal acts, based on the concept of "an eye for an eye."

libel   False and malicious publication of defaming, insulting materials exposing an individual to contempt, hatred, and scorn, or harming him or her in his business or profession.

libel, group   False and malicious material which exposes an ethnic, national, religious, or other defined group to hatred, ridicule, or public scorn.

libel, seditious   A criticism of the form, constitution, policies, laws, officers, symbols, or conduct of a sovereign government so severe as to excite hostility among that government's citizens or residents. *See also* SEDITION.

lie detector (polygraph)   An instrument that measures physiological reactions (blood pressure, pulse, breathing, electrodermal response) so that a trained examiner may determine with considerable probability whether a subject is telling the truth.

lineup   A group of people placed together in a line so that victims or eyewitnesses may attempt to pick out the perpetrator of a crime.

lockup   A short-term confinement facility or a jail; also, cells in a police station.

Lombrosian   Pertaining to the criminological views postulated by Cesare Lombroso (1836–1909) and to adherents of the positivist school of criminology, particularly as they related to Lombroso's view that some people are born criminals and others (called criminaloids) are born with criminal tendencies or predilections.

longitudinal study   Research involving the collection of data at two or more points in time, usually on the same individuals. It is sometimes called a follow-up study, panel study, or cohort study.

Mafia (originally called Camorra; often called Cosa Nostra)   A group of Italian-dominated organized-crime leaders and their followers that originated in Sicily in the early or middle nineteenth century. It flourished in the United States beginning in the late nineteenth century.   *See also* CRIME FAMILY; MOB; ORGANIZED CRIME.

magistrate   A lower-court judge, sometimes called a justice of the peace, municipal judge, or police judge who is usually assigned to arraignments, preliminary hearings, the setting of bail, and the disposition of minor offenses.

malfeasance   A wrongful act, usually committed by a public officer.   *See also* MISFEASANCE; NONFEASANCE.

malice   Originally, the term meant to act with a wicked state of mind; modernly, it is the state of mind when a perpetrator intentionally or recklessly causes a harmful result.   *See also* RECKLESSLY.

malicious mischief   Intentionally and wrongfully damaging, destroying, or defacing the property of another, without his or her consent.

malicious prosecution   Unsuccessful civil or criminal proceedings, prosecuted with malice and without probable cause.

malum in se ("wrong in itself"; pl. **mala in se**)   An act that is inherently evil and that is criminalized because it is wrong.

malum prohibitum ("wrong because prohibited"; pl. **mala prohibita**)   An act that is not thought of as inherently evil but that is wrong because it has been criminalized.

mandamus, writ of   A writ ordering or mandating that a public official perform an act (such as issuing a license or permit) that the law recognizes as his or her duty.

mandatory release   Release from prison at the completion of the entire sentence. This contrasts with parole, which is a discretionary release prior to the completion of the sentence.

manslaughter   The unlawful killing of a human being, without malice aforethought.   *See also* HOMICIDE; MURDER.

manslaughter, involuntary   Death resulting from a lawful or unlawful act committed with recklessness or criminal negligence.

manslaughter, negligent   Death resulting from failure to use ordinary care, or from being culpably careless and imprudent.

manslaughter, vehicular   Killing a human being while drunkenly, recklessly, or illegally operating a motor vehicle.

manslaughter, voluntary   The intentional killing of another in sudden heat of passion, as the result of adequate provocation.

martial law   Military law over a civilian population, imposed in times of war, rebellion, or rioting, and sometimes after a natural catastrophe, to prevent looting and other disorders.

maximum security   Security measures observed in a custodial institution where utmost efforts are made to prevent escapes. In maximum-security institutions, the freedom of inmates and of visitors to them is restricted more than in other prisons and correctional facilities.   *See also* MEDIUM SECURITY; MINIMUM SECURITY.

"max out"   A colloquial term often used to refer to the maximum expiration date of a sentence; the mandatory release which occurs when the entire sentence has been served.

mayhem   Originally, the malicious injury of another in such a manner as to impair his or her ability to defend himself or herself. Today mayhem refers to causing the loss, disablement, disfigurement of a limb, an eye, or any other bodily member.

medium security   Security measures observed in a correctional institution or detention facility where freedom of inmates and visitors is restricted and efforts are made to prevent escapes, but to a lesser extent than in institutions housing more dangerous criminals.   *See also* MAXIMUM SECURITY; MINIMUM SECURITY.

mens rea   The criminal intent or "guilty mind." The phrase is used in two distinct ways—in a broad sense and in a narrow sense. In its broad sense, mens rea is synonymous with a person's blameworthiness or, more precisely, those conditions that make a person's violation sufficiently blameworthy to merit the condemnation of criminal conviction. It its narrow (and more modern) sense, the mens rea of an offense consists of those elements of the offense definition that describe the required mental state of the defendant at the time of the offense, but does not include excuse defenses or other doctrines outside of the offense definition.   *See also* ACTUS REUS; CULPABILITY; INTENT.

military justice   The code of law and the judicial machinery established for the purpose of enforcing discipline and punishing crime in the armed forces.   *See also* UNIFORM CODE OF MILITARY JUSTICE.

minimum security   The security measures observed in a correctional institution or detention facility where relative freedom is granted to prisoners and visitors and where lesser emphasis is placed on preventing escapes.   *See also* MAXIMUM SECURITY; MEDIUM SECURITY.

minor   A juvenile, child, or infant; one who has not reached a legal age of adulthood; one who is accused of a criminal act and is tried as a juvenile.

Miranda **warnings (***Miranda* **rights)**   Warnings that must be given prior to interrogation of those arrested or held in custody, as a result of the decision of the United States Supreme Court in *Miranda v. Arizona* (1966). The required warnings are that the defendant has a right to remain silent, that anything he or she says can and will be used against him or her in court, that he or she has a right to consult with a lawyer and have the lawyer with him or her during interrogation, and that if he or she is indigent a lawyer will be appointed to represent him or her. If the warnings were not given or the defendant did not thereafter waive these rights, any statement obtained from him or her as a result of interrogation is inadmissible in evidence in the government's case-in-chief in a criminal trial.

miscarriage of justice   A gross error in the outcome of a criminal case, generally applied to the conviction and punishment of an innocent defendant.

misdemeanor   A prohibited act not amounting to a felony, with punishment limited to a fine or confinement in a local jail, or both; a crime less serious in terms of authorized sanctions than a felony, but more so than an infraction.   *See also* CRIME; FELONY; MALUM PROHIBITUM; OFFENSE; VIOLATION.

misfeasance   An incompetent, mistaken, or negligent act of a public officer in violation of his or her lawfully prescribed duties or responsibilities.   *See also* MALFEASANCE; NONFEASANCE.

misprision of felony   The obsolete crime of withholding knowledge that a person has committed a felony.

mistake of fact   A defense based on the grounds that a defendant did not know certain essential facts, that he or she could not have been expected to have known them, and that there could be no crime without such knowledge.

mistake of law   A defense, rarely recognized, offered by an accused that he or she did not know his or her act was criminal or did not comprehend the legal consequences of what he or she was doing.   *See also* IGNORANTIA LEGIS NON EXCUSAT.

mistrial   A trial terminated or declared void before a verdict is reached, because of some procedural defect, impediment, or error that will prejudice a jury; or because the jury has not been able to agree on a verdict. When there is a mistrial a new trial can be held without double jeopardy, unless the defendant has objected to the mistrial and an appellate court holds that the mistrial was improperly declared by the trial judge, that is, that it was neither necessary nor required by the interests of justice.

mitigating circumstance   Any circumstance that is thought sufficient to diminish the degree of guilt and merit a more lenient sentence, while not excusing the misconduct of the accused.

M'Naghten rule   The rule laid down by the House of Lords after the 1843 verdict of "not guilty by reason of insanity" in the case of Daniel M'Naghten. The rule stated that the perpetrator of a crime is not to be held criminally responsible if, at the time of the act, he or she suffered from a disease of the mind either making him or her unable to know the nature of the act he or she was perpetrating or, if he or she did know it, making him or her unable to realize that what he or she was doing was wrong.   *See also* CULPABILITY; EXCUSE; INSANITY; MENS REA.

mob   An underworld gang consisting of people involved in organized crime, and referred to collectively as "the mob."   *See also* CRIME FAMILY; MAFIA.

Model Penal Code   A criminal code proposed in 1962 by the American Law Institute, suggested as a model to states revising and overhauling their penal laws. Many provisions of the Model Penal Code have been adopted in various states.

Model Sentencing Act   A sentencing proposal drawn up in 1963 by the Advisory Council of Judges of the National Council on Crime and Delinquency.

modus operandi   The criminal "signature" method of crime investigation; it involves the analysis of crimes with a view toward identifying patterns associated with specific habitual offenders.

morals squad   *See* VICE SQUAD.

Mosaic Code   The law of the Old Testament, particularly as expressed in the Ten Commandments, proscribing such actions as murder, adultery, stealing, and bearing false witness.

motion   An application for a court order or ruling, for example, a pretrial motion to suppress evidence or to dismiss an indictment, or a motion for a directed verdict of acquittal.

motive   The impulse, emotion, drive, or reason that impels the perpetrator to commit a crime; examples are profit, revenge, or elimination of a rival.

murder   The unlawful killing of another human being with malice aforethought, usually but not exclusively meaning an intention to kill.   *See also* HOMICIDE; MANSLAUGHTER.

murder, first-degree   The most serious and severely punishable crime of killing, usually defined as (1) premeditated, deliberate, and intentional; or (2) carried out while committing another felony.   *See also* HOMICIDE; MANSLAUGHTER.

murder, second-degree   Murder that is not premeditated but that is carried out with malice aforethought. The punishment for second-degree murder is less severe than that for first-degree murder.   *See also* HOMICIDE; MANSLAUGHTER.

Napoleonic Code   The code of laws adopted in France by the regime of Napoleon Bonaparte in 1810 and revised in 1819. The Napoleonic Code became the basis for the criminal code in most continental European and Latin American countries.

necessity   The defense of justification of an otherwise criminal act on the ground that the perpetrator needed to commit it because a greater evil would have ensued had he or she failed to do so. Thus, one could plead necessity if he or she committed arson to destroy official documents that would otherwise have fallen into the hands of a wartime enemy.

neglected child   A juvenile who lacks proper care and guardianship from his or her parent. Neglected children sometimes fall under the jurisdiction of the juvenile court and sometimes are legally designated as "dependent children."   *See also* DEPENDENT CHILD.

negligence, criminal   Conduct sufficiently careless to constitute the basis of a crime which results in death, injury, or damage to property, and which becomes subject to prosecution as a crime.

negligence, gross   An act or omission in which the responsible individual did not use the slightest care to avoid injury to another, but in which intent to harm was absent.   *See also* NEGLIGENTLY.

negligently (or negligence)   The lowest level of criminal culpability under the Model Penal Code and most penal codes. A person acts negligently if he or she should be aware, but is not, of a substantial and unjustifiable risk that some circumstance exists (for example, that certain property is stolen) or that some injury will result from his or her conduct. The risk must be of such a grave nature that his or her failure to perceive the risk constitutes a gross deviation from the standard of care one would expect of a reasonable person. Negligence constitutes so-called objective fault. The critical distinction between negligence and higher levels of criminal culpability, all of which involve so-called subjective fault, is that one who only acts negligently is punished simply for his or her failure to live up to an external standard of due care, rather than for personally possessing a culpable state of mind.   *See also* CULPABILITY; KNOWINGLY; MENS REA; PURPOSELY; RECKLESSLY.

neoclassicism   A trend in history of criminal justice and criminology that flourished in the early nineteenth century in Europe. It modified the views of the classical school of criminology by introducing the concepts of diminished criminal responsibility and less severe punishment because of the age or mental condition of the perpetrator.

no bill (or no true bill)   A phrase employed when a grand jury that has been presented with evidence against a suspect refuses to vote an indictment.

no-knock entry   Police procedure permitted in certain raids to avoid giving suspects time to destroy evidence, escape, or prepare to resist.

nolle prosequi ("to be unwilling to pursue")   Withdrawal of a prosecution by the prosecutor, before or during a trial.

nolo contendere ("I do not wish to contest")   Alternative plea to not guilty, acceptable in federal district and some state courts. If the defendant makes this plea he or she can be sentenced as if he or she had pleaded guilty, but the plea cannot be used as an admission in a subsequent civil action.

nonfeasance   Failure or refusal of a public officer to perform a duty or responsibility required of him or her by law.   *See also* MALFEASANCE; MISFEASANCE.

notice   A formal communication, as to the defendant in a lawsuit, advising him or her of what further action is intended.

notice of alibi   *See* ALIBI, NOTICE OF.

oath   A sworn statement having the effect of making the person swearing to it liable to prosecution for perjury if anything material stated therein is later shown to be deliberately false.

objection   A statement made in court by prosecutor or defense counsel, asking the judge not to permit a witness to answer a question, or if it is already answered, to note that the response is not acceptable because of violation of the rules of criminal procedure. In making the objection, a lawyer calls upon the judge to prevent a reply, to discontinue a line of interrogation, to strike a question or answer from the official record, to instruct the jury to ignore what has been said, or to make some other appropriate decision.

obscenity That which is deemed by law to be disgusting, vile, and offensive, at a specific time and in a given society. Obscenity often refers to the explicitly sexual, but can refer to the nonsexual as well.

obstruction of justice Interference by act of omission with the proper performance of a judicial act, for example, an arrest or a lawful search, by such means as destroying records or giving false information.

offender One who has been convicted of a criminal offense; unless specifically stated otherwise, he or she is presumed to be an adult. *See also* CRIMINAL.

offender, adult A person who has committed a crime and has been tried as an adult rather than as a juvenile; also, a person who, having reached a legally stated age of adulthood, is convicted of a crime.

offender, first A person who has been convicted for the first time and who therefore might be treated leniently. Although the accused may have committed previous crimes, he or she is officially categorized as a first offender if he or she has not been convicted previously.

offender, youthful A term applied to a youth in late adolescence or early adulthood who has been convicted of a crime. Youthful offenders are sometimes deemed eligible for community supervision or segregated incarceration, often with rehabilitation programs not offered to older offenders. Successful completion of these programs can in some instances expunge the conviction of the youthful offender if he or she does not recidivate. The eligibility age for youthful-offender status differs from one jurisdiction to another. *See also* JUVENILE DELINQUENT.

offense An act in violation of the law, sometimes used to describe a violation less serious than a crime. *See also* INFRACTION.

omission A failure to act when there is a duty to act. Nonperformance of an act may constitute a specific statutory crime of omission (for example, failure to file income-tax returns), or it may serve as a basis for prosecution for an ordinary crime, such as criminal homicide, when nonperformance of a civil duty exists (for example, a parent's duty to protect his or her child), and harm ensues that could have been avoided by performance of the duty.

ordinance A statute enacted by a county, municipal government, or township, as distinct from laws enacted by federal or state legislative bodies.

organized crime (also called the **syndicate**) An ongoing, coordinated conspiracy, characterized by hierarchy and division of labor, and involving a relatively large number of criminals. Organized crime is in partial or total control of numerous illegal activities, such as usury, gambling, prostitution, pornography, drug traffic, extortion, and hijacking. It also controls many legal enterprises, such as restaurants and trucking firms, which are apparently used to conceal the sources of illegally obtained money and to accomplish other criminal purposes. *See also* CRIME FAMILY; MAFIA; MOB.

original jurisdiction The authority of a court to try a case at its beginning; this is the first court to which the case is brought for trial.

overcriminalization Passage of legislation making marginal acts criminal and resulting in more criminal laws than can be enforced or are necessary for the protection of society and the safety of life and property.

overcharging An indictment, information, or complaint that includes charges either more serious than are warranted by the criminal event, or more numerous, so as to place pressure on a defendant to plea bargain. *See also* GRAND JURY.

overt act An open act in furtherance of criminality (as opposed to an idea, a plan, or an omission) that may be necessary for a conviction of an uncompleted effort, a conspiracy, or treason.

pardon An act of clemency in which a crime allegedly committed by one found guilty is forgiven. A full pardon acts to annul a guilty verdict, restoring a defendant to a position of not having been convicted and of not being triable again for the same offense because of double jeopardy protection. A limited pardon frees the offender from further punishment but not from the conviction. A conditional pardon goes into effect only when a stated condition (conditions) is fulfilled. It can be revoked if the beneficiary violates the condition(s).

parens patriae ("parent of the country") Governmental assumption (in the United States, assumed by the states) of the responsibility of caring for children who are neglected, delinquent, or without competent parents.

parole The status of an offender conditionally released from a correctional institution before completion of his maximum prison sentence. A paroled offender is placed under supervision of an authorized agency and subjected to restrictions, violation of which may result in revocation of parole. *See also* CORRECTIONS, COMMUNITY; PROBATION; RELEASE, CONDITIONAL.

parole, revocation of Termination of parole and remand to prison for violation of the terms of a parole, usually, but not necessarily, for conviction of a new felony.

parole violation An act of a parolee (paroled offender) that violates the conditions of the parole and may result in its revocation.

parricide The killing of one's father, mother, or other close relative.

Part I Offenses Eight crimes whose incidence is reported by the F.B.I. in its annual Uniform Crime Reports as "most serious." These crimes are murder and non-negligent homicide, forcible rape, robbery, aggravated assault, burglary, motor vehicle theft, arson, and larceny-theft. These formerly were called "index" offenses.

Part II Offenses   Crimes defined by the F.B.I. Uniform Crime Reports as "less serious," and including most offenses other than Part I offenses and traffic offenses, such as simple assault, fraud, embezzlement, drug offenses, and juvenile status offenses.

particulars   *See* BILL OF PARTICULARS.

party-dominated process   A classical aspect of the adversary system that gives to the judge the passive role of umpire and allows the adversaries (prosecution and defense) to be the major forces in the trial. In a party-dominated process, the judge cannot initiate or continue proceedings; the parties control the factual, and to a large extent the legal, boundaries of a case.

patricide   The killing of one's father.

peculation   Embezzlement, or any wrongful or illegal appropriation of money or property assigned to one's care.

penal code   The criminal code of a jurisdiction. It defines criminal conduct and defenses thereto, and determines the punishment to be imposed.

penal colony   An area colonized in part or entirely by transported criminals and their guards and administrators.   *See also* PENAL SETTLEMENT; TRANSPORTATION.

penal sanction   *See* PENALTY.

penal servitude   Punishment for a crime by imprisonment with involuntary (usually hard) labor.

penal settlement   An area, usually in an overseas colony or a remote section of a country, to which prisoners were (or are) consigned and employed at arduous labor.   *See also* PENAL COLONY; TRANSPORTATION.

penalty (criminal sanction; legal penalty; sanction)   The punishment authorized by law for committing a specific offense within a jurisdiction.   *See also* PUNISHMENT.

penitentiary   A prison originally intended to keep the inmates in isolation both from society and one another, so that they could meditate on their evil past and be penitent. Later the word became synonymous with *prison*.   *See also* PRISON; REFORMATORY.

penology   The scientific study of corrections, including the justifications, rationalizations, theories, and aims of punishments, the types of punishment, and their effectiveness.

perjury   The act of deliberately testifying falsely, under oath, about a material fact.

personal recognizance   *See* RELEASE ON OWN RECOGNIZANCE.

Person in Need of Supervision (PINS)   One of several terms used to refer to juveniles who commit status offenses that would not be crimes if committed by adults, such as truancy, runaway, and incorrigibility.

petition   A formal request to an executive or judicial officer to perform some act within his or her power or authority, as to pardon, commute, reprieve, or adjudicate as delinquent.

piracy   The forcible seizure of a seagoing vessel. An authorized seizure in wartime is not piracy but an act of war. In recent decades, piracy has also come to be used to describe the seizure of aircraft in the air (skyjacking).

Piso's justice   A punishment that is legally and technically justifiable but not morally defensible.

plea   A defendant's formal answer in court to the charges brought against him or her in a complaint, information, or indictment.   *See also* NOLO CONTENDERE; PLEA OF NOT GUILTY.

plea, conditional   A plea of guilty or nolo contendere which is entered on the understanding that the defendant will still be allowed to appeal a prior adverse ruling which otherwise would be forfeited by entry of the plea (for example, a pretrial suppression motion).

plea, slow   A very short trial on stipulated evidence following the defendant's plea of not guilty, a procedure sometimes utilized to preserve for appeal issues which would be forfeited by a guilty plea.

plea bargaining (plea negotiating)   Discussions between the prosecutor and the defense concerning the giving of some apparent concession (a lower sentence, a reduction in the seriousness of the charge, or a reduction in the number of charges) to the defendant in exchange for his or her waiver of trial and plea of guilty.

plea of not guilty   A statement to a court by the defendant that he or she has rejected the alternative of a guilty plea (or, if available, a plea of nolo contendere) and instead wishes to go to trial and put the prosecution to its proof. Many defendants initially plead not guilty but later (usually after engaging in plea bargaining) change their pleas to guilty.

pleasure-pain principle   The utilitarian concept that people endeavor to maximize pleasure (profit) and minimize pain (loss); making the anticipated penalty greater than the expected gain is believed to deter rational people from committing crimes.   *See also* CLASSICAL SCHOOL.

police officer (law enforcement officer; policeman)   A government officer authorized to use physical force in order to maintain public order and safety; to prevent, detect, and investigate crime; and to apprehend and arrest suspected offenders.

police power   The right of state and local governments to legislate constraints on private rights for the purpose of ensuring the health, safety, morale, and general welfare of the citizenry.

police prosecution   System common in the United Kingdom and Ireland in which certain crimes are prosecuted by high-ranking police officers rather than by appointed or elected prosecutors.

polygraph   *See* LIE DETECTOR.

poor laws   Legislation passed in England beginning in the sixteenth century that gave local parishes the responsibility of supporting the needy. As a consequence of the laws, persons unable to work were confined to their own locality, and vagrants and wanderers were punished and returned to their place of origin.

positivist school (of criminology)   A major trend in criminological theory that flourished from the mid-nineteenth century through the early twentieth century. It had a highly determinist view of human behavior.   *See also* CLASSICAL SCHOOL; LOMBROSIAN.

possession   Custody and control over money or property assigned to one's care.   *See also* CRIMINAL POSSESSION.

post-conviction proceedings (post-conviction remedies)   Appeal of a conviction or a sentence; collateral attack by habeas corpus or statutory remedy; request for commutation, pardon, reprieve, or stay of execution.

postmortem examination   An autopsy (examination performed upon a body) conducted in order to determine the cause of death.

post-release care   Aftercare or parole supervision and support of prisoners discharged into the community before the expiration of their maximum terms.

predatory crime   Illegal activity, usually but not necessarily property crime, in which the offender preys upon, exploits, attacks, or in another way takes advantage of the victim.   *See also* CRIMES AGAINST PROPERTY.

predisposition report   Report given to the juvenile court judge by a probation or parole officer, prior to the disposition hearing, which describes the background of the juvenile and the circumstances of the offense and concludes with a recommendation about the disposition of the case. Comparable to the presentence investigation report (PSI) in criminal court.

prehearing investigation   An investigation made by a probation officer before the adjudication of a minor in a juvenile court. Its aim is to inform the judge of the given juvenile's background, the motivation for his or her behavior, and any other information that might be useful in judicial procedure.

preponderance of the evidence   The greater weight of the evidence presented by one side in an adversary proceeding. In a civil suit, a case is supposed to be decided by a fair preponderance of the credible evidence. In a criminal proceeding this is insufficient, and a defendant can be found guilty only if the guilt is established beyond a reasonable doubt.   *See also* ADVERSARY SYSTEM.

prerelease period   The period just before release from a penal institution, during which a specially developed program of reentry orientation is given in some institutions to lessen the difficulties of transition.

presentence report (presentence investigation report; PSI)   A statement drawn up by a probation officer that gives background information on an offender, including prior criminal record, social and personal history, results of interviews, and recommendations to the judge as to the sentence to be imposed. In the federal system and many state systems, the initial calculation of the appropriate sentencing range under the applicable sentencing guidelines is done by a probation officer in a presentence report.

presentment   A charge against an accused, issued by a grand jury. When such a charge is made by a grand jury upon submission of evidence by the prosecutor, it is known as an indictment; when made without request or submission of evidence by the prosecutor, it is a presentment.

presumption of innocence   The principle that in a criminal case a defendant is innocent unless and until proved guilty. The burden of proof is always on the prosecution to demonstrate guilt, and never upon the defendant to demonstrate innocence.

pretrial identification proceeding   Any proceeding, such as a lineup, photographic display, or individual confrontation, occurring prior to a trial, at which witnesses are called to identify an accused.

pretrial motion   Request made to the court before a trial that may cover such issues as change of venue, admissibility of a confession into evidence, ruling on privileged communication, or anything that might be material to the ensuing trial.

pretrial publicity   Information disseminated about a crime, a defendant, or a forthcoming trial that is sometimes claimed by the defense to be inordinate, prejudicial, and precluding a fair trial. It is often used by the defense in its request that the trial be continued until a later date or that the place of trial be moved (motion for a change of venue).

prevalence of crime   Criminality measured in a given population during a certain period of time. The prevalence of juvenile delinquency in a city or state in 1995, for example, refers to the number of juveniles in that area in 1995 who have ever been adjudicated delinquent, relative to the total number of juveniles in the city or state at that time.   *See also* INCIDENCE OF CRIME.

prima facie ("at first view")   So far as can be judged by first appearance and without hearing further evidence.

principal   A perpetrator of a crime, as distinguished from an accessory; one who does the acts constituting the crime, in contrast to one whose acts take the form of helping or influencing another to commit a crime (an accessory or accomplice).

prior restraint   A court of other government order forbidding or censoring printed matter before publication. Such restraints are almost never permitted under the First Amendment to the Constitution.

prison (adult correctional institution; penitentiary)   A correctional facility having custodial authority over adults sentenced to more than one year; any federal or state penal institution for confinement of adult felons.   *See also* JAIL; PENITENTIARY.

prisoner   A person confined in a prison; any inmate being held under color of law, including in a jail; also, one who is being transported or who is in court, while under the supervision of correctional officers.

prisoners' rights   Any rights to which convicts are entitled by law, usually as interpreted by the courts, such as freedom from cruel and unusual punishment, the right to receive visitors, or the right to prepare legal appeals.

prison reform   *See* CORRECTIONAL REFORM.

privilege A right or protection granted to persons in special statuses, and not extended to others. Privileges may be held by the defendant, defense counsel, the judge, the spouse of the accused, and others. *See also* PRIVILEGED COMMUNICATION; SELF-INCRIMINATION.

privilege, absolute A prohibition against prosecution for criminal libel, regardless of malice, generally limited to official participation in the governmental process. This prohibition is based on the belief that the public benefits by having officials at liberty to exercise their function with independence and without fear of litigation. *See also* LIBEL; PRIVILEGE, CONDITIONAL.

privilege, conditional A defense in criminal libel which contends that the defendant has made the allegedly libelous statement in order to fulfill a public or private duty to speak.

privilege against self-incrimination *See* SELF-INCRIMINATION.

privileged communication Information that may not be revealed in evidence over the objection of the person holding the privilege because it was communicated in the course of a special relationship, such as husband-wife, physician-patient, lawyer-client, or clergyman-penitent. *See also* INFORMATION, CONFIDENTIAL.

proactive policing Police work where the police take the initiative rather than responding to calls by the public. For example, in consensual crimes such as prostitution and drug dealing, most police work is proactive because no victim calls the police. *See also* REACTIVE POLICING.

probable cause Reasonable grounds to believe that items legitimately sought are located on a premises, thus justifying a search; or that a person has committed a crime, thus justifying an arrest or an indictment.

probation Supervision of a convicted offender within the community, imposed by the sentencing judge in lieu of a prison term (but sometimes combined with a jail term). Violation of the conditions of probation, or the commission of another crime, can result in revocation of probation and in confinement. *See also* CORRECTIONS, COMMUNITY; PAROLE.

probation officer One who is in charge of overseeing probationers (persons on probation).

problem-oriented policing Police work that addresses an entire problem situation rather than attempts to solve particular crimes that have occurred within that situation. For example, rather than focusing on the arrest of particular prostitutes or particular drug dealers, police may attempt to deal with the entire neighborhood situation that allows prostitutes and drug dealers to work the streets.

property crime *See* CRIMES AGAINST PROPERTY.

property theft Larceny, embezzlement, receiving and selling of stolen goods, or other criminal acts that fall into the category of thievery and involve property. Most theft is property theft (an exception is theft of services), and most crimes against property are thefts (exceptions are vandalism and arson). *See also* CRIMES AGAINST PROPERTY.

pro se ("on behalf of self") Acting as counsel for oneself, with or without co-counsel.

prosecution In a criminal case, the side (the state or federal government) that conducts the proceedings against the accused and attempts to establish the guilt of the defendant.

prosecution, mandatory A system of criminal procedure that limits the prosecutor's discretion not to prosecute. In Germany, for example, the prosecutor cannot decline to prosecute serious crimes if there is enough evidence to convict, and a prosecutor so deciding must notify the complainant, who may appeal. *See also* DISCRETION.

prosecution, private A system prevailing in England and some continental countries that allows the victim of a crime to initiate and conduct criminal proceedings. In practice, private prosecution is rare in most of these countries.

prosecutor (prosecuting attorney) An attorney, appointed or elected, charged with the official duty of initiating and maintaining criminal proceedings on behalf of the government (the people) against those accused of committing crimes.

prosecutorial discretion *See* DISCRETION.

prosecutorial waiver *See* CONCURRENT JURISDICTION.

psychopath (sociopath) A person who is not insane but who has a severe mental or personality disorder. The psychopath is deficient in capacity to feel guilt, accept love, and empathize with others.

public defender Legal counsel designated and reimbursed by the government and assigned to the defense of indigents in criminal cases. *See also* LEGAL AID.

punishment Any pain or deprivation imposed on a person by sentence of a court or by a lawful administrative authority (such as a prison disciplinary officer) because that person has been judged guilty of a violation of the law. *See also* PENALTY.

punishment, corporal Physical pain inflicted as punishment for a crime or offense, such as flogging.

punishment, cruel and unusual A phrase used in the Eighth Amendment to the United States Constitution but not defined with specificity by the Supreme Court; it generally refers to punishment for a given offense that is inflicted only rarely, is excessively brutal, and is highly disproportionate to what is deserved for the crime committed.

purposely A person acts purposely with respect to a result if his conscious object is to cause such a result. The highest level of culpability under the Model Penal Code. *See also* CULPABILITY; KNOWINGLY; MENS REA; NEGLIGENTLY; RECKLESSLY.

pyromania Psychoanalytic and popular term for a compulsive urge to set fires; in criminology, usually referred to as pathological firesetting.

quash To dismiss a charge or indictment.

racket An illegitimate enterprise made possible by coercion, threat, or bribery; most commonly extortion or fraud, but also various illegal or forced sales.

racketeering Obtaining money or other valuables by fraud, illegal use of political advantage, or threat of violence. The term is often associated with activities of organized crime.

rape   The traditional offense of rape required proof of five elements: penetration, force, resistance, non-consent, and a culpable state of mind (mens rea). Some states have abandoned the term "rape" and use instead a gender-neutral term, such as "sexual battery" or "sexual assault."   *See also* ASSAULT, SEXUAL; RAPE, STATUTORY.

rape, statutory   Consensual sexual intercourse between a male and a female who is under the age of consent. In some jurisdictions, the term also applies to consensual sexual intercourse between a custodian and a patient or a custodian and an inmate.

rape trauma syndrome   The behavioral, somatic, and psychological reactions of rape and attempted rape victims. The syndrome evidence has been offered in court for two primary reasons: (1) to prove lack of consent by the alleged victim, and (2) to explain post-incident conduct by the victim, such as delayed reporting of the incident, that the jury might perceive as inconsistent with the claim of rape.   *See also* RAPE.

reactive policing   Police activity that responds to a public request, such as the report of a crime by a victim or witness. Most policing is reactive.   *See also* PROACTIVE POLICING.

reasonable doubt   Lack of certainty as to the truth of a charge; belief that all other reasonable hypotheses, except that the defendant is guilty as charged, cannot be excluded. In a criminal case, a defendant can be found guilty only when no reasonable doubt exists in the minds of the jurors (or judge or judges, in a bench trial). That is, the case against the accused must be established beyond a reasonable doubt to justify a verdict of guilty.

reasonable suspicion   The degree of articulable suspicion, although short of the probable cause, needed to make a custodial arrest, which will suffice to justify the brief stopping of a person for investigation of pending, ongoing, or past criminal conduct or to frisk for weapons.

rebuttal   The introduction of evidence contradicting or refuting adverse testimony; the effort to demonstrate that the adversary's witnesses are mistaken or lack credibility. The rebuttal or rebuttal case is also the point in a trial at which such contradicting testimony is introduced.

recidivist (repeater)   A habitual or career criminal; one who, having been convicted and punished for a crime, commits the same or another offense.

recklessly (or reckless)   The third highest level of culpability under the Model Penal Code. A person acts recklessly if he or she consciously disregards a substantial and unjustifiable risk that some circumstance exists (for example, that certain property is stolen) or that some injury will result from his or her conduct. The risk must be of such as grave nature that disregard of the risk constitutes a gross deviation from the standard of care one would expect of a reasonable person. The narrow distinction between negligence and reckless-ness is that the risk-taking in the latter case, but not the former, is advertent. The narrow distinction between knowledge and recklessness lies in the probability of the circumstance existing or harm occurring—practical certainty versus substantial risk—of which the person is aware.   *See also* CULPABILITY; KNOWINGLY; MENS REA; PURPOSELY; NEGLIGENTLY.

recognizance   *See* RELEASE ON OWN RECOGNIZANCE.

reformatory   A correctional facility that was original-ly conceived of as a place where offenders would re-form or change their behavior, attitudes, and values. Nowadays, the term usually refers to juvenile institutions.   *See also* DETENTION CENTER, JUVENILE; INSTITU-TION, JUVENILE.

regulatory crime   A crime that violates an order of a federal or state regulatory agency, for example, the Food and Drug Administration or the Securities and Exchange Commission.   *See also* WHITE-COLLAR CRIME.

rehabilitation   The change of an offender's behavior, mental state, and values in such a way that he or she ceases committing criminal acts.

release   Conditional, temporary, or permanent discharge from custody.

release, conditional   Release of a convicted prisoner before termination of his or her maximum sentence, on condition that he or she live in the community according to specified rules and under the supervision of a parole officer.   *See also* PAROLE.

release, study (study furlough)   A program in which a convict is allowed to leave jail or prison for several hours at a time in order to attend classes and continue his education at a nearby college or technical institution.   *See also* RELEASE, WORK.

release, unconditional   Freedom after arrest or confinement without further correctional supervision, either because of dismissal of charges, a finding of not guilty, an executive order (as a pardon), or because a complete sentence has been served.   *See also* PAROLE; PROBATION.

release, work (work furlough)   A program that permits an incarcerated offender to leave the place of confinement during working hours, usually on weekdays, in order to work in a place of employment outside the prison. Work release is generally restricted to trusted and nonviolent offenders who are being readied for discharge.   *See also* SENTENCE, SPLIT.

release on own recognizance (ROR)   Pretrial release, or release pending sentencing or pending appeal from a guilty verdict, without bail or bond, on the promise of the accused that he or she will return to court or custody when so ordered.

remand   To send back, as when a higher court re-mands a case to a lower one for a new trial, resentencing, or different handling of an issue; or when a court remands to custody one who has been free.

rendition   Term commonly used for extradition of a person from one state to another.

repeater   *See* RECIDIVIST.

reprieve   A stay of execution of sentence.

residential treatment center A residence in which offenders are temporarily living, under conditions less confining than in a jail or prison, and where the major emphasis is on therapy.

res judicata; res adjudicata ("judged matter") A final judgment by a court having jurisdiction that is conclusive and binding on the litigating parties in any further proceedings involving the same matter that brought the case to court in the first instance.

responsibility (criminal responsibility) Duty, obligation, and accountability for a crime because the perpetrator is not a child and has the mental ability to distinguish right from wrong and to conform to the requirements of the law. *See also* CULPABILITY; EXCUSE; INSANITY; MENS REA.

restitution, community (community or compensatory service) Public work done for the community, in lieu of or in addition to other sanctions, as a punishment for crime or to repair public property damaged by the offender. *See also* RESTORATIVE JUSTICE.

restitution, victim An offender's restoring of money or other stolen valuables to the victim; his or her performing of any acts that may help restore the victim to the status prevailing before the crime. This may be done voluntarily, perhaps in hopes of obtaining a more lenient sentence, or it may be ordered by a court as part of a sentence or as a condition of probation. Restitution does not necessarily relieve an accused of the necessity of standing trial and facing criminal sanctions, but it often does so in practice, or it acts to placate a complainant and to reduce the severity of a sentence. *See also* RESTORATIVE JUSTICE.

restorative justice A sentence, juvenile disposition, or alternative to prosecution which emphasizes repairing the harm caused by the offense, rather than punishment for its own sake (retribution) or to prevent further crimes (however, the latter is also a goal of some restorative justice programs, particularly those which seek to identify and address underlying problems or conflicts which led to the offense). Examples of restorative justice measures include restitution and victim-offender mediation. *See also* RESTITUTION, COMMUNITY; RESTITUTION, VICTIM; VICTIM-OFFENDER MEDIATION.

restraint of trade Illegal action taken to prevent the free flow of goods in a market economy. Restraint of trade may take such forms as the holding back of improved products, the monopolistic control of raw materials, or agreement among corporations to fix prices and not to compete in given areas.

retentionist One who favors the retention or reinstitution of the death penalty, in contrast to the abolitionist, who favors its abolition.

retribution The just-deserts theory of punishment, which maintains that an offender should suffer to the extent deserved by the seriousness of the crime and the offender's culpability in committing the crime.

revenge A motive for punishment characterized by the urge to retaliate against the offender.

revolving-door justice The frequent sentencing of the same offender to short terms for such minor offenses as prostitution and public drunkenness. The offender adheres to the same pattern of behavior and goes in and out of confinement regularly.

right to counsel A right guaranteed by the Sixth Amendment to the Constitution, as interpreted by the Supreme Court, permitting or necessitating representation by counsel at trial and other critical stages of the criminal process, and requiring in most instances that indigent defendants be provided with counsel for that purpose.

riot A public disturbance created by a large number of persons engaging in tumultuous conduct out of control of the authorities, thereby causing risk of violence, injury to persons or property, or general public alarm.

robbery A theft from the person, attempted or carried out by the use or threat of bodily force, including the use or threatened use of a deadly or dangerous weapon such as a gun, knife, or blunt instrument.

role morality The theory that a professional role, like that of lawyer, morally requires or permits a person to do or fail to do something that would be immoral for someone not in such a professional role. For example, the theory of role morality explains why State Bars generally require lawyers to keep the secrets of their criminal defendant clients, even when ordinary people would have a moral obligation to reveal such secrets if they knew of them.

rule of strict construction (or rule of lenity) The requirement that ambiguous statutory language be construed narrowly in favor of the defendant; generally held by courts to be applicable to criminal statutes.

runaway A juvenile who leaves home without parental permission. *See also* STATUS OFFENSE.

runaway grand jury *See* GRAND JURY, RUNAWAY.

sanction (criminal sanction) *See* PENALTY.

scam Organized undercover police attempts to identify and apprehend persons engaging in a variety of crimes; also, such a crime itself, particularly a confidence game. *See also* ENTRAPMENT; STING.

Scotch verdict *See* VERDICT, SCOTCH.

Scotland Yard The popular name for the headquarters (since 1829) of the London Metropolitan Police. The office, originally located in a building at Whitehall Place, took its name from the building's back premises, Scotland Yard, through which the public had access to the building itself. The Metropolitan Police Office is now located on Victoria Street.

search and seizure Intrusion by government agents upon a justified expectation of privacy, and the assertion of control by such agents over a person, place, or thing. Examples include the entry and search of a home or the arrest and search of a person. *See also* EXCLUSIONARY RULE.

search warrant A written order authorizing the search of a designated premises or property and the seizure of specified items as possible evidence.

Secret Service A federal law enforcement agency that has primary responsibility for guarding the president of the United States and other high-ranking federal officials.

sedition An attempt, short of treason, to excite hostility against a sovereign government among its own citizens or other residents under its jurisdiction. *See also* LIBEL, SEDITIOUS.

self-defense and defense of others Defenses to a charge of criminal conduct in which the defendant concedes the transgression of a norm or statute against violence (e.g., assault or homicide), but maintains that under the circumstances the use of force was either not wrongful (justification) or was wrongful, but it would be unfair to impose punishment (excuse). Either as a justification or as an excuse, the defendant is completely exonerated. In contrast, "imperfect" or "incomplete" self-defense, where a significant element of the defense is absent, mitigates or reduces the charge, for example, from murder to manslaughter. *See also* EXCUSE; JUSTIFICATION.

self-incrimination Evidence presented, or testimony or other statements given, by a defendant or suspect, hurtful to himself and tending to indicate his guilt. In Anglo-American law and under the Fifth Amendment, involuntary self-incrimination is banned. *See also* ADMISSION; CONFESSION.

self-report studies Investigations of delinquency, criminality, and deviant behavior by means of questionnaires in which persons (who usually remain anonymous) are asked to indicate the nature, extent, and frequency of their illegal and deviant activities in the past.

self-representation *See* PRO SE.

sentence Any punishment meted out to a defendant who has been found guilty, pleaded guilty, or pleaded nolo contendere.

sentence, commutation of An act of clemency in which a sentence of death is changed to a term in prison, or in which a prison sentence is lessened, sometimes to time already served, in order to permit the convict's release without delay.

sentence, deferred A penalty whose imposition is not disclosed or imposed until a later time. A sentence may be deferred, for example, pending preparation of a presentence investigation report.

sentence, definite (fixed sentence; flat sentence) A sentence to a fixed time of incarceration, as ninety days or five years, with no possibility of early release.

sentence, determinate A prison term for a fixed time, with no possibility of early release on parole, but usually with eligibility for good time credits (time off for good behavior).

sentence, indefinite Often used interchangeably with *indeterminate sentence*, but sometimes meaning a term with no maximum, for example, from one year to life.

sentence, indeterminate A sentence for a range of years, for example, between one and ten years, the time actually served being determined by the correctional or parole authorities.

sentence, mandatory (mandatory penalty) A punishment, generally in the form of life imprisonment or a specified lesser term in prison, set by law for one found guilty of a given crime. If a sentence is mandatory, the trial judge does not have the discretion to impose any other.

sentence, mandatory minimum A minimum prison term specified by law for one found guilty of a given crime. When such a penalty applies, the trial judge may have discretion to impose a longer prison term, but may not impose a shorter one.

sentence, split A term in jail (sometimes in prison) with weekend furloughs to be spent with family, or weekday furloughs so that the offender can continue to work at his or her regular job. The time spent outside of jail or prison does not count as time served toward completion of the sentence. This term is also used to describe a sentence combining a short, uninterrupted term in jail followed by a period of release on probation. *See also* RELEASE, STUDY; RELEASE, WORK.

sentence, stay of A postponement of the initiation of carrying out a sentence, generally pending further judicial or executive hearings or decisions, but without a change of the sentence. A stay of sentence may be for a specific period of time, or for an indefinite period until a further decision is reached. *See also* SENTENCE, SUSPENDED.

sentence, suspended (stayed sentence) A sentence, such as a fine or prison term, that is not carried out (executed), but that may later be carried out in whole or in part at the discretion of the court if, during a specified period of time, the offender commits another crime or otherwise violates conditions of release. Sometimes the sentencing court places an offender on probation or another form of release without specifying the fine or prison term which would be imposed in case of violation of the conditions of release. Such a decision is called a stay of imposition of sentence (as opposed to a stay of execution, or suspended sentence); in case of violation, the court cannot impose and execute a specific sentence without holding a full sentencing hearing (including the right to counsel).

sentences, concurrent Two or more sentences to be served simultaneously. This device effectively reduces the severity of a sentence, while also ensuring the state the right to continue confinement if a court of appeals should overturn the guilty verdict on one of the charges.

sentences, consecutive Two or more sentences to be served in succession in a correctional institution.

sentencing, differential Unequal penalties imposed on different persons for the same or similar crimes. The inequalities may reflect such legally irrelevant reasons as race or sex, or different sentencing policies among judges or jurisdictions. *See also* SENTENCING DISPARITY.

sentencing, discretionary The power of the sentencing judge to decide upon the nature and severity of a sentence to be imposed after a plea or a finding of guilt.   *See also* SENTENCE, MANDATORY.

sentencing, uniform   Equal sentences imposed for crimes of equal seriousness in the same relevant circumstances.   *See also* SENTENCING, DIFFERENTIAL.

sentencing council   A group of judges who meet on a more or less regular basis to discuss sentencing decisions in pending cases in order to make nonbinding recommendations to the trial judge. The latter is usually a member of the council.

sentencing disparity   Unwarranted, inappropriate, and hence unjust variation in punishment from one offender to another. Disparities can be identified by comparing sentencing practices of judges and jurisdictions or by correlating sentences to offender characteristics (such as race and gender), characteristics of the victim, or any other statistical analysis, preferably multivariate, that can reveal inequalities of punishments for comparable offenses or offenders.

sentencing guidelines   A system adopted voluntarily by judges or imposed by statute in the federal system and many states in order to structure sentencing discretion. Legislatively-imposed guidelines are usually developed and monitored by an independent, appointed statewide sentencing commission. Guidelines reforms are often combined with the abolition of parole release discretion; in such systems, the guidelines sentence includes recommendations as to whether a prison term should be imposed for a given offense, and if so, of what duration, with early release based only on credits for good conduct in prison. Legislated guidelines may be either voluntary or "presumptive." The latter are legally binding on the sentencing judge unless the judge "departs" because of unusual aggravating or mitigating circumstances, and such a departure (or any sentence, in some systems) is appealable.

sequester   To keep a jury in custodial supervision (usually in a hotel) during a trial so as to prevent contact with the public or press; also, to separate prospective witnesses so that they cannot influence one another's testimony.

severance   The act of separating the trials of two or more defendants or of two or more charges against a single defendant, rather than holding one trial at which the defendants or charges are tried together.

sex crime (sex offense)   Prohibited and legally punishable behavior such as rape, sodomy, or carnal abuse of children.

sex psychopath (sex deviate)   A catchall name for those who repeatedly and compulsively violate sex laws; generally regarded as a stigmatizing label with little precise and scientifically reliable and valid predictive implication.

shelter   A place providing temporary care or custody for juveniles, battered wives, rape victims, and others. Shelters may be for children or juveniles in need of supervision, persons charged with minor offenses, or persons held pending adjudication of their cases.   *See also* DETENTION CENTER.

shelter care facility   An unlocked and non-secure facility for temporarily housing juveniles who are awaiting adjudication or disposition in the juvenile court. *See also* DETENTION CENTER.

sheriff   The highest police officer in a county, having responsibilities for enforcing the law in unincorporated areas; for operating the county jail; in many cases for providing bailiffs and maintaining order in county courts; and for cooperating with city and state police in crime prevention and law enforcement.

shock probation   Sentencing offenders to a brief time in an institutional setting, such as a boot camp, followed by a period of time on probation.

social control   All the formal and informal mechanisms utilized in a society to ensure obedience to its laws, mores, and prevailing norms.

social factors   Possible nonheritable influences on behavior that reflect environmental sources, such as socioeconomic status.   *See also* BIOLOGICAL FACTORS; GENETIC FACTORS.

socialization   The process by which one learns the nature, values, and forms of behavior in a culture, subculture, or new group into which one has been placed.

sodomy   Any sexual penetration other than penile-vaginal; sometimes restricted to anal penetration of male or female. In some jurisdictions the word is used to describe oral-genital relations, bestiality, and other sexual activities.

solicitation (incitement)   An attempt to persuade another to commit a crime that the solicitor desires and intends to have committed.

solicitor   In the United Kingdom and the British Commonwealth countries, a lawyer who handles wills, contracts, and property transactions, and who prepares cases for presentation in court by a barrister. *See also* COUNSEL.

speedy trial   A trial without unnecessary delay. A speedy trial is guaranteed by the Sixth Amendment to the United States Constitution and by federal and state statutes and is intended to protect an accused from long pretrial detention or from an interminable period of living under the shadow of charges not adjudicated.

standard of review   The amount of deference given by a reviewing court to the determinations of a lower court. Generally, factual determinations are reviewed deferentially on appeal, while legal determinations are reviewed *de novo*, or without deference.

Star Chamber   A seventeenth-century English administrative court with criminal jurisdiction. The term is now used pejoratively to denote court proceedings held in camera (without access by public or press) and without a publicly available transcript or record.

stare decisis ("to stand by decided matters")   Law by precedent, in which previous decisions and rulings are guides to be followed by courts in analogous cases.

state's evidence   Testimony by a codefendant, co-conspirator, or accomplice in a crime, against the defendant and for the prosecution. By turning state's evidence, a codefendant usually obtains leniency, if not complete dismissal of charges, and often requires governmental protection in a witness relocation program.

status offense An act declared by statute to be an offense when committed by a juvenile but not when committed by an adult. Examples are truancy, running away from home, age-specific curfew violation, sexual activity, or drinking of alcoholic beverages in a public place.

statute A duly enacted law, code, or ordinance, passed by an authorized legislative body and approved by the chief executive of the jurisdiction or passed over his veto.

stay A stoppage of a trial or other proceedings, by court order.

steal To commit an act of larceny, theft, or robbery; to take, without permission and legal authorization, anything to which one does not have title.

stigma An invidious or pejorative label that redounds to the disadvantage of the person so labeled.

sting A covert operation in which detectives and other officers of the law pose as criminals in order to obtain information, gather evidence, and make arrests of persons engaging in criminal activity. *See also* ENTRAPMENT; SCAM; SOLICITATION.

street patrol Supervision of the streets and neighborhoods by police, in patrol cars or on foot.

strict construction *See* RULE OF STRICT CONSTRUCTION.

strict liability The concept that one can be held responsible for some acts without the necessity of proving mens rea or blame, fault, or negligence. For example, the prosecution of a corporate executive for the adulteration of his products by careless employees, without his knowledge or consent, would constitute strict liability.

subculture A way of life of a group of considerable size that differs in some essential respects from the larger or dominant culture of the society as a whole. There are various types of subcultures, such as ethnic or criminal; it has been suggested that youth gangs, for example, constitute a subculture.

subculture of violence A way of life attributed to large sectors of the lower social classes. In it there is much dependence on force or the threat of force to establish identity and gain status. The subculture of violence may lead to criminality as a method of problem-solving.

subornation Secret enticement or encouragement; the term is generally used to describe efforts aimed at inducing another to commit perjury. *See also* SOLICITATION.

subpoena A written order demanding that a witness appear in a given court at a specified time to testify, or to bring specified material to court. *See also* BENCH WARRANT; SUMMONS.

subpoena duces tecum ("under penalty you shall bring with you") A court order requesting that a person appear and bring all documents and papers that might affect the outcome of a legal proceeding.

substantive criminal law Those sections of penal codes and other legislation that define crimes and prescribe punishments, as distinguished from procedural criminal law, which is concerned with rules governing the adjudication of the guilt or innocence of an accused.

suggestive Suggesting a particular answer or result; a term often used to challenge the fairness of identification procedures (i.e., "the lineup was suggestive") or the testimony of child witnesses (i.e., "the social worker's interview of the child was suggestive").

summons An order issued by a police officer (after or in lieu of arrest), or by an officer of a court, to appear in court at a given time. The summons may be an order to a suspect, defendant, witness, or juror. *See also* CITATION; SUBPOENA.

supreme court Usually the highest appellate court in a state system, but also used in some jurisdictions (as New York) to describe a trial court that hears felony cases.

Supreme Court of the United States The highest court (court of last resort) in the United States, consisting of nine Justices appointed for life. The Supreme Court has ultimate jurisdiction for deciding the constitutionality of all state and federal laws and for interpreting the Constitution and federal statutes.

suspect One who is under investigation or interrogation as a likely perpetrator of a crime but who has not yet been formally charged or placed under arrest.

SWAT (Special Weapons and Tactics teams) Special units in police departments that are trained and equipped to deal with situations of great public danger.

syndicate *See* ORGANIZED CRIME.

talesman One who is summoned to be added to a jury in order to compensate for a deficient number; by extension, any member of a panel from which a jury is to be chosen. *See also* JUROR, ALTERNATE.

team policing A term associated with community policing, in which there is group responsibility for managing crime in an area.

testimony Evidence offered in a trial by a witness, under oath.

theft *See* LARCENY.

time served The total period spent in confinement for a given offense or on a given charge, usually computed as time spent both before and after sentencing. In some instances, when persons are held without bail pending trial, the entire sentence is to time already served, thus permitting immediate discharge.

tort A noncriminal wrong or injury, resulting from a breach of legal duty, for which one can be sued for damages or an injunction.

training school A juvenile correctional facility, so named because it was originally intended to be not only a place of confinement but also a facility where youths would be given vocational and occupational training. *See also* DETENTION CENTER, JUVENILE; INSTITUTION, JUVENILE.

transcript   A verbatim record of the proceedings of a trial or ancillary proceedings, required for purposes of possible appeal.

transnational crime   Illegal activity involving more than one sovereign nation, or in which national borders are crossed, as in organized crime, international terrorism, smuggling of drugs, and illegal traffic in armaments.

transportation   The banishing or exiling of convicts to distant penal settlements. Prisoners were transported by czarist Russia to Siberia, by France to Devil's Island, and by England to Georgia, Australia, New Zealand, and Van Diemen's Land (Tasmania). *See also* PENAL COLONY.

trespass   Intrusion into or refusal to leave another's property, or interference with another's actual and peaceable possession of property.

trespass, criminal   Trespass which is made criminal. *See also* BREAKING AND ENTERING; BURGLARY.

trial   The proceedings which, in a criminal case, offer an opportunity for the prosecution and defense to present evidence and at which a verdict is rendered; such proceedings are distinct from the arraignment or the appeal.

trial, bench   A trial without a jury, in which the verdict is handed down by one or more judges.

trial, bifurcated (two-stage trial)   Procedure in capital cases (*see* CAPITAL CRIME) in which, after a finding of guilt by the trial jury, a second proceeding, before either the same or a new panel, is required to recommend or set the sentence.

trial, jury   A trial before a jury, which is the trier of fact and determiner of the guilt or lack thereof of the defendant.

trial, speedy   *See* SPEEDY TRIAL.

trial, summary   A judicial proceeding that is carried out rapidly and that dispenses with many formalities, such as an indictment or information. Summary trials are now used only for infractions and traffic offenses.

trial by ordeal   Proceedings held in ancient and medieval times at which the guilt or innocence of an accused was determined by his ability to withstand torture without confessing.

trial de novo   *See* DE NOVO.

tribal law   The rules of law, generally unwritten, in a tribe or tribelike subculture of a nation. These rules have official standing within the tribe so long as they do not conflict with those of the sovereign nation itself.

trier of fact   *See* FACT FINDER.

truant   A juvenile who does not attend school and has no valid excuse. *See also* STATUS OFFENSE.

true bill   An indictment by a grand jury, endorsing the charge of a prosecutor that a person has committed one or more crimes. *See also* NO BILL.

twin studies   Research that assesses the role of genetic and environmental influences on behavior by comparing the behaviors of two types of twins: twins who are genetically identical, or monozygotic (MZ), and twins who are not genetically identical, or dizygotic (DZ). To the extent that the similarity observed in MZ twins is greater than that in DZ twins, genetic influences may be implicated.

Uniform Code of Military Justice   The code of law for the armed forces of the United States.

Uniform Crime Reports (UCR)   A series of annual data compilations (*Crime in the United States*) published by the Federal Bureau of Investigation. The UCR include information on ages of offenders, geographic areas, and crime rates, along with other data. *See also* PART I OFFENSES; PART II OFFENSES.

United States Supreme Court   *See* SUPREME COURT OF THE UNITED STATES.

utilitarianism   An eighteenth- and nineteenth-century school of philosophy that thrived in England, according to which the rightness of conduct is determined by whether it maximizes pleasure and minimizes pain, and therefore produces the greatest happiness for the greatest number. Led by Jeremy Bentham (1748–1832), the utilitarian penologists were influenced by Cesare Beccaria. *See also* CLASSICAL SCHOOL; PLEASURE-PAIN PRINICIPLE.

utter   To declare that a counterfeit substance is genuine or to offer to pass it as genuine.

vacate a judgment   To reverse a verdict or other decision of a court; to render such a verdict or decision void.

vacate a plea   To withdraw or to render void a previously entered guilty plea.

vagueness doctrine (void for vagueness doctrine)   The principle that a statute written in an imprecise manner and capable of being invoked arbitrarily may violate due process and hence be unconstitutional, since it does not make clear what is and is not permitted.

venire   The panel of persons summoned to court from which a jury is selected.

venireman   One summoned to serve on a jury; a juror.

venue   The place in which a trial is held, usually the same locality as where the alleged crime occurred.

venue, change of   Removal of a trial from the location (venue) in which it would usually be tried to another location, to ensure a fair trial, avoid public pressures, select an unprejudiced jury, or for another reason stated in court.

verdict   The decision handed down by the jury in a trial; to be distinguished from the findings made by a judge at a trial without jury.

verdict, directed   A jury decision rendered by an order of a trial judge; in modern criminal procedure the directed verdict is always to acquit, although it may be limited to specific counts or specific defendants.

verdict, Scotch   A verdict rendered in Scotland, in which the charges against the defendant are declared not proved. A defendant is freed after a Scotch verdict, but he can be tried again, if new evidence is found, without violation of the double jeopardy rule.

vicarious liability Liability for the actions of another in the absence of fault, as where the person neither knew of, encouraged, nor assisted in the acts of the other. Usually imposed because of a person's general duty of supervision over another.

vice squad (morals squad) A police unit dealing with prostitution, pornography, indecent (sex-related) entertainments, and other offenses defined as detrimental to the morals of a community.

victim compensation Money or other assistance awarded by the state to the victim of a crime.

victimization survey A means of measuring the crime rate by interviewing selected samples of people regarding their victimization or that of members of their household, family, or business. Such surveys are used to correct errors in statistics on crimes known to the police by estimating from victim reports the frequency of various types of crimes, injuries, and losses, as well as to learn other information about the acts, the offenders, and the victims.

victimless crime (consensual crime) A violation of law committed by or between two or more adults with the voluntary consent of each participant, as in adultery, sodomy, or gambling.

victim-offender mediation A meeting or series of meetings between an offender and the victim or victims of the crime, which seeks to make offenders understand the impact the crime has had on the victim(s), and the ways in which the offender can repair the harms caused. Such meetings often also seek to help victims better understand why the offender committed the offense, while also encouraging acceptance of responsibility by the offender, victim and community restitution, victim forgiveness of the offender, victim-offender reconciliation, and measures which will help to prevent recurrence of the offense. Mediation can be imposed as a sentence, a juvenile disposition, or an alternative to adult or juvenile prosecution. *See also* RESTITUTION, COMMUNITY; RESTITUTION, VICTIM; RESTORATIVE JUSTICE.

victimology A subdiscipline of criminology that studies victims and victimization processes and techniques, victim-offender relationships, victim precipitation, victim vulnerability, restitution and compensation programs, and related subjects.

victim precipitation A criminal act in which the victim was responsible, at least in part, for initiating, encouraging, or escalating the altercation resulting in his or her own loss, injury, or death.

victim restitution *See* RESTITUTION, VICTIM.

victim-witness assistance program A program established in some jurisdictions to provide special services and support for victims, particularly of rape.

vigilantism Action taken by community, neighborhood, or other groups, without authorization by law, to frighten, contain, or take revenge on alleged, suspected, or would-be offenders.

violation An act contrary to law (such as failure to stop for a red light) but usually not serious enough to be punished or processed as a crime. In the United States, violations are generally contrary to local ordinances or to administrative codes (as the motor-vehicle and traffic code) rather than to state or federal penal codes. The word is also used to describe any lawbreaking act. *See also* INFRACTION; OFFENSE.

violence Physical force or its threat, directed against persons.

void for vagueness doctrine *See* VAGUENESS DOCTRINE.

voir dire ("to see and speak") The examination of prospective jurors to determine whether they are qualified to serve on a jury.

voluntariness The state of having autonomy over one's actions; it is allegedly diminished or negated by such conditions as physical duress, illness, hypnosis, or mental defect. *See also* EXCUSE; MENS REA.

waiver A voluntary relinquishment of one's rights, for example, the right to a trial by jury. Some rights may not be waived, such as the right not to suffer cruel and unusual punishment.

waiver of jurisdiction, juvenile The process by which a juvenile court judge relinquishes the jurisdiction of the juvenile court for a particular offense or offender, and thereby transfers that jurisdiction to the criminal court. That is, when juvenile court jurisdiction is waived, the juvenile will be tried in criminal court as an adult. *See also* CONCURRENT JURISDICTION; LEGISLATIVE EXCLUSION.

war crime An action ordered or authorized by leaders of a country engaged in a war, or carried out by its military personnel with or without such orders, that violates internationally accepted rules governing the conduct of war. War crimes include wanton killing of civilians; harsh treatment, torture, or killing of prisoners; and use of chemical and biological weapons banned by treaties and agreements.

warrant An order issued by a court and authorizing an arrest or a search. *See also* ARREST WARRANT; BENCH WARRANT; SEARCH WARRANT.

weapons charge Violation of local, state, or federal laws governing the carrying of weapons and the licensing requirements for the purchase, sale, or possession of a weapon.

white-collar crime Illegal activity committed by corporate executives or managers, people in high political office, or other members of the upper strata of society, particularly in the course of their occupational pursuits. Examples are bribery, price-fixing, environmental pollution, and consumer fraud.

wiretapping Surreptitious recording of telephone conversations. When this is done by the government without a court order it is illegal, and evidence obtained from an illegal wiretap is usually inadmissible in a criminal case. *See also* EAVESDROPPING.

witness Anyone called to testify by either side in a trial who is sworn in and who offers evidence deemed relevant to the case; also, one who has observed an event, such as a crime. *See also* EYEWITNESS.

witness, adverse A witness who is biased against or hostile to the party who has called him or her, and who therefore may be asked leading questions and cross-examined.

witness, alibi   Someone testifying in support of a defendant's alibi, usually claiming to have been with or to have observed the defendant in a place other than where the crime was committed at the time of its commission.

witness, character   A person of good repute brought to court by the defense to testify that, based on his or her knowledge of the defendant and the defendant's reputation in the community, it is unlikely that he or she would have committed the crime charged.

witness, expert   One who qualifies as specially knowledgeable in a scientific, technical, or professional field, as a psychiatrist, examiner of documents, or geologist, and who testifies in a case on an issue in which his special training, education, and experience are useful.

witness, protected   A government witness, usually in an organized-crime prosecution, who is provided with a new identity, financial assistance, and government protection against possible retaliation from those whose criminal acts he or she has revealed or against whom he or she has testified.

witness list   A list of all those intended to be called as witnesses by either side in a trial. It is usually demanded of the prosecution by the defense, so that counsel for the accused can prepare a case adequately and not be taken by surprise. In many jurisdictions the defense must furnish a list of alibi and expert witnesses it intends to call.

witness relocation program   A change of name, identity, and place of residence of a witness, usually a criminal who has turned state's evidence and assisted in the prosecution of an organized-crime figure, and who believes that he or she and his or her family are in jeopardy. The program, which involves a few thousand witnesses and members of their families, is administered by the marshals of the United States Department of Justice.

workhouse   A house of detention or a correctional facility for short-term confinement of minor offenders. *See also* JAIL; LOCKUP.

writ of error   A legal document by which appellate review is requested, on the ground that a lower-court decision was based on one or more errors.

writ of error coram nobis   An order to a lower court, commanding that its record of proceedings be sent to a higher court for appellate review.

youthful offender   A vague term sometimes used to refer to offenders who are legally juveniles (e.g., below the age of 18 in most states). Other times it is used to refer to older juvenile and younger adult offenders, such as from the ages 16 to 22, who are then grouped together. In particular, some "youthful offender" institutions house both juveniles who have been tried and convicted as adults in criminal court, and younger adult offenders.

EDWARD SAGARIN
DONAL E. J. MACNAMARA
THOMAS J. BERNARD
DEBORAH W. DENNO
JOSHUA DRESSLER
RICHARD S. FRASE
CAROL S. STEIKER

LEGAL INDEX

The following index is in two parts. The first, a Table of Cases, includes all the court decisions cited in this Encyclopedia; the second, arranged by topic, comprises all other legal documents cited therein. These are listed alphabetically within each topical category in the following order: national constitutions; treaties and other international agreements; federal (United States) and other national statutes; executive orders (United States); federal rules and regulations; American state constitutions, statutes, and rules and regulations; congressional resolutions; and proposed but unenacted international agreements and national laws. Unless otherwise indicated, (1) references are to American materials or jurisdictions, and (2) the statutes listed were in force as of July 2001. However, American state statutes dated before 1900 may be assumed to be no longer in effect, even where not so indicated.

TABLE OF CASES

C

D

LEGAL DOCUMENTS

Vol. 1: pp. 1–498; Vol. 2: pp. 499–935

VOL. 1: PP. 1–498; VOL. 2: PP. 499–935

GENERAL INDEX

Page references to entire articles are in **boldface.** References to figures and tables are denoted by *f* and *t.* Persons are indexed only when there is a substantial reference to them or a substantial quotation by them. In references to research work by three or more authors, as a rule only the first author is indexed.

American Federation of State,
  County, and Municipal
  Employees (AFSCME), 140
American Friends Service
  Committee (AFSC), 269
American Law Institute, 4,
  422–425
American Revolution
  criminal law reform, 414–416
  prisons, 1170
American Society for Industrial
  Security (ASIS), 1113
American Society of Criminology
  (ASC), 488
Ames, Oakes, 107
Amnesty, **56–60**
  antitrust offenses, 592
  Civil War, 57
  definition, 56
  truth commissions, 59
Amputation as punishment
  (Islam), 195
Ancient cultures, amnesty and
  pardon in, 56
Andaman Islanders' lack of law,
  200
Andenaes, Johannes, *contributor,*
  "Deterrence," **507–514**
Anderson, Elijah, *contributor,*
  "Delinquent and Criminal
  Subcultures," **499–506**
Anger management and rape
  treatment, 1304
Anglo-American adversary
  system, 27–30
Antebellum period and criminal
  law reform, 416–419
Anthropologic studies of law, 200
Anticorrupt practice acts,
  107–108
Anti-Saloon League, 46
Antisocial personality disorder
  (APD), 1006–1007, 1265,
  1266
Anti-stalking legislation,
  1500–1501, 1505–1507
Antitrust offenses, **590–599**
APD. *See* Antisocial personality
  disorder
Apostasy (Islam), 198
Appeal, **60–67,** 368
  bail pending, 62–63
  concurrent sentences, 63
  constitutional errors, 65
  courts, 61, 188, 380–381, 408
  death sentence review, 64
  double jeopardy, 553–554
  equal protection and due
    process, 61–62
  extraordinary writs, 63

Federal courts, 60–61
final-order requirements, 62
frivolous, 62
Great Britain, 188, 402
guilty plea convictions, 64
indigent appellants, 61–62
interlocutory, 63
juries' lack of sentence
  discretion, 1402
mootness, 63
plain error, 64–65
by prosecution, 63, 64
reversal of convictions, 65–66
right to counsel for
  discretionary, 274
Russia, 210, 213
scope of appellate review, 63–64
sentence, 64, 1459
shaming punishments, 1487
statistics, 387
by victim (Russia), 213
Aquinas, St. Thomas, 458
Archbold, Carol, *contributor,*
  "Police: Organization and
  Management," **1083–1092**
Architecture, jail, 854
Aristotle, 1, 457
Arizona, drug offenders in, 1201
Arraignment, **67–70**
  defects or delay in process,
    68–69
  definition, 67
  distinction from initial
    appearance, 67–68
  guilty pleas at, 751–752
  purpose of, 68
  See also Pretrial procedure
Arrest
  African Americans, 1603
  domestic violence, 545–546,
    1609
  use of force, 889–890
Arrestable offenses (Great
  Britain), 184–185
Arrest and stop. *See* Search and
  seizure
Arrestee Drug Abuse Monitoring
  Program (ADAM), 565
Arson, **70–76**
  behavioral and economic
    aspects, **70–73**
  common-law, 73–74
  degrees of, 75
  legal aspects, **73–76**
  model statutes, 75–76
  offender types, 70–71
  for profit, 71–72
  riots, 72
  statistics, 72–73
  statutory, 74–76

ART. *See* Aggression
  Replacement Training
Arum, Richard, *contributor,*
  "Education and Crime,"
  607–613
ASC. *See* American Society of
  Criminology
Aschaffenburg, Gustav, 41
ASI. *See* Addiction Severity Index
ASIS. *See* American Society for
  Industrial Security
Aspect causation, 158–159
Assassination, **76–81**
  assassins, 78, 80–81
  definition, 76–78
  extradition of assassins, 78
  impact, 81
  legal status of, 78
  psychology of assassins, 80–81
  socioeconomic conditions,
    78–80
  terrorism vs., 77, 1550
  treason, 78
Assault and battery, **82–85,** 1356
  aggravated battery, 83
  defenses to, 84
  domestic battery, 84
  elements of, 82–83
Assembly of States Parties, 823
Asset Forfeiture Program,
  715–716
Assigned counsel system, 144
Assisted suicide. *See* Euthanasia
  and assisted suicide
Association Against Prohibition
  Amendment (AAPA), 49
Assortative mating and crime
  causation, 318–319
Atavistic criminal, theory of the,
  461
Attachment theory and crime
  causation, 316–317
Attempt, **85–92**
  abandonment, 89
  actus reus, 87–88
  belated acceptance of principles,
    85
  equivocality approach, 88
  functions of punishment, 86–87
  impossibility, 89–90
  last-act test, 88
  lenient treatment, 90–91
  mens rea, 87
  Model Penal Code approach,
    88–89
  penalty ranges, 90–91
  preventive detention, 86–87
  proximity test, 88
Attempted battery, 83
Attempted larceny, 1558–1559

C

Escape, use of force to prevent, 892–893

Escort services. *See* prostitution

Espionage, 1398

Essays on Crimes and Punishment (Beccaria), 133

Estimator variables in eyewitness identification research, 665–666

Estrich, Susan, 708

Ethics and defense counsel, 280–283

European Court, 183, 191, 838–839

European Union

effect on cooperation among European police forces, 183

likelihood of single criminal justice system, 191

terrorism, 1551

unification of law, 398–399

Euthanasia and assisted suicide, **623–629**

Evidence

discovery, **533–540**

DNA, 1376–1377

evaluation of, 450–451, 866

gathering of, by police, 363

hearsay, 145–246, 491, 493, 1583

physical, 744, 1070

preliminary hearings, 1132

rape, 1312

scientific, **1373–1383**

sentencing, 1455, 1458

sufficiency test (Great Britain), 187

See also Admissibility of evidence; Exclusionary rules of evidence

Evolution and crime, 461

Examination of witnesses, 490–494, 1582

Excessive fines, forfeiture as, 718

Exchange theory and family abuse, 674

Excitement arsonists, 71

Exclusionary rules of evidence, **629–637**

applicability to states, 436–444, 631

China, 179–180

comparative-reprehensibility theory, 636

confessions obtained through police interrogation, 440–441

due process test, 635

equal protection clause, 635–636

exceptions, 632, 636

eyewitness identification, 635–636

Germany, 447–448

grand juries, 741

Italy, 447

mental abnormality evidence, 530–531

protection for the guilty, 443, 633

Russia, 211

self-incrimination, 439, 441–442, 635

sentencing, 1457

Spain, 447

tort remedies vs., 634–635

See also Admissibility of evidence; Evidence

Exculpatory mistakes, 1015–1017

Excuse, **637–661**

distinction from justification, 641, 883–884

retribution, 639–640

self-defense, 899

superior orders, claim of, 642

theory, **637–643**

See also Culpability; Duress; Infancy; Insanity; Intoxication; Justification; Liability

Execution. *See* Capital punishment

Executional requirements for electronic surveillance, 1681

Executive branch penal power, 427, 429–430

Executive clemency, 57–58

Executives, theft by, 615

Exemption from jury service, 875, 876

Ex-offenders' civil disabilities, 249–255

Experimental research in criminology, 474–475

Expert witnesses, 868

Explosives and arson law, 75

Express plea bargaining, 755

Expropriation, illegal, 586–587

External threats and research validity, 477

Extortion. *See* Blackmail and extortion; Bribery

Extradition, 78, 846–847

Extraterritorial jurisdiction, 861–863

Extreme emotional disturbance doctrine, 531–532

Extreme recklessness and murder, 789–790

Eyewitness identification, **661–669,** 1071

constitutional aspects, **661–664**

evidence, 635–636

psychological aspects, **664–669**

Eysenck, Hans, 319

F

Factual impossibility and attempt, 90

Factual legal guilt, 747–748

Fair cross-section requirement in jury selection, 876–877

Fair trial (China), 179–180

Fall, Albert, 107

False accusation of unlawful intercourse (Islam), 194

False pretenses and fraud, 1566–1570

False statement, 1050–1051

Families Against Mandatory Minimums (FAMM), 270

Family

conferences, 821

incarcerated mothers, 1197

influences on criminal behavior, 316–319

parenting, 317–318, 678–679, 682

relationships and crime, **677–684**

single-parent families, 316–317, 677–678

youth gangs and, 909

See also Domestic violence

FAMM. *See* Families Against Mandatory Minimums

Farrington, David P., *contributor,* "Crime Causation: Psychological Theories," **315–324**

F.B.I. *See* Federal Bureau of Investigation

Fear

of crime, **684–686,** 1064, 1066, 1277–1278

as element of robbery, 1355

Federal agencies

civil suits by, 161

law enforcement careers, 147

See also Specific agencies

Federal benefits, convicted persons' forfeiture of, 251–252

Federal Bureau of Investigation (F.B.I.)

careers, 147

computer crime, 226–227

H

Habeas corpus, **767–774**
  capital punishment, 772
  efforts to limit scope, 770–772
  federal review of state criminal convictions, 124
  nonretroactivity doctrine, 771
  post conviction review, 768–770
Hackers, computer, 222, 223
Hadd offenses (Islam), 193–195
Hagan, John, 171
Hague Convention violations, 829
Halfway houses. *See* Community residential centers
Halfway houses (liability), 1542–1543
Hall, Christopher Keith, *contributor,* "International Criminal Courts," **829–835**
Hamlet (Shakespeare), 982
Hand, Learned, 11, 602
Hands-off doctrine, 1161–1163
Hanna, Cheryl, *contributor,* "Domestic Violence," **543–549**
Hare Psychopathy Checklist Revised (Hare PCL-R), 1265–1266
Harm
  based crime theory, 289–290
  causation tests, 153, 157
  consensual sex crimes, 1465, 1466
  morality offenses, 352–353
Harmless error and appeal, 64–65
Hart, H. L. A., 350
Hart, Herbert, 159
Harvard Law School, 141
Hasan ibn-al-Sabbah, 76
Hasse, Ann Fingarette, *contributor,* "Excuse: Intoxication," **657–661**
Hassell, Kimberly, *contributor,* "Prevention: Police Role," **1155–1161**
Hastings, Warren, 106–107
Hate crimes, **774–779,** 1634
  controversy, 467–468
  definition, 774
  legislation (Russia), 216
Hate speech, 978
Hauptmann, Bruno Richard, 972
Hawkins, Gordon, *contributor*
  "Corporal Punishment," **255–258**
  "Crime Commissions," **334–340**
Haymarket anarchists, 129

Hearsay evidence, 245–246, 491, 493, 1583
Helpers in crime. *See* Accessories; Accomplices
Herman, Max, *contributor,* "Riots: Behavioral Aspects," **1346–1351**
Heroin use, 564–565
Hertz, Randy, *contributor,* "Excuse: Infancy," **648–650**
Heterogeneity and criminal careers, 343
Highway robbery (Islam), 195
Hinckley, John, Jr., 1503
Hirsch, Eric, 478
Hirschfield, Paul J., *contributor,* "Prevention: Community Programs," **1143–1148**
Hirschi, Travis, 517
  control theory, 608
  school performance/delinquency relationship, 609
Hispanics. *See* Race and ethnicity
Hiss, Alger, 1050
HITS. *See* Homicide Investigation and Tracking System
HIV/AIDS, **804–807**
  prisoners with, 1186
  prostitution, 1259–1260
  sexual regulation, 802
Hobbes, Thomas, 458–459, 646
Hobhouse, Leonard, 200
Holdover programs, juvenile, 919
Home detention, 919, 1230
Home Detention Curfew (Great Britain), 190
Homel, Ross, *contributor,* "Drinking and Driving," **555–560**
Homeless and the police, 1606
Homicide, **779–797**
  abortion, 2–3
  Africa, 516–517
  African Americans, 170
  behavioral aspects, **779–786**
  "born alive" standard of victims, 786
  categories, 788
  causation, 784, 787–788
  definition, 779
  developed countries, 1024
  developing countries, 516–518
  diminished capacity, 794
  excusable, 641–642
  historic homicide rates, 1515
  incapacitation, 813
  Islam, 196–198
  Latin America, 516–517

  legal aspects, **786–797**
  legal death, 786–787
  liability, 787–788
  necessity defense, 894
  negligent, 795–796
  noncriminal *vs.* criminal, 788
  population growth, 781–782
  provocation, 793–794
  sentencing, 796
  sociological explanations, 784
  statistics, 779–780, 780–782
  technology, 783–784
  vehicular, 795–796
  victim-offender relationship, 783
  women's rates, 782
  worldwide rates, 780–782
  See also Murder
Homicide Investigation and Tracking System, 1530–1531
Homosexuality
  crime and, **797–804**
  cross-cultural evidence of, 797–798
  domestic violence, 543–544
  legal recognition of same-sex couples, 802–803
  persecution, 800
  sexual orientation legislation, 802–803
  sodomy laws, 1470–1471
Honore, Tony, 159
Hoover, Herbert, 335
Hoover, J. Edgar, 688–691, 1056–1057
Horning, Donald N. M., *contributor*
  "Employee Theft: Behavioral Aspects," **613–616**
  "Employee Theft: Legal Aspects," **616–619**
Horton, Willie, 1123
Hospitalization for mental incompetency, 220
Hostage taking, 845
House arrest, 1417
Houses of refuge, 268, 911, 927–928
Howard, John, 133
Howard League for Penal Reform (Great Britain), 191
Howe, Scott W., *contributor,* "Publicity in Criminal Cases," **1269–1277**
Hubbard, F. Patrick, *contributor,* "Trespass, Criminal," **1576–1577**
Human capital model of crime causation, 304–305

Human immunodeficiency virus.
    See HIV/AIDS
Human rights
  European Union, 398–399
  international standards, 835,
      839–840
  truth commissions, 59
Human Rights Watch, 270, 933
Humanitarian law, 837
Hung juries, 1585
Hurst, James Willard, *contributor,*
    "Treason," **1573–1577**
Husak, Douglas, *contributor,* Drugs
    and Crime: Legal Aspects,
    566–572
Hyperides, 282
Hypnosis, 1071, 1374–1375

I

IAP. *See* Intensive Aftercare
    Program
ICPSR. *See* Inter-University
    Consortium for Political
    and Social Research
ICVS. *See* International Crime
    Victim Survey
Identification, eyewitness. *See*
    Eyewitness identification
ILC. *See* International Law
    Commission
I-Levels model, 1587
ILJ. *See* Institute for Law and
    Justice
Illicit marketeering and
    organized crime, 1044
Illinois
  capital punishment, 129
  extortion, 103
  moratorium on executions, 124
Immigrants and the temperance
    movement, 45–46
Imminence of threat and duress,
    645
Imminent danger, 887, 902–903
Immunity
  grand jury grants of, 744
  testimonial, 439, 441
Implicit plea bargaining, 755
Importation model of prison
    subcultures, 1188–1189
Impossibility and attempt, 89–90
Impulsiveness theories of crime
    causation, 320–321
Impulsivity management and
    rape treatment, 1305
Imwinkelried, Edward J.,
    contributor, "Scientific
    Evidence," **1373–1383**

Incapacitation, **809–818**
  criminal trajectory approach,
      815
  models of corrections,
      1213–1214
  punishment for, 427, 432–433,
      1287
  sexual predators, 815–816
  See also Deterrence; Prevention,
      crime
Incarceration
  crime rates, 471
  drug treatment vs., 816817
  gang members, 909
  incapacitation, **809–818**
  rates, 35–36
  sentencing guidelines and
      incarceration rates,
      1439–1441
  See also Corrections system;
      Jails; Prisons
Incendiarism. *See* Arson
Incentive in economic model of
    criminal behavior, 303
Incest, 520, 1468–1469
Inciardi, James A., *contributor*
    "Arson: Behavioral and
        Economic Aspects," **70–73**
    "Drugs and Crime: Behavioral
        Aspects," **560–566**
Incidence-based crime statistics,
    1528–1529
Incivilities and social
    disorganization, 580
Income as risk factor for family
    violence, 672
Income tax evasion. *See* Tax
    offenses
Incompetence. *See* Competence
Increasing crime rates,
    1519–1520
Inculpatory statements, 229–230
Independent living programs for
    youth, 922
Indeterminate sentences, 420,
    509, 1317–1319,
    1401–1403, 1425–1426,
    1449–1450
Index crimes, 1526–1527
India, codification of law in,
    406–407
Indictment
  grand jury proceedings,
      741–742
  prosecution of felonies by, 738,
      742
Indigent defendants
  appeal, 61–62
  bail, 98–99

right to counsel, 120, 143–144,
    273, 277, 440
Indirect costs of crime,
    1510–1511
Inducement and entrapment,
    620
Industrialization and criminality.
    See Development
    (economic) and crime
Inevitable accident, 641–642
Infancy, **648–650,** 911
    See also Excuse
Influenza as prenatal factor of
    violence, 297
Informal disposition, **818–823,**
    942*f*
Information technology and
    police, 1088–1089
Ingber, Stanley, *contributor,*
    "Libel, Criminal," **975–980**
Initial appearance as distinct
    from arraignment, 67–68
Inmates. *See* Prisoners
Innate drive theories of violence,
    1651
Innocence protection, 443
Innocent agency, 9
Inquisitorial system
  adversary system vs., 26–30,
      445–446, 450–451,
      1578–1579
  China, 177–178
  France, 450–451
  Germany, 451–452
  Italy, 452
  Spain, 452
  See also Accusatorial system;
      Adversary system
Insanity defense, 637, **650–657**
  abolition of, 655–656
  commitment of offenders,
      1010–1011
  guilty but mentally ill verdicts,
      652–653
  Russia, 214
  See also Excuse; Mentally
      disordered offenders
Instinct, violence and, 1651
Institute for Law and Justice
    (ILJ), 481
Institutional anomie theory of
    crime causation, 331
Institutional defects and criminal
    behavior, 311–312
Institutionalization of juvenile
    status offenders, 962
Institutions, juvenile justice,
    927–935
Insurance claims, arson for,
    70–71

geographic distribution of rates, 576–577

Great Britain, 402, 404

intelligence and crime studies, 824, 825

legal rights, 1076–1077

mediation programs, 541

National Advisory Committee for Juvenile Justice and Delinquency Prevention, 337

Office of Juvenile Justice and Delinquency Prevention (OJJDP), 485

police handling of, **1073–1083,** 1077–1081

prevention programs, 962, 1145, **1152–1154**

procedural protections, 365–366

proof standards, 915

rates, 946*f*

reduction programs, 138

religion, 1328–1329

right to constitutional criminal procedural protections, 162–163

school performance/crime relationship, 609

self-report surveys, 1535–1538

social disorganization, 330–331, 578–581

Society for the Prevention of Juvenile Delinquency (SPJD), 268

status offenders, **957–963**

status offenses, **957–963**

transfers to adult courts, 816, 942, 943*f*, **947–957**

treatment programs, 1322

typologies, 1587

violent offenders, **963–969**

See also Causation, crime; Criminal careers; Gangs, youth; Juvenile justice system; Subcultures, delinquent and criminal

Juvenile justice system, **911–947**

adjudication hearings, 941

aftercare, 922–923

Aggression Replacement Training (ART), 934

amenability to treatment, 949

benefits of smaller treatment programs, 931

caseload, 942–943, 944*f*, 945*t*

chronic offenders, 952–953

community treatment, **917–927**

concurrent jurisdiction for certain offenses, 949–950

Conditions of Confinement Report, 929–930

court records, 946

courts, 269, **937–947**

day treatment programs, 921

delinquency rates, 946*f*

denial of right to jury trials, 916

design of institutional facilities, 930–931

detention alternatives, 919

disposition of cases, 942–943

due process rights, 943–945

emergence of, 1318–1319

establishment of, 421

establishment of system of, 649

"get tough" policies, 950–951

history and philosophy, **911–917**

holdover programs, 919

home detention, 919

independent living programs, 922

institutions, 923–924, **927–935**

Intensive Aftercare Program, 923

judicial waiver, 947–955

juvenile courts, 269, 421, **937–947,** 1318–1319

legal rights of juveniles in confinement, 932–933

legislative offense exclusion, 949–950, 955

mental illness, 931–932

mentoring programs, 922

organization and structure of system, 1074–1075

overcrowding in institutions, 929–930

Performance-based Standards (PbS) Project, 930

personnel, 940

policing juveniles, 1604–1605

post-adjudication programs, 920–922

pre-adjudication community treatment, 919

prevention efforts, 1153–1154

prison-like facilities, 933

probation, 920–921

procedural rights, 914–916

process, 940–942

reform, 911, 912–914

Rehabilitative Ideal, 913–915

restitution and community service, 921

restorative justice, 924–925

reverse waiver, 951–952

sentencing, 945–946, 948–949

shelters, 919

staff training, 932

statistics, 920, 928–929, 942–943

structure and organization, 939–940

terminology, 941*f*

transfer of juveniles to adult system, 816, 942, 943*f*, **947–957,** 1077

turnover rates of staff, 932

waiver case dispositions, 952–953

waiver laws, 951, 955

wilderness and adventure programs, 922

wraparound services, 922

K

Kadish, Sanford H., *contributor,* "Conspiracy," **240–247**

Kahan, Dan M., *contributor*
"Arson: Legal Aspects," **73–76**
"Assault and Battery," **82–85**
"Attempt," **85–91**
"Bank Robbery," **101–102**
"Bribery," **105–111**
"Conspiracy," **240–247**
"Criminal Law Reform: Historical Development in the United States," **412–426**
"Forgery," **719–722**
"Homicide: Legal Aspects," **786–797**
"Riots: Legal Aspects," **1351–1354**
"Robbery," **1354–1359**
"Sedition and Domestic Terrorism," **1394–1400**
"Shaming Punishments," **1483–1489**
"Solicitation," **1491–1495**
"Theft," **1556–1573**
"Treason," **1573–1577**
"Trespass, Criminal," **1576–1577**
"White-Collar Crime," **1672–1677**

Kansas City Gun experiment, 1608

Karlan, Pamela S., *contributor,* "Counsel: Right to Counsel," **274–278**

Karmen, Andrew, *contributor,* "Vigilantism," **1645–1648**

Katz, Leo, *contributor,* "Excuse: Duress," **643–648**

Kefauver Senate committee on organized crime, 1038

V

Y

Z

ISBN 0-02-865323-8

9 780028 653235

90000